Red Hat® LINUX® Secrets®,
2nd Edition

Red Hat® LINUX® Secrets®, 2nd Edition

Naba Barkakati

IDG Books Worldwide, Inc.
An International Data Group Company

Foster City, CA ♦ Chicago, IL ♦ Indianapolis, IN ♦ New York, NY

Red Hat® LINUX® Secrets®, 2nd Edition

Published by
IDG Books Worldwide, Inc.
An International Data Group Company
919 E. Hillsdale Blvd., Suite 400
Foster City, CA 94404
www.idgbooks.com (IDG Books Worldwide Web site)

Cover: some images © 1998 PhotoDisk, Inc.

Library of Congress Catalog Card Number: 98-73783

ISBN: 0-7645-3175-1

Printed in the United States of America

10 9 8 7 6 5 4 3 2 1

1B/RV/RQ/ZY/FC

Distributed in the United States by IDG Books Worldwide, Inc.

Distributed by Macmillan Canada for Canada; by Transworld Publishers Limited in the United Kingdom; by IDG Norge Books for Norway; by IDG Sweden Books for Sweden; by Woodslane Pty. Ltd. for Australia; by Woodslane (NZ) Ltd. for New Zealand; by Addison Wesley Longman Singapore Pte Ltd. for Singapore, Malaysia, Thailand, Indonesia, and Korea; by Norma Comunicaciones S.A. for Colombia; by Intersoft for South Africa; by International Thomson Publishing for Germany, Austria, and Switzerland; by Toppan Company Ltd. for Japan; by Distribuidora Cuspide for Argentina; by Livraria Cultura for Brazil; by Ediciencia S.A. for Ecuador; by Ediciones ZETA S.C.R. Ltda. for Peru; by WS Computer Publishing Corporation, Inc., for the Philippines; by Unalis Corporation for Taiwan; by Contemporanea de Ediciones for Venezuela; by Computer Book & Magazine Store for Puerto Rico; by Express Computer Distributors for the Caribbean and West Indies. Authorized Sales Agent: Anthony Rudkin Associates for the Middle East and North Africa.

For general information on IDG Books Worldwide's books in the U.S., please call our Consumer Customer Service department at 800-762-2974. For reseller information, including discounts and premium sales, please call our Reseller Customer Service department at 800-434-3422.

For information on where to purchase IDG Books Worldwide's books outside the U.S., please contact our International Sales department at 650-655-3200 or fax 650-655-3297.

For information on foreign language translations, please contact our Foreign & Subsidiary Rights department at 650-655-3021 or fax 650-655-3281.

For sales inquiries and special prices for bulk quantities, please contact our Sales department at 650-655-3200 or write to the address above.

For information on using IDG Books Worldwide's books in the classroom or for ordering examination copies, please contact our Educational Sales department at 800-434-2086 or fax 317-596-5499.

For press review copies, author interviews, or other publicity information, please contact our Public Relations department at 650-655-3000 or fax 650-655-3299.

For authorization to photocopy items for corporate, personal, or educational use, please contact Copyright Clearance Center, 222 Rosewood Drive, Danvers, MA 01923, or fax 978-750-4470.

 is a trademark under exclusive license to IDG Books Worldwide, Inc., from International Data Group, Inc.

ABOUT IDG BOOKS WORLDWIDE

Welcome to the world of IDG Books Worldwide.

IDG Books Worldwide, Inc., is a subsidiary of International Data Group, the world's largest publisher of computer-related information and the leading global provider of information services on information technology. IDG was founded more than 25 years ago and now employs more than 8,500 people worldwide. IDG publishes more than 275 computer publications in over 75 countries (see listing below). More than 90 million people read one or more IDG publications each month.

Launched in 1990, IDG Books Worldwide is today the #1 publisher of best-selling computer books in the United States. We are proud to have received eight awards from the Computer Press Association in recognition of editorial excellence and three from *Computer Currents'* First Annual Readers' Choice Awards. Our best-selling *...For Dummies*® series has more than 50 million copies in print with translations in 38 languages. IDG Books Worldwide, through a joint venture with IDG's Hi-Tech Beijing, became the first U.S. publisher to publish a computer book in the People's Republic of China. In record time, IDG Books Worldwide has become the first choice for millions of readers around the world who want to learn how to better manage their businesses.

Our mission is simple: Every one of our books is designed to bring extra value and skill-building instructions to the reader. Our books are written by experts who understand and care about our readers. The knowledge base of our editorial staff comes from years of experience in publishing, education, and journalism — experience we use to produce books for the '90s. In short, we care about books, so we attract the best people. We devote special attention to details such as audience, interior design, use of icons, and illustrations. And because we use an efficient process of authoring, editing, and desktop publishing our books electronically, we can spend more time ensuring superior content and spend less time on the technicalities of making books.

You can count on our commitment to deliver high-quality books at competitive prices on topics you want to read about. At IDG Books Worldwide, we continue in the IDG tradition of delivering quality for more than 25 years. You'll find no better book on a subject than one from IDG Books Worldwide.

John Kilcullen
CEO
IDG Books Worldwide, Inc.

Steven Berkowitz
President and Publisher
IDG Books Worldwide, Inc.

Eighth Annual Computer Press Awards ≥1992

Ninth Annual Computer Press Awards ≥1993

Tenth Annual Computer Press Awards ≥1994

Eleventh Annual Computer Press Awards ≥1995

IDG Books Worldwide, Inc., is a subsidiary of International Data Group, the world's largest publisher of computer-related information and the leading global provider of information services on information technology. International Data Group publishes over 275 computer publications in over 75 countries. More than 90 million people read one or more International Data Group publications each month. International Data Group's publications include: **ARGENTINA:** Buyer's Guide, Computerworld Argentina, PC World Argentina; **AUSTRALIA:** Australian Macworld, Australian PC World, Australian Reseller News, Computerworld, IT Casebook, Network World, Publish, Webmaster; **AUSTRIA:** Computerwelt Osterreich, Networks Austria, PC Tip Austria; **BANGLADESH:** PC World Bangladesh; **BELARUS:** PC World Belarus; **BELGIUM:** Data News; **BRAZIL:** Annuário de Informática, Computerworld, Connections, Macworld, PC Player, PC World, Publish, Reseller News, Supergamepower; **BULGARIA:** Computerworld Bulgaria, Network World Bulgaria, PC & MacWorld Bulgaria; **CANADA:** CIO Canada; Client/Server World, ComputerWorld Canada, InfoWorld Canada, NetworkWorld Canada, WebWorld; **CHILE:** Computerworld Chile, PC World Chile; **COLOMBIA:** Computerworld Colombia, PC World Colombia; **COSTA RICA:** PC World Centro America; **THE CZECH AND SLOVAK REPUBLICS:** Computerworld Czechoslovakia, Macworld Czech Republic, PC World Czechoslovakia; **DENMARK:** Communications World Danmark, Computerworld Danmark, Macworld Danmark, PC World Danmark, Techworld Danmark; **DOMINICAN REPUBLIC:** PC World Republica Dominicana; **ECUADOR:** PC World Ecuador; **EGYPT:** Computerworld Middle East, PC World Middle East; **EL SALVADOR:** PC World Centro America; **FINLAND:** MikroPC, Tietoverkko, Tietoviikko; **FRANCE:** Distributique, Hebdo, Info PC, Le Monde Informatique, Macworld, Reseaux & Telecoms, WebMaster France; **GERMANY:** Computer Partner, Computerwoche, Computerwoche Extra, Computerwoche FOCUS, Global Online, Macwelt, PC Welt; **GREECE:** Amiga Computing, GamePro Greece, Multimedia World; **GUATEMALA:** PC World Centro America; **HONDURAS:** PC World Centro America; **HONG KONG:** Computerworld Hong Kong, PC World Hong Kong, Publish in Asia; **HUNGARY:** ABCD CD-ROM, Computerworld Szamitastechnika, Internetto online Magazine, PC World Hungary, PC-X Magazin Hungary; **ICELAND:** Tolvuheimur PC World Island; **INDIA:** Information Communications World, Information Systems Computerworld, PC World India, Publish in Asia; **INDONESIA:** InfoKomputer PC World, Komputek Computerworld, Publish in Asia; **IRELAND:** ComputerScope, PC Live!; **ISRAEL:** Macworld Israel, People & Computers/Computerworld; **ITALY:** Computerworld Italia, Macworld Italia, Networking Italia, PC World Italia; **JAPAN:** DTP World, Macworld Japan, Nikkei Personal Computing, OS/2 World Japan, SunWorld Japan, Windows NT World, Windows World Japan; **KENYA:** PC World East African; **KOREA:** Hi-Tech Information, Macworld Korea, PC World Korea; **MACEDONIA:** PC World Macedonia; **MALAYSIA:** Computerworld Malaysia, PC World Malaysia, Publish in Asia; **MALTA:** PC World Malta; **MEXICO:** Computerworld Mexico, PC World Mexico; **MYANMAR:** PC World Myanmar; **NETHERLANDS:** Computer! Totaal, LAN Internetworking Magazine, LAN World Buyers Guide, Macworld Netherlands, Net, WebWereld; **NEW ZEALAND:** Absolute Beginners Guide and Plain & Simple Series, Computer Buyer, Computer Industry Directory, Computerworld New Zealand, MTB, Network World, PC World New Zealand; **NICARAGUA:** PC World Centro America; **NORWAY:** Computerworld Norge, CW Rapport, Datamagasinet, Financial Rapport, Kursguide Norge, Macworld Norge, Multimediaworld Norge, PC World Ekspress Norge, PC World Nettverk, PC World Norge, PC World ProduktGuide Norge; **PAKISTAN:** Computerworld Pakistan; **PANAMA:** PC World Panama; **PEOPLE'S REPUBLIC OF CHINA:** China Computer Users, China Computerworld, China InfoWorld, China Telecom World Weekly, Computer & Communication, Electronic Design China, Electronics Today, Electronics Weekly, Game Software, PC World China, Popular Computer Week, Software Weekly, Software World, Telecom World; **PERU:** Computerworld Peru, PC World Profesional Peru, PC World SoHo Peru; **PHILIPPINES:** Click!, Computerworld Philippines, PC World Philippines, Publish in Asia; **POLAND:** Computerworld Poland, Computerworld Special Report Poland, Cyber, Macworld Poland, Networld Poland, PC World Komputer; **PORTUGAL:** Cerebro/PC World, Computerworld/Correio Informático, Dealer World Portugal, Mac*In/PC*In Portugal, Multimedia World; **PUERTO RICO:** PC World Puerto Rico; **ROMANIA:** Computerworld Romania, PC World Romania, Telecom Romania; **RUSSIA:** Computerworld Russia, Mir PK, Publish, Seti; **SINGAPORE:** Computerworld Singapore, PC World Singapore, Publish in Asia; **SLOVENIA:** Monitor; **SOUTH AFRICA:** Computing SA, Network World SA, Software World SA; **SPAIN:** Communicaciones España, Computerworld España, Dealer World España, Macworld España, PC World España; **SRI LANKA:** Infolink PC World; **SWEDEN:** CAP&Design, Computer Sweden, Corporate Computing Sweden, Internetworld Sweden, it.branschen, Macworld Sweden, MaxiData Sweden, MikroDatorn, Nätverk & Kommunikation, PC World Sweden, PCaktiv, Windows World Sweden; **SWITZERLAND:** Computerworld Schweiz, Macworld Schweiz, PCtip; **TAIWAN:** Computerworld Taiwan, Macworld Taiwan, NEW ViSiON/Publish, PC World Taiwan, Windows World Taiwan; **THAILAND:** Publish in Asia, Thai Computerworld; **TURKEY:** Computerworld Turkiye, Macworld Turkiye, Network World Turkiye, PC World Turkiye; **UKRAINE:** Computerworld Kiev, Multimedia World Ukraine, PC World Ukraine; **UNITED KINGDOM:** Acorn User UK, Amiga Action UK, Amiga Computing UK, Apple Talk UK, Computing, Macworld, Parents and Computers UK, PC Advisor, PC Home, PSX Pro, The WEB; **UNITED STATES:** Cable in the Classroom, CIO Magazine, Computerworld, DOS World, Federal Computer Week, GamePro Magazine, InfoWorld, I-Way, Macworld, Network World, PC Games, PC World, Publish, Video Event, THE WEB Magazine, and WebMaster; online webzines: JavaWorld, NetscapeWorld, and SunWorld Online; **URUGUAY:** InfoWorld Uruguay; **VENEZUELA:** Computerworld Venezuela, PC World Venezuela; and **VIETNAM:** PC World Vietnam.   5/7/98

Credits

Acquisitions Editor
Laura Lewin

Development Editors
Laura E. Brown
Luann Rouff

Technical Editor
Phil Hughes

Copy Editors
Luann Rouff
Anne Friedman
Colleen Dowling

Project Coordinator
Tom Debolski

**Graphics and
Production Specialists**
Hector Mendoza
Linda Marousek
Christopher Pimentel

Quality Control Specialists
Mick Arellano
Mark Schumann

Proofreader
Arielle Carole Mennelle

Indexer
Liz Cunningham

Packaging Coordinator
Cyndra Robbins

About the Author

Naba Barkakati is an expert programmer and successful computer-book author who has experience in a wide variety of systems, ranging from MS-DOS and Windows to UNIX and the X Window System. He bought his first personal computer — an IBM PC-AT — in 1984 after graduating with a Ph.D. in electrical engineering from the University of Maryland at College Park. While pursuing a full-time career in engineering, Naba dreamed of writing software for the emerging PC software market. As luck would have it, instead of building a software empire like Microsoft, he ended up writing successful computer books.

Over the past ten years, Naba has written 22 computer books on a number of topics ranging from Windows programming with Visual C++ to Linux. He had authored several best-selling titles such as *The Waite Group's Turbo C++ Bible*, *Object-Oriented Programming in C++*, *X Window System Programming*, *Visual C++ Developer's Guide*, and *Borland C++ 4 Developer's Guide*. Naba's books have been translated into many languages, including Spanish, French, Polish, Greek, Italian, Chinese, Japanese, and Korean. His most recent books are *UNIX Webmaster Bible* and *Discover Perl 5*, both published by IDG Books Worldwide.

Naba lives in North Potomac, Maryland, with his wife Leha and their children, Ivy, Emily, and Ashley.

To my wife Leha and our daughters, Ivy, Emily, and Ashley

Preface

If you are beginning to use Linux you need a practical guide. One that not only gets you going with the installation and setup of Linux, but also shows you how to use Linux for specific tasks, such as an Internet host or a software development platform.

The first edition of this book was a technical guide designed to address these needs. That book included Version 3.0 of the popular Slackware distribution of Linux on a CD-ROM with the standard installation and setup information.

A great deal has happened in the two years since the first edition was published. The Linux kernel, the core operating system, is now at release 2.0. New kernel features, as well as support, for new hardware continue to grow. A huge upsurge in user interest has occurred, as evidenced by the growing number of Linux books, especially those for beginners. In addition, newer Linux distributions — combinations of the operating system with applications and installation tools — have been developed to simplify the installation process.

In particular, the Red Hat Linux distribution has emerged as the choice of users who want a simpler installation process than that offered by Slackware Linux. Red Hat includes a number of graphical tools that run under the X Window System to help users with set up and configuration tasks. In addition to installation differences, Red Hat Linux also differs from Slackware Linux in the location and format of some system configuration files. Although experts argue over the relative merits of one arrangement of configuration files over another, the simpler installation steps afforded by the Red Hat Linux distribution certainly better serve the novice user. In any case, the core Linux operating system and the collection of applications are nearly identical in all Linux distributions.

Red Hat LINUX Secrets, 2nd Edition follows the successful model of the first edition with one significant change: it includes the latest release of Red Hat Linux (version 5.1, with the 2.0.34 kernel) on the companion CD-ROM. This book provides detailed technical information on installing and customizing Linux, including coverage of various types of computers and peripherals.

This book then goes a step beyond existing books and shows you how to use Linux as a solution to specific problems. In addition, it provides information on freely available software packages — such as news and mail, graphics, and text utilities — on the book's companion CD-ROM.

The unique aspects of *Red Hat LINUX Secrets, 2nd Edition* are the tips, techniques, shortcuts, and little-known facts about using Linux in various real-world tasks, ranging from simply learning UNIX to setting up a WWW server for your business.

By reading this book you get the following benefits:

- Learn how to install and set up Linux from the Red Hat Linux CD-ROM included with the book
- Learn how to use various peripherals (video cards, hard disks, and network cards) in Linux
- Learn about dial-up networking (with SLIP and PPP) under Linux
- Get tips, techniques, and shortcuts for specific uses of Linux, such as:
  - Learn how to use Linux as an Internet host (WWW server and anonymous FTP server)
  - Understand how Linux and DOS can coexist
  - Learn UNIX on Linux
  - Learn C and C++ programming on Linux
  - Learn Motif programming on Linux
- Receive many Linux tools and utilities
- Learn about Linux resources that can serve as continuing sources of information in the ever-changing world of Linux

Organization of the Book

Red Hat LINUX Secrets, 2nd Edition has 24 chapters, organized into four parts and four appendixes:

Part I: Configuring Your Linux System includes two chapters that essentially guide you through the steps of installing Linux from the CD-ROM bundled with the book. The second chapter in this part describes how to apply patches and reconfigure the Linux kernel as new revisions become available.

Part II: Running Linux focuses on how to run Linux after it has been installed. Part II includes six chapters that explain how to set up the graphical interface with *X*, how to use Linux commands (which essentially are UNIX commands), how to access DOS from Linux, and how to use the Tcl/Tk scripting language for quick-and-dirty programming.

Part III: Exploiting Your Hardware in Linux provides all the information you need to use various types of hardware in Linux. The hardware descriptions cover everything from the computer processor, memory, and bus to serial ports and PC cards (that use the PCMCIA interface).

Part IV: Using Linux for Fun and Profit has seven chapters that show how to use Linux for specific purposes such as setting up an Internet host, running a World Wide Web server, developing software, and preparing documents.

Appendix A: The Best of Linux Applications describes several popular Linux applications on the book's companion CD-ROM.

Appendix B: Linux Commands presents alphabetically arranged reference entries for the most important Linux commands.

Appendix C: Linux Resources lists resources on the Internet where you can obtain the latest information about Linux.

Appendix D: CD-ROM Installation Instructions summarizes how to install Linux from the book's companion CD-ROM.

If you are a new user, you should start in Part I with the installation of Linux from the CD-ROM. If you have already installed Linux, you might begin with Chapter 3 and learn how to make the most of Linux in everyday use. If you have specific hardware questions, you should go directly to a relevant chapter in Part III. Part IV is meant to describe specific Linux uses. Read the relevant chapters in Part IV to get going with specific tasks. When you need information on a specific Linux command, turn to Appendix B and look for that command in the alphabetically arranged reference entries.

Conventions Used in This Book

Red Hat LINUX Secrets, 2nd Edition uses a simple notational style. All listings, filenames, function names, variable names, and keywords are typeset in a `monospace font` for ease of reading. The first occurrences of new terms and concepts are in *italic*. Text you are directed to type is in **boldface**.

Each chapter starts with a short list of all the neat things you learn in that chapter. The summary at the end of the chapter tells you a bit more about what the chapter covered.

Following the time-honored tradition of the IDG Books *Secrets* series, I use icons to help you pinpoint useful information quickly. Following is what I had in mind for the icons:

Note

The Note icon marks an interesting fact — something I thought you'd like to know.

Tip

The Tip icon marks things you can do to make your job simpler — hints you can try.

Caution

The Caution icon highlights potential pitfalls. With this icon, I'm telling you: Watch out! This could hurt your system!

CD

The CD icon points to specific programs or documentation on this book's companion CD-ROM.

Cross-Reference

The Cross Reference icon points out paragraphs that lead you to other chapters in the book for a deeper discussion of a topic.

Secret

The Secret icon marks facts that are not well-documented but important to know. Once you know these facts, they may clear up many questions.

Wizard

The Wizard icon marks technical information of interest to an advanced user.

Sidebars

This is a sidebar. I use sidebars throughout the book to highlight interesting, but not critical, information. Sidebars explain concepts you may not have encountered before or give insight on a related topic. If you're in a hurry, you can safely skip the sidebars. On the other hand, if you find yourself flipping through the book looking for interesting information, searching for the sidebars is a good idea.

Red Hat Linux 5.1 CD-ROM

Red Hat LINUX Secrets, 2nd Edition addresses the needs of new users who want to put Linux to some productive use on their home or office PC. Because installation is one of the difficult phases in getting started with Linux, the editorial team and I decided to include a copy of Red Hat Linux 5.1 (with Linux kernel 2.0.34) on the companion CD-ROM. Red Hat Linux is easy to install and is well-supported by Red Hat (www.redhat.com).

Red Hat Linux 5.1 is a complete Linux distribution with the 2.0.34 kernel (operating system) plus a large selection of Linux software. In particular, the following software is on the Red Hat Linux 5.1 CD-ROM:

■ Linux kernel 2.0.34 with driver modules for all major PC hardware configurations including IDE/EIDE and SCSI drives, PCMCIA devices, and CD-ROMs

- Complete set of installation and configuration tools for setting up devices (such as keyboard and mouse) and services (network)

- Graphical user interface based on the XFree86 3.3.2 package with fvwm2 and AfterStep window managers

- Full TCP/IP networking for Internet, LANs, and intranets

- Tools for connecting your PC to your Internet service provider using PPP, SLIP, or dialup serial communications programs

- Complete suite of Internet applications including electronic mail (sendmail, elm, pine, mailx), news (inn, tin, trn), Internet Relay Chat (ircii), telnet, FTP, and NFS

- Apache Web server 1.2.6 to turn your PC into a Web server and Netscape Communicator 4.05 to surf the Net

- Samba 1.9 LAN Manager software for Microsoft Windows connectivity

- Several text editors (GNU Emacs 20.2, JED, Joe, vim)

- Graphics and image manipulation software such as XV, XPaint, Xfig, Gnuplot, Ghostscript, Ghostview, GIMP, ImageMagick, and xanim

- Programming languages (GNU C and C++ 2.7.2.3, Perl 5.004, Tcl/Tk 8.0.2, Python 1.5.1, GNU AWK 3.0.3) and software development tools (GNU Debugger 4.17, RCS 5.7, GNU Bison 1.25, flex 2.5.4a, TIFF, and JPEG libraries)

- Support for industry standard Executable and Linking Format (ELF) and Intel Binary Compatibility Specification (iBCS)

- Complete suite of standard UNIX utilities

- Tools to access and use DOS files and applications (DOSEMU 0.66.7, mtools 3.8)

- Text formatting and typesetting software (groff, TeX, and LaTeX)

- Games such as GNU Chess, xtetris, acm, colour-yahtzee, flying, fortune-mod, mysterious, paradise, xchomp, xevil, xgalaga, xgammon, xpilot

This long list of software shouldn't overwhelm you. You only have to learn to use what you need. Besides, this book shows you both how to install Linux and use most of this software.

If you have enough space available on your PC's hard disk (or, better yet, a spare second hard disk), Red Hat Linux installation can be as simple as creating a boot disk, booting the PC, and filling up information in a series of dialog boxes. But don't take my word for it — you can see for yourself!

Now it's time to begin your Linux adventure. Take out the companion CD-ROM, turn to Chapter 1, and let the fun begin. Before you know it, you'll be a Linux expert!

I hope you enjoy this book as much as I enjoyed writing it!

Acknowledgments

I am grateful to Laura Lewin for getting me started with this book.
Thanks to everyone else at IDG Books Worldwide who transformed my
raw manuscript into this well-edited and beautifully packaged book,
especially development editors Laura Brown and Luann Rouff, who
guided me through the manuscript submission process and kept
everything moving. I appreciate the guidance and support you both gave
me during this project. Also, thanks to Lenora Chin Sell for making the
necessary arrangements with Red Hat for the book's companion
CD-ROM.

I also want to thank Phil Hughes, publisher of *Linux Journal*
(www.linuxjournal.com), for reviewing the manuscript for technical
accuracy. Phil provided many useful suggestions for improving the
book's content.

Of course, if it were not for Linux, no reason would exist for this book.
For this, we have Linus Torvalds and the legions of Linux developers
around the world to thank.

Finally, and, as always, my greatest thanks go to my wife Leha for her
patience and understanding and for taking care of everything while I
stayed glued to my PCs the past few months. As I wrap up the book, my
daughters, Ivy, Emily, and Ashley are tracking my progress and counting
the days to the deadline. Thanks for being there!

Contents at a Glance

Contents

Introduction

Linux is truly amazing when you consider how it originated and how it continues to evolve. From its modest beginning as the hobby of one person—Linus Torvalds of Finland—Linux has grown into a full-fledged 32-bit operating system (64-bit on the DEC Alpha processor) with features that rival those of commercial x86 UNIX operating systems, such as Solaris and SCO UNIX. To top it off, Linux—with all its source code—is available free to anyone. All you must do is download it from an Internet site or get it on a CD-ROM for a nominal fee from one of many Linux CD vendors.

Linux certainly is an exception to the rule "you get what you pay for." Even though Linux is free, it is no slouch when it comes to performance, features, and reliability. The robustness of Linux has to do with the way it was developed. Many developers around the world collaborated over the Internet to add features. Incremental versions are continually being downloaded by users and tested in a variety of system configurations. Linux revisions go through much more rigorous beta testing than any commercial software does.

Since the release of Linux 1.0 on March 14, 1994, the number of Linux users around the world has grown exponentially. Based on data gathered by the Linux Counter (`http://counter.li.org/`), the estimated installed base is anywhere from 1 million to more than 5 million users worldwide. The same data provides some interesting statistics about Linux:

- Most Linux users are in United States, Canada, and Europe.

- The percentage of Linux users who use it at home is 87 percent; 35 percent use it at work; some use it both at work and home.

- The percentage of users who get Linux via FTP is 42 percent. About 40 percent of users buy Linux on a CD-ROM, typically from a vendor such as InfoMagic or Red Hat Linux.

- Slackware Linux continues to be the most popular Linux distribution: Red Hat and Debian are the other two prominent distributions.

- The percentage of users who run Linux on Intel 486 systems is 42 percent —30 percent on Pentium processors. Systems typically have 8 to 32MB of memory and 500MB to 1.5GB disk.

- The percentage of Linux systems that use an Ethernet network is 50 percent, while 34 percent use dial-up networking with SLIP and PPP.

- Most Linux systems have anywhere from one to eight users.

- The percentage of Linux systems that are used as Internet servers (World Wide Web, FTP, Mail, firewall, and even as router) is 61 percent.

The Linux distributions — Red Hat, Slackware, and Debian — differ in the way each handles the installation process. Because installation is the most difficult step in getting started with Linux, it helps to select a Linux distribution that makes installation easy. Red Hat Linux excels when it comes to the installation process. Red Hat provides an installation program that guides new users through the crucial parts of the installation process, including disk partitioning. The ease of installation makes Red Hat Linux a good choice for all users, especially new users.

Red Hat Linux comes with extensive online information on topics such as installing and configuring the operating system for a wide variety of PCs and peripherals. Although expert users can manage to install and run Linux with the online documentation alone, new users find consulting a book (such as this one) helpful for detailed guidance on Linux installation. Typically, users also move to Linux with some specific purpose in mind (such as setting up a World Wide Web server or learning X programming).

Part I:

Configuring Your Linux System

Chapter 1: Installing Linux

Chapter 2: Upgrading Linux

Chapter 1

Installing Linux

Starting with the Intel 80386 processor, continuing with the 80486, and now with the Pentium and Pentium II, the computing power of PC processors continues to grow steadily. Processor clock speeds have increased from the 16MHz 80386 of a few years ago to the 450MHz Pentium II processors of today. The IBM PC-AT-based Industry Standard Architecture (ISA) bus is being supplanted by the high-performance Peripheral Component Interconnect (PCI) bus. The hardware performance of a modern, run-of-the-mill PC clearly is on a par with that of workstations, such as those from Hewlett-Packard and Sun.

When it comes to operating systems, however, PCs have not kept up with workstations. Many PCs still run 16-bit operating systems, such as MS-DOS or Windows 3.1, which do not fully exploit the 32-bit processing capabilities of the PC's processors. Workstations, on the other hand, run UNIX — a multitasking and multiuser operating system (this means the operating system can run several programs simultaneously and support more than one user at a time). Typically, workstations also use the X Window System for a graphical user interface.

Differences between 16-bit and 32-bit operating systems

Intel 80386, 80486, and Pentium processors have 32-bit registers and can process data items 32 bits at a time. But 16-bit operating systems, such as MS-DOS and Windows 3.1, use only the 16 low-order bits of the 32-bit registers (see the figure) and work with data items in 16-bit chunks.

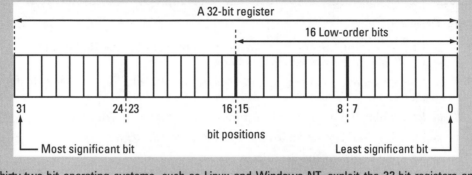

Thirty-two-bit operating systems, such as Linux and Windows NT, exploit the 32-bit registers and process data 32 bits at a time. You need a 32-bit operating system, such as Linux, to exploit the capabilities of your PC's 32-bit processor.

UNIX has been available for PCs for some time, but you had to pay nearly as much for a fully configured commercial PC UNIX operating system as you did for the PC itself. This situation changed when Linus Torvalds of the University of Helsinki in Finland decided to build a UNIX-like operating system for the PC. What started as a simple task-switching example, with two processes that printed AAAA... and BBBB... on a dumb terminal, has grown into a full-fledged multitasking and multiuser operating system that rivals commercially available UNIX systems for Intel 80×86 systems. Many programmers around the world contributed code and collaborated to bring Linux to its current state. With the release of Version 1.0 in March 1994, Linux became an operating system of choice for UNIX enthusiasts, as well as for people who are looking for a low-cost UNIX platform for a specific use, such as developing software or running an Internet host.

After you overcome your initial fear of the unknown and install Linux, you will see how you can use Linux to turn your PC into a UNIX workstation. The best part is you can get Linux free — just download it from one of several Internet sites. The best way for beginners and experts alike to get started, though, is to buy a book (such as this one) that comes with a Linux CD-ROM. This complete guide to Linux starts with installation and moves on to specific tasks (such as developing software or connecting to the Internet) that you may want to perform with your Linux PC.

Note

Installation can be one of the tricky steps in Linux, especially if you have a no-name IBM-compatible PC. You need some specific information about hardware, such as the type of disk controller, video card, and CD-ROM drive. Linux controls the hardware through drivers, so you need to make sure the current release of Linux includes drivers for your hardware. Because Linux is free, you cannot demand — or expect — support for some specific hardware. Linux is, however, continually growing through collaboration among programmers throughout the world. If your hardware is popular enough, a good chance exists that someone has developed a driver for it. In any case, the version of Red Hat Linux on the companion CD-ROM already supports such a wide variety of hardware that all your PC's peripherals probably are supported.

To get you started on your Linux experience, this chapter shows you how to install Linux from the companion CD-ROM. The chapter starts with an overview of the entire installation process; then it guides you step by step through the installation process.

Cross-Reference

If you have installed Linux already, Chapter 2 shows you how to configure and upgrade Linux to take advantage of fixes or enhancements for the Linux operating system.

Understanding the Linux Installation Process

Before starting a big job, I always find it helpful to visualize the entire sequence of tasks I must perform. The process is similar to studying a map before you drive to a place where you have never been. Linux installation can be a big job, especially if you run into snags. This section shows you the road map for the installation process. After reading this section, you should be mentally prepared to install Linux.

The exact steps for installing Linux may depend on the Linux *distribution* — the exact packaging of the operating system — you are using. This book shows you the installation steps for the companion Red Hat CD-ROM. Here are the general steps for installing Red Hat Linux:

1. Gather information about your PC's hardware before you install Linux. Linux accesses and uses various PC peripherals through software components called *drivers*. You have to make sure the version of Linux you are about to install has the necessary drivers for your system's hardware configuration. Conversely, if you do not have a system yet, look at the list of hardware supported by Linux and make sure you buy a PC with components that Linux supports.

2. You may have to perform a process known as *partitioning* to allocate parts of your hard disk for use by Linux. If you are lucky enough to have a spare hard disk, you may decide to keep MS-DOS and Windows on the first hard disk and install Linux on the second hard disk. With a spare

second disk you needn't worry about partitioning under DOS or Windows. If you have only one hard disk, however, you must partition that disk into several parts. Use a part for DOS and Windows, and leave the rest for Linux.

3. Under DOS or Windows, create a Linux boot disk (or just a boot disk). The *boot disk* is used to boot your PC and start an initial version of the Linux operating system. If you boot your PC under MS-DOS (it has to be MS-DOS only; not an MS-DOS window in Windows 95), you can skip this step — instead, you can boot Linux directly from the CD-ROM.

4. Boot your PC with the Linux boot disk (or start MS-DOS and run a command from the CD-ROM). This procedure automatically runs the Red Hat Linux installation program. From this point on, you will respond to a number of dialog boxes as the Red Hat installation program takes you through the steps.

5. Respond to a dialog box that asks you if you have a color monitor. From subsequent dialog boxes, you select the keyboard type and indicate where Red Hat Linux is located (in the CD-ROM drive).

6. Prepare the hard disk partitions where you plan to install Linux. If you have created space for Linux by reducing the size of an existing DOS partition, now you have to create the partitions for Linux. Typically, you need at least two partitions: one for the Linux files and the other for use as the *swap partition*, a form of virtual memory. To perform this step, the installation program gives you the option of using the Linux fdisk command or Red Hat's new disk management utility called *Disk Druid*.

7. Format the hard disk partitions, indicate which partition is the swap partition, and specify the partition where to install Linux (this is called the *root partition*). You also get a chance to mount other disk partitions. Mounting a partition associates a physical disk partition with a directory in the Linux file system.

8. Select various software components to install. Each component represents a part of Linux — from the base operating system to components such as the emacs editor, programming tools, the Perl scripting language, and the X Window System (a graphical windowing system). You simply select the components you need and let the Red Hat installation program do its job.

9. If you installed the X Window System, the installation program configures the mouse and then runs the Xconfigurator program that creates a configuration file (/etc/X11/XF86Config) used by the X Window System. In response to dialog boxes presented by the Xconfigurator program, you provide information about your video card and monitor.

10. If you installed the networking software, the installation program enables you to configure the network. You specify a number of parameters including an IP address, host name, and domain name.

11. Specify the local time zone.

12. Configure any printers you have. You can configure a printer connected directly to the PC or a remote printer on the network. Red Hat even enables you to configure a printer connected to a PC running Windows 95 or Windows NT.

13. Select a root password. The root user is the *super user*—a user who can do anything—in Linux.

14. Install the Linux Loader (LILO) program on your hard disk so you can boot Linux when you power up your PC after shutting it down.

15. If you find that Linux does not work properly with one or more of your system components (such as the CD-ROM drive or sound card), you may have to reconfigure the Linux operating system to add support for those system components.

The following sections guide you through the basic installation steps and the initial booting of Linux.

Note

Your PC must have a CD-ROM drive—one supported by Linux—to install Linux from this book's companion CD-ROM. If your PC does not have a CD-ROM drive, but your PC is on a network, you may use another PC's CD-ROM drive and install Linux over the network using NFS or FTP.

Preparing Your PC for Linux Installation

Before you install Linux, you should prepare your PC for the installation. You can be in either of two situations:

- You already have a PC that runs one of the popular PC operating systems, such as MS-DOS, Microsoft Windows 3.1, Windows 95, Windows NT, or OS/2.

- You are about to buy a PC and you plan to run Linux on that PC at least some of the time.

If you are about to purchase a PC, you are lucky, because you can get a PC configured with peripherals that Linux supports. To pick a Linux-compatible configuration, all you must do is consult the current list of hardware Linux supports and then select a PC that includes only supported hardware components. You may have to ask the vendor explicitly for detailed information about peripherals such as the video card, CD-ROM drive, and networking card to ensure you can use the peripherals under Linux. Selecting a PC with Linux-supported hardware greatly minimizes the potential for problems installing Linux. The next few sections list hardware Linux supports.

You can also buy a PC with Linux already installed. You'll find advertisements for such Linux workstations in the *Linux Journal* (see Appendix C).

If you want to install Linux on an existing PC, verify the latest Linux distribution supports all the hardware on your PC. In other words, you have to take an inventory of your PC's hardware components and determine whether Linux currently supports any of them.

Taking stock of your PC's components

Like many other operating systems, Linux supports various types of hardware through device drivers. For each type of peripheral device, such as a networking card or a CD-ROM drive, Linux needs a driver. In fact, each kind of peripheral needs a separate driver. Because Linux is available free (or relatively inexpensively) and because many programmers scattered throughout the world cooperate to develop Linux, you cannot demand support for a specific kind of hardware. Your best bet is to hope someone who can write a Linux driver has the same hardware you do. In all likelihood, this person will write a driver, which eventually will find its way into a version of Linux; then you can use that hardware under Linux.

Check the list of hardware the version of Linux on the companion CD-ROM supports (I summarize this list in the next few sections). You can install and run Linux even if no Linux drivers are available for certain peripherals. At minimum, however, to install Linux from the companion CD-ROM, you must have a Linux-compatible processor, bus type, hard disk, keyboard, and CD-ROM drive. If you want to run the X Window System, you also must ensure that XFree86 (the *X* server for Linux) supports the mouse, the video card, and the monitor. (Chapter 4 tells you all about *X*.)

The following sections provide an overview of the hardware the version of Linux on the companion CD-ROM supports.

Cross-Reference

Chapters 9 through 17 cover all PC hardware in detail. Turn to those chapters for more information on whether Linux supports your system's unique hardware configuration. In Chapters 9 through 17, you also can find information on how to get the most from your PC's hardware under Linux.

Processor

The *processor* is the central processing unit (CPU) — the integrated circuit chip that performs all the processing in the PC. At minimum, you need an Intel 80386 processor to run Linux. Any Intel 80386-, 80486-, and Pentium-compatible processor can run the Linux operating system. Among the compatibles, Linux can run on AMD K5, K6, and Cyrix and IBM processors.

Note

You cannot run Linux on an 80286 PC; the 80286 is not a 32-bit processor.

Bus

The *bus* is the standard electrical connection between the processor and its peripherals. Several types of PC buses exist. The most popular bus is the Industry Standard Architecture (ISA) bus, formerly called the *AT bus* because IBM introduced it in the IBM PC-AT computer in 1984. Other buses include Extended Industry Standard Architecture (EISA); VESA Local Bus (VLB); Micro Channel Architecture (MCA); and, most recently, Peripheral Component Interconnect (PCI).

Note

Linux currently supports all common PC buses. Support for the MCA bus (used in IBM PS/2 computers) first appeared in Linux kernel Version 2.0.7 (Chapter 2 explains the kernel version numbers).

Memory

Commonly referred to as *random access memory* (RAM), memory is not a factor in compatibility. You need at least 8MB of RAM to get good performance, however. Although you may be able to install and run Linux on a PC that has 4MB RAM, you cannot run the X Window System on that PC. The X Window System manages the graphical interface through an *X server*, which is a large program that needs a great deal of memory to run efficiently.

Secret

If you are buying a new PC, you should get at least 16MB of RAM. If you have an old PC with less than 8MB of RAM, you may want to add more memory to bring the total up to 16MB. The more physical memory a system has, the more efficiently it runs multiple programs because the programs can all fit in memory. Although Linux can use a part of the hard disk as virtual memory, such disk-based memory is much slower than physical memory. The amount of physical memory required depends on the size of the Linux operating system and any other software you have to run all the time, such as the *X* Window System. Although Linux alone would run on 4MB of memory, you need at least 8MB to run *X*. Add to this any applications (such as editor or compiler) that you might run and you'll soon see why you need at least 16MB of RAM for adequate performance.

Video card and monitor

Most PCs have what is known as *Super VGA* (Video Graphics Array) video cards. Linux works fine with all video cards in text mode. But when it comes to XFree86 — the Linux version of the X Window System — the story is quite different. If XFree86 does not support your video card explicitly, you have to work hard to get XFree86 configured for your video card.

The kind of monitor you use is not particularly critical, but it must be capable of displaying at the screen resolutions the video card uses, which are expressed in terms of the number of picture elements, or *pixels*, horizontally and vertically (such as 1024×768).

Generally, XFree86's support for a video card depends on the *video chipset* — the integrated circuit that controls the monitor and causes the monitor to display output. A video-card manufacturer, however, may use a video chipset in a nonstandard manner. In such a case, you need a special version of XFree86 to support that video card. To help you select a video card, following is a list of video cards XFree86 Version 3.3.1 (the version included on the companion CD-ROM) supports:

- ATI Mach8, ATI Mach32, and ATI Mach64
- ATI VGA Wonder series
- Compaq AVGA
- DEC 21030
- Diamond Viper VLB and Viper PCI
- Enhanced Graphics Adapter (EGA)
- Genoa GVGA

- Hercules monochrome

- Hyundai HGC-1280 monochrome

- IBM 8514/A, XGA, and XGA-II

- Matrox MGA2064W (Millennium) and Matrox MGA1064SG (Mystique)

- Number Nine Imagine I128

- NVidia NV1

- Orchid P9000

- Sigma LaserView PLUS monochrome

- Video 7 (also known as Headland Technologies HT216-32)

- Video cards based on the Advance Logic AL2101, 2228, 2301, 2302, 2308, and 2401 chipsets

- Video cards based on Alliance AP6422 and AT24 chipsets

- Video cards based on the ARK Logic ARK1000PV, ARK1000VL, ARK2000PV, and ARK2000MT chipsets

- Video cards based on the Chips & Technologies 64200, 64300, 65520, 65525, 65530, 65535, 65540, 65545, 65546, 65548, 65550, and 65554 chipsets

- Video cards based on the Cirrus Logic CLGD5420, 542x, 5430, 5434, 5436, 544x, 546x, 5480, 62x5, 6420, 6440, 754x, and 7555 chipsets (x is any digit)

- Video cards based on the IIT AGX-010, 014, 015, and 016 chipsets

- Video cards based on the MX68000 and MX68010 chipsets

- Video cards based on the NCR 77C22, 77C22E, and 77C22E+ chipsets

- Video cards based on the OAK OTI-067, OTI-077, and OTI-087 chipsets

- Video cards based on the RealTek RTG3106 chipset

- Video cards based on the S3 732 (Trio32), 764 (Trio64), Trio64V+, 801, 805, 864, 866, 868, 86C325 (ViRGE), 86C375 (ViRGE/DX), 86C385 (ViRGE/GX), 86C988 (ViRGE/VX), 911, 924, 928, 964, and 968 chipsets (see Chapter 4 for a list of supported S3 cards)

- Video cards based on the SGS-Thomson STG2000 chipset

- Video cards based on the SiS 86c201, 86c202, and 86c205 chipsets

- Video cards based on the Weitek P9000 chipset

- Video cards based on the Trident 8800CS, 8200LX, 8900x, 9000, 9000i, 9100B, 9200CXr, 9320LCD, 9400CXi, 9420, 9420DGi, 9430DGi, 9440, 96xx, and Cyber938x chipsets (x represents any digit)

- Video cards based on the Tseng ET3000, ET4000, ET4000AX, ET6000, W32, W32i, and W32p chipsets

- Video cards based on the Western Digital WD90C00, WD90C10, WD90C11, WD90C24, WD90C31 and WD90C33 chipsets

- Video Graphics Array (VGA)
- Western Digital Paradise PVGA1

For the basic Linux installation, you needn't worry about the video card. Detailed information about the video card becomes important when you want to configure XFree86.

Cross-Reference

Although you go through an *X* configuration step during Red Hat Linux installation, you can find further details on configuring XFree86 in Chapter 4.

Hard drive

Linux supports any hard drive your PC's Basic Input and Output System (BIOS) supports. In many older 386 and 486 PCs, you had to use a separate driver to access large hard drives — the system BIOS could not handle these drives. You can't install Linux on such systems. In short, Linux supports your hard drive only if the system BIOS supports the hard drive without any additional drivers with one significant restriction. To be able to boot Linux from a large hard drive (that's any drive with more than 1,024 cylinders), the Linux Loader (LILO), the Linux kernel, and the LILO configuration files must be located in the first 1,024 cylinders of the drive. This is because the Linux Loader uses BIOS to load the kernel and the BIOS cannot access cylinders beyond the first 1,024.

For hard drives connected to your PC through a SCSI controller card, Linux must have a driver that enables the SCSI controller to access and use the hard drive. A summary of supported SCSI controllers appears in the "SCSI Controllers" section of this chapter.

Tip

The only remaining decision about the hard drive is its capacity. If you have an old PC, you may have a relatively low-capacity hard drive — perhaps as low as 500MB. Although you can install Linux and X Window System within 400MB, doing so does not leave much room for Windows 95, should you want to keep it. Therefore, if your old PC has an IDE interface and one small hard disk (500MB or smaller), you may want to add a second hard drive because most IDE controllers can support two hard drives. If you have a SCSI card, you can connect up to seven SCSI devices to it.

If you are buying a new PC, remember a complete Linux installation (with the all the Red Hat packages) takes nearly 400MB of disk space. On top of that, you need some disk space for your work. Luckily, most new PCs nowadays come with disk sizes ranging anywhere from 1.6GB to 6GB. Any of these disk sizes is large enough, so you can keep Windows on one of the partitions and have the option of booting either Windows or Linux.

Tip

Consider buying a second hard drive for Linux. A second drive makes the installation process considerably less risky, because you needn't partition the drive on which Windows 95 may be installed.

The PC BIOS

All IBM-compatible PCs come with a BIOS built into read-only memory (ROM). The BIOS contains a set of input/output (I/O) functions for accessing the PC's peripheral devices, such as the keyboard, display, printer, serial port, and floppy disk or hard drive.

The BIOS is essentially software stored on ROM, and as such, PC vendors revise and update the BIOS just like any software. Typically, the BIOS is revised to handle new devices, such as new hard drives with much larger capacity than originally envisioned, or even new bus types, such as PCI. BIOS revisions may also improve performance by doing various tasks more efficiently.

Because the BIOS is a crucial element in getting Linux to work with a PC's peripherals, you might consider a BIOS upgrade to get Linux going on an older 386 or 486 PC. The upgrade process involves replacing a pair of chips with new ones — you must contact your PC's manufacturer to get new revisions of the BIOS chips compatible with your PC.

Another reason to upgrade your PC's BIOS (and probably the CMOS Real-Time Clock as well) is the Year 2000 problem where the PC fails to maintain the correct year once 2000 rolls in.

Floppy disk drive

As they do for the hard drive, Linux drivers use the PC BIOS to access the floppy disk drive. Therefore, your floppy disk drive is compatible with Linux. You may, though, have to boot Linux from a floppy disk during the installation. For this purpose, you need a high-density 5.25" (1.2MB-capacity) or 3.5" (1.44MB-capacity) floppy disk drive. You can avoid booting from a floppy provided you can boot your PC under MS-DOS (not an MS-DOS window under Windows 95) and you can access the CD-ROM from the DOS command prompt.

Keyboard and mouse

Linux supports any keyboard that already works with your PC, but the mouse needs explicit support in Linux. You need a mouse if you want to configure and run XFree86, the X Window System for Linux.

Linux supports the following popular mice:

- Microsoft serial mouse
- Mouse Systems serial mouse
- Logitech Mouseman serial mouse
- Logitech serial mouse
- Logitech bus mouse
- PS/2 (auxiliary device) mouse
- Microsoft bus mouse
- ATI XL Inport bus mouse
- QuickPort (C&T 82C710) mouse (used on TI Travelmate and Toshiba laptop PCs)

SCSI controller

The Small Computer System Interface, commonly called *SCSI* (and pronounced *scuzzy*), is a standard way of connecting many types of peripheral devices to a computer. SCSI is in many kinds of computers — from high-end UNIX workstations to PCs. To use a SCSI device on your PC, you need a SCSI controller card that plugs into one of the connector slots on your PC's bus.

Typically, you connect hard drives and CD-ROM drives through a *SCSI controller.* A single controller enables you to connect up to six SCSI devices to your PC. If you want to access and use a SCSI device under Linux, you have to make sure Linux supports your SCSI controller card.

The Linux release on the companion CD-ROM already supports the following popular SCSI controllers:

- Acculogic ISApport based on the NCR 53c406a chipset
- Adaptec AHA-1510 and AHA-152x (based on AIC-6260 or AIC-6360 chips; x is any digit) controllers for the ISA bus
- Adaptec AHA-154x (x is any digit) controllers for the ISA bus
- Adaptec AHA-174x (x is any digit) controllers for the EISA (Extended Industry Standard Architecture) bus
- Adaptec AHA-274x controller for the EISA bus and AHA-284x controller for the VLB (VESA Local Bus); both cards use AIC-7770 chips
- Adaptec AHA 2920 controller
- Adaptec AHA-2940 and AHA-3940 controllers for the PCI bus; these cards use the AIC-7870 chip
- Adaptec AVA-1505 and AVA-1515 controllers for the ISA bus (supported by the Adaptec 152x driver in Linux)
- Always IN2000
- AMI Fast Disk VLB/EISA (supported by the BusLogic driver in Linux)
- BusLogic SCSI controllers for ISA, EISA, VLB, and PCI (all models)
- DPT PM2001 and PM2012A controllers
- DPT Smartcache controllers for ISA, EISA, and PCI buses, including models PM2011, PM2021, PM2041, PM3021, PM2012B, PM2022, PM2122, PM2322, PM2042, PM3122, PM3222, PM3332, PM2024, PM2124, PM2044, PM2144, PM3224, and PM3334
- DTC 329x controller for the EISA bus (supported by the Adaptec 154x driver in Linux)
- Future Domain TMC-16x0 and TMC-3260 (PCI) SCSI controllers
- Future Domain TMC-8xx and TMC-950
- ICP-Vortex PCI-SCSI Disk Array Controllers including models GDT6111RP, GDT6121RP, GDT6117RP, GDT6127RP, GDT6511RP, GDT6521RP, GDT6517RP, GDT6527RP, GDT6537RP, and GDT6557RP

- ICP-Vortex EISA-SCSI Controllers including models GDT3000B, GDT3000A, GDT3010A, GDT3020A and GDT3050A

- Media Vision Pro Audio Spectrum 16 SCSI controller for ISA bus

- Media Vision Premium 3D SCSI based on the NCR 53c406a chipset

- NCR 5380 generic SCSI cards

- Qlogic FAS408 controller

- Quantum ISA-200S and ISA-200MG

- SCSI controllers based on the NCR 53c7x0 and 53c8x0 (for PCI bus) chipsets

- Seagate ST-01 and ST-02 controllers for ISA bus

- Sound Blaster 16 SCSI controller for ISA bus (supported by the Adaptec 152x driver in Linux)

- Tekram DC-390, DC-390W/U/F

- Trantor T128, T128F, and T228 controllers for ISA bus

- Trantor T130B based on the NCR 53c400 chipset (supported by the NCR 5380 driver)

- UltraStor 14F (for ISA bus), UltraStor 24F (for EISA bus), and UltraStor 34F (for VLB bus)

- Western Digital WD7000 SCSI controllers

Tip

This list keeps growing as Linux developers add support for new SCSI controllers. For a more complete list, check the online documentation included on the CD-ROM. The "Looking up the online documentation" section at the end of this chapter shows you how to find and use the online documentation.

CD-ROM drive

CD-ROM (Compact Disc Read-Only Memory) drives are popular because each CD-ROM can hold up to 650MB of data. This is a relatively large amount of storage compared to a floppy disk. CD-ROMs are reliable and inexpensive to manufacture. Vendors can use a CD-ROM to distribute a large amount of information at a reasonable cost.

This book provides Linux on a CD-ROM, so you need a CD-ROM drive to install the software. Most new PCs come with a CD-ROM drive. If the basic configuration does not include a CD-ROM drive, you can add one at a fraction of the cost of your PC — usually around a hundred U.S. dollars. If you have an older PC that doesn't have a CD-ROM drive, you need to buy one to install Linux from this book's companion CD-ROM.

CD-ROM drives became popular on PCs over the past few years as users went for the multimedia experience. As you may know, in the context of the PC, *multimedia* refers to the use of multiple media—sound, images, animation, and video—in software applications. The sound card and CD-ROM drive were the two common elements of all multimedia software.

The combination of sound cards and CD-ROM drives has been so popular that many sound cards (such as Creative Labs' Sound Blaster Pro) were sold with a CD-ROM drive. You had to connect the CD-ROM drive with a cable to the sound card, which included the appropriate hardware connector. Linux supports CD-ROM drives (such as the Sound Blaster Pro CD) that connect to a sound card.

Nowadays, most CD-ROM drives use the Enhanced Integrated Drive Electronics (EIDE) interface that also connects hard disk drives to the PC. Linux supports all EIDE CD-ROM drives.

Some CD-ROM drives are SCSI devices that connect to a SCSI controller card. Linux supports a SCSI CD-ROM drive as long as it has a driver for the SCSI controller.

Following are some of the common CD-ROM drives Linux supports:

- Any EIDE CD-ROM drive (also referred to as AT Attachment Packet Interface, or ATAPI drives)
- Any SCSI CD-ROM drive that can transfer data in blocks of 512 or 2,048 bytes (this includes most of the CD-ROM drives on the market)
- Aztech CDA268, Orchid CDS-3110, and Okano/Wearnes CDD-110, Conrad TXC, CyCDROM CR520ie, CyCDROM CR540ie, CyCDROM CR940ie
- Creative Labs CD-200(F)
- Funai E2550UA/MK4015
- GoldStar R420
- IBM External ISA CD-ROM drive
- Lasermate CR328A
- LMS Philips CM 206
- Longshine LCS-7260
- Matsushita/Kotobuki/Panasonic CD-ROM drive models CR-521, CR-522, CR-523, CR-562, and CR-563 (the CD-ROM drives bundled with the Sound Blaster Pro sound card)
- MicroSolutions Backpack parallel port drive
- Mitsumi CD-ROM drive (CR DC LU05S, FX001D/F)
- Optics Storage Dolphin 8000AT
- Sanyo H94A
- Sony CDU31A, CDU33A, CDU-510, CDU-515, CDU-531, and CDU-535 drives
- Teac CD-55A SuperQuad

Tip

The Sound Blaster 16 sound card features one of two CD-ROM interfaces: a proprietary interface and a SCSI interface. Linux supports both interfaces, but you need to know which interface your Sound Blaster 16 board provides. You should find this information in the manual that accompanies the Sound Blaster 16 board.

Note, you can connect an ATAPI CD-ROM drive to an IDE controller and treat it as a second hard drive. If you want a simple way to attach a CD-ROM drive to your PC and you don't need an additional hard drive, you might consider installing an ATAPI CD-ROM drive as a slave of the boot hard drive.

Sound card

On PCs, sound cards and CD-ROM drives go hand in hand because most CD-ROM-based multimedia programs include sound effects you can enjoy only if you have a sound card. Under Linux, you also can play sound on the sound card. If you have a sound card, you can play audio CDs or play Doom (a popular game) with full sound effects.

The version of Linux on the companion CD-ROM supports the following sound cards:

- 6850 UART (Universal Asynchronous Receiver Transmitter) MIDI (Musical Instrument Digital Interface)
- Adlib (OPL2) sound card
- ATI Stereo F/X (Sound Blaster-compatible)
- Audio Excell DSP16
- Aztech Sound Galaxy NX Pro
- Crystal CS4232 (PnP — Plug and Play) based cards
- ECHO-PSS (Orchid SW32 and Cardinal DSP16)
- Ensoniq SoundScape (but you must start DOS to initialize card)
- Gravis Ultrasound, Ultrasound MAX, and Ultrasound 16-bit sampling daughterboard
- Logitech SoundMan 16 (PAS-16 compatible), SoundMan Games, and SoundMan Wave (Jazz16/OPL4)
- MediaTriX AudioTriX Pro
- Media Vision Premium 3D Jazz16 (Sound Blaster Pro-compatible), Pro Audio Spectrum 16 (PAS-16), and Pro Sonic 16 Jazz
- Microsoft Sound System (AD1848)
- MPU-401 MIDI
- OAK OTI-601D cards (Mozart)
- OPTi 82C928/82C929 cards (MAD16/MAD16 Pro/ISP16/Mozart)

- Sound Blaster, Sound Blaster 16, and Sound Blaster Pro
- Sound Galaxy NX Pro
- ThunderBoard (Sound Blaster-compatible)
- Turtle Beach Wavefront cards (Maui, Tropez)
- WaveBlaster and other Sound Blaster 16 daughterboards
- Cards based on the ESS Technologies AudioDrive chips such as 688, 1688, and 1868

Network adapter

A network adapter is necessary only if you are going to connect your Linux PC to an Ethernet network. Linux supports a variety of Ethernet network adapters. Arcnet and IBM's Token Ring network are also supported.

Cross-Reference

See Chapter 16 for more information on Linux's support for token ring and other network adapters.

Following is a list of Ethernet cards Linux supports:

- 3Com 3C503, 3C505, 3C507, 3C509, 3C509B (ISA bus), and 3C579 (for EISA bus)
- 3Com Etherlink III Vortex Ethercards (3C590, 3C592, 3C595, 3C597) for PCI bus, 3Com Etherlink XL Boomerang Ethercards (3C900, 3C905) for PCI bus and 3Com Fast EtherLink Ethercard (3C515) for ISA bus
- Ethernet cards based on AMD LANCE (79C960) chip for ISA and PCI
- Accton parallel port Ethernet adapter
- Allied Telesis AT1500, AT1700, and LA100PCI-T
- Ansel Communications AC3200 EISA
- Apricot Xen-II
- AT&T GIS WaveLAN
- AT-Lan-Tec and RealTek parallel-port Ethernet adapter
- Cabletron E21xx (x is any digit)
- Cogent EM110
- D-Link DE600 and DE620 parallel-port Ethernet adapter
- Danpex EN-9400
- Digital Equipment Corporation (DEC) DEPCA, EtherWORKS, EtherWORKS 3, DE425 (EISA), DE434 (PCI), DE435 (PCI), DE450, DE500, DE450-XA, DE500-XA, and DEC QSilver
- Fujitsu FMV-181, FMV-182, FMV-183, FMV-184

- Hewlett-Packard HP J2405A, PCLAN (27245 and 27*xxx* series), PCLAN PLUS (27247B and 27252A), and 10/100VG PCLAN (J2577, J2573, 27248B, J2585) (ISA, EISA, and PCI)

- ICL EtherTeam 16i / 32 (EISA)

- Intel EtherExpress and EtherExpress Pro

- KTI ET16/P-D2, ET16/P-DC ISA

- New Media Ethernet

- Novell Ethernet NE1000, NE1500, NE2000, and NE2100 (all clones may not work)

- PureData PDUC8028 and PDI8023

- Racal-Interlan NI5210 (based on the i82586 Ethernet chip), NI6510 (uses the AMD 7990 LANCE chip and does not work with more than 16MB of memory)

- SEEQ 8005

- Schneider & Koch G16

- SMC (Western Digital) WD8003, WD8013, SMC Elite, SMC Elite Plus, SMC Elite 16 Ultra, SMC EtherEZ (ISA), SMC 9000 Series, SMC PCI EtherPower 10/100

- Zenith Z-Note and IBM ThinkPad 300 built-in Ethernet adapter

- Znyx 312 Etherarray

Tip

If you plan to use Linux on a stand-alone PC at home, you can use Serial Li Internet Protocol (SLIP) or Point-to-Point Protocol (PPP) to connect to the Internet over a dial-up connection through an Internet service provider (IS See Chapter 18 for details.

Making a hardware checklist

Now that you have seen a summary of various hardware peripherals Linux supports, you should have a rough idea of whether you have the right PC hardware to use Linux. If you are buying a new PC to run Linux, the hardware list should help you decide the hardware configuration of the new PC.

To summarize, go through the following checklist to see whether you are ready to install Linux from this book's companion CD-ROM:

- Does your PC have an 80386 or better processor, with the ISA, EISA, VLB, MCA, or PCI bus; at least 8MB of RAM; a high-density floppy disk drive; and a large hard drive (at least 500MB)? Remember, if you plan to run both Windows 95 and Linux on your PC, you need at least 1GB of disk space.

- Does your PC have a CD-ROM drive that Linux supports? (You need a CD-ROM drive to install Linux from this book's companion CD-ROM.)

Tip

If you don't know what kind of CD-ROM drive you have, you should watch the system boot up in DOS and watch the DOS driver load—the driver usually displays a message with the brand of the CD-ROM drive.

- Can you get a second hard drive? (If so, you can install Linux on that hard drive. Installing Linux on a second drive prevents you from messing up your first hard drive, which usually has MS-DOS or Windows loaded on it.)

- If you have a SCSI controller with any SCSI devices you want to use under Linux, is the SCSI controller supported by Linux?

- Is your video card supported by Linux? (If not, you won't be able to set up and run the X Window System.)

- Is your mouse supported by Linux? (If not, you won't be able to set up and run the X Window System.)

As the comments after the questions indicate, you do not necessarily have to answer each question Yes. You must answer the first two items Yes, however, because without that basic hardware configuration, Linux cannot run on your system.

Note

If you plan to install Linux on a second hard disk, you needn't go through the process of partitioning (dividing) your hard disk under MS-DOS. Skip the next few sections and proceed to create the Linux boot disk (see the section "Creating the boot disk"). Then you can boot Linux from the boot disk and partition the second hard drive for use under Linux.

Partitioning your hard drive under MS-DOS or Windows

If your PC has a single hard disk drive, chances are you have Microsoft Windows 95 (or Windows 3.1) installed on that drive. If your hard drive is at least 1GB, I recommend you keep Windows installed on your system even if you want to work mostly in Linux. After all, you have to perform some of the Linux installation steps under MS-DOS or Windows. Also, you can access the Windows files from Linux. You get the best of both worlds if you keep MS-DOS and Windows around when you install Linux.

Tip

If your new PC has one large hard disk (typically larger than 2GB) but there are two drives—C and D—this means the disk already has two partitions. In this case, you may simply want to use the extended partition for Linux.

Typically, your PC hard disk is set up as a single large drive, designated by the drive letter *C*. Unless you can scrounge up a second hard disk for your PC or if you already have a second disk you can spare, your first task is to divide your one and only hard disk to make room for Linux.

Working in MS-DOS or Windows before you install Linux

If you are a MS-DOS or Windows beginner, you may find it difficult to follow some of the Linux installation steps you must perform under MS-DOS. Following are some of the terms and concepts you should know to perform the necessary installation steps:

■ *Boot floppy drive.* The first floppy drive (A) is the boot floppy drive. If you put a floppy disk in the A drive and turn on the power, your PC automatically tries to start from the floppy. (Many new PCs enable you to set the boot device; however, by default, nearly all PCs come configured with the first floppy drive as the boot device.) This feature is built into the computer and does not depend on what operating system is installed on your system's hard disk. In most new systems, the A drive is a 3.5-inch floppy drive. Many older systems, however, use a 5.25-inch floppy drive as the A drive. To install Linux, you need a high-density boot floppy drive.

■ *Partitions.* A physical hard drive can be divided into several parts, each of which can be treated as a separate logical hard drive. Although most new PCs use the entire hard disk as a single drive, you can partition the disk into up to four sections, called the *four primary partitions*. To install Linux on your hard disk, you have to create at least two partitions for Linux—one partition for the Linux file system and the other for *swap space* (virtual memory in which the contents of the physical memory can be stored temporarily). If you want to keep Windows in one partition and also install Linux, you need three partitions.

■ *Repartitioning a hard disk.* If your hard disk has only one partition, the process of creating more partitions is referred to as *repartitioning*. To repartition a disk, you

have to back up its contents. Then use the MS-DOS FDISK command to delete the old partition and create several new ones, and finally restore the old contents to one of the partitions. The Red Hat Linux distribution (on this book's CD-ROM) includes an MS-DOS program called *FIPS*, which you can use to repartition a hard disk without destroying the contents of the old partition. This utility is not guaranteed to work perfectly, however, so you still need to back up your important files before attempting to repartition the hard disk with FIPS.

■ *Formatting a disk.* The MS-DOS FDISK program only defines a section of the physical disk to be used by an operating system such as MS-DOS. You still must prepare that section of disk before MS-DOS can use it to store files and directories. *Formatting* is the process of making a partition ready for a file system.

■ *Directories and files.* In MS-DOS, a drive is divided into directories. Each directory, in turn, can contain other directories and files. The file is where the actual information is stored. The directories help you organize your documents and programs. All files for the Windows operating system, for example, usually are in the C:\WINDOWS directory. The directory C:\WINDOWS\SYSTEM contains some special files Windows needs. As you see, the backslash character is used as a separator between names of directories. The directory C:\ is known as the root directory; WINDOWS is a subdirectory of the root directory, and SYSTEM is a subdirectory of WINDOWS. Therefore, C:\WINDOWS\SYSTEM is two levels down from the root directory.

- *Filenames.* An MS-DOS filename consists of a name of 1 to 8 characters, followed by a period and then an extension that can have 0 to 3 characters. README.TXT is an MS-DOS filename with the name README and the extension TXT. Executable programs have the COM or EXE extension, whereas DOC typically represents a document that can be opened by a word processing program.

- *MS-DOS commands.* You use MS-DOS through commands you enter at a prompt.

The MS-DOS command interpreter displays a prompt (usually the current drive and directory name, followed by a greater than sign, such as C:\>). MS-DOS commands often have options that start with a slash. You can use the /S option with the FORMAT command, for example, to format and copy the system files to a disk. Note, you can use the MS-DOS commands even under Windows 95 in an MS-DOS window.

Steps to repartition hard disk

In the following sections, I assume your PC has a single hard disk on which MS-DOS is already installed (Windows may be installed as well, but this doesn't matter in the task you are about to perform). To repartition the disk, you must perform the following tasks:

1. Back up the contents of your hard disk.

   If you bought a new PC, you are lucky, because the hard disk should not have much data to back up.

2. Create an MS-DOS boot disk (in Windows 95, create a startup disk by using the Add/Remove Programs option in the Control Panel).

   You use this disk to start your PC and partition the hard disk.

3. Run FDISK from the disk and create the new partitions.

4. Format the MS-DOS partition and restore the files from the backup you created in Step 1.

The next four sections guide you through these steps.

Partitioning your hard disk under Windows 95

If your PC runs Windows 95, you still must follow the same steps to partition the hard disk as you would have under MS-DOS. The only difference is you first have to create a startup disk by using the Add/Remove Programs option in the Control Panel and then boot the PC with that startup disk. After this, you can run the FDISK program to create the new partitions.

Back up your hard disk

Backing up the hard disk takes a long time, but no safe way to repartition the hard disk exists without a backup. Red Hat Linux, however, comes with the FIPS utility program, which can partition a hard disk without destroying the data currently on the disk.

How you back up your hard disk depends on what you have on your hard disk. If you have a new PC, the hard disk probably contains Windows and any other software the vendor bundled with the system. If you have the original disks for Windows and the bundled software, you may decide to skip the backup and reinstall everything after you create the new partitions. If you have an old PC, you may decide to back up only the directories you cannot reinstall from original floppy disks or CD-ROM. If you have a word processing program, for example, you don't have to back up that program's directory, because you can always reinstall the program. All you need to backup are the directories that contain documents you had created with the word processing program.

To back up your hard disk, you can use the backup utility that comes with MS-DOS. In DOS Versions 5.0 and earlier, use the BACKUP utility to back up all or some of the directories of your hard disk. In DOS Versions 6.0 and later, use the MSBACKUP utility.

Create a bootable disk for MS-DOS

Usually, you turn on your PC's power and the PC automatically loads the operating system (MS-DOS or Windows 95, for example) from the first hard drive: the C drive. If you put a disk in the A drive and power up the PC, however, the PC loads the operating system from the disk. If the disk does not contain the operating system, you get this familiar message:

```
Non-System disk or disk error
Replace and strike any key when ready
```

This message tells you the PC tried to load, but could not find operating system files on the floppy disk. Usually, you remove the disk and press a key, and the PC boots from the hard drive.

To change the hard drive partitions, you actually want to boot the PC from the A drive. This way, you can be sure the hard drive is not in use when you change its partitions. To create a bootable disk, perform these steps:

1. Put a floppy disk in your A drive, and type the command **FORMAT A: /S**.

    MS-DOS prompts you with the following message:

```
Insert new diskette for drive A
and press ENTER when ready...
```

Caution

The contents of the disk are destroyed when you format the disk.

2. Press Enter, because you already have the floppy disk in the A drive.

   MS-DOS formats the disk and places the necessary operating-system files on the disk (that's what the /S option of the FORMAT command does). DOS also prompts you for a Volume label; you can press Enter in response. Finally, DOS asks whether you want to format another disk; press **N** to indicate you are done with formatting.

3. Copy other necessary files to the A drive.

   At minimum, you need to copy the FDISK.EXE program to the disk so you can use it to partition the hard disk and the FORMAT.COM program to format the new DOS partition. Use the following commands to copy the FDISK.EXE program to the disk in the A drive (text in parentheses is my comment):

```
C:
CD \WINDOWS\COMMAND  (DOS commands are in this directory)
COPY FDISK.EXE A:
COPY FORMAT.COM A:
```

Caution

You also may need other programs to restore the backup you created earlier. Those programs needn't be on the boot disk; just make sure you have a copy of them on disk somewhere.

4. Test the boot disk.

   Close all running programs, put the newly created boot disk in the A drive, and press Ctrl+Alt+Delete to reboot your PC. MS-DOS should start and you should see an A:\> prompt.

Repartition hard disk with FDISK

Now that you have successfully backed up your hard disk and prepared a bootable MS-DOS disk, you can repartition your hard disk. To begin this procedure, put the MS-DOS boot disk in drive A, and restart your PC (press Ctrl+Alt+Delete. Or, turn the power off and then on). When you see the A:\> prompt, type **FDISK** and press Enter. FDISK runs and displays a message about enabling support for large disks using a new file system called FAT32. Because FAT32 file system is not supported by many operating systems, including older versions of Windows 95, you should not enable this feature of FDISK. Press Enter to accept the default answer of No. Then, FDISK displays the screen shown in Figure 1-1.

```
                        MS-DOS Version 6
                      Fixed Disk Setup Program
                  (C)Copyright Microsoft Corp. 1983 - 1993

                           FDISK Options

        Current fixed disk drive: 1

        Choose one of the following:

        1. Create DOS partition or Logical DOS Drive
        2. Set active partition
        3. Delete partition or Logical DOS Drive
        4. Display partition information
        5. Change current fixed disk drive


        Enter choice: [1]




        Press Esc to exit FDISK
```

Figure 1-1: FDISK's opening screen

Caution

Back up your hard disk before you use FDISK to repartition it (refer to the previous section "Back up your hard disk"). When you alter the partitions, you cannot access the old data on the disk. You can run FDISK, view the disk partitions, and exit without damaging your hard disk, but enter the commands carefully — you don't want to wipe out your hard disk's contents accidentally.

Tip

FDISK is available in all versions of MS-DOS and in Windows 95. (In Windows 95, you can start your PC in MS-DOS mode and use the FDISK command to repartition the disk.) In this session with FDISK, you delete a partition and create a smaller DOS partition, leaving some disk space for the Linux partitions.

Use the following strategy to repartition your hard disk:

1. Select FDISK menu Option 4 to look at your hard disk's current partition information.

2. Select FDISK menu Option 3 to delete the DOS partition.

3. Select FDISK menu Option 1 to create a new, smaller DOS partition that leaves enough space for Linux (I discuss the size of partitions in the "Create New DOS Partition" section).

4. Select FDISK menu Option 2 and mark the newly created DOS partition active.

Later, you partition the rest of the disk under Linux as described in the section "Partitioning Your Hard Disk under Linux."

Check your hard disk's current partitioning information

Before you delete the partition, press **4** and then press Enter to view the current partition information. Figure 1-2 shows the FDISK screen for a typical disk that contains a single DOS partition for the entire disk.

```
                    Display Partition Information

Current fixed disk drive: 1

Partition  Status   Type   Volume Label  Mbytes  System   Usage
  C: 1        A     PRI DOS  LNBPC-C        325    FAT16    100%




    Total disk space is  325 Mbytes (1 Mbyte = 1048576 bytes)






Press Esc to continue
```

Figure 1-2: FDISK screen showing typical partition information

Disk 1 refers to the first physical hard disk on your system. The PRI DOS entry in the Type field indicates the partition is a primary DOS partition — the partition that contains the files needed to boot MS-DOS. The entry in the Partition field tells you this is the C drive in MS-DOS. You probably have the same situation.

Delete the primary DOS partition

Press Esc to return to the FDISK main menu (refer to Figure 1-1). To delete the primary DOS partition, press **3** and then press Enter. FDISK displays another menu, shown in Figure 1-3.

```
              Delete DOS Partition or Logical DOS Drive

   Current fixed disk drive: 1

   Choose one of the following:

   1.   Delete Primary DOS Partition
   2.   Delete Extended DOS Partition
   3.   Delete Logical DOS Drive(s) in the Extended DOS Partition
   4.   Delete Non-DOS Partition


   Enter choice: [ ]




   Press Esc to return to FDISK Options
```

Figure 1-3: FDISK screen showing the options for deleting a partition

You can delete several kinds of partitions. An extended partition, for example, is simply a partition that can be further subdivided into logical drives. Typically, however, when an entire disk is devoted to Windows, you have only a primary DOS partition to delete.

To delete the primary DOS partition, press **1** and then press Enter. FDISK displays the screen shown in Figure 1-4, requesting confirmation that you really want to delete the partition.

```
                          Delete Primary DOS Partition

        Current fixed disk drive: 1

        Partition   Status    Type     Volume Label   Mbytes    System    Usage
           C: 1        A     PRI DOS    LNBPC-C          325     FAT16     100%




        Total disk space is   325 Mbytes (1 Mbyte = 1048576 bytes)




        WARNING! Data in the deleted Primary DOS Partition will be lost.
        What primary partition do you want to delete..? [1]


        Press Esc to return to FDISK Options
```

Figure 1-4: The FDISK screen is requesting confirmation before deleting the primary DOS partition.

Press Enter. FDISK deletes the partition and returns to the main screen shown in Figure 1-1.

Create a new DOS partition

In this step, you create the primary DOS partition again, but this time, you make it smaller. At this point you must decide how much disk space you want to leave aside for MS-DOS (and Windows) and how much you want to devote to Linux. The final choice depends on the total capacity of your hard disk and your planned use of Linux.

The following table shows a rough calculation of how much disk space you need:

Item	Disk Space (MB)
Complete Linux installation from companion CD-ROM	400
Linux swap space (for use in virtual memory)	16
User space for Linux (so you can work in Linux)	150
Windows	500
Total	1,066

Tip

If your PC has more than 16MB memory, make the swap space the same size as the amount of memory. Otherwise, set aside at least 16MB of disk space for swap space.

If you have a 1.2GB hard disk, allocate 500MB to the primary DOS partition and leave the rest for Linux. Unfortunately, with today's disk-hungry applications, you may find 500MB is inadequate for all your Windows applications. I assume you want to use Linux in earnest, so I recommend setting aside enough disk space for Linux.

If you have a bigger capacity disk (many new systems come with 2 or 4GB disks), remember these minimums and proportionately increase the sizes of the DOS and Linux partitions.

If you have an old PC with a smaller capacity disk — say, 500MB — you should either devote the entire disk to Linux or get a second disk, so you can keep Windows and still run Linux.

To create the new primary DOS partition, press **1** at the FDISK main screen (refer to Figure 1-1) and then press Enter. FDISK displays the menu shown in Figure 1-5.

```
              Create DOS Partition or Logical DOS Drive

   Current fixed disk drive: 1

   Choose one of the following:

   1. Create Primary DOS Partition
   2. Create Extended DOS Partition
   3. Create Logical DOS Drive(s) in the Extended DOS Partition



   Enter choice: [1]




   Press Esc to return to FDISK Options
```

Figure 1-5: FDISK screen with options for creating a partition

Press Enter to indicate you want to create a primary DOS partition. FDISK asks you for the partition's size, in megabytes. Specify the amount of space for the DOS partition and press Enter. FDISK creates the primary DOS partition and returns to the main screen shown in Figure 1-1.

Make the DOS partition active

To boot from the primary DOS partition, you have to make it active. From FDISK's main screen (refer to Figure 1-1), press **2** and then press Enter. FDISK asks you for the partition you want to make active. This should be the primary DOS partition you just created. Press Enter to make this partition active.

Press Esc to quit FDISK. FDISK informs you it will restart the PC. Leave the DOS boot disk in the A drive and press Enter. The PC reboots and you again see the A:\> prompt.

Restore the MS-DOS partition

The new primary DOS partition will be your PC's C drive. Before you can use this drive, however, you have to format it. To format the C drive, type **FORMAT C: /S**. The FORMAT program displays a warning message. You can ignore it because you are formatting a newly created partition on your hard disk.

After the new C drive is formatted, you have to restore the contents of the hard disk. If you had backed up only your files and not the Windows files, you have to start by installing Windows on your newly formatted C drive. Typically, you have to boot the PC from the first Windows installation disk and follow the instructions.

After you have Windows installed on the C drive, you can use your backup program to restore all the files you previously backed up from the hard disk. To complete this step, you must follow the appropriate instructions for the backup program you used. If you used the MSBACKUP program in DOS Versions 6.0 or later, for example, you can use the same program to restore the files from the backup floppy disks.

Repartitioning with FIPS

If you understand the partitions as being sections of the hard disk, you may wonder whether a way exists to cordon off the unused part of a hard disk and make a new partition out of the unused part without destroying any existing data. This idea is behind a utility program called *FIPS* (The *F*irst Nondestructive *I*nteractive *P*artition *S*plitting Program). FIPS can split an existing primary DOS partition into two partitions.

Tip

Although you have no guarantee FIPS will split a DOS partition successfully, you may consider using it to create room for Linux, especially if you have a brand-new PC with only DOS and Windows installed on the hard disk. In this case, even if something goes wrong with FIPS, you can reinstall Windows and the applications. I used FIPS to split the DOS partition on a new PC's hard disk and create room for Linux.

The FIPS.EXE program and related files are located in the \DOSUTIL subdirectory of the companion CD-ROM. To use FIPS, follow these steps:

1. For FIPS to work, all used areas of the disk must be contiguous or at least as tightly packed as possible. You can prepare the disk for FIPS by running a defragmenter. In MS-DOS 6.0 or later, use the program DEFRAG to defragment the disk. In Windows 95, click the right mouse button on the disk symbol in the Explorer window, select Properties from the pop-

up menu, then click the Properties tab, and click the `Defragment Now` button. You also should check the hard disk for errors by running a program such as Norton Disk Doctor (in Windows 95, use SCANDISK). If you happen to have it, use Norton Speed Disk to defragment the hard disk because it's significantly faster than the DEFRAG utility.

2. Create a bootable disk, using the command FORMAT A: /S.

3. Copy the following files from the CD-ROM to the formatted disk (the following example assumes D: is the CD-ROM drive):

```
COPY D:\DOSUTILS\FIPS.EXE A:
COPY D:\DOSUTILS\RESTORRB.EXE A:
COPY D:\DOSUTILS\FIPSDOCS\ERRORS.TXT A:
```

FIPS.EXE is the program that splits partitions. ERRORS.TXT is a list of FIPS error messages. You consult this list for an explanation of any error messages FIPS displays. RESTORRB.EXE is a program that enables you to restore certain important parts of your hard disk from a backup of those areas created by FIPS.

4. Leave the bootable disk in the A drive and press Ctrl+Alt+Delete to reboot the PC. The PC boots from A and displays the A\> prompt.

5. Type **FIPS**. The FIPS program runs and shows you information about your hard disk. FIPS gives you an opportunity to save backup copy of important disk areas before proceeding. After that, FIPS shows the first free cylinder where the new partition can start (as well as the size of the partition, in megabytes). Figure 1-6 shows the output of the FIPS program at this stage.

```
Sectors per FAT: 256
Sectors per track: 63
Drive heads: 255
Hidden sectors: 63
Number of sectors (long): 4192902
Physical drive number: 80h
Signature: 29h

Checking boot sector ... OK
Checking FAT ... OK
Searching for free space ... OK

Do you want to make a backup copy of your root and boot sector before
proceeding (y/n)? y
Do you have a bootable floppy disk in drive A: as described in the
documentation (y/n)? y

Writing file a:\rootboot.000

Enter start cylinder for new partition (17 - 260):

Use the cursor keys to choose the cylinder, <enter> to continue

Old partition       Cylinder      New Partition
  1059.0 MB           135            988.4 MB
```

Figure 1-6: The FIPS program is prompting the user for new partition size.

6. Use the left and right arrow keys to adjust the starting cylinder of the new partition (the one that results from splitting the existing partition) to change the partition size. Press the right arrow to increase the starting cylinder number (this leaves more room in the existing partition and reduces the size of the new partition you are creating).

7. When you are satisfied with the size of the new partition, press Enter. FIPS displays the modified partition table and prompts you to enter **C** to continue or **R** to reedit the partition table.

8. Press **C** to continue. FIPS displays some information about the disk and asks whether you want to write the new partition information to the disk.

9. Press **Y**. FIPS writes the new partition table to the hard disk and then exits.

Remove the disk from the A drive and reboot the PC. When the system comes up, everything in your hard disk should be intact, but the C drive will be smaller. You have created a new partition from the unused parts of the old C drive.

You needn't do anything with the newly created partition under DOS. Later, in the section "Partitioning Your Hard Disk under Linux," you learn how to use the new partition under Linux.

Creating the Red Hat boot disk

After you repartition the hard disk and make room on the hard disk for Linux, you can begin the next step of installing Linux from this book's CD-ROM: creating the Linux boot disk. (For this step, you should turn on your PC without any disk in the A drive and then run Windows as usual.)

Tip

You do not need a boot disk if you can start your PC under MS-DOS — not an MS-DOS window in Windows 95 — and access the CD-ROM from the DOS command prompt. If you run Windows 95, restarting the PC in MS-DOS mode is enough. However, the CD-ROM may not be accessible in MS-DOS mode because the startup files — AUTOEXEC.BAT and CONFIG.SYS — may not be configured correctly. Try restarting your PC in MS-DOS mode and see if the CD-ROM can be accessed. If you succeed, then skip this section and proceed to the section "Booting Linux for Installation."

Like the MS-DOS boot disk, the Linux boot disk is used to start your PC and start Linux. Once you have installed Linux, you no longer need the Linux boot disk except in an emergency (when you have to reinstall Linux from the CD-ROM).

The boot disk is the initial version of Linux you use to start Linux, prepare the hard disk, and load the rest of Linux. Creating the boot disk involves using a utility program called RAWRITE.EXE to copy a special file called the *Linux boot image* to a disk.

To create the Linux boot disk under Windows, follow these steps:

1. Open an MS-DOS window (select MS-DOS Prompt from the Programs area in the Start menu).

2. In the MS-DOS window, enter the following commands at the MS-DOS prompt (my comments are in parentheses and your input is in boldface):

```
D:    (use the drive letter for the CD-ROM drive)
CD \DOSUTILS
RAWRITE
Enter disk image source file name: \images\boot.img
Enter target diskette drive: A
Please insert a formatted diskette into drive A: and press -ENTER-
:
```

As instructed, you should put a formatted disk into your PC's A drive and then press **Enter**. RAWRITE copies the boot-image file to the disk.

After you see the DOS prompt, you can take the Linux boot disk out of the A drive and (if you haven't done so already) label it appropriately. A label such as *Linux Boot Disk* would be appropriate.

Creating the Red Hat supplementary install disk

If you have a device that uses the PCMCIA interface (commonly found on notebook PCs), you need a second disk besides the boot disk. The second disk is called a *supplementary install disk,* which has a Linux file system with a number of directories. The disk contains programs and files that may be needed under special circumstances, such as installing from a PCMCIA CD-ROM drive.

Tip

You should go ahead and create a supplementary install disk because you also need this disk to fix any problems you encounter with your Linux system after you complete the installation.

To create the supplementary disk, insert the Red Hat Linux CD-ROM in the CD-ROM drive and type the following commands in an MS-DOS window:

```
d:    (use the drive letter for the CD-ROM drive)
cd \images
\dosutils\rawrite
Enter disk image source file name: supp.img
Enter target diskette drive: a
Please insert a formatted diskette into drive A: and press -ENTER- :
```

Insert a formatted floppy disk into A drive and press Enter. When the DOS prompt returns, the supplementary install disk is ready.

Installing Linux over the network using NFS

You can install Linux from another system on a network provided both systems are on the network and the other system has the Red Hat distribution on a directory that's exported through the Network File System (NFS). To perform such an installation, you must be knowledgeable about NFS or ask the help of someone who manages the network. You have to create the boot floppy disk as usual. After you use the boot floppy, designate NFS as the installation method and provide information about your network card and the network, including the IP addresses of your PC, gateway, and name server. Next you specify the NFS server's name or IP address and the server's directory containing the Red Hat distribution. Then, you can proceed with the usual installation steps.

Booting Linux for Installation

The Red Hat Linux installation program runs under Linux — this means you need to run Linux on your PC before you can go through the installation steps. This initial version of Linux can come from a boot floppy or the CD-ROM itself. This initial Linux operating system, in turn, runs the installation program, which prepares the disk partitions and copies all necessary files from the CD-ROM to the disk.

You can boot your PC with an initial version of the Linux operating system in one of the following ways:

- Load Linux by executing the AUTOBOOT.BAT command file while your PC is running MS-DOS.

- Boot your PC from the Linux boot floppy you had created earlier.

The following sections describe the two approaches of booting Linux and initiating the Red Hat installation.

Starting Linux from the Red Hat CD-ROM

You can start Linux directly from the CD-ROM while your PC is running MS-DOS. An MS-DOS program called LOADLIN.EXE can load a Linux kernel into memory and begin running Linux. The Linux kernel itself is in another file. You needn't understand all the details of how LOADLIN starts Linux. In fact, the Red Hat CD-ROM provides a DOS batch file — AUTOBOOT.BAT — in the \DOSUTILS directory that runs LOADLIN with appropriate arguments.

Note

You can use AUTOBOOT to start Linux directly from CD-ROM only if your PC is running MS-DOS alone (not an MS-DOS window under Windows 95). Also, you must be able to use the CD-ROM from MS-DOS. If your PC runs Windows 95, select Shutdown from the Start menu and then click the button labeled

`Restart the Computer in MS-DOS mode`. From the DOS prompt, if you can see the directory of the CD-ROM (with the command DIR D: where *D* is the drive letter of the CD-ROM drive), then you can start Linux directly from the CD-ROM. Otherwise, you have to use a boot floppy.

To start Linux, place the Red Hat CD_ROM in the CD-ROM drive and use the following commands from the DOS prompt:

```
D:
cd \dosutils
autoboot
```

After Linux starts, the Red Hat installation program begins to run. The section "Installing Linux from the Red Hat CD-ROM" describes the installation steps in detail.

Booting from the Linux floppy

To start Linux for installation, put the Linux boot floppy in your PC's A drive and restart your PC (either press the reset button or press Ctrl+Alt+Delete). Your PC goes through its normal startup sequence, such as checking memory and running the ROM BIOS code. Then the PC loads Linux from the floppy and begins running the Red Hat installation program.

Watching the boot process

A few moments after you start the boot process, an initial screen appears — the screen displays a welcome message and ends with a `boot:` prompt. The welcome message tells you help is available by pressing one of the function keys — F1 through F4.

If you do want to read the help screens, press the function key corresponding to the help you want. If you do nothing for a minute, the boot process proceeds with the loading of the Linux kernel into the PC's memory. To start booting Linux immediately, press Enter. After the Linux kernel loads, it automatically starts the Red Hat Linux installation program.

Tip

As the Linux kernel begins to run, various messages appear onscreen. These messages tell you whether the Linux kernel has detected your hardware. The messages typically flash by too quickly for you to follow. Afterwards, the screen shows a message that asks you if you have a color monitor. At this point, press Shift+PgUp to scroll back and read the messages about your hardware. You should see messages corresponding to hardware in your PC. In particular, look for a message about the CD-ROM because the kernel has to detect the CD-ROM to proceed with the rest of the installation.

You can also view the messages by pressing Alt+F4 — this switches the display to another virtual screen where all kernel messages appear.

The following listing shows a typical sequence of messages displayed when I boot one of my PCs using the Red Hat Linux boot floppy (this particular PC has a 200MHz Pentium processor with 64MB memory, 4GB disk, an ATAPI CD-ROM drive, and an Iomega ZIP drive):

```
boot:
Loading initrd.img.................
Loading vmlinuz.........
Uncompressing Linux...done.
Now booting kernel
Console: 16 point font, 400 scans
Console: colour VGA+ 80x25, 1 virtual console (max 63)
pcibios_init : BIOS32 Service Directory structure at 0x000f69f0
pcibios_init : BIOS32 Service Directory entry at 0xfd7e0
pcibios_init : PCI BIOS revision 2.10 entry at 0xfd9df
Probing PCI hardware.
Calibrating delay loop.. ok - 299.01 BogoMIPS
Memory: 62188/65536K available (736k kernel code, 384k reserved, 1256k
data)
Swansea University Computer Society NET3.035 for Linux 2.0
NET3: Unix domain sockets 0.13 for Linux NET3.035.
Swansea University Computer Society TCP/IP for NET3.034
IP Protocols: IGMP, ICMP, UDP, TCP
VFS: Diskquotas version dquot_5.6.0 initialized
Checking 386/387 coupling... Ok, fpu using exception 16 error
reporting.
Checking 'hlt' instruction... Ok.
Linux version 2.0.34 (root@porky.redhat.com) (gcc version 2.7.2.3) #1
Fri May 8 16:05:57 EDT
Starting kswapd v 1.4.2.2
Serial driver version 4.1.3 with no serial options enabled
tty00 at 0x3f8 (irq = 4) is a 16550A
PS/2 auxiliary pointing device detected -- driver installed.
Real Time Clock Driver v1.07
Ramdisk driver initialized : 16 ramdisks of 4096K size
ide: i82371 PIIX (Triton) on PCI bus 0 function 57
    ide0: BM-DMA at 0xfcf0-0xfcf7
    ide1: BM-DMA at 0xfcf8-0xfcff
hda: ST34342A, 4130MB w/0kB Cache, CHS=523/255/63
hdc: Pioneer CD-ROM ATAPI Model DR-A24X 0105, ATAPI CDROM drive
hdd: IOMEGA ZIP 100 ATAPI, ATAPI FLOPPY drive
ide0 at 0x1f0-0x1f7,0x3f6 on irq 14
ide1 at 0x170-0x177,0x376 on irq 15
Floppy drive(s): fd0 is 1.44M
FDC 0 is a National Semiconductor PC87306
md driver 0.35 MAX_MD_DEV=4, MAX_REAL=8
scsi : 0 hosts.
scsi : detected total.
Partition check:
hda: hda1 hda2 hda3
ide-floppy: hdd: I/O error, pc = 5a, key = 5, asc = 24, ascq =  0
ide-floppy: Can't get drive capabilities
hdd: 98304kB, 96/64/32 CHS, 4096 kBps, 512 sector size, 2941 rpm
hdd: The drive reports both 100663296 and 0 bytes as its capacity
```

```
RAMDISK: Compressed image found at block 0
VFS: Mounted root (ext2 filesystem)
Welcome to Red Hat Linux
```

In this example, the message shows Linux has detected the ATAPI CD-ROM drive. The letters hdc refers to the device name Linux uses for the CD-ROM drive.

Installing Linux from the Red Hat CD-ROM

After you start the initial version of Linux following the procedures described in the section "Booting Linux for Installation," Linux runs the Red Hat Linux installation program from the CD-ROM. The rest of the installation occurs under the control of the installation program.

Interacting with the Red Hat installation program

The installation program uses a full-screen text-based interface. Figure 1-7 shows a typical Red Hat Linux installation screen.

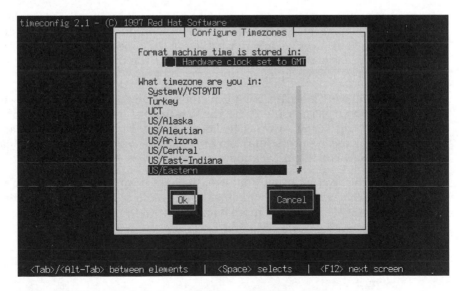

Figure 1-7: A typical installation screen with a dialog box

Each screen typically presents a dialog box with various elements such as lists of items from which you select items and buttons that you select to indicate action. Typically, the buttons are labeled OK and Cancel. The bottom of the screen displays a help message that tells you how to navigate around the text screen.

Instead of a mouse, you use specific keys to move the text cursor. Consult Table 1-1 for the keystrokes to use for specific actions.

Table 1-1	Interacting with the Red Hat installation program
Keystrokes	*Action*
Arrow keys	Moves from one item to the next in a dialog box.
Tab	Moves forward to the next item in a dialog box.
Alt+Tab	Moves backward to the previous item in a dialog box.
Spacebar	Selects the item on which the cursor rests. If the item is already selected, turns the selection off. Thus, the spacebar toggles the selection.
Enter	Presses the button on which the cursor rests. If the dialog box has a single button, pressing Enter is equivalent to pressing that button.
F12	Accepts current values and proceeds to the next dialog box. This is equivalent to pressing the OK button.

Monitoring the installation process

As the installation progresses, you are primarily responding to various dialog boxes, typing information the installation program needs. The installation program displays useful information on a number of virtual consoles — these are screens of text in memory you can view on the physical screen by pressing the key sequences shown in Table 1-2.

Tip

You will work mostly in the main console — virtual console 1. To switch to another virtual console, press the keystroke shown in Table 1-2. For example, to view the install log on virtual console 3, press Alt+F3. After you are done viewing the log, press Alt+F1 to return to the main console, so you can continue with the installation.

Typically, you get by without ever having to switch to the other screens but, if something should go wrong, you can switch to the install log screen by pressing Alt+F3 and get more information on the problem.

Table 1-2	Virtual consoles during Red Hat Linux installation	
Virtual Console	*Keystroke*	*Description*
1	Alt+F1	This is the main console where the installation program displays the text-based user interface through which you install Linux.
2	Alt+F2	This console displays a shell prompt where you can use Linux commands to monitor the progress of installation. The shell prompt appears only after you insert the CD-ROM and press Enter in response to a dialog displayed by the installation program.

Virtual Console	Keystroke	Description
3	Alt+F3	This is the install log. Messages from the installation program appear here.
4	Alt+F4	The Linux kernel displays its messages on this console. After Linux initially boots, you may want to switch to this console to see the kernel messages because they include information about hardware Linux detects in your PC.
5	Alt+F5	This console shows the outputs of any programs run during the installation process.

Understanding the Red Hat installation phases

Linux installation is a lengthy process with the following major phases:

1. *Getting Ready to Install:* Indicate the type of keyboard and specify where Red Hat Linux is located (for example, the CD-ROM). If your PC has a PC Card device with PCMCIA interface, this phase detects such devices and asks you for the supplementary install disk that contains files needed for PCMCIA support.

2. *Partitioning and Using the Hard Disk:* Answer questions about any SCSI devices you have and proceed to partition the disk. You also specify the partition to be used as swap area and which partition will hold the Linux root directory (represented by /). The partitions are also formatted before use. Red Hat includes the Disk Druid program to perform all the steps in this phase of installation.

3. *Selecting the Components to Install:* Select which components of Red Hat Linux — such as X Window System, Emacs editor, and Web server — you want to install. After you select the components, the installation program takes over and installs the selected components on the hard disk.

4. *Configuring Linux:* In this phase you set up the X Window System, the TCP/IP network, the time zone, and any printer. You also set a password for the root — the super user. You conclude the configuration step and the installation by specifying where the Linux Loader (LILO) should be stored.

If you have all configuration information (such as IP addresses and host names for the TCP/IP network configuration) handy and all goes well, installing Linux from the companion CD-ROM on a fast (166MHz or better) Pentium PC should take approximately an hour. For example, on my 200MHz Pentium PC with 64MB RAM and a 1GB disk partition devoted to Linux, the entire installation took about 40 minutes. On older 486 PCs, the installation process may take somewhat longer.

The Red Hat installation program probes — attempts to determine the presence of — specific hardware and tailors the installation steps accordingly. For example, if the installation program detects a PC Card device that uses PCMCIA interface, the program automatically asks for the supplementary install disk. This means you may see some variation in the sequence of steps depending on your specific hardware configuration.

The following sections describe each of the Red Hat Linux installation phases in detail.

Getting ready to install

In this phase, you go through the following steps before moving on to disk setup and actual installation of Linux:

1. The installation program displays a black-and-white dialog box to ask if you have a color monitor (see Figure 1-8). Press Tab to move between Yes and No. Once the cursor is on the correct button, press Enter.

```
Welcome to Red Hat Linux



                    ┤ Color Choices ├
                    Are you using a color monitor?

                    Yes ▌              No


```

Figure 1-8: The dialog box asks you whether you have a color monitor.

2. A welcome screen appears. The message tells you to visit the Red Hat Web site at:

   `http://www.redhat.com`

   Press Enter to continue the installation.

3. The installation program checks if there are any PC Card devices that use the PCMCIA interface. If any PCMCIA device is found, the installation program displays a dialog box that asks you to insert the Red Hat supplementary install disk. If you have a PCMCIA device (such as an Ethernet card on a portable PC for installing over the network), insert the supplementary install disk and then select OK.

4. The installation program displays a list of keyboard types, as shown in Figure 1-9.

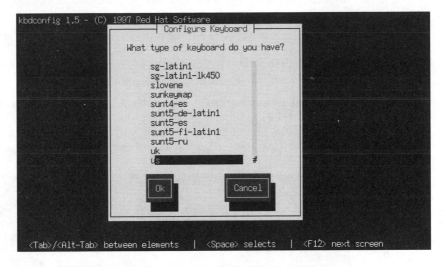

Figure 1-9: Selecting a keyboard type during Red Hat installation

Use the arrow keys to move up and down the list and press Spacebar. Select the keyboard type that matches what your system has. Then press F12 to proceed to the next step.

5. Specify where the Red Hat packages are located from the dialog box shown in Figure 1-10.

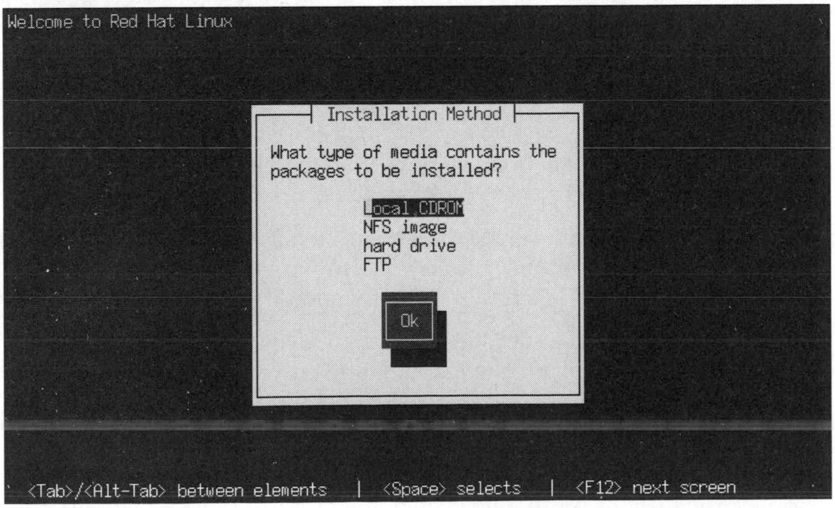

Figure 1-10: Specifying where the Red Hat Linux packages are located.

The Local CDROM option refers to the CD-ROM drive on your PC. Because you are installing from this book's companion CD-ROM, you should put the CD-ROM into the drive, select Local CDROM, and press Enter.

You can use the NFS and FTP options to install Red Hat Linux from another system over the network. The hard drive option refers to a way of installing Red Hat Linux from files you copy into another hard drive partition using an operating system such as Windows 95.

6. The installation program initializes the CD-ROM and displays a dialog box (see Figure 1-11) asking if you want to install a new system or upgrade an older Red Hat installation. Assuming you are installing for the first time, make sure the cursor is on the Install button and press Enter.

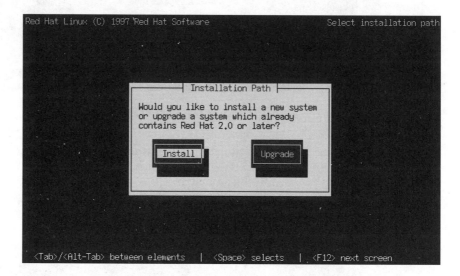

Figure 1-11: This is the dialog box to select whether you are installing or upgrading.

7. The installation program then displays the screen shown in Figure 1-12 that asks you if you have a SCSI adapter in your PC.

If you have any SCSI device, such as a SCSI hard drive, you must select Yes. Then, the installation program displays a list of SCSI adapters (see Figure 1-13) from which you should select the one on your system.

The installation program then loads the driver for the SCSI adapter. After this step you can install Linux on your SCSI hard drive.

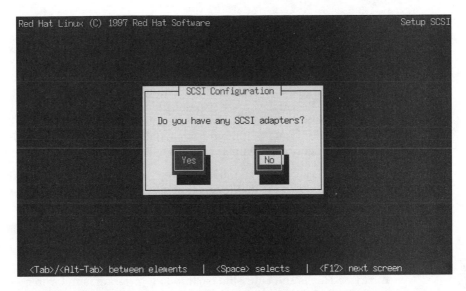

Figure 1-12: Select Yes if you have a SCSI adapter in your PC .

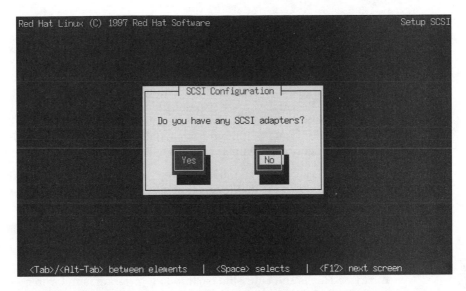

Figure 1-13: Selecting a driver for your PC's SCSI adapter, if any.

The next major phase of installation involves partitioning the hard disk for use in Linux.

Partitioning and using the hard disk

Like MS-DOS, Linux requires you to partition and prepare a hard disk before you can install Linux on the hard disk. You usually do not perform this step because, when you buy your PC from a vendor, the vendor takes care of preparing the hard disk and installing Windows and all other applications on the hard disk. Because you are installing Linux from scratch, however, you must perform this crucial step yourself. You have to prepare the hard disk partitions under Linux before you can install the rest of Linux. As you see in the following sections, this task is just a matter of following instructions.

When the Red Hat Linux installation program reaches the disk partitioning phase, it displays a text dialog box that gives you two options to partition and use the hard disk:

- **Disk Druid**: This is a Red Hat utility program that uses text dialogs to enable you to partition the disk and, at the same time, specify what parts of the Linux file system are to be loaded on which partition.

- fdisk: This is the Linux file partitioning program, similar in concept to the DOS FDISK command, but with many more capabilities than the DOS version. When you use the Linux fdisk program, you have to type cryptic one-letter commands to manipulate disk partitions. Once you learn the commands, though, you may find fdisk more powerful than Disk Druid. For example, Disk Druid does not enable you to change the type of a partition indicating what type of file system will be stored on the partition; but you can easily change the partition type with fdisk.

Cross-Reference

In this chapter, I explain how to use Disk Druid to prepare and use the disk partitions for Red Hat Linux installation. You can learn about fdisk in Chapter 11.

Before you start to use Disk Druid to partition your disk, you must know how to refer to the disk drives and partitions in Linux. Also, you should understand the terms *mount points* and *swap partition*. The next three sections describe these terms and concepts and then proceed to describe Disk Druid.

Disk names in Linux

The first step is to learn how Linux refers to the various disks. Linux treats all devices as files and has actual files that represent each device. In Linux, these *device files* are located in the /dev directory. If you are new to UNIX, you may not yet know about UNIX filenames, but you will learn more as you continue to use Linux. If you know how MS-DOS filenames work, you will find Linux filenames are similar, except it does not use drive letters (such as A and C) and substitutes the slash (/) for the MS-DOS backslash (\) as the separator between directory names.

Because Linux treats a device as a file in the /dev directory, the hard disk names start with /dev. Table 1-3 lists the hard disk and floppy drive names you may have to use.

Table 1-3	Hard disk and floppy drive names
Name	**Description**
/dev/hda	First Integrated Drive Electronics (IDE) drive (in DOS, usually the C drive)
/dev/hdb	Second IDE drive
/dev/sda	First Small Computer System Interface (SCSI) drive
/dev/sdb	Second SCSI drive
/dev/fd0	First floppy drive (the A drive in DOS)
/dev/fd1	Second floppy drive (the B drive in DOS)

When you use the Red Hat Disk Druid or Linux fdisk program to prepare the Linux partitions, you must identify the disk drive by its name such as /dev/hda.

Tip

When Disk Druid or fdisk displays the list of partitions, the partition names are of the form /dev/hda1, /dev/hda2, and so forth. Linux constructs each partition name by appending the partition number (1 through 4, for the four primary partitions on a hard disk) to the disk's name. Therefore, if your PC's single IDE hard drive has two partitions, you will notice the installation program uses /dev/hda1 and /dev/hda2 as the names of these partitions. Here are more examples of hard disk partition names in Linux:

Name	**Partition**
/dev/hda1	First primary partition of first IDE drive
/dev/hda2	Second primary partition of first IDE drive
/dev/hda3	Third primary partition of first IDE drive
/dev/hda4	Fourth primary partition of first IDE drive
/dev/hda5	First logical partition of first IDE drive
/dev/hda6	Second logical partition of first IDE drive
/dev/hdb1	First primary partition of second IDE drive
/dev/sda1	First primary partition of first SCSI drive
/dev/sda2	Second primary partition of first SCSI drive
/dev/sdb1	First primary partition of second SCSI drive
/dev/sdc1	First primary partition of third SCSI drive

Mount point

In Linux, you use a physical disk partition by associating with a specific part of the file system, which is a hierarchical arrangement of directories — a directory tree. If you have more than one disk partition (you may have a second disk with a Linux partition), you can use all of them in Linux. All you have to do is decide which part of the Linux directory tree should be located on each partition — a process known in Linux as *mounting a file system on a device* (the disk partition is a device).

Note

The term *mount point* refers to the directory you associate with a disk partition or any other device.

Suppose you have two disks on your PC and you have created Linux partitions on both disks. Figure 1-14 illustrates how you can mount different parts of the Linux directory tree (the file system) on these two partitions.

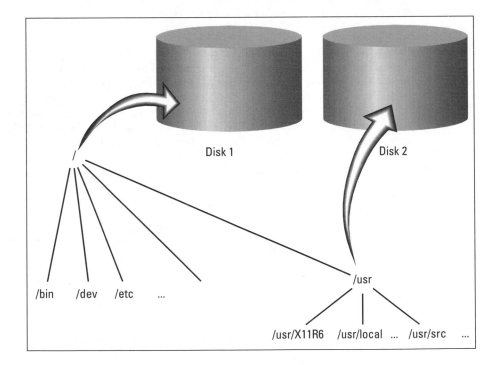

Figure 1-14: An example of mounting the Linux file system on two disk partitions

Swap partition

Most advanced operating systems support the concept of virtual memory, in which part of your system's hard disk is used as an extension of the physical memory (RAM). When the operating system runs out of physical memory, it can move (or swap out) the contents of currently unneeded parts of RAM to make room for a program that needs more memory. As soon as the time comes to access anything in the swapped-out data, the operating system has to find something else to swap out and then swap in the required data from disk. This process of swapping data back and forth between the RAM and the disk also is known as *paging*.

Because the disk is much slower than RAM, the system's performance is slower when the operating system has to perform a lots of paging, but virtual memory enables you to run programs you otherwise would be unable to run.

Linux supports virtual memory and can make use of a swap partition. When you create the Linux partitions, you should create a swap partition for Linux. With the Disk Druid utility program, described in the next section, it is simple to create a swap partition. Simply mark a partition type as swap device and Disk Druid will perform the necessary tasks.

Disk preparation

As you get ready to prepare the disk for Linux installation, you should see the Disk Setup dialog box with the button marked Disk Druid already selected, as shown in Figure 1-15. To use Disk Druid, press Enter.

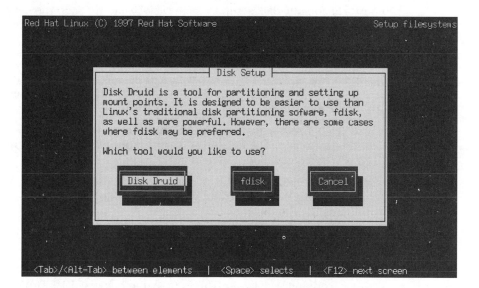

Figure 1-15: Disk Setup dialog box from Red Hat Linux installation program

Disk Druid gathers information about the hard drives on your system and displays a dialog box with the list of disk drives and the current partition information for one of the drives, as shown in Figure 1-16.

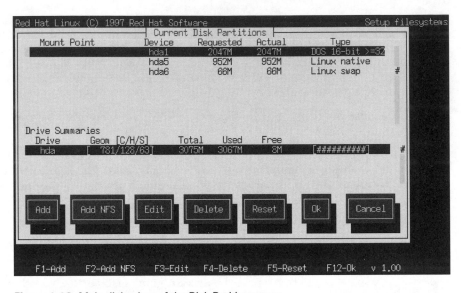

```
Red Hat Linux (C) 1997 Red Hat Software                    Setup filesystems
                        ┌─ Current Disk Partitions ─┐
        Mount Point       Device   Requested   Actual       Type
                           hda1        2047M     2047M    DOS 16-bit >=32
                           hda5         952M      952M    Linux native
                           hda6          66M       66M    Linux swap        #




   Drive Summaries
        Drive    Geom [C/H/S]      Total    Used    Free
         hda    [  781/128/63]     3075M    3067M     8M    [##########]     #




      ┌─────┐  ┌─────────┐  ┌──────┐  ┌────────┐  ┌───────┐  ┌────┐  ┌────────┐
      │ Add │  │ Add NFS │  │ Edit │  │ Delete │  │ Reset │  │ Ok │  │ Cancel │
      └─────┘  └─────────┘  └──────┘  └────────┘  └───────┘  └────┘  └────────┘


      F1-Add    F2-Add NFS   F3-Edit   F4-Delete   F5-Reset   F12-Ok    v 1.00
```

Figure 1-16: Main dialog box of the Disk Druid program

You perform specific disk setup tasks in Disk Druid through the seven buttons across the bottom of the dialog box. Specifically, the buttons perform the following actions:

- **Add** enables you to create a new partition, assuming enough free disk space is available to create a partition. When you press this button, another dialog box appears where you can fill in information necessary to create a partition.

- **Add NFS** is used to associate an NFS directory — a directory located on another system on the network — with a mount point on your system. The NFS directory mounted read-only.

- **Edit** enables you to alter the attributes of an existing partition. You make changes to the current attribute in another dialog box that appears when you press the Edit button.

- **Delete** is used to delete the partition currently highlighted in the Current Disk Partitions list (see Figure 1-16).

- **Reset** restores all partition information back to the way it was before you started running Disk Druid. This is possible because Disk Druid does not actually make changes to the partition table (which is stored on the hard drive) until after you exit by pressing the OK button.

- **OK** causes Disk Druid to ask you if you really want to update the partition tables on all the hard drives in your system. If you answer Yes, Disk Druid makes changes to the partition tables and exits.

- **Cancel** is used to exit Disk Druid without saving any changes you might have made.

Exactly what you do in Disk Druid depends on the hard drives in your PC and the partitions they already have. For my discussion, I assume you have created the necessary hard disk space for Linux by one of the following methods:

- You started with a single hard drive with a single partition (only C drive in Windows). Then you used FIPS to split that partition into two (see the section "Repartitioning with FIPS"). After partitioning, you end up with two DOS partitions.

- Your PC had a single large hard drive (greater than 2GB) that had two partitions (C and D drives in Windows). In this case, the second partition is an extended partition that contains the logical drive D. You want to install Linux on the extended partition that used to be the D drive in Windows.

Both of these situations call for the same sequence of steps:

1. Delete the DOS partition—the one with enough space for Linux installation, not the one where Windows is installed.

2. Create two Linux partitions out of the available disk space—one for swap space and the other for the Linux file system.

The next section shows the specific steps you will perform in Disk Druid to set up the minimum number of partitions Linux needs. You can prepare other disk partitions (if you have a second hard drive, for example) following the steps outlined in the next section.

**Cross-
Reference**

After you set up the partitions, you have to initialize the swap partition and format the partition meant for the Linux file system. These steps are described in the sections "Initializing the swap space" and "Formatting the partitions."

Setting up the partitions

To prepare an existing DOS partition for Linux, you have to perform the following steps in Disk Druid:

1. Delete the DOS partition you want to use for Linux. To do this, select the partition (this will typically be the one with Device name hda2) from the Current Disk Partitions list (see Figure 1-16) and then press the Delete button. As a shortcut, you may simply select the partition and press **F4**. Before deleting the partition, remember to note the partition's size from the Current Disk Partitions list.

2. Create a new partition for the Linux file system. To do this, press the Add button (or press **F1**). You will see the Edit New Partition dialog box (see Figure 1-17) where you should fill in / as the mount point and enter the size in megabytes. To compute the size, simply subtract the size of the swap space (32MB or the amount of RAM in your PC, whichever is more) from the original size of the partition. Select the OK button and then press **Enter** to complete this step and return to the Disk Druid's main dialog box.

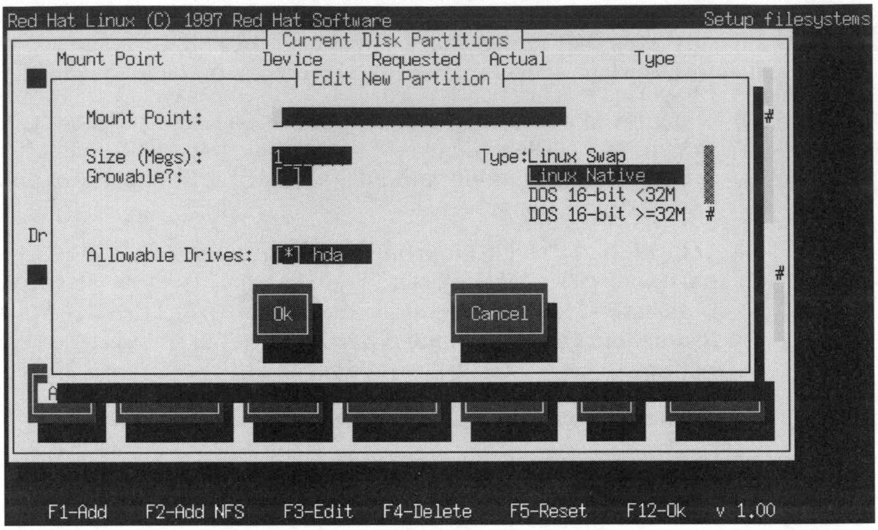

```
Red Hat Linux (C) 1997 Red Hat Software                    Setup filesystems
                    ┤ Current Disk Partitions ├
       Mount Point        Device   Requested   Actual        Type
  ■                       ┤ Edit New Partition ├                           #

       Mount Point:       _____

       Size (Megs):       1___        Type:Linux Swap
       Growable?:         [_]              Linux Native
                                           DOS 16-bit <32M
                                           DOS 16-bit >=32M    #
  Dr

       Allowable Drives:  [*] hda                              #
  ■

                         ┌────┐          ┌────────┐
                         │ Ok │          │ Cancel │
                         └────┘          └────────┘



    A

   F1-Add     F2-Add NFS    F3-Edit    F4-Delete    F5-Reset    F12-Ok    v 1.00
```

Figure 1-17: Edit New Partition dialog box where you fill in the attributes of a new partition

3. Create another new partition and set it as a Linux swap space. To do this, press F1 from the Disk Druid main dialog box (Figure 1-16). Then, in the Edit New Partition dialog box (Figure 1-17), enter the size of the partition. Press Tab to move to the list of partition types and use the arrow keys to select Linux Swap as the type—when you do so, the text Swap Partition appears in the Mount Point field. Next, press Tab to select the OK button and press Enter to define the new partition and return to the Disk Druid's main dialog box.

4. If you want to access the DOS partition under Linux, make sure you assign a mount point for this partition. Basically, you will assign a Linux directory name where the DOS partition will appear. For example, you can use /dosc as the mount point for the DOS partition; then you can access the DOS files in the /dosc directory in Linux. This mnemonic is good because the name dosc should remind you this drive is the C drive under DOS. To assign the mount point, select the DOS partition (typically, this is listed as Device hda1 in the Current Disk Partitions list) and press F3 to edit the attributes. The Edit Partition dialog box appears (see Figure 1-18). Type the mount point (for example, /dosc) and press Enter to return to the Disk Druid's main dialog box.

5. Make the changes permanent by pressing the OK button in the Disk Druid main dialog box (Figure 1-16).

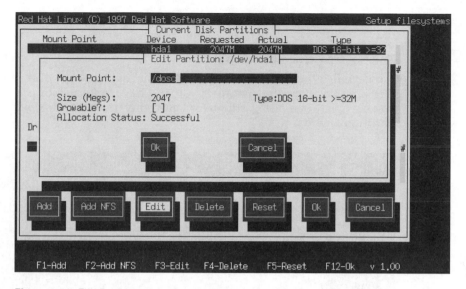

Figure 1-18: Edit Partition dialog box enables you to change the attributes of a partition.

Initializing the swap space

After you finish specifying the partitions in Disk Druid, the Red Hat installation program displays a dialog box (see Figure 1-19) that lists all partitions of type Linux Swap and asks you whether you want to initialize the swap spaces. If you created one swap partition, the list will include that single partition. You should go ahead and initialize the swap partition by pressing Tab until the OK button is selected and then pressing **Enter**.

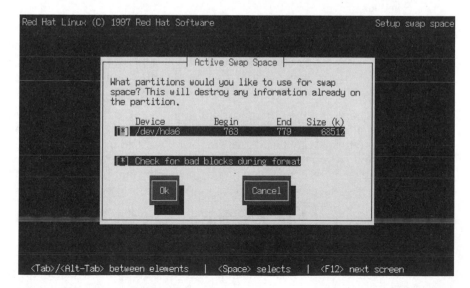

Figure 1-19: Dialog box that enables you to initialize the swap space

Tip

If the installation program does not find any swap partition, chances are you did not set the partition type to Linux Swap.

Formatting the partitions

After the Red Hat installation program initializes the swap space, it displays a dialog box that lists the partitions you may have to format for use in Linux. If you have only one disk partition for Linux, then the list shows only that partition (see Figure 1-20).

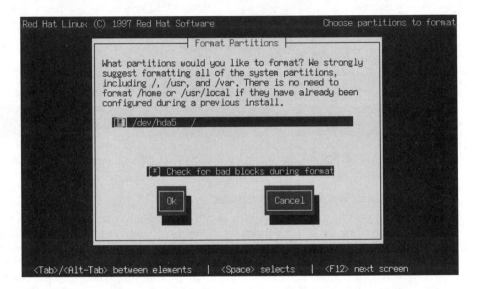

Figure 1-20: The Format Partitions dialog box enables you to format the partitions for use in Linux.

To format the partition, press Tab to move the cursor to the partition's name and then press Spacebar to select. You should also select the item marked Check for bad blocks during format so the formatting process marks any areas of the disk that may be physically defective.

Note

If you have multiple disk partitions mounted on different directories of the Linux file system and you are upgrading an existing installation, you do not have to format any partitions where you want to preserve existing data. For example, if you have all user directories on a separate disk partition mounted on the /home directory, you do not have to format that partition.

Selecting the components to install

After you select the partitions to format, the installation program does not immediately format the partitions. Instead, it asks you for the Red Hat Linux components you want to install. This way, after you have selected the components, you can go away for a cup of coffee and the Red Hat installation program can format the disk partition and copy all necessary files to that partition.

Red Hat uses special files called *packages* to bundle a number of files that make up a specific software. For example, all configuration files, documentation, and binary files for the Perl programming language comes in a Red Hat package. You use a special program called Red Hat Package Manager (RPM) to install, uninstall, and find out information about packages. Chapter 2 describes how to use RPM. For now, just remember a component is made up of several Red Hat packages.

Figure 1-21 shows the dialog box with the list of components you can elect to install. Each component is identified by a descriptive label with a square bracket ([ ]) prefix.

Figure 1-21: Dialog box from where you select the components to install

An asterisk (*) in the square bracket means the component is selected. When the dialog box first appears, many of the components are already selected, as indicated by the asterisks. You can think of the marked components as the minimal set of components recommended for installation by Red Hat. You can, however, choose to install any or all of the components. Use the arrow keys to move up and down in the scrolling list (Figure 1-21) and press Spacebar to select or deselect a component.

Table 1-4 shows the components included in the list. In the table, an asterisk prefix indicates the component is selected by default. In addition to these user-selectable components, the Red Hat installation program automatically installs a large number of packages needed to run Linux.

Tip

Each component requires specific packages to run. The Red Hat installation program automatically checks for any package dependencies and shows you a list of packages required, but that you have not selected. In this case, you should install the required packages.

Because each component is a collection of many different Red Hat packages, the installation program also gives you an option to select individual packages. If you select the item labeled "Select individual packages," that appears after the list in Figure 1-21 and then press the OK button, the installation program takes you to further dialog boxes to select individual packages. If you are installing Linux for the first time, however, you needn't go down to that level of detail to install specific packages. Simply pick from Table 1-4 the components you think you need. You can always install additional packages later on with the RPM utility program.

Table 1-4   List of components to install in Red Hat Linux

Component Name*	Description
Printer Support	Packages needed to print from the system. Includes utilities such as lpr and Ghostscript.
*X Window System	Packages that make up XFree86 3.3.1, the X Window System for Intel x86 systems. Includes all fonts, the fvwm2 window manager, Ghostscript, Tcl/Tk, Perl, and many utility programs. The actual X server package is selected by a configuration program when you configure X at a later phase of the installation.
*Mail/WWW/ News Tools	Packages such as elm, pine, and trn for reading e-mail and news groups. Also includes many packages for X Window System, Perl, Tcl/Tk, printer support.
DOS/Windows Connectivity	Packages such as dosemu, mtools, lha, zip, and unzip that are useful for accessing DOS and Windows files from Linux. Also includes many packages for the X Window System.
*File Managers	File managers such as mc (Midnight Commander) and xfm along with Perl, Tcl/Tk, and the X Window System.
Graphics Manipulation	Image manipulation packages such as ImageMagick, gimp, and Ghostscript along with all of X Window System.
X Games	The entire X Window System component plus the X game packages xbill, xboard, xboing, xchomp, xdemineur, xevil, xfishtank, xgalaga, xgammon, xgopher, xjewel, xlander, xpat2, xpilot, xpuzzles, xsnow, and xtrojka.
Console Games	Old UNIX games such as hangman and fish as well as new games such as yahtzee, Doom, gnuchess, trojka, and some card games.
*X Multimedia Support	Packages for sound and animation under X. Also includes all X Window System packages.
*Console Multimedia	Sound and animation support packages such as aumix, sndconfig, rhsound, cdp, maplay, and playmidi.

Component Name*	Description
Print Server	Packages needed to make the Linux system a print server.
*Networked Workstation	TCP/IP networking packages such as FTP (File Transfer Protocol), Telnet, and NFS (Network File System).
*Dialup Workstation	TCP/IP networking packages, as well as packages such as `ppp` and `dip` needed for dial-up networking. Also includes communication packages such as `minicom` and `lrzsz` (for sending and receiving files).
News Server	Perl and INN (Internet News server) packages needed to make the Linux system a server for news groups.
NFS Server	Packages such as `portmap` and `nfs-server` that make the Linux system a NFS server.
SMB (Samba) Connectivity	Packages such as `samba` and `smbfs` that are needed to use the Linux PC as a LAN Manager server. Includes many other packages, such as TCP/IP networking packages and printer support packages.
IPX/Netware (tm) Connectivity	Packages needed to use the Linux PC as a Novell Netware server. Includes much of the TCP/IP networking packages as well.
Anonymous FTP/ Gopher Server	The `wu-ftpd` and `anonftp` packages along with all TCP/IP networking packages needed to support anonymous FTP in Linux.
Web Server	The Apache Web server and other networking packages needed to use the Linux system as a Web server.
DNS Name Server	The `bind`, `bind-utils`, and `caching-nameserver` packages along with other support packages needed to provide Domain Name Service (DNS) on the Linux system.
Postgres (SQL) Server	The `postgresql`, `postgresql-data`, and `postgresql-devel` packages along with many support packages to implement the Postgres SQL server (a database) on the Linux system.
Network Management Workstation	Packages to support network management through SNMP (Simple Network Management Protocol) and IP firewall administration utility. Also includes many networking packages required by the network management tools.
TeX Document Formatting	Packages needed for the TeX (pronounced *tech,* as in *technology*) document-formatting system.
Emacs	Version of Emacs text editor that does not require *X.*
Emacs with X windows	GNU Emacs 20.2 that runs in *X.* Also includes the X Window System component and the version of Emacs that does not require *X.*
C Development	The GNU C compiler, the `gdb` debugger, Revision Control System (RCS), various header files, and other utilities for C programming.
Development Libraries	Various libraries needed for software development in Linux.

(continued)

Table 1-4 *(Continued)*

Component Name*	Description
C++ Development	The GNU C++ compiler and other associated files needed for C++ programming.
X Development	*X* header files and libraries as well as the X Window System needed for developing applications that use *X*.
Extra Documentation	Various online manual pages (called *man* pages in UNIX) as well as Linux HOWTO files and Frequently Asked Questions (FAQs) for many Linux software. You should go ahead and install this component.
Everything	Select this item to install all the components.

*Components marked with an asterisk (*) prefix are selected by default.

After you have selected the components to select, press Tab to move to the OK button in Figure 1-21 and then press Enter. The installation program displays an informative dialog box, as shown in Figure 1-22.

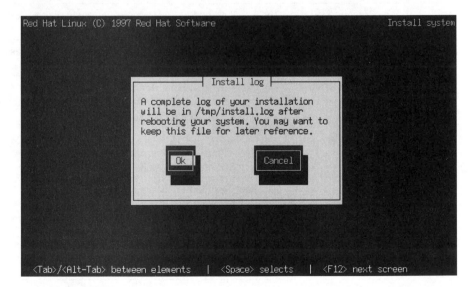

Figure 1-22: Informative message about install log just before the selected components are installed

The dialog box informs you a log of the installation will be in the /tmp/install.log file. This file will essentially list all the Red Hat packages installed in your system. Here are a few lines from the beginning of the /tmp/install.log file after I finished installing Red Hat Linux on a PC:

```
Installing setup.
Installing filesystem.
```

```
Installing basesystem.
Installing anonftp.
Installing AnotherLevel.
Installing ldconfig.
Installing termcap.
Installing libtermcap.
Installing glibc.
Installing grep.
Installing fileutils.
Installing bash.
Installing aout-libs.
Installing slang.
Installing newt.
Installing chkconfig.
Installing apache.
```

You can review the install log later and keep the file for future reference.

Press Enter to proceed with the installation. The Red Hat installation program formats the disk partitions and then installs the packages. As it installs packages, the installation program displays a status screen that shows the progress of the installation with information such as total number of packages to install, number installed so far, estimated amount of disk space needed, and estimated time remaining to install.

Tip

The formatting and installation takes a while — you can take a break and check back in ten minutes or so. When you come back, you should be able to get a sense for the time remaining from the status screen the installation program updates continually.

Configuring Linux

When the installation program finishes loading all the selected packages, it moves on to the configuration phase. Assuming you are installing the X Window System and the networking component, the configuration steps are as follows:

- Configure the mouse
- Configure *X*
- Configure the network
- Set the time zone
- Configure services
- Configure printers
- Set the root password
- Create a custom boot disk
- Install LILO

The following sections describe each of these configuration steps.

Configure the mouse

If you have installed the X Window System component (as described in the section "Selecting the Components to Install"), the Red Hat installation program runs the `mouseconfig` utility program to detect your PC's mouse. Figure 1-23 shows a typical outcome of the mouse detection.

Figure 1-23: Dialog box informing you of the type of mouse detected

In this case, the `mouseconfig` program found a mouse that uses a PS/2 style interface. Because this is simply meant as information for you, press Enter to proceed to the next step.

The mouse configuration program displays another dialog box (Figure 1-24) that gives you the option to emulate a 3-button mouse with a typical 2-button mouse on PCs.

If you select Yes, you can simulate a middle button click by pressing both buttons simultaneously. Because many *X* applications assume a 3-button mouse, you should go ahead and select the Yes button on the dialog box.

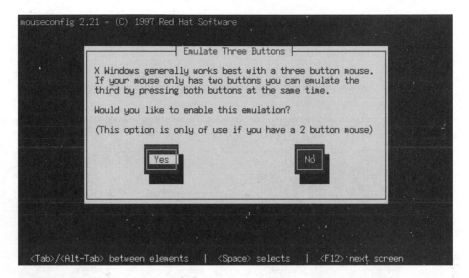

Figure 1-24: Dialog box asking you if you want to emulate a 3-button mouse

Configure *X*

If you selected the X Window System component (as described in the "Selecting the Components to Install" section), the Red Hat installation program now runs the Xconfigurator utility program to create a configuration file the *X* server needs.

The Xconfigurator program starts with a welcome dialog box, as shown in Figure 1-25.

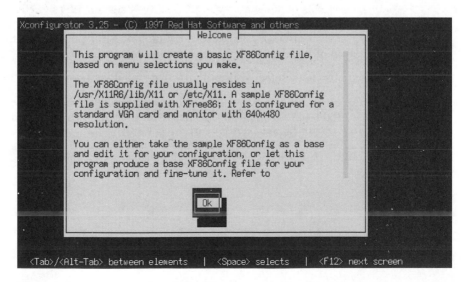

Figure 1-25: Welcome dialog box from the Xconfigurator program

To read the rest of the message in the dialog box, press the down arrow key to scroll down. After reading the message, press Enter to continue with the configuration process.

Xconfigurator **automatically detects the chipset used by your video card and displays a summary message, as shown in Figure 1-26.**

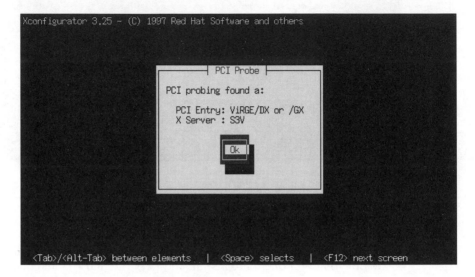

Figure 1-26: Result of probing the video card

In this case, Xconfigurator **finds a video card based on the S3 ViRGE/DX (or /GX) chipset and recommends the S3V X server. In fact, the message from** Xconfigurator **is somewhat cryptic. The S3V X server refers to the X server program with the full name** XF86_S3V **that will be installed in the** /usr/X11R6/bin **directory. Because the dialog box in Figure 1-26 is for your information only, press Enter to continue with the rest of the configuration.**

The next step is to select your monitor from a list, as shown in Figure 1-27.

Press the up and down arrow keys to browse through the list. If you find your monitor model listed, position the cursor on that monitor and then press Enter. Otherwise, select Custom and press Enter.

If you choose Custom, Xconfigurator **displays another dialog box, as shown in Figure 1-28.**

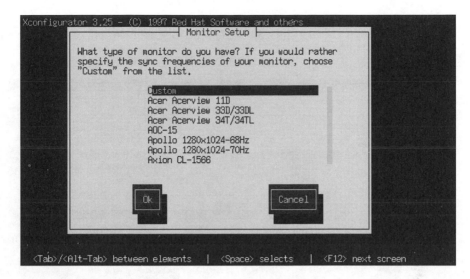

Figure 1-27: Selecting your monitor type

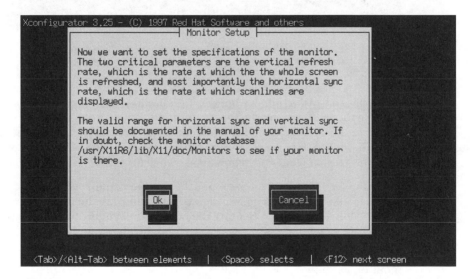

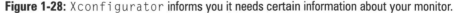

Figure 1-28: Xconfigurator informs you it needs certain information about your monitor.

As the dialog box (Figure 1-28) says, you have to provide two critical parameters of your monitor:

- Horizontal synchronization frequency—the number of times per second the monitor can display horizontal raster lines, in kilohertz (kHz)

- Vertical synchronization rate or vertical refresh rate—how many times a second the monitor can display the entire screen

You can find this information in your monitor's manual.

Press Enter in response to the dialog box of Figure 1-28 to continue.
Xconfigurator displays a list of predefined monitor capabilities, as shown in
Figure 1-29.

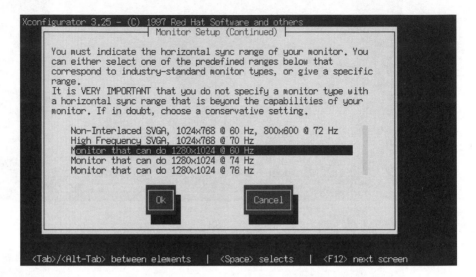

```
Xconfigurator 3.25 - (C) 1997 Red Hat Software and others
                   ┤ Monitor Setup (Continued) ├

    You must indicate the horizontal sync range of your monitor. You
    can either select one of the predefined ranges below that
    correspond to industry-standard monitor types, or give a specific
    range.
    It is VERY IMPORTANT that you do not specify a monitor type with
    a horizontal sync range that is beyond the capabilities of your
    monitor. If in doubt, choose a conservative setting.

       Non-Interlaced SVGA, 1024x768 @ 60 Hz, 800x600 @ 72 Hz
       High Frequency SVGA, 1024x768 @ 70 Hz
       Monitor that can do 1280x1024 @ 60 Hz
       Monitor that can do 1280x1024 @ 74 Hz
       Monitor that can do 1280x1024 @ 76 Hz


                 ┌──────┐              ┌────────┐
                 │  Ok  │              │ Cancel │
                 └──────┘              └────────┘


  <Tab>/<Alt-Tab> between elements  |  <Space> selects  |  <F12> next screen
```

Figure 1-29: List of predefined horizontal synchronization ranges displayed by
Xconfigurator

Caution

Typically, one of the items from this list should match your monitor's
specifications. If you need to guess your monitor's capabilities, be
conservative. Do not specify a horizontal synchronization range that is
beyond the capabilities of your monitor. A wrong value of horizontal
synchronization frequency can damage your monitor.

For example, if your monitor's manual says it is capable of displaying
1,280×1,024 resolution at 60Hz, then you should pick the item that matches
this specification. After selecting the horizontal synchronization capabilities,
press Enter.

Xconfigurator now prompts for the vertical synchronization rate of your
monitor, as shown in Figure 1-30.

Pick the vertical synchronization range nearest to your monitor's
specifications and press Enter.

Xconfigurator displays a dialog box (see Figure 1-31) informing you the *X*
server will be run to gather information about your video card.

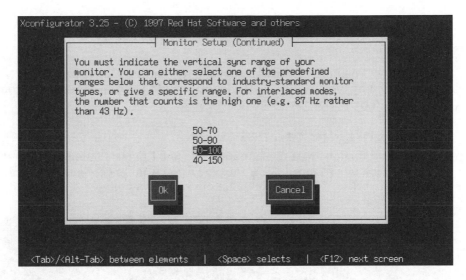

Figure 1-30: List of vertical synchronization ranges displayed by Xconfigurator

Figure 1-31: Message prior to video card probing by Xconfigurator

Because the message is meant as information to you, read the message and then press Enter to proceed.

The screen blinks a few times and then XConfigurator displays a default video mode—in terms of resolution such as 1,024×768 and color such as 8 bit. To accept the default setting, press Enter.

Xconfigurator then writes the XF86Config file in the /etc/X11 directory and displays a dialog box telling you that you are done. Press Enter to exit the *X* configuration step.

Tip After you finish the installation and reboot the PC to restart Linux, you can try *X* by typing startx at the Linux prompt. For now, you have to continue with the rest of the configuration steps.

Configure the network

After completing *X* configuration, the Red Hat installation program displays a dialog box (Figure 1-32) asking you if you want to configure the local area network (LAN) parameters for your Linux system.

Figure 1-32: Dialog box asking you if you want to configure the local area network

As the dialog box points out, this step is not for configuring the dial-up networking. You need to perform this step if your Linux system is connected to a TCP/IP LAN, through an Ethernet card.

If your system is on a LAN, even if it is a LAN that is not connected to the Internet, you should select the Yes button. The Red Hat installation program then displays a dialog box where you have to enter certain parameters for TCP/IP configuration (Figure 1-33).

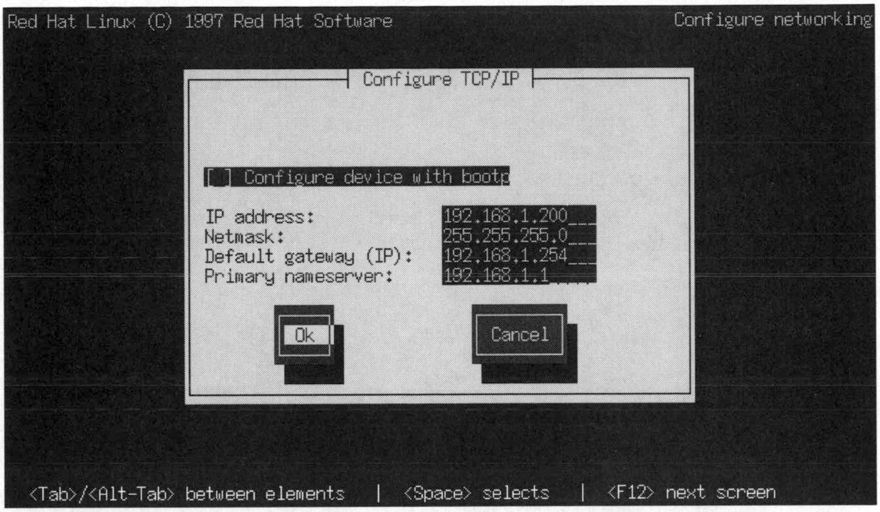

```
Red Hat Linux (C) 1997 Red Hat Software                    Configure networking

                        ┤ Configure TCP/IP ├

                  [ ] Configure device with bootp

                  IP address:            192.168.1.200___
                  Netmask:               255.255.255.0___
                  Default gateway (IP):  192.168.1.254___
                  Primary nameserver:    192.168.1.1_____

                          Ok                Cancel

       <Tab>/<Alt-Tab> between elements  |  <Space> selects  |  <F12> next screen
```

Figure 1-33: TCP/IP configuration dialog where you enter IP addresses for a TCP/IP LAN (sample values filled in)

The dialog box asks for four key parameters:

- IP address of the Linux system (the one you are installing)
- Network mask
- IP address of the gateway (the system through which you might go to any outside network)
- IP address of the name server

Cross-Reference

If you have a private LAN (one not directly connected to the Internet), you may use an IP address from a range that has been designated for private use. A common IP address for private LANs are the addresses in the range 192.168.1.1 through 192.168.1.254. You learn more about TCP/IP networking and IP addresses in Chapter 16.

After you enter the requested parameters, press Tab to select OK and then press Enter. The installation program then displays another dialog box (Figure 1-34) that asks for more information about the TCP/IP LAN.

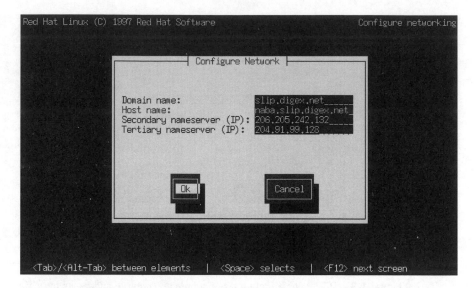

Figure 1-34: Dialog box for further network information (sample values filled in)

This time you have to enter the following information:

■ Domain name of your LAN

■ The host name for your Linux system (for a private LAN, you can assign your own host name)

■ IP address of a secondary name server

■ IP address of a tertiary name server

After you enter the requested information, select OK and press Enter.

Set the time zone

After completing the network configuration, you must select the *time zone* — the difference between the local time and the current time at Greenwich, England, which is the standard reference time (also known as Greenwich Mean Time, or GMT). The installation program shows you a list of time zones (Figure 1-35), in terms of country or regions.

You see time zones for many countries organized by the continents and for many regions of the United States. Press the up and down arrow keys to select your location. If you live on the East Coast of the United States, for example, you would select USA/Eastern. If your country is not listed, select one of the entries that designates the difference between your local time and GMT. After you select your time zone, press **Enter**.

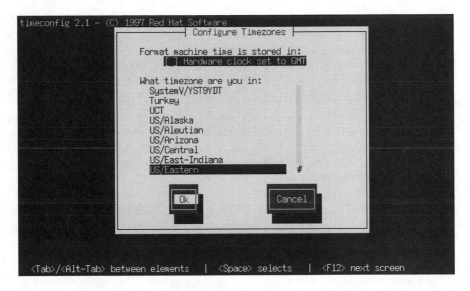

Figure 1-35: Dialog box where you select your time zone

Configure services

After time zone selection, the Red Hat installation program proceeds to set up the services that should run automatically every time you start your Linux system. You have to select the desired services from the list shown in the dialog box of Figure 1-36.

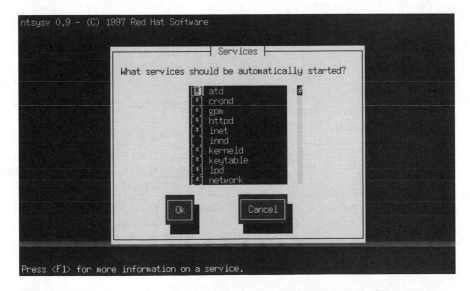

Figure 1-36: Dialog box where you select the services to start automatically

Each line in the list shows the name of a service with a square bracket prefix ([ ]). An asterisk (*) in the square bracket indicates the service is selected to run. When the dialog box first appears, many services are already selected. You can use the up and down arrow keys to move around in the list and press the Spacebar to select or deselect a service. After making your selections, press Tab to select OK and then press Enter.

Table 1-5 shows a list of the services along with a brief description of each one. The first column shows the name of the service, which is the same as the name of the program that must run to provide the service. The names with an asterisk in the second column are the ones preselected by the installation program.

Table 1-5   Services configured to start automatically in Linux

Service Name	Pre-selected	Description
atd	*	Runs commands scheduled by the `at` and `batch` commands.
crond	*	Runs user-specified programs according to a periodic schedule set by the `crontab` command.
gpm	*	Enables use of mouse in text-mode screens.
httpd	*	This is the Apache World Wide Web (WWW) server.
inet	*	This is the Internet super server, also known as `inetd`. It starts other Internet services, such as Telnet and FTP, whenever they are needed.
innd		This is the Internet News server you can use to support local new groups on your system.
kerneld	*	Automatically loads kernel modules as Linux needs these modules. You should always run the `kerneld` service because the Linux operating system needs it.
keytable	*	Loads selected keyboard map as specified in the file `/etc/sysconfig/keyboard`. You should leave this service running on your system.
lpd	*	Server that manages the queue of print jobs and sends the print jobs to the printer. You need this server if you want to do any printing from the Linux system.
mars-nwe		This is a Novell Netware compatible MARS file and print server. Run this server if you want to use your Linux system as a Netware server.
named		This is the Domain Name Server (DNS) that translates host names into IP addresses. You can run a copy on your system, if you want.

Service Name	Pre-selected	Description
network	*	This server enables you to activate or deactivate all network interfaces configured to start at system boot time.
nfs	*	Exports file systems using the Network File System (NFS) protocol so that other systems (running NFS) can share files from your system.
nfsfs	*	Server to mount or unmount NFS file systems.
portmap	*	Server used by any software that relies on Remote Procedure Calls (RPC). NFS requires the portmap service.
postgresql	*	Starts stops the PostgreSQL server that handles database requests (PostgreSQL is a free database that comes with Red Hat Linux).
random	*	Server needed to generate high-quality random numbers on the Linux system.
routed		Updates IP routing tables using the RIP protocol. You needn't enable this service unless you need to route IP packets between multiple networks in your organization.
rusersd		Enables users on any system on the network to find out who is logged in at a system.
rwhod		Enables remote users get a list of all users on the Linux system running the rwhod service.
sendmail	*	Moves mail messages from one machine to another. Start this service if you want to send mail from your Linux system.
smb	*	Starts and stops the Samba smbd and nmbd services used to support LAN Manager services on a Linux system.
snmpd	*	Simple Network Management Protocol (SNMP) service used for network management functions.
sound	*	Saves certain sound card settings at system shutdown and restores them at startup.
syslog	*	Service used by many other programs (including other services) to log various error and status messages in a log file (usually, the /var/log/messages file). You should always run this service.
ypbind		Service needed for Network Information System (NIS). You needn't start ypbind unless you are using NIS.

Configure printers

After setting up the services, the Red Hat installation program displays a dialog box (Figure 1-37) that asks whether you want to configure a printer. If you intend to do any printing from the Linux system, select Yes from this dialog box.

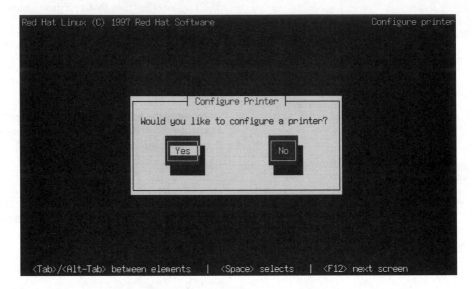

Figure 1-37: This dialog box asks if you want to configure a printer.

You should select Yes from the dialog box of Figure 1-37 even if you do not have any printer directly connected to the Linux system. You have to configure a printer even if you plan to print on a remote printer. This step enables you to select a shared printer connected to another Linux system or a Windows 95 system.

After you select Yes and press Enter, the installation program asks you about the type of printer connection, as shown in Figure 1-38.

You can select from three types of printer connections:

- **Local**: Refers to a printer connected directly to the PC where you are installing Linux.

- **Remote lpd**: Refers to a printer physically connected to another Linux system on the local network.

- **LAN Manager**: Refers to a printer connected to another PC on the local network and that runs the LAN Manager protocol (typically used to share resources such as disks and printers among PCs running Windows 95 or Windows NT).

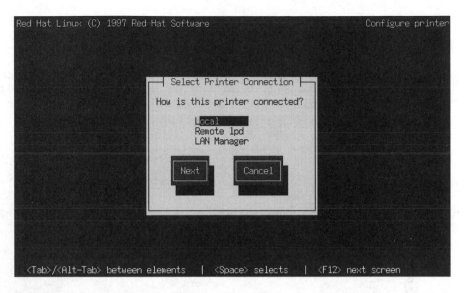

Figure 1-38: Selecting the type of printer connection

You should specify the printer connection that applies to your configuration. After you select a connection type, the installation program displays a dialog box showing two standard printer options, as shown in Figure 1-39.

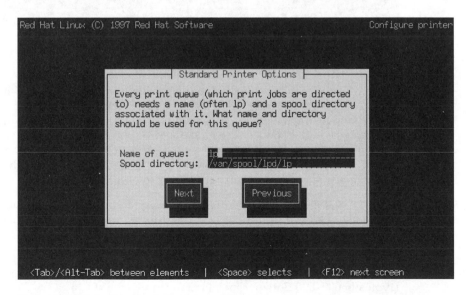

Figure 1-39: Selecting standard printer options

These are called standard options because they are needed no matter what type of printer connection you have. You needn't change these standard printer options; simply select the Next button and press Enter.

The next configuration step depends on the type of printer connection you specified in the dialog box of Figure 1-38. If you had selected a local printer, the installation program displays a dialog box (Figure 1-40) asks you to specify the printer port to which your printer is physically connected.

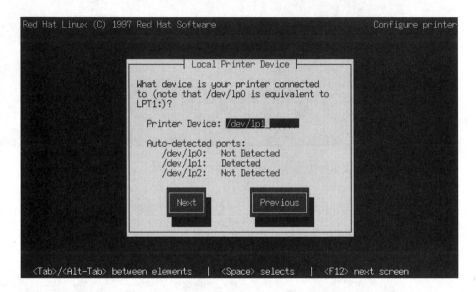

Figure 1-40: Printer port for local printer

Usually, the printer is connected to the parallel port of the PC. In Windows, the parallel ports are referred to as LPT1, LPT2, and so on. In Linux, the corresponding device names are /dev/lp0, /dev/lp1, and so on. As the dialog box of Figure 1-40 shows, the installation program tells you which parallel ports it has detected and fills in the most likely port name in a text-entry area. You should verify that the information is correct (and enter the correct port name, if necessary); then press Enter to continue configuring the printer.

The next dialog box (Figure 1-41) requires you to identify your printer type from a list of known printers. Select the printer type and then press **Enter** to continue with the printer configuration.

Next the installation program displays another dialog box (Figure 1-42) requesting information on the paper size and the resolution of the printer (typically 600×600 dots per inch in many modern laser printers). You should select the appropriate values.

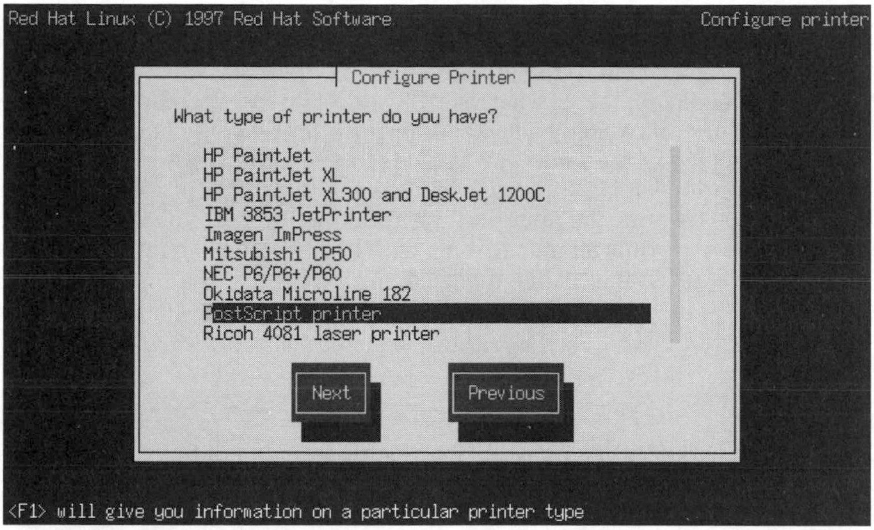

Figure 1-41: Selecting the printer type

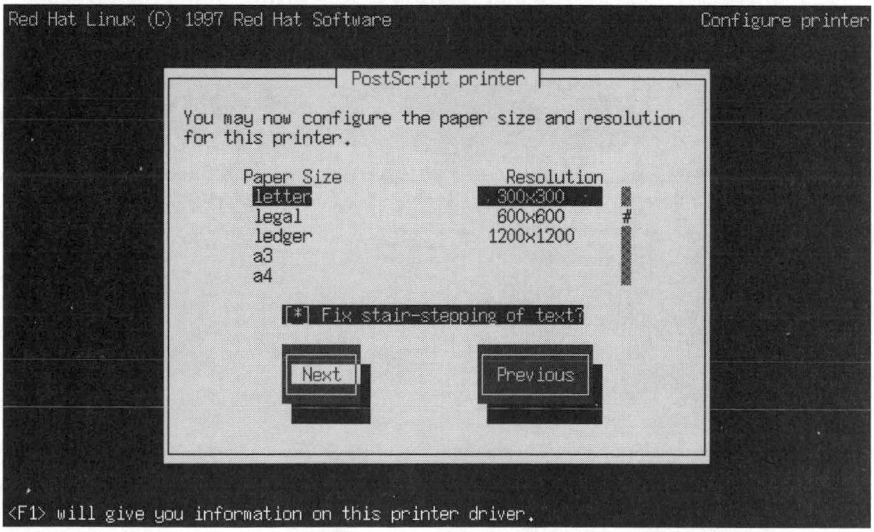

Figure 1-42: Dialog box to select paper size and resolution of selected printer

Another item in the dialog box of Figure 1-42 is an option labeled `Fix stair-stepping of text`. This refers to a problem that occurs when text files from Linux are sent to the printer — in Linux text files each line ends with a single linefeed character whereas DOS and Windows end each line with a carriage return followed by a linefeed. The printer reacts to carriage return and linefeed in the same way as old-fashioned typewriters — linefeed advances to next line and carriage return moves to beginning of a line. When printing a DOS text file, the lines print one after another, as you would expect. When the printer prints a Linux text file with lines ending in a linefeed only, however, the output looks something like this:

```
Line 1 ends here
                Line 2 here
                            and so on
                                        like a staircase.
```

To avoid this staircase effect or stair-stepping of text, just check the box marked `Fix stair-stepping of text` in the dialog box of Figure 1-42 and Linux will take care of the problem by sending a carriage return before each linefeed whenever you print a text file.

After you select the options in Figure 1-42 and press Enter, the installation program shows you all the options in another dialog box (Figure 1-43) so you can verify the printer configuration.

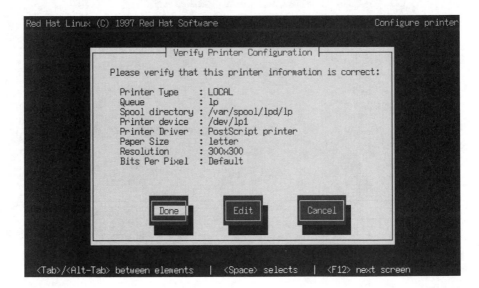

Figure 1-43: Verifying the printer settings

After confirming the settings are correct, press Enter to proceed to the next configuration step.

Set the root password

After completing the printer configuration, the installation program prompts you for a root password, as shown in Figure 1-44.

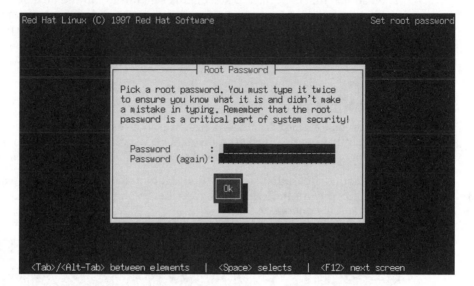

Figure 1-44: A dialog box enables you to set the root password.

The root user is the super user in Linux. Because the super user can do anything in the system, you should assign a password you can remember, but that others cannot guess easily. Typically, you would make the password at least eight characters long, include a mix of letters and numbers, and, for good measure, throw in some special characters such as + or *.

Type the password on the first line and then re-enter the password on the next line. The password does not appear onscreen. You have to type the password in twice and both entries must match before the installation program accepts the password. This ensures you did not make any mistakes in typing. After you type the password twice, select OK and press Enter to proceed to the next configuration step.

Create a custom boot disk

After you specify a root password, the installation program displays a dialog box that asks if you want to create a custom boot disk. You can use this disk to boot your Linux system if the Linux kernel on the hard disk is damaged or if the Linux Loader (described in the next section) does not work. Press Enter to answer Yes. The installation program then asks you to insert a formatted floppy into your PC's A drive. You should place a formatted floppy in the A drive and press Enter (note, all data on the floppy will be destroyed).

The installation program copies the Linux kernel and some other files to the floppy. After the setup program prepares the custom boot disk, remove the floppy from the A drive, label it appropriately, and save it for future use.

You can use this boot disk to start Linux on your PC. In the next section, you see how to place a Linux Loader program on your PC's C drive. That process, however, involves altering a critical part of the hard disk. If you do not feel comfortable with altering the hard disk or if the Linux Loader somehow fails to work, you can always boot Linux from the custom boot disk you just created.

Install LILO

LILO stands for *Linux Loader* — a program that resides on your hard disk and starts Linux from the hard disk. If you have Windows or OS/2 on your hard disk, you can configure LILO to load any of these operating systems as well.

In the last configuration step, the Red Hat installation program displays a dialog box (Figure 1-45) that asks you where you want to install LILO, also known as the *bootloader*.

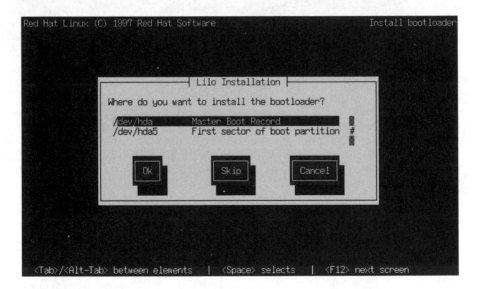

Figure 1-45: Specifying where to install LILO

The dialog box gives you the option to install LILO in one of two locations:

■ Master Boot Record (MBR), which is located in the first sector of your PC's hard disk (the C drive)

■ First sector of the partition where you loaded Linux

Select a location — preferably the Master Boot Record — press Tab to select OK, and then press **Enter**.

Caution

Although a Skip button enables you to skip LILO installation, you need to install LILO, or you will be unable to start Linux after you finish the installation. At the same time, though, you should know installing LILO in the Master Boot Record can be risky. If LILO is not configured properly, your PC may be unable to boot from the hard disk. Unfortunately, the Red Hat installation program does not offer any other option for booting Linux. You have to wait until you have started Linux for the first time before you can prepare a boot disk to start Linux from your PC's A drive.

After you select the location for LILO installation, the installation program displays another dialog box (Figure 1-46) that enables you to enter any special options that may be needed by Linux as it boots.

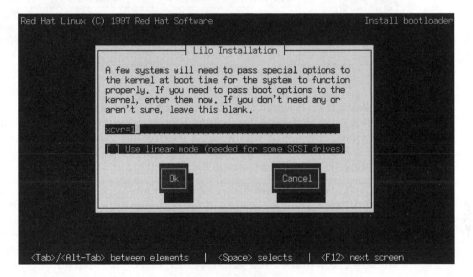

Figure 1-46: Entering boot-time options for Linux

Whether you need any special options depends on what hardware you have. For example, on my system, I have a 3Com 3C503 Ethernet card connected to the local Ethernet using an external transceiver. When Linux loads the driver software for the 3Com 3C503 card, I need to specify the option xcvr=1 to make sure the driver uses the external transceiver. I enter this option on the first line of the dialog box, as shown in Figure 1-46.

After you enter any necessary options, select the OK button, and press Enter to continue with LILO installation. The Red Hat installation program displays another dialog box (Figure 1-47) that gives you the option to make other disk partitions bootable.

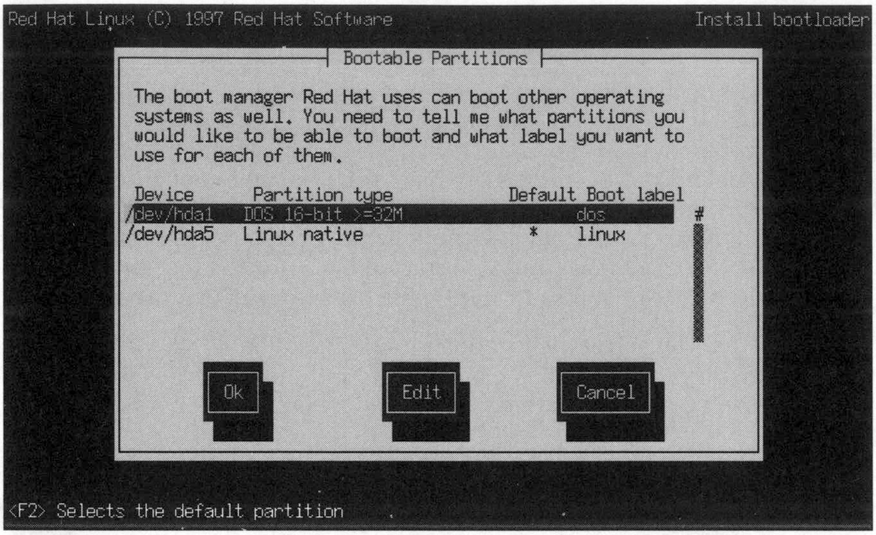

```
Red Hat Linux (C) 1997 Red Hat Software                    Install bootloader

                    ┤ Bootable Partitions ├

        The boot manager Red Hat uses can boot other operating
        systems as well. You need to tell me what partitions you
        would like to be able to boot and what label you want to
        use for each of them.

        Device      Partition type            Default Boot label
        /dev/hda1   DOS 16-bit >=32M                   dos      #
        /dev/hda5   Linux native              *        linux




              Ok              Edit              Cancel



<F2> Selects the default partition
```

Figure 1-47: Making other partitions bootable under LILO

The dialog box shows a table that lists the Linux partition and any other partitions that may contain another operating system. On my system, the table includes two entries: the Linux partition and the DOS partition (that actually has Windows 95 installed on it). Each entry in this table is an operating system LILO can boot.

After you install LILO, whenever your PC boots from the hard disk, LILO runs and displays a prompt. At the prompt, you may type the name of an operating system to boot — the last column of the table in Figure 1-47 shows the names you may enter at the LILO prompt. In this case, you type linux to boot Linux and dos to boot from the DOS partition (which should start Windows 95, if that's what you have installed on that partition).

If you enter nothing at the LILO prompt, it waits for a few seconds and boots the default operating system. The default operating system is the one with an asterisk in the Default column in Figure 1-47 (in this case Linux is the default).

If you want to change any of the entries, select Edit and then press Enter. If you accept the choices as shown in the dialog box of Figure 1-47, press Tab to select OK and then press Enter. This installs LILO and completes the Red Hat Linux installation.

Starting Linux for the First Time

After you finish installing LILO, the Red Hat Linux installation program automatically reboots the system. The PC goes through its normal power-up sequence and loads LILO from the C drive and the following prompt appears:

```
LILO boot:
```

When you install LILO, if you specified the Linux partition as the default one, you can simply wait; after a few seconds, LILO boots Linux.

If you want to boot from another partition (such as DOS), press the Tab key. LILO displays the names of the available bootable partitions. For example, a typical display might be:

```
linux dos
```

You can then type the name of the partition you want to boot (or press Enter to boot from the first partition).

After LILO boots Linux, you should see a long list of opening messages, including the names of the devices Linux detects. One of the first few messages says `Calibrating delay loop.. ok - 299.01 BogoMIPS`; the number that precedes `BogoMIPS` depends on your system's processor type. *BogoMIPS* is a Linux jargon term that is the subject of countless discussions in various USENET newsgroups devoted to Linux. (*Usenet* is a loose collection of computers that exchange electronic mail and news. You learn more about Usenet in Chapters 18 and 19.) Linux uses the BogoMIPS measurement in situations in which the operating system has to wait for a specified period.

At the end of all the messages, you see the Linux login prompt, as follows:

```
Red Hat Linux release 5.1 (Manhattan)
Kernel 2.0.34 on an i586
hostname login:
```

where `hostname` is the name you assigned to your system when you configured the network. If you do not configure the network, `localhost` is used as the system name.

Because there are no other users at this point, type **root** and press Enter. Then type the root password (the one you set during installation) to log in as the super user. Now you can perform a few initial chores and learn how to shut down your Linux system.

What is BogoMIPS?

When your Linux system boots, you notice a message such as `Calibrating delay loop.. ok - 299.01 BogoMIPS`, with some number before `BogoMIPS`. BogoMIPS is one of those words that confound new Linux users. This sidebar explains what BogoMIPS means.

As you may know, *MIPS* stands for *millions of instructions per second* — a measure of how fast your computer runs programs. (As such, MIPS is not a good measure of performance, because comparing the MIPS of different types of computers is difficult.) *BogoMIPS* is *bogus MIPS*, which refers to an indication of the computer's speed. Linux uses the BogoMIPS number to calibrate a delay loop, in which the computer processes some instructions repeatedly until a specified amount of time has passed.

The BogoMIPS numbers can range anywhere from 1 to 300 or more, depending on the type of processor (386, 486, or Pentium). A typical 33MHz 80386DX system has a BogoMIPS of about 6, whereas a 66MHz 80486DX2/66 system shows a *BogoMIPS* of about 33. The BogoMIPS for older Pentium systems is on par with (or slightly less than) that of 80486 processors, because the *BogoMIPS* calculation does not take advantage of any advanced features (such as the capability to execute instructions in parallel) of the Pentium. On my 75MHz Pentium system, Linux reports a *BogoMIPS* of 30.22. On a more recent 200MHz Pentium MMX system, however, the *BogoMIPS* is 299.01.

Recovering from a forgotten root password

If you forget the root password, you can follow these steps to set a new root password:

1. Power up your PC as usual. At the LILO boot prompt, type the name of the Linux boot partition followed by the word `single`, as follows (you type the text shown in boldface):

   `LILO boot: `**`linux single`**

   This causes Linux to start up as usual, but run in a single-user mode that does not require you to log in. After Linux starts, you see the following command-line prompt:

   `bash#`

2. Use the `passwd` command to change the root password as follows:

   `bash# `**`passwd`**
   `New UNIX password:`

   Type the password you want to use (it won't appear onscreen) and then press Enter. Linux asks for the password again, as follows:

   `Retype new UNIX password:`

   Type the password again, and press Enter. If you enter the same password both times, the `passwd` command changes the password and displays a message:

   `passwd: all authentication tokens updated successfully`

3. Now you reboot the PC by pressing Ctrl+Alt+Delete. After Linux starts, it displays the familiar login prompt again. Now you should be able to log in as root with the new password.

Creating a boot floppy disk

After you successfully start Linux and log in as root, you should immediately create a Linux boot floppy disk. You can use this floppy disk to boot your Linux system if the Linux kernel on the hard disk is damaged. You should also have the boot floppy disk before you do anything to the Linux kernel, such as upgrade it to a new version following the procedures outlined in Chapter 2.

To create the boot floppy disk, follow these steps:

1. Insert a formatted floppy disk into your PC's A drive. If you have an unformatted floppy, you can format it with the following command:

```
fdformat /dev/fd0H1440
Double-sided, 80 tracks, 18 sec/track. Total capacity 1440 kB.
Formatting ... done
Verifying ... done
```

2. Copy the file vmlinuz from the /boot directory to the floppy disk. (The vmlinuz file happens to be the Linux kernel.) Use the following command:

```
cd /boot
cp vmlinuz /dev/fd0
cp: overwrite `/dev/fd0'? y
```

3. Determine the kernel's root device — the disk partition where the root file system is located — with the following command:

```
rdev
/dev/hda3 /
```

In this case, the root device is /dev/hda3; the device name may be different on your system.

4. Set the kernel's root device. Use the device reported by the rdev command in the previous step. For example, to set the root device to /dev/hda3, I type:

```
rdev /dev/fd0 /dev/hda3
```

5. Mark the root device as read-only. Use the following command:

```
rdev -R /dev/fd0 1
```

This causes Linux initially to mount the root file system as read-only. Then Linux checks the file system for any errors and, if no errors exist, the file system is mounted in read-write mode. By setting the root device as read-only, you avoid several warning and error messages.

After you prepare the boot floppy disk, you should try it. Go through the next four sections. Then, when you are ready to shutdown the system, put the boot floppy disk in the A drive and type the following command:

```
/sbin/shutdown -r now
```

After the PC reboots, Linux should start as usual and you should see a login prompt. If it does not work, remove the floppy disk from the A drive and press **Ctrl+Alt+Delete** to boot from the hard disk. Then, you can repeat the procedure for creating the boot floppy disk.

Starting X

In one of the Red Hat Linux installation steps, you configured the X Window System. The configuration step creates a file that contains information about your mouse, keyboard, video card, and monitor. (You learn all about the X configuration file in Chapter 4.) For now, you should quickly start X and see if the configuration file works. To start X, type the following command at the Linux prompt:

```
startx
```

You will see a number of messages flash across the screen as the X server starts.

Caution

If the screen goes crazy, press Ctrl+Alt+Backspace to kill X. If this does not stop X, press the reset button of your computer. Otherwise, your monitor may be damaged.

If the configuration file does not work at all, you will see a number of error messages: one saying the X server is aborting and then a message about being unable to connect to the X server that goes something like this:

```
_X11TransSocketUNIXConnect: Can't connect: errno = 111
giving up.
xinit:  Connection refused (errno 111): unable to connect to X server
xinit:  No such process (errno 3): Server error.
```

Cross-Reference

Although the error messages seem to refer to sockets and connections, the reason is usually problems with the configuration file — the X server could not start because it had problems with some of the settings in the X configuration file. One common problem is the X server could not find a suitable video mode (screen resolution) for your monitor and video card. Consult Chapter 10 to learn more about the X configuration file and what settings might help you get X running on your system.

If all goes well, the screen will turn gray for a time and you will see a cursor shaped like an X. After a little while, the screen background changes and a number of windows appear, as shown in Figure 1-48.

Cross-Reference

Depending on your video card and monitor, your screen layout may be different from Figure 1-48. In particular, your screen might show only a small part of a larger virtual screen; then you have to move the mouse down to see the toolbar. For now you can ignore these nuances. Chapter 5 explains the layout of various elements onscreen and how you may customize them.

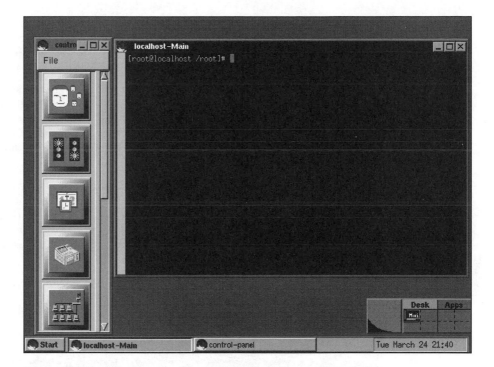

Figure 1-48: Successfully starting *X* for the first time

Look at the initial *X* window screen as it appears in Figure 1-48. You should note three key items on the screen:

- Along the left edge, you see a control panel — a window with a number of large buttons, each with a picture on it. These icons represent tools (computer programs) you can start by clicking each icon. Chapter 6 shows you how to use the control panel tools to perform some Linux system administration chores.

- To the right of the control panel — occupying much of the screen space — is a terminal window. You can type Linux commands in this window. Chapter 6 introduces you to some Linux commands and Appendix B lists many commonly used Linux commands.

- A task bar, similar to the one in Windows 95, appears along the bottom edge of the screen. As in Windows 95, the task bar has a Start button and a button for each of the open windows. The right edge of the task bar shows the current date and time.

Adding user accounts

While you have the *X* graphical interface up and running, you might as well perform one key system administration function — add other user accounts to the system.

Tip A good idea is to create another user account besides root. Even if you are the only user of the system, logging in as a less-privileged user is good practice, because this way, you cannot damage any important system files inadvertently. When necessary, you can log in as root and perform any system administration tasks.

As a convenience, Red Hat Linux includes several graphical system administration tools that appear as icons in a control panel (see the tall window on the left-hand side of the screen in Figure 1-48). If you move the mouse over each icon, a pop-up help message shows you the name of this tool. The first icon, with the picture of a face, is meant for adding user accounts.

To add myself as a new user, for example, I would follow these steps:

1. Click the first icon in the control panel. This brings up the User Configurator tool, as shown in Figure 1-49.

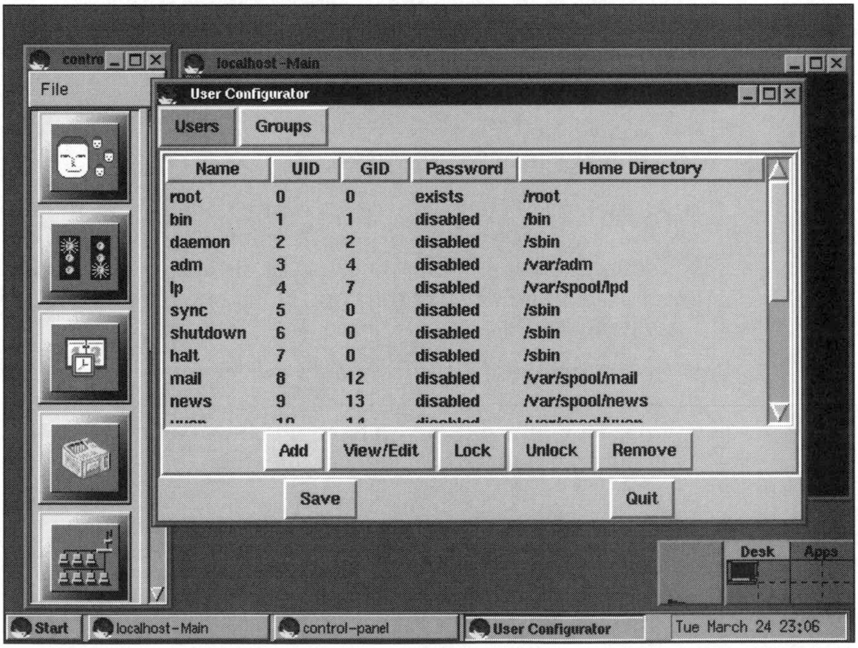

Figure 1-49: Main window of the User Configurator tool

2. Click the Add button in the main window of Figure 1-49. This brings up the Edit User Definition dialog box, as shown in Figure 1-50.

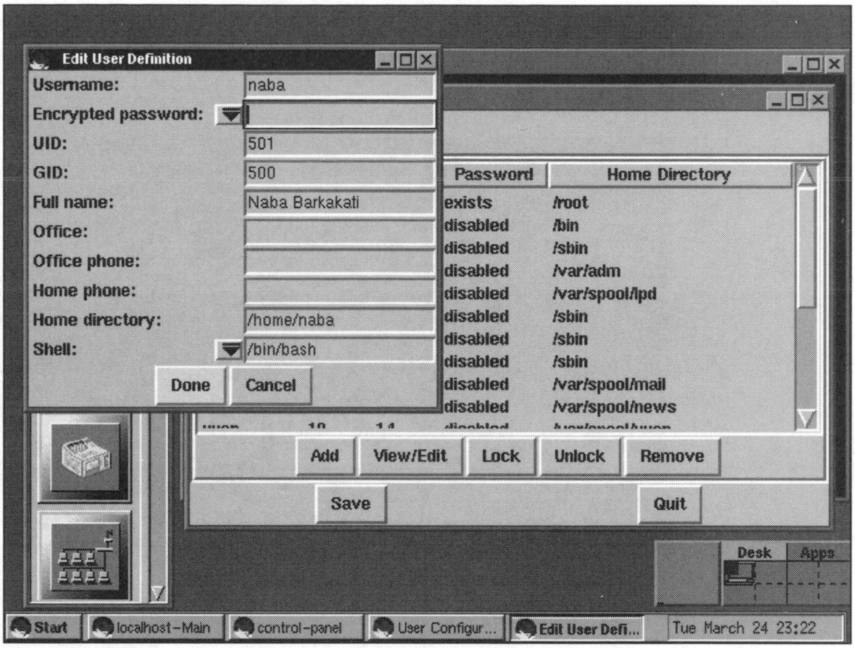

Figure 1-50: Entering information for a new user account

3. Fill in the requested information. In particular, you must enter the user name, password and the home directory. For my account, I use /home/naba as the home directory. You can use a similar home directory for your account. After you fill in all the fields, click the Done button. This returns you to the main window of the User Configurator tool (Figure 1-49).

4. Click the Quit button. A dialog box asks for confirmation. Click Save and Quit button to save the new user information and exit the tool.

Quitting X

Now that you have tried *X* and used one of the graphical tools under *X,* you should learn how to quit *X*. To shut down the X Window System, follow these steps:

1. Click the Start button on the task bar (at the bottom-left corner of the screen). The Start menu pops up (similar to Windows 95).

2. Move the mouse to the `Exit Fvwm` item (*Fvwm* refers to the window manager — you have to exit the window manager to shut down *X*). Another menu appears.

3. Click the `Yes, Really Quit` button (see Figure 1-51). The *X* screen disappears and you return to the text screen. You can now see some of the messages the *X* server printed when it had first started.

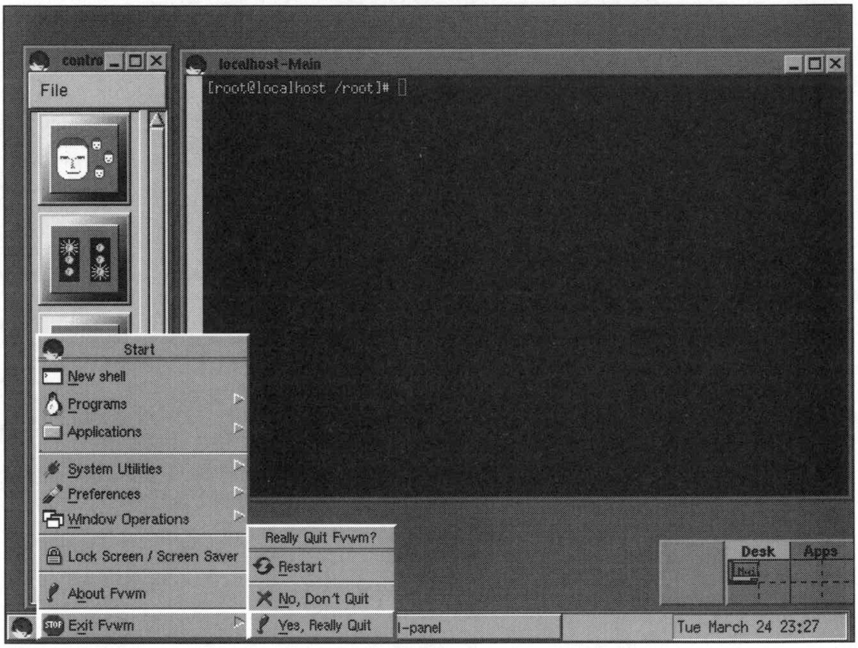

Figure 1-51: Shutting down the X Window System

Looking up the online documentation

You should know an important source of information in Linux. Every so often, you see instructions asking you to enter a Linux command. After a while, you are bound to get to the point at which you vaguely recall a command's name, but you cannot remember the exact syntax of what you are supposed to type. This situation is where the Linux online manual pages can come to your rescue.

You can view the manual page — commonly referred to as the *man page* — for a command by using the man command. (You do have to remember this command to be able to look up online help.) To view the man page for the `passwd` command, for example, type the following command:

```
man passwd
```

Linux displays the information page by page. Press the Spacebar to move to the next page. When you finish, press **q** to return to the Linux command prompt.

Having touted the usefulness of the online help pages, I must point out the term *Linux command* refers to any executable file, ranging from a script file that contains other Linux commands to standard Linux executable programs. Although man pages exist for most standard programs, many programs do not have any online help. For example, if you type `help` at a Linux command prompt, you get a list of commands that are defined internally to the command processor (called a *shell*). When you type **man help**, however, Linux responds as follows:

```
No manual entry for help
```

Nevertheless, whenever you are at a loss about some command, using the man command is worthwhile to see whether any online help for that command exists.

Another form of online documentation is the HOWTO files in the /usr/doc/HOWTO directory of your system (these files are installed if you select the Extra Documentation component during installation). The HOWTO files all have a `-HOWTO.gz` suffix in the file name. Each file is a text file that has been compressed using the `gzip` command.

Each HOWTO file contains information about some area of Linux, such as the hardware it supports or how to create a boot disk. Table 1-6 lists the HOWTO files that should be in the `/usr/doc/HOWTO` directory of your Linux system provided you had installed the Extra Documentation component.

To view any of these files, go to the `/usr/doc/HOWTO` directory and use the `zcat` command as follows:

```
cd /usr/doc/HOWTO
zcat topic-name-HOWTO.gz | more
```

where `topic-name` is the first part of the filename excluding the `-HOWTO.gz` suffix. Thus, to view the `Bootdisk-HOWTO.gz` file, type:

```
zcat Bootdisk-HOWTO.gz | more
```

Tip

You needn't type the long filename; just type `zcat Bootd` and then press Tab. The Linux command processor—the shell—automatically completes the filename that matches what you typed. Then you can type `| more` to complete the command line.

Table 1-6   Linux HOWTO files in `/usr/doc/HOWTO` **directory**

HOWTO file name	*Contents*
`3Dfx-HOWTO.gz`	How to configure Linux to support the 3Dfx graphics accelerator chip.
`AX25-HOWTO.gz`	How to install and configure Linux to support for AX.25 packet radio protocol used by Amateur Radio Operators worldwide.
`Access-HOWTO.gz`	How to make Linux useable by persons with disabilities.
`Alpha-HOWTO.gz`	Overview of Digital Equipment Corporation's 64-bit RISC architecture Alpha CPU (Linux runs on the Alpha).
`Assembly-HOWTO.gz`	How to program in assembly language in Linux.
`Benchmarking-HOWTO.gz`	How to benchmark a Linux system — measure how fast the system completes a computing task.
`BootPrompt-HOWTO.gz`	A list of arguments that can be passed to Linux at boot time (at the `LILO boot:` prompt).
`Bootdisk-HOWTO.gz`	How to create boot, root, and other utility disks for Linux.
`CD-Writing-HOWTO.gz`	How to record a CD-ROM using a CD Recorder installed in a Linux system.
`CDROM-HOWTO.gz`	How to install, configure, and use CD-ROM drives with Linux.
`Chinese-HOWTO.gz`	How to configure Linux for use with Chinese character set and Chinese version of X Window System.
`Commercial-HOWTO.gz`	A list of commercial software for Linux.
`Consultants-HOWTO.gz`	A list of consultants or consulting firms that provide support for Linux.
`Cyrillic-HOWTO.gz`	How to typeset and print documents in the Russian language on a Linux system.
`DNS-HOWTO.gz`	How to set up Domain Name Service (DNS) on a Linux system.
`DOS-to-Linux-HOWTO.gz`	How to apply your knowledge of MS-DOS in Linux.
`DOSEMU-HOWTO.gz`	How to set up and use the MS-DOS Emulator, DOSEMU.
`Danish-HOWTO.gz`	How to configure Linux for use with the Danish character set.
`Database-HOWTO.gz`	How to set up the PostgreSQL Relational Database System on Linux (PostgreSQL comes with Red Hat Linux on the companion CD-ROM).
`Disk-HOWTO.gz`	How best to use multiple disks and partitions in a Linux system.

HOWTO file name	Contents
Distribution-HOWTO.gz	A list of Linux distributions with particular focus on commercial CD-ROM distributions.
ELF-HOWTO.gz	How to compile and run programs in the ELF (Executable and Linking Format) binary format (the version of Linux on the companion CD-ROM is already configured to run ELF binaries).
Emacspeak-HOWTO.gz	How to support blind users using Emacspeak, an Emacs subsystem that provides feedback through synthesized speech.
Ethernet-HOWTO.gz	How to configure and use Ethernet network adapters with Linux.
Finnish-HOWTO.gz	How to set up Linux for the Finnish language (except for the initial paragraph, the HOWTO itself is in Finnish).
Firewall-HOWTO.gz	How to set up an Internet firewall on a Linux system.
French-HOWTO.gz	How to set up Linux for the French language (this HOWTO is in French).
Ftape-HOWTO.gz	How to set up and use floppy tape drives (QIC-40, QIC-80, QIC-3010, and QIC-3020 compatible tape drives that connect to your PC through the floppy disk controller) in Linux.
GCC-HOWTO.gz	How to set up and use the GNU C compiler and development libraries in Linux.
German-HOWTO.gz	How to use Linux with the German character set (this HOWTO is in German).
Glibc2-HOWTO.gz	How to install and use the GNU C Library Version 2 (libc 6) on Linux systems.
HAM-HOWTO.gz	Information about amateur radio software for Linux.
Hardware-HOWTO.gz	A list of hardware known to work with Linux and how to locate any necessary drivers.
Hebrew-HOWTO.gz	How to support Hebrew character set in X Window System and text-mode screens.
IPX-HOWTO.gz	How to obtain, install, and configure various software that use the Linux support for IPX protocol (IPX is used by Novell Netware).
ISP-Hookup-HOWTO.gz	How to connect a Linux system to an Internet service provider (ISP) via a dial-up modem connection.
Installation-HOWTO.gz	How to obtain and install Linux.
Intranet-Server-HOWTO.gz	How to use a Linux system in an Intranet Intranet that ties together UNIX, Novell Netware, Windows NT, and Windows 95 systems.

(continued)

Table 1-6 *(Continued)*

HOWTO file name	Contents
Italian-HOWTO.gz	How to set up Linux for the Italian language (this HOWTO is in Italian).
Java-CGI-HOWTO.gz	How to develop and use Java programs in Linux.
Kernel-HOWTO.gz	How to upgrade and rebuild the Linux kernel.
Keyboard-and-Console-HOWTO.gz	How to use various Linux utilities to configure the keyboard and the console (the text-mode screen).
MGR-HOWTO.gz	How to use the MGR (ManaGeR) graphical windowing system in Linux.
MILO-HOWTO.gz	How to set up and use the Miniloader (MILO) for Linux on Alpha AXP based systems (just as LILO loads and starts Linux on Intel-based PCs, MILO loads Linux on Alpha systems).
Mail-HOWTO.gz	How to set up and maintain Electronic Mail (e-mail) on a Linux system.
NET-3-HOWTO.gz	How to install and configure TCP/IP networking in Linux.
NFS-HOWTO.gz	How to set up NFS (Network File System) server and client in Linux.
NIS-HOWTO.gz	How to configure NIS (Network Information Service) in Linux.
News-HOWTO.gz	How to set up and maintain USENET news (discussion groups) in Linux.
Optical-Disk-HOWTO.gz	How to install and configure optical disk drives in Linux (includes detailed coverage of the Panasonic LF1000 PD Phase change optical drive with the SCSI-II interface).
PCI-HOWTO.gz	Information on Linux's support for the PCI (Peripheral Component Interconnect) bus architecture.
PCMCIA-HOWTO.gz	How to install and use PCMCIA (Personal Computer Memory Card International Association) Card Services in Linux.
PPP-HOWTO.gz	How to set up and use Point-to-Point Protocol (PPP) networking in Linux.
Pilot-HOWTO.gz	How to use the 3Com (U.S. Robotics) Palm Pilot personal digital assistant (PDA) with a Linux system.
Polish-HOWTO.gz	How to set up Linux for the Polish language (this HOWTO is in Polish).
Printing-HOWTO.gz	How to set up printing in Linux.
Printing-Usage-HOWTO.gz	How to use the print spooling system in Linux.
RPM-HOWTO.gz	How to use the Red Hat Package Manager (RPM) in Linux.

HOWTO file name	*Contents*
Reading-List-HOWTO.gz	List of books useful for a Linux user.
SCSI-HOWTO.gz	Information about support for SCSI devices in Linux.
SCSI-Programming-HOWTO.gz	Information on programming the SCSI device driver in Linux (useful for programmers who want to add support for a new SCSI device in Linux).
SMB-HOWTO.gz	How to use the Server Message Block (SMB) protocol, also called the NetBIOS or LAN Manager protocol, with Linux.
SRM-HOWTO.gz	How to boot an Alpha-based Linux system using the SRM (System Reference Manual) firmware, which is the firmware normally used to boot DEC UNIX on Alpha.
Serial-HOWTO.gz	How to set up serial communication devices in Linux.
Serial-Programming-HOWTO.gz	How to program the serial port in Linux.
Shadow-Password-HOWTO.gz	How to obtain, install, and configure the password Shadow Suite in Linux (password shadowing provides for more secure passwords than the ones stored in the /etc/passwd file).
Slovenian-HOWTO.gz	How to configure Linux for Slovenian users (this HOWTO is in Slovenian).
Sound-HOWTO.gz	How to enable support for sound hardware in Linux.
Sound-Playing-HOWTO.gz	Lists many sound file formats and the applications that can be used to play sound in Linux.
Spanish-HOWTO.gz	How to configure Linux for Spanish-speaking users (this HOWTO is in Spanish).
TeTeX-HOWTO.gz	How to install and use the teTeX TeX (pronounced *tech* as in technology) and LaTeX document formatting software in Linux.
Thai-HOWTO.gz	How to set up Linux for the Thai language.
Tips-HOWTO.gz	Hints and tips to make Linux more useful and fun.
UMSDOS-HOWTO.gz	How to install and use the UMSDOS file system that enables you to install Linux in an MS-DOS directory (not included in Red Hat Linux).
UPS-HOWTO.gz	How to use an uninterruptable power supply (UPS) with Linux.
UUCP-HOWTO.gz	How to set up and use the UNIX-to-UNIX Copy (UUCP) software in Linux.
User-Group-HOWTO.gz	How to establish and run a Linux User Group.
VAR-HOWTO.gz	Lists Linux Value Added Resellers (VARs).

(continued)

Table 1-6 *(Continued)*	
HOWTO file name	**Contents**
VMS-to-Linux-HOWTO.gz	How to transition from VMS to Linux (VMS is an operating system that runs on VAX systems from Digital Equipment Corporation).
XFree86-HOWTO.gz	How to install and configure the XFree86 (X Window System Version 11 Release 6 — X11R6) in Linux.
XFree86-Video-Timings-HOWTO.gz	How to create a modeline in the *X* configuration file for a specific video card (see Chapter 10 for a description of modeline and format of the X configuration file).

Shutting down Linux

When you are ready to shut down Linux, you should do so in an orderly manner. Even if you are the sole user of a Linux system, several other programs usually are running in the background. Also, operating systems such as Linux try to optimize the way they write data to the disk. Because disk access is relatively slow (compared with the time needed to access memory locations), data usually is held in memory and written to the disk in large chunks. If you simply turn the power off, therefore, you run the risk that some files won't be updated properly.

To shut down Linux, use the shutdown command. You have to log in as root to execute this command. If you are already logged in using another user name, you can become super user by typing the following command (your input is shown in boldface; my comments are in italic):

```
su
Password:     (type the root password and press Enter)
```

After you become super user, type the following command to halt the system:

```
/sbin/shutdown -h now
```

The following message appears:

```
The system is going down for system halt NOW !!
```

After a few moments, you see a many more messages about processes being stopped. Finally, you see the message:

```
System halted
```

Now you can safely turn the power off.

If you want to reboot the system instead of halting it, use the `shutdown` command with the `-r` option, as follows:

```
/sbin/shutdown -r now
```

Tip

Another way to restart the system quickly is to press Ctrl+Alt+Delete — the same key combination you use to reboot a PC under DOS. Anyone can use the Ctrl+Alt+Delete sequence to reboot a Linux system from the console (this means the PC's keyboard, not a terminal connected to the serial port).

Summary

Linux is a UNIX-like operating system for Intel 80×86, Pentium, and compatible systems. The CD-ROM that accompanies this book includes the latest version of the popular Red Hat Linux distribution. This chapter guides you through the process of installing Linux on your PC. The next chapter shows you how to keep your Linux kernel current and how to install new packages using the Red Hat Package Manager (RPM).

The detailed information in this chapter includes:

▶ Information about your PC that you should gather before installing Linux

▶ The overall process of installing Red Hat Linux (including the X Window System) from the companion CD-ROM

▶ Steps you perform under MS-DOS or Microsoft Windows before installing Linux

▶ How to boot Linux initially, partition the hard disk, and load the various software components from the companion CD-ROM using the Red Hat installation program.

▶ How to start and shut down a Linux system

Chapter 2

Upgrading Linux

One reason Linux is so exciting is many programmers are constantly improving it. Some programmers, for example, write drivers that add support for new hardware, such as a new CD-ROM drive or a new networking card. Other programmers add support for more video cards to run the X Window System. The Linux development community makes all these innovations available to you in the form of fixes, known as *patches,* or through new versions of Linux.

Although you needn't upgrade or modify the Linux operating system — the kernel — every time a new patch or a new version becomes available, sometimes you need to upgrade simply because the new version corrects some problems or supports your hardware better.

You may want to rebuild the kernel even when there are no fixes or enhancements. The Linux kernel on the companion CD-ROM is a generic kernel that uses modules to support all types of hardware. You may want to build a new kernel that links in the drivers for only those devices actually installed on your system. In particular, if you have a SCSI hard disk, you definitely want to create a kernel that supports your SCSI adapter. Depending on your needs, you may also want to change some of the kernel configuration options, such as turning on IP forwarding, so you can use your Linux system as an Internet gateway for your local area network (LAN).

Many of the fixes and improvements are provided by Red Hat — these updates are in the form of Red Hat Packages distributed from Red Hat's FTP server (ftp://ftp.redhat.com/). To install these packages, you have to use the Red Hat Package Manager.

This chapter starts with a brief tutorial about rpm — the Red Hat Package Manager program. Then it shows you how to apply a kernel patch and how to rebuild the Linux kernel.

Using the Red Hat Package Manager

A significant innovation of Red Hat is the *Red Hat Package Manager* (RPM) —
a system for packaging all the necessary files for a software product in a
single file. Red Hat Linux is distributed in the form of a large number of RPMs.
When you install Red Hat Linux from the companion CD-ROM, the installation
program uses the rpm command to unpack the packages and copy the files to
appropriate locations on the disk.

Although you needn't understand the internal structure of an RPM file, you
should know how to use the rpm command to work with RPM files.
Specifically, you may want to perform one or more of the following tasks with
RPMs:

- Find out the version number and other information about RPMs installed
  on your system.

- Install a new software package from an RPM. For example, you might
  install a package you had skipped during the initial installation. In
  particular, you have to install the source files for Linux kernel before you
  can rebuild the kernel.

- Remove (uninstall) unneeded software you previously installed from an
  RPM. You might uninstall a package to reclaim the disk space if you find
  you never use the package.

- Upgrade an older version of an RPM with a new one. You might upgrade
  after you download a new version of a package from Red Hat's FTP
  server. Often, you must upgrade an RPM to benefit from the fixes in the
  new version.

- Verify an RPM is in working order. You can verify a package to check if all
  necessary files are in the correct locations.

You can perform all these tasks with the rpm command — it's all a matter of
using different options. The next few sections briefly introduce you to the rpm
command.

Tip

If you ever forget the rpm options, type the following command to see a list:

```
rpm --help | more
```

You will be amazed by the number of options rpm has!

Understanding RPM filenames

An RPM contains a number of files, but it appears as a single file on your
Linux system. By convention, the RPM filenames have a specific structure.
To see the names of RPM files that come on the companion CD-ROM, use
the following steps:

1. Place the CD-ROM in the CD-ROM drive and mount it with a command such as the following:

```
mount /dev/hdc /cdrom
mount: block device /dev/hdc is write-protected, mounting read-only
```

   Make sure you use the device name for your CD-ROM drive in place of /dev/hdc.

2. Go to the directory in which the RPMs are located and view a listing:

```
cd /cdrom/RedHat/RPMS
ls *.rpm | more
AnotherLevel-0.5-2.noarch.rpm
BRU2000-15.0P-1.i386.rpm
BRU2000-X11-15.0P-1.i386.rpm
ElectricFence-2.0.5-5.i386.rpm
ImageMagick-3.9.1-1.i386.rpm
ImageMagick-devel-3.9.1-1.i386.rpm
MAKEDEV-2.3.1-1.noarch.rpm
SysVinit-2.71-3.i386.rpm
X11R6-contrib-3.3.1-1.i386.rpm
XFree86-100dpi-fonts-3.3.1-14.i386.rpm
XFree86-3.3.1-14.i386.rpm
XFree86-75dpi-fonts-3.3.1-14.i386.rpm
(rest of the listing deleted)
```

As you might guess from the listing, all RPM files end with a .rpm extension. To understand the various parts of the file name, consider the following RPM:

```
XFree86-3.3.1-14.i386.rpm
```

This file name has the following parts separated by dashes (-):

- *Package name*: XFree86

- *Version number*: 3.3.1

- *Release number*: 14 (this is a Red Hat-assigned release number)

- *Architecture*: i386 (that means this package is for Intel 80386-compatible processors)

Usually, the package name is descriptive enough for you to guess what the RPM might contain. The version number is the same as that of the software package's current version number (even when it is distributed in some other form such as a tar file). Red Hat assigns the release number to keep track of changes. The architecture should be i386 or noarch for the RPMs you want to install on a PC with an Intel x86-compatible processor.

Finding out about RPMs

As it installs packages, the `rpm` command builds up a database of installed RPMs. You can use the `rpm -q` command to query this database to determine information about packages installed on your system.

For example, to find out the version number of the Linux kernel installed on your system, type the following `rpm -q` command:

```
rpm -q kernel
kernel-2.0.31-7
```

The response is the name of the RPM for the kernel (this is the executable version of the kernel; not the source files). The name is the same as the RPM file name except the last part — `.i386.rpm` — is not shown. In this case, the version part of the RPM tells you the kernel is 2.0.31.

If you are going to compile the kernel, you might want to know the version of the GNU C compiler (`gcc`) installed on your system. To see the `gcc` version number, type

```
rpm -q gcc
gcc-2.7.2.3-8
```

The response tells you that you have `gcc` Version 2.7.2.3.

You can see a list of all installed RPMs with the following command:

```
rpm -qa
```

You see a long list of RPMs scroll by your screen. To view the list one screen at a time, type

```
rpm -qa | more
```

If you want to search for a specific package, feed the output of `rpm -qa` to the `grep` command. For example, to see all packages with `kernel` in their names, type:

```
rpm -qa | grep kernel

kernel-2.0.31-7
kernel-headers-2.0.31-7
kernel-modules-2.0.31-7
kernelcfg-0.4-7
kernel-source-2.0.31-7
```

You can query much more than a package's version number with the `rpm -q` command. By adding single letter options, you can find out other useful information about a package. For example, try the following command to see the files in the kernel package:

```
rpm -ql kernel
/boot/System.map-2.0.31
/boot/module-info-2.0.31
/boot/vmlinuz-2.0.31
/sbin/installkernel
```

Following are several useful forms of `rpm -q` commands to query information about a package (to use any of these `rpm -q` commands, type the command followed by the package name):

`rpm -qc`	Lists all configuration files in a package.
`rpm -qd`	Lists all documentation files in a package. These are usually the online manual pages (also known as *man* pages).
`rpm -qi`	Displays detailed information about a package including version number, size, installation date, and a brief description.
`rpm -ql`	Lists all the files in a package. For some packages this can be a long list.
`rpm -qs`	Lists the state of all files in a package.

Installing an RPM

To install an RPM, you have to use the `rpm -i` command. You must provide the name of the RPM file as the argument. A typical example would be to install an RPM from the CD-ROM. As usual, you have to mount the CD-ROM first and then change to the directory in which the RPMs are located. Then, use the `rpm -i` command to install the RPM.

For example, to install the kernel-source RPM (which contains the source files for the Linux operating system) from my CD-ROM, I type the following commands:

```
mount /dev/hdc /cdrom
mount: block device /dev/hdc is write-protected, mounting read-only
cd /cdrom/RedHat/RPMS
rpm -i kernel-source*
```

Tip

Note, you needn't type the full RPM file name — you can use a few characters from the beginning of the name followed by an asterisk. Make sure you type enough of the name to uniquely identify the RPM file.

If you try to install an RPM that is already installed, the `rpm` command displays an error message. For example, here is what happens when I try to install the Emacs editor on my system:

```
rpm -i emacs-20*
package emacs-20.2-4 is already installed
error: emacs-20.2-4.i386.rpm cannot be installed
```

To force the `rpm` command to install a package even if there are errors, just add `—force` to the `rpm -i` command as follows:

```
rpm -i --force emacs-20*
```

Removing an RPM

You might want to remove—uninstall—a package if you realize you don't need the software. For example, if you installed the X Window System development package, but you are uninterested in writing any *X* applications, you can easily remove the package by using the rpm -e command.

You need the name of the package before you can remove it. One good way to find the name is to use rpm -qa in conjunction with grep to search for the appropriate RPM file. For example, to locate the X Window System development RPM, you might try:

```
rpm -qa | grep XFree
XFree86-3.3.1-14
XFree86-75dpi-fonts-3.3.1-14
XFree86-devel-3.3.1-14
XFree86-libs-3.3.1-14
```

In this case, XFree86-devel happens to be the package name you need. To remove the package, type:

```
rpm -e XFree86-devel
```

Note, you do not need the full RPM file name; all you need is the package name—the first part of the file name up to the dash (-) before the version number.

The rpm -e command does not remove a package other packages need. For example, when I try to remove the kernel-headers package, I get the following error message:

```
rpm -e kernel-headers
removing these packages would break dependencies:
        kernel-headers is needed by glibc-devel-2.0.5c-10
        kernel-headers = 2.0.31 is needed by kernel-source-2.0.31-7
```

Upgrading an RPM

Use the rpm -U command to upgrade an RPM. You must provide the name of the RPM file that contains the new software. For example, if I have Version 1.2.4 of the Apache Web server installed on my system, but I want to upgrade to Version 1.2.5., I download the RPM file apache-1.2.5-1.i386.rpm from Red Hat's FTP server (ftp://ftp.redhat.com/pub/redhat/updates/5.0/i386) and then use the following command:

```
rpm -U apache-1.2.5-1.i386.rpm
```

The rpm command performs the upgrade by first removing the old version of the apache package and then installing the new RPM.

Tip

Whenever possible, you should upgrade rather than remove the old package and then install the new version. Upgrading automatically saves the old configuration files, which saves you the hassle of configuring the software after a fresh installation.

Caution

When you are upgrading the kernel and the kernel module packages that contain a ready-to-run Linux kernel, you should go ahead and install it with the `rpm -i` command (instead of the `rpm -u` command). This way, you won't overwrite the current kernel. See the section "Upgrading with a Red Hat Kernel RPM" to learn how to install a new kernel extracted from a kernel RPM.

Verifying an RPM

You may not do this often, but if you suspect a software package is not properly installed, use the `rpm -V` command to verify the package. For example, to verify the kernel package, type the following:

```
rpm -V kernel
```

This causes rpm to compare size and other attributes of each file in the package against the original files. If everything verifies correctly, the rpm -V command does not print anything. If any discrepancies exist, you will see a report of the discrepancies. For example, I modified the configuration files for the Apache Web server. Here is what I see when I verify the apache package:

```
rpm -V apache
S.5....T c /etc/httpd/conf/access.conf
S.5....T c /etc/httpd/conf/httpd.conf
S.5....T c /etc/httpd/conf/srm.conf
```

In this case, the output from `rpm -V` shows three configuration files have changed. Each line of output consists of three parts:

- The line starts with eight characters; each character indicates the type of discrepancy found. For example, S means the size is different and T means the time of last modification is different. Table 2-1 shows each character and its meaning. A period means that specific attribute matches with the original.

- For configuration files, a c appears next; otherwise, this field is blank. That's how you can tell whether a file is a configuration file. Typically, you won't worry if a configuration file has changed because you probably made the changes yourself.

- The last part of the line is the full pathname of the file. From this part, you can tell exactly where the file is located.

Table 2-1	Characters used in RPM verification reports
Character	*Meaning*
S	Size has changed
M	Permissions and file type are different
5	The checksum computed with the MD5 algorithm is different
D	Device type is different
L	Symbolic link is different
U	File's user is different
G	File's group is different
T	File modification time is different

Applying Kernel Patches

Like any major software product, Linux has a version number that changes as new features are added. Typically, the version number has two parts: the *major version number* and the *minor version number*. MS-DOS 6.2, for example, has a major version number of 6 and a minor version number of 2. The minor version number changes as incremental improvements are made to the software. The major version number changes only when a significant change occurs.

In addition to the customary major and minor version numbers, Linux includes a third number that denotes the current patch level. Patches typically are corrections — changes made to code to fix errors.

When you boot Linux, the welcome message shows you the Linux version number and the patch level. You may, for example, see the following line:

```
Kernel 2.0.31 on an i586
```

What is a kernel patch?

The term *kernel* refers to the core Linux operating system — it is the program that makes your PC a Linux PC. The term *patch* refers to corrections. Putting the two together, you can see *kernel patch* refers to corrections to the Linux operating system itself.

Linux comes with the source code, so patches are alterations to the source code. When you apply a kernel patch, you change the Linux operating system's source code. After you make the changes, you have to rebuild Linux to put the changes into effect. Rebuilding involves compiling the kernel source code.

This message tells you the Linux version is 2.0 and the patch level is 31. Kernel Version 2.0.31 was originally included on the initial Red Hat Linux 5.0 CD-ROM. In later copies of Red Hat Linux 5.0, however, Red Hat had upgraded the kernel to Version 2.0.32.

You can also use the `uname` command to determine the current kernel version number. To see how it works, type:

```
uname -r
2.0.31
```

The output shows the version number of the Linux kernel. The `uname` command works on any UNIX system.

Although the version number changes relatively slowly, a version such as 2.0 may contain many patches. You generally can find out about patches if you keep up with Linux developments by periodically reading USENET newsgroups devoted to Linux (such as `comp.os.linux.announce` and `comp.os.linux.setup`).

Cross-Reference

You need access to the Internet to read the USENET newsgroups. Consult Chapters 18 and 19 for more information on connecting your Linux system to the Internet.

Installing the kernel source

To apply any patches to the kernel, you need the kernel source files installed on your system. The Red Hat Linux installation program does not install the kernel source files. These files are available in the form of a Red Hat Package on the companion CD-ROM.

Use the following steps to install the kernel source package on your system:

1. Log in as `root` and insert the Red Hat Linux CD-ROM into the CD drive.

2. Use the `mount` command to mount the CD-ROM drive on a directory in the file system. The exact format of the command depends on the CD-ROM device name and the mount directory. For example, type the following command to mount an IDE CD-ROM drive (attached to the secondary IDE interface corresponding to the Linux device `/dev/hdc`) on the `/cdrom` directory:

```
mount /dev/hdc /cdrom
mount: block device /dev/hdc is write-protected, mounting read-only
```

Replace `/dev/hdc` with the device name for your CD-ROM drive. If the `/cdrom` directory does not exist, type the `mkdir /cdrom` command to create the directory.

3. Change directory to the `RedHat/RPMS` directory on the CD-ROM and use RPM to install the kernel source files. Use the following commands:

```
cd /cdrom/RedHat/RPMS
rpm -ivh kernel-source*
kernel-source
##################################################
```

RPM indicates progress by displaying a series of hash marks (#). After RPM finishes installing the kernel source package, the necessary source files will be in the /usr/src/linux **directory.**

Getting the patches

If you read about a kernel patch that fixes some problem you may have had with Linux, typically you also learn about the patch number. When you ask for help with some Linux problem by posting a message in a newsgroup (such as "I am running kernel Version 2.0.31 and my brand-new SCSI controller does not seem to work"), you may get replies saying you should bring the kernel up to 2.0.33 because that new SCSI controller is supported at patch level 2.0.33.

To go from 2.0.31 to 2.0.33, you have two options:

■ If it's available, get the complete Linux 2.0.33 kernel source and install it.

■ Get patches 32 and 33 and apply them to the source files for kernel Version 2.0.31.

Tip

Typically, the entire kernel distribution is a large file (around 6MB in Version 2.0.31) even in compressed form, whereas most patch files are less than 100KB (although some can be as large as 1MB). Downloading and applying only the required patches makes sense, therefore. You have to get the patches over the Internet by using FTP (File Transfer Protocol).

Cross-Reference

If you do not have Internet access, Chapters 18 and 19 explain how you can connect your system to the Internet using a modem (you must sign up with an Internet service provider for the access).

Note

To explain the process of getting the patch files, I assume your system is connected to the Internet and you can use the ftp command to access any computer on the Internet.

The Linux kernel patches (as well as the latest versions of the kernel) are available from the FTP site ftp.funet.fi in Finland. This FTP site organizes the Linux kernels and associated patches by version number. All files for Linux Version 2.0, for example, are in the /pub/Linux/kernel/src/v2.0 directory. The kernel files and patches for Version 2.0 are named as follows (only a few representative names are shown):

```
linux-2.0.31.tar.gz (compressed file containing the complete kernel
for Linux 2.0.31)
patch-2.0.32.gz (compressed file containing patch 32 for Version 2.0)
patch-2.0.33.gz (compressed file containing patch 33 for Version 2.0)
```

Linux files are distributed in compressed format to minimize the amount of data you must transfer over the Internet. The .gz at the end of the file name tells you this file was compressed with the gzip command. As you see later, you can decompress such a file by using the gunzip command (or the gzip -d command).

The best way to learn how to get and apply a patch is to see an example. Following is an example of how to get the relevant patch files to go from Linux Version 2.0.31 to 2.0.33. The following sample session with the `ftp` program is based on my system's dial-up connection to the Internet (at a modem speed of 28,800 bits per second because my Internet service provider does not yet support 56Kbps modems):

```
ftp ftp.funet.fi
Connected to nic.funet.fi.220-Hello UNKNOWN at
dcc0xxxx.slip.digex.net,220-220-Welcome to the FUNET archive,  Please
login as `anonymous' with
220-your E-mail address as the password to access the archive.
220-See the README file for more information about this archive.
220-
220-  All anonymous transfers are logged with your host name and
whatever you
220-  entered for the password. If you don't like this policy,
disconnect now!
220-
220-
220-nic.funet.fi FTP server (Version 4.1452 problems@ftp.funet.fi)
ready.
220-There are 90 (max 250) archive users in your class at the moment.
220-Assuming 'login anonymous', other userids do vary.)
220-Local time is Sat Apr  4 02:25:26 1998 EET DST
220-
220 You can do "get README" even without logging in!
Name (ftp.funet.fi:naba): anonymous
331 Guest login ok, give your E-mail address for password.
Password:
230-Guest `naba@access.digex.net' login ok.
230-
230-        Finnish University and Research network FUNET
230-                  Archive FTP.FUNET.FI
230-
230-Most important file name suffixes are described at
README.FILETYPES
230-News about this system can be looked at README.NEWS
230-
230-Welcome, you are 84th archive user in your class (max 250).
230-Your class is named: The known world outside NORDUnet region
230-There are 125 users in all classes (max 765)
230-Your data-transfer rate has no limitations.
230-
230-Local time is Sat Apr  4 02:26:33 1998 EET DST
230-
230-We have special access features, see file README
230-  It was last updated Wed Nov 12 22:15:21 1997 - 142.1 days ago
230
Remote system type is UNIX.
Using binary mode to transfer files.
ftp> cd /pub/Linux/kernel/src/v2.0
250 CWD command successful.
```

```
ftp> ls
200 PORT command successful.
150 Opening ASCII mode data connection for .
-r--r--r--   1 mirror    mirror       26373 Aug 30  1996 Changes
-r--r--r--   1 mirror    mirror           0 Dec 16 22:55 LATEST-IS-
2.0.33
-r--r--r--   1 mirror    mirror       16335 Jun  8  1996 Logo.gif
-r--r--r--   1 mirror    mirror         561 Jun  8  1996 Logo.txt
-r--r--r--   1 mirror    mirror     5859566 Jul  2  1996 linux-
2.0.1.tar.gz
-r--r--r--   1 mirror    mirror     5940281 Jul 26  1996 linux-
2.0.10.tar.gz
... (a portion of the listing is deleted)
-r--r--r--   1 mirror    mirror     6199356 Apr  7  1997 linux-
2.0.30.tar.gz
-r--r--r--   1 mirror    mirror     6558735 Oct 17 21:25 linux-
2.0.31.tar.gz
-r--r--r--   1 mirror    mirror     6567164 Nov 18 02:34 linux-
2.0.32.tar.gz
-r--r--r--   1 mirror    mirror     6573183 Dec 16 22:55 linux-
2.0.33.tar.gz
-r--r--r--   1 mirror    mirror     5926911 Jul  7  1996 linux-
2.0.4.tar.gz
-r--r--r--   1 mirror    mirror     5927899 Jul  9  1996 linux-
2.0.5.tar.gz
... (a portion of the listing is deleted)
-r--r--r--   1 mirror    mirror      293692 Apr  7  1997 patch-
2.0.30.gz
-r--r--r--   1 mirror    mirror      999854 Oct 17 21:25 patch-
2.0.31.gz
-r--r--r--   1 mirror    mirror       41721 Nov 18 02:34 patch-
2.0.32.gz
-r--r--r--   1 mirror    mirror       38497 Dec 16 22:55 patch-
2.0.33.gz
-r--r--r--   1 mirror    mirror       47797 Jul  7  1996 patch-
2.0.4.gz
-r--r--r--   1 mirror    mirror       14118 Jul  9  1996 patch-
2.0.5.gz
-r--r--r--   1 mirror    mirror        6545 Jul 11  1996 patch-
2.0.6.gz
-r--r--r--   1 mirror    mirror        9657 Jul 14  1996 patch-
2.0.7.gz
-r--r--r--   1 mirror    mirror       40335 Jul 19  1996 patch-
2.0.8.gz
-r--r--r--   1 mirror    mirror       27966 Jul 25  1996 patch-
2.0.9.gz
drwxr-xr-x  35 mea       mirror        8192 Feb  2 00:47 patch-html
226 Transfer complete.
ftp> binary
200 Type set to I.
ftp> get patch-2.0.32.gz
local: patch-2.0.32.gz remote: patch-2.0.32.gz
200 PORT command successful.
150 Opening BINARY mode data connection for
/pub/Linux/kernel/src/v2.0/patch-2.0.32.gz (41721 bytes).
226 Transfer complete.
```

```
41721 bytes received in 16 secs (2.6 Kbytes/sec)
ftp> get patch-2.0.33.gz
local: patch-2.0.33.gz remote: patch-2.0.33.gz
200 PORT command successful.
150 Opening BINARY mode data connection for
/pub/Linux/kernel/src/v2.0/patch-2.0.33.gz (38497 bytes).
226 Transfer complete.
38497 bytes received in 14.6 secs (2.6 Kbytes/sec)
ftp> bye
221-Goodbye, and thank you for using the FUNET archive.
221 You transferred 83 KBytes during this session.
```

Common practice is to use the login name *anonymous* when downloading software from an FTP site. Providing your e-mail address as the password also is customary. Then you follow these straightforward steps:

1. Use the cd command to change directory to the location where the files for the current version of Linux reside.

2. Type ls -l to see a listing of files in that directory. Look for file names beginning with *patch*; these are the patch files.

3. Type binary to set file-transfer mode to binary.

4. Use the get command to download the necessary patch files one by one.

5. Type bye to quit the ftp program.

Next, you have to unpack the patch files and apply the patches.

Applying the patches

After you download the patches, you first have to decompress the file and then you can apply the patches. Follow these steps to apply the patches:

1. Copy the patch files to the /usr/src directory.

2. Type the following commands to go to the /usr/src directory and decompress the patch files:

```
cd /usr/src
gunzip patch*.gz
```

3. Use the patch command to apply the patches one by one, as follows:

```
patch -p0 < patch-2.0.32 2> err.32
patch -p0 < patch-2.0.33 2> err.33
```

The first command runs the patch command with the file patch-2.0.32 as input and sends all output messages (including any error reports) to the file err.32.

After the commands have finished, check the err.32, and err.33 files to see whether any of the patches failed. One good way is to use the text-search tool grep to look for any occurrence of the string *fail*, as follows:

```
grep fail err.*
```

If `grep` finds any occurrence of the string *fail*, the patch was not successful, perhaps because the kernel source files were already modified from their original form.

For now, just try the `grep` command as is. In Chapter 6, you learn more about `grep` and other Linux commands.

If they work without any errors, the `patch` commands change the source code of the Linux operating system to reflect any changes that the developers have made since Version 2.0.31. After the last patch, the Linux source code should be at level 2.0.33. All you have to do next is rebuild the kernel and then your Linux system will be at Version 2.0.33.

Unfortunately, these straightforward steps may not work with Red Hat Linux because Red Hat has modified some of the kernel files. For example, the original version of Red Hat Linux 5.0 came with kernel 2.0.31, but some of the files seem to have been modified for Version 2.0.32. When you try to apply the 2.0.32 patches to the 2.0.31 source files, many of the patches will appear to be already installed. The `patch` command then prompts you as follows:

```
Reversed (or previously applied) patch detected!  Assume -R? [y]
```

The -R option is meant to handle cases in which the old and new file names are inadvertently mixed up. You can answer No and skip the patch. When this happens, it means the patches may not apply correctly.

If the `patch` command fails, you can still upgrade the kernel to newer versions — you just have to get the newer kernels from Red Hat's FTP server. You can also download the entire kernel from the `ftp.funet.fi` FTP server and rebuild the kernel as explained in the following section.

Rebuilding the kernel

Rebuilding the kernel refers to the task of creating a new binary file for the core Linux operating system. This binary file is the file that runs when Linux boots. You may have to build the kernel for various reasons:

- After you apply kernel patches (as described in the preceding section), the operating system's source files are updated and you must rebuild the kernel and reboot the system to use the new kernel.

- After you initially install Linux, you may want to create a new kernel that includes support for only the hardware actually installed on your system. In particular, if you have a SCSI adapter, you may want to create a kernel that links in the SCSI driver. The kernel in the companion CD-ROM includes the SCSI driver as an external module that must be loaded at start up.

- After you add support for a new device (a sound card, for example), you must configure the kernel and rebuild it. In this case, you select appropriate options to enable the sound driver for your sound card.

Caution

Before you rebuild the kernel, prepare an emergency boot floppy (see "Preparing an emergency boot disk" in Chapter 1 for details). If the system does not boot after you rebuild the kernel, you can use that emergency boot floppy to start the system and repeat the kernel build process.

To rebuild the Linux kernel, you need the kernel source files. The kernel source files are not normally installed. If you have not done so already, you should install these files following the steps outlined earlier in "Installing the kernel source."

Building the kernel involves the following key phases:

- Configure the kernel
- Make the kernel
- Make the modules
- Install the kernel and other required files

The next section describes the use of modules versus linking in hardware support directly into the kernel. Subsequent sections describe the phases of kernel building.

Using the kernel and modules

Before you start configuring the kernel, you should understand you have two options for the device drivers needed to support various hardware devices in Linux:

- *Link in support*: You can link the drivers for all hardware on your system into the kernel. As you might imagine, the size of the kernel grows as device driver code is incorporated into the kernel. A kernel that links in all necessary support code is called a *monolithic kernel*.

- *Use modules*: You can create the necessary device drivers in the form of modules. A *module* is a block of code the kernel can load after it starts running. A typical use of modules is to add support for a device without having to rebuild the kernel for each new device. Modules needn't be device drivers; they can be also be used to add new functionality to the kernel. A kernel that uses modules is called a *modular kernel*.

You do not have to create a fully monolithic or fully modular kernel. In fact, common practice is to link in some support directly into the kernel, whereas infrequently used device drivers may be built in the form of modules.

Tip

When you create a custom kernel for your hardware configuration, you may link in all required device drivers into the kernel. You can keep the size of such a monolithic kernel under control because you only link in device drivers for the hardware actually installed on your system.

For a company such as Red Hat, a modular kernel is the best choice. Red Hat provides a generic kernel along with a large number of modules to support all types of hardware. Then, the installation program configures the system to load only those modules needed to support the hardware installed in a user's system.

As you configure the kernel, you must select how to include support for specific devices. Typically, for each configuration option, you have to respond with one of the following choices:

- y to link in the support into the kernel
- m to use a module
- n skip the support for that specific device

If a device does not have a modular device driver, you won't see the **m** option.

Configuring the kernel

To configure the kernel, log in as `root`. Then change directory to `/usr/src/linux` by using the following command:

```
cd /usr/src/linux
```
To configure the kernel, you must indicate what features and device drivers you want to include in your Linux system. In essence, you are building a copy of Linux with the mix-and-match features you want.

Red Hat Linux provides three ways for you to configure the kernel:

- Type `make menuconfig` to enter kernel configuration parameters through a text-based interface, similar to the one used by the Red Hat installation program.

- Type `make xconfig` to use an X Window-based configuration program to configure the kernel. You must be running *X* to use this configuration program with a graphical interface.

- Type `make config` to use a program that prompts you for each configuration option one by one. You can use this configuration program from the Linux command prompt.

Each of these programs achieve the same end result — each stores your choices in a text file named `.config` located in the `/usr/src/linux` directory. Because the file name starts with a period, you won't see it when you use the `ls` command to list the directory. Type `ls -a` to see the file in the directory listing.

All the kernel configuration step does is capture your choices in the `.config` file. The kernel file does not change until you actually compile the kernel with the `k` command. This means you can go through the kernel configuration option as many times as you want.

Here are some lines from the .config file on my system (after I configured the kernel):

```
more .config
#
# Automatically generated make config: don't edit
#

#
# Code maturity level options
#
# CONFIG_EXPERIMENTAL is not set

#
# Loadable module support
#
CONFIG_MODULES=y
# CONFIG_MODVERSIONS is not set
CONFIG_KERNELD=y

#
# General setup
#
# CONFIG_MATH_EMULATION is not set
CONFIG_NET=y
# CONFIG_MAX_16M is not set
CONFIG_PCI=y
CONFIG_SYSVIPC=y
CONFIG_BINFMT_AOUT=y
CONFIG_BINFMT_ELF=y
CONFIG_KERNEL_ELF=y
# CONFIG_M386 is not set
# CONFIG_M486 is not set
CONFIG_M586=y
# CONFIG_M686 is not set
(rest of the file not shown)
```

Essentially, each configuration option has a name and each one is assigned a value. The name begins with CONFIG_ followed by a word that identifies the option. Each selected option has a value of y (to link in support for that feature) or m (to use a module for that feature). Lines beginning with # are comments. Comment lines list features that have not been selected.

In the sample .config file, CONFIG_PCI is set to y, which means the kernel should include support for PCI (Peripheral Component Interconnect) bus. On the other hand, CONFIG_MATH_EMULATION is not set—this means the kernel needn't include code to emulate a math coprocessor (386 and 486SX processors needed a separate math coprocessor, but newer processors such as Intel Pentium and AMD K6 have the math coprocessor built in).

Tip

I describe the configuration process through the `make config` command. Although this approach is somewhat tedious because it walks you through each option one by one, it is ideal as a learning tool. As you step through the groups of configuration options, I provide notes explaining what they mean. You can then use any configuration tool (`make xconfig`, `make menuconfig`, or `make config`) to perform the configuration.

To start configuring the kernel, type:

```
make config
rm -f include/asm ( cd include ; ln -sf asm-i386 asm)
/bin/sh scripts/Configure arch/i386/config.in
#
# Using defaults found in arch/i386/defconfig
#
```

The first question asks if you want to try any experimental code or device drivers:

```
** Code maturity level options*Prompt for development and/or
incomplete code/drivers (CONFIG_EXPERIMENTAL) [Y/n/?] n
```

Unless you are adventurous, you can safely answer No to this question.

Tip

The possible answers to each prompt appears in square brackets with the default answer in uppercase. Thus, [Y/n/?] means the default answer is Yes, and two other possible answers are n and ?. To accept the default, press Enter.

The next group of options asks you about support for loadable modules (a loadable module is like a DOS TSR — terminate and stay resident — program):

```
*
* Loadable module support
*
Enable loadable module support (CONFIG_MODULES) [Y/n/?] y
Set version information on all symbols for modules
(CONFIG_MODVERSIONS) [Y/n/?] n
Kernel daemon support (e.g. autoload of modules) (CONFIG_KERNELD)
[Y/n/?] y
```

You want to include support for modules, so answer Yes.

The next question asks about including version information in each module. If modules have version information, the module is checked for compatibility with the current kernel version. Because it is easy to unload a module that does not work, I tend to answer No to this option. However, you may safely accept the default and press Enter.

The third question asks about kernel daemon — a program that runs continuously and loads any module the kernel might need. You should answer Yes to this option.

Next comes a set of general options, starting with the following question:

```
*
* General setup
*
Kernel math emulation (CONFIG_MATH_EMULATION) [Y/n/?] n
```

If you have an older 386 or 486SX PC that does not have a math coprocessor, you can answer Yes to this question and have the kernel perform floating-point arithmetic in software.

The next option asks you about turning on networking support:

```
Networking support (CONFIG_NET) [Y/n/?] y
```

You should answer Yes even if you don't have a network card or plan to connect the system to the Internet. The reason is programs running on your system may use an internal networking connection to communicate. You need that internal networking support so everything works properly.

A question about limiting your system's memory to 16MB follows:

```
Limit memory to low 16MB (CONFIG_MAX_16M) [N/y/?] n
```

This question appears because many older PCs could not handle more than 16MB memory. If you have an old system (or if your system's memory is less than 16MB), you may answer Yes. For newer PCs, it is safe to answer No.

The next configuration option lets you enable support for the PCI bus:

```
PCI bios support (CONFIG_PCI) [Y/n/?] y
```

If your PC has a PCI bus (most new Pentium PCs have PCI bus), answer Yes.

The next prompt asks about System V Inter Process Communication (IPC) support:

```
System V IPC (CONFIG_SYSVIPC) [Y/n/?] y
```

As with the networking support, System V (which refers to UNIX System V) IPC is used by programs to communicate with one another. You should enable this support by answering Yes.

The next few questions deal with the format of binary files and the processor type:

```
Kernel support for a.out binaries (CONFIG_BINFMT_AOUT) [Y/m/n/?] y
Kernel support for ELF binaries (CONFIG_BINFMT_ELF) [Y/m/n/?] y
Compile kernel as ELF - if your GCC is ELF-GCC (CONFIG_KERNEL_ELF)
[Y/n/?] y
Processor type (386, 486, Pentium, PPro) [386] Pentium
  defined CONFIG_M586
```

The a.out format refers to an older format for executable files (also called *binary files*). You should select Yes because you may have to run some older programs that use the a.out format.

ELF (Executable and Linking Format) is a new standard format for executable programs. You would definitely want the kernel to support ELF binaries.

The kernel itself should be compiled and stored as ELF, so you can safely answer Yes to the third question.

The last question of the set queries about your system's processor type. If you answer 386, the compiled kernel can run on any other processor, such as a 486 or a Pentium. If you are creating a kernel specifically for your system, though, enter your processor type.

The next set of questions is about the floppy drive and the hard drive. The first question asks if you want floppy drive support:

```
*
* Floppy, IDE, and other block devices
*
Normal floppy disk support (CONFIG_BLK_DEV_FD) [Y/m/n/?] y
```

Because most PCs do have a floppy drive, your answer will probably be Yes.

You should answer Yes to the next question if you have one or more IDE (Integrated Drive Electronics) drives:

```
Enhanced IDE/MFM/RLL disk/cdrom/tape/floppy support
(CONFIG_BLK_DEV_IDE) [Y/n/?] y
*
* Please see Documentation/ide.txt for help/info on IDE drives
*
```

Tip

By the way, the note in the previous listing refers to the file `/usr/src/linux/Documentation/ide.txt`. Many useful help files (these are all text files) are in the `/usr/src/linux/Documentation` directory.

The next question refers to an old IDE driver that supports disks only (newer IDE drivers also support other devices such as CD-ROMs). You should answer No unless you have an old PC with only a hard disk connected to the IDE interface:

```
    Use old disk-only driver on primary interface
(CONFIG_BLK_DEV_HD_IDE) [N/y/?] n
```

If you have an IDE CD-ROM drive, answer Yes to the following question (*ATAPI* is another name for the enhanced IDE interface):

```
    Include IDE/ATAPI CDROM support (CONFIG_BLK_DEV_IDECD) [Y/n/?] y
```

If you have a tape drive connected to the IDE interface, you should answer Yes to the following question. I do not have a tape drive, so my answer is No:

```
    Include IDE/ATAPI TAPE support (CONFIG_BLK_DEV_IDETAPE) [Y/n/?] n
```

If you have an IDE floppy drive such as an Iomega Zip drive, answer Yes to the following question:

```
    Include IDE/ATAPI FLOPPY support (new) (CONFIG_BLK_DEV_IDEFLOPPY)
[Y/n/?] y
```

The next option enables you to use a SCSI driver to access a device connected to the IDE interface. You should normally answer No to this question:

```
SCSI emulation support (CONFIG_BLK_DEV_IDESCSI) [N/y/?] n
```

You can enable support for IDE interfaces built on PC Cards with the following option. You should answer No unless you have a such a PC Card:

```
Support removable IDE interfaces (PCMCIA)
(CONFIG_BLK_DEV_IDE_PCMCIA) [Y/n/?] n
```

The next two options correct some known problems with specific chipsets used in IDE interfaces. You can safely answer Yes to both questions:

```
CMD640 chipset bugfix/support (CONFIG_BLK_DEV_CMD640) [Y/n/?] y
  CMD640 enhanced support (CONFIG_BLK_DEV_CMD640_ENHANCED) [Y/n/?] y
RZ1000 chipset bugfix/support (CONFIG_BLK_DEV_RZ1000) [Y/n/?] y
```

The next question applies to a PCI bus system with an IDE hard drive that also uses the Intel Triton I/II IDE interface chipset. If you do not know that level of detail about your system, you can safely answer Yes to this question:

```
Intel 82371 PIIX (Triton I/II) DMA support (CONFIG_BLK_DEV_TRITON)
[Y/n/?] y
```

Answer Yes to the following question if you want to enable support for various IDE chipsets used in PC motherboards. This support may be necessary for Linux to access third or fourth IDE drives. If you have more than two IDE drives, you might want to turn on this option. I answer No because I have only two IDE drives — one disk drive and a CD-ROM drive:

```
Other IDE chipset support (CONFIG_IDE_CHIPSETS) [N/y/?] n
```

The next option enables support for the loopback device — this lets Linux manipulate an entire file system inside a single large file. You can usually answer No to this option:

```
*
* Additional Block Devices
*
Loopback device support (CONFIG_BLK_DEV_LOOP) [M/n/y/?] n
```

If you want to combine several hard disk partitions into a single logical device, answer Yes to the following option. If you are unsure, just answer No:

```
Multiple devices driver support (CONFIG_BLK_DEV_MD) [Y/n/?] n
```

If you want to use a portion of your system's memory as a disk capable of storing a file system, answer Yes to the following question. Typically, a RAM disk is used only during system startup when the hard disk may not be available yet. You can answer m to include RAM disk support in the form of a module:

```
RAM disk support (CONFIG_BLK_DEV_RAM) [Y/m/n/?] m
```

Answer Yes to the following question only if your PC uses an old hard disk controller of the type first used in the IBM XT computer around mid 1980s:

```
XT harddisk support (CONFIG_BLK_DEV_XD) [N/y/m/?] n
```

The next set of options deal with networking. How you answer depends on how you want to use your Linux system in a network. Here are some guidelines:

- Answer Yes to enable CONFIG_FIREWALL if you want to use your Linux system as a firewall — an intermediary system that controls information flowing between a local area network (LAN) and the Internet. You should turn on this option if you want to use IP masquerading, which allows many systems on a private LAN to access the Internet through a Linux system with a valid IP address. You also have to turn on CONFIG_IP_FORWARD. Chapter 16 explains IP masquerading.

- If you answer Yes to CONFIG_NET_ALIAS, you can assign multiple IP addresses to a single network interface card.

- You should always enable CONFIG_INET for TCP/IP networking.

- By turning on IP forwarding (CONFIG_IP_FORWARD), you can use your Linux system as a *router* — a gateway between two LANs.

- You should turn on CONFIG_IP_MULTICAST if you use the Linux system as a router.

- You can enable CONFIG_SYN_COOKIES if you want Linux to resist a type of attack known as SYN flooding, which can overwhelm the network connection.

- Say Yes to CONFIG_IP_ACCT only if you want to use your Linux system as a router.

- If you are using the system as a router, enable CONFIG_IP_ROUTER.

  *You can safely answer No to the IP tunneling (CONFIG_NET_IPIP) option. You need to address this option only in certain situations, such as moving a laptop from one network to another without changing its IP address.

Here is how I opt to answer these questions on one of my systems (which is not being used as a router):

```
*
* Networking options
*
Network firewalls (CONFIG_FIREWALL) [Y/n/?] n
Network aliasing (CONFIG_NET_ALIAS) [Y/n/?] n
TCP/IP networking (CONFIG_INET) [Y/n/?] y
IP: forwarding/gatewaying (CONFIG_IP_FORWARD) [Y/n/?] n
IP: multicasting (CONFIG_IP_MULTICAST) [Y/n/?] n
IP: syn cookies (CONFIG_SYN_COOKIES) [Y/n/?] y
IP: accounting (CONFIG_IP_ACCT) [Y/n/?] n
IP: optimize as router not host (CONFIG_IP_ROUTER) [N/y/?] n
IP: tunneling (CONFIG_NET_IPIP) [M/n/y/?] n
```

The next set of options is also for networking. As the comment indicates, you can simply accept the default choices for these options (press Enter to accept the default):

```
*
* (it is safe to leave these untouched)
*
IP: PC/TCP compatibility mode (CONFIG_INET_PCTCP) [N/y/?] n
IP: Reverse ARP (CONFIG_INET_RARP) [M/n/y/?] m
IP: Disable Path MTU Discovery (normally enabled)
(CONFIG_NO_PATH_MTU_DISCOVERY) [N/y/?] n
IP: Drop source routed frames (CONFIG_IP_NOSR) [Y/n/?] y
IP: Allow large windows (not recommended if <16Mb of memory)
(CONFIG_SKB_LARGE) [Y/n/?] y
```

With the next four options, you can enable support for other networking protocols besides TCP/IP. You can support IPX (the protocol used by Novell Netware), Appletalk, and packet radio (AX.25). The fourth option is for a network link between the kernel and other processes. I disable all these options because I don't need them on my system:

```
*
*
*
The IPX protocol (CONFIG_IPX) [M/n/y/?] n
Appletalk DDP (CONFIG_ATALK) [M/n/y/?] n
Amateur Radio AX.25 Level 2 (CONFIG_AX25) [N/y/?] n
Kernel/User network link driver (CONFIG_NETLINK) [N/y/?] n
```

Next follows an entire set of options that have to do with SCSI devices. If your system has a SCSI adapter, you should start by answering Yes to the CONFIG_SCSI option. After that, you have to answer questions about the types of devices (disk, tape, CD-ROM) connected to the SCSI adapter. Finally, you have to enable support for the specific SCSI adapter model on your system.

Tip

If your system has a SCSI adapter, always press y to all the needed SCSI options. Do not press m to create SCSI modules. You must go through several extra steps to install a kernel that has to load modular SCSI device drivers. The easiest approach is simply to link in the SCSI support by answering y to options such as CONFIG_SCSI, CONFIG_BLK_DEV_SD, and the configuration option corresponding to your SCSI adapter (see the next listing).

The following listing shows my choices for SCSI support (for an Adaptec AHA 1542 adapter):

```
*
* SCSI support
*
SCSI support (CONFIG_SCSI) [N/y/m/?] y
*
* SCSI support type (disk, tape, CD-ROM)
*
SCSI disk support (CONFIG_BLK_DEV_SD) [N/y/m/?] (NEW) y
SCSI tape support (CONFIG_CHR_DEV_ST) [N/y/m/?] (NEW) n
SCSI CD-ROM support (CONFIG_BLK_DEV_SR) [N/y/m/?] (NEW) n
```

```
SCSI generic support (CONFIG_CHR_DEV_SG) [N/y/m/?] (NEW) y
*
* Some SCSI devices (e.g. CD jukebox) support multiple LUNs
*
Probe all LUNs on each SCSI device (CONFIG_SCSI_MULTI_LUN) [N/y/?]
(NEW) n
Verbose SCSI error reporting (kernel size +=12K)
(CONFIG_SCSI_CONSTANTS) [N/y/?] (NEW) n
*
* SCSI low-level drivers
*
7000FASST SCSI support (CONFIG_SCSI_7000FASST) [N/y/m/?] (NEW)
Adaptec AHA152X/2825 support (CONFIG_SCSI_AHA152X) [N/y/m/?] (NEW)
Adaptec AHA1542 support (CONFIG_SCSI_AHA1542) [N/y/m/?] (NEW) y
Adaptec AHA1740 support (CONFIG_SCSI_AHA1740) [N/y/m/?] (NEW)
Adaptec AIC7xxx support (CONFIG_SCSI_AIC7XXX) [N/y/m/?] (NEW)
AdvanSys SCSI support (CONFIG_SCSI_ADVANSYS) [N/y/m/?] (NEW)
Always IN2000 SCSI support (CONFIG_SCSI_IN2000) [N/y/m/?] (NEW)
AM53/79C974 PCI SCSI support (CONFIG_SCSI_AM53C974) [N/y/m/?] (NEW)
BusLogic SCSI support (CONFIG_SCSI_BUSLOGIC) [N/y/m/?] (NEW)
DTC3180/3280 SCSI support (CONFIG_SCSI_DTC3280) [N/y/m/?] (NEW)
EATA-DMA (DPT, NEC, AT&T, SNI, AST, Olivetti, Alphatronix) support
(CONFIG_SCSI_EATA_DMA) [N/y/m/?] (NEW)
EATA-PIO (old DPT PM2001, PM2012A) support (CONFIG_SCSI_EATA_PIO)
[N/y/m/?] (NEW)
EATA ISA/EISA/PCI (DPT and generic EATA/DMA-compliant boards) support
(CONFIG_SCSI_EATA) [N/y/m/?] (NEW)
Future Domain 16xx SCSI support (CONFIG_SCSI_FUTURE_DOMAIN) [N/y/m/?]
(NEW)
Generic NCR5380/53c400 SCSI support (CONFIG_SCSI_GENERIC_NCR5380)
[N/y/m/?] (NEW)
NCR53c406a SCSI support (CONFIG_SCSI_NCR53C406A)[N/y/m/?] (NEW)
NCR53c7,8xx SCSI support (CONFIG_SCSI_NCR53C7xx) [N/y/m/?] (NEW)
NCR53C8XX SCSI support (CONFIG_SCSI_NCR53C8XX) [N/y/m/?] (NEW)
IOMEGA Parallel Port ZIP drive SCSI support (CONFIG_SCSI_PPA)
[N/y/m/?] (NEW)
PAS16 SCSI support (CONFIG_SCSI_PAS16) [N/y/m/?] (NEW)
Qlogic FAS SCSI support (CONFIG_SCSI_QLOGIC_FAS) [N/y/m/?] (NEW)
Qlogic ISP SCSI support (CONFIG_SCSI_QLOGIC_ISP) [N/y/m/?] (NEW)
Seagate ST-02 and Future Domain TMC-8xx SCSI support
(CONFIG_SCSI_SEAGATE) [N/y/m/?] (NEW)
Tekram DC-390(T) SCSI support (CONFIG_SCSI_DC390T) [N/y/m/?] (NEW)
Trantor T128/T128F/T228 SCSI support (CONFIG_SCSI_T128) [N/y/m/?]
(NEW)
UltraStor 14F/34F support (CONFIG_SCSI_U14_34F) [N/y/m/?] (NEW)
UltraStor SCSI support (CONFIG_SCSI_ULTRASTOR) [N/y/m/?] (NEW)
```

GDT SCSI Disk Array Controller support (CONFIG_SCSI_GDTH) [N/y/m/?] (NEW)Answer Yes to the next question if you have a network card in your system:

```
*
* Network device support
*
Network device support (CONFIG_NETDEVICES) [Y/n/?] y
```

The next option, when enabled, creates a dummy network device that is needed for inactive dial-up networking such as SLIP (Serial Line IP) or PPP (Point-to-Point Protocol). You should answer Yes if you plan to use PPP or SLIP:

```
Dummy net driver support (CONFIG_DUMMY) [M/n/y/?] y
```

If you have two phone lines with two modems, you can enable *serial line load balancing,* which allows your Linux system to use two phone lines as a single higher-capacity connection. Naturally, this works only if a similar arrangement exists at the other end of the phone lines. Typically, you can answer No to this option:

```
EQL (serial line load balancing) support (CONFIG_EQUALIZER) [M/n/y/?] n
```

The next option lets you enable PLIP, which refers to Parallel Port Internet Protocol, a way to network two Linux PCs by connecting the two parallel ports:

```
PLIP (parallel port) support (CONFIG_PLIP) [M/n/y/?] n
```

Answer Yes to the next question if you plan to connect your Linux PC to an Internet service provider (ISP) using the PPP:

```
PPP (point-to-point) support (CONFIG_PPP) [M/n/y/?] y
*
* CCP compressors for PPP are only built as modules.
*
```

You can enable support for SLIP with the next option, but currently most PCs use PPP to connect to the Internet (there is no harm in enabling SLIP support even if you use PPP):

```
SLIP (serial line) support (CONFIG_SLIP) [M/n/y/?] y
```

The next option is for packet radios. If you have a packet radio interface, answer Yes; otherwise, answer No:

```
Radio network interfaces (CONFIG_NET_RADIO) [N/y/?] n
```

If you have an Ethernet card in your system, answer Yes to the next question:

```
Ethernet (10 or 100Mbit) (CONFIG_NET_ETHERNET) [Y/n/?] y
```

Now you have to select the exact model of network card installed on your system. Here is how I indicate my PC has an old 3Com 3C503 card:

```
3COM cards (CONFIG_NET_VENDOR_3COM) [Y/n/?] y
3c501 support (CONFIG_EL1) [M/n/y/?] n
3c503 support (CONFIG_EL2) [M/n/y/?] y
3c509/3c579 support (CONFIG_EL3) [M/n/y/?] n
3c590/3c900 series (592/595/597/900/905) "Vortex/Boomerang" support
(CONFIG_VORTEX) [M/n/y/?] n
AMD LANCE and PCnet (AT1500 and NE2100) support (CONFIG_LANCE) [Y/n/?] n
Western Digital/SMC cards (CONFIG_NET_VENDOR_SMC) [Y/n/?] n
Other ISA cards (CONFIG_NET_ISA) [Y/n/?] n
EISA, VLB, PCI and on board controllers (CONFIG_NET_EISA) [Y/n/?] n
```

```
Pocket and portable adaptors (CONFIG_NET_POCKET) [Y/n/?] n
Token Ring driver support (CONFIG_TR) [Y/n/?] n
FDDI driver support (CONFIG_FDDI) [N/y/?] n
ARCnet support (CONFIG_ARCNET) [M/n/y/?] n
```

The next option enables you to include support for Integrated Services Digital Network (ISDN), a digital telephone line you can use to connect the Linux system to the Internet. You should answer Yes only if you have ISDN installed:

```
*
* ISDN subsystem
*
ISDN support (CONFIG_ISDN) [M/n/y/?] n
```

If you have a common type of CD-ROM drive — IDE or SCSI — then you should answer No to the following question:

```
*
* CD-ROM drivers (not for SCSI or IDE/ATAPI drives)
*
Support non-SCSI/IDE/ATAPI CDROM drives (CONFIG_CD_NO_IDESCSI) [Y/n/?]
n
```

The next set of options enables you to turn on support for specific types of file systems. You can make your choices based on the following guidelines:

Option	*Description*
CONFIG_QUOTA	Turns on disk quota so you can limit each user's disk space. Answer **y** only if your system has many users and you want to implement disk quota.
CONFIG_MINIX_FS	Supports the Minix file system — the original file system of Linux. This simple file system is still used on floppy disks, so you should answer **m** to include support in the form of a module.
CONFIG_EXT_FS	Enables support for extended file system, which is no longer in use. You can safely answer **n** for this option.
CONFIG_EXT2_FS	Enables support for the second extended file systems — the current standard file system for Linux. You should definitely answer **y** to turn on this option.
CONFIG_XIA_FS	Supports the XIA file system, another old file system no one uses anymore. Select **n** to disable this option.
CONFIG_FAT_FS	Turns on support for any File Allocation Table (FAT)-based file system (examples are MS-DOS and Windows 95 VFAT file systems). Answer **y** if you want to access MS-DOS or VFAT files.

Option	Description
CONFIG_MSDOS_FS	Supports MS-DOS file systems. Press **y** if you want to read an MS-DOS partition on the hard disk or an MS-DOS floppy.
CONFIG_VFAT_FS	Supports Windows 95 VFAT file system. Answer **y** if your system has partitions with VFAT file systems.
CONFIG_UMSDOS_FS	Supports the UMSDOS file system, which stores Linux files in an MS-DOS partition. You can safely answer **n**.
CONFIG_PROC_FS	Turns on support for the /proc virtual file system through which you can get information about the kernel. The /proc file system does not exist on the disk; files are created when you access them. You should answer **y** to enable this option because it is useful and some system programs rely on /proc.
CONFIG_NFS_FS	Enables you to mount Network File System (NFS) directories from other systems on a network. Answer **y** if you want to access NFS directories.
CONFIG_ROOT_NFS	Allows your Linux system to mount its entire file system from another system running NFS (useful if your Linux system does not have any hard disk at all). Most people answer **n** to this option.
CONFIG_SMB_FS	Enables your Linux system to access shared directories from networked PCs running Windows 95 or Windows for Workgroups. Answer **y** if you want to access shared directories on Windows systems.
CONFIG_SMB_WIN95	Allows your Linux system to work around some bugs in the Windows 95 shared directories. Answer **y** if you turned on CONFIG_SMB_FS.
CONFIG_ISO9660_FS	Turns on support for the standard ISO 9660 file system used on CD-ROMs (this was also known as the High Sierra File System and referred to as hsfs on some UNIX workstations). If you have a CD-ROM drive, answer **y** here.
CONFIG_HPFS_FS	Enables your Linux system to access an OS/2 HPFS file system. Answer **y** if you have an OS/2 partition on your hard disk.
CONFIG_SYSV_FS	Turns on support for the System V file system used by SCO, Xenix, and Coherent variants of UNIX for Intel PCs. If you need to access a System V file system, answer **y** here.
CONFIG_UFS_FS	Allows your Linux system to read (but not write to) theUFS file system used by the BSD (Berkeley Software Distribution) variants of UNIX (such as SunOS, FreeBSD, NetBSD and NeXTstep). Answer **y** if you need to access any UFS file system.

The following listing shows my choices for these file system configuration options:

```
*
* Filesystems
*
Quota support (CONFIG_QUOTA) [Y/n/?] n
Minix fs support (CONFIG_MINIX_FS) [M/n/y/?] m
Extended fs support (CONFIG_EXT_FS) [M/n/y/?] n
Second extended fs support (CONFIG_EXT2_FS) [Y/m/n/?] y
xiafs filesystem support (CONFIG_XIA_FS) [M/n/y/?] n
DOS FAT fs support (CONFIG_FAT_FS) [Y/m/n/?] y
MSDOS fs support (CONFIG_MSDOS_FS) [Y/m/n/?] y
VFAT (Windows-95) fs support (CONFIG_VFAT_FS) [M/n/y/?] n
umsdos: Unix like fs on top of std MSDOS FAT fs (CONFIG_UMSDOS_FS)
[M/n/y/?] n
/proc filesystem support (CONFIG_PROC_FS) [Y/n/?] y
NFS filesystem support (CONFIG_NFS_FS) [M/n/y/?] y
   Root file system on NFS (CONFIG_ROOT_NFS) [N/y/?] (NEW) n
SMB filesystem support (to mount WfW shares etc..) (CONFIG_SMB_FS)
[M/n/y/?] y
SMB Win95 bug work-around (CONFIG_SMB_WIN95) [N/y/?] y
ISO9660 cdrom filesystem support (CONFIG_ISO9660_FS) [M/n/y/?] y
OS/2 HPFS filesystem support (read only) (CONFIG_HPFS_FS) [M/n/y/?] n
System V and Coherent filesystem support (CONFIG_SYSV_FS) [M/n/y/?] n
UFS filesystem support (read only) (CONFIG_UFS_FS) [M/n/y/?] n
```

You would typically answer Yes to the next option because you need this if you use the PC's serial port in any way (such as connecting a modem):

```
*
* Character devices
*
Standard/generic serial support (CONFIG_SERIAL) [Y/m/n/?] y
```

The next few options are needed if you have any multiport serial interface cards that enable you to connect multiple terminals or other devices to your Linux system. Answer No if you do not have any such devices on your system. In between these multiport serial devices is a question about parallel printer support (CONFIG_PRINTER). If you plan to connect a printer to the parallel port, answer Yes to this option.

```
Digiboard PC/Xx Support (CONFIG_DIGI) [N/y/?] n
Cyclades async mux support (CONFIG_CYCLADES) [M/n/y/?] n
Stallion multiport serial support (CONFIG_STALDRV) [Y/n/?] n
SDL RISCom/8 card support (CONFIG_RISCOM8) [M/n/y/?] n
Parallel printer support (CONFIG_PRINTER) [M/n/y/?] y
Specialix IO8+ card support (CONFIG_SPECIALIX) [M/n/y/?] n
```

If you have a bus mouse or a PS/2 style mouse, answer Yes to the next option:

```
Mouse Support (not serial mice) (CONFIG_MOUSE) [Y/n/?] y
```

Next answer Yes to the option that refers to the specific brand of mouse on your system:

```
ATIXL busmouse support (CONFIG_ATIXL_BUSMOUSE) [Y/m/n/?] n
Logitech busmouse support (CONFIG_BUSMOUSE) [Y/m/n/?] n
Microsoft busmouse support (CONFIG_MS_BUSMOUSE) [Y/m/n/?] m
PS/2 mouse (aka "auxiliary device") support (CONFIG_PSMOUSE) [Y/m/n/?]
y
C&T 82C710 mouse port support (as on TI Travelmate)
(CONFIG_82C710_MOUSE) [Y/n/?] n
```

If you want support for other devices, such as light pens and touch screens, answer Yes to the next question:

```
Support for user misc device modules (CONFIG_UMISC) [N/y/?] n
```

If you have a non-SCSI tape drive, you should answer Yes to the next question; otherwise, answer No:

```
QIC-02 tape support (CONFIG_QICO2_TAPE) [N/y/?] n
```

If you have a tape drive connected to your floppy controller, answer y or m to the next option (note the comment about setting certain parameters in a specific source file):

```
Ftape (QIC-80/Travan) support (CONFIG_FTAPE) [M/n/y/?] m
*
* Set IObase/IRQ/DMA for ftape in ./drivers/char/ftape/Makefile
*
```

The next option applies to battery-powered laptops, for which it is important to save power. If you are not installing Linux on a laptop, answer No here:

```
Advanced Power Management BIOS support (CONFIG_APM) [N/y/?] n
```

The following option enables a watchdog feature — if after creating a certain file it is not updated once every minute, the system reboots. You typically do not need this option, so it is best to answer No:

```
Watchdog Timer Support (CONFIG_WATCHDOG) [N/y/?] n
```

If you enable the next option, you can access your PC's real-time clock through a special device file. If you are running a Symmetric Multi Processing (SMP) version of Linux, you should enable this option; otherwise, answer No:

```
Enhanced Real Time Clock Support (CONFIG_RTC) [Y/n/?] n
```

The next set of options are for sound card support. If you have a sound card installed, start by answering y or m to the CONFIG_SOUND option. After that, you have to answer a number of questions about various sound cards. You can always answer m to build the sound support in the form of modules that can be loaded when needed. Here is a typical listing of sound-related options:

```
*
* Sound
*

Sound card support (CONFIG_SOUND) [M/n/y/?] m
/dev/dsp and /dev/audio support (CONFIG_AUDIO) [Y/n/?] y
MIDI interface support (CONFIG_MIDI) [Y/n/?] y
FM synthesizer (YM3812/OPL-3) support (CONFIG_YM3812) [M/n/?] m
ProAudioSpectrum 16 support (CONFIG_PAS) [M/n/?] n
Sound Blaster (SB, SBPro, SB16, clones) support (CONFIG_SB) [M/n/?] m
Generic OPL2/OPL3 FM synthesizer support (CONFIG_ADLIB) [M/n/?] m
Gravis Ultrasound support (CONFIG_GUS) [M/n/?] n
PSS (ECHO-ADI2111) support (CONFIG_PSS) [M/n/?] n
MPU-401 support (NOT for SB16) (CONFIG_MPU401) [M/n/?] n
6850 UART Midi support (CONFIG_UART6850) [M/n/?] n
MPU-401 UART Midi support (CONFIG_UART401) [M/n/?] n
Microsoft Sound System support (CONFIG_MSS) [M/n/?] n
Ensoniq SoundScape support (CONFIG_SSCAPE) [M/n/?] n
MediaTrix AudioTrix Pro support (CONFIG_TRIX) [M/n/?] n
Support for MAD16 and/or Mozart based cards (CONFIG_MAD16) [M/n/?] n
Support for Turtle Beach Wave Front (Maui, Tropez) synthesizers
(CONFIG_MAUI) [M/n/?] n

Audio DMA buffer size 4096, 16384, 32768 or 65536 (DSP_BUFFSIZE)
[65536]
make[1]: Entering directory `/usr/src/linux-2.0.31/drivers/sound'
Compiling Sound Driver v 2 for Linux
rm -f configure
gcc -I/usr/src/linux-2.0.31/include -o configure configure.c
./configure fixedlocal > local.h
./configure fixeddefines > .defines
make[1]: Leaving directory `/usr/src/linux-2.0.31/drivers/sound'
Additional low level drivers (CONFIG_LOWLEVEL_SOUND) [N/y/?] n
```

The next and final option enables you to profile the kernel—find out how much time the kernel spends in various functions. Most users answer No to disable this option:

```
*
* Kernel hacking
*
Kernel profiling support (CONFIG_PROFILE) [N/y/?] n

The linux kernel is now hopefully configured for your setup.
Check the top-level Makefile for additional configuration,
and do a 'make dep ; make clean' if you want to be sure all
the files are correctly re-made
```

The kernel configuration session ends with a message you should proceed by typing the commands make dep and then make clean, before building the kernel.

Building the kernel

You should initiate the next three tasks with a single command line (Linux enables you to enter multiple semicolon-separated commands on the same line) so you can type the line, press Enter and then take a break because this part takes a while.

Depending on your system, making a new kernel can take anywhere from a few minutes to over an hour. Type the following on a single line to initiate the process:

```
make dep; make clean; make boot
```

The `make dep` command determines which files have changed and what needs to be compiled again. The `make clean` command deletes old, unneeded files (such as old copies of the kernel). Finally, `make boot` creates the new kernel.

As the kernel is built, you see a lot of messages onscreen. When it's all over, a new kernel will be in the form of a compressed file named `zImage` in the `/usr/src/linux/arch/i386/boot` directory.

To use the new kernel, you have to copy the kernel to the `/boot` directory and edit the `/etc/lilo.conf` file to set up LILO — the Linux Loader. You learn these steps in the section "Installing the kernel." Before you proceed with the kernel installation, however, you have to build and install the modules.

Building and installing the modules

If you selected any modules during the kernel configuration, you must build the modules and install them. Perform these tasks with the following steps:

1. Type the following commands to build the modules:

   ```
   cd /usr/src/linux
   make modules
   ```

2. The current set of modules in a directory is named after the version of Linux kernel your system is running. For example, if your system runs kernel Version 2.0.31, the modules are in

   ```
   /lib/modules/2.0.31
   ```

   Move the module directory to a new location, as follows:

   ```
   mv /lib/modules/2.0.31 /lib/modules/2.0.31-old
   ```

3. Install the new modules with the following command:

   ```
   make modules_install
   ```

Now you can install the kernel and make it available for booting by LILO.

Installing the new kernel

Red Hat Linux uses LILO to load the Linux kernel from the disk. The configuration file /etc/lilo.conf lists the kernel binary that LILO runs. You can examine the contents of the LILO configuration file by typing the following command:

```
cat /etc/lilo.conf
```

Here is what I see when I try this command on one of my systems with a SCSI adapter:

```
boot=/dev/hda
map=/boot/map
install=/boot/boot.b
prompt
timeout=50
image=/boot/vmlinuz-2.0.31
        label=linux
        root=/dev/hda1
        initrd=/boot/initrd-2.0.31.img
        read-only
```

You learn more about LILO and its configuration file (/etc/lilo.conf) in Chapter 11. For now, you should note the following:

- The last five lines define a specific kernel file that LILO can boot. You can make LILO boot another kernel by adding a similar five-line section to the configuration file.

- The image=/boot/vmlinuz-2.0.31 line identifies the kernel that LILO loads. In this case, the kernel file is vmlinuz-2.0.31, located in the /boot directory.

- The label=linux line gives a name to the kernel. In this case, you can type linux at the boot: prompt to make LILO boot this particular kernel.

- The root=/dev/hda1 line specifies the disk partition where the root Linux file system is located. This may be different on your system.

  *The initrd=/boot/initrd-2.0.31.img line specifies a file that contains an initial RAM disk image that serves as a file system before the disks are available. You see the initrd line only if your system has a SCSI adapter and the kernel uses a modular SCSI driver. In this case, the kernel uses the RAM disk—a block of memory used as a disk—to get started initially; then it loads the SCSI driver module and begins using the SCSI hard disk. You do not need the initrd line if you create a kernel with the SCSI adapter support built into the kernel.

On systems with an MS-DOS partition, the LILO configuration file might include another section with details for the operating system (perhaps Windows 95) on that partition.

To configure LILO to boot yet another kernel (the one you have just built), follow these steps:

1. Copy the new kernel binary to the /boot directory. The new binary file is /usr/src/linux/arch/i386/boot/zImage. I simply copy it to the /boot directory with the same name:

   ```
   cp /usr/src/linux/arch/i386/boot/zImage /boot
   ```

   If you choose, you can give the new file a different name (especially if another older zImage is already in that directory).

2. Use your favorite text editor to edit the /etc/lilo.conf file to add the following lines just after the timeout line in the file (if you need help with a text editor, consult Chapter 24 to learn about vi and Emacs — two popular text editors for Linux):

   ```
   image=/boot/zImage
           label=new
           root=/dev/hda1
           read-only
   ```

   On your system, you should make sure the root line is correct — instead of /dev/hda1 you should list the correct disk partition where the Linux root directory (/) is located.

   Note, I am not showing the initrd line anymore because I assume you are no longer using a modular SCSI driver even if your system has a SCSI adapter.

3. Save the lilo.conf file and exit the editor.

4. Install LILO again by using the following command:

   ```
   /sbin/lilo
   ```

Now you are ready to reboot the system and try out the new kernel.

Rebooting the system

After you finish configuring and installing LILO and you are back at the Linux prompt, type the following command to reboot the system:

```
reboot
```

When you see the LILO boot: prompt, type the name you assigned to the new kernel in the /etc/lilo.conf file. You needn't type anything if you added the new kernel description before all other operating systems in the LILO configuration file.

After the system reboots, you should see the familiar login prompt. To see proof you are, indeed, running the new kernel, log in as a user and type:

```
uname -srv
Linux 2.0.31 #4 Fri Apr 10 21:17:07 EDT 1998
```

The last part of the message shows you the date and time this kernel was built — this should be the time when you rebuilt the kernel.

Tip

If the system *hangs* (which means nothing seems to happen — there is no output on the screen and no disk activity), you may have skipped a step during the kernel rebuild. You can power the PC off and on to reboot again. This time, enter `linux` (the old working kernel's name) at the LILO `boot:` prompt.

If you cannot boot the older version of Linux either, use an emergency boot disk (containing an earlier, but working, version of Linux) to start the system. Then you can repeat the kernel rebuild and installation process making sure you follow all the steps correctly.

Upgrading with a Red Hat Kernel RPM

As mentioned in "Applying kernel patches," you may get errors when applying kernel patches because of differences between Red Hat's version of the kernel files and the standard kernel source. In this case, you can get newer versions of kernels directly from Red Hat's FTP server. Red Hat distributes all software updates, including new versions of kernels, in the form of RPM files.

The basic steps to accomplish the kernel upgrade are as follows:

1. Download the kernel RPM file from Red Hat's FTP server. You also have to download the `kernel-modules` RPM. In addition, if you want to rebuild the kernel, you must download the `kernel-source` and `kernel-headers` corresponding to the new version of kernel.

2. Install the RPMs using the `rpm -i` command.

3. If you have a SCSI adapter on your system, create a new initial RAM disk by running the `/sbin/mkinitrd` command.

4. Reconfigure LILO to boot the new kernel.

5. Try out the new kernel by rebooting the system.

The next few sections further describe these steps.

Downloading new kernel RPMs

Red Hat makes software updates available in the form of RPMs — packages — at their FTP server `ftp.redhat.com`. For Red Hat Linux Version 5.0, the updates are located in the `/pub/redhat/updates/5.0/i386` directory. For Red Hat Linux Version 5.1, the updates are located in the `/pub/redhat/updates/5.1/i386` directory.

The following FTP session shows how I downloaded the necessary kernel upgrade RPMs from Red Hat's FTP server (anything I typed appears in boldface):

```
ftp ftp.redhat.com
Connected to ftp.redhat.com.
220-
220-              Red Hat Software Proudly Presents:
220-
220-      Red Hat 5.0 -- Hurricane,
ftp://ftp.redhat.com/pub/redhat/redhat-5.0/
220-      Red Hat Contrib -- ftp://ftp.redhat.com/pub/contrib/
220-
220 gonzales.redhat.com FTP server (Version wu-2.4.2-academ[BETA-
15](1) Fri Dec 12 20:41:30 EST 1997) ready.
Name (ftp.redhat.com:naba): anonymous
331 Guest login ok, send your complete e-mail address as
Password:
230 Guest login ok, access restrictions apply.
Remote system type is UNIX.
Using binary mode to transfer files.
ftp> cd /pub/redhat/updates/5.0/i386
250-Please read the file README.kernl
250-  it was last modified on Wed Dec 17 14:05:51 1997 - 109 days ago
250 CWD command successful.
ftp> ls kernel*
200 PORT command successful.
150 Opening ASCII mode data connection for /bin/ls.
-rw-r--r--  1 root     root        482029 Nov 26 11:31 kernel-
2.0.32-2.i386.rpm
-rw-r--r--  1 root     root        446095 Nov 26 11:31 kernel-headers-
2.0.32-2.i386.rpm
-rw-r--r--  1 root     root       1229707 Nov 26 11:31 kernel-modules-
2.0.32-2.i386.rpm
-rw-r--r--  1 root     root       6195859 Nov 26 11:32 kernel-source-
2.0.32-2.i386.rpm
226 Transfer complete.
ftp> binary
200 Type set to I.
ftp> prompt
Interactive mode off.
ftp> mget kernel*
local: kernel-2.0.32-2.i386.rpm remote: kernel-2.0.32-2.i386.rpm
200 PORT command successful.
150 Opening BINARY mode data connection for kernel-2.0.32-2.i386.rpm
(482029 bytes).
226 Transfer complete.
482029 bytes received in 240 secs (2 Kbytes/sec)
local: kernel-headers-2.0.32-2.i386.rpm remote: kernel-headers-
2.0.32-2.i386.rpm
200 PORT command successful.
150 Opening BINARY mode data connection for kernel-headers-
2.0.32-2.i386.rpm (446095 bytes).
```

```
226 Transfer complete.
446095 bytes received in 260 secs (1.7 Kbytes/sec)
local: kernel-modules-2.0.32-2.i386.rpm remote: kernel-modules-
2.0.32-2.i386.rpm
200 PORT command successful.
150 Opening BINARY mode data connection for kernel-modules-
2.0.32-2.i386.rpm (1229707 bytes).
226 Transfer complete.
1229707 bytes received in 565 secs (2.1 Kbytes/sec)
local: kernel-source-2.0.32-2.i386.rpm remote: kernel-source-
2.0.32-2.i386.rpm
200 PORT command successful.
150 Opening BINARY mode data connection for kernel-source-
2.0.32-2.i386.rpm (6195859 bytes).
226 Transfer complete.
6195859 bytes received in 2.35e+03 secs (2.6 Kbytes/sec)
```

In this session, I downloaded the following RPM files:

RPM file name	Description
kernel-2.0.32-2. i386.rpm	Includes the kernel file for Version 2.0.32
kernel-modules-2.0. 32-2.i386.rpm	Includes all the modules needed by kernel Version 2.0.32
kernel-headers-2.0. 32-2.i386.rpm	Contains the header files for Linux Version 2.0.32 (needed if you want to rebuild the kernel)
kernel-source-2.0. 32-2.i386.rpm	Contains the source files for Linux Version 2.0.32 (needed if you want to rebuild the kernel)

Installing the kernel RPMs

To install the kernel and the modules, follow these steps:

1. Make sure you are in the directory where the RPM files (the ones you downloaded from Red Hat's FTP server) are located.

2. Type the following command to install the kernel RPM:

```
rpm -ivh kernel-2.0.32-2.i386.rpm
kernel
###########################################################
```

This step creates the new kernel file vmlinuz-2.0.32 in the /boot directory.

3. Install the new kernel-modules RPM with the following command:

```
rpm -ivh kernel-modules-2.0.32-2.i386.rpm
kernel-modules
###########################################################
```

This step creates a `/lib/modules/2.0.32` directory and places the module files in this directory.

You need to install the `kernel-source` and `kernel-headers` RPMs only if you want to build a new kernel. Use the following `rpm -i` commands to install these packages:

```
rpm -i kernel-source-2.0.32-2.i386.rpm
rpm -i kernel-headers-2.0.32-2.i386.rpm
```

Making new initial RAM disk

If you have a SCSI adapter in your system and you are using a SCSI device driver module, you have to make a new *initial RAM disk image* — a file that can be copied into a block of memory and used as a memory-resident disk.

To see if you have any SCSI driver modules, try the following command:

```
grep scsi /etc/conf.modules
```

Tip

If this command produces no output, your system is not using a SCSI module and does not need an initial RAM disk. You can skip this step and proceed to reconfigure LILO.

On one of my systems with an Adaptec AHA 1542 SCSI adapter, I get the following result when I search using the `grep` command:

```
grep scsi /etc/conf.modules
alias scsi_hostadapter aha1542
```

In this case, I had to create the initial RAM disk using the `mkinitrd` command. Usually, the initial RAM disk image is stored in a file whose name begins with `initrd`. As you might guess, `initrd` is a shorthand for initial RAM disk, and the `mkinitrd` command is so named because it makes an `initrd` file.

To create the initial RAM disk image for kernel Version 2.0.32, type the following command:

```
/sbin/mkinitrd /boot/initrd-2.0.32.img 2.0.32
```

This creates the file `initrd-2.0.32.img` in the `/boot` directory. You will refer to this `initrd` file in the LILO configuration file (`/etc/lilo.conf`).

Reconfiguring LILO

After you install the RPMs and, if necessary, create the initial RAM disk image, you have to reconfigure LILO so it can boot the new kernel. This reconfiguration step is like the procedure described earlier in "Installing the new kernel." The only difference is the need to include an `initrd` line if your system needs the SCSI driver module.

Use a text editor such as vi or Emacs to edit the /etc/lilo.conf file. Add the following lines near the beginning of this file, right after the timeout line:

```
image=/boot/vmlinuz-2.0.32
        label=linux-new
        root=/dev/hda1
        initrd=/boot/initrd-2.0.32.img
        read-only
```

Caution

On the root=/dev/hda1 line, change /dev/hda1 to the correct device name for the disk partition where your Linux system's root directory (/) is located.

After editing and saving the /etc/lilo.conf file, reinstall LILO with the following command:

```
/sbin/lilo
```

Now you can reboot the system and try out the new version of kernel.

Trying out new kernel

You are ready to try the new kernel after you have installed the kernel and kernel-modules RPMs, created the initial RAM disk file, and reconfigured LILO. From the Linux prompt, type the following:

```
reboot
```

When the system reboots and you see the LILO boot: prompt, type linux-new to boot the new kernel. If you added the new kernel description before all other operating systems in the LILO configuration file, that kernel should boot even if you don't type anything at the boot: prompt.

After Linux starts, you should see the following message before the login prompt:

```
Red Hat Linux release 5.0 (Hurricane)
Kernel 2.0.32 on an i586
```

Now your Linux system is running kernel Version 2.0.32.

Summary

Linux was developed through the efforts of many programmers scattered around the globe. These programmers (and many new ones) continue to enhance Linux and to release bug fixes and new versions. You may occasionally have to get some updates or bug fixes and rebuild the Linux kernel. This chapter provides detailed information on how to apply the fixes (known as patches) and how to build a new kernel. It also shows you how to download and install new updates from Red Hat in the form of Red Hat Package Manager (RPM) files. The next chapter steps back from the installation and configuration details and provides an overview of Linux and what you can do with your Linux PC.

By reading this chapter, you learn the following:

▶ The term *kernel* refers to the core Linux operating system — this is the program that makes your PC a Linux PC.

▶ The Linux kernel is improved continually to correct errors (these are the bug fixes) or add new functionality. Such updates are distributed in the form of patches — changes to specific Linux source files. You have to apply the patches and rebuild the kernel to benefit from any enhancements to the kernel.

▶ You can get the patches via FTP from `ftp.funet.fi` in the `/pub/Linux/kernel/src` directory. Look under the current version number (for example, v2.0 for Version 2.0) for specific patches.

▶ The patches are distributed in compressed form — recognizable by the `.gz` suffix in the file name. You must use the `gunzip` command to uncompress the patches.

▶ Copy the patches to the `/usr/src` directory and then use the `patch` command to apply the patches. This alters the kernel's source code in the `/usr/src/linux` directory.

▶ Before rebuilding the kernel, you should prepare an emergency boot disk so you can restart the system if something goes wrong with the kernel rebuild process.

▶ To rebuild the kernel, change directory to `/usr/src/linux` and then use the `make` command. You must follow the sequence `make config; make dep; make clean; make boot` (in that order). You also have to use the commands `make modules` and `make modules_install`.

▶ To make a new kernel available for booting, you must copy the new kernel file to the `/boot` directory and edit the LILO configuration file `/etc/lilo.conf` so it includes information about the new kernel file. Then you must run `/sbin/lilo` to reinstall LILO.

▶ In addition to applying patches, you can also upgrade to a new version of kernel by downloading and installing new updates from Red Hat's FTP server. These updates are distributed in the form of Red Hat Package Manager (RPM) files that package all necessary files for a software package in a single file. You have to use the `rpm` command to install and use RPM files.

▶ You can download updates for Red Hat Linux via ftp from `ftp.redhat.com` in the `/pub/redhat/updates/5.1/i386` directory.

Part II:

Running Linux

Chapter 3

An Overview of Linux

Now that you have successfully installed and configured Linux, you are ready to explore and use your Linux system. You probably had a specific use in mind when you first decided to install Linux on your PC. Whether you want to use Linux to develop software or you just want to surf the Net, this book is your personal guide in your journey through the Linux maze. Even though you have a specific use in mind, you will find it useful to get a detailed overview of Linux, complete with its high points and pitfalls. When you know more about Linux, you can be a smart user, employing Linux in ways you may have thought impossible.

Accordingly, this chapter provides a broad brushstroke picture of Linux and describes how you can get the most out of the built-in capabilities of Linux, such as networking, developing software, and running applications.

Linux Versions

After Linux Version 1.0 was released on March 14, 1994, the loosely organized
Linux development community adopted a version number scheme. Versions
1.*x.y* and 2.*x.y,* wherein *x* is an even number, are stable versions. The number
y is the *patch level,* which is incremented as problems are fixed.

Versions 2.*x.y* with an odd *x* number are beta releases for developers only.
They may be unstable, so you should not use these versions for daily use.
Developers add new features to these odd versions of Linux.

When this book was written, the latest stable version of Linux was 2.0.34, and
developers were working on Version 2.1.1069 (note, a link to information
about the latest version of the Linux kernel always exists at
`http://www.linuxresources.com/what.html`). This book's companion CD-ROM
contains the latest stable version of Linux available as of fall 1998.

**Cross-
Reference**

If you hear about a later version of Linux or about *patches* (corrections) to
the current version that may help you, you can obtain the patches and
rebuild the kernel easily by following the instructions in Chapter 2.

Linux as a UNIX Platform

Like other UNIX systems, Linux is a multiuser, multitasking operating system,
which means Linux enables multiple users to log in and run more than one
program at the same time.

Linux is designed to comply with IEEE Std 1003.1-1990 (POSIX.1). This
standard defines the functions that applications written in the C programming
language use to access the services of the operating system — for tasks
ranging from opening a file to allocating memory. On March 8, 1996, the
Computer Systems Laboratory of the National Institute of Standards and
Technology (NIST) — a U.S. Government agency — validated that Linux
Version 1.2.13, as packaged by Open Linux Ltd., conforms to the POSIX.1
standard. To see a list of POSIX validated products, point your World Wide
Web browser to `ftp://nemo.ncsl.nist.gov/pub/posix/151-2reg`.

Along with POSIX conformance, Linux includes many features of other UNIX
standards, such as the System V Interface Document (SVID) and the Berkeley
Software Distribution (BSD) version of UNIX. Linux takes an eclectic approach,
picking the most needed features of several standard flavors of UNIX.

The POSIX standard

POSIX stands for *Portable Operating System Interface* (abbreviated as POSIX to make it sound like UNIX). The Institute of Electrical and Electronics Engineers (IEEE) began developing the POSIX standards to promote the portability of applications across UNIX environments. POSIX is not limited to UNIX, though. Many other operating systems, such as DEC VMS and Microsoft Windows NT, implement POSIX — in particular, IEEE Std. 1003.1-1990, or POSIX.1, which provides a source-level C-language Application Programming Interface (API) to the services of the operating system, such as reading and writing files. POSIX.1 has been accepted by the International Standards Organization (ISO) and is known as the ISO/IEC IS 9945-1:1990 standard.

Incidentally, the term POSIX is used interchangeably with the term P1003, which is how IEEE refers to the POSIX activities. Thus, POSIX.1 is the same as P1003.1.

In addition to POSIX.1, the POSIX family of standards includes standards ranging from POSIX.2 through POSIX.22, summarized as follows:

POSIX.1 — already a widely accepted standard for source-level portability. POSIX.1 provides a C-language Application Programming Interface (API) to the operating system. The IEEE and ISO have approved this standard. Over the past few years, POSIX.1 was expanded to include several other areas: POSIX.1a (system interface extensions), POSIX.1b (real-time), POSIX.1c (threads), POSIX.1d (real-time extensions), POSIX.1e (security), POSIX.1f (transparent file access), POSIX.1g (protocol independent services), POSIX.1h (fault tolerance).

POSIX.2 — a standard for shell and tools, which are, respectively, the command processor and the utility programs an operating system must provide. The IEEE has approved this standard.

POSIX.3 — a standard for testing and verification for POSIX compliance. The IEEE has approved this standard.

POSIX.4 — a standard for real-time programming and *threads,* concurrently executing blocks of code within a program. This proposed standard has been incorporated into POSIX.1 as POSIX.1b (real-time), POSIX.1c (threads), and POSIX.1d (real-time extensions). POSIX.1b and POSIX 1.c have been approved by the IEEE.

POSIX.5 — an Ada-language API corresponding to POSIX.1. The IEEE and ISO have approved this standard.

POSIX.6 — a standard for system security. This standard has been moved to POSIX.1e and it's still work in progress.

POSIX.7 — a standard for system administration. This standard is now in a new area known as P1387.

POSIX.8 — a standard for network interfaces, including (a) transparent file access, (b) protocol-independent network interface, (c) Remote Procedure Calls (RPC), and (d) protocol-dependent application interfaces for open system interconnect. This standard has been moved to POSIX.1f and it's not yet approved.

POSIX.9 — a FORTRAN language API corresponding to POSIX.1. The IEEE and ISO have approved this standard.

POSIX.10 — a standard for the supercomputing Application Environment Profile (AEP). The IEEE has approved this standard.

POSIX.11 — a proposed standard for Transaction Processing AEP. It has been removed from consideration.

POSIX.12 — a standard for protocol-independent services. This has been moved to POSIX.1g. (Work in progress.)

(continued)

(continued)

POSIX.13 — a standard for real-time application environment profile. (Work in progress.)

POSIX.14 — a standard for multiprocessing application environment profile. (Work in progress.)

POSIX.15 — a standard for batch processing. (Work in progress.)

POSIX.16 — a defunct standard.

POSIX.17 — a standard for directory services (X.400and X.500). This has been moved to P1224.2, P1326.2, P1327.2, and P1328.2 (IEEE has approved these standards).

POSIX.18 — is the POSIX profile. (Work in progress.)

POSIX.19 — used to be the Fortran 90 binding for POSIX.1, but it has been deleted.

POSIX.20 — a standard for real-time extensions in Ada; it has been moved to POSIX.5b. (Work in progress)

POSIX.21 — a standard for real-time distributed system communication. (Work in progress.)

POSIX.22 — a security framework guide. (Work in progress.)

For the latest information on the POSIX standards, point your World Wide Web browser to the home page of the Portable Application Standards Committee (PASC) at `http://www.pasc.org` (the page says the site is powered by Red Hat Linux and Apache).

In addition to POSIX.1 compliance, Linux supports POSIX.2 (shell and utilities). POSIX.2 focuses on the operating system's command interpreter (commonly referred to as the *shell*), and a standard set of utility programs. If you know UNIX or you've had some exposure to it, you know UNIX takes a tools-oriented view of the operating system. A tool is available for almost anything you want to do and the shell enables you to combine several tools to perform tasks more complicated than those handled by the basic tools. The POSIX.2 standard maintains this tools-oriented view, providing the following features:

- A shell with a specified set of built-in commands and a programming syntax that can be used to write *shell programs* or scripts.

- A standard set of utility programs — such as `sed`, `tr`, and `awk` — that can be called by shell scripts and applications. Even the `vi` editor and the `mail` electronic-mail program are part of the standard set. You learn more about these utilities in Chapter 6.

- A set of C functions, such as `system` and `getenv`, that applications can use to access features of the shell.

- A set of utilities for developing shell applications (there is a C compiler for POSIX.2 called `c89`).

The default Linux shell is called *Bash*, which stands for *Bourne-Again Shell* — a reference to the *Bourne shell*, which has been the standard UNIX shell since its early days. Bash incorporates many of the features required by POSIX.2 and then some. Bash essentially inherits the features and functionality of the

Bourne shell. In case of any discrepancy between the Bourne shell and POSIX.2, Bash follows POSIX.2. For stricter POSIX.2 compliance, Bash even includes a POSIX mode.

All in all, Linux serves as a good platform for learning UNIX because it offers a standard set of UNIX commands (the POSIX.2 standard as well as the best features of both System V and BSD UNIX).

Linux's support for POSIX.1 and other common UNIX *system calls* (the functions applications call) make it an excellent system for software development. Another ingredient of modern workstation software — the X Window System — also is available in Linux, in the form of Xfree86.

The availability of common productivity software — such as word processing, spreadsheet, and database applications — is an area in which Linux was lacking. This situation is changing, though The Applixware Office Suite (sold by Red Hat Software, Inc.) is a good example of productivity software for Linux. Other recent entries are WordPerfect 7 for Linux from Corel Corporation and Star Office from Star Division (http://www.stardivision.com/). Additionally, many existing software packages (designed for UNIX workstations with the X Window System) can be readily ported to Linux, thanks to Linux's support for portable standards such as POSIX.1 and the X Window System.

Note

Another exciting development is support for the Intel Binary Compatibility Standard (iBCS) in Linux. The iBCS standard provides binary compatibility between applications developed on various UNIX systems meant for Intel x86 processors. For example, iBCS support enables you to run WordPerfect for SCO UNIX on your Linux PC.

The iBCS support comes in the form a loadable module (a *loadable module* is like a DOS TSR — terminate and stay resident — program), which you can load after booting Linux with a command of the following form:

```
/sbin/insmod -f /lib/modules/2.0.31/misc/iBCS
```

The Red Hat Linux distribution on the companion CD-ROM includes the iBCS module and related documentation in an RPM. You can install that RPM from the Red Hat Linux CD-ROM using the following steps:

1. Insert the Red Hat Linux CD in the CD-ROM drive and mount it:

   ```
   mount /dev/hdc /cdrom
   ```

   Remember to replace /dev/hdc with the device name for your CD-ROM drive. If the /cdrom directory does not exist, create it with the mkdir /cdrom command.

2. Change directory to /cdrom/RedHat/RPMS and then use the rpm-U command to install the iBCS module as follows:

   ```
   cd /cdrom/RedHat/RPMS
   rpm -U iBCS*
   ```

According to the README file in the /usr/doc/iBCS-2.0 directory, the current iBCS module can load and run binary files from the following operating systems:

- SCO UNIX (including SCO OpenServer 5)
- Solaris (x86 version)
- System V Release 4 UNIX for Intel processors (such as UnixWare, Dell UNIX, and Interactive UNIX)
- Wyse V/386 UNIX
- Xenix V/386
- Xenix 286

Support for other operating systems such as 386BSD, FreeBSD, NetBSD, and BSDI/386 are also in the works.

The X Window System in Linux

Let's face it — typing cryptic UNIX commands on a terminal is boring. Those of us who know the commands by heart may not realize it, but the installed base of UNIX is not going to increase significantly if we don't make the system easy to use. This is where the X Window System, or *X,* comes to the rescue.

X provides a standard mechanism for displaying device-independent bitmapped graphics. *X* also is a windowing system, enabling applications to organize their output in separate windows.

Although *X* provides the mechanism for windowed output, it does not offer any specific look or feel for applications. The look and feel comes from graphical user interfaces (GUIs), such as OSF/Motif and OPEN LOOK, which are based on the X Window System. Of these two GUIs, Motif has taken the lion's share of the market, but the OPEN LOOK interface continues to be available on workstations from Sun Microsystems.

Cross-Reference

The Red Hat Linux distribution on this book's CD-ROM comes with the X Window System in the form of Xfree86 3.3.1 — an implementation of X11R6 (X Window System Version 11, release 6, which is the latest release of *X*) for 80×86 systems. A key feature of Xfree86 is its support for a wide variety of video cards available for today's PCs. As you learn in Chapter 4, Xfree86 supports literally hundreds of PC video cards, ranging from the run-of-the-mill Super Video Graphics Adapter (SVGA) to accelerated graphics cards such as the ones based on the S3, Mach64, and Weitek P9000 video chipsets.

As for the GUI, Linux includes several *window managers* — special X programs that manage the windows in which other *X* programs display their output. The window managers typically add a border and a title bar to an *X* application's window.

Although Motif is the dominant GUI in the UNIX marketplace, it does not come with Linux because the Open Software Foundation does not give away Motif free. Motif has a look and feel similar to that of Microsoft Windows and includes the Motif Window Manager (mwm), and the Motif toolkit for programmers. You can get Motif for Linux from several commercial vendors for under $150.

Although you have to pay extra to get Motif, if you need it for a project, a Linux PC with a copy of Motif is still an economical way to set up a software-development platform. If you have a consulting business or if you want to develop *X* and Motif software at home, Linux definitely is the way to go.

Unlike Microsoft Windows or the Macintosh System software, Linux does not come with a powerful graphics file manager, so you may be unable to escape the need to learn UNIX commands and use a terminal window under *X* to do your work. You can, however, use Linux and Xfree86 to develop graphical software that's easy for everyone to use.

In the Linux distribution, you can see a sample of some graphical applications that run under *X*. The most noteworthy programs relate to image display and editing. The first is the shareware program XV, by John Bradley; the other one is `xpaint`, by David Koblas; another one is GIMP, a program with capabilities on a par with Adobe Photoshop.

Another important aspect of the X Window System is you can run applications across the network. For example, you might run a graphical application on a server on the network, but view that application's output and interact with it from your Linux desktop. In other words, with *X,* your Linux PC becomes a gateway to all the other systems on the network.

Cross-Reference

Chapter 4 shows you how to set up Xfree86 on your system, and Chapter 23 explains how to develop X applications on a Linux system.

Linux Networking

Networking refers to all aspects of data exchange between one or more computers, ranging from the physical connection to the protocol for the actual data exchange. A *network protocol* is the method agreed upon by the sender and receiver for exchanging data across a network.

Different network protocols are used at different levels of the network. At the physical level — the level at which the data bits travel through a medium, such as a cable — protocols such as Ethernet and token-ring are used. Application programs don't really work at this physical level, though. Instead, they rely on protocols that operate on blocks of data. These protocols include Novell's Internet Packet Exchange (IPX) and the well-known Transmission Control Protocol/Internet Protocol (TCP/IP).

Cross-Reference

The different levels of network protocols can be represented by a networking model, such as the seven-layer Open Systems Interconnection (OSI) reference model, developed by the International Standards Organization (ISO). Chapter 16 includes a discussion of this model.

Standard network protocols such as TCP/IP have been key to the growth of interconnected computers, resulting in local as well as wide area networks (WANs). Protocols have allowed interconnection of these smaller networks and we now have interconnected networks that form an internetwork: the Internet.

TCP/IP

Networking has been a strength of UNIX since its early days. In particular, the well-known TCP/IP protocol suite has been an integral part of UNIX ever since TCP/IP appeared in BSD UNIX around 1982. By now, TCP/IP is the WAN protocol of choice in the global Internet.

Linux supports the TCP/IP protocol suite and includes all common network applications, such as `telnet`, `ftp`, and `rlogin`. At the physical network level, Linux includes drivers for many Ethernet cards. Token ring is also an integral part of the Linux kernel source. All you have to do is rebuild the kernel and enable support for token-ring.

Cross-Reference

You might say Linux's support for TCP/IP—the dominant protocol suite of the Internet—comes naturally. The rapid development of Linux itself would not have been possible without the collaboration of so many developers from Europe and America. This collaboration, in turn, has been possible only because of the Internet. In Chapter 19, you learn how to set up TCP/IP networking and use the network software.

Linux also includes the Berkeley Sockets (so named because the socket interface was introduced in Berkeley UNIX around 1982)—a popular interface for network programming in TCP/IP networks. For those of you with C programming experience, the Sockets interface consists of several C header files and several C functions you call to set up connections and to send and receive data.

You can use the Berkeley Sockets programming interface to develop Internet tools such as World Wide Web browsers. Because most TCP/IP programs (including those available free at various Internet sites) use the Sockets programming interface, getting these programs up and running on Linux is easy because Linux includes the Sockets interface.

PPP and SLIP

Not everyone has an Ethernet connection to the Internet—especially those of us who use Linux on our home PCs. A way exists, though, to connect to the Internet and communicate by using the TCP/IP protocol over a phone line and modem. What you need is a *server*—a system with an Internet connection, which accepts a dial-in connection from your system.

Nowadays, commercial outfits known as *Internet service providers* (ISPs) offer this type of service for a fee. If you don't want to pay for such a connection, find out whether a computer at your business provides this access. This option may not be unreasonable, especially if you are doing UNIX software development (for your company) on your Linux PC at home.

When you access the Internet through a server, that server runs one of two protocols:

■ Serial Line Internet Protocol (SLIP)

■ Point-to-Point Protocol (PPP)

Both protocols support TCP/IP over a dial-up line. SLIP is a simpler and older protocol than PPP, which has more features for establishing a connection. Nearly everyone uses PPP nowadays, though. To establish a connection, your system must run the same protocol as the ISP's system.

Cross-Reference

Linux supports both SLIP and PPP for dial-up Internet connections. You can turn your Linux system into a SLIP or PPP server so other computers can dial into your computer and establish a TCP/IP connection over the phone line. Chapter 18 explains how to set up SLIP and PPP on your Linux system.

File sharing with NFS

In the MS-DOS and Microsoft Windows world, you may be familiar with the concept of a *file server*—a system that maintains important files and allows all other systems on the network to access those files. Essentially, all PCs on the network share one or more central disks. In DOS and Windows, users see the file server's disk as being just another drive, with its own drive letter (such as *U*). In PC networks, file sharing typically is implemented with Novell NetWare or Microsoft LAN Manager protocols.

The concept of file sharing exists in UNIX as well. The *Network File System* (NFS) provides a standard way for a system to access another system's files over the network. To the user, the remote system's files appear to be in a directory on the local system.

Cross-Reference

NFS is available in Linux. You can share your Linux system's directories with other systems that support NFS. The other systems that access your Linux system's files via NFS do not necessarily have to run UNIX. In fact, NFS is available for DOS and Windows, too, so you can use a Linux PC as the file server for a small workgroup of PCs that run DOS and Windows. Chapter 21 further explores this use of a Linux PC as a file server.

UUCP

An old but important data-exchange protocol is UUCP (UNIX-to-UNIX Copy). For some systems, this protocol continues to be a means of exchanging electronic mail and news. Usenet news—the bulletin board system (BBS) of the Internet—originated with UUCP. Computers that were connected to each other over phone lines and modems used UUCP to exchange mail messages, news items, and files. Essentially, the messages and news were relayed from one computer to another. That system was a low-cost way to deliver news and mail. Although today much of the e-mail and news travel over permanent network connections of the Internet, UUCP still allows many distant systems to be part of the Internet community, as far as USENET news and e-mail go.

Linux includes UUCP. If your Linux system has a modem and if you want to exchange files with another system via a dial-up connection, you can use UUCP. However, with the proliferation of Internet service providers, chances are good you will probably connect your Linux PC to the Internet through an ISP.

Linux System Administration

System administration refers to tasks that must be performed to keep a computer system up and running properly. Because almost all computers are networked now, another set of tasks is needed to keep the network up and running. These tasks are collectively called *network administration*. A site with many computers probably has a full-time *system administrator,* someone who takes care of all system and network administration tasks. Large sites may have separate system administration and network administration personnel. If you are running Linux on a home PC or on a few systems in a small company, you probably are both the system administrator and the network administrator.

Cross-Reference

Linux includes all the basic commands and utilities needed for system and network administration. Chapter 6 briefly covers some of these commands. Chapters 18 and 19 describe the network-administration tools.

System administration tasks

As a system administrator, your typical tasks include the following:

- *Installing, configuring, and upgrading the operating system and various utilities.* You learned how to install Linux and other software packages in Chapter 1. Chapter 2 shows you how to upgrade the operating system and Chapter 4 covers the installation of the X Window System.

- *Adding and removing users.* As shown in "Adding user accounts" in Chapter 1, you can use Red Hat's graphical User Configurator tool to add a new user after you install Linux. If a user forgets the password, you have to use the `passwd` command to change the password.

- *Installing new software.* For the typical Linux software, which you get in source-code form, this task involves using tools such as `gunzip` (to uncompress the software), `tar` (to unpack the archive), and `make` (to build the executable programs). For software distributed by Red Hat in Red Hat Package Manager (RPM) files, you must use the `rpm` command to install the software. Chapter 2 describes RPM.

■ *Making backups*. You can use the `tar` program to archive one or more directories and to copy the archive to a floppy disk (if the archive is small enough) or to a tape (if you have a tape drive).

■ *Mounting and unmounting file systems*. When you want to read an MS-DOS floppy disk, for example, you have to mount that disk's MS-DOS file system on one of the directories of the Linux file system. You must use the `mount` command to accomplish this task.

■ *Monitoring the system's performance*. You have to use a few utilities, such as `top` (to see where the processor is spending most of its time) and `free` (to see the amount of free and used memory in the system).

■ *Starting and shutting down the system*. Although starting the system typically involves nothing more than powering up the PC, you must take some care when you want to shut down your Linux system. You should use the `shutdown` command to stop all programs before turning off your PC's power switch.

Network administration tasks

Typical network-administration tasks include the following:

■ *Adding network support to the kernel*. You may have to configure and build the Linux kernel so it includes support for specific network adapters, as well as for PPP and SLIP. Chapter 2 guides you through the steps needed to configure and build the kernel.

■ *Maintaining the network configuration files*. In Linux (as well as in other UNIX systems), the TCP/IP network is configured through several text files you may have to edit in to make networking work. You may have to edit one or more of the following files: `/etc/hosts`, `/etc/networks`, `/etc/host.conf`, `/etc/resolv.conf`, `/etc/HOSTNAME`, `/etc/hosts.allow`, `/etc/hosts.deny`, and the scripts in the `/etc/sysconfig/network-scripts` directory.

■ *Setting up PPP and SLIP*. You use tools — such as `chat` and `dip` — to set up PPP and SLIP connections.

■ *Monitoring network status*. You have to use tools such as `netstat` (to view information about active network connections), `/sbin/ifconfig` (to check the status of various network interfaces), and `ping` (to make sure a connection is working).

■ *Configuring UUCP* (if you want to dial-up another system and exchange e-mail or news). You may not use UUCP at all because most systems now exchange e-mail and news with the TCP/IP protocol on the Internet.

DOS and Linux

As you probably know, MS-DOS and Microsoft Windows are the most popular operating systems for 80386, 80486, and Pentium PCs. Because Linux started on 80386/80486 PCs, a connection between DOS and Linux has always existed. Typically, you start the Linux installation with some steps in DOS.

Linux has maintained its connection to DOS in several ways:

■ Linux supports the MS-DOS file system. From Linux, you can access MS-DOS files on the hard disk or on a floppy disk.

■ Linux includes a set of tools (called mtools) that manipulate MS-DOS files from within Linux.

■ Work is progressing on an MS-DOS emulator (commonly referred to as *DOSEMU*) that uses the virtual 8086 mode of 80386 or better processors, much as Windows 95 provides the capability to run a DOS session within a window.

The DOSEMU project has already shown some success and many DOS applications (including WordPerfect 5.1 and FoxPro 2.0) have been shown to run under the DOS emulator.

An ongoing project called WINE is attempting to develop a Windows emulator for the X Window System under Linux. Actually, WINE enables you to use your existing Windows 3.1 installation and run Windows 3.1 programs you have installed on your PC's DOS partition.

Cross-Reference

Chapter 7 describes how you can access DOS from Linux. The chapter also explains the use of the mtools utilities and provides information about DOSEMU.

Software Development in Linux

Of all the potential uses of Linux, software development fits Linux perfectly. Software-development tools, such as the compiler and the libraries are included, because you need them anyway when you rebuild the Linux kernel. If you are a UNIX software developer, you already know UNIX, so you will feel right at home in Linux.

As far as the development environment goes, you have the same basic tools (such as an editor, a compiler, and a debugger) you might use on other UNIX workstations, such as those from Hewlett-Packard (HP), Sun Microsystems, IBM, or Digital Equipment Corporation (DEC). So if you work by day on one of the mainstream UNIX workstations, you can use a Linux PC at home to duplicate that development environment at a fraction of the cost. Then you can either complete work projects at home or devote your time to software that you write for fun and then share on the Internet.

Just to give you a sense of Linux's software-development support, following is a list of various features that make Linux a productive software-development environment:

- GNU's C compiler, `gcc`, which can compile ANSI-standard C programs.

- GNU's C++ compiler (`g++`), which has support for AT&T C++ 3.0 features.

- The GNU debugger, `gdb`, which enables you to step through your program to find problems and to determine where and how a program failed. (The failed program's memory image is saved in a file named core; `gdb` can examine this file.)

- The GNU profiling utility, `gprof`, enables you to determine the degree to which a piece of software uses your computer's processor time.

- GNU `make` and `imake` utilities, which enable you to manage the compiling and linking of large programs.

- Revision Control System (RCS), which maintains version information and control access to the source files so two programmers don't inadvertently modify the same source file.

- GNU Emacs editor, which prepares source files and even launches a compile-link cycle to build the program.

- Perl scripting language, which is used to write scripts that tie together many smaller programs with UNIX commands to accomplish a specific task.

- The Tool Command Language and its X toolkit (Tcl/Tk), which enables you to prototype *X* applications rapidly.

- Dynamically linked shared libraries, which allow the actual program files to be much smaller, because all the library code that several programs may use is shared, with only one copy loaded in the system's memory.

- POSIX.1 and POSIX.2 header files and libraries, which enable you to write portable programs.

Cross-Reference

Chapter 22 covers software development in Linux. Read Chapter 8 first to learn about Tcl/Tk programming.

Linux as an Internet On-Ramp

Many of you already have access to the Internet and have experienced what the Internet has to offer:

Electronic mail, newsgroups, and the World Wide Web (*WWW* or *the Web*). Whether you are in the "Been there, done that" camp or the "What's the Web?" camp, you may be happy to learn that a Linux PC includes everything you need to access the Internet. In fact, your PC can becomes a first-class citizen of the Internet, with its own Web server, on which you can publish any information you want.

Although Linux includes TCP/IP and supporting network software with which you can set up your PC as an Internet host, one catch exists: First, you have to obtain a physical connection to the Internet. Your Linux PC has to be connected to another *node* (which can be another computer or a networking device, such as a router) on the Internet. This requirement is the stumbling block for many people—an Internet connection costs money, with the price proportional to the data-transfer rate.

Many commercial ISPs provide various forms of physical connections to the Internet. In the U.S., if you are willing to spend between $15 and $30 a month, you can get an account on a PPP server. Then you can run PPP software on your Linux system; dial in, via a modem; and connect to the Internet at data-transfer rates ranging from 28,800 bits per second (bps) to 56,000 bps, depending on your modem.

Although a dial-up connection is adequate for using your Linux system to access the Internet and to receive e-mail and read news, it may not be appropriate if you want your system to provide information to other people through the Web or FTP (file transfer protocol). For this purpose, you need a connection available 24 hours a day, because other systems may try to access your system at any time of day. For a few hundred dollars a month, you can get a dedicated SLIP or PPP connection and make your system a permanent presence on the Internet.

Another option for a small business—or for anyone who has a few networked PCs—is connecting a local area network (LAN) to the Internet. You can run Linux on one of the PCs to accomplish this task. Typically, you would have an Ethernet LAN running TCP/IP connected to all of the PCs on the network, including the Linux machine. The Linux PC sets up a SLIP or PPP connection to the Internet (via a dial-up or dedicated connection). You then can set up the Linux PC to act as a gateway between the Ethernet LAN and the Internet so the PCs on your LAN can access other systems on the Internet.

Cross-Reference

In Chapter 19, you learn how to configure your Linux system to access the Internet. More important, you learn how to use a Linux PC as the gateway for your local network and the Internet.

Summary

Once you get Linux going on your PC, you can turn your attention to the work you plan to do with Linux. Whether you want to develop software or set up your PC as an Internet host, you can use Linux wisely if you know its overall capabilities. Accordingly, this chapter provides an overview of various aspects of Linux, ranging from software development to networking and system administration. The next chapter turns to another configuration task—it shows you how to configure and run the X Window System on your Linux PC. After you get *X* running, you have a graphical user interface for Linux.

By reading this chapter, you learn the following:

▶ Linux developers use a version number scheme to help you understand what the various versions mean. Versions 2.*x.y*, wherein *x* is an even number, are stable versions. The number *y* is the *patch level*, which is incremented as problems are fixed. Versions 2.*x.y* with an odd *x* are beta releases for developers only; they may be unstable.

▶ POSIX stands for *Portable Operating System Interface* (abbreviated as POSIX to make it sound like UNIX). The Institute of Electrical and Electronics Engineers (IEEE) began developing the POSIX standards to promote the portability of applications across UNIX environments.

▶ Linux is a UNIX look-alike operating system that conforms to the POSIX.1 standard. As such, Linux is ideal as a low-cost UNIX system.

▶ The Linux distribution on the companion CD-ROM also includes an Intel Binary Compatibility Standard (iBCS) module you can install with the `rpm` command and then load with the `/sbin/insmod` command. With the iBCS module, Linux can run binaries from other Intel x86 UNIX systems, such as UnixWare, SCO UNIX, Dell UNIX, Interactive UNIX, Xenix V/386, and Xenix 286.

▶ This book's Linux distribution comes with the XFree86 (X Window System Version 11 Release 6, or X11R6) software. After you install XFree86, you have a graphical user interface for Linux. In addition, *X* enables you to run applications across the network—which means you could run applications on another system on the network and have the output appear on your Linux PC's display.

▶ Linux supports TCP/IP networking well. TCP/IP is the networking protocol of choice on the Internet. A Linux PC, therefore, is ideal as an Internet host providing various Internet services such as FTP and the World Wide Web. You can also use the Linux PC as your Internet ramp—connecting to an Internet service provider through a dial-up TCP/IP connection and running a Web browser to surf the Net.

▶ The Linux distribution includes all the software development tools necessary to write UNIX and *X* applications. You'll find the GNU C and C++ compiler for compiling source files, `make` for automating the compiling, the `gdb` debugger for finding bugs and the Revision Control System (RCS) for managing various revisions of a file. Thus, a Linux PC serves as an ideal software developer's workstation.

Chapter 4

Secrets of X under Linux

In This Chapter

▶ Introducing the X Window System

▶ Setting up XFree86 under Linux

▶ Configuring XFree86

▶ Starting *X*

▶ Trying different video modes

▶ Quitting *X*

If you have used the Macintosh System software or Microsoft Windows, you are familiar with the convenience of graphical user interfaces. In the world of UNIX workstations, the GUI is not an integral part of the operating system. Instead, UNIX workstations typically provide Motif as the GUI. *Motif,* in turn, is built on a windowing system called the *X Window System,* or *X.* Linux also supports *X*—a version of *X* called XFree86, which is designed to work with your PC's video cards. For the GUI, Linux offers several window managers.

Cross-Reference

This chapter explains the X Window System and provides the details you need to help you install XFree86 on your Linux system. The companion CD-ROM contains the XFree86 software, which you installed on your hard disk during the installation process shown in Chapter 1. At that time, you also configured XFree86. This chapter revisits the XFree86 configuration file and shows you how to start *X* on your Linux PC.

Understanding the X Window System

The term *X Window System* is loosely applied to several components that facilitate window-based graphics output on a variety of bitmapped displays.

At the heart of *X* is the *X server*—a process (computer program) running on a computer that has a bitmapped display, a keyboard, and a mouse. Applications—*X clients*—that need to display output do so by communicating with the X server via one of several possible interprocess communication mechanisms. The communication between the X clients and the X server follow a well-defined protocol: the *X protocol.* In addition to the X server, the clients, and the X protocol, the term *X* encompasses a library of routines known as *Xlib*, which constitutes the C-language interface to the facilities of the X server.

Bitmapped graphics displays

Bitmapped graphics displays have two distinct components:

- A *video monitor* — usually, a cathode-ray tube (CRT) on which the graphics output appears. The monitor often is referred to as the *display screen* or simply the *screen*.

- A *video card* (or *graphics card*) — either a plug-in card or some circuitry built into the system's motherboard that causes the output to appear by sending the appropriate signals to the monitor.

In a bitmapped graphics display, the monitor shows an array of dots (known as *pixels,* or *picture elements*), and the appearance of each pixel corresponds to the contents of a memory location in the video card (that's the *video memory*). For a black-and-white display in which each pixel is either bright or dark, a single bit of memory can store the state of a pixel. The term *bitmapped* refers to this correspondence between each bit in memory and a pixel onscreen.

For color displays, each pixel may have anywhere from 4 to 24 bits of memory. The number of bits per pixel also is referred to as the *depth*. The depth determines the number of colors that can be displayed on the monitor simultaneously. An 8-bit depth, for example, provides 256 simultaneous colors, because $2^8 = 256$.

PC video cards can work in different *video modes*, each with a specific depth. Most PC video cards support an 8-bit depth and are usually capable of 24-bit depth.

Bitmapped graphics are also called *raster graphics*, because the graphics that appear on the monitor are constructed from a large number of horizontal lines known as *raster lines*. These raster lines are generated by an electron beam sweeping across a phosphor-coated screen. Because each dot of phosphor, corresponding to a pixel, glows in proportion to the intensity of the beam, each line of the image can be generated by controlling the intensity of the beam as it scans across the screen. A monitor creates the illusion of a steady image by drawing the raster lines repeatedly. Most monitors redraw an entire screen of raster lines 50 to 90 times a second.

Color displays represent any given color by using a combination of the three primary colors: red (R), green (G), and blue (B). The term *RGB value* often is used to specify a color in terms of the intensities of the primary colors. A color monitor uses three electron beams — one for each primary color. The screen of a color monitor has a repeated triangular pattern of red, green, and blue phosphor dots. Each phosphor glows in its color when the electron beam impinges on it. The video card sends signals to vary the intensity of the electron beams, thereby causing many shades of colors to be displayed on the monitor.

Clients and servers

When you work with a typical *X* display, the X server runs on your computer and controls the monitor, keyboard, and mouse. The server responds to commands sent by X clients that open windows and draw in those windows. This arrangement is known as the *client/server model*. As the name implies, the server provides a service the client requests. Usually, clients communicate with the server through a network, with client and server exchanging data using a protocol that both understand.

You may already have seen the client/server model in action. A *file server*, for example, stores files and enables clients to access and manipulate those files. Another common application, the *database server*, provides a centralized database from which clients retrieve data by sending queries. Similarly, the X display server offers graphics-display services to clients that send X protocol requests to the server.

One major difference exists between the X server and other servers, such as file and database servers. Whereas file servers and database servers usually are processes executing on remote machines, the X server is a process executing on the computer where the monitor is located. The X clients may run locally or on remote systems.

 In the PC LAN's client/server model, applications are typically stored on a central server. Users access these server-based applications from client PCs. When you run an application from a PC, the application executes in your PC's processor. In the X client/server model, the situation is different. When you run an application, it actually runs in the server's processor — only the output appears on your Linux PC (which runs the X server). In other words, the X server runs at a location you typically associate with the client (as in client PC in a PC LAN). Remember this distinction when you work with the *X* client/server model.

Graphical user interfaces and *X*

An application's user interface determines its appearance (look) and behavior (feel). When the user interface uses graphic objects, such as windows and menus, we call it a *graphical user interface* (many call it GUI, pronounced *GOO-EY*, for short) a point-and-click user interface, because users generally interact with a GUI by moving the mouse pointer onscreen and clicking the mouse button. To verify the closing of a file, for example, the user may click the mouse button while the mouse pointer is inside a box labeled OK.

Graphical user interfaces were developed at the Xerox Palo Alto Research Center (PARC). Subsequently, Apple Computer made such interfaces popular in its Lisa and Macintosh systems. Today, GUIs are available for most systems. Microsoft Windows is available for most IBM-compatible PCs with 386 or better processors; Presentation Manager, for OS/2; and OSF/Motif and OPEN LOOK (built on *X*), for UNIX.

Most GUIs, including Motif and OPEN LOOK, have four components::

- A window system
- A window manager
- A toolkit
- A style guide

The graphical *window system* organizes graphics output on the display screen and performs basic text and graphics-drawing functions.

The *window manager* enables the user to move and resize windows. The window manager also is partly responsible for the appearance of the windows, because it usually adds a decorative frame to them. Another important aspect of the window manager is the management of *input focus*: the mechanism by which the user can select one of several windows onscreen and make that one the current *active window* (the window with which the user intends to interact). This process is called giving the input focus to a window. For GUIs based on the X Window System, a window manager is an X client, just like any other *X* application.

The third component, the *toolkit*, is a library of routines with a well-defined programming interface. This toolkit is primarily of interest to programmers because it enables programmers to write applications that use the facilities of the window system and have a consistent look and feel.

At first glance, you would think these three components — the window system, the window manager, and the toolkit — are enough for a GUI. They are not. Unless programmers follow a common set of guidelines, the look and feel of applications built with a GUI may not be consistent. Therefore, a GUI has a crucial fourth component: the *style guide*, which specifies the appearance and behavior of an application's user interface.

You may believe the requirement of following a style guide robs programmers of their creativity, but the style guide applies only to the common elements of applications' user interface. The guide establishes basic conventions, such as the relative locations of the File, Edit, and Help pull-down menus and the meaning of mouse-button bindings (*binding* refers to the association of a button click to a specific action, such as the appearance of a pop-up menu when a user clicks the right mouse button). The GUI does not impose any restrictions on the specific functions an application performs. Programmers have ample opportunity to be creative in designing these application-specific parts.

A short history of X

The development of the X Window System started in 1984 at the Massachusetts Institute of Technology (MIT), under the auspices of the MIT Laboratory for Computer Science and MIT/Project Athena. From the beginning, *X* had industry support because DEC and IBM were involved in Project Athena. By early 1986, DEC introduced the first commercial implementation of *X* running on the VAXstation-II/GPX under the Ultrix operating system: X Version 10, release 3 (X10R3). Soon *X* attracted the attention of other prominent workstation vendors, such as Hewlett-Packard, Apollo Computer (Apollo has since merged with Hewlett-Packard), Sun Microsystems, and Tektronix.

Feedback from users of X10 urged project members to start a major redesign of the X protocol. While the design of what would become X Version 11 (X11) proceeded, X10R4 was released in December 1986. X10R4 was the last release of X Version 10.

In January 1987, during the first *X* technical conference, 11 major computer vendors announced a joint effort to support and standardize on X11. The first release of X11—X11R1—became available in September 1987. To ensure the continued evolution of *X* under the control of an open organization, the MIT X Consortium was formed in January 1988. Under the leadership of Robert W. Scheifler, one of the principal architects of *X*, the consortium has been a major reason for the success of *X*. Since then, control of the X Window System has been passed on to the X Consortium, Inc., a nonprofit corporation.

In March 1988, release 2 of X11—X11R2—became available. X11 release 3—X11R3—appeared in late October 1988. In January 1990, the MIT X Consortium released X11R4; X11R5 followed in August 1991.

As *X* takes root in the workstation world, the X Consortium continues to improve *X* in several areas, including support for *X* programming by means of the C++ programming language and the addition of an object-based toolkit named Fresco, which was part of X11R6 (released in April 1994). Throughout these releases, the X11 protocol has remained unchanged. All enhancements have been made through the X11 protocol's capability to support extensions. At the time this book was written, the most prevalent version of *X* was X11R6.

X on Linux

The X Window System for Linux comes from the XFree86 project—a cooperative project of programmers who bring *X* to the PC. As a result, the Linux version of *X* is called XFree86.

The X server is responsible for displaying output on the monitor. As such, the server must access and use the video card. The PC world has such a wide variety of video cards, creating an X server that can work with all video cards is difficult. But common chipsets—integrated circuits—are used in many video cards. The XFree86 project provides several servers, each capable of working with a specific chipset.

Unfortunately, even when several vendors build video cards based on the same chipset, the vendors can configure the chipsets in unique ways. Therefore, the XFree86 servers still have to be tuned to handle each specific brand of video card. For this purpose, the XFree86 developers need detailed information about the video cards. For a while, several well-known video-card vendors refused to release information about their cards. The growing installed base of Linux users, however, persuaded these vendors to release the necessary information to the XFree86 project, so XFree86 Version 3.3.1 includes support for a large number of previously unsupported video cards.

Note

The version of XFree86 on the companion CD-ROM supports the commonly found Diamond SpeedStar and Diamond Stealth series of video cards. The support became available once Diamond agreed to release technical information about the video cards to XFree86 developers.

Setting Up *X* on Linux

You want to get *X* set up and going quickly — without *X*, Linux has no GUI. If you are used to other graphical environments (perhaps on another UNIX workstation or on a PC running Microsoft Windows), you probably want a similar graphical environment on Linux.

If you plan to develop software on your Linux system, chances are good your software has a graphical component that must be implemented and tested under *X*. You must set up and run *X* to do this.

No matter what your purpose, if you want to set up XFree86, you have to prepare a special configuration file, named `XF86Config`, that contains information about your hardware. XFree86 3.1.2 comes with a utility program called `xf86config` (same name as the configuration file, but in lowercase) that can help you create the `XF86Config` file.

The next few sections guide you through the process of configuring XFree86 and starting *X* on your Linux PC.

Knowing your hardware before configuring XFree86

To configure XFree86, you must know the hardware *X* must access and use. From this chapter's brief introduction to *X*, you know the X server controls the following hardware:

- The video card
- The monitor
- The keyboard
- The mouse

The X server needs information about these components to work properly.

The monitor

XFree86 controls the monitor through the video card. As such, an XFree86 server can cause a video card to send a wide range of signals to the monitor (to control how fast a raster line is drawn, for example, or how often the entire screen is redrawn). If a video card causes the monitor to perform some task beyond its capabilities (drawing each raster line much faster than it was designed to do, for example), the monitor may actually be damaged. To ensure the signals from the video card are within the acceptable range for a monitor, XFree86 needs information about some key characteristics of the monitor.

At minimum, you have to provide the following information about the monitor:

- The range of acceptable horizontal synchronization frequencies. A typical range might be 30–64 kilohertz (kHz).

- The range of allowable vertical synchronization rates (also known as *vertical refresh rates*), such as 50–90 Hertz (Hz).

- If available, the bandwidth, in megahertz, such as 75MHz.

Typically, the monitor's documentation includes all this information. If you bought your PC recently, you may still have the documentation. If you lost your monitor's documentation, one way to find the information might be from your Microsoft Windows setup. If your system came with a Windows driver for the display, that driver may display information about the monitor. Also, the Norton System Information tool may also provide this information. Another possibility is to visit your computer vendor's Web site and look for the technical specification of the monitor. I was able to locate useful information about my system's monitor from the vendor's Web site.

The video card

XFree86 already provides X servers designed to work with a particular video chipset (the integrated circuit chips that generate the signals needed to control the monitor). To select the correct X server, you have to indicate what video chipset your video card uses.

Even within a family of video cards based on a specific chipset, many configurable parameters may vary from one card to another. Therefore, you also must specify the vendor name and the model of your video card.

At minimum, you have to provide the following information about the video card:

- Video chipset, such as S3 or ATI Mach64

- Vendor name and model, such as Diamond Stealth 64 VRAM, Number Nine GXE64, or ATI Graphics Xpression

- Amount of video RAM (random-access memory), such as 1MB or 2MB

Most PC vendors indicate only the make and model of the video card in advertisements; the ads rarely mention the video chipset. You should ask explicitly about the video chipset and for as much information as the vendor can provide about the video card's model.

If you are going to use an old PC to run Linux, you could try to find this information by opening your computer's case and looking at the video card. The vendor name and model number may be inscribed on the card. For the video chipset, you must look at the markings on the different chips on the video card and try to guess. On a video card, you may find a chip with the following markings (only part of the markings are shown here):

```
S3 Trio 64 (GACC 2)
86C764 - P
```

You might guess this card uses the S3 chipset. In fact, markings on the chip show the 86C764 number as well (either in the full form or as 764). Now, if you can locate the vendor name and model of this card, you may be all set to configure the X server to run properly on your PC.

The mouse

The *mouse* is an integral part of a GUI, because users indicate choices and perform tasks by pointing and clicking. The X server moves an onscreen pointer as you move the mouse. Also, the X server monitors all mouse clicks and sends these mouse-click events to the appropriate X client application — the one whose window contains the mouse pointer.

Although you may have set up the mouse during Linux installation, you still have to provide information about the mouse to the X server. The XFree86 X server needs a mouse to start; if the X server cannot access and control the mouse, it won't start.

To specify the mouse, you need to know the following things:

- The mouse type, such as Microsoft, Logitech, BusMouse, or PS/2-style mouse

- The type of connection between your mouse and the system — serial or bus.

- The mouse device name. You can leave this as the generic name /dev/mouse, because the Red Hat installation program sets up a link between /dev/mouse and the actual mouse device; the actual device name depends on the type of mouse and where it is connected — the exact serial port for a serial mouse, for example.

You should not have any problem with the mouse as long as the mouse type and device names are correct.

Caution

If you have a bus mouse, you should know that running the gpm program (the program that enables you to cut and paste text in text-mode display) may interfere with *X*. If you have a bus mouse, do not run gpm before starting *X*. To check if gpm is running, use the following command and look for a gpm process in the output:

```
ps ax | grep gpm
```

If gpm is running, use the gpm -k command to stop the program before you start *X*.

Using the XF86Config program

The XFree86 X servers read and interpret the XF86Config file to find detailed information about your PC's monitor, video card, keyboard, and mouse. In addition, the XF86Config file specifies the types of video modes you want to use.

You use a utility program called xf86config to generate a usable XF86Config file. The xf86config program asks you questions that you answer. You must have some information about your PC's video card and monitor to answer these questions.

To run `xf86config`, log in as root and type `xf86config` at the Linux command prompt. The `xf86config` program displays a screen of text that includes the following information:

- The `XF86Config` file is in `/etc` or `/usr/X11R6/lib/X11` directory. A sample file named `XF86Config.eg` is located in `/usr/X11R6/lib/X11`, which is configured for a standard Video Graphics Array (VGA) card and a monitor with 640×480 resolution.

- You can edit the sample `XF86Config` file or create a new one by continuing with `xf86config`.

- The file `/usr/X11R6/lib/X11/doc/README.Config` describes the configuration process.

- `README` files for specific video chipsets are located in the `/usr/X11R6/lib/X11/doc` directory.

- Before continuing with `xf86config`, you should know your video chipset and the amount of video memory.

After reading the preceding section, you should have found out all you could about your video card and monitor. Now press Enter to continue.

The `xf86config` program asks you to make sure the directory `/usr/X11R6/bin` is present in your `PATH` environment variable (the setting of this environment variable determines the order in which Linux searches for files). If you installed XFree86 from the companion CD-ROM, the directory name `/usr/X11` is a symbolic link—an alias—to the `/usr/X11R6` directory, which means you can use the directory name `/usr/X11/bin` to refer to `/usr/X11R6/bin`.

The `xf86config` program also shows you the current setting of the `PATH` environment variable. You see the `PATH` contains `/usr/X11R6/bin`, so you can press Enter to proceed to the next step.

The `xf86config` program asks you to specify a mouse protocol that determines how the X server communicates with the mouse. The program shows you the following list of options:

```
1.  Microsoft compatible (2-button protocol)
2.  Mouse Systems (3-button protocol)
3.  Bus Mouse
4.  PS/2 Mouse
5.  Logitech Mouse (serial, old type, Logitech protocol)
6.  Logitech MouseMan (Microsoft-compatible)
7.  MM Series
8.  MM HitTablet
9.  Microsoft IntelliMouse
```

Press the number that corresponds to your mouse type. If your mouse is connected to a PS/2-style port, for example, select **4**. Press the appropriate number and then press Enter.

The `xf86config` **program then asks the following:**

```
Please answer the following question with either 'y' or 'n'.
Do you want to enable Emulate3Buttons?
```

If your mouse has two buttons, `xf86config` suggests you enable Emulate3Buttons. Press **y** and then press Enter. If you enable Emulate3Buttons, you can simulate a middle button click by pressing both buttons simultaneously. Many X applications assume the mouse has three buttons, so this feature comes in handy in the PC world, where a mouse typically has two buttons.

Next, you must specify the full device name for the mouse. During Linux installation, when you configured the mouse, the installation program created a link between your mouse device and the standard name `/dev/mouse`; so you can press Enter. Otherwise, you should enter the device name for your mouse. For a serial mouse, use one of the following names:

- `/devttyS0` **for a mouse connected to COM1**

- `/devttyS1` **for a mouse connected to COM2**

- `/devttyS2` **for a mouse connected to COM3**

- `/devttyS3` **for a mouse connected to COM4**

For a bus mouse, use one of these names:

- `/dev/atibm` **for ATI bus mouse**

- `/dev/logibm` **for Logitech bus mouse**

- `/dev/inportbm` **for Microsoft bus mouse**

- `/dev/psaux` **for any mouse connected to PS/2-style auxiliary port**

Type the device name that corresponds to your mouse, and press Enter. You can enter an exact device name even if there is a link between `/dev/mouse` and your actual mouse device.

The xf86config program asks if you want to use XKEYBOARD extension (a feature of X11R6) to manage the keyboard layout (the layout determines what character is associated with each physical key on the keyboard):

```
Please answer the following question with either 'y' or 'n'.
Do you want to use XKB? n
```

If you answer Yes, you must select one of several predefined keyboard layouts. You can safely press **n**; then you must use the `xmodmap` program to alter your keyboard layout.

The `xf86config` program then asks whether you want to generate special characters when you work in *X*. To do this, you can bind the left Alt key to Meta and the right Alt key to ModeShift. (*Meta* and *ModeShift* are the standardized names of special keys used in *X;* you can associate the keys with any physical key on the keyboard.)

The program then asks the following:

```
Please answer the following question with either 'y' or 'n'.
Do you want to enable these bindings for the Alt keys? y
```

There is no harm in enabling these keys, so press **y** and then press Enter to continue with the configuration.

Next, xf86config informs you it needs two critical parameters of your monitor:

- Horizontal synchronization frequency—the number of times per second the monitor can display a horizontal raster line, in kilohertz (kHz)

- Vertical synchronization rate—how many times a second the monitor can display the entire screen, in Hertz (Hz)

You can find this information in your monitor's manual.

Press Enter to continue. The xf86config program offers you the following options:

```
    hsync in kHz; monitor type with characteristic modes
 1  31.5; Standard VGA, 640x480 @ 60Hz
 2  31.5 - 35.1; Super VGA, 800x600 @ 56Hz
 3  31.5, 35.5; 8514 Compatible, 1024x768 @ 87 Hz interlaced (no
800x600)
 4  31.5, 35.15, 35.5; Super VGA, 1024x768 @ 87 Hz interlaced, 800x600
@ 56Hz
 5  31.5 - 37.9; Extended Super VGA, 800x600 @ 60 Hz, 640x480 @ 72Hz
 6  31.5 - 48.5; Non-Interlaced SVGA, 1024x768 @ 60 Hz, 800x600 @ 72Hz
 7  31.5 - 57.0; High Frequency SVGA, 1024x768 @ 70 Hz
 8  31.5 - 64.3; Monitor that can do 1280x1024 @ 60 Hz
 9  31.5 - 79.0; Monitor that can do 1280x1024 @ 74 Hz
10  31.5 - 82.0; Monitor that can do 1280x1024 @ 76 Hz
11  Enter your own horizontal sync range
```

You can enter the number that corresponds to your monitor or type **11** to specify a range.

Caution

Do not specify a horizontal synchronization range beyond the capabilities of your monitor. A wrong value can damage the monitor.

Many monitor manuals provide a range of values for the horizontal synchronization rate. To enter a range of values, type **11** and then press Enter. The program prompts you for the range. Enter the range as two values separated by a minus sign (-). My monitor's documentation, for example, says the horizontal synchronization range is 30–64 kHz, so I enter the following:

```
Horizontal sync range: 30-64
```

Next, xf86config prompts you for the vertical synchronization rate and gives you the following options:

```
1  50-70
2  50-90
```

```
3   50-100
4   40-150
5   Enter your own vertical sync range
```

If you know the range, press **5** and then press Enter. At the next prompt, enter the range for the vertical synchronization. My monitor's documentation shows this range to be 55–90 Hz, so I enter the following:

```
Vertical sync range: 55-90
```

Next, you have to enter an identifier for your monitor's definition. Typically, you can enter your monitor's make and model. You can enter anything here, because this information is simply used as an identifier in references to the monitor in another part of the XF86Config configuration file (the following section describes that file's layout). For my system's monitor, I respond as follows:

```
Enter an identifier for your monitor definition: Dell VS15X
Enter the vendor name of your monitor: Dell
Enter the model name of your monitor: VS15X
```

The next task is to configure the video-card settings. The xf86config program displays an explanatory message and asks this question:

```
Do you want to look at the card database? y
```

Press **y** and then press Enter. The program then displays a list of 381 cards. Press Enter after each screen to see the entire list. The complete list appears after this paragraph. The make, model, and chipset of the video card are crucial pieces of information you need to select the correct XFree86 X server and configure it properly. You want to browse through this list to see whether *X* will work with your video card.

```
0    2 the Max MAXColor S3 Trio64V+           S3 Trio64V+
1    928Movie                                 S3 928
2    AGX (generic)                            AGX-014/15/16
3    ALG-5434(E)                              CL-GD5434
4    ASUS PCI-AV264CT                         ATI-Mach64
5    ASUS PCI-V264CT                          ATI-Mach64
6    ASUS Video Magic PCI V864                S3 864
7    ASUS Video Magic PCI VT64                S3 Trio64
8    ATI 3D Pro Turbo                         ATI-Mach64
9    ATI 3D Xpression                         ATI-Mach64
10   ATI 3D Xpression+ PC2TV                  ATI-Mach64
11   ATI 8514 Ultra (no VGA)                  ATI-Mach8
12   ATI All-in-Wonder                        ATI-Mach64
13   ATI Graphics Pro Turbo                   ATI-Mach64
14   ATI Graphics Pro Turbo 1600              ATI-Mach64
15   ATI Graphics Ultra                       ATI-Mach8
16   ATI Graphics Ultra Pro                   ATI-Mach32
17   ATI Graphics Xpression with 68875 RAMDAC ATI-Mach64

Enter a number to choose the corresponding card definition.
Press Enter for the next page; press q to continue configuration.

18   ATI Graphics Xpression with AT&T 20C408 RAMDAC  ATI-Mach64
19   ATI Graphics Xpression with CH8398 RAMDAC       ATI-Mach64
```

```
20  ATI Graphics Xpression with Mach64 CT (264CT)         ATI-Mach64
21  ATI Graphics Xpression with STG1702 RAMDAC            ATI-Mach64
22  ATI Mach64                                            ATI-Mach64
23  ATI Mach64 3D RAGE II+, Internal RAMDAC               ATI-Mach64
24  ATI Mach64 3D RAGE II, Internal RAMDAC                ATI-Mach64
25  ATI Mach64 CT (264CT), Internal RAMDAC                ATI-Mach64
26  ATI Mach64 GT (264GT), aka 3D RAGE, Internal RAMDACATI-Mach64
27  ATI Mach64 VT (264VT), Internal RAMDAC                ATI-Mach64
28  ATI Mach64 with AT&T 20C408 RAMDAC                    ATI-Mach64
29  ATI Mach64 with CH8398 RAMDAC                         ATI-Mach64
30  ATI Mach64 with IBM RGB514 RAMDAC                     ATI-Mach64
31  ATI Ultra Plus                                        ATI-Mach32
32  ATI Video Xpression                                   ATI-Mach64
33  ATI Win Boost with AT&T 20C408 RAMDAC                 ATI-Mach64
34  ATI Win Boost with CH8398 RAMDAC                      ATI-Mach64
35  ATI Win Boost with Mach64 CT (264CT)                  ATI-Mach64
```

Enter a number to choose the corresponding card definition.
Press Enter for the next page; press **q** to continue configuration.

```
36  ATI Win Boost with STG1702 RAMDAC                     ATI-Mach64
37  ATI Win Turbo                                         ATI-Mach64
38  ATI Wonder SVGA                                       ATI vgawonder
39  ATrend ATC-2165A                                      ET6000
40  Actix GE32+ 2MB                                       S3 801/805
41  Actix GE32i                                           S3 805i
42  Actix GE64                                            S3 864
43  Actix ProStar                                         CL-GD5426/5428
44  Actix ProStar 64                                      CL-GD5434
45  Actix Ultra                                           S3 928
46  Acumos AVGA3                                          CL-GD5420/2/4/6/8/9
47  Alliance ProMotion 6422                               AP6422
48  Ark Logic ARK1000PV (generic)                         ARK1000PV
49  Ark Logic ARK1000VL (generic)                         ARK1000VL
50  Ark Logic ARK2000MT (generic)                         ARK1000MT
51  Ark Logic ARK2000PV (generic)                         ARK1000PV
52  Avance Logic 2101                                     Avance Logic
53  Avance Logic 2228                                     Avance Logic
```

Enter a number to choose the corresponding card definition.
Press Enter for the next page; press **q** to continue configuration.

```
54  Avance Logic 2301                                     Avance Logic
55  Avance Logic 2302                                     Avance Logic
56  Avance Logic 2308                                     Avance Logic
57  Avance Logic 2401                                     Avance Logic
58  Binar Graphics AnyView                                ET6000
59  Boca Vortex (Sierra RAMDAC)                           AGX-015
60  California Graphics SunTracer 6000                    ET6000
61  Canopus Co. Power Window 3DV                          S3 ViRGE
62  Canopus Total-3D                                      Verite 1000
63  Cardex Challenger (Pro)                               ET4000/W32(i/p)
64  Cardex Cobra                                          ET4000/W32(i/p)
65  Cardex Trio64                                         S3 Trio64
66  Cardex Trio64Pro                                      S3 Trio64
67  Chips & Technologies CT64200                          ct64200
```

```
68   Chips & Technologies CT64300                      ct64300
69   Chips & Technologies CT65520                      ct65520
70   Chips & Technologies CT65525                      ct65525
71   Chips & Technologies CT65530                      ct65530
```

Enter a number to choose the corresponding card definition.
Press Enter for the next page; press **q** to continue configuration.

```
72   Chips & Technologies CT65535                      ct65535
73   Chips & Technologies CT65540                      ct65540
74   Chips & Technologies CT65545                      ct65545
75   Chips & Technologies CT65546                      ct65546
76   Chips & Technologies CT65548                      ct65548
77   Chips & Technologies CT65550                      ct65550
78   Chips & Technologies CT65554                      ct65554
79   Chips & Technologies CT65555                      ct65555
80   Chips & Technologies CT68554                      ct68554
81   Cirrus Logic GD542x                               CL-GD5420/2/4/6/8/9
82   Cirrus Logic GD543x                               CL-GD5430/5434
83   Cirrus Logic GD544x                               CL-GD544x
84   Cirrus Logic GD5462                               CL-GD5462
85   Cirrus Logic GD5464                               CL-GD5464
86   Cirrus Logic GD62xx (laptop)                      CL-GD6205/15/25/35
87   Cirrus Logic GD64xx (laptop)                      CL-GD6420/6440
88   Cirrus Logic GD754x (laptop)                      CL-GD7541/42/43/48
89   Colorgraphic Dual Lightning                       ET4000/W32(i/p)
```

Enter a number to choose the corresponding card definition.
Press Enter for the next page; press **q** to continue configuration.

```
90    Creative Labs 3D Blaster PCI (Verite 1000)       Verite 1000
91    Creative Labs Graphics Blaster 3D                CL-GD5464
92    Creative Labs Graphics Blaster MA201             CL-GD544x
93    Creative Labs Graphics Blaster MA202             CL-GD544x
94    Creative Labs Graphics Blaster MA302             CL-GD5462
95    Creative Labs Graphics Blaster MA334             CL-GD5464
96    DFI-WG1000                                       CL-GD5420/2/4/6/8/9
97    DFI-WG5000                                       ET4000/W32(i/p)
98    DFI-WG6000                                       WD90C33
99    DSV3325                                          S3 ViRGE
100   DSV3326                                          S3 Trio64V+
101   DataExpert DSV3325                               S3 ViRGE
102   DataExpert DSV3365                               S3 Trio64V+
103   Dell S3 805                                      S3 801/805
104   Dell onboard ET4000                              ET4000
105   Diamond Edge 3D                                  nv1
106   Diamond Multimedia Stealth 3D 2000               S3 ViRGE
107   Diamond Multimedia Stealth 3D 2000 PRO           S3 ViRGE/DX
```

Enter a number to choose the corresponding card definition.
Press Enter for the next page; press **q** to continue configuration.

```
108   Diamond SpeedStar (Plus)                         ET4000
109   Diamond SpeedStar 24                             ET4000
110   Diamond SpeedStar 24X (not fully supported)      WD90C31
111   Diamond SpeedStar 64                             CL-GD5434
```

```
112   Diamond SpeedStar HiColor                            ET4000
113   Diamond SpeedStar Pro (not SE)                       CL-GD5426/28
114   Diamond SpeedStar Pro 1100                           CL-GD5420/2/4/6/8/9
115   Diamond SpeedStar Pro SE (CL-GD5430/5434)            CL-GD5430/5434
116   Diamond SpeedStar64 Graphics 2000/2200               CL-GD5434
117   Diamond Stealth 24                                   S3 801/805
118   Diamond Stealth 32                                   ET4000/W32(i/p)
119   Diamond Stealth 3D 2000                              S3 ViRGE
120   Diamond Stealth 3D 2000 PRO                          S3 ViRGE/DX
121   Diamond Stealth 3D 3000                              S3 ViRGE/VX
122   Diamond Stealth 64 DRAM SE                           S3 Trio32
123   Diamond Stealth 64 DRAM with S3 SDAC                 S3 864
124   Diamond Stealth 64 DRAM with S3 Trio64               S3 Trio64
125   Diamond Stealth 64 VRAM                              S3 964
```

Enter a number to choose the corresponding card definition.
Press Enter for the next page; press **q** to continue configuration.

```
126   Diamond Stealth 64 Video VRAM (TI RAMDAC)            S3 968
127   Diamond Stealth Pro                                  S3 928
128   Diamond Stealth VRAM                                 S3 911/924
129   Diamond Stealth Video 2500                           Alliance AT24
130   Diamond Stealth Video DRAM                           S3 868
131   Diamond Stealth64 Graphics 2001 series               ARK2000PV
132   Diamond Stealth64 Graphics 2xx0 series (864 + SDAC)S3 864
133   Diamond Stealth64 Graphics 2xx0 series (Trio64)      S3 Trio64
134   Diamond Stealth64 Video 2001 series (2121/2201)      S3 Trio64V+
135   Diamond Stealth64 Video 2120/2200                    S3 868
136   Diamond Stealth64 Video 3200                         S3 968
137   Diamond Stealth64 Video 3240/3400 (IBM RAMDAC)       S3 968
138   Diamond Stealth64 Video 3240/3400 (TI RAMDAC)        S3 968
139   Diamond Viper PCI 2Mb                                Weitek 9000
140   Diamond Viper VLB 2Mb                                Weitek 9000
141   EIZO (VRAM)                                          AGX-014/15/16
142   ELSA Gloria-4                                        S3 968
143   ELSA Gloria-8                                        S3 968
```

Enter a number to choose the corresponding card definition.
Press Enter for the next page; press **q** to continue configuration.

```
144   ELSA Victory 3D                                      S3 ViRGE
145   ELSA Victory 3DX                                     S3 ViRGE/DX
146   ELSA WINNER 1000/T2D                                 S3 Trio64V2
147   ELSA Winner 1000AVI (AT&T 20C409 version)            S3 868
148   ELSA Winner 1000AVI (SDAC version)                   S3 868
149   ELSA Winner 1000ISA                                  S3 805i
150   ELSA Winner 1000PRO with S3 SDAC                     S3 864
151   ELSA Winner 1000PRO with STG1700 or AT&T RAMDAC      S3 864
152   ELSA Winner 1000PRO/X                                S3 868
153   ELSA Winner 1000TRIO                                 S3 Trio64
154   ELSA Winner 1000TRIO/V                               S3 Trio64V+
155   ELSA Winner 1000TwinBus                              S3 928
156   ELSA Winner 1000VL                                   S3 928
157   ELSA Winner 2000                                     S3 928
158   ELSA Winner 2000AVI                                  S3 968
159   ELSA Winner 2000AVI/3D                               S3 ViRGE/VX
```

```
160   ELSA Winner 2000PRO-2                              S3 964
161   ELSA Winner 2000PRO-4                              S3 964
```

Enter a number to choose the corresponding card definition.
Press Enter for the next page; press **q** to continue configuration.

```
162   ELSA Winner 2000PRO/X-2                            S3 968
163   ELSA Winner 2000PRO/X-4                            S3 968
164   ELSA Winner 2000PRO/X-8                            S3 968
165   ELSA Winner 3000                                   S3 ViRGE/VX
166   ELSA Winner 3000-L-42                              S3 ViRGE/VX
167   ELSA Winner 3000-M-22                              S3 ViRGE/VX
168   ELSA Winner 3000-S                                 S3 ViRGE
169   ET3000 (generic)                                   ET3000
170   ET4000 (generic)                                   ET4000
171   ET4000 W32i, W32p (generic)                        ET4000/W32(i/p)
172   ET4000/W32 (generic)                               ET4000/W32
173   ET6000 (generic)                                   ET6000
174   ExpertColor DSV3325                                S3 ViRGE
175   ExpertColor DSV3365                                S3 Trio64V+
176   Generic VGA compatible                             Generic VGA
177   Genoa 5400                                         ET3000
178   Genoa 8500VL(-28)                                  CL-GD5426/28
179   Genoa 8900 Phantom 32i                             ET4000/W32(i/p)
```

Enter a number to choose the corresponding card definition.
Press Enter for the next page; press **q** to continue configuration.

```
180   Genoa Phantom 64i with S3 SDAC                     S3 864
181   Genoa VideoBlitz III AV                            S3 968
182   Hercules Dynamite                                  ET4000/W32
183   Hercules Dynamite 128/Video                        ET6000
184   Hercules Dynamite Power                            ET4000/W32(i/p)
185   Hercules Dynamite Pro                              ET4000/W32(i/p)
186   Hercules Graphite HG210                            AGX-014
187   Hercules Graphite Power                            AGX-016
188   Hercules Graphite Pro                              AGX-015
189   Hercules Graphite Terminator 64                    S3 964
190   Hercules Graphite Terminator 64/DRAM               S3 Trio64
191   Hercules Graphite Terminator Pro 64                S3 968
192   Hercules Stingray                                  ALG-2228/2301/2302
193   Hercules Stingray 64/V with ICS5342                ARK2000MT
194   Hercules Stingray 64/V with ZoomDAC                ARK1000PV
195   Hercules Stingray Pro                              ARK1000PV
196   Hercules Stingray Pro/V                            ARK1000PV
197   Hercules Terminator 3D/DX                          S3 ViRGE/DX
```

Enter a number to choose the corresponding card definition.
Press Enter for the next page; press **q** to continue configuration.

```
198   Hercules Terminator 64/3D                          S3 ViRGE
199   Hercules Terminator 64/Video                       S3 Trio64V+
200   Integral FlashPoint                                ET4000/W32(i/p)
201   Intel 5430                                         CL-GD5430
202   Interay PMC Viper                                  ET6000
```

```
203   JAX 8241                                      S3 801/805
204   Jaton Video-58P                               ET6000
205   Jaton Video-70P                               CL-GD5464
206   Jazz Multimedia G-Force 128                   ET6000
207   LeadTek WinFast 3D S600                       S3 ViRGE
208   LeadTek WinFast S200                          ET4000/W32(i/p)
209   LeadTek WinFast S430                          S3 968
210   LeadTek WinFast S510                          S3 968
211   MELCO WGP-VG4S                                S3 ViRGE
212   MELCO WGP-VX8                                 S3 ViRGE/VX
213   Matrox Comet                                  ET4000/W32(i/p)
214   Matrox Marvel II                              ET4000/W32(i/p)
215   Matrox Millennium (MGA)                       mga2064w
```

Enter a number to choose the corresponding card definition.
Press Enter for the next page; press **q** to continue configuration.

```
216   Matrox Millennium II                          mga2164w
217   Matrox Mystique                               mga1064sg
218   MediaVision Proaxcel 128                      ET6000
219   Mirage Z-128                                  ET6000
220   Miro Crystal 10SD with GenDAC                 S3 801/805
221   Miro Crystal 12SD                             S3 Trio32
222   Miro Crystal 16S                              S3 928
223   Miro Crystal 20SD PCI with S3 SDAC            S3 868
224   Miro Crystal 20SD VLB with S3 SDAC (BIOS 3.xx)  S3 864
225   Miro Crystal 20SD with ICD2061A (BIOS 2.xx)   S3 864
226   Miro Crystal 20SD with ICS2494 (BIOS 1.xx)    S3 864
227   Miro Crystal 20SV                             S3 964
228   Miro Crystal 22SD                             S3 Trio64
229   Miro Crystal 40SV                             S3 964
230   Miro Crystal 80SV                             S3 968
231   Miro Crystal 8S                               S3 801/805
232   Miro MiroVideo 20TD                           ET4000/W32(i/p)
233   Miro Video 20SV                               S3 968
```

Enter a number to choose the corresponding card definition.
Press Enter for the next page; press **q** to continue configuration.

```
234   NeoMagic (laptop/notebook)                    NeoMagic 128/V/ZV
235   Number Nine FX Motion 331                     S3 Trio64V+
236   Number Nine FX Motion 332                     S3 ViRGE
237   Number Nine FX Motion 531                     S3 868
238   Number Nine FX Motion 771                     S3 968
239   Number Nine FX Vision 330                     S3 Trio64
240   Number Nine GXE Level 10/11/12                S3 928
241   Number Nine GXE Level 14/16                   S3 928
242   Number Nine GXE64                             S3 864
243   Number Nine GXE64 Pro                         S3 964
244   Number Nine GXE64 with S3 Trio64              S3 Trio64
245   Number Nine Imagine I-128 (2-8MB)             I128
246   Number Nine Imagine I-128 Series 2 (2-4MB)    I128
247   Number Nine Visual 9FX Reality 332            S3 ViRGE
248   Oak (generic)                                 Oak-067/77/87
249   Ocean (octek) VL-VGA-1000                     ARK1000VL
```

```
250   Orchid Celsius (AT&T RAMDAC)                          AGX-015
251   Orchid Celsius (Sierra RAMDAC)                        AGX-015
```

Enter a number to choose the corresponding card definition.
Press Enter for the next page; press **q** to continue configuration.

```
252   Orchid Fahrenheit 1280                                S3 801
253   Orchid Fahrenheit VA                                  S3 801/805
254   Orchid Fahrenheit-1280+                               S3 801/805
255   Orchid Kelvin 64                                      CL-GD5434
256   Orchid Kelvin 64 VLB Rev A                            CL-GD5434
257   Orchid Kelvin 64 VLB Rev B                            CL-GD5434
258   Orchid P9000 VLB                                      Weitek 9000
259   Orchid Technology Fahrenheit Video 3D                 S3 ViRGE
260   Paradise Accelerator Value                            Oak OTI-087
261   Paradise/WD 90CXX                                     WD90CXX
262   Rendition Verite 1000                                 Verite 1000
263   S3 801/805 (generic)                                  S3 801/805
264   S3 801/805 with ATT20c490 RAMDAC                      S3 801/805
265   S3 801/805 with ATT20c490 RAMDAC and ICD2061A         S3 801/805
266   S3 801/805 with Chrontel 8391                         S3 801/805
267   S3 801/805 with S3 GenDAC                             S3 801/805
268   S3 801/805 with SC1148{2,3,4} RAMDAC                  S3 801/805
269   S3 801/805 with SC1148{5,7,9} RAMDAC                  S3 801/805
```

Enter a number to choose the corresponding card definition.
Press Enter for the next page; press **q** to continue configuration.

```
270   S3 864 (generic)                                      S3 864
271   S3 864 with ATT 20C498 or 21C498                      S3 864
272   S3 864 with SDAC (86C716)                             S3 864
273   S3 864 with STG1703                                   S3 864
274   S3 868 (generic)                                      S3 868
275   S3 868 with ATT 20C409                                S3 868
276   S3 868 with ATT 20C498 or 21C498                      S3 868
277   S3 868 with SDAC (86C716)                             S3 868
278   S3 86C325 (generic)                                   S3 ViRGE
279   S3 86C375 (generic)                                   S3 ViRGE/DX
280   S3 86C385 (generic)                                   S3 ViRGE/GX
281   S3 86C764 (generic)                                   S3 Trio64
282   S3 86C765 (generic)                                   S3 Trio64V+
283   S3 86C775 (generic)                                   S3 Trio64V2
284   S3 86C785 (generic)                                   S3 Trio64V2
285   S3 86C801 (generic)                                   S3 801/805
286   S3 86C805 (generic)                                   S3 801/805
287   S3 86C864 (generic)                                   S3 864
```

Enter a number to choose the corresponding card definition.
Press Enter for the next page; press **q** to continue configuration.

```
288   S3 86C868 (generic)                                   S3 868
289   S3 86C911 (generic)                                   S3 911/924
290   S3 86C924 (generic)                                   S3 911/924
291   S3 86C928 (generic)                                   S3 928
292   S3 86C964 (generic)                                   S3 964
293   S3 86C968 (generic)                                   S3 968
```

294	S3 86C988 (generic)	S3 ViRGE/VX
295	S3 911/924 (generic)	S3 911/924
296	S3 924 with SC1148 DAC	S3 924
297	S3 928 (generic)	S3 928
298	S3 964 (generic)	S3 964
299	S3 968 (generic)	S3 968
300	S3 Trio32 (generic)	S3 Trio32
301	S3 Trio64 (generic)	S3 Trio64
302	S3 Trio64V+ (generic)	S3 Trio64V+
303	S3 Trio64V2 (generic)	S3 Trio64V2
304	S3 Trio64V2/DX (generic)	S3 Trio64V2
305	S3 Trio64V2/GX (generic)	S3 Trio64V2

Enter a number to choose the corresponding card definition.
Press Enter for the next page; press **q** to continue configuration.

306	S3 ViRGE (S3V server)	S3 ViRGE
307	S3 ViRGE (generic)	S3 ViRGE
308	S3 ViRGE/DX (generic)	S3 ViRGE/DX
309	S3 ViRGE/GX (generic)	S3 ViRGE/GX
310	S3 ViRGE/VX (generic)	S3 ViRGE/VX
311	S3 Vision864 (generic)	S3 864
312	S3 Vision868 (generic)	S3 868
313	S3 Vision964 (generic)	S3 964
314	S3 Vision968 (generic)	S3 968
315	SNI PC5H W32	ET4000/W32(i/p)
316	SNI Scenic W32	ET4000/W32(i/p)
317	SPEA Mercury 64	S3 964
318	SPEA Mirage	S3 801/805
319	SPEA/V7 Mercury	S3 928
320	SPEA/V7 Mirage P64	S3 864
321	SPEA/V7 Mirage P64 with S3 Trio64	S3 Trio64
322	SPEA/V7 Mirage VEGA Plus	ALG-2228
323	SPEA/V7 ShowTime Plus	ET4000/W32(i/p)

Enter a number to choose the corresponding card definition.
Press Enter for the next page; press **q** to continue configuration.

324	STB Horizon	CL-GD5426/28
325	STB Horizon Video	CL-GD5440
326	STB LightSpeed	ET4000/W32(i/p)
327	STB LightSpeed 128	ET6000
328	STB MVP-2	ET4000
329	STB MVP-2 PCI	ET4000/W32(i/p)
330	STB MVP-2X	ET4000/W32(i/p)
331	STB MVP-4 PCI	ET4000/W32(i/p)
332	STB MVP-4X	ET4000/W32(i/p)
333	STB Nitro (64)	CL-GD5434
334	STB Nitro 3D	S3 ViRGE/GX
335	STB Nitro 64 Video	CL-GD5446
336	STB Pegasus	S3 928
337	STB Powergraph 64	S3 Trio64
338	STB Powergraph 64 Video	S3 Trio64V+
339	STB Powergraph X-24	S3 801/805
340	STB Systems Powergraph 3D	S3 ViRGE
341	STB Systems Velocity 3D	S3 ViRGE/VX

Enter a number to choose the corresponding card definition.
Press Enter for the next page; press **q** to continue configuration.

```
342   STB Velocity 64 Video                    S3 968
343   SiS SG86C201                             SIS86C201
344   Sierra Screaming 3D                      Verite 1000
345   Sigma Concorde                           ET4000/W32
346   Sigma Legend                             ET4000
347   Spider Black Widow                       AGX-015
348   Spider Black Widow Plus                  AGX-016
349   Spider Tarantula 64                      S3 964
350   Spider VLB Plus                          CL-GD5428
351   TechWorks Thunderbolt                    ET4000/W32
352   Techworks Ultimate 3D                    CL-GD5464
353   Trident 8900/9000 (generic)              TVGA8900/9000
354   Trident 8900D (generic)                  TVGA8900D
355   Trident TGUI9400CXi (generic)            TGUI9400CXi
356   Trident TGUI9420DGi (generic)            TGUI9420DGi
357   Trident TGUI9430DGi (generic)            TGUI9430DGi
358   Trident TGUI9440 (generic)               TGUI9440
359   Trident TGUI9660 (generic)               TGUI9660
```

Enter a number to choose the corresponding card definition.
Press Enter for the next page; press **q** to continue configuration.

```
360   Trident TGUI9680 (generic)               TGUI9680
361   Trident TVGA9200CXr (generic)            TVGA9200CXr
362   Unsupported VGA compatible               Generic VGA
363   VI720                                    CL-GD5434
364   VL-41                                    S3 801/805
365   VidTech FastMax P20                      S3 864
366   VideoLogic GrafixStar 300                S3 Trio64
367   VideoLogic GrafixStar 400                S3 Trio64V+
368   VideoLogic GrafixStar 500                S3 868
369   VideoLogic GrafixStar 550                CL-GD5464
370   VideoLogic GrafixStar 600                ET6000
371   VideoLogic GrafixStar 700                S3 968
372   ViewTop PCI                              ET4000/W32(i/p)
373   WD 90C24 (laptop)                        WD90C24
374   WD 90C24A or 90C24A2 (laptop)            WD90C24A
375   WinFast 3D S600                          S3 ViRGE
376   WinFast S200                             ET4000/W32(i/p)
377   WinFast S430                             S3 968
```

Enter a number to choose the corresponding card definition.
Press Enter for the next page; press **q** to continue configuration.

```
378   WinFast S510                             S3 968
379   XGA-1  (ISA bus)                         XGA-1
380   XGA-2  (ISA bus)                         XGA-2
381   miro miroMedia 3D                        S3 ViRGE
```

Enter a number to choose the corresponding card definition.
Press Enter for the next page, press **q** to continue configuration.

Select your video card by typing the appropriate number. One of my PCs, for example, has a Number Nine GXE64 video card with the S3-Trio64 chipset. For this PC, I type **244** and press Enter.

Tip

Each new release of XFree86 supports more video cards. The list in this section shows the cards XFree86 3.3.1 supports (as a point of reference, in Version 3.1.2 the list had only 124 entries; now there are 381 supported cards). If your video card's vendor and model do not appear in the list, but you know the video chipset, try selecting the entry that corresponds to the generic ship set. If you have a video card based on the S3-Trio64 chipset, for example, but you do not know the make and model of the card, select card number 301 from the list.

After you enter your selection, xf86config displays some information (and any appropriate instructions) about the video card you selected. When I select card number 244, for example, xf86config displays the following:

```
Your selected card definition:

Identifier: Number Nine GXE64 with S3-Trio64
Chipset:    S3-Trio64
Server:     XF86_S3
Do NOT probe clocks or use any Clocks line.

Press Enter to continue or ctrl-c to abort.
```

Tip

Notice the instruction that I should not probe clocks or use any Clocks line. If you see any instruction like this, remember it as you continue with xf86config. If the program offers to probe clocks, for example, you should answer No. You needn't understand what the instruction means. Simply follow it and you should have an XF86Config file that works properly.

After you press Enter to continue, xf86config displays the following message, asking you to select an X server:

```
Now you must determine which server to run. Refer to the manpages and other
documentation. The following servers are available (they may not all be
installed on your system):

1  The XF86_Mono server. This a monochrome server that should work on any
   VGA-compatible card, in 640x480 (more on some SVGA chipsets).
2  The XF86_VGA16 server. This is a 16-color VGA server that should work on
   any VGA-compatible card.
3  The XF86_SVGA server. This is a 256 color SVGA server that supports
   a number of SVGA chipsets. On some chipsets it is accelerated or
   supports higher color depths.
4  The accelerated servers. These include XF86_S3, XF86_Mach32, XF86_Mach8,
   XF86_8514, XF86_P9000, XF86_AGX, XF86_W32, XF86_Mach64, XF86_I128 and
   XF86_S3V.

These four server types correspond to the four different "Screen" sections in
XF86Config (vga2, vga16, svga, accel).
```

```
5  Choose the server from the card definition, XF86_S3.
```

```
Which one of these screen types do you intend to run by default (1-5)? 5
```

If you specified your video card correctly, you should press **5** so the server corresponds to the video card. The xf86config program then displays the following message and question:

```
The server to run is selected by changing the symbolic link 'X'. For
example,'rm /usr/X11R6/bin/X; ln -s /usr/X11R6/bin/XF86_SVGA
/usr/X11R6/bin/X' selects the SVGA server.

Please answer the following question with either 'y' or 'n'.
Do you want me to set the symbolic link?
```

Press **y** to answer Yes to this question.

Next, xf86config asks how much video memory your video card has:

```
How much video memory do you have on your video card:
1  256K
2  512K
3  1024K
4  2048K
5  4096K
6  Other
```

Most current video cards have either 2MB (2,048KB) or 4MB (4,096KB) of video memory. You need at least 1MB of video memory to display 256 colors at 1,024×768 resolution (1,024 pixels horizontally by 768 pixels vertically). Type the number that corresponds to the amount of memory in your video card and then press Enter.

Now you have to provide an identifier for your video card. Type the appropriate information for your card. Following is what I enter for my PC's video card:

```
Enter an identifier for your video card definition: Number Nine GXE64
Enter the vendor name of your video card: Number Nine.
Enter the model (board) name of your video card: GXE64
```

The xf86config program then prompts you for some technical information especially useful for the accelerated servers. First, the program asks for a RAMDAC setting; press **q** and then press Enter to continue. Then the program asks for a clock chip setting. If you do not know this information, press Enter to continue.

Next comes the Clocks line, which is a list of clock frequencies the X server uses when it starts. Without a Clocks line, the X server determines the clock frequencies every time it starts. The X server can run in a *probeonly mode* (when started with the command X -probeonly), in which the server determines and displays the clock frequencies. Then you can place this information on a line in the XF86Config file. In fact, the xf86config program can run the X server in probeonly mode and get the clock values.

Before you decide to proceed, check to see whether your video card needs a Clocks line (recall the instructions that xf86config displays when you select a video card). Many video chipsets do not need a Clocks line. When I specify an S3 video card, for example, I get the following message:

```
The card definition says NOT to probe clocks.
Do you want me to run 'X -probeonly' now? n
```

Naturally, I press **n** to answer no. On the other hand, if your card can use a Clocks line, go ahead and press **y** to answer yes. The xf86config program runs the X server in probeonly mode, gets the clock values, and adds an appropriate Clocks line to the configuration file.

Next, the xf86config program displays several modes and asks you to make a selection, as follows:

```
For each depth, a list of modes (resolutions) is defined. The default
resolution the server will start-up with will be the first listed
mode that can be supported by the monitor and card.
Currently it is set to:

"640x480" "800x600" "1024x768" for 8bpp
"640x480" "800x600" for 16bpp
"640x480" for 24bpp
"640x400" for 32bpp

Note: 16, 24, and 32bpp are only supported on a few configurations.
Modes that cannot be supported due to monitor or clock constraints
will be automatically skipped by the server.

1  Change the modes for 8bpp (256 colors)
2  Change the modes for 16bpp (32K/64K colors)
3  Change the modes for 24bpp (24-bit color, packed pixel)
4  Change the modes for 32bpp (24-bit color)
5  The modes are OK, continue.

Enter your choice: 5
```

The abbreviation bpp stands for *bits per pixel*. The depth of a mode is expressed by values such as 8bpp and 16bpp. You can safely select the last option and continue. Press **5** and then press Enter to accept the choices and proceed.

This step completes your session with xf86config. The program displays the following message, asking whether it can write the XF86Config file in the current directory:

```
I am going to write the XF86Config file now. Make sure you don't
accidentally
overwrite a previously configured one.

Do you want it written to the current directory as 'XF86Config'? n

Please give a filename to write to: /etc/X11/XF86Config
```

Answer **n** in response to the first question and then type /etc/X11/XF86Config and press Enter. The xf86config program writes the configuration file and exits.

If you are lucky, the XF86Config file generated by xf86config may be all you need to run *X* with your PC's video card and monitor. Because of the potential for monitor damage if you make wrong settings in the XF86Config file, though, you should use an editor to look through the configuration file (Chapter 24, Text Processing in Linux, describes the vi and GNU Emacs editors).

Checking the XF86Config file

When you run the xf86config program, you create a XF86Config file; you also select an X server appropriate for your video card. The XF86Config file describes your video card, monitor, and mouse to the X server. By default, the X server first looks for the configuration file in the /etc/X11 directory (/etc/X11/XF86Config), which is where you should save the configuration file.

If you study the example XF86Config file, you see the configuration file consists of several sections. Each section has the following format:

```
# This a comment
Section "SectionName"
    EntryName   EntryValue
    ...
    ...
    Subsection "SubsectionName"
        EntryName EntryValue
        ...
        ...
    EndSubsection
EndSection
```

Sections consist of a sequence of entries; each entry has a name and a value. A section may contain one or more subsections. A pound sign (#) at the beginning of a line marks a comment line.

The XF86Config file contains one or more of the following seven sections:

- *Files*. This section lists the *pathnames* (full directory names) of font files and the file that contains the color database, called the *RGB file*. RGB stands for red, green, and blue — the three primary components of color.

- *ServerFlags*. This section lists various X server options, such as DontZap (which means "do not allow the Ctrl+Alt+Backspace keystroke to terminate the X server") and DontZoom (which means "do not accept special keystrokes to change screen resolution").

- *Keyboard*. This section specifies the type of keyboard and characteristics, such as auto-repeat delay and rate.

- *Pointer*. This section lists information about the mouse, including its device name. (In the X Window System's terminology, the mouse is known as the *pointer*.)

- *Monitor*. This section includes the specifications of a monitor (such as horizontal and vertical synchronization rates) and a list of video modes the monitor supports.

- *Device*. This section describes the characteristics of a video card (*graphics device*). The configuration file may have more than one Device section.

- *Screen*. This section describes a combination of a video card and monitor to be used by the X server. Typically, the configuration file has several Screen sections.

For the most part, you should not have to learn all the details of these sections; the XF86Config file should be your starting point. The next few sections summarize some of the important sections of the configuration file and give you guidelines on changes you may have to make.

The Files section

The Files section lists the location of some files the X server needs. These files include the following:

- A file that contains the color definitions (this file is called the *RGB file*)

- The locations of the fonts (each location is a directory)

You needn't change the name of the RGB file. As for the font locations, make sure each directory exists. The directories should exist, provided you installed all the fonts during Linux installation. If a font directory does not exist, you have to remove that line from the configuration file or type # at the beginning of that line.

ServerFlags section

In this section, you can have one of the flags listed in Table 4-1; just place the word on a line by itself.

Table 4-1   Serverflags section flags

Flag	Meaning
NoTrapSignals	Used only for debugging.
DontZap	Causes the X server to ignore Ctrl+Alt+Backspace, which usually causes the X server to exit.
DontZoom	Causes the X server to ignore the Ctrl+Alt+Keypad + and Ctrl+Alt+Keypad – key combinations that otherwise would change the video modes. (*Keypad* + and *Keypad* – refer to the plus and minus keys in the numeric keypad.)

The configuration file generated by xf86config does not use any of these flags, so you should leave this section as is. Later, you will find the Ctrl+Alt+Backspace combination to be useful when the X server does not work or hangs up somehow. The Ctrl+Alt+Keypad + and Ctrl+Alt+Keypad − combinations are useful when you want to try different video modes without having to restart the X server.

The Monitor section

The Monitor section is a crucial section of the XF86Config file because it lists some important technical data about the monitor. If you recently purchased your PC, you probably received a manual for the monitor. In this manual, you should find a Technical Specifications page. You need data from that page to fill out the Monitor section.

Make sure the section contains an Identifier entry. Following is a typical entry:

```
Identifier  "Dell VS15X"
```

The Screen section, described later in this chapter, refers to this monitor by the name Dell VS15X.

Two other entries — HorizSync and VertRefresh — are important. The HorizSync entry should specify the range of horizontal synchronization values. Simply enter the range as specified in the monitor's manual. The unit for horizontal synchronization is kilohertz (kHz).

For VertRefresh, you should provide the range of vertical refresh frequencies (also listed as vertical synchronization in monitor manuals). The unit for vertical synchronization is hertz (Hz).

For the Dell VS15X, the HorizSync and VertRefresh settings (obtained from the monitor's manual) are as follows:

```
# NOTE: THE VALUES HERE ARE EXAMPLES ONLY. REFER TO YOUR MONITOR'S #
USER MANUAL FOR THE CORRECT NUMBERS.
    HorizSync   30-64
    VertRefresh 55-90
```

Following these two critical values, you see a large number of ModeLine entries. That list is a set of standard modelines; the X server picks the best standard mode from that set. You needn't edit those lines.

The Device section

The Device section specifies the video card and gives it a name (through the Identifier entry). The xf86config program generates a configuration file that contains a standard Device section for a VGA card. You should check the Device section created with the input you provided to xf86config. This section should contain a proper Identifier entry, such as the following:

```
Identifier  "Number Nine GXE64 with S3-Trio64"
```

The Screen section refers to this video card by the name shown in the Identifier entry. For many video cards, this section may not contain much more information, because the X server (for that card) can automatically configure and use the card properly.

Tip

For some video cards, the Device section of the XF86Config file requires a Clocks entry that has a sequence of floating-point numbers as the value. These clocks are among the hardest things to fill in (although some video chipsets — such as S3-Trio64 — do not need clocks). One way to get the clocks is to run the X server with the command X -probeonly. In fact, the xf86config program runs *X* this way and gets the clocks for you. All you have to do is press **y** when you see the following question:

```
Do you want me to run 'X -probeonly' now?
```

If your video card needs clocks in the Device section, this method is the easiest way to get the necessary values.

Screen section

Each Screen section specifies a Monitor and a Device to be used with a specific X server. You specify the Monitor and Device by the names shown in the respective Identifier entries. A Driver entry identifies the X server.

The xf86config program generates several Screen sections in the configuration file. Each Screen section is meant for a different X server, identified by the Driver entry. Table 4-2 lists the options.

Table 4-2	Driver entries
Entry	*Purpose*
accel	X server for accelerated video chipsets (S3, Mach32, Mach64, P9000, 8514, AGX, and W32)
svga	X server for SuperVGA cards
vga16	X server for generic 16-color VGA cards
vga2	X server for monochrome VGA cards

Each Screen section also lists several Display subsections, which indicate the video modes (such as 640×480, for 640 pixels horizontally by 480 pixels vertically; 800×600; and 1024×768). Each Display subsection also has a Depth entry that specifies the number of bits used for each pixel — bits per pixel, or depth.

The current X server selects the Screen section whose Driver entry matches the X server's type (Super VGA or Accelerated, for example). You specify the X server during your session with the xf86config program.

Running *X*

After you have a complete XF86Config file, you are ready to start the X server and some X applications. To start *X,* run the startx script, which is a file that contains Linux commands. This script is in the /usr/X11/bin directory, but this directory should be in your PATH environment variable. To run this script, type startx.

The startx script looks for another script file, named .xinitrc, in your home directory. If startx does not find any .xinitrc file in your home directory, it runs the xinit command with the default script /usr/X11R6/lib/X11/xinit/xinitrc. Notice, unlike the .xinitrc file in your home directory, the default script file does not have a period as the first character of its name.

The result of running startx depends on the commands in .xinitrc in your home directory, if you have one. Otherwise, the result depends on the commands in the /usr/X11R6/lib/X11/xinit/xinitrc file. With the default version of this file, when you run startx as a normal user (not root), your screen should appear as shown in Figure 4-1.

Cross-Reference

Now you can enter Linux commands at the prompt in the xterm window (the large window in the middle of the screen). You learn more about customizing the *X* display in Chapter 5.

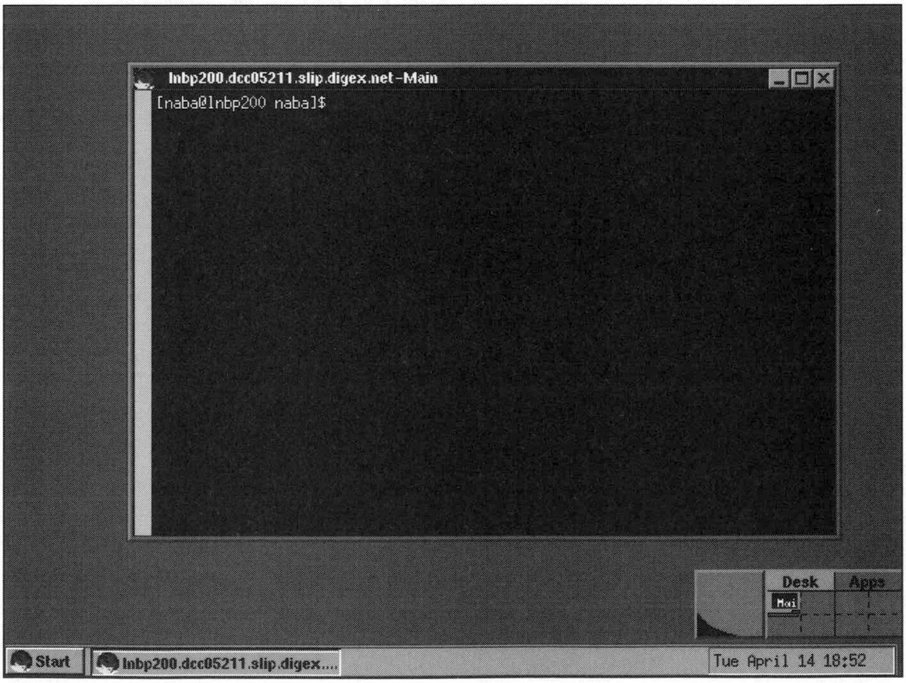

![Figure 4-1 screenshot showing the initial X display with a terminal window titled "lnbp200.dcc05211.slip.digex.net - Main" and a taskbar at the bottom with a Start button and "Tue April 14 18:52"]

Figure 4-1: The initial *X* display

The X server quits when the startx script ends. The startx script, in turn, ends when its last command finishes. Usually, the window manager (such as fvwm2) is the last command, so you can stop *X* and return to the text screen by quitting the window manager.

Aborting with Ctrl+Alt+Backspace

If your monitor and video card are not properly specified in the XF86Config file, chances are good when you start *X* with the startx command, you do not see the *X* display shown in Figure 4-1. If you have problems such as a distorted display or if the system appears to lock up, press Ctrl+Alt+Backspace to kill the X server and return to the text display. (In UNIX, the term *kill* refers to abnormally exiting a program. UNIX even has a kill command that stops errant programs.)

After you stop the X server, you can go through the XF86Config file again and try to determine what may be wrong.

Trying different screen modes

In your XF86Config file, if you look at the Screen section that applies to your X server, you notice several Display subsections. Each Display subsection lists the video modes supported for a specific depth — the number of bits in each pixel's value. An X server typically supports a depth of 8, which means each pixel has an 8-bit value and the server can display up to $2^8 = 256$ distinct colors. The Display subsection lists the video modes in terms of the display resolution, which, in turn, is expressed in terms of the number of pixels horizontally and vertically.

The Screen section for the accelerated X server I use for my S3-Trio64 video card, for example, shows the following Display subsection for the 8-bits-per-pixel depth:

```
# The accelerated servers (S3, Mach32, Mach8, 8514, P9000, AGX, W32,
Mach64)
Section "Screen"
    Driver      "accel"
    Device      "Number Nine GXE64 with S3-Trio64"
    Monitor     "Dell VS15X"
    Subsection "Display"
        Depth       8
        Modes       "640x480" "800x600" "1024x768"
        ViewPort    0 0
        Virtual     1024 768
    EndSubsection
    ...
EndSection
```

When the X server starts, it configures the video card at the resolution (in this case, 640×480, or 640 pixels horizontally by 480 pixels vertically) that corresponds to the first mode shown in the Modes entry, as follows:

```
Modes        "640x480" "800x600" "1024x768"
```

You can try the other modes without having to exit the X server. Press Ctrl+Alt+Keypad+ (*Keypad+* means the plus key in the numeric keypad). The X server switches to the next mode — in this case, 800×600. Press Ctrl+Alt+Keypad+ again and the X server switches to 1,024×768 mode. When you press Ctrl+Alt+Keypad+, therefore, the X server cycles forward to the next mode listed in the Modes entry.

Tip Press Ctrl+Alt+Keypad+ several times and make sure the X server works in all video modes.

To cycle backward to the preceding mode, press Ctrl+Alt+Keypad– (*Keypad–* means the minus key in the numeric keypad). Therefore, if the X server is displaying in 800×600 mode and you press Ctrl+Alt+Keypad–, the server switches to 640×480 mode.

You can make the X server start in any of the supported modes. If you want the X server to start at the highest-resolution mode, simply change the Modes entry in the Screen section that corresponds to your X server (the Driver entry in the Screen section indicates the X server type) to the following:

```
Modes        "1024x768" "800x600" "640x480"
```

This change makes *X* start in 1,024×768 mode, which gives you much more screen area than 640×480 mode.

The screen resolutions in the Modes entry determine the following:

- The first resolution is the default resolution (the resolution in which the X server starts).

- When you alter screen resolutions, the X server scrolls through the resolutions in the order shown in the Modes entry. When you press Ctrl+Alt+Keypad+, the X server changes resolutions in the left to right order. The order is reversed when you press Ctrl+Alt+Keypad-.

Quitting from window manager

To exit the X display and return to the text screen, you must exit the last program the `startx` script file started. This program is the window manager — in this case, the `fvwm2` window manager.

To quit the `fvwm2` window manager, place the mouse pointer in a background area of the X display and click the left mouse button. The window manager displays a pop-up menu. Several of the menu items have arrows that point to the right. If you place the mouse pointer on one of these arrows, a cascade menu pops up.

Move the mouse pointer to the item labeled Exit fvwm, which has an arrow pointing to the right. The `fvwm2` window manager displays a submenu, as shown in Figure 4-2.

Place the pointer on the item labeled Yes, Really Quit, and release the mouse button. The `fvwm2` window manager quits, which, in turn, causes the `startx` script to end and then the X server exits. You should be back at the text screen, with a Linux command prompt.

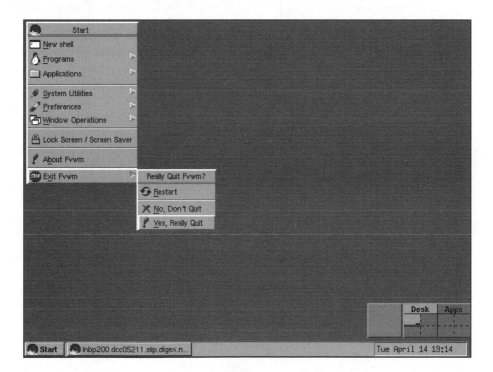

Figure 4-2: Quitting the `fvwm2` window manager

Summary

The X Window System, or *X,* is a popular window system that serves as the basis of graphical user interfaces and graphical output on most UNIX workstations. XFree86 is a free implementation of *X* for Intel 80×86 and compatible PCs. XFree86 works with a variety of video cards, but you must configure it to use the appropriate parameters for your video card and monitor. This chapter shows you how to configure and run *X* on your Linux system. The next chapter turns to the subject of customizing and using the graphical user interface *X* and the window manager provides.

By reading this chapter, you learn the following:

- X Window System is a network-transparent windowing system based on the client/server model. The X server, running on a workstation with a bit-mapped graphics display, manages regions of screen known as windows, where the output from X client applications appear. The X clients often run on remote systems, but their output appears on the local X display.

- The term graphical user interface (GUI) describes a user interface that makes use of windows, menus, and other graphical objects, so users can interact with the application by pointing and clicking mouse buttons. From an application developer's point of view, a GUI is a combination of a window manager, a style guide, and a library of routines (toolkit) that can be used to build the user interface.

- *X* provides the basic functions that can be used to build a GUI. Many GUIs are built upon *X.* Motif and OPEN LOOK are examples of such GUIs. Motif is one of the most popular GUIs.

- XFree86 is the X Window System for Linux PCs and it comes on this book's companion CD-ROM. When you install Linux from the CD-ROM, you also install XFree86.

- XFree86 3.3.1 supports a wide variety of video cards, including the commonly found Diamond-brand video cards.

- Before you start *X* on your Linux PC, you must configure XFree86 to work with your PC's video card, monitor, mouse, and keyboard.

- To configure XFree86, you should run the `xf86config` program. This program prompts you for some technical information about your PC's video card, monitor, and mouse.

- You should specify the correct information about your monitor because incorrect information may cause damage to the monitor.

- The `xfree86config` program creates the configuration file `/etc/X11/XF86Config`. You must have this file ready before you start *X.*

▶ To start *X,* all you have to do is type `startx`. To start an initial set of X applications automatically, you should include commands to start these applications in a file named `.xinitrc` in your home directory.

▶ If the X server seems to hang your system, press Ctrl+Alt+Backspace to kill the X server.

▶ You can switch between different modes (screen resolutions such as 1024×768 and 800×600) by pressing special key combinations: Ctrl+Alt+Keypad+ and Ctrl+Alt+Keypad-.

Chapter 5

Customizing Your Linux Startup

In This Chapter

▶ Understanding the steps in Linux startup

▶ Getting a graphical login prompt with xdm

▶ Learning how to customize *X* applications through resources

▶ Understanding the fvwm2 window manager

By now, you have installed Linux and *X,* and you have had your first taste of Linux. You probably still log in at a text screen, however, and then start the X Window System manually. If you have any experience with the current generation of UNIX workstations or Microsoft Windows, you are familiar with the convenience of a graphical interface. You also can set up Linux so you work completely in the graphical environment provided by the X Window System.

This chapter explains how you can make your login prompt appear in a graphical window. You also learn about fvwm2 — a popular window manager in Linux.

Cross-Reference

If you have not installed Linux and *X* yet, turn to Chapter 1 to install Linux and *X.* Then return to this chapter to try the techniques shown in this chapter.

Starting *X* Automatically at Login

Right now, you have to log in at a text prompt and then type startx to start the X Window System. If you always log in and immediately switch to the graphical screen with the startx command, you can automate this task easily by adding the startx command to a special file the Linux command processor — the shell — executes automatically when you log in.

The default command processor in Linux is called *Bash,* which stands for *Bourne again shell.* When Bash starts, it reads and executes the commands in a file named /etc/profile. After processing the /etc/profile file, Bash processes one more file in your home directory, using the following logic:

1. If a file named `.bash_profile` exists in your home directory, Bash processes it.

2. If Bash does not find the `.bash_profile` file, it looks for and then processes the file named `.bash_login`, provided that the file exists.

3. If your home directory does not have `.bash_profile` or `.bash_login`, Bash looks for and processes the file named `.profile`.

Thus, to ensure *X* starts automatically, you can place the `startx` command in the file named `.bash_profile` in your home directory. One problem exists with this solution, though. If your Linux system is on a network, you can log into your system over the network. When you log in over the network, however, you would not want to start *X,* because *X* will run at your monitor's location, even though you're not there.

When you log into your Linux PC from the PC's keyboard (as opposed to logging in over the network), an environment variable named `TERM` is set to the string `linux`. To ensure Bash executes the `startx` command only when you log in at the *console* (the term refers collectively to the PC's monitor and keyboard), you can put in the appropriate commands to have Bash run `startx` only when the `TERM` variable is set to `linux`. You learn more about Bash commands in Chapter 6, but the following shows what you need in `.bash_profile` to start *X* when you log in at the console:

```
if [ "$TERM" = "linux" ]; then
  startx
fi
```

A more interesting setup is staying entirely in a graphical environment. Even the login prompt is a dialog box. The next section explains how you can set up your Linux system to provide a graphical login screen.

The environment variable

An *environment variable* is simply a way to associate a name with a string. The shell has a standard set of environment variables. The environment variable named HOME, for example, is set to your home directory. How you define an environment variable depends on the shell you use. In Bash (the default shell in Linux), you set an environment variable by using the following syntax:

```
NAME=Value; export NAME
```

NAME is the name of the environment variable and *Value* is a string that denotes the value associated with *NAME*. A shorter way to define and use an export variable is to use the following syntax:

export *NAME=Value*

Setting Up a Graphical Login

To log in on many UNIX workstations (such as those from Hewlett-Packard or IBM), you have to type the name and password in a login dialog window. Setting up your Linux workstation so it displays a graphical login screen is easy. In fact, the Linux CD-ROM comes with the X Display Manager (xdm) program, which is designed to handle user logins through a graphical interface.

The X Display Manager (xdm)

The xdm program is similar to the processes getty and login, which are commonly used in UNIX systems (including Linux) to enable a user to log into the system.

When xdm runs, it reads various configuration parameters from a file named xdm-config, which usually is in the directory /etc/X11/xdm. One of the parameters in this file is the name of another file, which specifies the displays on which xdm displays the login dialog window. This list usually is in the file /etc/X11/xdm/Xservers.

The name of a display also indicates whether it is local or remote. Suppose you want to use xdm to access your workstation from the local display. In this case, Xservers should contain the following line:

```
:0 local /usr/X11R6/bin/X
```

You specify the local display by the local keyword that follows the display number. In this case, you have to provide the complete pathname of the X server program.

Processes

In UNIX, the term *process* refers to a program executing in memory and its associated environment. The environment includes the input and output files that belong to the program and a collection of environment variables. Essentially, you create a process whenever you type a command at the shell prompt. Of course, the shell (the command interpreter of the operating system) itself is just another process — one that creates new processes at your command.

For the default configuration (after you install Linux and *X* from the companion CD-ROM), xdm manages the login session as follows:

1. xdm starts the X server and executes the Xsetup_0 script from the /etc/X11/xdm directory. The default Xsetup_0 script runs the xconsole program that opens a window in which all console messages appear.

2. `xdm` displays a dialog window containing fields in which the user can enter a name and a password.

3. After a user enters a name and password and presses Enter, `xdm` verifies the password and executes the startup script `/etc/X11/xdm/GiveConsole`.

4. `xdm` runs the `Xsession` script from the `/etc/X11/xdm` directory. That script typically looks for another script file, named `.xsession`, in the user's home directory. This file is similar to the `.xinitrc` file `xinit` uses after it starts the X server. The `.xsession` file should list the commands for starting selected X applications. Typically, this list includes the `xterm` terminal emulator. If no `.xsession` file exists, the `Xsession` script runs the script `/etc/X11/xinit/xinitrc`.

5. From this point, the user can interact with the system through the X display and through the window manager (started by the `.xsession` file or the systemwide script `/etc/X11/xinit/xinitrc`).

6. When the user exits *X* (by quitting the window manager), `xdm` runs the `/etc/X11/xdm/TakeConsole` script. At the end of this script, `xdm` returns to the login dialog window display and waits for another user to log on.

Although this brief description of `xdm` does not show you all the details, `xdm` provides a user-friendly interface for user login. Also, like many other X utility programs, `xdm` is highly configurable. For example, the names of the script files in the preceding list are the typical ones, but you can specify other names through the file named `xdm-config`, which, by default, also resides in the `/etc/X11/xdm` directory.

When you install Linux and *X* from the companion CD-ROM, `xdm` is already configured to display a login dialog on your PC's monitor. If you want to experiment with `xdm`, you can log in as root and type `xdm -nodaemon` at the shell prompt. This command starts `xdm`, which, in turn, displays the login dialog window. At this point, you or any other user can log in by typing the user name and password in the dialog window. But you still do not have an arrangement in which `xdm` runs automatically as soon as Linux boots. You can create such an arrangement easily enough, but first you must understand about the way Linux runs programs after it boots.

The init process

As you know from the installation steps in Chapter 1, when Linux boots, it loads and runs the core operating-system program from the disk. The core operating system, however, is designed to run other programs. A process named `init` is responsible for starting the initial set of processes on your Linux system.

What the `init` process starts depends on the following:

- The *run level*, which designates a system configuration in which only a selected group of processes exists

- The `/etc/inittab` file, a text file that specifies the processes to start at different run levels

Secret

The current run level, together with the contents of the /etc/inittab file, controls which processes init starts. Linux, for example, has seven run levels: 0, 1, 2, 3, 4, 5, and 6. By convention, some of these levels indicate specific processes that run at that level. Run level 1, for example, denotes a single-user, stand-alone system. Run level 0 means the system halted and run level 6 means the system is being rebooted. Run levels 2 through 5 are multiuser modes with various levels of capabilities.

The initial default run level is 3. As the following section explains, you can change the default run level by editing a line in the /etc/inittab file.

The /etc/inittab file

The /etc/inittab file is the key to understanding the processes that init starts at various run levels. You can look at the contents of the file (you do not have to log in as root to do this) by using this command:

```
more /etc/inittab
```

Following are a few selected lines from the default /etc/inittab file:

```
#
# inittab       This file describes how the INIT process should set up
#               the system in a certain run-level.
#
# Author:       Miquel van Smoorenburg,
<miquels@drinkel.nl.mugnet.org>
#               Modified for RHS Linux by Marc Ewing and Donnie Barnes
#

# Default runlevel. The runlevels used by RHS are:
#   0 - halt (Do NOT set initdefault to this)
#   1 - Single user mode
#   2 - Multiuser, without NFS (The same as 3, if you do not have
networking)
#   3 - Full multiuser mode
#   4 - unused
#   5 - X11
#   6 - reboot (Do NOT set initdefault to this)
#
id:3:initdefault:

# System initialization.
si::sysinit:/etc/rc.d/rc.sysinit

l0:0:wait:/etc/rc.d/rc 0
l1:1:wait:/etc/rc.d/rc 1
l2:2:wait:/etc/rc.d/rc 2
l3:3:wait:/etc/rc.d/rc 3
l4:4:wait:/etc/rc.d/rc 4
l5:5:wait:/etc/rc.d/rc 5
l6:6:wait:/etc/rc.d/rc 6

# Things to run in every runlevel.
ud::once:/sbin/update
```

```
# Trap CTRL-ALT-DELETE
ca::ctrlaltdel:/sbin/shutdown -t3 -r now

# When our UPS tells us power has failed, assume we have a few minutes
# of power left.  Schedule a shutdown for 2 minutes from now.
# This does, of course, assume you have power installed and your
# UPS connected and working correctly.
pf::powerfail:/sbin/shutdown -f -h +2 "Power Failure; System Shutting
Down"

# If power was restored before the shutdown kicked in, cancel it.
pr:12345:powerokwait:/sbin/shutdown -c "Power Restored; Shutdown
Cancelled"


# Run gettys in standard runlevels
1:12345:respawn:/sbin/mingetty tty1
2:2345:respawn:/sbin/mingetty tty2
3:2345:respawn:/sbin/mingetty tty3
4:2345:respawn:/sbin/mingetty tty4
5:2345:respawn:/sbin/mingetty tty5
6:2345:respawn:/sbin/mingetty tty6

# Run xdm in runlevel 5
x:5:respawn:/usr/bin/X11/xdm -nodaemon
```

Lines that start with a pound sign (#) are *comments*. The first *noncomment* line in the /etc/inittab file specifies the default run level as follows:

```
id:3:initdefault:
```

Even though you do not know the syntax of the /etc/inittab file (and you really do not have to learn the syntax), you probably can guess the 3 in that line denotes the default run level. Thus, if you want your system to be at run level 5 after startup, all you have to do is change 3 to 5.

Tip

Type **man inittab** to see the detailed syntax of the entries in the inittab file. The rest of this section briefly describes the inittab file format.

Each entry in the /etc/inittab file specifies a process that init should start at one or more specified run levels — you simply list all the run levels at which the process should run. Each entry in the inittab file has four fields — separated by colons — in the following format:

```
id:runlevels:action:process
```

The fields have the following meanings:

- The *id* field is a unique one- or two-character identifier. The init process uses this field internally. You can use any identifier you want, as long as you do not use the same identifier on more than one line.

- The *runlevels* field is a sequence of zero or more characters, each denoting a run level. The line with the identifier 1, for example, applies to run levels 1 through 5, so the *runlevels* field for this entry is 12345.

- The *action* field tells the init process what to do with that entry. If this field is initdefault, for example, init interprets the *runlevels* field as the default run level. If this field is set to wait, init starts the process specified in the *process* field and waits until that process exits.

- The *process* field specifies the process init has to start. Of course, some settings of the *action* field require no process field. (When *action* is initdefault, for example, no need exists for a *process* field.)

The process often is specified in terms of a shell script, which, in turn, can start several processes. The 13 entry, for example, is specified as follows:

```
13:3:wait:/etc/rc.d/rc 3
```

This entry specifies init should execute the file /etc/rc.d/rc with 3 as an argument. If you look at the file /etc/.rc.d/rc, you notice it is a script file. After you learn more about writing shell scripts in Chapter 6, you can study the file /etc/rc.d/rc to see how it starts for run levels 1 through 5.

Getting back to the subject of starting xdm for a graphical login, you can see an explicit reference to xdm in the last line of the /etc/inittab file, which is defined as follows:

```
x:5:respawn:/usr/bin/X11/xdm -nodaemon
```

This command runs xdm. Because of a symbolic link, /usr/X11/bin/xdm and /usr/X11R6/bin/xdm refer to the same program.

To start xdm automatically after Linux boots, all you must do is edit the /etc/inittab file and change 3 in the following line to 5 (thereby changing the default run level to 5):

```
id:3:initdefault:
```

Caution

Before you edit the /etc/inittab file, you should know any errors in this file may prevent Linux from starting up to a point at which you can log in. If you cannot log in, you cannot use your system. As the following section explains, you should try run level 5 with an init 5 command before you actually change the default run level in the /etc/inittab file.

The init command

To try a new run level, you do not necessarily have to change the default run level in the /etc/inittab file. If you log in as root, you can change the run level (and, consequently, the set of processes that run in Linux) with the init command, which has the following format:

```
init runlevel
```

Here, *runlevel* must be a single character denoting the run level you want. To put the system in single-user mode, for example, you would type the following:

```
init 1
```

Thus, if you want to try run level 5 (and see whether xdm works) without changing the /etc/inittab file, enter the following command at the shell prompt:

```
init 5
```

The system should end all current processes and enter run level 5. By default, the init command waits 20 seconds before stopping all current processes and starting the new processes for run level 5.

To switch to run level 5 immediately, type the command init -t0 5. (The number after the -t option indicates the number of seconds that init waits before changing the run level.)

The init process switches to run level 5 and starts xdm. The xdm program in turn starts *X* and displays a graphical login dialog, as shown in Figure 5-1.

Figure 5-1: The xdm program displays a graphical login dialog

The text-entry cursor (it looks like a vertical bar) appears in the login: field. Type your login name and press Enter. The text cursor moves to the Password: field. Type your password and press Enter to complete the login process.

After you log in from the xdm login window, *X* starts as usual and runs the applications specified in the Xclients file located in the /etc/X11/xinit directory. If you want to start your own set of applications, use a text editor to prepare a file named .Xclients in your home directory and include in that file commands to start various applications such as xterm and the fvwm2 window manager.

The initial X desktop produced by the commands in the /etc/X11/xinit/ Xclients file includes an xterm terminal window and the fvwm2 window manager with a task bar and some buttons, as shown in Figure 5-2.

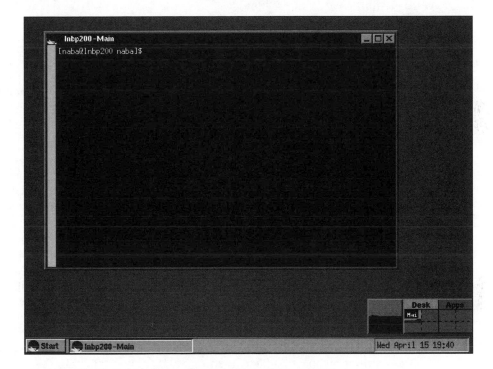

Figure 5-2: The initial *X* desktop with the default configuration files

Customizing *X*

You can customize almost all aspects of the X display, ranging from the screen's background color to the default font for all applications. The basic philosophy of *X* (and of UNIX, as well) is users should have the freedom to configure the software to suit their taste. Thus, X applications load various settings from a resource file. Each X application also accepts a set of standard command-line options. This section shows you the general techniques for customizing X applications. The section also provides specific information about the xterm terminal emulator and the fvwm window manager.

Root-window appearance

In *X,* the entire display screen is called the *root window.* A utility program named xsetroot enables you to tailor the appearance of the root window. With xsetroot, you can customize the screen as follows:

- Use the -solid option to set the screen to a solid color. You can specify the color by name; the color names are in the text file /usr/lib/X11/rgb.txt.

- Use the -bitmap option to set the background to a bitmapped graphic file.

- Use the -cursor or the -cursor_name options to specify a cursor shape when the mouse pointer rests anywhere on the root window.

- Use the -gray option to set the background to gray.

To customize the root window, you should run xsetroot from the command prompt and experiment with various options until you find an appearance you like. Then you can put the appropriate xsetroot commands in your .Xclients file.

If you have experience with the Macintosh or Windows 95 graphical environments, you can see the tasks performed by the xsetroot command are similar to customizing your desktop from the Control Panel. Of course, in the Macintosh and Windows 95, you use a GUI to customize the desktop. In *X,* you have to settle for a command-line program (xsetroot).

Screen color

You can set the screen's background color with the xsetroot program. To set the background to a solid SteelBlue color, for example, type the following command at a shell prompt in an xterm window:

```
xsetroot -solid SteelBlue
```

To try more colors, you have to know the names of the colors. The color definitions are in a text file named /usr/lib/X11/rgb.txt. To see a list of the color names, open that file with an editor or type the following command in an xterm window:

```
more /usr/lib/X11/rgb.txt
```

Following are some of the lines from the rgb.txt file:

```
255 255 255 white
  0   0   0 black
190 190 190 gray
 65 105 225 RoyalBlue
 70 130 180 SteelBlue
218 165  32 goldenrod
184 134  11 DarkGoldenrod
233 150 122 DarkSalmon
255 160 122 LightSalmon
```

As you might guess, the three numbers indicate the intensity levels of the red (R), green (G), and blue (B) components of the color. The intensity levels range between 0 and 255.

Wizard

In addition to using the descriptive name for a color, you can specify a color as a hexadecimal number of six hexadecimal digits, which works out to two digits for each of the three components of a color: red (R), green (G), and blue (B). The digits in a six-digit hexadecimal RGB value of a color are interpreted from left to right, with the most significant pair of digits being assumed for R, the middle pair for G, and the least significant pair for B. The character # precedes the hexadecimal digits to signify a color specification in hexadecimal format. When you specify a color this way, you have to put the hexadecimal color value within quotation marks. You can use the hexadecimal format to specify any color you want.

Table 5-1 lists some common colors expressed in hexadecimal format:

Table 5-1	Common colors in hexadecimal
Color	**Hexadecimal value**
black	#000000
red	#ff0000
green	#00ff00
blue	#0000ff
yellow	#ffff00
cyan	#00ffff
magenta	#ff00ff
white	#ffffff

Now that you know how to specify any arbitrary color in hexadecimal RGB format, you can experiment with new colors. You can try a strange color for the screen background, for example, by using the following command:

```
xsetroot -solid "#ccb0b0"
```

If you want a simple gray background (which can be quite pleasing to the eye, if a bit unadventurous), you can get it by using this command:

```
xsetroot -gray
```

Hexadecimal numbers

Even though you may be unfamiliar with the terminology, you're familiar with one number system from your everyday experience — the decimal number system. We express decimal numbers using the digits 0 through 9, and when writing values, we use the concepts of ones, tens, hundreds, and thousands. For example, consider the number 3,495. Using the concept of ones, tens, hundreds, and thousands, we can write this as:

3,495 = 3 Thousands + 4 Hundreds + 9 Tens + 5 Ones

or

$3,495 = 3\times10^3 + 4\times10^2 + 9\times10^1 + 5\times10^0$

The last form represents the number in powers of 10, which is the base or radix of the decimal number system.

The hexadecimal number system is similar to the decimal number system, except the base is 16. To write a number in hexadecimal, you need 16 digits representing the values from 0 through 15 just as the decimal system uses the 10 digits 0 through 9. Here are the sixteen hexadecimal digits:

Hexadecimal Digit	Decimal Value of Digit
0	0
1	1
2	2
3	3
4	4
5	5
6	6
7	7
8	8
9	9
a	10
b	11
c	12
d	13
e	14
f	15

As you can see, the letters a through f are used to represent the values 10 through 15, respectively. You can use either lowercase or uppercase letters for the hexadecimal digits.

Knowing the similarity between the decimal and hexadecimal number systems, you can easily find the decimal equivalent of a hexadecimal number. For example, 1b in hexadecimal is $1\times16^1 + 11\times16^0 = 16 + 11 = 27$ in decimal.

Screen-background image

You needn't settle for a solid color as the screen background. You can use xsetroot with the -bitmap option to tile a monochrome bitmap image over the screen background (tiling means copies of the bitmap are laid out one next to the other until the whole screen is covered — similar to the way you would cover a floor with physical tiles). You can use the -fg and the -bg options to draw the image in the foreground color and fill the background with a selected background color.

Try the following command to set the screen background to an interesting pattern of the *X* logo:

```
xsetroot -bitmap /usr/include/X11/bitmaps/xlogo64 -fg "#cccccc" -bg
"#c0c0c0"
```

The /usr/include/X11/bitmaps directory contains many more bitmap files you can try as background images.

Although `xsetroot` cannot display a color image as the screen background, you can use the `xv` program to display an image file of your choice as the background. The `xv` program can handle quite a few image formats, including the popular formats GIF, PCX, BMP, JPEG, and TIFF. Suppose you have a favorite image file called `sunset.gif`, which shows a beautiful sunset and you want to use this image as the backdrop on your X display. To accomplish this task, include the following command in your `.xsession` file:

```
xv -quit -root -max /usr/local/sunset.gif
```

This command assumes the image file `sunset.gif` is in the `/usr/local` directory.

Tip

Avoid using colorful images as screen background; other X programs will run out of colors if you display a too colorful image as the background. Remember, the typical 8-bit video card can display at most 256 colors. If the background image has more than 16 colors, you may run into problems as you run other programs. In particular, programs like the Netscape Navigator Web browser also need colors to display all those images most Web pages have.

In addition to causing *X* to run out of colors, a color image background also uses up resources of the X server and may affect the system's performance. Therefore, the safe solution is to use a solid color background for the screen background.

Cursor shape and color

With the `xsetroot` program, you can set the shape and color of the cursor when the pointer is resting anywhere on the root window. Inside an application's windows, the application controls the cursor shape and color.

Although you can use two bitmap files to define an arbitrarily shaped cursor, a simpler method is to select one of the predefined cursor shapes. You can use the `-cursor_name` option of the `xsetroot` program to specify a cursor. The cursor names are defined in the file `/usr/include/X11/cursorfont.h`. The names are meant for use in X programs and each cursor name has an `XC_` prefix. You have to leave out the `XC_` prefix when you use the cursor name with the `xsetroot` program.

Following are a few cursor names:

`X_cursor`	A cursor shaped like an *X* (the default cursor)
`arrow`	An arrow pointing to the upper-right corner
`left_ptr`	An arrow pointing to the upper-left corner

The default cursor is a black `X_cursor`. To change the cursor to a white left arrow, type the following command:

```
xsetroot -cursor_name left_ptr -fg white -bg black
```

In the Macintosh and Windows 95 graphical environments, the cursor is a left-pointing arrow. If you are familiar with those environments, you might want to change the cursor to the left arrow.

X resources

Most X applications are highly configurable. You can alter the appearance and, to some extent, even the behavior of an X application in two ways:

- Alter the application's default behavior through options you specify in the command line that starts the application.

- Specify values for options in a text file called a *resource file*. (X programmers use the term *resource* to refer to any user-configurable option in an application.)

For small UNIX utilities, a handful of command-line options may be enough to specify all user-configurable parameters of the program. X applications tend to have a large number of variables the user can set, however. An X application may have several windows, each of which may have a border, a background color, and a foreground color. Although an X application provides default values for these parameters, the user can override most of these values. In addition, the user can change the font for any text to be displayed in windows. X applications simply have too many variables for the user to set through command-line options alone. The creators of *X* recognized this problem and devised a database of resources.

In an X application, the term *resource* refers to any parameter that affects the application's behavior or appearance. Accordingly, foreground and background colors, fonts, and size and placement of windows are typical resources. A resource does not have to be a parameter related to *X;* it can be anything that controls the behavior of an application and that can be specified by the user. An application might have a parameter named `verbose`, which, when set, enables printing of detailed information as it runs. In addition to the application's window size and location, `verbose` qualifies as a resource of this application.

The resource file

You have to specify the resources for an X application in a text file known as a *resource file* or a *resource database*. The X resource database is a simple text file in which you can specify the value of various parameters in a well-defined format.

X resource files are not as complicated and sophisticated as a traditional database. The X resource database contains specifications of the form "all foreground colors are white," "`xterm`'s background is light cyan," and so on.

X applications use a set of utility routines — collectively known as the *X resource manager* — to extract the value of precisely identified individual parameters from this rather imprecise database. Consider the query "what is the foreground color of the `xterm` application?" If you specified the foreground color of `xterm` in the resource file, the resource manager returns this value. If, however, the only specification for foreground color in the database is the general statement "all foreground colors are black," the value returned for `xterm`'s foreground color is black.

X's resource-naming convention

To specify an X application's resource values, such as foreground color, you must know how to name a resource and how to specify the value for a resource.

The name of a resource depends on the name of the application and the names of its components, which usually are the major child windows. For applications built with the *X toolkit* (essentially, a library of user interface components), the components would be the names of widgets used to build the application.

Note

A *widget* is nothing more than a user interface component such as a push button, a list box, or a dialog box. An X toolkit, such as the Motif toolkit, provides the functions programmers can use to create and use widgets in their programs.

The names of the application and its components can be of two types: *class name* and *instance name*. The class name indicates the general category of the application or component, whereas each individual copy has its own instance name.

Consider a concrete example: the xterm application. This application is of the class XTerm, and the instance goes by the name xterm. The xterm application uses a component named vt100 of class VT100 (the VT100 component emulates a VT102, but the internal name is VT100), which contains a component named scrollbar of the class Scrollbar. Now consider the following resources: the foreground color of the VT100 window and the visibility of the scrollbar in that window. In xterm, as in most X applications, the foreground color resource has the class name Foreground and the instance name foreground. The scrollbar's visibility is controlled by a Boolean variable named on.

Most X applications follow this convention of naming the class of a resource by capitalizing the first letter of its instance name. Names of applications also follow this convention, which promotes some consistency among applications. The naming of the application, its components, and the resources, though, are entirely under the control of the application. (Toolkit-based applications, however, are somewhat constrained by the built-in names of predefined widgets.)

Now you can give these resources unique names in xterm and specify values for them. You can assign values for the foreground color of the VT100 window and the on variable of its scrollbar in the following manner:

```
xterm.vt100.foreground:    yellow
xterm.vt100.scrollbar.on:   true
```

This example illustrates the syntax of naming resources and giving their values. The name of a resource starts with the name of the application, followed by names of the components, each of which is separated from the next by a period (.). The resource name comes last and the value of the resource follows a colon (:). You specify the value as a text string; it is up to the application to interpret that string. The resource manager has utility routines that can help the programmer with this task.

The names illustrated so far in this section are full instance names, showing the application and all its components. You also can have full class names, which for `xterm.vt100.foreground` is `XTerm.VT100.Foreground`. You obtain this name by replacing the instance name of each component with the corresponding class name.

Partial names for resources

The preceding section explains how to specify a resource by its full name, but the resource specification can be imprecise. You might indicate, for example, that all components of class VT100 should have a yellow foreground. You can accomplish this task by making the following entry in the resource database:

```
*VT100.Foreground:  yellow
```

Because there is no application name, this specification of the foreground color applies to the VT100 component used in any application. Similarly, to specify the background color of every component of the `xterm` application be Navy, you would include the following line in the resource file:

```
xterm*background:Navy
```

To understand the resource-naming scheme, you have to know something about the inner workings of the X resource manager. By now, you probably have guessed the X resource manager locates a resource's value by matching a precisely specified resource name with the imprecise entries in the resource database. The search algorithm used by the resource manager follows certain rules for matching a full resource name with the partial names in the resource database. Knowing the following rules can help you understand what kind of specification for a resource is precise enough to suit your needs:

- An asterisk (*) matches zero or more components of the name. Therefore, the query for `xterm.vt100.foreground` matches this entry:

  ```
  xterm*foreground:  yellow
  ```

- After the asterisk is accounted for, the application name, the component names, and the resource name (class or instance) must match the items present in the entry. Therefore, a query for `XTerm.VT100.Scrollbar.Background` matches this entry:

  ```
  xterm.vt100.scrollbar.background: Navy
  ```

  but not

  ```
  xterm.vt100.scrollbar.on: true
  ```

- More specific resource specifications take precedence over less specific settings. Entries with a period (.) take precedence over ones with an asterisk (*). If you specify the following, everything in `xterm` has a navy background, but the scrollbar has a white background:

```
xterm*background: Navy
xterm.vt100.scrollbar.background: white
```

- Instance names take precedence over class names. Thus, the specific entry `xterm*background` will override the one that uses class names: `XTerm*Background`.

- An entry with a class name or an instance name takes precedence over one that uses neither. In `xterm`, the value given in the entry `XTerm*Foreground` overrides that under the more general entry `*Foreground`.

- Names are matched from left to right, because the hierarchy of components of a resource name goes from left to right. In other words, when looking for the resource named `xterm.vt100.scrollbar.background`, the resource manager matches the entry

```
xterm.vt100*background: white
```

instead of

```
xterm*scrollbar.background: Navy
```

because `vt100` appears to the left of `scrollbar`.

The location of resource files

Most X applications load resource settings from several sources in a specific order. First, the applications look for a file named `/usr/lib/X11/app-defaults/AppClass`, in which `AppClass` is the class name of the application. Thus, `xterm` looks for its resources in `/usr/lib/X11/app-defaults/XTerm`.

Next, the application looks for a string named `RESOURCE_MANAGER`, which is attached to (associated with) the root window of the display in which the application's window appears. In *X,* a string associated with the root window is known as a *property* of the root window.

Tip

You can use the utility program `xprop` to see whether this property exists on your display's root window. Simply type **xprop -root** and look for an entry labeled `RESOURCE_MANAGER(STRING)` in the output. The `xprop` utility also can read a resource file and load the contents into this property (as a long string).

If the `RESOURCE_MANAGER` property does not exist, the application reads the resource specifications from the `.Xdefaults` file in your home directory. Next, the application loads the resources (if any) specified by the file indicated by the environment variable `XENVIRONMENT`. If this variable is not set, the next source for resources is a file named `.Xdefaults-hostname` in your home directory. In this file, *hostname* is the name of the system on which the application is running.

You can, of course, override any of the resource specifications through command-line options.

If you want to see the effect of resources, following is an example of how you might do it. In your current `xterm` window, use an editor to create the file `xttest`, containing the following lines:

```
xterm.vt100.scrollBar:       true
*VT100.Foreground:           yellow
xterm.vt100.background:          navy
xterm.vt100.scrollbar.background: white
```

Now type the following command, run the `xrdb` utility program, and load these settings into the `RESOURCE_MANAGER` property of the root window:

```
xrdb -load xttest
```

Type **xprop -root** to verify the resources are loaded. Notice the contents of the resource file are stored internally in the property `RESOURCE_MANAGER` as a long string. Now start another `xterm` session with the command **xterm &**. You should see a new `xterm` window that has yellow characters on a navy background except for the scrollbar, which has a white background.

Standard X resources

By convention, all X applications have a standard set of resources. These resources include parameters such as foreground and background colors, window size and location (collectively known as *geometry*), and font. Table 5-2 lists some of the standard X resources.

Table 5-2   Standard X resources

Instance Name	Class Name	Command-Line Option	Specifies
background	Background	-bg -background	Background color
borderColor	BorderColor	-bd -border	Border color
borderWidth	BorderWidth	-bw -borderwidth	Border width (in pixels)
display	Display	-d -display	Name of display
foreground	Foreground	-fg -foreground	Foreground color
font	Font	-fn -font	Font name
geometry	Geometry	-geometry	Size and location
title	Title	-title	Title string

Command-line options in X applications

In addition to resource databases, X applications accept command-line arguments. Table 5-2 shows the common command-line options for X applications. This section summarizes a few important command-line options.

The -display option

You use `-display` to specify the display on which the application's output should appear. (An X application can run on one system and display its output on a display connected to another system on a network.) If you are logged into a remote computer, for example, and you want to run the client `xclock` on that system, you can start it with a command like the following:

```
xclock -display sysname:0 &
```

Here, `sysname` is the name of your system (the name you see when you type the command **hostname** on your system).

The -geometry option

Another common option is `-geometry`, which you use to specify the size and location of an application's window. You have to specify the geometry in a standard format, as follows:

```
widthxheight[+-]xoffset[+-]yoffset
```

In this format, `width`, `height`, `xoffset`, and `yoffset` are numbers, and you have to pick one of the two signs shown in the brackets. The `width` and `height` values specify the size of the window, in pixels (except for `xterm`, for which you specify these values in number of columns and rows of text). The `xoffset` and `yoffset` values are also in pixels. The meaning of these two numbers depends on the application. In `xterm`, for example, a positive `xoffset` indicates the number of pixels by which the left side of the window is offset from the left side of the screen. A negative `xoffset`, on the other hand, specifies the number of pixels by which the right edge of the window is offset from the right edge of the screen. Similarly, positive and negative `yoffset` indicate the offsets of the top and bottom edges of the window, respectively.

You would type the following command to place an 80-character by 25-line `xterm` window at the upper-right corner of your screen, with a 16-pixel gap between the window's frame and the screen's top and right edges:

```
xterm -geometry 80x25-16+16 &
```

Options for window appearance

Several other command-line options determine the appearance of an application's window. These options specify the foreground color (`-fg`); the background color (`-bg`); the border color (`-bd`); and the border width (`-bw`), in pixels. You specify the colors by names that appear in the `/usr/lib/X11/rgb.txt file`. To start `xterm` with yellow characters on a navy background, use the following command:

```
xterm -bg navy -fg yellow &
```

If a color name includes embedded space, enter the name in quotes. To specify `light blue` as the background for `xterm`, use the following command:

```
xterm -bg "light blue" &
```

As explained in the "Screen color" section earlier in this chapter, you also can specify the color as a hexadecimal number with six hexadecimal digits. The digits in a six-digit hexadecimal RGB value of a color are interpreted from left to right, with the most significant pair of digits assumed for red (R), the middle pair for green (G), and the least significant pair for blue (B). You must place the # character in front of the hexadecimal digits to signify the color specification is in hexadecimal format. You can try a strange color for `xterm`'s background by using the following command:

```
xterm -bg "#ccb0b0" &
```

Font specification

The font resource of an application controls the appearance of the text output. Like colors, fonts are specified by names. In *X,* font names are very descriptive. Following is an example:

```
-adobe-courier-medium-r-normal--12-120-75-75-m-60-iso8859-1
```

For this font, `adobe` is the maker, `courier` is the family, and the font is of `medium` weight (it can be `bold`, for example). The `r` value indicates the font is roman. An `i` at this position indicates italic,and an `o` indicates oblique. The `normal` value is a parameter for character-width and spacing between characters; it also can be `condensed`, `narrow`, or `double`.

The numbers that follow the two dashes (- -) indicate the font's size. `12` indicates the pixel size of the font, and `120` gives the size in tenths of a printer's point. The next two numbers, `75-75`, give the horizontal and vertical resolution for which the font is designed. The letter that follows the resolution (`m`) is the spacing; this value can be `m` for monospace or `p` for proportional. The next number, `60`, is the average width of all characters in this font, measured in tenths of a pixel (in this case, 6 pixels). The string `iso8859-1` identifies the character set of the font, as specified by the International Standards Organization (ISO). In this case, the character set is ISO Latin 1, a superset of the ASCII (American Standard Code for Information Interchange) character set.

Tip

You needn't give the entire name when you specify a font in a resource file. You can use asterisks (*) for fields that can be arbitrary. Suppose you want the VT100 window in `xterm` to use a medium-weight 12-point `courier` font. With a judicious sprinkling of asterisks, you can specify this font in the resource file as follows:

```
*VT100*Font: *courier-medium-r-normal--*120*
```

Using the fvwm2 Window Manager

A *window manager* is a special X client that takes care of interactions among windows for various clients onscreen. You need a window manager to control the placement and size of each client's window. Without a window manager, you cannot change a window's location or alter its size.

To see why a window manager is necessary, consider the case of two clients —A and B—that are displaying on the same screen. Neither client has any idea of the other's needs. Suppose you run client B after A and B takes over the entire screen (the root window) as its output window. At this point, A's window is obscured beneath B's and you have no way to reach A's window.

A window manager provides you the means to switch from B to A, even when B is ill-behaved (for example, if B's window fills the entire screen, you have no way of accessing A's window without a window manager). The fvwm2 window manager adds a decorative frame to the main window of each application. This frame enables you to move and resize the windows. You can click-and-drag a corner of the frame to shrink B's window. The default window manager in Linux— fvwm2 —shows an outline of the window that changes in size as you move the mouse. This outline enables you to make the topmost window smaller to expose windows underneath it. In addition, with fvwm2, you can get a pull-down menu by clicking the upper-left corner of the window's frame (see Figure 5-3). This menu contains options that enable you to resize a window, reduce the window to an icon, and quit the application.

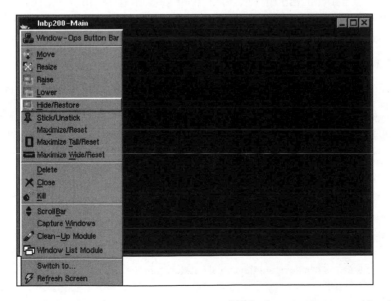

Figure 5-3: The fvwm2 window manager adds the frame and menu to this window.

AnotherLevel and fvwm2

The `fvwm2` program is in the `/usr/X11R6/bin` directory — the older version of this window manager was called `fvwm`; Version 2 has such extensive changes that it is distributed as a new program with the name `fvwm2`.

The default `Xclients` script in the `/etc/X11/xinit` directory starts `fvwm2` with an appropriate set of options. These options indicate which configuration files `fvwm2` should load. What `fvwm2` loads by default is a set of custom `fvwm2` configuration files called `AnotherLevel`. These configuration files are located in the `/etc/X11/AnotherLevel` directory. They are text files; if you are curious, you can browse them with the `more` command. For example, type `more /etc/X11/AnotherLevel/fvwm2rc.m4` to view the main configuration file.

Caution

The `AnotherLevel` configuration files are quite complicated — they are written in the m4 macro language. You should not edit them unless you know m4.

With the default `AnotherLevel` configuration, when `fvwm2` runs, it provides an initial X desktop, as shown in Figure 5-2. It adds a frame (with a 3D appearance) around each onscreen window.

The next few sections discuss several other features of `fvwm2`. As you read the following discussion of `fvwm2`, remember these descriptions correspond to the default settings of `fvwm2` as defined by the configuration files in the `/etc/X11/AnotherLevel` directory. If Red Hat updates these files in a later version, the look and feel of `fvwm2` might change. Therefore, do not be surprised if you find that `fvwm2` in your system does not behave exactly as described in this section.

The Virtual Desktop

The v in `fvwm2` stands for *virtual* ; `fvwm2` provides a virtual desktop larger than the physical dimensions of your system's screen. By default, `fvwm2`'s virtual desktop has eight pages, organized into two groups of four (labeled `Desk` and `Apps`) Each page has an area equal to the size of the X display screen. To help you navigate the virtual desktop, `fvwm2` displays a small pager window in one corner of the screen, as shown in Figure 5-4.

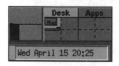

Figure 5-4: You can navigate the virtual desktop with the pager window.

To go to a specific page, click that page in the pager window. The *pager window* is a constant fixture on each page, because it is a sticky window. In `fvwm`, a sticky window always appears on each virtual screen page. You can turn any window into a *sticky window* by selecting Stick/Unstick from its window menu (see Figure 5-3).

Secret Even though you get many virtual screen pages, fvwm2's need for memory depends only on the number of windows. The size of the virtual desktop makes no difference in the amount of memory fvwm2 uses. So you can use the virtual-desktop feature of fvwm2 without worrying about wasting memory.

The task bar

Another key feature of fvwm2 is the Windows 95 style task bar (see Figure 5-5) that appears along the bottom edge of the screen.

Figure 5-5: The fvwm2 window manager displays a Windows 95 style task bar.

The task bar displays a Start menu and buttons for each window (in any page of the virtual desktop). The right-hand edge of the task bar displays the current date and time.

The start menu

If you click the left mouse button on the Start button on the task bar, fvwm2 displays the Start menu. The same menu appears if you click the left mouse button while the mouse pointer is anywhere in the root window. Typically, this menu lists items that start an application. Some of the menu items have an arrow. A submenu appears when you place the mouse pointer on an item with an arrow. Figure 5-6 shows the Start menu on my system.

Figure 5-6: Click the left mouse button on the root window to view the Start menu.

You should explore all the items in the Start menu to see all the tasks you can perform from this menu. In particular, you should move the mouse over the Preferences item to see the submenu (see Figure 5-7) that lists your options for changing the appearance of the desktop.

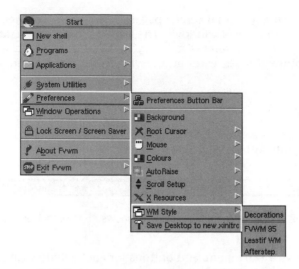

Figure 5-7: The Preferences submenu enables you to change the appearance of the desktop.

As Figure 5-7 shows, the Preferences submenu enables you to change the root window's background, the cursor shape, and many other elements of the desktop.

Other desktop styles

One of the most intriguing items in the Preferences submenu is the WM Style option, which is selected in Figure 5-7. You can change the entire desktop style by selecting items from that submenu. The default style is FVWM 95, which mimics the Windows 95 desktop to some extent.

You have two other options in the WM Style submenu:

- Lesstif WM provides a Motif-style layout.
- Afterstep is a NextStep style-desktop layout.

To try the Motif layout, select the Lesstif WM item from the WM Style submenu shown in Figure 5-7. The Windows 95-style task bar vanishes and the window decorations change to the distinctive Motif style, as shown in Figure 5-8.

You can still get the Start menu (see Figure 5-8) — just click the left mouse button with the pointer anywhere in the root window. If you want to switch back to the Windows 95-style desktop or try the Afterstep desktop, move the pointer to the Preferences item and then to WM Style. From the WM Style menu, pick the desktop style you want.

For example, if you pick the Afterstep style, the desktop takes on the appearance shown in Figure 5-9.

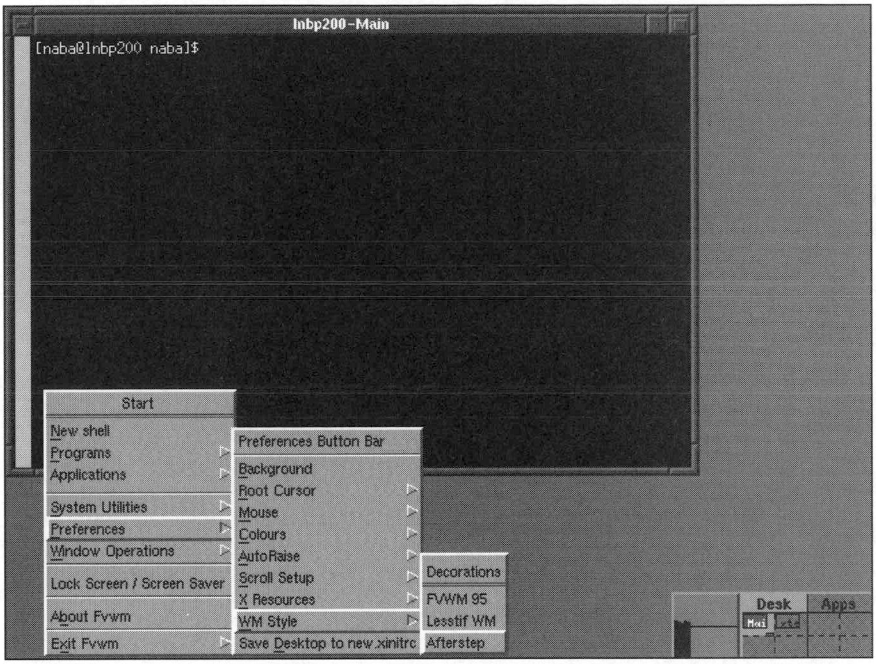

Figure 5-8: A typical Motif-style desktop with `fvwm2` window manager

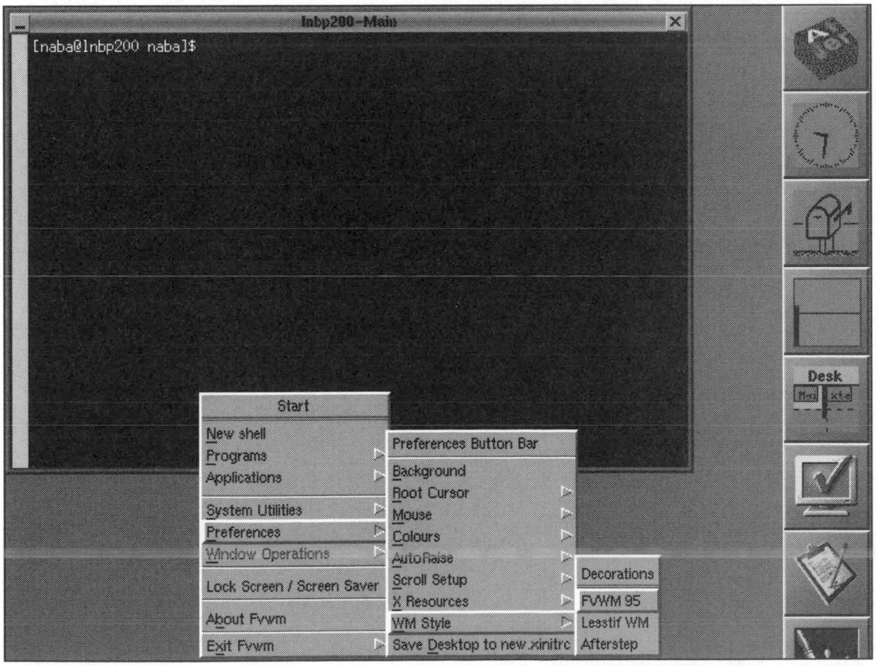

Figure 5-9: The Afterstep desktop with `fvwm2` window manager

The window decorations look different and the right-hand edge has a column of buttons, each of which enables you to perform a specific task such as starting a text editor or opening a terminal window.

Tip

As Figure 5-9 shows, you can still get the Start menu if you click the left mouse button with the pointer on the root window. By selecting Preferences ⇨ WM Style ⇨ FVWM 95, you can switch back to the Windows 95-style desktop.

Summary

Newcomers and old-timers alike can benefit from a graphical point-and-click user interface. This chapter shows you how to set up Linux to start in a graphical mode so you can stay in the graphical environment.

By reading this chapter, you learn the following:

▶ The X Window System includes a program named X Display Manager (xdm), which provides a graphical login prompt. When you understand how processes start in Linux, you can have xdm run every time you boot Linux.

▶ After Linux boots, a process named init starts all the other processes. The exact set of initial processes depends on the run level, which typically is a number ranging from 0 to 6. The /etc/inittab file specifies the processes that start in each run level.

▶ The /etc/inittab file specifies the X Display Manager (xdm) program starts at run level 5. Therefore, you can start xdm running with the command init 5. This command is a good way to try xdm.

▶ You can easily customize most X applications. The customizable aspects of an X application are known as *resources*. You can specify the values of resources in the .Xresources file in your home directory. Through resources, you can specify parameters such as background color, foreground color, and fonts.

▶ The window manager controls much of the look and feel of the X Window System's graphical environment. The fvwm2 window manager is highly customizable; in Red Hat Linux, its configuration is controlled by the AnotherLevel configuration files in the /etc/X11/AnotherLevel directory. The fvwm2 menus let you customize many aspects of the desktop's appearance.

Chapter 6

Secaets of Linux Commands

In This Chapter

▶ Understanding shells: the command interpreters of Linux

▶ Looking at Bash (the Bourne Again Shell)

▶ Understanding the Linux directory structure

▶ Using Linux commands to work with files

▶ Writing shell scripts

▶ Automating common chores with a shell script

▶ Understanding the basics of Perl programming

You saw how to work within a graphical environment in Linux in Chapter 5. Unfortunately, you can't do everything from the graphical environment. It's not impossible to design a graphical interface that enables you to perform most chores, but Linux does not come with such a comprehensive graphical user interface. Therefore, even in the graphical environment of *X,* you often have to work in an xterm window, where you can use Linux commands to accomplish specific tasks.

You can have a variety of command interpreters, or *shells*, in Linux. This chapter introduces you to *Bash,* the Bourne Again Shell, which is the default shell in Linux. You learn some important shell commands and also see how to write simple *shell scripts*, a collection of shell commands stored in a file. When it comes to writing scripts, a language called *Perl* is popular among UNIX system administrators. Because you probably are the system administrator of your Linux system, this chapter also introduces you to Perl.

Cross-Reference

I defer coverage of Tcl/Tk, another popular scripting language you can use to build applications with a graphical interface, to Chapter 8.

The Bash Shell

If you have used MS-DOS, you may be familiar with COMMAND.COM, the DOS command interpreter, the program that displays the infamous C:\> prompt. Linux provides a command interpreter similar to COMMAND.COM in DOS. In UNIX, the command interpreter traditionally is referred to as a *shell*. The original UNIX shell was called the *Bourne shell* and its executable program was named sh. The default Linux shell is Bash and its program name is bash (you find it in the /bin directory). Bash is compatible with the original sh but includes many desirable features of other well-known shells, such as the C shell and the Korn shell. For example, Bash lets you recall commands you entered previously; it even completes partial commands.

The purpose of a shell such as Bash is to display a prompt and execute the command you type at the keyboard. Some commands, such as cd (change directory) and pwd (print working directory), are built into Bash. Many more commands, such as cp (copy) and ls (list directory), are separate programs (meaning a file representing these commands resides in one of the directories on your system). As a user, however, you needn't know or care whether some command is built in or whether it is in the form of a separate executable program.

In addition to the standard Linux commands, Bash can execute any program stored in an executable file. Bash can even execute a shell script (a text file containing one or more commands). As you learn later in the section "Shell Scripts in Bash" of this chapter, you can actually use the shell's built-in commands to write programs (also known as *shell scripts*).

The next few sections give you a sense of the various features of a shell, ranging from the general command syntax to the basics of shell programming. After you go through the overview, you can read more about selected topics in later sections.

The discussions in this chapter assume you are using Bash as your shell because Bash is the shell you get when you install Linux from the CD-ROM that accompanies this book.

Command syntax

Because a shell interprets what you type, knowing how the shell processes the text you enter is important. All shell commands have the following general format:

```
command option1 option2 ... optionN
```

A single line of command is commonly referred to as a *command line*. On a command line, you enter a command followed by one or more options (or *arguments*) known as *command-line options* (or *command-line arguments*).

One basic rule is you must use a space or a tab to separate the command from the options. You must also separate options with a space or a tab. If you want to use an option that contains embedded spaces, you have to put that option inside quotation marks. To search for my name in the password file, for example, I would enter the `grep` command as follows:

```
grep "Naba Barkakati" /etc/passwd
```

When `grep` prints the line with my name, it looks like this:

```
naba:Lgb7sOywtVswx:500:100:Naba Barkakati:/home/naba:/bin/bash
```

That line contains a great deal of information, the most interesting information (for the purposes of this discussion) being the field that follows the last colon (:). That field shows the name of the shell I am running.

The number and the format of the command-line options, of course, depend on the actual command. When you learn more about the commands, you see the command-line options that control the behavior of a command are of the form *X* , in which *X* is a single character.

If a command is too long to fit on a single line, you can press the backslash (\) key, followed by Enter. Then you can continue entering the command on the next line. Or, you can concatenate several shorter commands on a single line; just use the semicolon (;) as a separator between the commands. For example, when rebuilding the Linux kernel (as explained in Chapter 2) you can complete three sequential tasks by typing the following commands on a single line:

```
make dep; make clean; make boot
```

Command combinations

Linux follows the UNIX philosophy of giving the user a toolbox of many simple commands. You can, though, combine these simple commands to create a more sophisticated command. Suppose you want to determine whether a device file named `sbpcd` resides in your system's `/dev` directory. You look for the file because some documentation tells you that for a Sound Blaster Pro CD-ROM drive, you need that device file. You could use the command `ls /dev` to get a directory listing of the `/dev` directory and see whether anything containing `sbpcd` appears in the listing. Unfortunately, the `/dev` directory has a great many entries and it may be difficult to locate any item that has `sbpcd` in its name. You can combine the `ls` command with `grep` and come up with a command that does exactly what you want:

```
ls /dev | grep sbpcd
```

The shell sends the output of the `ls` command (the directory listing) to the `grep` command, which searches for the string `sbpcd`. That vertical bar (|) is known as a *pipe,* because it acts as a conduit between the two programs; the output of the first command becomes the input of the second one.

Note

Most Linux commands are designed in a way that allows the output of one command to be fed into the input of another. All you have to do is concatenate the commands, placing pipes between them.

I/O redirection

Linux commands that are designed to work together have a common feature: they always read from the *standard input* (usually, the keyboard) and write to the *standard output* (usually, the screen). If you want a command to read from a file, you can redirect the standard input to come from that file. Similarly, to save the output of a command in a file, you can redirect the standard output to a file. These features of the shell are called *input* and *output redirection,* or *I/O redirection*.

Using the following command, for example, you can search through all files in the /usr/include directory for the occurrence of the string typedef and then save that list in a file called typedef.out:

```
grep typedef /usr/include/* > typedef.out
```

This command also illustrates another feature of Bash. When you use an asterisk (*), Bash replaces the asterisk with a list of all the filenames in the specified directory. Thus, /usr/include/* means all the files in the /usr/include directory.

Shell programs

If you are not a programmer, you may feel apprehensive about programming. But shell programming can be as simple as storing a few commands in a file. In fact, you can have a useful shell program that has a single command.

While writing this book, for example, I had to capture screens from the X Window System and use the screen shots in figures. I used the X screen-capture program, xwd, to store the screen images in the X Window Dump (XWD) format. The book's production team, however, wanted the screen shots in PCX format. So I used the Portable Bitmap (PBM) toolkit to convert the XWD images to PCX format. To convert each file, I had to run two programs and delete a temporary file, as follows:

```
xwdtopnm < file.xwd > file.ppm
ppmtopcx < file.ppm > file.pcx
rm file.ppm
```

These commands assume the programs xwdtopnm and ppmtopcx are in one of the directories listed in the PATH environment variable. By the way, xwdtopnm and ppntopcx are two programs in the PBM toolkit.

After converting a few XWD files to PCX format, I got tired of typing the same sequence of commands for each file. At that point, I prepared a file named topcx and saved the following lines in it:

```
xwdtopnm < $1.xwd > $1.ppm
ppmtopcx < $1.ppm > $1.pcx
rm $1.ppm
```

Then I made the file executable, using this command:

```
chmod +x topcx
```

The `chmod` command enables you to change the permission settings of a file. One of those settings determines whether the file is executable. The `+x` option means you want to mark the file as an executable file. You need to do this because Bash will run only executable files.

Finally, I converted the file `figure1.xwd` to `figure1.pcx` by using the following command:

```
topcx figure1
```

The `topcx` file is called a *shell program*. When you run this shell program with the command `topcx figure1`, the shell substitutes `figure1` for each occurrence of $1.

In a nutshell, this is why you might create shell programs: to have your Linux system perform repetitive chores.

Here is another interesting example of a shell program. Suppose you occasionally have to use MS-DOS text files on your Linux system. Although you might expect to use a text file on any system without any problem, there is one catch: DOS uses a carriage return followed by a linefeed to mark the end of each line, whereas Linux (and other UNIX systems) use only a linefeed. As a result, if you use the `vi` editor to open a DOS text file, you see ^M at the end of each line. That ^M stands for *Ctrl-M,* which is the carriage-return character.

On your Linux system, you can easily rid the DOS text file of the extra carriage returns by using the `tr` command with the `-d` option. Essentially, to convert the DOS text file *filename.dos* to a Linux text file named *filename.linux*, you type the following:

```
tr -d '\015' < filename.dos > filename.linux
```

In this command, `'\015'` denotes the ASCII code for the carriage-return character in octal notation.

Note

You can use the `tr` command to translate or delete characters from the input. When you use `tr` with the `-d` option, it deletes all occurrences of a specific character from the input data. Following the `-d` option, you must specify the character to be deleted. Like many UNIX utilities, `tr` reads the standard input and writes its output to standard output. As the sample command shows, you must use input and output redirection to use `tr` to delete all occurrences of a character in a file and to save the output in another file.

If you don't want to remember all this information every time you convert a DOS file to UNIX, store the following in a file named `dos2unix`:

```
tr -d '\015' < $1 > $2
```

Then make the file executable by using this command:

```
chmod +x dos2unix
```

That's it! Now you have a shell program named `dos2unix` that converts a DOS text file to a UNIX text file. If you have the MS-DOS partition mounted as `/dosc`, you can try the `dos2unix` shell program with the following command:

```
dos2unix /dosc/autoexec.bat aexec.bat
```

The command creates a file named `aexec.bat` in the current directory. If you open this file with the `vi` editor, you should not see any `^M` characters at the ends of lines.

If you are familiar with MS-DOS, you'll note shell scripts are a lot like MS-DOS batch files. Except for some syntax differences, shell scripts are similar to DOS batch files.

Environment variables

The shell and other Linux commands need information to work properly. If you type a command that isn't one of that shell's built-in commands, the shell must locate an executable file (whose name matches the command you typed). The shell needs to know which directories to search for those files. Similarly, a text editor such as `vi` needs to know the type of terminal (even if the terminal happens to be `xterm`, which essentially emulates a terminal in a window).

One way to provide this kind of information to a program is through command-line options. If you use this approach, however, every time you start a program, you may have to enter many options. UNIX provides an elegant solution through environment variables.

An *environment variable* is nothing more than a name associated with a string. On my system, for example, the environment variable named `PATH` is defined as follows:

```
PATH=/usr/local/bin:/bin:/usr/bin:.:/usr/X11R6/bin
```

The string to the right of the equal sign is the value of the `PATH` environment variable. By convention, the `PATH` environment variable is a sequence of directory names, each name separated from the preceding one by a colon (:). The period in the list of directories also denotes a directory; it represents the current directory.

When the shell has to search for a file, it simply searches the directories listed in the `PATH` environment variable. The shell searches the directories in `PATH` in order of their appearance. If two programs have the same name, therefore, the shell executes the one it finds first.

In a fashion similar to the shell's use of the `PATH` environment variable, an editor such as `vi` uses the value of the `TERM` environment variable to determine how to display the file you are editing with `vi`. To see the current setting of `TERM`, type the following command at the shell prompt:

```
echo $TERM
```

If you type this command in an `xterm` window, the output is as follows:

```
xterm
```

To define an environment variable in Bash, use the following syntax:

```
export NAME=Value
```

Here, `NAME` denotes the name of the environment variable, and `Value` is the string representing its value. Therefore, you set `TERM` to the value `xterm` by using the following command:

```
export TERM=xterm
```

With an environment variable like `PATH`, you typically want to append a new directory name to the existing definition, rather than define the `PATH` from scratch. The following example shows how you can accomplish this task:

```
export PATH="$PATH:/usr/games"
```

This command appends the string `:/usr/games` to the current definition of the `PATH` environment variable. The net effect is to add `/usr/games` to the list of directories in `PATH`.

`PATH` and `TERM` are only two of a handful of common environment variables. Table 6-1 lists some of the useful environment variables in Bash.

Table 6-1   Useful Bash environment variables

Environment variable	Contents
DISPLAY	The name of the display on which the X Window System displays output (typically set to `:0.0`)
HOME	Your home directory
LOGNAME	Your login name
PATH	The list of directories in which the shell looks for programs
PS1	The shell prompt (the default is `bash$` for all users except `root`; for `root`, the default prompt is `bash#`).
SHELL	Your shell (`SHELL=/bin/bash` for Bash)
TERM	The type of terminal

Processes

Every time the shell acts on a command you type, it starts a *process*. The shell itself is a process; so are any scripts or programs the shell executes. An example of such a program is the fvwm2 window manager. You can use the ps command to see a list of processes. When you type ps, for example, Bash shows you the current set of processes. Following is a typical report I get when I enter the ps command in an xterm window:

```
ps
PID TTY STAT   TIME COMMAND
  344   1 S     0:00 /bin/login -- naba
  352   1 S     0:00 -bash
  363   1 S     0:00 sh /usr/X11R6/bin/startx
  364   1 S     0:00 xinit /usr/X11R6/lib/X11/xinit/xinitrc --
  367   1 S     0:00 fvwm2 -cmd FvwmM4 -debug
/etc/X11/AnotherLevel/fvwm2rc.m4
  436   1 S     0:00 /usr/X11R6/lib/X11/fvwm2//FvwmTaskBar 9 4
/tmp/fvwmrca00376
  437   1 S     0:00 /usr/X11R6/lib/X11/fvwm2//FvwmButtons 11 4
/tmp/fvwmrca0037
  440   1 S N   0:00 xload -nolabel -geometry 32x20+0+0 -bg grey60 -
update 5
  441   1 S     0:00 /usr/X11R6/lib/X11/fvwm2//FvwmPager 11 4
/tmp/fvwmrca00376
  442  p0 S     0:00 bash
  501  p0 R     0:00 ps
```

In the default output format, the COMMAND column shows the commands that created the processes. This list shows the bash shell and the ps command as the processes. Other processes include all the programs the shell started when I typed startx to run *X*. In particular, the list include the fvwm2 (window manager) process.

The default ps command does not provide all the processes running on a Linux system. What ps shows are the commands you started, either directly or indirectly (through shell scripts that run automatically when you log in). To see the full complement of processes, use the a option of the ps command together with the x option, as follows:

```
ps ax
```

I won't show the output of the command because quite a few processes are running even when you are the only user on the system. You should expect to see anywhere from 30 to 45 processes in the list.

Secret

If you study the output of the ps command, you find the first column has the heading PID and it shows a number for each process. *PID* stands for *process ID* (identification), which is a sequential number assigned by the Linux kernel. If you look through the output of the ps ax command, you should see the init command is the first process; it has a PID or process number of 1. That's why init is referred to as the *mother of all processes*.

Tip

The process ID or process number is useful when you have to stop an errant process forcibly. Look at the output of the ps ax command and note the PID of the offending process. Then use the kill command with that process number. To stop process number 123, for example, type **kill -9 123**.

Secret

UNIX systems, including Linux, use signals to notify a process that a specific event has occurred. The kill command enables you to send a signal to a process (identified by a process number). The -9 part of the kill command indicates the signal to be sent; 9 is the number of the SIGKILL signal that causes a process to exit.

Background commands and virtual terminals

When you use MS-DOS, you have no choice but to wait for each command to complete before you enter the next command. (You can type ahead a bit, but the MS-DOS system can hold only a few characters in its internal buffer.) Linux, however, can handle multiple tasks at the same time. The only problem you may have is the terminal or console will be tied up until a command completes.

If you are working in an xterm window and a command takes too long to complete, you can open another xterm window and then continue to enter other commands and do your work. If you are working in text mode, however, and some command seems to take too long, you need another way to access your system.

You can continue working in several ways while your Linux system handles a lengthy task:

- You can start a lengthy command *in the background*, which means the shell starts the process corresponding to a command and immediately comes back to accept more commands. The shell does not wait for the command to complete; the command runs as a distinct process in the background. To start a process in the background, all you must do is place an ampersand (&) at the end of a command line. When I want to run the topcx shell script to convert a large image file named image1.xwd to PCX format, for example, I run the script in the background by using the following command:

```
topcx image1 &
```

- If a command (that you did not run in the background) seems to be taking a long time, press Ctrl-Z to stop it; then type **bg** to put that process in the background.

- Use the *virtual-terminal* feature of Linux. Even though your Linux system has only one physical terminal (the combination of monitor and keyboard is called the *terminal*), it gives you the appearance of having multiple terminals. The initial text screen is the first virtual terminal. Press Alt-F2 to get to the second virtual terminal, Alt-F3 for the third virtual terminal, and so on. From the X Window System, you have to press Ctrl-Alt-F1 to get to the first virtual terminal, Ctrl-Alt-F2 for the second one, and so on.

Tip

To get back to the X display, press Ctrl-Alt-F7. You can use one of the virtual terminals to log in and kill processes that may be causing your X display screen to become unresponsive (if the mouse stops responding, for example).

Command completion in Bash

Many commands take a filename as an argument. When you want to browse through a file named `/etc/X11/XF86Config`, for example, you type the following:

```
more /etc/X11/XF86Config
```

That entry causes the `more` command to display the file `/etc/X11/XF86Config` one screen at a time. For the commands that take a filename as an argument, Bash includes a feature that enables you to type short filenames. All you must type is the bare minimum—just the first few characters—to identify the file uniquely in its directory.

To see an example, type `more /etc/X11/XF`, but don't press Enter yet; press Tab instead. Bash automatically completes the filename, so the command becomes `more /etc/X11/XF86Config`. Now press Enter to run the command.

Tip

Whenever you type a filename, press Tab after the first few characters of the filename. Bash probably can complete the filename, so you needn't type the entire name. If you have not entered enough characters to identify the file uniquely, Bash beeps. Just type a few more characters and press Tab again.

Wildcards

Another way to avoid typing too many filenames is to use *wildcards*, special characters, such as the asterisk (*) and question mark (?), that match zero or more characters in a string. If you are familiar with MS-DOS, you may have used commands such as COPY *.* A: to copy all files from the current directory to the A drive. Bash accepts similar wildcards in filenames. In fact, Bash provides many more wildcard options than MS-DOS does.

Bash supports three types of wildcards:

- The asterisk (*) character matches zero or more characters in a filename. Therefore, * denotes all files in a directory.

- The question mark (?) matches any single character.

- A set of characters in brackets match any single character from that set. The string [xX]*, for example, matches any filename that starts with x or X.

Wildcards are handy when you want to perform a task on a group of files. To copy all the files from a directory named /mnt to the current directory, for example, type the following:

```
cp /mnt/* .
```

Bash replaces the wildcard character * with the names of all the files in the /mnt directory. The period at the end of the command stands for the current directory.

You can use the asterisk with other parts of a filename to select a more specific group of files. Suppose you want to use the grep command to search for the string typedef struct in all files in the /usr/include directory that meet the following criteria:

- The filename starts with s.
- The filename ends with .h.

The wildcard specification s*.h denotes all filenames that meet these criteria. Thus, you can perform the search with the following command:

```
grep "typedef struct" /usr/include/s*.h
```

The string contains a space you want the grep command to find, so you have to enclose that string in quotation marks. This method ensures that Bash does not try to interpret each word in the string as a separate command-line argument.

Although the asterisk (*) matches any number of characters, the question mark (?) matches a single character. Suppose you have four files — image1.pcx, image2.pcx, image3.pcx, and image4.pcx — in the current directory. To copy these files to the /mnt directory, use the following command:

```
cp image?.pcx /mnt
```

Bash replaces the single question mark with any single character and copies the four files to /mnt.

The third wildcard format — [...] — matches a single character from a specific set. Typically, you combine this format with other wildcards to narrow the matching filenames to a smaller set. To see a list of all filenames in the /etc/X11/xdm directory that start with x or X, type the following command:

```
ls /etc/X11/xdm/[xX]*
```

When expanding the [...] wildcard format, if Bash does not find any filenames matching the format, it leaves the wildcard specification intact.

Command history

To make it easy for you to repeat long commands, Bash stores up to 500 old commands. Essentially, Bash maintains a *command history* (a list of old commands). To see the command history, type `history`. Bash displays a numbered list of the old commands, including those you entered during previous logins. That list may resemble the following:

```
1  cd
2  ls -a
3  more /etc/X11/XF86Config
4  history
```

If the command list turns out to be too long, you may choose to see only the last few commands. To see the last ten commands only, type this command:

```
history 10
```

To repeat a command from the list the `history` command shows, all you must do is type an exclamation point (!), followed by that command's number. To repeat command number 3, type !3.

You also can repeat an old command without knowing its command number. Suppose you typed `more /usr/lib/X11/xdm/xdm-config` a while ago and now you want to look at that file again. To repeat the previous `more` command, simply type the following:

```
!more
```

Often, you want to repeat the last command you typed, perhaps with a slight change. You may, for example, have displayed the contents of the directory by using the `ls -l` command. To repeat this command, type two exclamation points, as follows:

```
!!
```

Sometimes, you want to repeat the previous command, but add extra arguments to it. Suppose `ls -l` shows too many files. You can simply repeat that command but pipe the output through the `more` command, as follows:

```
!! | more
```

Bash replaces the two exclamation points with the previous command and then appends | `more` to that command.

Tip

An easy way to recall previous commands is to press the up-arrow key, which causes Bash to go backward in the list of commands. To move forward in the command history, press the down-arrow key.

Command editing

After you recall a command, you needn't settle for the command as is; you can edit the command. Bash supports a wide variety of command-line editing commands. These commands are similar to those used by the `emacs` and `vi` editors.

Suppose you want to look at the file `/etc/X11/XF86Config`, but you typed the following:

```
more /etc/X11/XF86config
```

After you press Enter and see an error message saying no such file exsts, you realize the `c` in `config` should have been uppercase. Instead of typing the entire line, you can type the following editing command to fix the problem:

```
^con^Con
```

Bash interprets this command to mean it should replace the string `con` with `Con` in the previous command.

By default, Bash enables you to edit the command line using a small subset of commands supported by the `emacs` editor.

I am already familiar with `emacs`, so I use the `emacs` commands to edit commands. To bring back a previous command line, for example, I press Ctrl-P. Then I commonly use the following keystrokes to edit the command line:

Ctrl-B to go backward a character

Ctrl-F to go forward a character

Ctrl-D to delete the character on which the text cursor rests

To insert text, I type the text. Although `emacs` has a huge selection of editing commands, you can edit Bash command lines adequately with the preceding small set.

Aliases

While configuring the Linux kernel and creating a new Linux boot floppy, I changed the directory to `/usr/src/linux/arch/i386/boot` quite a few times. After typing that directory name twice, I immediately set up a shortcut, using Bash's alias feature:

```
alias goboot='cd /usr/src/linux/arch/i386/boot'
```

I intentionally did not use any underscore characters or uppercase letters in `goboot`, because I wanted the alias to be quick and easy to type (and it had to mean something to me only). After I defined the alias, I could go to that directory by typing the following at the Bash prompt:

```
goboot
```

As you can see, an *alias* is simply an alternative (and, usually, shorter) name for a lengthy command. Bash replaces the alias with its definition and performs the equivalent command.

Tip

If you type the same long command often, you should define an alias for that command. To make sure the alias is available whenever you log in, place the definition in the `.bash_profile` file in your home directory.

Many users use the alias feature to give more familiar names to common commands. If you are a DOS user and you are used to the `dir` command to get a directory listing, you can simply define `dir` as an alias for `ls` (the Linux command that displays the directory listing), as follows:

```
alias dir=ls
```

Now you can type `dir` whenever you want to see a directory listing.

Another good use of an alias is to redefine a dangerous command, such as `rm`, to make it safer. By default, the `rm` command deletes one or more specified files. If you type `rm *` by mistake, `rm` deletes all files in your current directory. I learned this the hard way one day when I wanted to delete all files that ended with `.xwd`. (These files were old screen images I no longer needed.) I intended to type `rm *.xwd` but, somehow, I ended up typing `rm * .xwd`. I got the following message:

```
rm: .xwd: No such file or directory
```

At first I was puzzled by the message from `rm`, so I typed **ls** to see the directory's contents again. When the listing showed nothing, I realized I had an extra space between the `*` and `.xwd`. All the files in that directory, of course, were gone forever.

The `rm` command provides the `-i` option, which asks for confirmation before deleting a file. To make this option a default, add the following `alias` definition to the `.bash_profile` file in your home directory:

```
alias rm='rm -i'
```

That's it! From now on, when you use `rm` to delete a file, the command first asks for confirmation, as follows:

```
rm .bash_profile
rm: remove `.bash_profile'? n
```

Press **y** to delete the file; otherwise, press **n**.

Linux Commands

The shell enables you to run any Linux command, but you need to know the commands before you can run them. Because Linux is a UNIX clone, all Linux commands essentially are UNIX commands. Some of the most important commands are for moving around the Linux file system. This section summarizes these important commands. You can try these commands at the shell prompt in an `xterm` window.

Cross-Reference

Consult Appendix B for a Linux command reference to learn about many more Linux commands.

Linux directory layout

Like any other operating system, Linux organizes information in files. The files are, in turn, contained in directories. A directory can have subdirectories, giving rise to a hierarchical structure. Unlike MS-DOS, in which you see individual drives, the Linux file system starts with a root directory; a single slash (/) denotes the root directory. Figure 6-1 shows the basic layout of the Linux file system, including the root directory and several important subdirectories.

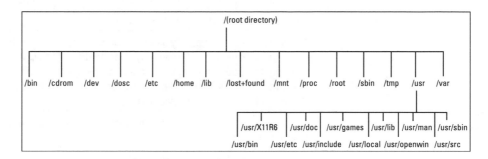

Figure 6-1: The Linux directory structure

Many directories have specific purposes. If you know the purpose of specific directories, finding your way around the Linux directories is easier. Another benefit of knowing the typical use of directories is you can guess where to look for specific types of files when you face a new situation. Table 6-2 briefly describes the directories in a Linux system:

Table 6-2 Linux system directories

Directory	Description
/	The root directory that forms the base of the file system. All files and directories are logically contained in the root directory, regardless of their physical locations.
/bin	Contains the executable programs that are part of the Linux operating system. Many Linux commands, such as cat, cp, ls, more, and tar, are located in /bin.
/boot	Contains the Linux kernel and other files needed by the LILO boot manager.
/mnt/cdrom	Directory where the CD-ROM drive typically is mounted.
/dev	Contains all device files. Linux treats each device as being a special file and all such files are located in the device directory /dev.
/dosc	Directory where the MS-DOS partition is typically mounted (provided your system's hard disk has an MS-DOS partition).

(continued)

Table 6-2 *(Continued)*

Directory	*Description*
/etc	Contains most system configuration files and the initialization scripts (in the /etc/rc.d subdirectory).
/home	Conventional location of the home directories of all users. User naba's home directory, for example, is /home/naba.
/lib	Contains library files for C and other programming languages.
/lost+found	Directory for lost files. Every disk partition has a lost+found directory.
/mnt	An empty directory, typically used to mount devices such as floppy disks and disk partitions temporarily. Also contains the /mnt/floppy directory for mounting floppy disks and the /mnt/cdrom directory for mounting the CD-ROM drive (of course, you can also mount the CD-ROM drive on another directory).
/proc	A special directory that contains information about various aspects of the Linux system.
/root	The home directory for the root user.
/sbin	Contains executable files representing commands typically used for system-administration tasks. Commands such as mount, halt, umount, and shutdown reside in the /sbin directory.
/tmp	Temporary directory any user can use as a scratch directory (meaning the contents of this directory are considered to be unimportant and are usually deleted every time the system boots).
/usr	Contains the subdirectories for many important programs, such as the X Window System and the online manual.
/var	Contains various system definition files, as well as directories for holding transient information.

The /usr directory also contains a host of useful subdirectories. Table 6-3 lists a few of the important subdirectories in /usr.

Table 6-3 Important /usr subdirectories

Subdirectory	*Description*
/usr/X11R6	Contains the XFree86 (X Window System) software.
/usr/bin	Contains executable files for many more Linux commands, including utility programs commonly available in Linux, but not part of the core Linux operating system.
/usr/doc	Contains the documentation files for the Linux operating system, as well as many utility programs (such as the Bash shell, mtools, the xfm File Manager, and the xv image viewer).

Subdirectory	Description
/usr/games	Contains the Linux game collection, which includes games such as doom, dungeon, hangman, and snake.
/usr/include	Contains the header files (files with names ending in .h) for the C and C++ programming languages. Also includes the X11 header files in the /usr/include/X11 directory.
/usr/lib	Contains the libraries for C and C++ programming languages; also contains the libraries for X and Tcl.
/usr/local	Contains local files. The /usr/local/bin directory, for example, is supposed to be the location of any executable program developed on your system.
/usr/man	Contains the online manual (which you can read by using the man command).
/usr/sbin	Contains many administrative commands, such as commands for electronic mail and networking.
/usr/src	Contains the source code for the Linux kernel (the core operating system).

Directory navigation

In Linux, when you log in as root, your home directory is /root. For other users, the home directory is usually in the /home directory. My home directory (when I log in as naba), for example, is /home/naba.

By default, only you have permission to save files in your home directory, but you can create subdirectories in your home directory to organize your files further.

A Linux shell such as Bash supports the concept of a *current directory*, which is the directory on which all file and directory commands operate. After you log in, for example, your current directory is the home directory. To see the current directory, use the pwd command.

To change the current directory, use the cd command. To change the current directory to /usr/doc, type the following:

```
cd /usr/doc
```

Then, to change the directory to the bash-1.14.7 subdirectory in /usr/doc, type this command:

```
cd bash-1.14.7
```

Now, if you use the pwd command, that command shows /usr/doc/bash-1.14.7 as the current directory. Therefore, you can refer to a directory's name in two ways:

■ An absolute pathname (such as /usr/doc) that specifies the exact directory in the directory tree

■ A relative directory name (such as bash-1.14.7, which means the bash-1.14.7 subdirectory of the current directory)

If you type cd bash-1.14.7 in /usr/doc, the current directory changes to /usr/doc/bash-1.14.7, but the same command in /home/naba tries to change the current directory to /home/naba/bash-1.14.7.

Tip

Use the cd command without any arguments to change the current directory to your home directory. Actually, the lone cd command changes the current directory to the directory listed in the HOME environment variable, but that environment variable contains your home directory by default.

Notice the tilde character (~) also refers to the directory specified by the HOME environment variable. Thus, the command cd ~ changes the current directory to whatever directory the HOME environment variable specifies.

Wizard

You can use a shortcut to refer to any user's home directory. Prefix a user's login name with a tilde (~) to refer to that user's home directory. Therefore, ~naba refers to the home directory of the user naba and ~root is the home directory of the root user. If your system has a user with the login name emily, you would type cd ~emily to change to Emily's home directory.

The directory names . and .. have special meanings. A single period (.) indicates the current directory, whereas two periods (..) indicate the parent directory. If the current directory is /usr/doc, for example, you can change the current directory to /usr by using this command:

```
cd ..
```

Directory listings and permissions

As you move around the Linux directories, you want to know the contents of a directory. You can get a directory listing by using the ls command. By default, the ls command, without any options, displays the contents of the current directory in a compact four-column format. If you log in as root and type ls, the ls command lists the contents of the /root directory in the following manner:

```
Mail        Xrootenv.0
```

From this listing, you cannot really tell whether an entry is a file or a directory. To see the complete details of a directory's contents, use the -l option with ls, as follows:

```
ls -l
```

For the /root directory, a typical output from ls -l is the following:

```
total 2
drwx------    2 root      root          1024 Jan 26 00:32 Mail
-rw-r--r--    1 root      root           345 Apr  5 01:07 Xrootenv.0
```

This listing shows considerable information about each directory entry, which can be a file or another directory. Looking at a line from the right column to the left, you see the rightmost column shows the name of the directory entry. The date and time before the name show the date and time of the last modification to that file. Before the date and time is the size of the file, in bytes.

The file's group and owner appear to the left of the column that shows the file's size. The next number indicates the number of links to the file. Finally, the leftmost column shows the file's *permission settings*, which determine who can read, write, or execute the file.

The first letter of the leftmost column has a special meaning, as the following list shows:

- If the first letter is `l`, the file is a symbolic link to another file.

- If the first letter is `d`, the file is a directory.

- If the first letter is a dash (-), the file is a normal file.

After that first letter, the leftmost column shows a sequence of nine characters, which appears as `rwxrwxrwx` when each letter is present. Each letter indicates a specific permission and a hyphen in place of a letter indicates no permission for a specific operation on the file. Think of these nine letters as three groups of three letters (`rwx`), interpreted as follows:

- The leftmost group of `rwx` controls the read, write, and execute permission of the file's owner. In other words, if you see `rwx` in this position, the file's owner can read (`r`), write (`w`), and execute (`x`) the file. A hyphen in the place of a letter indicates no permission. Thus, the string `rw-` means the owner has read and write permission but no execute permission. Typically, executable programs (including shell programs) have execute permission.

- The middle three `rwx` letters control the read, write, and execute permission of any user belonging to that file's group.

- The rightmost group of `rwx` letters controls the read, write, and execute permission of all other users (collectively referred to as the *world*).

Thus, a file with the permission setting `rwx` is accessible only to the file's owner, whereas the permission setting `rwxr-r` makes the file readable by everyone.

Use the `chmod` command to change the permission setting of a file. A shell program (or shell script), for example, typically is a text file you prepare with a text editor. After saving the file, you have to make the file executable before you can run the script. To add execute permission to a script file named `convert_images`, for example, type the following:

```
chmod +x convert_images
```

This command adds the execute permission for owner, group, and world.

An interesting feature of the `ls` command is it does not list any file whose name begins with a period. To see these files, you must use the `ls` command with the `-a` option, as follows:

```
ls -a
```

Tip

The example of the `ls` command shows an interesting feature of Linux commands: Most Linux commands take single-character options, each with a minus sign (you might think of this sign as being a hyphen) as prefix. When you want to use several options, type a hyphen and concatenate the option letters one after another. Therefore, `ls -al` is equivalent to `ls -a -l`.

File manipulation

You may often copy files from one directory to another. Use the `cp` command to perform this task. To copy the file `/usr/X11R6/lib/X11/fvwm2/system.fvwm2rc` to the `.fvwm2rc` file in another directory (such as your home directory), type the following:

```
cp /usr/X11R6/lib/X11/fvwm2/system.fvwm2rc  .fvwm2rc
```

If you want to copy a file to the current directory and retain the same name, use a period (.) as the second argument of the `cp` command. Thus, the following command copies the `XF86Config` file from the `/etc/X11` directory to the current directory:

```
cp /etc/X11/XF86Config
```

The `cp` command makes a new copy of a file and leaves the original intact.

Another Linux command, `mv`, moves a file to a new location. The original copy is gone and a new copy appears at the specified destination. One use of `mv` is to rename a file. If you want to change the name of the `today.list` to `old.list`, use the `mv` command, as follows:

```
mv today.list old.list
```

On the other hand, if you want to move the `today.list` file to the subdirectory named `saved`, use this command:

```
mv today.list saved
```

Wizard

An interesting feature of `mv` is you can use it to move entire directories —with all their subdirectories and files—to a new location. If you have a directory named `data` that contains many files and subdirectories, you can move that entire directory structure to `old_data` by using this command:

```
mv data old_data
```

Another common file operation is deleting a file. Use the `rm` command to delete a file. To delete a file named `old.list`, for example, type the following command:

```
rm old.list
```

Caution

Be careful with the `rm` command, in particular when you are logged in as `root`. Inadvertently deleting important files with `rm` is easy. (See the "Aliases" section earlier in this chapter to learn how you can avoid accidentally clobbering files with the `rm` command.)

In addition to copying, renaming, and deleting files, you may want to view a file's contents. Use the `more` command to look at a text file one page at a time. To view the file `/etc/X11/XF86Config`, for example, use this command:

```
more /etc/X11/XF86Config
```

The `more` command pauses after each page and you must press the spacebar to move to the next page. Press Enter to move forward one line at a time in the file.

Another useful Linux command for file viewing is `less`. (The name is a play on words, because `less` does more than `more`.) Whereas `more` enables you to move forward one page at a time, the `less` command enables you to move forward and backward through a file.

Directory manipulation

To organize files in your home directory, you have to create new directories. Use the `mkdir` command to create a directory. To create a directory named `images` in the current directory, type the following:

```
mkdir images
```

After you create the directory, you can use the `cd images` command to change to that directory.

When you no longer need a directory, use the `rmdir` command to delete it. You can delete a directory only when the directory is empty.

File finder

The `find` command locates files (and directories) that meet specified search criteria. The `find` command is one of the most useful Linux commands. The Linux version of the `find` command comes from GNU and it has more extensive options than the standard UNIX version. I show the syntax for the standard UNIX `find` command, however, because that syntax works in Linux and you can use the same format on other UNIX systems.

I must admit, when I began using UNIX many years ago (I started with Berkeley UNIX in the early 1980s), I was confounded by the `find` command. I must have stayed with one basic syntax of `find` for a long time before graduating to more complex forms. The basic syntax I learned first was for finding a file anywhere in the file system.

Suppose you want to find any file or directory with a name that starts with `fvwm`. You can use `find` to perform this search, as follows:

```
find / -name "fvwm*" -print
```

This command tells `find` to start looking at the root directory (/), to look for filenames that match `fvwm*`, and to display the full pathname of any matching file.

The `-print` option and the double quotation marks around the search string are not necessary in Linux as long as no files exist in the current directory that start with `fvwm`. You could have typed the preceding command as follows:

```
find / -name fvwm*
```

No harm exists in using the longer form, however, because that's how you must use `find` in other UNIX systems. I continue to show you `find` with the standard UNIX syntax.

You can use variations of this simple form of `find` to locate a file in any directory (as well as subdirectories contained in the directory). If you forget where in your home directory you stored all files named `y2k*` (names that start with the string `y2k`), you can search for the files by using the following command:

```
find ~ -name "y2k*" -print
```

When you become comfortable with this syntax of `find`, you can start using other options of `find`. To find only specific types of files (such as directories), use the `-type` option. The following command displays all top-level directory names in your Linux system:

```
find / -type d -maxdepth 1 -print
```

You probably do not have to use the complex forms of `find` in a typical Linux system, but you can always look up the rest of the `find` options by using this command:

```
man find
```

Shell Scripts in Bash

The fundamental philosophy of UNIX is to give the user many small and specialized commands, along with the necessary plumbing to connect these commands. By *plumbing,* I mean the way one command's output is used as a second command's input. Bash, the default shell in Linux, provides this plumbing in the form of I/O redirection and pipes. Bash also includes features such as the `if` statement, which runs commands only when a specific condition is True and the `for` statement, which repeats commands a specified number of times. You can use these features of Bash to write programs called *shell scripts.*

Shell scripts are popular among system administrators. If you are a system administrator, you can build up a collection of custom shell scripts that help you automate tasks you perform often. If the disk seems to be getting full, for example, you may want to find all files that exceed some size (say, 1MB) and that have not been accessed in the past 30 days. In addition, you may want to send an e-mail message to all users who have large files, requesting they try to archive and clean up those files. You can perform all these tasks with a shell script. You might start with the following `find` command to identify the large files:

```
find / -type f -atime +30 -size +1000k -exec ls -l {} \; > /tmp/largefiles
```

This command creates a file named `/tmp/largefiles`, which contains detailed information about the old files that are taking up too much space. After you get a list of the files, you can use a few other Linux commands — such as `sort`, `cut`, and `sed` — to prepare and send mail messages to users who have large files they should try to clean up.

The following sections provide an overview of Bash programming.

Caution

As you try simple shell programs, don't name your sample programs `test`. Linux includes an important program named `test` (`/usr/bin/test`). This program is used in shell scripts to test for various conditions, such as whether a file exists and whether a file is readable. If you create a sample program named `test`, some scripts may end up calling your program instead of the system's `test` program.

A simple shell script

Earlier in this chapter, the section "Shell Programs" discussed how you can simply place often-used commands in a file and use the `chmod` command to make the file executable. Voila — you have a shell script. Just as most Linux commands accept command-line options, a Bash script accepts command-line options. Inside the script, you can refer to the options as `$1`, `$2`, and so on. The special name `$0` refers to the name of the script itself.

Consider the following Bash script:

```
#!/bin/sh
echo "This script's name is: $0"
echo Argument 1: $1
echo Argument 2: $2
```

The first line causes Linux to run the `/bin/sh` program, which subsequently processes the rest of the lines in the script. The name `/bin/sh` traditionally refers to the Bourne shell — the first UNIX shell. In Linux, `/bin/sh` is a symbolic link to `/bin/bash`, which is the executable program for Bash. Therefore, in Linux, Bourne shell scripts are run by Bash (which happens to be compatible with the Bourne shell).

If you save this simple script in a file named `simple` and you make that file executable with the command `chmod +x simple`, you can run the script as follows:

```
simple
This script's name is: ./simple
Argument 1:
Argument 2:
```

Learning more about shell programming

Although these sections provide an overview of shell programming, there is much more to learn about shell programming than this single chapter can cover. *UNIX Power Tools*, coauthored by several UNIX gurus, is a good source of information on all aspects of UNIX commands in general and shell programming in particular.

The script file's name appears relative to the current directory, which is represented by a period. Because you ran the script without any arguments, the script does not display any arguments.

Now try running the script with a few arguments, as follows:

```
simple "This is one argument" second-argument third
This script's name is: ./simple
Argument 1: This is one argument
Argument 2: second-argument
```

As this example shows, the shell treats the entire string within double quotation marks as a single argument. Otherwise, the shell uses spaces as separators between arguments on the command line.

Bash programming overview

Like any programming language, Bash includes the following features:

- Variables that store values, including special built-in variables for accessing command-line arguments passed to a shell script and other special values

- The capability to evaluate expressions

- Control structures that enable you to loop over several shell commands or to execute some commands conditionally

- The capability to define functions that can be called in many places within a script. Bash also includes many built-in functions that you can use in any script.

The next few sections illustrate some of Bash's programming features through simple examples. Because you are already running Bash, you can try the examples by typing them at the shell prompt in an xterm window.

Variables

Define variables in Bash just as you define environment variables. Thus, you might define a variable this way:

```
count=12  # note no embedded spaces allowed
```

To use a variable's value, prefix the variable's name with a dollar sign ($). $PATH, for example, is the value of the variable PATH (yes, the famous PATH environment variable). To display the value of the variable named count, you would use the following command:

```
echo $count
```

Bash has some special variables for accessing command-line arguments. In a shell script, $0 refers to the name of the shell script. The variables $1, $2, and so on, refer to the command-line arguments. The variable $* stores all the command-line arguments as a single variable and $? contains the exit status of the last command executed by the shell.

You also can prompt the user for input and use the read command to read the input into a variable. Following is an example:

```
echo -n "Enter value: "
read value
echo "You entered: $value"
```

The -n option stops the echo command from automatically adding a new line at the end of the string it displays.

Control structures

In Bash scripts, the control structures — such as if, case, for, and while — depend on the exit status of a command to decide what to do next. When any command executes, it returns an *exit status*, a numeric value that indicates whether the command was successful. By convention, an exit status of zero means the command succeeded. (Yes, you read it right: zero indicates success.) A nonzero exit status indicates something went wrong with the command.

You might use a script that makes a backup copy of a file before opening it by using the vi editor in the following manner:

```
#!/bin/sh
if cp "$1" "#$1"
then
    vi "$1"
else
    echo "Failed to create backup copy"
fi
```

This script illustrates the syntax of the *if-then-else* structure and also shows how the exit status of the cp command is used by the if structure to decide the next action. If cp returns zero, the script invokes vi to edit the file; otherwise, the script displays a message and exits.

Don't forget the final fi that terminates the if structure. Forgetting fi is a common source of errors in Bash scripts.

Bash includes the test command to enable you to evaluate any expression and use the expression's value as the exit status of the command. Suppose you want a script that enables you to edit an existing file. Using test, you might write such a script as follows:

```
#!/bin/sh
if test -f "$1"
then
    vi "$1"
else
    echo "No such file"
fi
```

A shorter form of the test command leaves out test and places the command's options in brackets. Using this notation, you would write the preceding script as follows:

```
#!/bin/sh
if [ -f "$1" ]
then
    vi "$1"
else
    echo "No such file"
fi
```

Another common control structure is the for loop. The following script adds the numbers one through ten:

```
#!/bin/sh
sum=0
for i in 1 2 3 4 5 6 7 8 9 10
do
    sum=`expr $sum + $i`
done
echo "Sum = $sum"
```

This example also illustrates the use of the expr command to evaluate an expression.

Built-in functions in Bash

Bash has more than 50 built-in functions, including common functions such as cd and pwd, as well as many others that are not used frequently. You can use these built-in functions in any Bash script. This chapter does not have enough space to cover the built-in functions, but you can learn more about them from the online manual for Bash by using the man bash command.

Perl as a Scripting Language

Officially, *Perl* stands for *Practical Extraction Report Language*. Perl was created by Larry Wall to extract information from text files and then use that information to prepare reports. Programs written in Perl, the language, are interpreted and executed by `perl`, the program. This book's companion CD-ROM includes the `perl` program; it should be installed on your system in the `/usr/bin` directory.

Perl is available on a wide variety of computer systems because, like Linux, Perl can be distributed freely. Also, Perl is popular among many users and system administrators as a scripting language, which is why this section introduces Perl and shows its strengths. In Chapter 8, you learn about another scripting language (Tcl/Tk) that provides the capability to create graphical user interfaces for the scripts.

As you know by now, the term *script* simply is a synonym for *program*. Unlike programs written in programming languages such as C and C++, Perl programs needn't be compiled; the `perl` program simply interprets and executes the Perl programs. The term *script* often is used for such interpreted programs written in a shell's programming language or in Perl. (Strictly speaking, `perl` does not simply interpret a Perl program; it converts the Perl program to an intermediate form before executing the program.)

Note

If you are familiar with shell programming or the C programming language, you can pick up Perl quickly. If you have never programmed, becoming proficient in Perl may take a while. I encourage you to start with a small subset of Perl's features and ignore anything you do not understand. Then you can slowly add Perl features to your repertoire.

Do I have Perl?

Before you proceed with the Perl tutorial, check to see whether you have `perl` installed on your system. Type the following command:

```
which perl
```

The `which` command tells you whether it finds a specified program in the directories listed in the `PATH` environment variable. If `perl` is installed, you should see the following output:

```
/usr/bin/perl
```

If the `which` command complains that no such program exists in the current `PATH`, this message does not necessarily mean you don't have `perl` installed. You may not have the `/usr/bin` directory in `PATH`. Check to ensure `/usr/bin` is in PATH: either type echo $PATH or look at the message displayed by the which command (this message includes the directories in PATH). If /usr/bin is not in PATH, use the following command to redefine PATH:

```
PATH=$PATH:/usr/bin; export PATH
```

Now try the which perl command again. If you still get an error, you may not have installed perl. You can always install Perl from the companion CD-ROM with the following steps:

1. Log in as root.

2. Insert the companion CD-ROM is in the CD-ROM drive and mount the CD-ROM using the following command:

   ```
   mount /dev/hdc /mnt/cdrom
   ```

   Replace /dev/hdc with the device name for your CD-ROM drive.

3. Type the following command to change directory to the location where the Red Hat packages are located:

   ```
   cd /mnt/cdrom/RedHat/RPMS
   ```

4. Type the following rpm (Red Hat Package Manager) command to install Perl:

   ```
   rpm -i perl*
   ```

If you have perl installed on your system, type the following command to see its version number:

```
perl -v
```

Following is typical output from that command:

```
This is perl, version 5.004_01

Copyright 1987-1997, Larry Wall

Perl may be copied only under the terms of either the Artistic License
or the GNU General Public License, which may be found in the Perl 4.0
source kit.
```

This output tells you that you have Perl Version 5.004, patch level 01, and Larry Wall, the originator of Perl, holds the copyright. Perl is freely distributed under the GNU General Public License, however.

The companion CD-ROM has Version 5.004_01 of Perl. You can get the latest version of Perl by pointing your Web browser to the Comprehensive Perl Archive Network (CPAN). The following address connects you to the CPAN site nearest to you:

```
http://www.perl.com/CPAN/
```

Your first Perl script

Perl has many features of C and, as you may be aware, most books on C start with an example program that displays Hello, World! on your terminal. Because Perl is an interpreted language, you can accomplish this task directly from the command line. If you enter:

```
perl -e 'print "Hello, World!\n";'
```

the system responds:

```
Hello, World!
```

This command uses the -e option of the perl program to pass the Perl program as a command-line argument to the Perl interpreter. In this case, the following line constitutes the Perl program:

```
print "Hello, World!\n";
```

To convert this line to a script, all you must do is place the line in a file and start the file with a directive to run the perl program (as you do in the shell scripts, in which you place a line such as #!/bin/sh to run the Bourne shell to process the script).

To try a Perl script, follow these steps:

1. Use a text editor, such as vi or emacs, to save the following lines in the file named hello:

   ```
   #!/usr/bin/perl
   # This is a comment.
   print "Hello, World!\n";
   ```

2. Make the hello file executable by using the following command:

   ```
   chmod +x hello
   ```

3. Run the Perl script by typing the following at the shell prompt:

   ```
   hello
   Hello, World!
   ```

That's it! You've just written and tried your first Perl script.

Secret

Notice the first line of a Perl script starts with #!, followed by the full pathname of the perl program. If the first line of a script starts with #!, the shell simply strips off the #!, appends the script file's name to the end, and runs the script. Thus, if the script file is named hello and the first line is #!/usr/bin/perl, the shell executes the following command:

```
/usr/bin/perl hello
```

More on Perl

This chapter devotes a few sections to give you an overview of Perl and show a few simple examples. This discussion doesn't do justice to Perl, though. If you want to use Perl as a tool, consult one of the following books on Perl:

Larry Wall, Tom Christiansen, and Randal L. Schwartz, *Programming Perl, 2nd Edition* (O'Reilly & Associates, 1996)

Randal L. Schwartz, *Learning Perl* (O'Reilly & Associates, 1993)

Naba Barkakati, *Discover Perl 5* (IDG Books Worldwide, 1997)

The book by Perl originator Larry Wall and Randal Schwartz is the authoritative guide to Perl (although it may not be the best resource for learning Perl). The later book by Randal Schwartz focuses more on teaching Perl programming. My recent book teaches Perl with step-by-step instructions backed by short, but complete, example programs.

A Perl overview

Most programming languages, including Perl, have some common features:

- *Variables* to store different types of data. You can think of each variable as a placeholder for data — kind of like a mailbox, with a name and room to store data. The content of the variable is its value.

- *Expressions* that combine variables by using *operators*. An expression might add several variables; another might extract a part of a string.

- *Statements* that perform some action, such as assigning a value to a variable or printing a string

- *Flow-control statements* that allow statements to be executed in various orders, depending on the value of some expression. Typically, flow-control statements include `for`, `do-while`, `while`, and `if-then-else` statements.

- *Functions* (also called *subroutines* or *routines*) that enable you to group several statements and give them a name. This feature enables you to execute the same set of statements by invoking the function that represents those statements. Typically, a programming language provides some predefined functions.

The next few sections provide an overview of these major features of Perl and illustrate the features through simple examples.

Basic Perl syntax

Perl is free-form, like C; no constraints exist on exact placement of any keyword. Perl programs often are stored in files with names that end in `.pl`, but there is no restriction on the filenames you can use.

As in C, each Perl statement ends with a semicolon (;). A pound sign (#) marks the start of a comment. The `perl` program disregards the rest of the line beginning with the pound sign.

Groups of Perl statements are enclosed in braces ({...}). This feature also is similar to C.

Variables

You don't have to declare Perl variables before using them, as you do in C. You can easily recognize a variable in a Perl script because each variable name begins with a special character: an at symbol (@), a dollar sign ($), or a percent sign (%). This special character denotes the variable's type. The three variable types are

- *Scalar variables*, which represent the basic data types: integer, floating-point number, and string. A dollar sign ($) precedes a scalar variable. Following are some examples:

```
$maxlines = 256;
$title = "Linux Secrets, Second Edition";
```

- *Array variables*, which are collections of scalar variables. An array variable has an at symbol (@) as a prefix. Thus, the following are arrays:

```
@pages = (62, 26, 22, 24);
@commands = ("start", "stop", "draw", "exit");
```

- *Associative arrays*, which are collections of key-value pairs in which each key is a string and the value is any scalar variable. A percent-sign (%) prefix indicates an associative array. You can use associative arrays to associate a name with a value. You might store the amount of disk space used by each user in an associative array such as the following:

```
%disk_usage = ("root", 147178, "naba", 28547, "emily", 55, "ivy", 60);
```

Because each variable type has its own special character prefix, you can use the same name for different variable types. Thus, %disk_usage, @disk_usage, and $disk_usage can appear within the same Perl program.

Scalars

Scalar variables are the basic data type in Perl. Each scalar's name starts with a dollar sign ($). Typically, you start using a scalar with an assignment statement that initializes it. You can even use a variable without initializing it. The default value for numbers is zero and the default value of a string is an empty string. If you want to see whether a scalar is defined, use the defined function as follows:

```
print "Name undefined!\n" if !(defined $name);
```

The expression (defined $name) is 1 if $name is defined. You can actually "undefine" a variable by using the undef function. You can undefine $name, for example, as follows:

```
undef $name;
```

Variables are evaluated according to context. Following is a script that initializes and prints a few variables:

```
#!/usr/bin/perl
$title = "Linux SECRETS, Second Edition";
$count1 = 550;
$count2 = 375;

$total = $count1 + $count2;

print "Title: $title -- $total pages\n";
```

When you run this Perl program, it produces the following output:

```
Title: Linux SECRETS, Second Edition -- 925 pages
```

As the Perl statements show, when the two numeric variables are added, their numeric values are used, but when the $total variable is printed, its string representation is displayed.

Another interesting aspect of Perl is it evaluates all variables in a string within double quotation marks ("..."). On the other hand, if you write a string inside single quotation marks ('...'), Perl leaves that string untouched. If you were to write

```
 print 'Title: $title -- $total pages\n';
```

with single quotes instead of double quotes, Perl would display

```
Title: $title -- $total pages\n
```

and not even generate a new line.

A useful Perl variable is $_ (dollar sign followed by the underscore character). This special variable is known as the *default argument*. The Perl interpreter determines the value of $_ depending on the context. When the Perl interpreter reads input from the standard input, $ holds the current input line. When the interpreter is searching, $_ holds the default search pattern.

Arrays

An *array* is a collection of scalars. The array name starts with an at symbol (@). As in C, array subscripts start at zero. You can access the elements of an array with an index. Perl allocates space for arrays dynamically.

Consider the following simple script:

```
#!/usr/bin/perl
@commands = ("start", "stop", "draw" , "exit");

$numcmd = @commands;
print "There are $numcmd commands. The first command is:
$commands[0]\n";
```

When you run the script, it produces the following output:

```
There are 4 commands. The first command is: start
```

As you can see, equating a scalar to the array sets the scalar to the number of elements in the array. The first element of the @commands array is referenced as $commands[0] because the index starts at zero. Thus, the fourth element in commands is $commands[3].

Two special scalars are related to an array. The $[variable is the current base index, which is zero by default. The scalar $#*arrayname* (in which *arrayname* is the name of an array variable) has the last array index as the value. Thus, for the @commands array, $#commands is 3.

You can print an entire array with a simple print statement like this:

```
print "@commands\n";
```

When Perl executes this statement, it displays the following output:

```
start stop draw exit
```

Associative arrays

Associative array variables, which are declared with a percent-sign (%) prefix, are unique features of Perl. Using associative arrays, you can index an array with a string such as a name. A good example of an associative array is the %ENV array that Perl automatically defines for you. In Perl, %ENV is the array of environment variables you can access by using the environment-variable name as an index. The following Perl statement prints the current PATH environment variable:

```
print "PATH = $ENV{PATH}\n";
```

When Perl executes this statement, it prints the current setting of PATH. In contrast to regular arrays, you must use braces to index into an associative array.

Perl has many built-in functions — such as delete, each, keys, and values — that enable you to access and manipulate associative arrays.

Predefined variables in Perl

Perl has several predefined variables that contain useful information you may need in a Perl script. Following are a few important predefined variables:

`@ARGV` is an array of strings that contains the command-line options to the script. The first option is `$ARGV[0]`, the second one is `$ARGV[1]`, and so on.

`%ENV` is an associative array that contains the environment variables. You can access this array by using the environment-variable name as a key. Thus, `$ENV{HOME}` is the home directory and `$ENV{PATH}` is the current search path the shell uses to locate commands.

`$$` is the script's process ID.

`$<` is the user ID of the user who is running the script.

`$?` is the status returned by the last `system` call.

`$_` is the default argument for many functions.

`$0` is the name of the script.

Operators and expressions

Operators are used to combine and compare Perl variables. Typical mathematical operators are addition (+), subtraction (-), multiplication (*), and division (/). Perl provides nearly the same set of operators C has. When you use operators to combine variables, you end up with *expressions*. Each expression has a value.

Following are some typical Perl expressions:

```
error < 0
$count == 10
$count + $i
$users[$i]
```

These expressions are examples of the *comparison operator* (the first two lines), the *arithmetic operator*, and the *array-index operator*.

Caution

In Perl, don't use the `==` operator to find out whether two strings match; the `==` operator works only with numbers. To test the equality of strings, Perl includes the FORTRAN-style `eq` operator. Use `eq` to see whether two strings are identical, as follows:

```
if ($input eq "stop") { exit; }
```

Other FORTRAN-style string comparison operators include `ne` (inequality), `lt` (less than), `gt` (greater than), `le` (less than or equal), and `ge` (greater than or equal). You also can use the `cmp` operator to compare two strings. The return value is –1, 0, or 1, depending on whether the first string is less than, equal to, or greater than the second one.

Perl also provides the following unique operators. C lacks an exponentiation operator, which FORTRAN includes; Perl uses ** as the exponentiation operator. Thus, you can enter the following:

```
$x = 2;
$y = 3;
$z = $x**$y;  # z should be 8 (2 raised to the power 3)
$y **= 2;  # y is now 9 (3 raised to the power 2)
```

You can initialize an array to null by using ( ) — the *null-list operator* — as follows:

```
@commands = ();
```

The dot operator (.) enables you to concatenate two strings, as follows:

```
$part1 = "Hello, ";
$part2 = "World!";
$message = $part1.$part2;  # Now $message = "Hello, World!"
```

A curious but useful operator is the *repetition operator*, denoted by x=. You can use the x= operator to repeat a string a specified number of times. Suppose you want to initialize a string to 65 asterisks (*). The following example shows how you can initialize the string with the x= operator:

```
$marker = "*";
$marker x= 65;  # Now $marker is a string of 65 asterisks
```

Another powerful operator in Perl is the *range ope*rator, represented by two periods (..). You can initialize an array easily by using the range operator. Following are some examples:

```
@numerals = (0..9); # @numerals is the list 0, 1, 2, 3, 4, 5, 6, 7, 8
, 9
@alphabet = ('A'..'Z'); # @alphabet is the list of capital letters A
through Z
```

Regular expressions

If you have used UNIX for a while, you probably know about the grep command, which enables you to search files for a pattern of strings. Following is a typical use of grep to locate all files with any occurrences of the string blaster or Blaster on any line of all files with names that end in .c:

```
cd /usr/src/linux/drivers/cdrom
grep "[bB]laster" *.c
```

These commands produce this output on my system:

```
cdu31a.c:   { 0x230,    0 },   /* SoundBlaster 16 card */
sbpcd.c: *           Works with SoundBlaster compatible cards and with
"no-sound"
sbpcd.c:        0x230, 1, /* Soundblaster Pro and 16 (default) */
sbpcd.c:        0x250, 1, /* OmniCD default, Soundblaster Pro and 16 */
sbpcd.c:        0x270, 1, /* Soundblaster 16 */
```

```
sbpcd.c:          0x290, 1, /* Soundblaster 16 */
sbpcd.c:static const char *str_sb = "SoundBlaster";
sbpcd.c:static const char *str_sb_l = "soundblaster";
sbpcd.c: *              sbpcd=0x230,SoundBlaster
sbpcd.c:            msg(DBG_INF," LILO boot: ...
sbpcd=0x230,SoundBlaster\n");
sjcd.c: * the SoundBlaster/Panasonic style CDROM interface. But today, the
```

As you can see, grep found all occurrences of blaster and Blaster in the files whose names end in .c.

The grep command's "[bB]laster" argument is known as a *regular expression*, a pattern that matches a set of strings. You construct a regular expression with a small set of operators and rules similar to the ones for writing arithmetic expressions. A list of characters inside brackets ([...]), for example, matches any single character in the list. Thus, the regular expression "[bB]laster" is a set of two strings, as follows:

```
blaster    Blaster
```

Perl supports regular expressions just as the grep command does. Many other UNIX programs, such as the vi editor and sed (stream editor), also support regular expressions. The purpose of a regular expression is to search for a pattern of strings in a file. This is why editors support regular expressions.

Perl enables you to construct complex regular expressions, but the rules are fairly simple. Essentially, the regular expression is a sequence of characters in which some characters have special meaning. Table 6-4 lists the basic rules of interpreting the characters.

Table 6-4	Rules for interpreting regular expression characters
Expression	**Meaning**
.	Matches any single character except a new line
$x*$	Matches zero or more occurrences of the character x
$x+$	Matches one or more occurrences of the character x
$x?$	Matches zero or one occurrence of the character x
[...]	Matches any of the characters inside the brackets
$x\{n\}$	Matches exactly n occurrences of the character x
$x\{n,\}$	Matches n or more occurrences of the character x
$x\{,m\}$	Matches zero or, at most, m occurrences of the character x

Expression	Meaning
x{n,m}	Matches at least n occurrences, but no more than m occurrences of the character x
$	Matches the end of a line
\0	Matches a null character
\b	Matches a backspace
\B	Matches any character that's not at the beginning or the end of a word
\b	Matches the beginning or end of a word — (when not inside brackets)
\cX	Matches Ctrl-X (where X is any alphabetic character)
\d	Matches a single digit
\D	Matches a nondigit character
\f	Matches a form feed
\n	Matches a new-line (line-feed) character
\ooo	Matches the octal value specified by the digits ooo (where each o is a digit between 0 and 7)
\r	Matches a carriage return
\S	Matches a nonwhite-space character
\s	Matches a white-space character (space, tab, or new line)
\t	Matches a tab
\W	Matches a nonalphanumeric character
\w	Matches an alphanumeric character
\xhh	Matches the hexadecimal value specified by the digits hh (where each h is a digit between 0 and f)
^	Matches the beginning of a line

If you want to match one of the characters $, |, *, ^, [,], \, and /, you have to place a backslash before them. Thus, you would type these characters as \$, \|, *, \^, \[, \], \\, and \/. Regular expressions often look confusing because of the preponderance of strange character sequences and the generous sprinkling of backslashes. As with anything else, though, you can start slowly and use only a few of the features in the beginning.

So far, this section has summarized the syntax of regular expressions, but you haven't yet seen how to use regular expressions in Perl. Typically, you place a regular expression within a pair of slashes and use the match (=~) or not-match (!~) operators to test a string. You can write a Perl script that performs the same search as the one done with grep earlier in this section. Follow these steps to complete this exercise:

1. Use an editor to type and save the following script in a file named `lookup`:

```
#!/usr/bin/perl

while (<STDIN>)
{
    if ( $_ =~ /[bB]laster/ ) { print $_; }
}
```

2. Make the `lookup` file executable by using the following command:

```
chmod +x lookup
```

3. Try the script, using the following command:

```
cat /usr/src/linux/drivers/cdrom/sbpcd.c | lookup
```

My system responds with this:

```
*               Works with SoundBlaster compatible cards and with
"no-sound"
        0x230, 1, /* Soundblaster Pro and 16 (default) */
        0x250, 1, /* OmniCD default, Soundblaster Pro and 16 */
        0x270, 1, /* Soundblaster 16 */
        0x290, 1, /* Soundblaster 16 */
static const char *str_sb = "SoundBlaster";
static const char *str_sb_l = "soundblaster";
 *               sbpcd=0x230,SoundBlaster
            msg(DBG_INF,"   LILO boot: ...
sbpcd=0x230,SoundBlaster\n");
```

The `cat` command feeds the contents of a specific file (which, as you know from the `grep` example, contains some lines with the regular expression) to the lookup script. The script simply applies Perl's regular expression-match operator (`=~`) and prints any matching line.

The `$_` variable in the script needs some explanation. The `<STDIN>` expression gets a line from the standard input and, by default, stores that line in the `$_` variable. Inside the `while` loop, the regular expression is matched against the `$_` string. All the `lookup` script's work is done with this single Perl statement:

```
if ( $_ =~ /[bB]laster/ ) { print $_; }
```

This example illustrates how you might use a regular expression to search for occurrences of strings in a file.

After you use regular expressions for a while, you can better appreciate their power. The trick is to determine exactly what regular expression performs the task you want. Following is a search that looks for all lines beginning with exactly seven spaces and ending with a right parenthesis:

```
while (<STDIN>)
{
    if ( $_ =~ /\)\n/ && $_ =~ /^ {7}\S/ )  { print $_; }
}
```

Flow-control statements

So far, you have seen Perl statements that are meant to execute in a serial fashion — one after another. Perl also includes statements that enable you to control the flow of execution of the statements. You have already seen the `if` statement and a `while` loop. Perl includes a complete set of flow-control statements just like those in C, but with a few extra features.

In Perl, all conditional statements take the following form:

```
conditional-statement
{ Perl code to execute if conditional is true }
```

Notice you *must* enclose within braces ({...}) the code following the conditional statement. The conditional statement checks the value of an expression to determine whether to execute the code within the braces. In Perl, as in C, any nonzero value is considered true, whereas a zero value means false.

The following sections briefly describe the syntax of the major conditional statements in Perl.

if and unless

The Perl `if` statement is similar to the C `if` statement. For example, an `if` statement might check a count to see whether the count exceeds a threshold, as follows:

```
if ( $count > 25 ) { print "Too many errors!\n"; }
```

You can add an `else` clause to the `if` statement, as follows:

```
if ($user eq "root")
{
    print "Starting simulation...\n";
}
else
{
    print "Sorry $user, you must be \"root\" to run this program.\n";
    exit;
}
```

If you know C, you can see Perl's syntax looks like C. Conditionals with the `if` statement can have zero or more `elsif` clauses to account for more alternatives, such as the following:

```
print "Enter version number:"; # prompt user for version number
$os_version = <STDIN>;          # read from standard input
chop $os_version;               # get rid of the newline at the end of
the line
# Check version number
if ($os_version >= 10 ) { print "No upgrade necessary\n";}
```

```
elsif ($os_version >= 6 && $os_version < 9) { print "Standard
upgrade\n";}
elsif ($os_version > 3 && $os_version < 6) { print "Reinstall\n";}
else { print "Sorry, cannot upgrade\n";}
```

The `unless` statement is unique to Perl. This statement has the same form as `if`, including the use of `elsif` and `else` clauses. The difference is `unless` executes its statement block only if the condition is False. You could, for example, use the following:

```
unless ($user eq "root")
{
    print "You must be \"root\" to run this program.\n";
    exit;
}
```

In this case, unless the string `user` is `"root"`, the script exits.

while

Use Perl's `while` statement for *looping* — repeating some processing until a condition becomes false. To read a line at a time from standard input and to process that line, you might use the following:

```
while ($in = <STDIN>)
{
# Code to process the line
    print $in;
}
```

If you read from the standard input without any argument, Perl assigns the current line of standard input to the `$_` variable. Thus, you can write the preceding `while` loop as follows:

```
while (<STDIN>)
{
# Code to process the line
    print $_;
}
```

Perl's `while` statements are more versatile than those in C, because you can use almost anything as the condition to be tested. If you use an array as the condition, for example, the `while` loop executes until the array has no elements left, as in the following example:

```
# Assume @arg has the current set of command arguments
while (@arg)
{
    $arg = shift @arg;        # extract one argument
# Code to process the current argument
    print $arg;
}
```

The `shift` function removes the first element of an array and returns that element.

You can skip to the end of a loop with the `next` keyword; the `last` keyword exits the loop. The following `while` loop adds the numbers from 1 to 10, skipping 5:

```
while (1)
{
    $i++;
    if($i == 5) { next;}   # Jump to the next iteration if $i is 5
    if($i > 10) { last;}   # When $i exceeds 10, end the loop
    $sum += $i;            # Add the numbers
}
# At this point $sum should be 50
```

for and foreach

Perl's `for` statement has a similar syntax to C's `for` statement. Use the `for` statement to execute a statement any number of times, based on the value of an expression. The syntax is as follows:

```
for (expr_1; expr_2; expr_3) { statement block }
```

expr_1 is evaluated one time, at the beginning of the loop, and the statement block is executed until expression *expr_2* evaluates to zero. The third expression, *expr_3*, is evaluated after each execution of the statement block. You can omit any of the expressions, but you must include the semicolons. Also, the braces around the statement block are required. Following is an example that uses a `for` loop to add the numbers from 1 to 10:

```
for($i=0, $sum=0; $i <= 10; $sum += $i, $i++) {}
```

In this example, the actual work of adding the numbers is done in the third expression, and the statement controlled by the `for` loop is an empty block ({}).

The `foreach` statement is most appropriate for arrays. Following is the syntax:

```
foreach Variable (Array) { statement block }
```

The `foreach` statement assigns to *Variable* an element from the *Array* and executes the statement block. The `foreach` statement repeats this procedure until no array elements are left. The following `foreach` statement adds the numbers from 1 to 10:

```
foreach $i (1..10) { $sum += $i;}
```

Notice I declare the array with the range operator (..). You also can use a list of comma-separated items as the array.

If you omit the *Variable* in a `foreach` statement, Perl implicitly uses the `$_` variable to hold the current array element. Thus, you could use the following:

```
foreach (1..10) { $sum += $_;}
```

goto

The `goto` statement transfers control to a statement label. Following is an example that prompts the user for a value and repeats the request if the value is not acceptable:

```
ReEnter:
print "Enter offset: ";
$offset = <STDIN>;
chop $offset;
unless ($offset > 0 && $offset < 512)
{
    print "Bad offset: $offset\n";
    goto ReEnter;
}
```

Access to Linux

You can execute any Linux command from Perl in several ways:

- Call the `system` function with a string that contains the Linux command you want to execute.

- Enclose a Linux command within *backquotes* (`` ` ``), which also are known as *grave accents*. You can run a Linux command this way and capture its output.

- Call the `fork` function to copy the current script and process new commands in the child process (if a process starts another process, then the new process is known as a *child process*).

- Call the `exec` function to overlay the current script with a new script or Linux command.

- Use `fork` and `exec` to provide shell-like behavior (monitor user input and process each user-entered command through a child process). This section presents a simple example of how to accomplish this task.

The simplest way to execute a Linux command in your script is to use the `system` function with the command in a string. After the `system` function returns, the exit code from the command is in the `$?` variable. You can easily write a simple Perl script that reads a string from the standard input and processes that string with the `system` function. Follow these steps:

1. Use a text editor to enter and save the following script in a file named `rcmd.pl`:

    ```
    #!/usr/bin/perl
    # Read user input and process command

    $prompt = "Command (\"exit\" to quit): ";
    print $prompt;

    while (<STDIN>)
    {
    ```

```
        chop;
        if ($_ eq "exit") { exit 0;}

    # Execute command by calling system
        system $_;
        unless ($? == 0) {print "Error executing: $_\n";}
        print $prompt;
    }
```

2. Make the `rcmd.pl` file executable, using the following command:

   ```
   chmod +x rcmd.pl
   ```

3. Run the script by typing `rcmd.pl` at the shell prompt. Following is some sample output from the `rcmd.pl` script (the output depends on what commands you enter):

   ```
   Command ("exit" to quit): ps
   PID TTY STAT  TIME COMMAND
     415  p0 S    0:00 /bin/login -h lnb486 -p
     416  p0 S    0:00 -bash
     585  p0 S    0:00 perl ./rcmd.pl
     586  p0 R    0:00 ps
   Command ("exit" to quit): exit
   ```

Another way to run UNIX commands is to use `fork` and `exec` in your Perl script. Following is an example script — `psh.pl` — that uses `fork` and `exec` to execute commands entered by the user:

```
#!/usr/bin/perl

# This is a simple script that uses "fork" and "exec" to
# runs a command entered by the user

$prompt = "Command (\"exit\" to quit): ";
print $prompt;

while (<STDIN>)
{
    chop;      # remove trailing newline
    if($_ eq "exit") { exit 0;}

    $status = fork;
    if($status)
    {
# In parent... wait for child process to finish...
        wait;
        print $prompt;
        next;
    }
    else
    {
        exec $_;
    }
}
```

The following example shows how the `psh.pl` script executes the `ps` command:

```
Command ("exit" to quit): ps
  PID TTY STAT   TIME COMMAND
  415 p0 S      0:00 /bin/login -h lnb486 -p
  416 p0 S      0:00 -bash
  589 p0 S      0:00 perl ./psh.pl
  590 p0 R      0:00 ps
Command ("exit" to quit): exit
```

UNIX shells, such as Bash, use the `fork` and `exec` combination to run commands.

File access

You may have noticed the `<STDIN>` expression in various examples in this chapter. This is Perl's way of reading from a file. In Perl, a file is identified by a *file handle*, which is just another name for an identifier. Usually, file handles are in uppercase characters. `STDIN` happens to be a predefined file handle that denotes the standard input — by default, the keyboard. `STDOUT` and `STDERR` are the other two predefined file handles. `STDOUT` is used for printing to the terminal and `STDERR` is used for printing error messages.

To read from a file, you write the file handle inside angle brackets (`<>`). Thus, `<STDIN>` reads a line from the standard input.

You can open other files by using the `open` function. The following example shows you how to open the `/etc/passwd` file for reading and how to display the lines in that file:

```
open (PWDFILE, "/etc/passwd");   # PWDFILE is the file handle
while (<PWDFILE>) { print $_;}   # By default, input line is in $_
close PWDFILE;                   # Close the file
```

By default, the `open` function opens a file for reading. You can add special characters at the beginning of the filename to indicate other types of access. A > prefix opens the file for writing, whereas a > prefix opens a file for appending. Following is a short script that reads the `/etc/passwd` file and creates a new file, named `output`, with a list of all users without any shell (the password entries for these users has a : at the end of the line):

```
#!/usr/bin/perl
# Read /etc/passwd and create list of users without any shell

open (PWDFILE, "/etc/passwd");
open (RESULT, ">output");                    # open file for writing

while (<PWDFILE>)
{
    if ($_ =~ /:\n/) {print RESULT $_;}
}

close PWDFILE;
close RESULT;
```

After you execute this script, you should find a file named `output` in the current directory. Following is what the output file contains when this script is run on my Linux system:

```
bin:*:1:1:bin:/bin:
daemon:*:2:2:daemon:/sbin:
adm:*:3:4:adm:/var/adm:
lp:*:4:7:lp:/var/spool/lpd:
mail:*:8:12:mail:/var/spool/mail:
news:*:9:13:news:/var/spool/news:
uucp:*:10:14:uucp:/var/spool/uucp:
operator:*:11:0:operator:/root:
games:*:12:100:games:/usr/games:
gopher:*:13:30:gopher:/usr/lib/gopher-data:
ftp:*:14:50:FTP User:/home/ftp:
nobody:*:99:99:Nobody:/:
```

One interesting filename prefix is the *pipe character*—the vertical bar (|). If you call `open` with a filename that begins with |, the rest of the filename is treated as a command. The Perl interpreter executes the command and you can use `print` calls to send input to this command. The following Perl script sends a mail message to a list of users:

```perl
#!/usr/bin/perl
# Send mail to a list of users

foreach ("root", "naba")
{
    open (MAILPIPE, "| mail -s Greetings $_");
    print MAILPIPE "Remember to send in your weekly report today!\n";
    close MAILPIPE;
}
```

If a filename ends with a pipe character (|), that filename is executed as a command, and you can read that command's output with the angle brackets, as shown in the following example:

```perl
open (PSPIPE, "ps -ax |");
while (<PSPIPE>)
{
# Process the output of the ps command—this example simply echoes
each line
    print $_;
}
```

Subroutines

Although Perl includes a large assortment of built-in functions, you can add your own code modules, in the form of subroutines. In fact, the Perl distribution comes with a large set of subroutines. Following is a simple script that illustrates the syntax of subroutines in Perl:

```perl
#!/usr/bin/perl
sub hello
{
```

```
# Make local copies of the arguments from the @_ array
    local ($first,$last) = @_;

    print "Hello, $first $last\n";
}

$a = Jane;
$b = Doe;

&hello($a, $b);     # Call the subroutine
```

When you run this script, it displays the following output:

```
Hello, Jane Doe
```

Following are some points to note about subroutines:

- The subroutine receives its arguments in the array @_ (the at symbol, followed by an underscore character).

- Variables used in subroutines are global by default. Use the local function to create a local set of variables.

- Call a subroutine by placing an ampersand (&) before its name. Thus, subroutine hello is called by &hello.

If you want, you can put a subroutine in its own file. The hello subroutine, for example, can be in a file named hello.pl. When you place a subroutine in a file, remember to add a return value at the end of the file—just type **1;** at the end to return 1. Thus, the hello.pl file would be as follows:

```
sub hello
{
# Make local copies of the arguments from the @_ array
    local ($first,$last) = @_;

    print "Hello, $first $last\n";
}
1;        # return value
```

Then you have to write the script that uses the hello subroutine, as follows:

```
#!/usr/bin/perl
require 'hello.pl';   # include the file with the subroutine
definition

$a = Jane;
$b = Doe;

&hello($a, $b);     # Call the subroutine
```

This script uses the require function to include the hello.pl file that actually contains the definition of the hello subroutine.

Built-in functions in Perl

Perl has nearly 200 built-in functions (also referred to as *Perl functions*), including functions similar to the ones in the C Run-Time Library, as well as functions that access the operating system. You need to go through the list of functions to see the breadth of capabilities available in Perl. This chapter doesn't have enough space to cover these functions, but you can learn about the Perl functions by pointing your Web browser to the following address:

```
ftp://ftp.digital.com/pub/plan/perl/CPAN/doc/manual/html/perlfunc.html
```

Summary

At heart, Linux is still UNIX, and you must learn to use a shell — a command interpreter — to perform many common tasks. Even when you use a graphical interface, you usually have to open an `xterm` terminal window and type commands at the shell prompt. This chapter focuses on Bash — the Bourne Again Shell — as well as the scripting language Perl.

By reading this chapter, you learn the following:

▶ Even when you stay in the graphical environment of the X Window System, you have to type Linux commands in an `xterm` window to perform many routine tasks.

▶ A shell is a program that runs commands for you. Bash is the default shell in Linux. Bash is compatible with the Bourne shell that comes with all other UNIX systems.

▶ The Linux directory structure is logically organized as a single tree, regardless of the physical location of subdirectories. Linux includes many commands for navigating directories and manipulating files.

▶ The `find` command provides a powerful way to locate all files that meet specific search criteria.

▶ A shell script is nothing more than a sequence of Linux commands in a file. Typically, you have to place a special line at the beginning of the script file and make it executable. Then you can run the script by typing its name at the shell prompt.

▶ Perl is a popular scripting language that comes on this book's companion CD-ROM. You can use Perl to write powerful scripts on your Linux system.

▶ Perl contains features comparable to those of other programming languages, such as C. A powerful feature of Perl is its capability to use regular expressions and to search files for occurrences of a search pattern.

Chapter 7

Secrets of DOS Under Linux

In This Chapter

▶ Accessing a DOS partition from Linux

▶ Using the `mtools` utility programs to access and use DOS floppy disks

▶ Exploring the capabilities of the DOSEMU DOS emulator

Typically, you install Linux on a PC that previously had DOS and Microsoft Windows installed on it. If you happen to work in DOS and Windows as well as in Linux, you probably want to access the DOS files from Linux. This chapter shows you how to mount and access MS-DOS disks, including floppy disks.

You also learn about a package called `mtools`, which enables you to access and use (copy, delete, and format) MS-DOS files (typically, on a floppy disk) in Linux.

Mounting a DOS File System

If you have MS-DOS and Microsoft Windows installed on your hard disk, you probably already have the DOS partition mounted under Linux. During installation (see Chapter 1), the Red Hat installation program runs the Disk Druid program, which asks whether you want to access any DOS hard disk partition under Linux. Disk Druid finds these DOS partitions (as well as OS/2 partitions) by checking the hard disk's partition table.

Through the Disk Druid program you can specify where you want to mount each DOS partition. (Mounting makes the DOS directory hierarchy appear as part of the Linux file system.) A common choice is to mount the first DOS partition as `/dosc`, the second one as `/dosd`, and so on. If you specify these mount points, Disk Druid performs the necessary steps to ensure the DOS partitions are mounted automatically whenever you boot Linux.

To see whether you already have your DOS hard disk partition mounted automatically, follow these steps (you needn't be the `root` user to do this):

1. Use the `grep` command to look for the string `msdos` in the file `/etc/fstab`. Here is the result I get with `grep` on one of my Linux PCs:

```
grep msdos /etc/fstab
/dev/hda1  /dosc  msdos   defaults   0 0
```

   I explain the file `/etc/fstab` in the "The `/etc/fstab` file" section of this chapter.

2. If the output shows one or more lines that contain `msdos`, your Linux system already mounts DOS hard disk partitions automatically. In this example, the output shows a matching line whose first field is the partition name `/dev/hda1` (the first partition on the first IDE disk); the second field, `/dosc`, shows where that partition is mounted.

3. If the `grep` command does not show any lines that contain the string `msdos` in `/etc/fstab`, your system does not mount any DOS hard disk partitions automatically. An explanation, of course, may be your hard disk does not have any DOS partitions.

Another quick way to find out about the mounted devices is to type `mount` (without any arguments) at the shell prompt. Following is the output of the `mount` command on my system:

```
/dev/hda3 on / type ext2 (rw)
/dev/hda1 on /dosc type msdos (rw) (MS-DOS partition mounted on /dosc)
```

If you see any `msdos` in the output, those lines indicate MS-DOS file systems mounted on Linux. In this case, an MS-DOS partition is mounted on the Linux directory `/dosc`.

The following sections explain how the DOS partitions are mounted automatically. Even if you don't have any DOS partitions on your hard disk, you may want to learn how to access a DOS file system from Linux, because someday you may have to access a DOS floppy disk under Linux. Understanding the concept of mounting is the key to using a DOS file system under Linux.

The mount command

As Chapter 6 explains, Linux has a single file system that starts at the root directory, denoted by a single slash (/). Even if you have a separate hard disk (or multiple hard disk partitions on a single disk), the contents of those hard disks appear logically somewhere in the Linux file system. *Mounting* is the operation you must perform to cause a physical storage device (be it a hard disk partition or a CD-ROM) to appear as part of the Linux file system.

Many Linux systems have a small disk partition mounted on the root directory (/) and a larger partition mounted on the /usr directory. A larger partition is used for /usr because many software packages, including the X Window System, are installed under /usr.

You can use the `mount` command to mount a device manually on the Linux file system at a specified directory. This directory is referred to as the *mount point*. You can use any directory as the mount point. If you mount a device on a nonempty directory, though, you lose the ability to access the files in that directory until you unmount the device with the `umount` command. Therefore, you should always use an empty directory (such as `/mnt`) as the mount point.

Like any UNIX command, `mount` has numerous options. At the same time, you can get by with only a few options.

Because mounting makes a physical device part of the Linux file system, by default only the `root` user is allowed to run the `mount` command. However, the `root` user can set up entries in the `/etc/fstab` file to enable any user to mount a device. Consult the section "Mounting DOS floppy disks" to learn how you can enable any user to mount DOS floppy disks. If you try to mount a device when you are not logged in as `root` and you get the message

```
mount: only root can do that
```

this means you must log in as `root` first.

If you are not already logged in as `root`, use the `su` command to become `root`. When you type **su** without any argument, the shell assumes you want to become `root` and prompts you for the root password, as follows:

```
[naba@lnbp200 naba]$ su   (Become the root user)
Password:                 (Enter root password)
[root@lnbp200 naba]#      (Now you are root)
```

After you enter the root password, the prompt changes to indicate you are `root`.

As `root`, suppose you want to mount the CD-ROM device (the name is `/dev/cdrom`) on the mount point `/mnt/cdrom` (which should already exist on your system). To do so, type the following command:

```
mount /dev/cdrom /mnt/cdrom
```

The `mount` command will report an error if the CD-ROM device is mounted already. Otherwise, the mount operation succeeds and you can access the CD-ROM's contents through the `/mnt/cdrom` directory.

To mount a DOS partition, you use a similar format for the `mount` command, but you also should specify the type of file system on the DOS partition. If your DOS partition is the first partition on your IDE (Integrated Drive Electronics) drive and you want to mount it on `/dosc`, use the following `mount` command:

```
mount -t msdos /dev/hda1 /dosc
```

The `-t msdos` part of the `mount` command specifies the device you are mounting — `/dev/hda1` — has an MS-DOS file system. Linux has built-in support for MS-DOS files. Figure 7-1 illustrates the effect of this `mount` command.

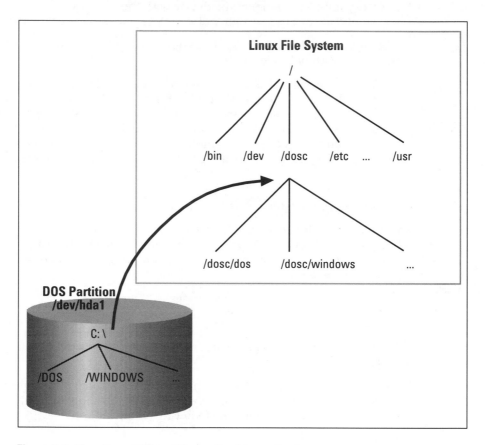

Figure 7-1: Mounting a DOS partition on the `/dosc` directory

Figure 7-1 also shows how directories in your DOS partition are mapped to the Linux file system. What used to be the `C:\DOS` directory under DOS becomes `/dosc/dos` under Linux. Similarly, `C:\WINDOWS` now is `/dosc/windows`. You probably can see the pattern now. To convert a DOS filename to Linux (for this specific case when you mount the DOS partition on `/dosc`), do the following:

- Change the DOS names to lowercase.

- Change `C:\` to `/dosc/`.

- Change all backslashes (\) to slashes (/).

DOS floppy disks

Just as you can mount a DOS hard disk partition under Linux, you can mount a DOS floppy disk. Usually, you must log in as `root` to mount a floppy, but you can follow the steps shown in the latter part of this section and set up your system so any user can mount a DOS floppy disk. You also need to know the device name for the floppy drive. By default, Linux defines two generic floppy device names:

- `/dev/fd0`, which is the A drive (the first floppy drive)

- `/dev/fd1`, which is the B drive (the second floppy disk drive, if you have one)

As for the mount point, an existing directory named `/mnt/floppy` is specifically meant for this type of temporary mount operation. Thus, you can mount the DOS floppy disk on the `/mnt/floppy` directory with the following command:

```
mount -t msdos /dev/fd0 /mnt/floppy
```

After the floppy is mounted, you can copy files to and from the floppy using Linux's copy command (`cp`). To copy the file `xtmenu1.pcx` from the current directory to the floppy, type the following:

```
cp xtmenu1.pcx /mnt/floppy
```

Similarly, to see the contents of the floppy disk, type the following:

```
ls /mnt/floppy
```

When you want to remove the floppy disk from the drive, you should first dismount the floppy drive. This action removes the association between the floppy disk's file system and the mount point on the Linux file system. Use the `umount` command to dismount a device, as follows:

```
umount /dev/fd0
```

You can set up your Linux system so any user can mount a DOS floppy disk. All you have to do is log in as `root` and add a line in the `/etc/fstab` file. For example, to enable users to mount a DOS floppy in the A drive on the `/a` directory, perform the following steps:

1. Log in as `root`.

2. Create the `/a` directory, with the following command:

   ```
   mkdir /a
   ```

3. Edit the `/etc/fstab` file in a text editor (such as `vi` or Emacs), insert the following line, save the file, and quit the editor:

   ```
   /dev/fd0     /a     msdos     noauto,user     0 0
   ```

You learn more about the /etc/fstab file in the next section; the user option (which appears next to noauto) enables all users to mount DOS floppy disks. The first field in that line is the device name (/dev/fd0), the second field is the mount directory (/a), and the third field shows the type of file system (msdos).

4. Log out and log in as a normal (not root) user.

5. To test that you can mount a DOS floppy disk without being root, insert a DOS floppy in the A drive and type the following command:

```
mount /a
```

Notice you use the mount directory as an argument for the mount command. The mount operation should succeed and you should see a listing of the DOS floppy when you type the command ls /a.

6. To unmount the DOS floppy, type umount /a.

The /etc/fstab file

In Linux, the /etc directory contains many text files that have configuration information for the system. As you learned in Chapter 5, for example, the /etc/inittab files contains information about what processes to start after Linux boots. The /etc/fstab file is one such configuration file—a text file containing information the mount and umount commands use. Each line in the /etc/fstab file provides information about a device to be mounted on a directory in the Linux file system.

Following is the /etc/fstab file from a typical Linux system:

```
/dev/hda3     /              ext2     defaults    1 1
/dev/hda1     /dosc          msdos    defaults    0 0
/dev/hda5     /dosd          msdos    defaults    0 0
/dev/hda4     swap           swap     defaults    0 0
/dev/fd0      /mnt/floppy    ext2     noauto      0 0
/dev/cdrom    /mnt/cdrom     iso9660  noauto,ro   0 0
none          /proc          proc     defaults    0 0
```

The first field on each line shows a device name, such as hard disk partition. The second field is the mount point and the third field indicates the type of file system on the device. You can ignore the last three fields for now.

The sample /etc/fstab file shows the /dev/hda4 device (the fourth partition on the first IDE hard disk) is used as a swap device for virtual memory, which is why both the mount point and the file-system type are set to swap. The last line shows another special file system—the proc file system—which Linux uses to store system information. The line on which msdos appears is the file-system type and specifies the DOS partition /dev/hda1 should be mounted on /dosc.

Secret

The contents of the `/etc/fstab` file are used to mount various file systems in Linux automatically. During Linux startup, the `init` process executes a shell script that invokes `mount` with the `-a` option. This script causes `mount` to read the `/etc/fstab` file and mount all listed file systems (except those with the `noauto` option). To mount a DOS partition automatically, therefore, you should add to the `/etc/fstab` file a line that contains the necessary information for mounting that partition. If you want to mount the DOS file system in the first partition of the first Small Computer System Interface (SCSI) disk on `/dosd`, for example, add the following line to `/etc/fstab`:

```
/dev/sda1    /dosd    msdos    defaults  0  0
```

The fourth field on each line of the `/etc/fstab` file shows a comma-separated list of options that apply to a specific device. Typically, you will find the `defaults` option in this field. The defaults option implies, among other things, that the device is mounted at boot time, only the root user can mount the device, and the device is mounted for reading and writing. If the options include `noauto`, the device is not automatically mounted when the system boots. Another useful option is user. Any user can mount a device in the `/etc/fstab` file that has the `user` option. For example, if you want to allow any user to mount the CD-ROM, log in as root and add the user option to the `/dev/cdrom` line in `/etc/fstab` as follows:

```
/dev/cdrom    /mnt/cdrom    iso9660 noauto,ro,user  0  0
```

With this line in place, any user can mount a CD-ROM with the following command:

```
mount /mnt/cdrom
```

Using mtools

The preceding sections show you one way to access the MS-DOS file system: mount the DOS hard disk or floppy disk using the `mount` command and then use regular Linux commands, such as `ls` and `cp`. This approach to mounting a DOS file system is fine for hard disks. Linux can mount the DOS partition automatically at startup and you can access the DOS directories on the hard disk whenever necessary.

If you want to get a quick directory listing of a DOS floppy disk, however, mounting can be tedious. First, you must mount the floppy drive, then you have to use the `ls` command, and, finally, you must use the `umount` command before taking the floppy disk out of the drive.

This is where the `mtools` package comes to the rescue. The `mtools` package implements most common DOS commands. The commands have the same names as in DOS, except you add an `m` prefix to each command. Thus, the command for getting a directory listing is `mdir`, and `mcopy` copies files. The best part of `mtools` is that you needn't mount the floppy disk to use the `mtools` commands.

Because the `mtools` commands write to and read from the physical device (floppy disk), you must log in as `root` to perform these commands. If you want any user to use the `mtools` commands, you must alter the permission settings for the floppy drive devices. Use the following command to enable anyone to read from and write to the first floppy drive:

```
chmod o+rw /dev/fd0
```

Do I have mtools?

The `mtools` package comes with the Red Hat Linux distribution on this book's companion CD-ROM. When you installed Linux, `mtools` was installed automatically as part of the base Linux. The `mtools` executable files are in the `/usr/bin` directory. To see whether you have `mtools` installed, type `ls /usr/bin/mdir` at the shell prompt. If the `ls` command shows this file exists, you should have `mtools` available on your system.

You can also type the following `rpm` command to verify `mtools` is installed on your system:

```
rpm -q mtools
mtools-3.6-4
```

If `mtools` is installed, the output shows you the full name of the `mtools` package. The sample output shows `mtools` Version 3.6 is installed on the system.

To try `mtools`, follow these steps:

1. Log in as `root`; or, type **su** and then enter the root password.

2. Place a MS-DOS floppy disk in your system's A drive.

3. Type **mdir**. You should see the directory of the floppy disk (in the standard DOS directory listing format).

The /etc/mtools.conf file

The `mtools` package should work with the default setup, but if you get any errors, you should check the `/etc/mtools.conf` file. This file contains the definitions of the drives (such as A, B, and C) that the `mtools` utilities see. Following are a few lines from a typical `/etc/mtools.conf` file:

```
drive a: file="/dev/fd0" exclusive
drive b: file="/dev/fd1" exclusive

# First IDE hard disk partition
drive c: file="/dev/hda1"

# First SCSI hard disk partition
# drive c: file="/dev/sda1"
```

The pound sign (#) starts comments. Each line defines a drive letter, the associated Linux device name, and some keywords that indicate how the device is accessed. In this example, the first two lines define drives A and B. The third noncomment line defines drive C as the first partition on the first IDE drive (/dev/hda1). If you have other DOS drives (for example, D), you can add another line that defines drive D as the appropriate disk partition.

If your system's A drive is a high-density 3.5-inch drive, you do not have to change anything in the default /etc/mtools.conf file.

Typically, you use the mtools utilities to access the floppy disks. Although you can define C and D drives for your DOS hard disk partitions, you may want to access those partitions by mounting them with the Linux mount command. Because the hard disk partitions can be mounted automatically at startup, accessing them through the Linux commands should be just as easy.

The mtools commands

As explained earlier in this chapter, the mtools package is a collection of utilities. So far, you have seen the command mdir — the mtools counterpart of the DIR command in DOS.

Tip

If you know the MS-DOS commands, using the mtools commands is easy. Type the DOS command in lowercase letters and remember to add m in front of each command. Because the Linux commands and filenames are case-sensitive, you must use all lowercase letters when you type mtools commands.

Table 7-1 summarizes the 13 commands available in mtools.

Table 7-1	The mtools commands	
mtools *utility*	*MS-DOS command*	*Action*
mattrib	ATTRIB	Changes MS-DOS file-attribute flags
mcd	CD	Changes an MS-DOS directory
mcopy	COPY	Copies files between MS-DOS and Linux
mdel	DEL or ERASE	Deletes an MS-DOS file
mdir	DIR	Displays an MS-DOS directory listing
mformat	FORMAT	Places an MS-DOS file system on a low-level formatted floppy disk (use fdformat to low-level-format a floppy in Linux)
mlabel	LABEL	Initializes an MS-DOS volume label
mmd	MD or MKDIR	Creates an MS-DOS directory
mrd	RD or RMDIR	Deletes an MS-DOS directory

(continued)

Table 7-1 *(Continued)*		
mtools *utility*	**MS-DOS** *command*	*Action*
mread	COPY	Copies an MS-DOS file to a Linux file
mren	REN or RENAME	Renames an existing MS-DOS file
mtype	TYPE	Displays the contents of an MS-DOS file
mwrite	COPY	Copies a Linux file to MS-DOS

You can use the mtools commands just as you would use the corresponding DOS command. For example, the mdir command works like the DIR command in DOS. The same goes for all the other mtools commands shown in Table 7-1. Regarding wildcard characters (such as *), you must remember the Linux shell is the first program to see your command. If you do not want the shell to expand the wildcard character, therefore, you should use quotation marks around filenames containing any wildcard characters. To copy all *.txt files from the A drive to your Linux directory, for example, use this command:

```
mcopy "a:*.txt".
```

If you leave off the quotation marks, the shell tries to expand the string a:*.txt with filenames from the current Linux directory and then it tries to copy those files (if any) from the DOS floppy disk.

On the other hand, when you want to copy files from the Linux directory to the DOS floppy disk, you *do* want the shell to expand any wildcard characters. To copy all *.pcx files from the current Linux directory to the DOS floppy disk, for example, invoke mcopy this way:

```
mcopy *.pcx a:
```

The mtools utilities let you use the backslash character (\) as the directory separator, just as you would under DOS. Whenever you have a filename that contains the backslash character, you must enclose the string in double quotation marks. The following command copies a file from a subdirectory on the A drive to the current Linux directory:

```
mcopy "a:\test\sample.dat".
```

How to format a DOS floppy

Suppose you run Linux on your home PC and you no longer have MS-DOS installed on your system, but you have to copy some files on an MS-DOS floppy disk and take the disk to your office. If you already have a formatted MS-DOS floppy, you can simply mount that floppy disk and copy the file to the floppy using the Linux cp command. What if you don't have a formatted DOS floppy? The mtools package again comes to the rescue.

The `mtools` package provides the `mformat` utility, which can format a floppy disk for use under MS-DOS. Unlike the DOS `format` command that formats a floppy in a single step, the `mformat` command requires you to follow a two-step process to prepare the floppy disk:

1. Use the `fdformat` command (a Linux command) to low-level-format a floppy disk. The `fdformat` command expects the floppy device name to be the argument; the device name includes all the parameters necessary for formatting the floppy disk.

   Figure 7-2 illustrates the device-naming convention for the floppy drive device. Based on the information shown in Figure 7-2, to format a 3.5-inch high-density floppy disk in your system's A drive, you use the following command:

   ```
   fdformat /dev/fd0H1440
   Double-sided, 80 tracks, 18 sec/track. Total capacity 1440 kB.
   Formatting ... done
   Verifying ... done
   ```

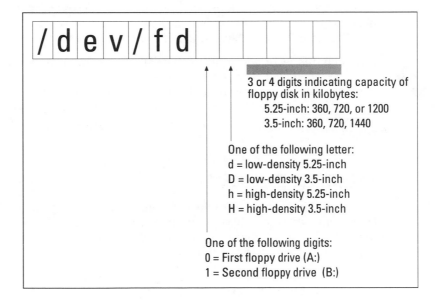

Figure 7-2: Naming convention for the floppy disk drive in Linux

2. Use the `mformat` command to put an MS-DOS file system on the low-level-formatted floppy disk. If the floppy is in drive A, type the following command:

   ```
   mformat a
   ```

Using DOSEMU

Accessing DOS file systems with the Linux `mount` command or through the `mtools` utilities enables you to exchange files with MS-DOS, but that capability does not help if you want to run a DOS program under Linux. As you might expect, Linux comes with a solution to this problem — you can use DOSEMU to create an MS-DOS environment within Linux.

Secret

Although DOSEMU stands for *DOS emulator*, it is really not an emulator. In fact, DOSEMU uses the same capabilities of the Intel 80×86 processor that Microsoft Windows uses to run MS-DOS in a window. Beginning with the 80386, Intel 80×86 and Pentium processors support a virtual-86 mode, in which multiple virtual 8086 machines can exist on the same 80×86 processor. As you may recall, the 8086 is the 16-bit microprocessor that originally ran MS-DOS. Because DOSEMU uses virtual-86 mode, it can run DOS programs in their native form, without any need to emulate the 80×86 instruction set. You need a copy of MS-DOS (any version from 3.3 to 6.2) to run DOSEMU.

DOSEMU must simulate a DOS environment for DOS applications that want to access the system's resources directly, such as the keyboard, printer, serial port, display, and disk. A configuration file, `/etc/dosemu.conf`, controls the way that DOSEMU accesses various system resources.

Caution

Although this section introduces DOSEMU, you should know DOSEMU is still under development. The DOSEMU version currently is 0.66 (it was not considered to be mature enough to have a 1.0 version number). Although DOSEMU is safe enough to try, you should be prepared to reboot your Linux system if anything goes wrong. Back up your important files before you try DOSEMU.

Installing DOSEMU

When you install Linux from the companion CD-ROM, if you select the DOS/Windows Connectivity component, the installation program installs DOSEMU. If you did not install DOSEMU during the initial installation, follow these steps to install DOSEMU now:

1. If you are not already logged in as `root`, type the **su** command and provide the root password to become `root`.

2. Make sure the companion CD-ROM is in the CD-ROM drive. If the CD-ROM is not mounted already, mount it by using the following command:

   ```
   mount /dev/cdrom /mnt/cdrom
   ```

3. Change the current directory to the CD-ROM directory in which the Red Hat packages are located, as follows:

   ```
   cd /mnt/cdrom/RedHat/RPMS
   ```

4. Type the following command to install DOSEMU:

   ```
   rpm -i dosemu*
   ```

   All the files necessary for running DOSEMU should be installed in the appropriate directories after this `rpm` command completes.

Reading the manual

After you install DOSEMU, you should read the documentation for information on how to set up and run it. You should start with the QuickStart file (a text file) in the /usr/doc/dosemu* directory. (The exact directory name depends on the version of DOSEMU you are using.) Use the following commands to browse this file:

```
cd /usr/doc/dosemu*
less QuickStart
```

Tip

The less command enables you to view the file one page at a time. less is similar to more, except less enables you to go backward as well as forward.

Following are the key points explained in the QuickStart file:

- The file /etc/dosemu.users contains the names of users who are allowed to run DOSEMU and what operations each user may perform in DOSEMU.

- You must edit the DOSEMU configuration file /etc/dosemu.conf to reflect your system's configuration.

- You need a hard disk *image file* (a Linux file DOSEMU treats as a DOS drive). This file is present when you install DOSEMU from this book's companion CD-ROM.

- To set up DOSEMU for the first time, you need a MS-DOS boot floppy that contains the files FDISK.EXE and SYS.COM. You can create this floppy under DOS, which must have come with your PC.

The following section shows you how to use the DOS floppy disk to set up the hard disk image. (This image file is used as the C drive under DOSEMU.)

Configuring DOSEMU

The DOSEMU distribution on this book's companion CD-ROM comes nearly ready to run. You do have to go through some configuration steps, however, before you can run DOSEMU. The following sections cover these tasks.

Editing /etc/docemu.conf

You must be logged in as root when you perform these configuration tasks. The first task is to edit the /etc/dosemu.conf file. Like most Linux configuration files, /etc/dosemu.conf is a text file. Comments start with a pound sign (#). The file already contains many commented lines, as well as instructions for each section.

To begin, you should note the following items in the configuration file:

1. Search for the string hdimage, and make sure no comment symbol (#) is at the beginning of that line, so it appears as follows:

```
disk { image "/var/lib/dosemu/hdimage" }    # use diskimage file.
```

This line refers to a Linux file `/var/lib/dosemu/hdimage` that serves as a disk under DOSEMU. The name `hdimage` stands for *hard disk image*. The first `disk` line in the `/etc/dosemu.conf` line defines the C drive under DOSEMU. When you install DOSEMU, the installation program also creates a `/varlib/dosemu/hdimage` file you can use as the hard disk image.

2. If you have a DOS partition you want to access under DOSEMU, uncomment an appropriate line (or add a new one with the correct name of your DOS partition). My system's DOS partition is `/dev/hda1`, so I have the following disk line uncommented in `/etc/dosemu.conf`:

```
disk { partition "/dev/hda1" readonly }    # 1st partition on 1st IDE.
```

This partition will then become the D drive under DOSEMU.

3. Search for `fd0` and make sure the floppy disk devices `/dev/fd0` (first floppy drive) and `/dev/fd1` (second floppy drive) are the correct size (`threeinch` or `fiveinch`). My system has only one 3.5-inch floppy drive, so I have only one uncommented line in the FLOPPY DISKS section of the `/etc/dosemu.conf` file:

```
floppy { device /dev/fd0 threeinch }
```

The `/etc/dosemu.conf` file contains many more options, but you needn't configure everything right now. The first step is to get DOSEMU running. Then you can turn to specific items, such as how to make the printer work and how to access the serial port under DOSEMU.

Initializing the hard disk image

You can think of the hard disk image as being a raw hard disk: you have to format it and make it bootable before DOSEMU can boot off that hard disk image. To do this, you need a real MS-DOS boot floppy disk. You can create the boot floppy by using the MS-DOS installation that came with your PC.

To create a DOS boot floppy, you first have to boot your system under MS-DOS (or Windows 95) and then perform these steps:

1. Put a floppy disk in your A drive (all previous contents of the floppy will be destroyed when you format it) and type the command `FORMAT A: /S`. MS-DOS prompts you with the following message:

```
Insert new diskette for drive A:
and press ENTER when ready...
```

2. Press Enter, because you already have the floppy disk in the A drive. MS-DOS formats the disk and places the necessary operating-system files on it (that's what the `/S` option of the `FORMAT` command does).

3. MS-DOS also prompts you for a Volume label. You can simply press Enter in response.

4. DOS asks whether you want to format another floppy disk. Type `N` to indicate you are done formatting.

5. Copy `FDISK.EXE` and `SYS.COM` files to the floppy disk. You need these two programs to initialize the hard disk image under DOSEMU. Use the following commands to copy the `FDISK.EXE` and `SYS.COM` programs to the floppy in the A drive:

```
c:
cd \windows\command (typically, the MS-DOS files are in this
directory)
copy fdisk.exe a:
copy sys.com a:
```

After you prepare the DOS boot floppy, restart Linux on your system, using your favorite method (LILO or a Linux boot floppy). Then log in as `root`.

Next, put the DOS boot floppy in the A drive and type the following command at the shell prompt:

```
dos -A
```

After a brief pause, DOSEMU should boot off the A drive and you are left with an `A:\>` prompt, as shown in Figure 7-3.

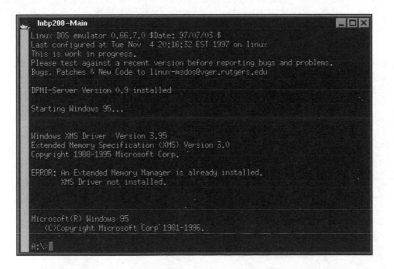

Figure 7-3: Starting DOSEMU for the first time from a DOS boot floppy disk

Type the following DOS command:

```
A:\> dir c:
```

DOSEMU should display the contents of the C drive—actually, the hard disk image file DOSEMU treats as the C drive. Your next task is to make this C drive bootable. To initialize the hard disk image (the C drive), perform these steps:

1. To initialize the master boot record of the C drive, type the following command:

   ```
   A:\> fdisk /mbr
   ```

You might get a few warning messages; you can ignore those messages.

2. Next, transfer the necessary system files to the hard disk image using the following command:

   ```
   A:\> sys c:
   System transferred
   ```

After these two steps, the hard disk image (C drive in DOSEMU) should be bootable. Before you can test the hard disk image, exit DOSEMU by using this command:

```
A:\> c:\exitemu
```

Starting DOSEMU from the hard disk image

After you get your hard disk image file set up properly, you should be able to boot directly from that image. Remove the DOS boot floppy from your system's A drive and type **dos** at the shell prompt. DOSEMU should boot from the hard disk image and display the familiar C:\> prompt, as shown in Figure 7-4.

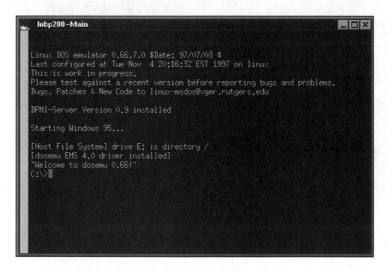

Figure 7-4: Booting DOSEMU from the hard disk image

In Figure 7-4, you see DOSEMU displaying some information and then booting from drive C. You get the C:\> prompt, from which you can type DOS commands.

If you type dir, you see the hard disk image that works as the C drive is about 1MB. That's adequate, though, because you can access your real DOS partition as well as your Linux partition. The C drive is used only to boot MS-DOS.

Tip

The initial DOSEMU message indicates the drive letter assigned to the Linux file system (the / directory). For example, the message in Figure 7-4 says the / directory is drive E. This means if you type dir e:, you should see the contents of the Linux root (/) directory.

If you have a DOS partition on your hard disk and you added an appropriate disk line in the /etc/dosemu.conf file, that partition should be the D drive under DOSEMU. Try the command dir d: and see what DOSEMU shows you. You should be able to run some simple DOS programs (such as the MS-DOS editor) from your hard disk's DOS partition. Type d:\windows\command\edit sample.txt to start the MS-DOS editor and edit the sample.txt file. Figure 7-5 shows the MS-DOS editor running under a DOSEMU session in an xterm window.

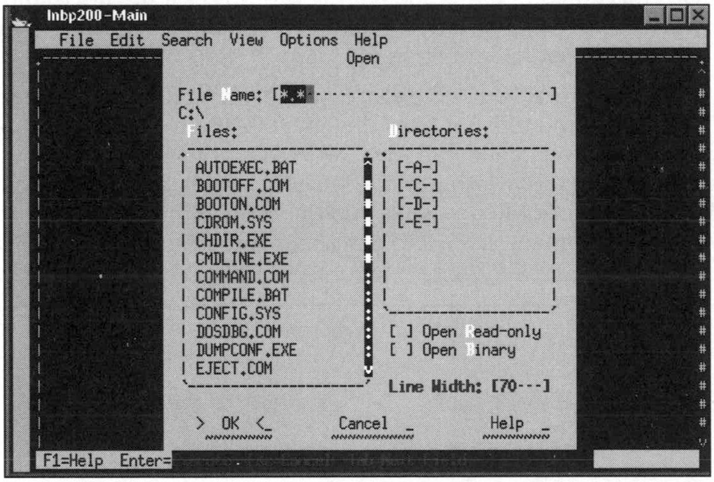

Figure 7-5: The Open dialog box of the MS-DOS editor running under DOSEMU in an xterm window

Figure 7-5 shows the editor's Open dialog box (press Alt+F and then type *o* to open this dialog). To quit the editor, press Alt+F and then type *x*.

You can get a DOS-like screen if you start DOSEMU from a text-mode console instead of from an xterm window.

When you are ready to quit DOSEMU, type **c:\exitemu** at the DOS prompt.

Summary

If your PC has a DOS partition in addition to the Linux partition or if you work with DOS floppy disks, you can access the DOS files directly from Linux. You also can use the `mtools` utility program's to format and use a DOS floppy disk directly from Linux. In addition, an ongoing project — DOSEMU — provides a DOS emulator that enables you to run DOS programs directly in Linux.

By reading this chapter, you learn the following:

▶ Linux has built-in support for the MS-DOS file system. You can use the `mount` command to access a DOS partition or a DOS floppy from Linux. After mounting a DOS file system at a directory in your Linux system, you can use Linux commands such as `ls` and `cp` to manipulate the DOS files.

▶ When you installed Linux, following the directions in Chapter 1, you also installed a set of utility programs known as `mtools`. The `mtools` programs provide a convenient way to access MS-DOS files, especially floppy disks, because you can use `mtools` commands without first having to mount the floppy disk. The `mtools` utilities include commands such as `mdir` and `mcopy` that work like the DOS commands `DIR` and `COPY`.

▶ This book's companion CD-ROM also includes a preliminary release of the DOSEMU DOS emulator that uses the Intel 80×86 processor's virtual-86 mode to run MS-DOS. You can install DOSEMU when you install Linux. Otherwise, you can install DOSEMU from the CD-ROM by using the `rpm -i` command. You need an MS-DOS boot floppy to set up DOSEMU. Although it is in its early stages of development, DOSEMU can run many existing DOS programs.

Chapter 8

Scripting in Linux with Tcl/Tk

In This Chapter

▶ Looking at Tcl/Tk

▶ Understanding Tcl syntax

▶ Writing Tcl scripts

▶ Building graphical interfaces for Tcl scripts with Tk

▶ Learning to use Tcl/Tk through examples

If you are already a C and X Window System programmer, you will be surprised by the ease with which you can create graphical applications with (Tool Command Language (Tcl) and its associated X toolkit, Tk — collectively referred to as *Tcl/Tk* (pronounced *tickle/tee kay*). Tcl is a scripting language like Perl. The biggest strength of Tcl is its X toolkit, Tk, which enables you to develop scripts with graphical user interfaces.

When I started using Tcl/Tk, I was pleasantly surprised by how few lines of Tcl/Tk it takes to create a functioning graphical interface. To a newcomer, a Tcl/Tk script still looks rather complicated, but if you have used C-based toolkits such as Xt and Motif to write programs, you can appreciate the high-level nature of Tk. Creating a user-interface component such as a button is much simpler in Tk than in Motif. You still must tend to many details, such as how to lay out the components of the user interface, but you can see results faster than with a C program that calls the Motif library.

Tip

If you have never programmed, don't avoid this chapter out of fear. The examples in this chapter teach you the basics of Tcl and Tk. You are bound to become a believer in Tcl/Tk after you see how quickly you can use Tcl/Tk's interpreter to create applications with graphical interfaces.

Whence Tcl/Tk?

John Ousterhout created Tcl and Tk when he was at the University of California at Berkeley. Tcl first appeared in 1989; Tk followed in 1991. Tcl/Tk are both freely available for unrestricted use, including commercial use. At this writing, the Tcl version is 8.0; Tk is 8.0. This book's companion CD-ROM includes Tcl/Tk.

Introducing Tcl

The creator of Tcl, John Ousterhout, intended Tcl to be a simple scripting language whose interpreter could be linked with any C program so the C program could use Tcl scripts. The term *embeddable* refers to this property of Tcl: the capability of any C program to use the Tcl interpreter and run Tcl scripts.

The following sections provide an overview of Tcl, its syntax, and some of its important commands. Because Tcl underlies the Tk toolkit, you should become familiar with Tcl before jumping into Tk (Tk is undoubtedly more fun because you can use it to create graphical interfaces).

Your first Tcl script

In Chapter 6, you saw how to write shell scripts and Perl scripts. You write Tcl scripts the same way. Unlike Perl, Tcl includes a shell — an interactive interpreter of Tcl commands. The Tcl shell program's name is `tclsh`; it should be in the `/usr/bin` directory.

When you log in, the `PATH` environment variable should include the `/usr/bin` directory. Thus, you can start the Tcl shell by typing `tclsh`. A percent sign (%) appears on the next line; this is the Tcl shell program's prompt. To see the version of Tcl you have, type **info tclversion** at the Tcl shell prompt. The Tcl shell program responds by printing the version of Tcl:

```
tclsh
% info tclversion
8.0
%
```

Now you can interactively try the following Tcl program, which prints `Hello, World!` on the standard output (the display screen):

```
% puts "Hello, World!"
Hello, World!
%
```

Type `exit` to quit the Tcl shell (`tclsh`).

Note

I didn't show the shell prompt in previous chapters, but I show the Tcl prompt (%) in this chapter's listings. This is because the Tcl prompt looks different from the Bash prompt. This should tell you that you aren't working in Bash.

The Tcl shell immediately processes the Tcl command you enter and displays the results; then it prompts you for the next input. At this point, you can type **exit** to quit the Tcl shell.

To prepare and run a Tcl script, follow these steps:

1. Use a text editor to enter and save the following lines in a file named `hellotcl` (this file will be the Tcl script):

```
#!/usr/bin/tclsh
# A simple Tcl script
puts "Hello, World!"
```

2. Type the following command at the shell prompt to make the `hellotcl` file executable (that's what the `+x` in the `chmod` command means):

```
chmod +x hellotcl
```

3. To run the `hellotcl` script, type the following at the shell prompt:

```
hellotcl
Hello, World!
```

You use these basic steps to create and run any Tcl script. You still have to learn the nuances of Tcl syntax, of course—as well as many rules. This section gets you started with an overview of Tcl.

More on Tcl/Tk

This chapter provides an overview of Tcl and Tk, highlights many key points, and shows simple examples. But there isn't enough room in this chapter to list all the information you must know to exploit the power of Tcl and Tk fully. Because of Tcl/Tk's popularity, you can find quite a few resources about it, ranging from books to Internet sites. Following is a short list of Tcl/Tk resources:

Books. Two prominent books on Tcl/Tk are available. The first is *Tcl and the Tk Toolkit,* by John K. Ousterhout, the originator of Tcl and Tk. John's book provides a broad overview of Tcl and Tk, including an explanation of the way Tcl command strings are parsed. The other book is *Practical Programming in Tcl and Tk, Second Edition,* by Brent B. Welch. This book provides more Tcl and Tk examples. Another recent addition to the list of Tcl/Tk books is *Tcl/Tk for Dummies* (IDG Books Worldwide, 1997) by Tim Webster and Alex Francis.

Internet resources. Several FTP and Web sites contain the latest Tcl/Tk distributions and information about Tcl/Tk development. The following list uses Uniform Resource Locator (URL) syntax. You can use a Web browser (such as Netscape, Mosaic, or Lynx) and enter the URL as shown. The browser then displays appropriate information about the contents of the site.

ftp://ftp.smli.com/pub/tcl *(Tcl/Tk master distribution site)*

http://www.scriptics.com/ *(John Ousterhout's new company)*

http://www.tclconsortium.org/ *(Tcl/Tk consortium)*

http://www.neosoft.com/tcl/ *(Tcl contributed sources archive)*

Other FTP sites with Tcl/Tk distributions:

ftp://ftp.ibp.fr/pub/tcl/distrib

ftp://sunsite.doc.ic.ac.uk/packages/tcl/

ftp://ftp.luth.se/pub/unix/tcl/ftp.smli.com_mirror/

ftp://ftp.funet.fi/pub/languages/tcl/

Tcl overview

True to its name (Tool Command Language), Tcl consists of a set of commands you can combine according to a set of rules. To write Tcl scripts, you have to understand two broad subjects:

- *Tcl syntax*. Tcl syntax is the set of rules the Tcl command interpreter follows when it interprets a *command string* (a line that contains a command and its arguments).

- *Tcl commands*. Although the syntax is the same for all commands, each individual Tcl command is meant to perform a specific task. To exploit Tcl fully, you must know what commands are available and what each command does. The Tcl command set can be extended by applications. In fact, Tk itself is an extension of Tcl; Tk adds commands that manipulate components of graphical user interfaces.

Start by learning the Tcl syntax, a handful of rules that determine the way each Tcl command is parsed. Because Tcl has many commands, learning all the commands can take a while. Even after you become proficient in the Tcl syntax and a small set of commands, you may need to keep a reference manual nearby so you can check the exact format of the arguments each command requires.

Tcl commands include the following basic programming facilities that you expect from any programming language:

- *Variables* that store data. Each variable has a name and a value. Tcl also enables you to define arrays of variables.

- *Expressions* that combine values of variables with operators. An expression might add two variables, for example. Tcl uses the `expr` command to evaluate expressions.

- *Control-flow commands* that allow commands to be executed in various order, depending on the value of some expression. Tcl provides commands such as `for`, `foreach`, `break`, `continue`, `if`, `while`, and `return` to implement flow control in Tcl scripts.

- *Procedures* that let you group several commands and give them a name. Procedures also accept arguments. Tcl provides the `proc` command to enable you to define procedures. You can use a procedure to execute the same set of commands (usually, with different arguments) by invoking the procedure that represents those commands.

The next few sections provide an overview of the Tcl syntax and the core Tcl commands.

Basic Tcl syntax

To understand the basic Tcl syntax, you must know a bit about how the Tcl interpreter processes each command string. The steps are as follows:

1. The Tcl interpreter *parses* (breaks down) the command string into words.

2. The Tcl interpreter applies rules to substitute values of variables and replace certain commands with their results.

3. The Tcl interpreter executes the commands, taking the first word as the command name and calling a command procedure to execute the command. That command procedure receives the rest of the words as strings.

When writing Tcl command strings, you must use *white space* (space or tab) to separate a command's name from its arguments. A new line or a semicolon (;) marks the end of a command string. You can put two commands on the same line, provided you insert a semicolon after the first command. Thus, you can use the following:

```
puts Hello, ; puts World!
Hello,
World!
```

The resulting output appears on separate lines, because the `puts` command adds a new line by default.

Use a backslash at the end of a line to continue that command string on the next line. Thus, you could write a command string to print `Hello, World!` as follows:

```
puts "Hello, \
World!"
```

Substitutions

The Tcl interpreter replaces certain parts of the command string with an equivalent value. If you precede a variable's name with a dollar sign ($), for example, the interpreter replaces that word with the variable's value. As you learn in the "Variables" section, you can define a variable in a Tcl script by using the `set` command, as follows:

```
set count 100
```

This command defines a variable named `count` with the value `100`. Now suppose you type the following:

```
puts $count
```

The interpreter first replaces `$count` with its value, which is 100. Thus, that command string becomes

```
puts 100
```

When the interpreter executes the `puts` command, it prints 100. This is an example of *variable substitution*.

In all, the Tcl interpreter supports three kinds of substitutions:

- *Variable substitution.* As the preceding example shows, if the Tcl interpreter finds a dollar sign ($), it replaces the dollar sign as well as the following variable name with that variable's value.

- *Backslash substitution.* You can embed special characters, such as new line and tab, in a word by using backslash substitution. You simply type a backslash, followed by one or more characters; the interpreter replaces that sequence with a nonprintable character. These sequences are patterned after ANSI Standard C's escape sequences. Table 8-1, which follows this list, summarizes the backslash sequences the Tcl interpreter understands.

- *Command substitution.* This type of substitution refers to the mechanism that enables you to specify a command be evaluated and replaced by its result before the interpreter processes the command string. The command `string length "Hello, World!"`, for example, returns 13, which is the length of the string. To set a variable named `len` to the length of this string, type the following:

```
set len [string length "Hello, World!"]
```

The interpreter processes the command inside the square brackets and replaces that part of the command string with the value of the command. Thus, this command becomes

```
set len 13
```

and the `set` command sets the `len` variable to 13.

Table 8-1   Backslash sequences in Tcl

Sequence	Replacement character *
\a	The bell character (0x7)
\b	Backspace (0x8)
\f	Form feed (0xc)
\n	New line (0xa)
\r	Carriage return (0xd)
\t	Horizontal tab (0x9)
\v	Vertical tab (0xb)
\<newline>	Replace the new line and white space on next line with a single space

Sequence	Replacement character *
\\	Interpret as a single backslash (\)
\"	Interpret as double quotation marks (")
\ooo	Use the value specified by the octal digits (up to three)
\xhh	Use the value specified by the hexadecimal digits (up to two)

* Hexadecimal values shown in parentheses

Comments

A pound sign (#) marks the start of a comment; the Tcl interpreter disregards the rest of the line, beginning with the pound sign. Tcl does, however, have a peculiar requirement on comments: you cannot start a comment within a command. The command string must end before you start a comment.

To understand this problem, try the following Tcl command at the `tclsh` prompt:

```
% puts "Hello, World!" # This is a comment
wrong # args: should be "puts" ?-nonewline? ?field? string
```

Essentially, the `puts` command processes the remainder of the line and complains about the number of arguments. The solution is to put a semicolon just before the pound sign (#), as follows:

```
% puts "Hello, World!" ;# This is a comment
Hello, World!
```

Tip

If you put comments at the end of a Tcl command, remember to precede the pound sign (#) with a semicolon (;). The semicolon terminates the preceding command and enables you to start a comment.

Braces and double quotation marks

You can use braces ({...}) and double quotation marks ("...") to group several words. Use double quotes to pass arguments that contain an embedded space or a semicolon, which otherwise ends the command. The quotes are not part of the group of words; they simply serve to mark the beginning and end of a group of words. Following are some examples of using double quotes to group words:

```
% puts "Hello, World!"
Hello, World!
% puts "Enter 1; otherwise file won't be saved!"
Enter 1; otherwise file won't be saved!
```

When you group words with double quotes, all types of substitutions still take place, as illustrated by the following example:

```
% puts "There are [string length hello] characters in 'hello'"
There are 5 characters in 'hello'
```

The Tcl interpreter replaces everything inside the brackets with the result of the `string length hello` command, whose return value is the number of characters in `hello` (5).

You also can use braces to group words. The Tcl interpreter does not perform any substitution when you group words with braces (if you enclose words in double quotes, the interpreter does perform substitution). Consider the preceding example with braces instead of double quotes:

```
% puts {There are [string length hello] characters in 'hello'}
There are [string length hello] characters in 'hello'
```

As the result shows, the Tcl interpreter simply passes everything, unchanged, as a single argument.

Tip

Use braces as a grouping mechanism when you have to pass expressions to control commands, such as `while` loops, `for` loops, or procedures.

Variables

Everything is a string in Tcl. Variable names as well as values are stored as strings. To define a variable, use the built-in Tcl command `set`. The following commands, for example, define the variable `book` as "Linux SECRETS, Second Edition"; the variable `year` as 1998; and the variable `price` as $49.99:

```
set book "Linux SECRETS, Second Edition"
set year 1998
set price \$49.99
```

To refer to the value of a variable, append a dollar sign ($) to the variable's name. To print the variable `book`, therefore, use the following format:

```
% puts $book
Linux SECRETS, Second Edition
```

If you use `set` with a single argument, `set` returns the value of that argument. Thus, `set book` is equivalent to `$book`, as the following example shows:

```
% puts [set book]
Linux SECRETS, Second Edition
```

Expressions

You can write expressions by combining variables with mathematical operators, such as + (add), - (subtract), * (multiply), and / (divide). Here are some examples of expressions:

```
set count 1
$count+1
$count + 5 - 2
2 + 3.5
```

You can use numbers as well as variable names in expressions. Use white space to enhance readability. And use parentheses to specify how you want an expression to be evaluated.

In addition to the basic mathematical operators, Tcl includes several built-in mathematical functions such as `sin`, `cos`, `tan`, `log`, and `sqrt`. Call these functions just as you do in C, with arguments in parentheses, as follows:

```
set angle 1.5
2*sin($angle)
```

You also can use Boolean operators, such as `!` (not), `&&` (and), and or (`||`). Comparison operators — such as `<` (less than), `>` (greater than), `<=` (less than or equal to), `==` (equal to), and `!=` (not equal to) — also are available. Expressions that use Boolean or comparison operators evaluate to 1 if true and 0 if false. You can write expressions such as the following:

```
count == 10
angle < 3.1415
```

Expressions are not commands by themselves. You can use expressions as arguments only for commands that accept expressions as arguments. The `if` and `while` commands, for example, expect expressions as arguments.

Tcl also provides the `expr` command to evaluate an expression. The following example shows how you might evaluate an expression in a Tcl command:

```
% set angle 1.5
1.5
% puts "Result = [expr 2*sin($angle)]"
Result = 1.99499
```

Although Tcl stores everything as a string, you have to use numbers where numbers are expected. If `book` is defined as `"Linux SECRETS, Second Edition"`, for example, you cannot write an expression `$book+1`, because it does not make sense.

Control-flow commands

Tcl's control-flow commands enable you to specify the order in which the Tcl interpreter executes commands. You can use the `if` command to test the value of an expression and, if the value is true (nonzero), you can make the interpreter execute a set of commands. Tcl includes control-flow commands similar to those in C, such as `if`, `for`, `while`, and `switch`. This section provides an overview of the control-flow commands.

A Tcl control-flow command typically has a *command block* (a group of commands) that the control-flow command executes after evaluating an expression. To avoid substitutions (such as replacing variables with their values), you must enclose the entire command block in braces. The following `if-else` control-flow commands illustrate the style of braces that works properly:

```
if { expression } {
# Commands to execute when expression is true
    command_1
    command_2
} else {
# Commands to execute when expression is false
# ...
}
```

You should follow this style of braces religiously in Tcl scripts. In particular, remember to include a space between the control-flow command (such as if) and the left brace ({) that follows the command.

The if command

In its simplest form, Tcl's if command evaluates an expression and executes a set of commands if that expression is nonzero (true). You might compare the value of a variable with a threshold as follows:

```
if { $errorCount > 25 } {
    puts "Too many errors!"
}
```

You can add an else clause to process commands if the expression evaluates to zero (false). Following is an example:

```
if { $user == "root" } {
    puts "Starting system setup ..."
} else {
    puts "Sorry, you must be \"root\" to run this program!"
}
```

Tcl's if command can be followed by zero or more elseif commands if you need to perform more complicated tests, such as the following:

```
puts -nonewline "Enter version number: "   ;# prompt user
set version [gets stdin]                    ;# read version number

if { $version >= 10 } {
    puts "No upgrade necessary"
} elseif { $version >= 6 && $version < 9} {
    puts "Standard upgrade"
} elseif { $version >= 3 && $version < 6} {
    puts "Reinstall"
} else {
    puts "Sorry, cannot upgrade"
}
```

The while command

The while command executes a block of commands until an expression becomes false. The following while loop keeps reading lines from the standard input until the user presses Ctrl+D:

```
while { [gets stdin line]  != -1 } {
    puts $line
# Do whatever you need to do with $line
}
```

Although this `while` command looks simple, you should realize it has two arguments inside two sets of braces. The first argument is the expression; the second argument contains the Tcl commands to be executed if the expression is true. You must always use braces to enclose both of these arguments. The braces prevent the Tcl interpreter from evaluating the contents; the `while` command is the one that processes what's inside the braces.

If you use a variable to keep count inside a `while` loop, you can use the `incr` command to increment that variable. You can skip to the end of a loop by using the `continue` command; the `break` command exits the loop. The following Tcl script uses a `while` loop to add all the numbers from 1 to 10 except 5:

```
#!/usr/bin/tclsh

set i 0
set sum 0

while { 1 } {
    incr i                       ;# increment i
    if {$i == 5} { continue }    ;# skip if i is 5
    if {$i > 10} {break }        ;# end loop if i exceed 10
    set sum [expr $sum+$i]       ;# otherwise, add i to sum
}
puts "Sum = $sum";
```

When you run this script, it should display the following result:

```
Sum = 50
```

The for command

Tcl's `for` command takes four arguments, which you should type in the following manner:

```
for {expr_1} { expr_2} { expr_3} {
    commands
}
```

The `for` command evaluates *expr_1* once at the beginning of the loop and executes the commands inside the final pair of braces until the expression *expr_2* evaluates to zero. The `for` command evaluates the third expression — *expr_3* — after each execution of the commands. You can omit any of the expressions, but you must use all the braces. The following example uses a `for` loop to add the numbers from 1 to 10:

```
#!/usr/bin/tclsh
for {set i 0; set sum 0} {$i <= 10} {set sum [expr $sum+$i]; incr i} {
}
puts "Sum = $sum";
```

When you run this script, it displays the following result:

```
Sum = 55
```

The foreach command

You may not have seen a command like `foreach` in C, but `foreach` is handy when you want to perform some action for each value in a list of variables. You can add a set of numbers with the `foreach` command as follows:

```
set sum 0
foreach i { 1 2 3 4 5 6 7 8 9 10} {
    set sum [expr $sum+$i]
}
puts "Sum = $sum"
```

If you have a list in a variable, you can use that variable's value in place of the list shown within the first pair of braces. Following is a `foreach` loop that echoes the strings in a list:

```
set users "root naba"
foreach user $users {
    puts "$user"
}
```

The switch command

Tcl's `switch` command is different from C's `switch` statement. Instead of evaluating a mathematical expression, Tcl's `switch` command compares a string with a set of patterns and executes a set of commands, depending on which pattern matches. The pattern is often expressed in terms of a regular expression.

Cross-Reference

See Chapter 6 for an introduction to regular expressions.

The following script illustrates the syntax and a typical use of the `switch` command:

```
#!/usr/bin/tclsh
# This script reads commands from the user and processes
# the commands using a switch statement

set prompt "Enter command (\"quit\" to exit): "

puts -nonewline "$prompt"; flush stdout

while { [gets stdin cmd]  != -1 } {
    switch -exact -- $cmd {
        quit    { puts "Bye!"; exit}
        start   { puts "Started"}
        stop    { puts "Stopped"}
        draw    { puts "Draw.."}
```

```
            default { puts "Unknown command: $cmd" }
    }
# prompt user again
    puts -nonewline $prompt; flush stdout
}
```

Following is a sample session with this script (user input is in boldface):

```
Enter command ("quit" to exit): help
Unknown command: help
Enter command ("quit" to exit): start
Started
Enter command ("quit" to exit): stop
Stopped
Enter command ("quit" to exit): quit
Bye!
```

As this example shows, the `switch` statement enables you to compare a string with a set of other strings and then to activate a set of commands, depending on which pattern matches. In this example, the string is `$cmd` (which is initialized by reading the user's input with a `gets` command) and the patterns are literal strings: `quit`, `start`, `stop`, and `draw`. Following is a case of an exact match, as indicated by the `-exact` flag on the first line of the `switch` command:

```
switch -exact -- $cmd {
  ...
}
```

The two hyphens (`--`) immediately after the `-exact` flag mark the end of the flags. When you use the `switch` command, always use the double hyphens at the end of the flag to prevent the test string from matching a flag inadvertently.

You can use the `switch` command with the `-regexp` flag to compare a string with a regular expression, as in the following example:

```
# Assume that $cmd is the string to be matched

switch -regexp -- $cmd {
    ^q.*    { puts "Bye!"; exit}
    ^x.*    { puts "Something x..."}
    ^y.*    { puts "Something y..."}
    ^z.*    { puts "Something z..."}
    default { puts "Unknown command: $cmd" }
}
```

In this example, each regular expression has a similar form. The pattern `^z.*` means any string that starts with a single `z`, followed by any number of other characters.

Tcl procedures

You can use the `proc` command to add your own commands. Such commands are called *procedures*; the Tcl interpreter treats them just as though they were built-in Tcl commands. The following example shows how easy it is to write a procedure in Tcl:

```
#!/usr/bin/tclsh

proc total items {
    set sum 0
    foreach i $items {
        set sum [expr $sum+$i]
    }
    return $sum
}

set counts "5 4 3 5"
puts "Total = [total $counts]"
```

When you run this script, it prints the following:

```
Total = 17
```

In this example, the procedure's name is `total` and it takes a list of numbers as the argument. The procedure receives the arguments in the variable named `items`. The body of the procedure extracts each item and returns a sum of the items. Thus, to add the numbers from 1 to 10, you have to call the `total` procedure as follows:

```
set sum1_10 [total {1 2 3 4 5 6 7 8 9 10}]
```

Secret

In a Tcl procedure, the argument name `args` has a special significance; if you use `args` as the argument name, you can pass a variable number of arguments to the procedure. If you change the `total` procedure's argument name from `items` to `args`, for example, you can call `total` this way:

```
set sum1_10 [total 1 2 3 4 5 6 7 8 9 10]   ;# notice variable number
of arguments
```

If you want to access a *global variable* (a variable defined outside a procedure) in the Tcl procedure, you have to use the `global` command inside the procedure. The `global` command makes a global variable visible within the scope of a procedure. If a variable named `theCanvas` holds the current drawing area in a Tk (Tcl's X toolkit) program, a procedure that uses the `theCanvas` must include the following command:

```
global theCanvas
```

Built-in Tcl commands

You have seen many Tcl commands in the preceding examples. Knowing the types of commands available in Tcl helps you decide which commands are most appropriate for the task at hand. Although this chapter cannot cover all Tcl commands, Table 8-2 summarizes Tcl's built-in commands.

 Tip

To get online help on any Tcl command listed in Table 8-2, type **man n**, followed by the command name. To get online help on Tcl's `file` command, for example, type **man n file**.

Table 8-2	Built-in Tcl commands
Command	**Action**
append	Appends an argument to a variable's value.
array	Performs various operations on an array variable.
break	Exits a loop command (such as `while` and `for`).
catch	Executes a script and traps errors to prevents errors from reaching the Tcl interpreter.
cd	Changes the current working directory.
close	Closes an open file.
concat	Joins two or more lists in a single list.
continue	Immediately begins the next iteration of a `for` or `while` loop.
eof	Checks to see whether end-of-file is reached in an open file.
error	Generates an error.
eval	Concatenates lists (as `concat` does) and then evaluates the resulting list as a Tcl script.
exec	Starts one or more processes that execute the command's arguments.
exit	Terminates the Tcl script.
expr	Evaluates an expression.
file	Checks filenames and attributes.
flush	Flushes buffered output to a file.
for	Implements a `for` loop.
foreach	Performs a specified action for each element in a list.
format	Formats output and stores it in a string (as the `sprintf` function in C does).
gets	Reads a line from a file.
glob	Returns the names of files that match a pattern (such as `*.tcl`).
global	Accesses global variables.

(continued)

Table 8-2	*(Continued)*
Command	**Action**
history	Provides access to the *history list* (the list of past Tcl commands).
if	Tests an expression and executes commands if the expression is true (nonzero).
incr	Increments the value of a variable.
info	Returns internal information about the Tcl interpreter.
join	Creates a string by joining all items in a list.
lappend	Appends elements to a list.
lindex	Returns an element from a list at a specified index. (Index 0 refers to the first element.)
linsert	Inserts elements into a list before a specified index.
list	Creates a list comprised of the specified arguments.
llength	Returns the number of elements in a list.
lrange	Returns a specified range of adjacent elements from a list.
lreplace	Replaces elements in a list with new elements.
lsearch	Searches a list for a particular element.
lsort	Sorts a list in a specified order.
open	Opens a file and returns a file identifier.
pid	Returns the process identifier (ID).
proc	Defines a Tcl procedure.
puts	Sends characters to a file.
pwd	Returns the current working directory.
read	Reads a specified number of bytes from a file. (You can read the entire file in a single read.)
regexp	Matches a regular expression with a string.
regsub	Substitutes one regular expression pattern for another.
rename	Renames or deletes a command.
return	Returns a value from a Tcl procedure.
scan	Parses a string, using format specifiers patterned after C's sscanf function.
seek	Changes the *access position* (where the next input or output operation occurs) in an open file.
set	Sets a variable's value or returns its current value.
source	Reads a file and processes it as a Tcl script.
split	Breaks a string into a Tcl list.

Command	Action
string	Performs various operations on strings.
switch	Processes one of several blocks of commands, depending on which pattern matches a specified string.
tell	Returns the current access position for an open file.
time	Returns the total time needed to execute a script.
trace	Executes a specified set of Tcl commands whenever a variable is accessed.
unknown	Handles any unknown command. (The Tcl interpreter calls this command whenever it encounters any unknown command.)
unset	Removes the definition of one or more variables.
uplevel	Executes a script in a different context.
upvar	References a variable outside a procedure. (Used to implement the pass-by-reference style of procedure call, in which changing a procedure argument changes the original copy of the argument.)
while	Implements a `while` loop that executes a set of Tcl commands repeatedly as long as an expression evaluates to a nonzero value (true).

String manipulation in Tcl

If you browse through the Tcl commands listed in Table 8-2, you find quite a few — such as `append`, `join`, `split`, `string`, `regexp`, and `regsub` — that operate on strings. This section summarizes a few string-manipulation commands.

When you set a variable to a string, the Tcl interpreter considers that string a single entity, even if that string contains any embedded spaces or special characters. Sometimes, you need to access the string as a list of items. The `split` command is a handy way to separate a string into its components. The lines in the /etc/passwd file, for example, look like this:

```
root:NpYzwIedcGAO.:0:0:root:/root:/bin/bash
```

The line is composed of fields separated by colons (:). Suppose you want to extract the first field from each line (because that field contains the login name). You can read the file a line at a time, split each line into a list, and extract the first element (the item at index 0) of each list. Following is a Tcl script that does this:

```
#!/usr/bin/tclsh

set fid [open "/etc/passwd" r]         ;# Open password file for read-
only access

while { [gets $fid line] != -1 } {
    set fields [split $line ":"]       ;# this command splits the string
into a list
# Just print out the first field
```

```
    puts [lindex $fields 0]              ;# lindex extracts an item at a
specified index
}
```

When you run this script, it should print all the login names from your system's /etc/passwd file.

The join command is the opposite of split; you can use it to create a single string from the items in a list. Suppose you have a list of six items, defined as follows:

```
set x {1 2 3 4 5 6}
```

When you join the elements, you can select what character you want to use between fields. To join the elements without anything in between them, use the following format:

```
set y [join $x ""]
```

Now the y string is "123456".

The string command is actually a group of commands for working with strings, because the first argument of string specifies the operation to be performed. The string compare command, for example, compares two strings, returning zero when the two strings are identical. A return value of –1 indicates the first string argument is lexicographically less than the second one, meaning it appears before the second one in a dictionary. Similarly, a 1 return value indicates the first string is lexicographically greater than the second one. Thus, you might use string compare in an if command as follows:

```
if { [string compare $command "quit"] == 0} {
    puts "Exiting..."
    exit 0
}
```

Table 8-3 lists the operations you can perform with Tcl's string command.

Table 8-3 Operations you can perform with String in Tcl

String command	Description
string compare string1 string2	Returns -1, 0, 1 after comparing strings
string first string1 string2	Returns index of the first occurrence of string1 in string2
string index string charIndex	Returns the character at index charIndex
string last string1 string2	Returns index of the last occurrence of string1 in string2
string length string	Returns the length of the string
string match pattern string	Returns 1 if the pattern matches the string, and 0 if it does not

String command	Description
`string range string first last`	Returns a range of characters from `string`
`string tolower string`	Returns the string in lowercase characters
`string toupper string`	Returns the string in uppercase characters
`string trim string chars`	the string after trimming the leading or trailing characters
`string trimleft string chars`	Returns the string after trimming the leading characters
`string trimright string chars`	Returns the string after trimming the trailing characters

Arrays

In Tcl, an *array* is a variable with a string index. An array contains elements; the string index of each element is called the *element name*. In other words, you can access an element of an array by using its name. Internally, Tcl implements arrays with an efficient data structure known as a *hash table*, which allows the Tcl interpreter to look up any array element in a relatively constant period of time.

You declare an array variable by using the `set` command. The following example shows how you might define the `disk_usage` array that holds the amount of disk space used by a system's users:

```
set disk_usage(root)      147178
set disk_usage(naba)      28574
set disk_usage(emily)     55
set disk_usage(ivy)       60
```

After you define the array, you can access its individual elements by element name, as in the following example:

```
set user "naba"
puts "Disk space used by $user = $disk_usage($user)K"
```

Environment variables

Tcl provides the environment variables in a predefined global array named `env`, with the environment-variable names used as element names. In other words, you can look up the value of an environment variable by using the variable name as an index. The following command prints the current PATH:

```
puts "$env(PATH)"
```

You can manipulate the environment variable array just as you do any other variables. You can add a new directory to PATH, for example, as follows:

```
set env(PATH) "$env(PATH):/usr/sbin"
```

Any changes to the environment variable do not affect the parent process (for example, the shell from which you started the Tcl script). Any new processes created by the script by means of the exec command, however, inherit the altered environment variable.

File operations in Tcl

Most of the examples presented so far in this chapter use Tcl's puts command to display output. By default, puts writes to the standard output: the xterm window, when you use *X*. You can write to a file, however, by providing a file identifier as the first argument of puts. To get a file identifier, you first have to open the file, using Tcl's open command. The following example shows how you would open a file, write a line of text to the file, and close the file:

```
set fid [open "testfile" w]   ;# open file named testfile for write
operations
puts $fid "Testing 1..2..3"   ;# use file ID with puts to write to this
file
close $fid                    ;# close the file
```

When you use puts to display a string on the standard output, you needn't provide any file-identifier argument. Also, puts automatically appends a new-line character at the end of the string. If you do not want the new line, use puts with the -nonewline argument, as follows:

```
puts -nonewline "Command> "   ;# -nonewline is good for command prompts
flush stdout ;# make sure output appears right away
```

You have seen the use of the gets command to read a line of input from the standard input. The following invocation of gets, for example, reads a line from the standard input (the command returns when you press Enter):

```
set line [gets stdin]  ;# read a line from standard input
```

The keyword stdin is a predefined file identifier that represents the standard input, which by default is your keyboard. Other predefined file IDs are stdout, for the standard output; and stderr, for the standard error-reporting device. By default, both stdout and stderr are connected to the display screen.

Following is a different way to call gets and read a line of input into a variable named line:

```
gets stdin line        ;# read a line of input into the line variable
```

To read from another file, you first should open the file for reading and then use gets with that file's ID. To read all lines from /etc/passwd and display them on the standard output, for example, you would use the following:

```
set fpass [open "/etc/passwd" r]      ;# open /etc/passwd for reading
while { [gets $fpass line] != -1} {    ;# read the lines in a while loop
    puts $line                        ;# and print each line
}
```

The gets command is good for reading text files because it works one line at a time; in fact, it looks for the new-line character as a marker that indicates the end of a line of text. If you want to read binary data, such as an image file, you should use the read command instead. To read and process a file in 2,048-byte chunks, you might use read in the following manner:

```
# Assume fid is the file ID of an open file
while { ![eof $fid]} {                ;# Until end-of-file is reached
    set buffer [read $fid 2048] ;# read up to 2048 bytes into buffer
# process the data in buffer     ;# and process the buffer
}
```

The second argument of the read command is the maximum number of bytes to be read. If you leave out this argument, the read command reads the entire file. You can use this feature to process entire text files. After reading the contents of the file, use the split command to separate the input data into lines of text. Following is an example:

```
set fid [open "/etc/passwd" r] ;# open file for reading
set buffer [read $fid 100000]   ;# read entire file into buffer
split $buffer "\n"              ;# split buffer into lines
foreach line $buffer {
    puts $line                     ;# do whatever you want with each line
}
```

If you want to process several files (such as all files whose names end with .tcl), use the glob command to expand a filename, such as *.tcl, into a list. Then you can use the open command to open and process each file in the following manner:

```
foreach filename [glob *.tcl] { ;# use glob to create list of
filenames
    puts -nonewline $filename    ;# display the filename (just for
testing)
    set file [open $filename r] ;# open that file
    gets $file line               ;# read the first line
    puts $line                    ;# and print it (this is only for
testing)
# process rest of the file as necessary
    close $file                   ;# remember to close the file
}
```

This is a good example of how to use the glob command in a script.

Executing Linux commands

Instead of duplicating the large number of Linux commands, Tcl simply provides the mechanism to run any Linux command. If you know Linux commands, you can use them directly in Tcl scripts.

You use the `exec` command to execute a Linux command in a Tcl script. In the command's simplest form, you provide the Linux command as an argument of `exec`. To show the current directory listing, for example, type the following:

```
exec ls
```

The output appears on the standard output (the monitor) just as it does when you enter the `ls` command at the shell prompt.

When you run Linux commands from the shell, you can redirect the input and output by using special characters, such as < (redirect input), > (redirect output), and | (pipe). These options are available in Tcl as well, because the `exec` command accepts a complete command line, including any input or output redirections. Thus, you can send the directory listing to a file named `dirlist` as follows:

```
exec ls > dirlist
```

Secret

Tcl's `exec` command does not expand wildcard characters (such as an asterisk) in filenames passed to a Linux command. If you use wildcards in filenames, you have to perform an additional step: you must process the filename specification through the `glob` command to expand it properly before providing the command to `exec`. In addition, you must pass the entire `exec` command to `eval` as an argument. To see a list of all files with names that end in `.tcl`, for example, you must use the `exec` command with `glob` and feed the entire command to `eval` as follows:

```
eval exec ls [glob *.tcl]          ;# this is equivalent to the Linux
command "ls *.tcl"
```

Introducing Tk

Tk (pronounced *tee kay)* is an extension of Tcl. Tk provides an X Window System-based toolkit you can use in Tcl scripts to build graphical user interfaces. As you might expect, Tk provides a set of Tcl commands beyond the core built-in set. You can use these Tk commands to create windows, menus, buttons, and other user-interface components, and to provide a graphical user interface for your Tcl scripts.

Tk uses the X Window System for its graphic components, which are known as widgets. A *widget* represents a user-interface component, such as a button, scrollbar, menu, list, or even an entire text window. Tk widgets provide a Motif-like three-dimensional appearance.

Note

If you are familiar with the Motif widgets, you may know Motif relies on Xt Intrinsics — an X toolkit used to build widgets. Unlike Motif, the Tk toolkit is not based on any other toolkit; it uses only Xlib, which is the C-language library for the X Window System. The upshot is you need only the freely available X Window System to use Tk.

As with anything new, you can best learn Tk through examples, which the following sections provide.

"Hello, World!" in Tk

Tk is a major-enough extension to Tcl to warrant its own shell, called wish (the *wi*ndowing *sh*ell). The wish shell interprets all built-in Tcl commands, as well as the Tk commands. You must start *X* before you can run wish; after all, wish enables you to use *X* to create graphical interfaces.

The wish program should be in the /usr/bin directory, which should be in your PATH environment variable by default. To start wish, all you have to do is type the following at the shell prompt in an xterm window:

```
wish
%
```

The wish program displays its prompt (the percent sign) and also a small window, as shown in the upper-right corner of Figure 8-1.

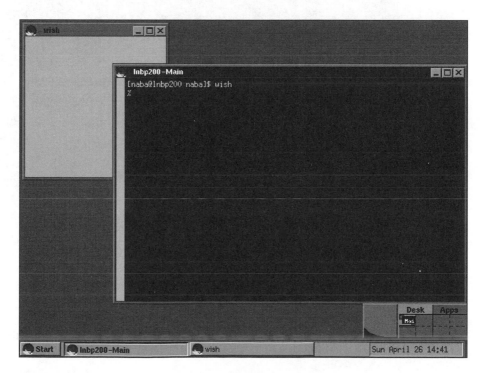

Figure 8-1: The result of running wish from an xterm window

Therefore, `wish` provides an interactive prompt where you can enter Tk commands to create a graphical interface. As `wish` interprets the commands, it displays the resulting graphical interface in the window.

To see how this interactive creation of graphical interface works, try the following commands at the `wish` prompt (type the part shown in boldface):

```
% label .msg -text "Hello, World!"
.msg
% button .bye -text "Bye" -command { exit }
.bye
% pack .msg .bye
%
```

Figure 8-2 shows the result of these commands; `wish` displays a `Hello, World!` label with a `Bye` button below it.

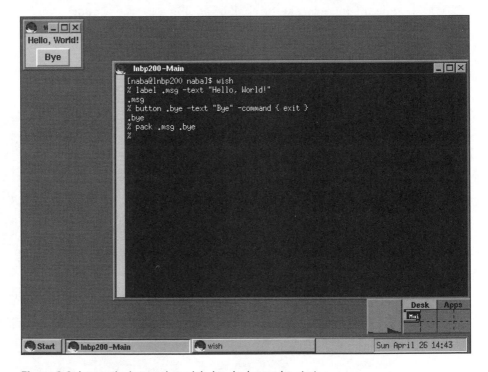

Figure 8-2: Interactively creating a label and a button in `wish`

Notice the label and the button do not appear until you enter the `pack` command. Also, the `wish` window shrinks to a size just large enough to hold the label and the button.

Click the Bye button; the wish program exits. This is because the -command { exit } argument of the button command associates the Tcl command exit with a click of the Bye button.

To create a Tk program or script that displays the Hello, World! label and the Bye button, all you must do is place the Tk commands in a file and add a special line at the beginning to ensure the wish shell processes the file. To do so, follow these steps:

1. Use a text editor to enter and save the following lines in a file named hellotk:

```
#!/usr/bin/wish -f
# A simple Tk script
label .msg -text "Hello, World!"
button .bye -text "Bye" -command { exit }
pack .msg .bye
```

Note

Notice the -f option in the first line. In Tk versions earlier than 4.0, you have to start wish with that option to make sure it processes the script file. The flag is optional in Tk Version 4.0 and later.

2. Type the following command at the shell prompt to make the hellotk file executable (that's what the +x in the chmod command means):

```
chmod +x hellotk
```

3. To run the hellotk script, type the following at the shell prompt in an xterm window:

```
hellotk
```

Figure 8-3 shows the window with a Hello, World! label and the Bye button that should appear when you run the hellotk script. Click the Bye button to close the window and end the script.

Figure 8-3: The result of running the hellotk script

As this example shows, the basic steps for writing a Tk script are the same as those for creating and running any Tcl script. The only difference is the Tk commands generate graphical output.

Tk widget basics

Now that you have been exposed to Tcl, you can begin writing Tk scripts. What you need to know are the Tk commands used to create and configure widgets.

Note

The term *widget* has the same meaning in Tk as it does in an X toolkit such as Motif — it is a user-interface component such as a push button, list box, or dialog box.

In the example in the preceding section, you used a label and a button widget. The command for creating a widget is the same as the widget's name. Therefore, the button command creates a button widget, label creates a label, and so on.

Tk has 13 other widget-creation commands, which are listed in Table 8-3.

Table 8-3   Tk commands for creating widgets

Command	Action
button	Creates a button widget.
canvas	Creates a canvas widget where you can display text, bitmaps, lines, boxes, polygons, and other widgets.
checkbutton	Creates a toggle button and associates it with a Tcl variable.
entry	Creates a one-line text-entry widget.
frame	Creates a frame widget capable of holding other widgets.
label	Creates a read-only, one-line label widget.
listbox	Creates a list-box widget capable of scrolling lines of text.
menu	Creates a menu.
menubutton	Creates a menu-button widget that pops up an associated menu when clicked.
message	Creates a read-only, multiple-line message widget.
radiobutton	Creates a radio-button widget linked to a Tcl variable.
scale	Creates a scale widget that can adjust the value of a variable.
scrollbar	Creates a scrollbar widget you can link to another widget.
text	Creates a text widget where the user can enter and edit text.
toplevel	Creates a *top-level widget* (a widget whose window is a child of the X Window System's root window).

As you create a widget, you can specify many of its characteristics as arguments of the command. You can, for example, create a blue button with a red label (test) and display the button by using the following commands:

```
button .b -text test -fg red -bg blue
pack .b
```

The `pack` command does not create a widget; rather, it positions a widget in relationship to others. Table 8-4 lists all the widget-manipulation commands.

Tip

To look up online help on any Tk command listed in Tables 8-3 and 8-4, type `man n`, followed by the command name. To get online help on the `bind` command, for example, type `man n bind`.

Table 8-4	Tk commands for manipulating widgets
Command	*Action*
after	Executes a command after a specified amount of time elapses.
bind	Associates a Tcl command with an X event so the Tcl command is automatically invoked whenever the X event occurs.
destroy	Destroys one or more widgets.
focus	Directs keyboard events to a particular window (gives that window the input focus).
grab	Confines pointer and keyboard events to a specified widget and its children.
lower	Lowers a window in the stacking order (the *stacking order* refers to the order in which various windows overlap one another on the display screen).
option	Provides access to the *X* resource database.
pack	Automatically positions widgets in a frame, based on specified constraints.
place	Allows manual positioning of a widget relative to another widget.
raise	Raises a window's position in the stacking order.
selection	Manipulates the X PRIMARY selection (the standard name of a selection in *X*).
send	Sends a Tcl command to a different Tk application (used for interprocess communications).
tk	Provides information about the internal state of the Tk interpreter.
tkerror	Handles any error that occurs in Tk applications (the interpreter calls this command when errors occur in Tk applications).
tkwait	Waits for an event such as the destruction of a window or a change in the value of a variable.
update	Processes all pending events and updates the display.
winfo	Returns information about a widget.
wm	Provides access to the window manager. (You can send commands to the window manager, requesting a size for your top-level window, for example.)

Naming widgets

From the example that created a label and a button, you may have guessed the argument that follows the widget-creation command is the widget's name. If you wonder why all the names start with a period, which is required at the beginning of a widget's name, this is because widgets are organized in a hierarchy.

Suppose you have a main window that contains a menu bar, a text area, and a scrollbar. The menu bar has two buttons, labeled File and Help. Figure 8-4 shows this widget hierarchy as it appears onscreen and also shows how the widget names relate to this hierarchy.

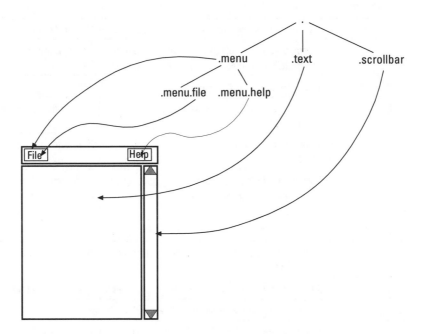

Figure 8-4: Relationship between widget names and widget hierarchy

The root of the hierarchy is the main window of the application; a single period (dot) is used to denote the main window. This main window is a child of the root window of the X display. Each child of the main window has a name that begins with a dot. Thus, .menu is a child of the main window.

The names of other widgets depend on their positions in the hierarchy. The buttons in the menu bar have names — .menu.file and .menu.help — indicating they are child widgets of the .menu widget. As you create widgets, you specify the name of each widget, in turn, defining the widget hierarchy.

If you think about it, you can see the widget-naming scheme is similar to the pathname of a file in Linux. The period (.) in the widget names is analogous to the slash (/) in a file's pathname. In fact, the Tk documentation and online manual pages use the term *Tk pathname* to indicate the widget hierarchy.

All widget names must start with a lowercase letter or a number. The name cannot include a period, because the period indicates the widget's location in the hierarchy. Names that start with a uppercase letter denote a class used in specifying resources. The meaning of the term *resources* is the same as in *X*.

See Chapter 6 for a discussion of X resources and how they are specified.

Configuring widgets

Tk treats each widget name as a command name. You can perform operations on a specific widget by using this widget's name followed by arguments that make sense for this widget. If you have a button named `.b`, for example, use the following command to set that button's background to blue:

```
.b config -fg blue
```

You can change the button's label to Goodbye! by using the following command:

```
.b config -text Goodbye!
```

The pairs of arguments `-fg blue` and `-text Goodbye!` specify the attributes of a widget. Each attribute name begins with a hyphen (-), as in `-text`. The next argument is that attribute's value.

Displaying widgets

Tk does not display a widget until you use a command to position the widget in the main window. You have to use a *geometry manager* — a Tk procedure that arranges one or more child widgets in a parent widget. Tk provides two geometry-management commands:

- The `place` command, which enables you to position a widget at a fixed location in the window of a designated master widget (this needn't be a parent widget). The master widget is used as a reference — other widgets are positioned relative to the master widget. You also can specify relative positions, such as a horizontal position that is half the width of the master widget.

- The `pack` command, which arranges child widgets around the edges of the master window. You can specify which side of the parent on which the child widget is placed, as well as any extra space you want to use around the child. As the name suggests, the `pack` command packs widgets together as tightly as possible.

Although the `pack` and `place` commands take many different options, their basic use is straightforward. My advice is you start `wish`, create a few widgets, and try the `place` and `pack` commands to see their effects. After that, you can consult the online manual for the exact options whenever you need them.

Tip

The `pack` and `place` commands have a form — `pack forget` and `place forget` — that you can use to hide a widget. If you want to hide a button named `.btn1`, for example, use the command `pack forget .btn1`. To make the button reappear, use the `pack .btn1` command again.

The pack command

The `pack` command is the most commonly used geometry-management command in Tk. As some of the simple examples in this chapter show, to make a button named `.btn1` appear, you use `pack` as follows:

```
pack .btn1
```

You can specify several widget names on the same `pack` command line. To display the buttons `.btn1`, `.btn2`, and `.btn3`, arranged in a vertical line in that order, use the following:

```
pack .btn1 .btn2 .btn3
```

Table 8-5 summarizes the `pack` command's syntax. As Table 8-5 shows, you can position widgets and get information about the widget hierarchy. If you want a more complicated layout of widgets, you have to use the packing options shown in Table 8-6.

Table 8-5   Different forms of the pack command

Command	Description
pack *widgetNames options*	Packs the listed widgets according to the specified options (same as `pack configure`). Table 8-6 shows the list of available options.
pack configure *widgetNames options*	Packs the listed widgets according to the specified options.
pack forget *widgetNames*	Hides (*unpacks*) the specified widgets.
pack info *widget*	Returns the *packing configuration* (a list of options and values) of the specified *widget*.
pack propagate *widget boolean*	If *boolean* is 1, enables geometry propagation for the specified widget; otherwise, disables propagation. (When geometry propagation is enabled, the size of a widget's window is determined by the sizes of the widgets contained in that window.)
pack slaves *widget*	Returns the list of widgets managed by a specified *widget*.

Table 8-6   Options for packing widgets

Option	Description
`-after` *widgetName*	Places the widget being packed after the widget specified by *widgetName*.
`-anchor` *anchorPos*	Determines where the managed widget is placed. (Applies only when the containing widget is larger than the managed widget.) The *anchorPos* value can be center, e, n, ne, nw, s, se, sw, or w; the default is center.
`-before` *widgetName*	Places the widget being packed before the widget specified by *widgetName*.
`-expand` *boolean*	If *boolean* is 1, the contained widget expands to use any space left over in the containing widget.
`-fill` *style*	Indicates how to expand the containing widget if it gets bigger than what the widgets contained in it require. The *style* value can be both, none, x, or y.
`-in` *widgetName*	Indicates the widget in which the widgets specified in the pack command line are placed. You needn't use this option; widgets are packed in their parent widget (f.b is packed in .f).
`-ipadx` *amount*	Specifies extra horizontal space inside the widget being packed (in addition to the space t already needs). The *amount* value is a number, in screen units.
`-ipady` *amount*	Specifies extra vertical space inside the widget being packed (in addition to the space it already needs). The *amount* value is a number, in screen units.
`-padx` *amount*	Specifies extra horizontal space outside the border of the widget being packed. The *amount* value is a number, in screen units.
`-pady` *amount*	Specifies extra vertical space outside the border of the widget being packed. The *amount* value is a number, in screen units.
`-side` *sideName*	Packs against the specified side. The *sideName* value is bottom, left, right, or top; the default is top.

Tip

If you are wondering how to remember all these options, my advice is that you *not* remember them. You usually can get by with just a few of these options and, after a while, you will begin to remember them. To become familiar with what each option does, start wish, create a few widgets, and try packing them with different options. From then on, whenever you need the exact syntax of an option, consult the online manual by typing **man n pack** or simply **man pack**.

The place command

The place command is a simpler way to specify the placement of widgets, but you must position all the windows yourself. It is simpler than pack because the place command gives you direct control of the widget positions. On the other hand, direct control of widget placement is fine for a few windows, but it can get tedious in a hurry when you have many widgets in a user interface.

Using place, you can position a widget at a specific location. To place .btn1 at the coordinate (100, 50) in its parent widget, use the following command:

```
place .btn1 -x 100 -y 50
```

A good use of place is to center a widget within its parent widget. For this purpose, you use the -relx and -rely options of place. If .f is a *frame widget* (a widget containing other widgets), you can display it at the center of the parent window by using the following commands:

```
frame .f
button .f.b1 -text Configure
button .f.b2 -text Quit
pack .f.b1 .f.b2 -side left
place .f -relx 0.5 -rely 0.5 -anchor center
```

As the code fragment shows, the buttons inside the frame are packed with the pack command. Only the frame, .f, is positioned with the place command. The -relx and -rely options enable you to specify the relative positions in terms of a fraction of the containing widget's size. A zero value for -relx means the left edge; 1 is the right edge; and 0.5 means the middle.

Like pack, the place command has several forms, which are listed in Table 8-7. Also, place takes several options, which are summarized in Table 8-8. Use these options with the plain place command or place configure command.

Table 8-7 Forms of the place command

Command	Description
place *widgetNames options*	Positions the listed widgets according to the specified options (same as place configure). Table 8-8 shows the list of available options.
place configure *widgetNames options*	Positions the listed widgets according to the specified options.
place forget *widgetNames*	Stops managing the specified widgets and unmaps (hides) them.
place info *widget*	Returns the list of options and their values for the specified *widget*.
place slaves *widget*	Returns the list of widgets managed by the specified *widget*.

Table 8-8   Options for placing widgets

Option	Description
-anchor *anchorPos*	Specifies which point of the managed widget is placed in the specified position in the managing window. The *anchorPos* value can be center, e, n, ne, nw, s, se, sw, or w; the default is nw (upper-left corner).
-bordermode *bmode*	Indicates how the managing widget's borders are used when the managed widgets are positioned. The *bordermode* value must be ignore, inside, or outside.
-height *size*	Specifies the height of the managed widget.
-in *widgetName*	Indicates the widget relative to which of the positions of the widgets specified in the place command line are specified. If you do not use this option, widgets are placed relative to their parent widgets (.f.b is positioned relative to .f).
-relheight *fraction*	Specifies the height of the managed widget as a fraction of the managing widget. The fraction is a floating-point value.
-relwidth *fraction*	Specifies the width of the managed widget as a fraction of the managing widget. The fraction is a floating-point value.
-relx *fraction*	Specifies the horizontal position of the managed widget as a fraction of the managing widget's width. The fraction is a floating-point value: 0.0 means the left edge and 1.0 means the right edge.
-rely *fraction*	Specifies the vertical position of the managed widget as a fraction of the managing widget's height. The fraction is a floating-point value: 0.0 means the top edge and 1.0 means the bottom edge.
-x *coord*	Specifies the horizontal position of the managed widget's anchor point in the managing widget. The *coord* value is in screen coordinates.
-y *coord*	Specifies the vertical position of the managed widget's anchor point in the managing widget. The *coord* value is in screen coordinates.
-width *size*	Specifies the width of the managed widget.

Binding actions to events

When you write a program that has a graphical user interface, various program actions are initiated by events such as the user clicking a button in the user interface. In a Tk script, you indicate what the program does by associating actions with events. In this case, an *action* is simply a Tcl script that performs some task. In the case of a Quit button, for example, a logical action is the Tcl command exit that ends the Tk script.

For buttons, a simple way to form this association is with a click of the button. Use the -command option of the button command to specify a Tcl command to be executed when the user clicks the button. The exit command is associated with the Quit button as follows:

```
button .b -text Quit -command { exit }
```

Tip

The curly braces are not necessary when you have only one Tcl command, but you can place more than one command inside the braces.

The bind command is the most common way to associate an action with an event. Following is the general syntax of the bind command:

```
bind widgetName <eventSpecification> TclCommand
```

The widgetName argument is usually the pathname of a widget, although you can bind an event to a class of widgets, such as all buttons. Typically, you have to consult online help to specify eventSpecification. (In this section, I show you an example and then explain event specifications.) The last argument — TclCommand — refers to the Tcl commands you want to execute when the specified event occurs. These Tcl commands can be any Tcl script, ranging from a simple puts command to a complete Tcl script stored in a separate file.

To see a more detailed example of how to bind an action to an event, consider this scenario. You may have noticed many Microsoft Windows applications sport a toolbar — essentially, a collection of buttons, each of which is meant to perform a specific task. Typically, each button bears an icon that indicates its purpose. To help users learn the meaning of a button quickly, many Windows applications have a feature called *tool help*. If you place the mouse pointer on a button, a small window pops up, displaying a short help message that tells you what the button does.

You can use Tk to implement a similar tool-help feature. Follow these steps:

1. Create the button.

2. Prepare the help message as a label (preferably with a bright background, such as yellow).

3. When the mouse pointer enters a button, an Enter event occurs. Bind the Enter event to a command that makes the help label visible. Use the place command to position the label relative to the button so the tool-help label always appears near the associated button.

The following example shows how `bind` is used to associate the `place` command (shown within braces) with the `Enter` event:

```
bind .f.b <Enter> { place .bh -in .f.b -relx 0.5 -rely 1.0 }
```

4. When the mouse pointer leaves the button, a `Leave` event occurs. Bind the `Leave` event to the `place forget` command to hide the help message, as follows:

```
bind .f.b <Leave> { place forget .bh }
```

The following sample `toolhelp` script demonstrates how to implement tool help in Tk:

```
#!/usr/bin/wish -f
# Demonstrates a "tool help" window that appears when you
# place the mouse pointer inside the "File" button.

wm geometry . 100x60

frame .f
button .f.b -text File
label .bh -text "Open file"
.bh config -bg yellow

bind .f.b <Enter> { place .bh -in .f.b -relx 0.5 -rely 1.0 }
bind .f.b <Leave> { place forget .bh }

button .f.q -text Quit -command { exit }

pack .f.b .f.q -side left
pack .f -fill x
```

Make the `toolhelp` script file executable by using the `chmod +x toolhelp` command. Then run that script by typing **toolhelp** at the shell prompt in an `xterm` window. Figure 8-5 shows the window that results after you place the mouse pointer on the File button.

Figure 8-5: A Tk script that demonstrates how to implement tool-help messages

When you use `bind` to associate a Tcl script with an event, you must know how to specify the event. Most events are either keyboard events or mouse events. A smaller number of events are related to the state of a widget's window. `<Map>` and `<Unmap>` events, for example, occur when a widget is managed or unmanaged (when you use `pack forget` or `place forget`).

Keyboard events

There are two keyboard events:

- `<KeyPress>` occurs when you press a key.

- `<KeyRelease>` occurs when you release the key.

You can specify a keyboard event for a specific key by appending that key's *keysym* (which is the X Window System's standard name for a key) to the string `KeyPress-` and enclosing everything in angle brackets. The event associated with pressing the q key, for example, is specified by `<Keypress-q>`. Tk provides a shorter format for keyboard events. You can simply place the keysym inside angle brackets, as follows:

`<q>`

For most key presses, the event specification is straightforward. If you want to exit when the user presses Ctrl+C inside a widget named `.text`, use the `bind` command as follows:

```
bind .text <Control-c> exit
```

Following are some other commonly used keysyms:

```
BackSpace  comma  Down  dollar  Escape  exclam  Left  numbersign
period  Return  Right  Tab  Up
```

Tip

Inside the Tcl commands bound to a key event, use the `%A` keyword to refer to the printable character the user presses. For any nonprintable character, `%A` is replaced by `{}` (a pair of empty braces). The `%W` keyword is replaced by the name of the widget that receives the keypress. Thus, you can use the following code to insert text into a text widget:

```
# Assume .text1 is a text widget
bind .text <KeyPress> {
    if { "%A" != "{}"} { %W insert insert %A}
}
```

Remember, a widget's name itself is a command and the command's argument depends on the type of widget. For a text widget, the command `%W insert insert %A` inserts the character into the text widget.

Mouse events

Use `<ButtonPress>` and `<ButtonRelease>` to denote mouse-button click and release events, respectively. You must append the button number to make the event specific. Thus, the action of clicking the left mouse button (which is Button 1 in *X* terminology) is denoted by `<ButtonPress-1>`. A shorthand notation for button presses is to leave out `Press`; thus, you can write `<Button-1>` to denote the event generated by clicking the left mouse button.

Tip

In the Tcl commands bound to a mouse event, the keywords %x and %y denote the *x* and *y* coordinates of the mouse pointer (relative to the widget's window) at the time of the mouse event. Thus, you can track the position of a widget's mouse click as follows:

```
bind .text1 <Button-1> { puts "Click at (%x, %y) on widget: %W"}
```

Other mouse events include the Enter and Leave events, which occur when you move the mouse pointer into or out of a widget, respectively. These two events are denoted by <Enter> and <Leave>. The toolhelp example shown in "Binding actions to events" earlier in this chapter illustrates a way to use the <Enter> and <Leave> events.

Another event related to the mouse pointer is the <Motion> event, which occurs when you move the mouse pointer within a widget.

Window events

In addition to keyboard and mouse events, *X* includes many events that occur when a window is manipulated. The X server generates <Map> and <Unmap> events, for example, when a widget is displayed or hidden (by the pack or place command).

A <Configure> event occurs when the user resizes a window. Thus, you can bind a <Configure> event to a redisplay procedure that redraws the contents of a widget, based on the new size.

A <Destroy> event occurs when a window is about to be destroyed. You bind a procedure to the <Destroy> event and intercept requests to delete a window.

More information on the X Window System

Tk enables you to intercept many more X events. For information on these X events and other aspects of the X Window System, consult one of the following books:

■ *Graphical Applications with Tcl and Tk, Second Edition*, Eric Foster-Johnson, M&T Books, 1997.

■ *X Window System Programming, Second Edition*, Naba Barkakati, SAMS, 1994

■ *Volume 1: Xlib Programming Manual*, O'Reilly & Associates, 1993

■ *Volume 2: Xlib Reference Manual*, O'Reilly & Associates, 1993

Summary

The combination of Tool Command Language (Tcl) and its X Window System –based graphical toolkit, Tk, is ideal for quickly developing applications with a graphical interface. This chapter introduces Tcl/Tk through simple examples.

By reading this chapter, you learn the following:

▶ Tcl is an interpreted language with a set of commands you can combine according to a set of rules. Tcl comes with the Red Hat Linux distribution on the companion CD-ROM. You can install Tcl at the same time you install Linux (see Chapter 1 for more information).

▶ You can learn the Tcl syntax and develop Tcl scripts interactively by running the Tcl command interpreter, `tclsh`, and entering Tcl commands at the `tclsh` prompt.

▶ Tcl includes built-in commands for most routine tasks, such as reading and writing files, manipulating strings, and running any Linux command. In addition, Tcl includes control-flow commands — such as `if`, `for`, and `while` — that enable you to control the sequence of commands processed by the interpreter. Finally, you can use Tcl's `proc` command to write new Tcl commands that use combinations of existing commands.

▶ Tk, the Tcl toolkit, is an extension of Tcl that uses the X Window System to enable you to build graphical user interfaces. Tk provides the three-dimensional appearance of Motif, but Tk does not require the Motif toolkit or any other X toolkit. Tk is built on Xlib, the C-language Application Programming Interface (API) for *X*.

▶ Tk includes commands for creating many common widgets (user-interface elements), such as buttons, labels, list boxes, and scrollbars. A widget-naming convention specifies the widget hierarchy (the organization of the widgets).

▶ To make the graphical interface active, you must use the `bind` command to associate Tcl commands with specific keyboard and mouse events.

▶ You can interactively experiment with and create Tk programs by running `wish`, the windowing shell that can interpret all Tcl and Tk commands.

Part III:

Exploiting Your Hardware in Linux

Chapter 9

Computers

Typically, after you install Linux by following the instructions in Chapter 1, you can begin using it without ever worrying about the details of your PC's architecture. You must pay attention to the make and model of your computer and its internal details only if you run into problems during installation. At minimum, you may have to understand your PC's hardware architecture — whether it uses a PCI bus or a VLB bus, for example — to successfully install and use Linux on your PC. At worst, you may have to know specific details about your system's motherboard (the main circuit board in your system) — information such as the type of Integrated Drive Electronics (IDE) controller used on the motherboard. Other peripherals, such as the hard disk and the display, are equally important; I cover these hardware components in subsequent chapters.

In a sense, the title of this chapter is misleading, because the term *computer* includes everything from the processor to the hard drive and the display. This chapter's goal is to provide you information about the compatibility of Linux with specific processor and bus types (the *bus* is a standard physical connection method for peripherals). Because a laptop computer is a more tightly integrated system than a desktop computer, this chapter also provides information on running Linux on several popular brands of laptop computers.

Basic Processor and Bus Types

As you move from a simple operating system, such as MS-DOS, to a more complex one, such as Linux, the exact details of your computer's hardware become more important because the operating system tries to make use of all the hardware's features. Most operating systems — including Linux — use device drivers to access and use hardware devices. Some hardware, such as the system's processor and associated circuitry, however, must be supported by the Linux kernel — the core operating system.

Linux was developed for Intel 80386 or better processors; the program uses what is known as the *protected mode* of the processor. MS-DOS uses the processor's *real mode*, in which the amount of addressable memory is limited to 1MB. In protected mode, 386 and better processors can access a large amount of memory (theoretically, up to 4GB).

Typical 386 architecture often limits 386-based PCs to run with, at most, 16MB of RAM. If you want to install more than 16MB RAM on a 386 PC, you may need a BIOS (Basic Input and Output System) ROM (Read-Only Memory) upgrade. For this, you must contact your PC's manufacturer and get the new ROM chips. Then, you have to remove the old ROM BIOS chips and install the new ones before you install Linux. Because Linux runs quite well on a 386 with enough memory, upgrading the BIOS can be a worthwhile exercise to put your old 386 PCs to good use.

You need at least an 80386 system to run Linux. Linux runs on all variants of the 80386, 80486, and Pentium processors. Thus, you can run Linux on 386SX, 386DX, 386SL, 386SLC, 486SX, 486DX, 486SL, 486DX2, 486DX4, Pentium, and Pentium II processors from Intel. (This list does not include all variants of the 386 and 486 processors, but you get the idea.) Collectively, these processors are often referred to as the 80×86 family of processors. Linux also runs on 80×86-compatible processors from other vendors, such as Cyrix and AMD.

The 80×86 family of processors use a *floating-point processor* (also known as a *math coprocessor*) to speed floating-point computations. In many 486 and Pentium processors, the floating-point processor is part of the basic processor. Linux uses the hardware floating-point processor, if available. Otherwise, Linux emulates the floating-point processor with software that is part of the Linux kernel.

Linux on other processors

Although the most widely distributed version of Linux is for Intel 80×86 and Pentium processors, Linux is also available for systems based on other processors, such as the Motorola 68000 family, Digital Equipment Corporation's (DEC) Alpha AXP processor, Sun SPARC processor, Hewlett-Packard's HP PA-RISC processor, the PowerPC processor, and the MIPS R4x00 processor. You can find further information on these versions of Linux on the Internet. Start by pointing your Web browser at one or more of the following Web sites:

Linux for systems with Motorola 68000 processors:

```
http://www.clark.net/pub/lawrencc/
linux/
```

Linux for DEC Alpha systems:

```
http://www.azstarnet.com/~axplinux/
ftp://ftp.redhat.com/pub/redhat/
redhat-5.1/alpha/
```

Linux for Sun SPARCstations:

```
http://www.geog.ubc.ca/s_linux.
html
ftp://ftp.redhat.com/pub/redhat/
redhat-4.2/sparc/
```

Linux for systems with HP PA-RISC processors:

```
http://www.osf.org/mall/os/
pa-mklinux/index.html
```

Linux for systems with the MIPS processor:

```
http://lena.fnet.fr/
```

Linux for systems with the PowerPC processor:

```
http://www.linuxppc.org/
http://www.mklinux.apple.com/
```

Bus types

The term *bus* refers to the collection wires that carry signals between the PC's processor and any peripheral devices. After the processor, the bus is a critical hardware characteristic of a PC. Each type of bus specifies the meaning of various signals and the *protocol* (the order and timing of signals) for transferring data over the bus.

Each bus has a maximum rate of data transfer, which depends on how many bits of data the bus can carry at a time and on the *clock rate* — how many times a second the signal can change between two states (0 and 1). Like a processor's internal clock rate, the bus clock rate is expressed in megahertz (MHz). 1MHz means a million times a second.

Each bus type specifies the physical dimensions of the controller card, the number and purpose of the connectors, and the slot on the motherboard where you plug in the card. Your system's hard disk, for example, is connected to the motherboard by means of a disk-controller card that is compatible with the bus type of that motherboard.

Following are several popular bus types:

- The *Industry Standard Architecture (ISA) bus* was the most widely used bus (until the PCI bus came along). This bus was used in the original IBM PC-AT. The ISA bus can transfer data 16 bits at a time. It operates at an 8-MHz clock rate, which is slow compared with today's processors which have clock rates in the 200-300MHz range. Typically, the ISA bus can achieve a data-transfer rate of 5MB/sec (that's 5 megabytes per second).

- The *Video Electronics Standard Association (VESA) Local Bus*, or VLB, was designed for high-performance data transfer between the processor and the video card. The typical VLB transfer rate is 30MB/sec. Early VLB systems often have a nonstandard implementation of the VESA local bus, which may cause problems with Linux.

- The *Micro Channel Architecture (MCA) bus* is IBM's proprietary bus, which first appeared in the PS/2 PCs. IBM designed this bus as a high-speed bus, but its proprietary nature kept it from being widely used in PCs.

- The *Extended Industry Standard Architecture (EISA) bus* came about as an alternative to the MCA bus with performance comparable to that of the MCA. The EISA bus is not widely used because the EISA bus peripheral cards are more expensive than their ISA bus counterparts. EISA bus performance is comparable with that of the VLB, transferring data at rates of 30MB/sec.

- The *Peripheral Component Interconnect (PCI) bus* is the latest high-performance bus; it operates at a clock rate of 33MHz and can transfer up to 64 bits of data at a time. When a PCI bus is used to transfer 32 bits at a time, the 33MHz clock rate implies the bus can transfer data at the rate of 33×4 = 132MB per second (notice 32 bits = 4 bytes). PCI is the up-and-coming standard. The current crop of Pentium PCs use the PCI bus but also offer ISA bus slots, so you can continue to use ISA cards. Typically, the PCI bus achieves a data-transfer rate of 60MB/sec.

Linux supports ISA, VLB, EISA, and PCI buses; the version of Linux on the companion CD-ROM can be installed and run on systems that have any of these buses. Because a bus is meant for connecting peripherals to the system, the support for a bus implies you can use peripherals that use controller cards of that bus type.

Of course, not all peripheral hardware (such as the graphics card and disk controller) for all these buses works under Linux. Each peripheral requires a driver, and the driver may not yet exist for some newer graphics cards or disk controllers. You can find more information about specific devices in Chapters 10 through 17.

Caution

The Linux kernel in this book's Red Hat Linux distribution CD-ROM does not support IBM PS/2 systems that have the Micro Channel Architecture (MCA) bus. The primary problem in supporting a bus such as MCA is someone must develop the driver software needed to access peripherals such as disk drives and video cards. Some Linux developers are working on supporting the MCA bus. You can find more information about Linux for MCA systems at `http://glycerine.cetmm.uni.edu/mca/`.

PCI-bus support in Linux

The PCI bus is rapidly becoming the bus of choice in all new Pentium-based PCs. One attraction is the high throughput of the bus. In addition, the bus is processor-independent; a PCI interface card should work on a Pentium PC as well as on a DEC Alpha system, as long as both systems use the PCI bus. The PCI bus design also makes it easy to build PCI components that can go directly on the motherboard, thereby minimizing the cost of additional *glue logic* (extra electronic components required to make everything work) other buses require.

Note

Among the current crop of PCI motherboards, the emerging standard seems to be the ones based on the Intel Triton chipset. This chipset supports a special type of memory called EDO (Extended Data Out) DRAM (Dynamic Random Access Memory), which includes a cache within the memory chip. Most current Pentium PCs use Intel Triton motherboards with EDO DRAM together with an external 512K cache. Typically, a PCI motherboard also has a built-in PCI video chipset and an IDE (Integrated Drive Electronics) interface for connecting IDE hard disks to the system. The PCI IDE interface is described further in Chapter 11.

XFree86 supports many PCI video cards — such as the ATI Graphics Pro Turbo, Diamond Viper PCI, and Number Nine GXE Pro PCI — as well as integrated video chipsets, such as S3 Trio32/Trio64.

CD

The version of Linux on the companion CD-ROM includes PCI Probe code, which collects information about PCI devices on your system as Linux boots. You can see this information by issuing a `cat /proc/pci` command. (The `/proc` file system is explained in the "Information from the `/proc` File System" section of this chapter.)

Some specific problems

When you have problems installing or configuring Linux on a PC, most of those problems have to do with specific peripherals — disk controllers, video cards, the CD-ROM drive interface, and so on. A few problems, however, are directly related to the processor or the basic hardware architecture of the PC. This section points out a few such problems and suggests some solutions.

System slowdown after memory is added

This problem occurs when you add extra memory to your PC (go from 16MB to 32MB, for example) and expect a significant performance gain; instead, the system slows dramatically. The reason for this strange behavior is the fact that when you add memory, you also must make sure that the new memory is being cached.

Cache memory is fast (and expensive) memory that keeps the processor working at full speed. (The *speed* of memory, incidentally, refers to how quickly the processor can get data in and out of that memory.) Typically, a system may have 256K or 512K of cache memory.

Ordinary memory (the kind you have in amounts of 16, 32, or 64MB) is too slow to keep up with today's fast processors. The cache memory acts as intermediate storage between the ordinary memory and the processor.

Secret

When you add memory, you have to make sure the cache memory works with the new memory. The exact solution depends on your motherboard. Sometimes, the solution is a matter of running your PC's setup program and turning on an option to cache the new memory area, which may be switched off.

On some systems, you must install the memory in specific physical sockets to ensure all the memory is cached. Yet another solution may be to set *jumpers*—connectors between pins on the motherboard—to enable the caching.

Some motherboards cache a certain amount of memory, based on the amount of cache memory. Usually, a motherboard with a 256K cache should be able to handle the caching needs of the system. Even with a 256K cache, you still may have to set some jumpers or turn on some options to enable caching for all the memory. Check your system's documentation for any clues; a small motherboard manual may provide this information.

Secret

If you add memory beyond 64MB, the system slowdown occurs because Linux cannot determine the exact amount of memory in your PC. At system startup, Linux uses BIOS calls to determine the amount of installed memory. Unfortunately, the original BIOS calls can only report up to 64MB of installed memory. If you have more than 64MB of memory, you have to specify the amount of memory through a LILO boot option. For example, if your PC has 96MB of memory, add the following option at the boot prompt:

```
mem=96M
```

You may also add this line to the LILO configuration file /etc/lilo.conf.

Secret

When you specify the amount of memory at boot time, remember some PCs may use the last 384KB of memory to cache the BIOS (essentially, the BIOS code is copied to this area). To be safe, you may want to specify an amount that's 1MB less than the actual. Thus, for a PC with 96MB of memory, you would use the option mem=95M.

Cyrix 6×86 system has some problems

The Cyrix 6×86 family of processors is a clone of the Intel x86 family of processors with performance comparable to Intel Pentium processors. As such, Linux works on Cyrix 6×86 systems. Some known problems exist with the Cyrix 6×86, however.

Secret

A short sequence of instructions can cause the Cyrix 6×86 processor to stop responding to all interrupts. Essentially, the system freezes up. You can learn more about this problem at http://www.tux.org/~balsa/linux/cyrix/p11. html. The solution is to enable the NO_LOCK bit in the CCR1 configuration register. A program called set6×86 is available to correct the problem. This program can also enable a feature of the 6×86 processor that cuts down on the power consumption when the processor is idle.

A few other minor problems exist, such as wrong computation of BogoMips on Cyrix 6×86 processors. For more information on Linux and the Cyrix 6×86 processors, visit http://www.tux.org/~balsa/linux/cyrix/ on the Web. At this site, you also find any patches you need for the Cyrix 6×86 processors.

Information from the /proc File System

You can find out a great deal about your computer by consulting the contents of a special file system known as the /proc file system. To use the /proc file system, of course, you must have Linux installed and running on your system. Still, knowing about the /proc file system is useful, because it can help you determine exact information about your PC (at least, about what Linux thinks your PC has) in case you are adding a new device or rebuilding the kernel and trying to decide what types of features you should enable in the kernel.

The /proc file system is not a real directory on the disk, but a collection of data structures in memory, managed by the Linux kernel, that appears to the user to be a set of directories and files. The purpose of /proc (also called the *process file system*) is to enable users to access information about the Linux kernel and the processes currently running on your system.

You can access the /proc file system just as you access any other directory, but you must know the meaning of various files to interpret the information. Typically, you can use the cat or more command to view the contents of a file in /proc; the file's contents provide information about some aspects of the system.

As with any directory, you may want to start by looking at a detailed directory listing of /proc. To do so, type ls -l /proc. The following is typical output from my system:

```
ls -l /proc
total 0
dr-xr-xr-x    3 root      root             0 May  3 06:13 1
dr-xr-xr-x    3 root      root             0 May  3 06:13 1623
dr-xr-xr-x    3 pekkle16  users            0 May  3 06:13 1624
dr-xr-xr-x    3 pekkle16  users            0 May  3 06:13 1625
dr-xr-xr-x    3 root      root             0 May  3 06:13 1636
dr-xr-xr-x    3 root      root             0 May  3 06:13 1637
dr-xr-xr-x    3 root      root             0 May  3 06:13 1670
dr-xr-xr-x    3 root      root             0 May  3 06:13 1702
dr-xr-xr-x    3 naba      users            0 May  3 06:13 1703
dr-xr-xr-x    3 naba      users            0 May  3 06:13 1704
dr-xr-xr-x    3 root      root             0 May  3 06:13 1719
dr-xr-xr-x    3 root      root             0 May  3 06:13 1720
dr-xr-xr-x    3 nobody    nobody           0 May  3 06:13 1783
dr-xr-xr-x    3 nobody    nobody           0 May  3 06:13 1784
dr-xr-xr-x    3 nobody    nobody           0 May  3 06:13 1785
dr-xr-xr-x    3 nobody    nobody           0 May  3 06:13 1786
dr-xr-xr-x    3 nobody    nobody           0 May  3 06:13 1787
dr-xr-xr-x    3 nobody    nobody           0 May  3 06:13 1788
dr-xr-xr-x    3 nobody    nobody           0 May  3 06:13 1789
dr-xr-xr-x    3 nobody    nobody           0 May  3 06:13 1790
```

```
dr-xr-xr-x   3 nobody    nobody          0 May   3 06:13 1791
dr-xr-xr-x   3 nobody    nobody          0 May   3 06:13 1792
dr-xr-xr-x   3 root      root            0 May   3 06:13 187
dr-xr-xr-x   3 root      root            0 May   3 06:13 196
dr-xr-xr-x   3 root      root            0 May   3 06:13 2
dr-xr-xr-x   3 root      root            0 May   3 06:13 2000
dr-xr-xr-x   3 daemon    root            0 May   3 06:13 207
dr-xr-xr-x   3 root      root            0 May   3 06:13 218
dr-xr-xr-x   3 root      root            0 May   3 06:13 22
dr-xr-xr-x   3 root      root            0 May   3 06:13 230
dr-xr-xr-x   3 root      root            0 May   3 06:13 241
dr-xr-xr-x   3 root      root            0 May   3 06:13 252
dr-xr-xr-x   3 root      root            0 May   3 06:13 267
dr-xr-xr-x   3 root      root            0 May   3 06:13 279
dr-xr-xr-x   3 root      nobody          0 May   3 06:13 290
dr-xr-xr-x   3 root      root            0 May   3 06:13 3
dr-xr-xr-x   3 postgres  postgres        0 May   3 06:13 316
dr-xr-xr-x   3 root      root            0 May   3 06:13 332
dr-xr-xr-x   3 root      root            0 May   3 06:13 341
dr-xr-xr-x   3 root      root            0 May   3 06:13 382
dr-xr-xr-x   3 root      root            0 May   3 06:13 383
dr-xr-xr-x   3 root      root            0 May   3 06:13 384
dr-xr-xr-x   3 root      root            0 May   3 06:13 385
dr-xr-xr-x   3 root      root            0 May   3 06:13 386
dr-xr-xr-x   3 root      root            0 May   3 06:13 387
dr-xr-xr-x   3 root      root            0 May   3 06:13 389
-r--r--r--   1 root      root            0 May   3 06:13 cmdline
-r--r--r--   1 root      root            0 May   3 06:13 cpuinfo
-r--r--r--   1 root      root            0 May   3 06:13 devices
-r--r--r--   1 root      root            0 May   3 06:13 dma
-r--r--r--   1 root      root            0 May   3 06:13 filesystems
-r--r--r--   1 root      root            0 May   3 06:13 interrupts
-r--r--r--   1 root      root            0 May   3 06:13 ioports
-r--------   1 root      root     16781312 May   3 06:13 kcore
-r--------   1 root      root            0 Apr  28 03:39 kmsg
-r--r--r--   1 root      root            0 May   3 06:13 ksyms
-r--r--r--   1 root      root            0 May   3 02:39 loadavg
-r--r--r--   1 root      root            0 May   3 06:13 locks
-r--r--r--   1 root      root            0 May   3 06:13 mdstat
-r--r--r--   1 root      root            0 May   3 06:13 meminfo
-r--r--r--   1 root      root            0 May   3 06:13 misc
-r--r--r--   1 root      root            0 May   3 03:49 modules
-r--r--r--   1 root      root            0 May   3 06:13 mounts
dr-xr-xr-x   2 root      root            0 May   3 03:49 net
-r--r--r--   1 root      root            0 May   3 04:23 pci
-r--r--r--   1 root      root            0 May   3 06:13 rtc
dr-xr-xr-x   3 root      root            0 May   3 06:13 scsi
lrwxrwxrwx   1 root      root           64 May   3 06:13 self -> 2000
-r--r--r--   1 root      root            0 May   3 06:13 stat
dr-xr-xr-x   5 root      root            0 May   3 06:13 sys
-r--r--r--   1 root      root            0 May   3 06:13 uptime
-r--r--r--   1 root      root            0 May   3 06:13 version
```

The first set of directories (indicated by the letter d at the beginning of the line) represents the processes currently running on your system. Each directory that corresponds to a process has the process ID (a number) as its name.

Notice the large file named /proc/kcore; this file represents the entire physical memory of your system. As the next few sections show, the files in the /proc file system can help you find out a great deal about your system.

The /proc/cpuinfo file

Several files in /proc contain interesting information about your system's hardware. The /proc/cpuinfo file, for example, lists the key characteristics of your system, such as processor type and floating-point processor information.

On one of my systems, when I want to check out the /proc/cpuinfo file, I type cat /proc/cpuinfo and get the following output:

```
cat /proc/cpuinfo
processor       : 0
cpu             : 586
model           : Pentium 75+
vendor_id       : GenuineIntel
stepping        : 5
fdiv_bug        : no
hlt_bug         : no
fpu             : yes
fpu_exception   : yes
cpuid           : yes
wp              : yes
flags           : fpu vme de pse tsc msr mce cx8
bogomips        : 30.00
```

This output is from a Dell Dimension P75 (75MHz Pentium) system from Dell Computer Corporation. The listing shows many interesting characteristics of the processor. Notice the line that starts with fdiv_bug. Remember the infamous Pentium floating-point-division bug? The bug is in an instruction called fdiv (for *floating-point division*). Thus, the fdiv_bug line indicates whether this particular Pentium has the bug (fortunately, my system's processor does not).

CPU naming convention

The term *CPU* stands for *central processing unit*. In the days of the mainframe and the minicomputer, the CPU was a unit — like a cabinet. For a PC, however, the CPU is the microprocessor — the 486 or Pentium chip that's at the heart of the PC. Thus, the file containing information about the processor (CPU) is named cpuinfo — a name derived from concatenating *cpu* with *info* (the short form of *information*). I am explaining this thought process because that's how programmers typically create short, cryptic names. After you see some of these names, you'll begin to guess their meanings more readily.

Cross-Reference

The last line in the /proc/cpuinfo file shows the BogoMips (for more information on BogoMips, see the "What is BogoMips?" sidebar in Chapter 1) for the processor, as computed by the Linux kernel when it boots. BogoMips is something Linux uses internally to time delay loops.

The /proc/pci file

If you have a PCI system (which most new Pentium systems are apt to be), you can check the /proc/pci file for information about the PCI devices on your system. As usual, type cat /proc/pci to see the information. Following is what I find on a Dell Pentium system with a PCI motherboard:

```
PCI devices found:
  Bus  0, device  13, function  0:
    IDE interface: CMD 640 (buggy) (rev 2).
      Medium devsel.  IRQ 14.
  Bus  0, device  10, function  0:
    VGA compatible controller: S3 Inc. Trio32/Trio64 (rev 0).
      Medium devsel.  IRQ 255.
      Non-prefetchable 32 bit memory at 0xfe000000.
  Bus  0, device   1, function  0:
    ISA bridge: VLSI 82C593-FC1 (rev 1).
      Medium devsel.  Fast back-to-back capable.  Master Capable.  No bursts.
  Bus  0, device   0, function  0:
    Host bridge: VLSI 82C592-FC1 (rev 1).
      Medium devsel.  Fast back-to-back capable.  Master Capable.  Latency=16.
```

As the listing shows, the system has four PCI devices. Of the four devices, the first two are of particular interest—the other two are related to interfaces between the PCU and ISA bus.

Note

The first PCI device is the interface to Integrated Drive Electronics (IDE) that are built into each IDE disk drive. (The name *Integrated Drive Electronics* means the electronics needed to control a drive are built into the drive itself.)

The second device is the video-display controller. This controller is a video card (or graphics card) that is built into the motherboard as a PCI device. Essentially, the motherboard contains the chips necessary to drive the monitor.

For each device, the /proc/pci file also shows the make and model of the device. The video controller, for example, is a S3 Trio32/Trio64 chipset. You can use information about the video chipset when you are configuring XFree86 to run on your system.

Secret

As the /proc/pci file shows, this Pentium system's IDE interface is the CMD 640A, which is known to have some problems (that's why the listing says it's *buggy*). The system's disk and CD-ROM drive are connected to the CMD640A. Although my system did not have any problems with the disk or the CD-ROM drive, some people have reported problems with the CMD 640 IDE controllers for the PCI bus. In particular, the CMD640 interface reportedly does not work reliably when drives are attached to the second interface. The version of Linux on the companion CD-ROM has the appropriate fixes to work around the buggy CMD 640A interface.

Other information in the /proc file system

All peripheral devices (such as the hard disk, sound card, CD-ROM drive, modem, and printer) in your system need access to some system resources. Each device typically needs the following resources:

■ *Interrupt Request (IRQ) number*, which the device uses to get the attention of the system's processor. You can think of the IRQ as being the direct line between a device and the processor. A limited number of IRQ lines are available, so a good possibility of conflict exists if you have too many peripheral devices in your system.

■ *Input/Output Port address (I/O address)*, which the processor uses to send data to and receive data from the peripheral device. A device typically needs a range of unique I/O addresses to work properly.

■ *Direct Memory Access (DMA) channel*, which the device uses to access the system's memory directly, rather than going through the processor.

Some devices do not need DMA channels, but most devices need an IRQ number and the required range of I/O addresses.

Even Linux needs these resources — IRQ, I/O address, and DMA channel — for each device, because the underlying hardware architecture dictates the need for these resources. Typically, if you have this information available for all hardware in your system, you can avoid problems that occur because of conflicting assignments of IRQ, I/O address, or DMA channel.

When you rebuild the kernel (as explained in Chapter 2) to add support for a specific device, such as a particular sound card, you have to provide the necessary IRQ, DMA, and I/O addresses to configure Linux properly. For some devices, Linux can probe the device and determine this information.

In addition to `/proc/cpuinfo` and `/proc/pci`, three files in the `/proc` file system contain information about the IRQ, DMA, and I/O addresses being used in your system. These files are:

■ `/proc/interrupts`, which contains information about the IRQs being used

■ `/proc/dma`, which shows the DMA channels being used

■ `/proc/ioports`, which lists the I/O port address ranges being used

As an example, following is the `/proc/interrupts` file for my system:

```
 0:    773590    timer
 1:        10    keyboard
 2:         0    cascade
 4:    337181 +  serial
 8:         1 +  rtc
10:      5447    3c509
11:      2062    aha1542
12:         0    PS/2 Mouse
13:         1    math error
14:     77969 +  ide0
15:         0 +  ide1
```

The first number on each line is the IRQ (interrupt request number). A colon follows this number; then you see the total number of interrupts (for this IRQ) that have occurred so far. The text at the end of the line indicate the device that uses this IRQ. The device `3c509` refers to the 3Com 3C509 Ethernet card, and `aha1542` is the Adaptec AHA1542 SCSI (Small Computer System Interface) controller card.

Following is the `/proc/dma` file for my system:

```
4: cascade
7: aha1542
```

As the listing shows, only two DMAs are in use. Many devices do not use direct memory access.

The `/proc/ioports` file contains more entries, because each device needs I/O port addresses. The following listing shows the `/proc/ioports` file for my system (my comments are in italic):

```
0000-001f : dma1          Direct Memory Access (DMA) controller 1
0020-003f : pic1          Programmable Interrupt Controller (PIC) 1
0040-005f : timer
0060-006f : keyboard      Keyboard
0070-007f : rtc           Real-time clock
0080-009f : dma page reg  DMA page register
00a0-00bf : pic2          Programmable Interrupt Controller (PIC) 2
00c0-00df : dma2          Direct Memory Access (DMA) controller 1
00f0-00ff : npu           Floating-point processor (numeric processor
                          unit)
0170-0177 : ide1          Integrated Drive Electronics interface 1
01f0-01f7 : ide0          Integrated Drive Electronics interface 0
0210-021f : 3c509         3Com 3C509 Ethernet card
02f8-02ff : serial(auto)  Second serial port (COM2)
0330-0333 : aha1542       Adaptec AHA1542 SCSI controller
0376-0376 : ide1          Integrated Drive Electronics interface 1
03c0-03df : vga+          Video controller (graphics card)
03f0-03f5 : floppy        Floppy drive
03f6-03f6 : ide0          Integrated Drive Electronics interface 0
03f7-03f7 : floppy DIR    Floppy drive
03f8-03ff : serial(auto)  First serial port (COM1)
```

Linux on Laptops

Laptops are more integrated than desktops are. A laptop's video card, monitor, and hard disk are all built into a compact package. In other words, you cannot easily mix and match components in laptops as you do in desktop systems, so you must make sure Linux supports all components of your laptop system.

Most laptops with Intel 80386 or better processors should be able to run plain Linux. If you want to install XFree86 (X Window System), however, you may have some trouble, because the video card (on a laptop, video circuitry is built into the motherboard) and the pointing device have to be supported by XFree86.

More about Linux on laptops

This chapter barely touches upon the subject of how to run Linux on laptops. As users have installed and run Linux on a variety of laptops, the user community's cumulative experience of Linux on laptops continues to grow. Much of this information is summarized and made available on the Web. For detailed information on how to install and run Linux on laptops, point your Web browser to the following Web site:

Linux on laptops Home Page:

http://www.cs.utexas.edu/users/kharker/linux-laptop/

This page includes links to many more Web pages, each documenting the details of how to install and run Linux on a specific laptop. In particular, you learn if you must do anything special to get Linux and *X* running on the laptop.

Chapters 10 through 17 of this book cover individual components, such as the video card and monitors. This section provides some information about running Linux on laptop PCs.

PCMCIA

Laptops have a unique type of interface known as PCMCIA, which stands for Personal Computer Memory Card International Association. The version of Linux on the companion CD-ROM supports PCMCIA. The current PCMCIA drivers support many common PCMCIA controllers, such as Databook TCIC/2, Intel i82365SL, Cirrus PD67xx, and Vadem VG-468 chipsets.

Cross-Reference

Consult Chapter 17 for more information on PCMCIA support in Linux.

Advanced power management

Another laptop-specific feature is *power management,* which refers to the capability of a laptop to suspend its activities to conserve battery power. Laptops with Advanced Power Management (APM) capability can suspend and resume power-consuming components (such as the display and hard drive), as well as provide information on battery life.

CD

The version of Linux on the companion CD-ROM can support APM, provided you enable the feature when you build the kernel (see Chapter 2 for information on how to build the kernel).

You can learn more about how to support APM under Linux by visiting the Web site at http://www.cs.utexas.edu/users/kharker/linux-laptop/apm.html.

Sound on laptops

Many high-end laptops come with built-in sound. Using the sound capabilities under Linux is a straightforward process, provided you can figure out what type of sound card you have in the laptop. Chapter 12 covers sound cards in detail.

The type of sound card can vary even among laptop models from the same vendor. The NEC Versa P, for example, comes with a Sound Blaster Pro-compatible card. The NEC versa M, on the other hand, has a Microsoft Sound System (MSS) card, which is not compatible with Sound Blaster.

As you learn in Chapter 12, the typical setup for Sound Blaster Pro is I/O address 0x220 (that's 220 in hexadecimal notation; the 0x prefix indicates hexadecimal in the C programming language), IRQ 5, and DMA 1. Thus, on the NEC Versa P, you should configure the Linux kernel with a Sound Blaster Pro at I/O address 0x220, IRQ 5, and DMA 1. The Texas Instruments TravelMate 4000M has a built-in sound card that needs similar settings.

On the NEC Versa M, try the Microsoft Sound System at I/O address 0x530, IRQ 9, and DMA 3. As usual, you should check your laptop's documentation for clues about the make and model of the sound card before you set up sound support.

The bottom line is you can set up Linux to support sound on a laptop the same way you would for a desktop PC. The first step is finding out what type of sound card your laptop has. Of course, many laptops simply do not have sound capability, so this point may be moot for some laptop users.

X on laptops

Users have reported success in running Linux together with XFree86 on many 386, 486, and Pentium laptops. Until recently, to run *X* on a laptop, you had settle for the standard 16-color VGA server (XF86_VGA16), because XFree86 did not support many of the popular video chipsets used in laptops. Many laptops support 640×480 resolution LCD screens with 256 colors, but the 16-color VGA server does not exploit the 256-color capability. You must be able to run the Super VGA X server (XF86_SVGA) to use 256 colors on a laptop.

To learn more about running *X* on laptops, point your Web browser to http://www.castle.net/X-notebook. On this page, you can also find a link that leads you to a list of video chipsets used in laptops. Most laptops use the following types of video chipsets:

- Western Digital WD90C24 series chips
- Chips & Technology 655xx series chips
- Cirrus Logic CL-GD6235, CL-GD6440 and CL-GD7543

The XF86_SVGA server in XFree86 3.3.2 supports all of these chipsets, as follows:

- Western Digital WD90C24 series chips

- Chips & Technologies 65520, 65525, 65530, 65535, 65540, 65545, 65546, 65550, and 65554 chipsets

- Cirrus Logic CL-GD6225, CL-GD6235, CL-GD6420, CL-GD6440, CL-GD754x, and CL-GD7555 chipsets

XFree86 3.3.1 supports most of the Cirrus Logic chipsets. The Chips & Technologies 65550 is popular on high-end laptops, such as NEC Versa 6200MMX. This chipset supports the Super VGA mode of 1,280×768 resolution with 64,000 colors.

Tip

If you plan to run X on a laptop, your best bet is to buy a laptop with the WD90C24, 65550, or CL-GD6440 chipsets. These chipsets are recent and XFree86 3.3.1 supports them well.

Summary

Linux is much more dependent on the details of your PC's hardware than DOS is. To install and use Linux, you need to make sure that Linux supports various parts of your PC. The chapter focuses on Linux's compatibility with the most important part of your PC: the motherboard, which contains the processor and the bus, where you connect the peripheral devices, such as the hard disk, video card, and CD-ROM drive.

By reading this chapter, you learn the following:

▶ Linux was designed for the Intel 80386 processor and it currently supports all variants of 386, 486, Pentium, and Pentium II processors, including any compatible processors such as the ones from Cyrix and AMD. Linux has also been ported to other processors, such as DEC Alpha AXP, Sun SPARC, HP PA-RISC, MIPS, and PowerPC.

▶ A *bus* is a standard set of wires through which a peripheral device connects to the PC's motherboard. Several bus types exist: ISA, EISA, MCA, VLB, and PCI. Linux supports each of these bus types. The PCI bus is the emerging standard as the high-performance bus for new Pentium PCs.

▶ Linux includes the /proc file system as a convenient way for users to access information about the system. You can find out much about your system by looking at the files in /proc. The /proc/devices file, for example, lists all devices in your system, and /proc/pci shows the PCI devices in a PCI system.

▶ Laptops are a special breed of computer, because all parts of a laptop—from the hard disk to the video card—are tightly integrated. Linux runs on many laptops. The main problem is support for laptop-specific features, such as Advanced Power Management (APM) and PCMCIA or PC Card interfaces. Another problem is running X on a laptop, because laptop video chipsets are not as well-supported by XFree86 as are desktop PCs' video cards. Nevertheless, Linux and X run on a wide variety of laptops.

Chapter 10

Video Cards and Monitors

When you install Linux on a PC, the video card and the monitor do not matter much if you work only with text. The specific details of the video card and monitor become important if you want to use the graphical interface provided by the X Window System — *X,* for short. If you want to benefit from the ease of use afforded by graphical interfaces, you want to install *X.* When you install *X,* you need detailed information about your video card and monitor to make *X* work on your PC.

This chapter describes various common video cards and monitors, their attributes, and the nuances of getting *X* to work with the video card and monitor. You also learn how to specify some video-card and monitor parameters needed to configure *X* for Linux.

Video Cards and Monitors

The video card or graphics adapter contains the electronics that control the monitor. On most systems, the video card is in the form of a circuit board that plugs into a slot on your PC's motherboard. On many new systems, however, the motherboard contains the necessary graphics chipsets.

Raster-scan display

All video cards operate on the same principle: they store an image in video memory (also called *video RAM* or *VRAM* for short) and generate the appropriate signals to display the image on the monitor's screen.

The *monitor* is the physical device that contains the display screen, where the graphic and text output appears. The *display screen* typically is a phosphor-coated glass tube on which an electron beam traces the output image. On laptop computers, the display screen is a Liquid Crystal Display (LCD) screen. More expensive laptops use active matrix display screens.

The image that appears on the monitor is made up of a large number of horizontal lines known as *raster lines*. An electron beam in the monitor generates the raster lines by sweeping back and forth on a phosphor-coated screen, as illustrated in Figure 10-1.

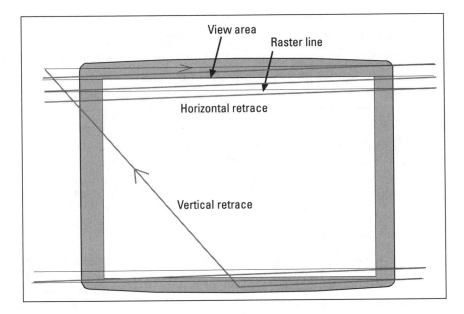

Figure 10-1: A typical raster scan display

The phosphor on the screen glows in proportion to the intensity of the electron beam. The glowing dot on the screen represents a picture element or *pixel*. Thus, a line of the image is generated by controlling the intensity of the beam as it scans across the screen. The phosphor fades in a while, but if the lines are redrawn repeatedly, our persistence of vision creates an illusion of a steady image. Most PC monitors redraw an entire screenful of raster lines 50 to 90 times a second.

As Figure 10-1 shows, the electron beam scans an area larger than the actual view area of the display screen, but the electron beam is active only when the beam is in the viewable area. Also, after reaching the end of a line, the beam has to return to the start of the next raster line. This part of the beam's motion is known as the *horizontal retrace*. Similarly, when the beam reaches the bottom of the screen, it must return to the first line to start another cycle of drawing. This period is known as the *vertical retrace*. The beam's intensity is reduced (the beam is blanked) during horizontal and vertical retrace, so those lines do not appear onscreen.

The video card generates the signals necessary to sweep the electron beam across the display and to refresh the display at a rapid rate. Two types of refresh exist: *interlaced* and *noninterlaced*. In interlaced refresh, each screen is drawn in two steps. First the electron beam sweeps across the screen drawing all odd-numbered raster lines. Then the electron beam goes back to the beginning of the screen and draws all even-numbered raster lines. Broadcast television uses interlaced refresh. Noninterlaced refresh involves drawing all raster lines in a single step. Most video cards refresh the screen 60 times or more per second and use a noninterlaced refresh.

Color display

Color display screens represent any color with a combination of the three primary colors: red (R), green (G), and blue (B). Most color displays use three electron beams, one for each primary color.

The screen in a color display has a repeated triangular pattern of red, green, and blue phosphor dots. Each phosphor glows in its color when the electron beam impinges on it. A perforated metal screen, known as a *shadow mask*, ensures each electron beam strikes the correct colored phosphor. The video card varies the intensity of the red, green, and blue electron beams, thereby displaying many colors.

Color palette and resolution

Typically, a video card allows a palette of 256 colors, in which case each pixel's color is stored in an 8-bit value. The actual color (in terms of R, G, B components) that corresponds to a pixel's 8-bit value is determined by consulting a color lookup table or *colormap*.

Today's high-performance video cards allow 3 bytes of storage per pixel, so each pixel's value can directly specify the RGB components that determine that pixel's color. These so-called 24-bit video cards provide true color display, but require more video memory to store the entire image.

Note

The resolution of a display screen is expressed in terms of the number of visible dots (pixels) across a raster line and the total raster lines. A common resolution is 640 dots across by 480 lines vertically, which is commonly expressed as 640×480. Other common screen resolutions are 800×600, 1,024×768, and 1,280×1,024.

Video RAM

The video card stores the contents of the pixels in random access memory (RAM) known as video RAM. The number of colors and the display resolution supported by a video card depend on the amount of video RAM. To store the information content of a 256-color 1,024×768 display screen, for example, the video card needs 1,024×768, or 786,432 bytes of video RAM (because an 8-bit pixel value represents 256 colors and 1 byte = 8 bits). On the other hand, to display 24-bit color at 1,024×768 resolution, the video card needs three times as much video RAM; 3×786,432 = 2,359,296 bytes or about 2.3MB of video RAM (because 24 bit = 3 bytes).

Typical video cards have 1MB, 2MB, or 4MB of video RAM. A video card with 1MB of video RAM can comfortably handle a 256-color, 1,024×768-resolution display.

Dot clock

You will run across the term *dot clock* when you configure a video card to work with XFree86 (the X Window System). *Dot clock* refers to the rate at which the video card can traverse the raster lines that make up a complete display screen. The value of dot clock is expressed in terms of the number of dots drawn per second.

Wizard

To get a rough idea of the dot clock, consider a 640×480 display, which has 640×480 = 307,200 dots (at least, the visible ones). To produce the appearance of a steady display, these dots should be repainted at least 72 times a second. Thus, the video card has to paint 640×480×72 = 22,118,400 dots a second. This rate amounts to approximately 22 million dots a second, which is expressed as a dot clock of 22MHz (1MHz = a million times a second).

In reality, an even higher dot clock is required for a 640×480 display refreshed at 72Hz (which means 72 times a second), because the electron beam cannot turn around on a dime. As illustrated in Figure 10-1, the electron beam must traverse a scan line beyond the visible number of dots before it can snap back to the beginning of the next line. The required dot clock for a 640×480 display at a 72-Hz refresh rate, for example, is 25.2MHz.

As you must realize by now, a higher-resolution display requires even higher dot clocks. A 1,024×768 display at a 72Hz refresh rate implies 1,024×768×72 = 56,623,104 dots per second, at minimum. Thus, you can tell the dot clock necessary for a 1,024×768 display will be somewhat higher than 56.6MHz.

Older video cards support a fixed set of dot clocks, but many advanced video cards include a programmable dot clock. When a video card has a programmable dot clock, the X server can set the video card to operate at any dot clock that lies in a range of acceptable values. For a video card with programmable dot clock, however, you may need to specify the name of the chip that controls the dot clock (known as the *clock chip*).

Importance of video card and monitor

Linux will work with any video card–monitor combination in text mode. If a video card and monitor work under MS-DOS or Windows, the combination will also work under Linux in text mode. The story is different when you install XFree86, the X Window System for Linux. Because XFree86 controls the video card directly (MS-DOS typically uses standard predefined modes of the video card), getting XFree86 running with a specific video card takes more work.

The monitor also is important for XFree86. Electrical signals from the video card control the monitor, so the monitor must be compatible with the video card. The output on the monitor is due to a rapidly moving electron beam that the video card's signals control. A monitor's compatibility with a video card has to do with how fast the video card attempts to move the electron beam on the display screen.

The resolutions supported by a video card–monitor combination depend on the amount of video memory on the card and on how fast the monitor's electron beam can move.

XFree86 gets the necessary information about the monitor and the video card from a special file named `XF86Config`, which usually is in the `/etc/X11` directory.

X-Server Selection

XFree86 comes with several *X* servers, each of which is designed for a specific set of video cards. To select the *X* server to run, you need to know the type of video card your PC has. For a new system, you can find this information by asking the PC's manufacturer. Ideally, you get information about the video card before you order the PC, so you can be sure Linux supports that video card.

If you have an older PC, determining the type of video card may be difficult. At minimum, you need to know what video chipset your system's video card uses. Even better is to know the manufacturer and model of the video card.

Tip

If you don't know anything about your system's video card, you still can run *X*. Assuming your PC is of recent enough vintage, chances are that its video card can emulate the original 16-color Video Graphics Array (VGA) video card. If you have run Microsoft Windows with the VGA driver, for example, you know your video card works as a generic VGA. XFree86 includes an X server named XF86_VGA16, which is designed specifically for the generic 16-color, 640×480 VGA video mode. Although the 16-color VGA mode may not exploit the full capabilities of your system's video card, you can at least get going and use *X*.

XFree86 Version 3.3.2 includes the following X servers (each of which is in the form of a separate executable program):

■ XF86_8514 for video cards based on the IBM 8514/A.

■ XF86_AGX for video cards that use the AGX video chipset.

■ XF86_Mach32 for video cards that use the ATI Mach32 video chipset.

■ XF86_Mach64 for video cards that use the ATI Mach64 video chipset.

■ XF86_Mach8 for video cards that use the ATI Mach8 video chipset.

■ XF86_Mono for a video card operating in the monochrome video mode or 2-color VGA mode.

■ XF86_P9000 for video cards that use the Weitek P9000 chipset. Diamond Viper and Orchid P9000 video cards use this chipset.

■ XF86_S3 for video cards that use the S3 chipset. Notice not all S3-based video cards are supported. You still must have a card this server explicitly supports.

■ XF86_SVGA for a video card operating in Super VGA mode. This category includes a large selection of video cards based on many chipsets.)

■ XF86_VGA16 for a video card operating in 16-color VGA mode. You can use this X server with most video cards, including older VGA and EGA (Enhanced Graphics Adapter) cards.

■ XF86_W32 for video cards that use the Tseng ET4000/W32 video chipset.

This list of servers may grow in future versions of XFree86. You should check the README files in the /usr/X11/lib/X11/doc directory for the latest information about specific video cards.

Cross-Reference

As explained in Chapter 4, you should run the xf86config utility program to set up XFree86 on your system. At that time, when you specify a video card, the xf86config program enables you to select an X server to run. After you select a specific X server, the xf86config program sets up /usr/X11R6/bin/X as a symbolic link to the actual X server binary. To use the XF86_S3 server, for example, the xf86config utility executes the following command:

```
ln -s /usr/X11R6/bin/XF86_S3 /usr/X11R6/bin/X
```

When you start *X* with the startx script or using xdm (as explained in Chapter 5), the X server that is symbolically linked to /usr/X11R6/bin/X is the one that gets started. When the X server starts, it reads the contents of the XF86Config file (from the /etc/X11 directory) to configure the video card and the monitor.

XF86Config File Revisited

When the X server starts, it finds information about the video card, monitor, keyboard, and mouse from the XF86Config file (usually in the /etc/X11 directory). In Chapter 4, I provided an overview of /etc/X11/XF86Config, but I did not fully describe how to fill in several important sections of the file. This section examines the XF86Config file in terms of providing the appropriate information for specific video cards and monitors.

As you learned in Chapter 4, XF86Config consists of several sections. Three sections in XF86Config deal with the video card and monitor:

- The Screen section combines a video card and monitor with the video modes to be used by a specific X server. Typically, XF86Config contains several Screen sections, one for each type of X server.

- The Device section describes the characteristics of a video card (also known as a *graphics device*). The configuration file may have several Device sections.

- The Monitor section lists the technical specifications of a monitor (such as the horizontal and vertical synchronization rates) and includes a list of video modes the monitor supports.

As explained in Chapter 4, you can create the XF86Config file by running the xf86config utility program. If you have your monitor's technical specifications handy and your video card appears in the list xf86config displays, the generated XF86Config file may work as is. You typically run into problems only when you attempt to use the full capabilities of advanced video cards. Later sections of this chapter describe how to use XFree86 with specific advanced video cards.

Screen section

The X server decides the settings of the video card and the monitor from the Screen section meant for that server. The X servers are grouped in four categories with the following names:

- vga2 refers to a video card – monitor combination operating in 2-color mode.

- vga16 means 16-color standard VGA mode.

- svga refers to Super VGA (originally this meant the 256-color, 640×480 mode, but the Super VGA X server supports nearly all video cards and even supports accelerated graphics on many video cards).

- accel refers to all accelerated X servers. (The specific X server depends on the exact chipset. You select the server when you run the xf86config utility program.)

The `Screen` section specifies the X server that can use that section, as well as the names of a `Device` (video card) and a `Monitor`. Following is a `Screen` section meant for an accelerated X server:

```
# Screen for accelerated servers (S3, Mach32, Mach8, 8514, P9000, AGX,
W32, Mach64)
Section "Screen"
  Driver    "accel"
  Device    "Number Nine GXE64 with S3-Trio64"
  Monitor   "Dell VS15X"
  Subsection "Display"
    Depth     8
    Modes     "640x480" "800x600" "1024x768"
    ViewPort  0 0
    Virtual   1024 768
  EndSubsection
  Subsection "Display"
    Depth     16
    Modes     "640x480" "800x600"
    ViewPort  0 0
    Virtual   800 600
  EndSubsection
  Subsection "Display4"
    Depth     32
    Modes     "640x400"
    ViewPort  0 0
    Virtual   640 400
  EndSubsection
EndSection
```

Comment lines start with the pound sign (#). The section's definition is enclosed in the `Section . . . EndSection` block.

The `Driver` line identifies the X server that should use this `Screen` section. Following the `Device` and `Monitor` names are several `Display` subsections. Each `Display` subsection applies to a specific `Depth` (the number of bits of storage per pixel, which also determines the number of colors that can be displayed at a time).

The X server automatically uses the first `Display` subsection in the `Screen` definition, but you can start the server with command-line options that specify a different `Depth`. If you start the X server with the `startx` command, you can use a `Depth` of 24 by issuing the following command:

```
startx -- -bpp 24
```

The `-bpp` option stands for bits per pixel, which is the same as `Depth`. Selecting a value for the `Depth` works provided the video card and the monitor are capable of supporting that `Depth`.

The `Modes` line in the `Display` subsection lists the names of video modes the monitor and video card can support. The names of these modes appear in the `Monitor` section of the `XF86Config` file.

If the video card has more memory than is needed to hold the information for all visible pixels in a specific mode, the X server can use the leftover memory to give the appearance of a much larger array of pixels than the 640×480 or 1,024×768 that may be specified by a video mode. In other words, you get a large virtual screen from which you can select a smaller area to view. The Virtual line indicates the size of this virtual screen, whereas ViewPort specifies which part of the virtual screen is mapped to the physical display.

Device section

The Device section of the XF86Config file provides information about the video card. For the standard VGA mode, XF86Config has a Device section that looks like this:

```
# Standard VGA Device:
Section "Device"
   Identifier   "Generic VGA"
   VendorName   "Unknown"
   BoardName    "Unknown"
   Chipset   "generic"
#   VideoRam  256
#   Clocks  25.2 28.3
EndSection
```

Each line in the section provides some information about the video card. In this case, the Identifier indicates the type of video card. This identifier is used in the Screen section to refer to a specific video card.

VendorName, BoardName, and Chipset further specify the type of video card and the video chipset. For the standard VGA mode, the VendorName, BoardName, and Chipset do not matter. Neither do you have to specify the amount of video RAM (on the VideoRam line) or the allowable dot clocks (on the Clocks line). Thus, they are commented out by the # at the beginning of these lines.

For many video cards that do not have a programmable dot clock, the most important line in the Device section is the Clocks line. The values in this line indicate the dot clocks the video card supports.

If you want, the xf86config program can run the X server with a special option (-probeonly), determine the dot clocks the video card supports, and fill in the Clocks line in the Device section. All you must do is answer Yes when the xf86config program asks whether you want to run *X* in -probeonly mode. When the X -probeonly command is executed, the X server consults the XF86Config file. The X server does not probe for dot clocks if a Clocks line already exists. Also, the configuration file must have the Keyboard and Pointer sections specified correctly so the X server can get to the point of probing the video card. In particular, if an error exists in the type of mouse device, X -probeonly fails.

In addition to the Clocks line, you can specify one or more flags meant for the X server for the type of video card you are specifying in the Device section.

Monitor section

The Monitor section lists the technical specifications of the monitor: the horizontal synchronization (or *horizontal sync*, for short) frequency and vertical refresh rate. You can get these values from your monitor's manual.

Wizard

The horizontal-sync signal occurs at the end of each raster line; this signal moves the electron beam from the end of one line to the beginning of the next raster line. The horizontal-sync frequency essentially is the number of times per second the monitor can trace a raster line on the display screen. If the monitor can display 480 lines (at 640×480 resolution, for example) and repaint the screen 72 times a second (a vertical refresh rate of 72Hz), the horizontal-sync frequency is at least 480×72 = 34,560 times a second = 34,560Hz = 34.56kHz. The actual value is higher because the monitor always has to display more lines than are visible.

Caution

You must be careful with the values of horizontal sync and vertical refresh because the X server uses these values to select what signals are sent from the video card. A monitor may be physically damaged if the video card sends signals beyond the monitor's specifications.

When you use the xf86config program to create the XF86Config file, the xf86config program gives you the option to select the horizontal-synchronization frequencies from a general list, such as standard VGA or a super VGA monitor. If you have no information about a monitor, you may want to start with a conservative setting for the horizontal sync, such as the value for a standard VGA monitor. (You needn't enter the exact value of horizontal sync — just select the monitor type.)

Most new monitors are multisync monitors that support a range of horizontal-synchronization frequencies (as opposed to a fixed value). If you have the monitor's manual, you can specify the range of frequencies for the horizontal sync.

The most important entries in the Monitor section are the Modelines lines, which list the video modes suitable for use with the monitor. Typically, most new users have questions about what to put in Modelines. You needn't actually do much about the Modelines; the xf86config utility program generates a XF86Config file that includes a standard set of mode timings. As long as you specify the monitor's horizontal-sync and vertical-refresh rates (*vertical refresh rate* refers to how often the screen is redrawn each second correctly), the X server automatically selects the best video mode your monitor and video card can support at a given resolution.

Following is a typical Monitor section (with most of the Modelines deleted):

```
Section "Monitor"

    Identifier "Dell VS15X"
    VendorName "Dell"
    ModelName  "VS15X"
```

```
# HorizSync is in kHz unless units are specified.
# HorizSync may be a comma separated list of discrete values, or a
# comma separated list of ranges of values.
# NOTE: THE VALUES HERE ARE EXAMPLES ONLY. REFER TO YOUR MONITOR'S
# USER MANUAL FOR THE CORRECT NUMBERS.

    HorizSync   30-64

#  HorizSync   30-64      # multisync
#  HorizSync   31.5, 35.2 # multiple fixed sync frequencies
#  HorizSync   15-25, 30-50 # multiple ranges of sync frequencies

# VertRefresh is in Hz unless units are specified.
# VertRefresh may be a comma separated list of discrete values, or a
# comma separated list of ranges of values.
# NOTE: THE VALUES HERE ARE EXAMPLES ONLY. REFER TO YOUR MONITOR'S
# USER MANUAL FOR THE CORRECT NUMBERS.

    VertRefresh 55-90

# Modes can be specified in two formats. A compact one-line format, or
# a multi-line format.

# These two are equivalent

#   ModeLine "1024xi" 45 1024 1048 1208 1264 768 776 784 817 Interlace

#   Mode "1024x768i"
#     DotClock   45
#     HTimings   1024 1048 1208 1264
#     VTimings   768 776 784 817
#     Flags      "Interlace"
#   EndMode

# 640x400 @ 70 Hz, 31.5 kHz hsync
Modeline "640x400"   25.175 640 664 760 800   400 409 411 450
# (Modelines deleted)
EndSection
```

The `Monitor` section's `Identifier` field gives a name to this monitor; this name is used in the `Screen` section to refer to this monitor. You should fill in the `HorizSync` and `VertRefresh` lines with information from the monitor's manual (or select conservatively from the typical values that the `xf86config` program displays).

Modeline computation

Although you can live with the standard `Modeline`s that `xf86config` generates, you may want to know the details of that line, in case you have to define a unique mode for a video card – monitor combination.

You typically specify a `Modeline` on a single line with the following syntax:

```
Modeline "name"  CLK  HRES HSS HSE HTOT  VRES VSS VSE VTOT flags
```

You must fill in all arguments that appear in italic except the last argument, which is an optional keyword that indicates the type of the mode. The *flags* field, for example, can be Interlace for an interlaced mode (alternative raster lines are drawn through the image each time) or DoubleScan (each scan line is doubled). Other flags indicate the polarity of the sync signal. The values can be +HSync, -HSync, +VSync, or -VSync, depending on the polarities you specify.

The meanings of the arguments on the Modeline are as follows:

- "*name*" is the name of this mode, in double quotes. Usually, the resolution of the mode is used as its name. Thus, you see mode names, such as "640×480" and "1024×768". These mode names are used in the Display subsection of the Screen section.

- *CLK* is the dot clock to be used for this mode. For a video card with a fixed set of dot clocks, the dot clock should be one of the values on the Clocks line in the Device section of the XF86Config file.

- HRES HSS HSE HTOT are the horizontal timing parameters. HRES is the horizontal resolution in terms of the number of pixels visible on a raster line. As Figure 10-1 shows, the actual number of pixels on a raster line exceeds the number of visible pixels. HTOT is the total pixels on the line. HSS is where the horizontal-sync signal begins and HSE is the pixel number where the horizontal-sync signal ends. The horizontal-sync signal moves the electron beam from one line to the next. For a 640×480 video mode, these four parameters might be 640 680 720 864. This sequence of numbers says 864 pixels are on the raster lines but only 640 are visible. The horizontal-sync signal begins at pixel 680 and ends at pixel 864.

- VRES VSS VSE VTOT are the vertical timing parameters. VRES is the vertical resolution in terms of the number of visible raster lines on the display screen. As Figure 10-1 shows, the actual number of raster lines exceeds the number of visible raster lines. VTOT is the total raster lines. VSS is the line number where the vertical-sync signal begins and VSE is the line number where the vertical-sync signal ends. The vertical-sync signal moves the electron beam from the bottom of the screen to the beginning of the first line. For a 640×480 video mode, these four parameters might be 480 488 491 521.

From a monitor's manual, you can get two key parameters: the vertical refresh rate (in Hz) and the horizontal synchronization frequency (in kHz). The monitor's manual provides these two values as ranges of valid values. The vertical refresh rate typically is between 50Hz and 90Hz; the horizontal sync frequency can be anywhere from 30kHz to 135kHz. Following are two equations that define the relationship between the dot clock and some of the horizontal and vertical timing parameters on the Modeline:

```
CLK = RR * HTOT * VTOT
CLK = HSF * HTOT
```

In these equations, RR is a screen refresh rate within the range of vertical refresh rate of the monitor and HSF is a horizontal-scan frequency supported by the monitor. Remember to convert everything to a common unit (for example, make sure all values are in Hz) when you apply these formulas.

To define a mode, you can start with a desired refresh rate (RR), such as 72Hz. For a given dot clock, you then can compute the product HTOT * VTOT from the first equation. Next, plug in a value for HSF within the range of supported horizontal-scan frequencies for the monitor. Because the dot clock is already known, you can compute HTOT from the second equation. After you know HTOT, you can determine VTOT because you already computed the product of HTOT * VTOT.

At this point, you know HTOT and VTOT. What you have to select are the arguments HSS, HSE, VSS, and VSE, which you need for the Modeline. Unfortunately, determining these four parameters requires some trial and error. You can pick the HRES and VRES values first (HRES and VRES determine the resolution of the mode). Then you have to select HSS and HSE to lie between HRES and HTOT and HSE > HSS. Similarly, VSS and VSE should be between VRES and VTOT and VSE > VSS.

If the display area looks small or not centered, you must alter the values HSS, HSE, VSS, and VSE to tweak the display. Given that the default XF86Config file already includes the Modelines for many common video modes, you should simply provide the allowable ranges of vertical refresh rates and horizontal-sync frequencies for your monitor and settle for one of the predefined modes.

Common Video Cards

XFree86 supports a wide variety of common video cards. Although the video card's brand name can be important, the video chipset is what matters most to the X server. XFree86 3.3.2 provides the XF86_SVGA server, which supports video cards based on the following chipsets:

- Tseng ET3000, ET4000AX, ET4000/W32, and ET6000

- Western Digital/Paradise PVGA1

- Western Digital WD90C00, WD90C10, WD90C11, WD90C24, WD90C30, WD90C31, and WD90C33

- Genoa GVGA

- Trident TVGA8800CS, TVGA8900B, TVGA8900C, TVGA8900CL, TVGA9000, TVGA9000i, TVGA9100B, TVGA9200CX, TVGA9320, TVGA9400CX, TVGA9420, TGUI9420DGi, TGUI9430DGi, TGUI9440AGi, TGUI9660XGi, and TGUI9680

- ATI 18800, 18800-1, 28800-2, 28800-4, 28800-5, 28800-6, 68800-3, 68800-6, 68800AX, 68800LX, 88800GX-C, 88800GX-D, 88800GX-E, 88800GX-F, 88800CX, 264CT, 264ET, 264VT, 264VT2, and 264GT

- NCR 77C22, 77C22E, and 77C22E+

- Cirrus Logic CLGD5420, CLGD5422, CLGD5424, CLGD5426, CLGD5428, CLGD5429, CLGD5430, CLGD5434, CLGD5436, CLGD5440, CLGD5446, CLGD5462, CLGD5464, CLGD6205, CLGD6215, CLGD6225, CLGD6235, CLGD6410, CLGD6412, CLGD6420, and CLGD6440

- Chips & Technologies 65520, 65530, 65540, 65545, 65520, 65530, 65540, 65545, 65546, 65548, 65550, and 65554

- Compaq AVGA

- OAK OTI067, OTI077, and OTI087

- Alliance AP6422

- Avance Logic ALG2101, ALG2228, ALG2301, ALG2302, ALG2308, ALG2401

- ARK Logic ARK1000PV, ARK1000VL, ARK2000PV, and ARK2000MT

- Matrox MGA2064W and Mystique cards

- MX MX68000 and MX680010

- NVidia/SGS Thomson NV1, and STG2000

- RealTek RTG3106

- SiS 86C201, 86C202, and 86C205

- Video 7/Headland Technologies HT216-32

The XF86_SVGA server uses these video cards in Super VGA (SVGA) mode, typically at resolutions up to 1,024×768, with 256 colors.

For late-breaking news on specific video chipsets, consult the following files in the /usr/X11/lib/X11/doc directory:

README.ati describes the XF86_SVGA server's support for ATI VGA Wonder series video cards.

README.cirrus describes the XF86_SVGA server's support for Cirrus Logic's video chipsets, including support for some accelerated graphics capabilities. The file also describes the options that relate to the Cirrus chipsets.

README.trident describes the XF86_SVGA server's support for Trident video chipsets including any options that affect the Trident chipsets.

README.Video7 describes the XF86_SVGA server's support for the Headland Technologies HT216-32 chipset.

README.WstDig describes the XF86_SVGA server's support for Western Digital video chipsets, including the WD90C31 and WD90C33, with accelerated graphics capabilities.

Accelerated Video Cards

If you want faster graphics under *X,* you need an accelerated video card that uses special video chipsets. Quite a few accelerated video chipsets are available and more will appear as PCs move to graphical operating systems such as Microsoft Windows and X Window System.

Following are some of the popular accelerated video chipsets:

- S3 chipsets (86C911, 86C924, 86C801, 86C805, 86C805i, 86C928, 86C864, 86C964, 86C732 or Trio32, 86C764 or Trio64, 86C765, 86C868, 86C968, 86C325, and 86C988) are used in a wide variety of brand name video cards, such as Diamond Stealth 24 VLB, Diamond Stealth 64, Number Nine GXE64, Number Nine GXE64 PCI, and SPEA Mirage P64. These chipsets are supported by the XF86_S3 server.

- S3 ViRGE (86C325), S3 ViRGE/DX (86C375), S3 ViRGE/GX (86C385) and S3 ViRGE/VX (86C988) chips are used in many new video cards such as Diamond Stealth 3D 2000, ELSA Winner 3000, Hercules Terminator 3D, and STB Nitro 3D. These newer S3 chips are supported by the XF86_S3V server.

- The Weitek P9000 chipset is used in video boards such as Diamond Viper VLB, Diamond Viper PCI, and Orchid P9000. The chipset is supported by the XF86_P9000 server.

- ATI Mach8, Mach32, and Mach64 chipsets are used in ATI-brand video cards, such as ATI Graphics Xpression Mach64. These chipsets are supported by the XF86_Mach8, XF86_Mach32, and XF86_Mach64 server.

- Tseng ET4000/W32 chipsets are used by video cards such as Hercules Dynamite Pro VLB and Mirage ET4000/W32 VLB. These chipsets are supported by the XF86_W32 server.

- IBM 8514/A chipsets (and clones) are used by video cards such as IBM 8514/A and Western Digital WD9510-AT. These chipsets are supported by the XF86_8514 server.

- IIT AGX-014, AGX-015, and AGX-016 chipsets are used in video cards such as the Hercules Graphite series. These chipsets are supported by the XF86_AGX server.

- The accelerated features of the Cirrus Logic CLGD5420, CLGD5422, CLGD5424, CLGD5426, CLGD5428, CLGD5429, CLGD5430, CLGD5434, CLGD6205, CLGD6215, CLGD6225, and CLGD6235 chipsets are primarily used in the video cards integrated into laptops. These chipsets are supported directly by the XF86_SVGA server.

- The accelerated features of the Western Digital WD90C31 and WD90C33 chipsets are supported directly by the XF86_SVGA server.

- The accelerated features of the Oak OTI-087 chipset are supported directly by the XF86_SVGA server.

XFree86 includes a separate server for each accelerated chipset except the Cirrus, Western Digital, and Oak chipsets. These chipsets are directly supported by the XF86_SVGA server.

The following sections describe a few popular accelerated video cards and video chipsets. For late-breaking news on specific video chipsets, consult the following files in the /usr/X11/lib/X11/doc directory:

README.agx describes the XF86 AGX server, which supports a wide variety of video cards based on the IIT AGX video chipset.

README.Oak describes the XF86_SVGA server's support for video cards based on Oak Technologies Inc.'s OTI067, OTI077, and OTI087 chipsets.

README.P9000 describes the XF86_P9000 server's support for the Weitek P9000 video chipset.

README.S3 describes the XF86_S3 server that supports a wide variety of video cards based on the S3 video chipset.

README.S3V describes the XF86_S3V server that supports a wide variety of video cards based on the S3 ViRGE video chipset.

README.W32 describes the XF86_W32 server's support for video cards based on the ET4000/W32 series of chipsets.

Diamond Viper and Orchid P9000

Two versions of the Diamond Viper video card are available: Viper VLB for Video Local Bus and Viper PCI for PCI systems. The Diamond Viper and Orchid P9000 video cards are based on the Weitek Power 9000 (P9000) video chipset, which the XF86_P9000 accelerated X server supports.

The XF86_P9000 server expects to find the name of the vendor on the Chipset line in the Device section of the XF86Config file. The server recognizes the following Chipset lines:

```
Chipset "viperpci"      # Diamond Viper PCI
Chipset "vipervlb"      # Diamond Viper VLB
Chipset "orchid_p9000"  # Orchid P9000
```

Historically, Linux did not support Diamond Video cards because Diamond did not freely provide technical information about its card. You had to sign a nondisclosure agreement to obtain such information. Since late 1994, however, Diamond has provided detailed technical information about its video cards to XFree86 developers without any restrictions. The net result is that all new Diamond video cards now are supported by XFree86.

ATI Mach8, Mach32, and Mach64

ATI Mach8 and Mach32 are IBM 8514/A-compatible accelerated video chipsets. The XF86_Mach8 and XF86_Mach32 accelerated X servers support the ATI Mach8 and Mach32 based video cards, respectively.

ATI Mach64 is a more recent high-performance video chipset. Several brands of ATI video cards, such as ATI Graphics Pro Turbo and ATI Graphics Xpression, use the Mach64 video chipset. Many Pentium PCI systems use the ATI Graphics Xpression video card. The version of XFree86 on the companion CD-ROM includes the XF86_Mach64 server that supports the Mach64 video card.

Secret

Some ATI video cards, such as the ATI Graphics Ultra and Ultra Pro, come with a mouse port. This mouse port conforms to the Logitech bus mouse protocol. If you have a mouse connected to the ATI card's mouse port, you should install the Logitech bus mouse driver.

S3 video cards

The S3 chipset is a popular accelerated video chipset used in many video cards. Table 10-1 shows the specific video cards (brand names) the XF86_S3 server supports in XFree86 3.3.2 — the latest release of XFree86. The bits-per-pixel (BPP) column shows the maximum BPP supported for that card. When the BPP column shows 32, for example, the 8- and 16-BPP modes are also supported.

Table 10-1 also includes video cards based on the S3 ViRGE chipset. The XF86_S3V server supports these video cards.

Table 10-1	S3-based video cards supported by XFree86 3.3.2	
S3 chipset	**Bits per pixel (bpp)**	**Cards**
801/805	16	Actix GE 32, Orchid Fahrenheit 1280+, STB PowerGraph X.24, JAX 8231, SPEA Mirage, STB PowerGraph X.24
805	16	Miro 10SD VLB/PCI, SPEA Mirage VLB
805	8	Diamond Stealth 24 VLB
928	16	Actix Ultra, SPEA Mercury VLB
928	32	ELSA Winner 1000 ISA/VLB/EISA, STB Pegasus VL, Number Nine GXE Level 10/11/12, Number Nine GXE Level 14/16
864	32	Actix GE 64 VLB, Miro 20SD (BIOS 1.x, BIOS 2.x, BIOS 3.x), ELSA Winner 1000 PRO VLB/PCI, ELSA Winner 1000 PRO, SPEA Mirage P64 DRAM (BIOS 4.x), Diamond Stealth 64 DRAM, Genoa Phantom 64i , Miro Crystal 20SD VLB (BIOS 3.x), Number Nine GXE64 PCI

(continued)

S3 chipset	Bits per pixel (bpp)	Cards
864	16	SPEA Mirage P64 DRAM (BIOS 3.x)
964	32	Miro Crystal 20SV PCI, Diamond Stealth 64, SPEA Mercury 64, Number Nine GXE64 Pro VLB/PCI, Miro Crystal 40SV, Hercules Graphite Terminator 64
964	8	ELSA Winner 2000 PRO PCI
868	32	ELSA Winner 1000AVI, Miro Crystal 20SD PCI
968	32	ELSA Winner 2000PRO/X, Diamond Stealth 64 Video VRAM, Genoa VideoBlitz III AVI, Hercules Terminator Pro 64, STB Velocity 64V, Number Nine FX Motion 771, Diamond Stealth 64 Video 3240/3400
732 (Trio32)	32	Diamond Stealth 64 DRAM SE, all Trio32-based cards
764 (Trio64)	32	SPEA Mirage P64 (BIOS 5.x), Diamond Stealth 64 DRAM, Diamond Stealth 64 Graphics 2000, Number Nine FX Vision 330, STB PowerGraph 64, all Trio64-based cards
ViRGE/DX/ GX/VX	32	Diamond Multimedia Stealth 3D 2000, Diamond Stealth 3D 2000, Diamond Stealth 3D 2000 PRO, Diamond Stealth 3D 3000, ELSA Winner 3000-S, Hercules Terminator 64/3D, Number Nine FX Motion 332, Orchid Tech. Fahrenheit Video 3D, STB systems Powergraph 3D, STB Nitro 3D

Table title (above): **Table 10-1** *(Continued)*

Although many video cards use the same S3 chipset, they differ in two significant areas:

- The clock chip that generates the dot clocks
- A chip, known as RAMDAC, that converts the contents of the video memory to analog signals sent to the monitor

Secret

When you select one of the supported S3-based video cards, you needn't specify the clock chip or RAMDAC. If you come across a new S3-based video card whose name does not appear in the list of supported cards, you may be able to get the XF86_S3 or XF86_S3V server to work with that card by specifying its clock chip and RAMDAC in the Device section of the XF86Config file.

Most RAMDACs are detected automatically by the X server, but if you have a video card with the AT&T 20C490 RAMDAC, you should include the following line in the Device section of the XF86Config file:

```
RamDac "att20c490"
```

Table 10-2 lists the supported clock chips and the ClockChip line you can use to specify the chip in the Device section of the Xf86Config file.

Table 10-2	Supported clock chips and the ClockChip LINE
Clock chip	ClockChip *line in* XF86Config
AT&T 20C409	ClockChip "att20c409"
Chrontel 8391	ClockChip "ch8391"
DCS2824-0 (Diamond, ICD2061A-compatible)	ClockChip "dcs2824"
IBM RGB 5xx	ClockChip "ibm_rgb5xx"
ICD2061A	ClockChip "icd2061a"
ICS2595	ClockChip "ics2595"
ICS5300 GENDAC (86c708-compatible)	ClockChip "ics5300"
ICS5342 GENDAC	ClockChip "ics5342"
ICS9161A (ICD2061A-compatible)	ClockChip "ics9161a"
S3 86c708 GENDAC	ClockChip "s3gendac"
S3 86c716 SDAC	ClockChip "s3_sdac"
Sierra SC11412	ClockChip "sc11412"
STG 1703	ClockChip "stg1703"
TI3025	ClockChip "ti3025"
TI3026	ClockChip "ti3026"

Commercial X Servers for XFree86

If XFree86 does not support your high-performance video card, you may have to look at a commercial X server. The price is between $100 and $200, but you get an X server that supports more cards than XFree86 does. For cards XFree86 already supports, the commercial version may provide better performance than XFree86 does.

Following are two well-known commercial X servers are:

■ Metro-X from Metro Link, Inc. For information, send e-mail to sales@metrolink.com or visit the company's Web site at http://www.metrolink.com/.

■ Accelerated-X from Xi Graphics, Inc. For information, send e-mail to sales@xig.com or try the company's Web page at http://www.xig.com/.

Following are examples of video cards supported by commercial X servers:

- ATI 3D RAGE PRO
- Matrox MGA Millenium II
- NeoMagic MagicGraph 128
- Number Nine Imagine 128, 9FX Vision330, and Revolution 3D
- Compaq QVision 2000
- Weitek P9100 chipset (used in video cards such as Diamond Viper Pro)
- Chips & Technologies 82C45x, 82C48x, and F655xx video chipsets

Many Pentium PCs are sold with these high-performance video cards. Although XFree86 probably will begin supporting at least some of these cards in the future, right now, these commercial products enable you to exploit these video cards under *X* and Linux.

The commercial X servers also do a better job of supporting 16-, 24-, and 32-bits-per-pixel (bpp) modes better than the XFree86 servers do. These modes essentially refer to the number of colors you can display on a monitor simultaneously. The 24-bpp mode allows 1 byte each for the RGB (red, green, and blue) components of color. The 32-bpp mode essentially is the 24-bpp mode, but the RGB value for a single pixel is stored in a 32-bit word, with 1 byte wasted (but 32 bit data transfer is more efficient than 24-bit data transfer). The term *24 bpp* is used to refer to the case in which the 24-bit RGB values are stored without wasting any space. As a result, the 24-bpp mode often is referred to as 24-bpp packed-pixel mode.

Summary

Video cards and monitors don't matter much if you use Linux in text mode only. If you want to use the XFree86 X Window System, however, you must pay attention to the video card and monitor. This chapter describes how XFree86 is configured and what types of video cards and monitors it supports.

By reading this chapter, you learn the following:

▶ In a PC, the video card stores the array of pixels that constitutes the image you see onscreen. The video card converts the pixel values to analog signals that drive the red (R), green (G), and blue (B) electron guns in a monitor. These RGB electron beams, in turn, paint the color image on the phosphor-coated display screen. The combination of the video card and monitor is important to the X Window System because the X server controls the video card directly and because the monitor must be capable of handling the signals the video card generates.

▶ XFree86 includes several X servers, each designed for a specific category of video cards, ranging from the generic VGA to accelerated cards such as ATI Mach64 and S3. You must select the X server based on the type of video card in your system, so you need to know what card you have before setting up XFree86.

▶ When the X server runs, it consults a configuration file named `XF86Config` (usually in the `/etc` directory) to select an appropriate video mode and to configure the video card and monitor for proper operation. Computing the valid video-mode parameters is complicated. As long as you know the technical specification of your monitor (such as horizontal-synchronization frequency and refresh rate), you needn't compute the video-mode information.

▶ Video cards fall into two broad groups. All Super VGA cards are controlled by the XF86_SVGA server and the accelerated video cards have custom X servers, such as XF86_S3 and XF86_Mach64.

▶ XFree86 supports most of the popular high-performance video cards, but if your favorite video card is not on the supported list, you must turn to a commercial vendor. For a small price, you can buy an X server for newer video cards, such as Number Nine Imagine 128 and Matrox MGA Millenium II.

Chapter 11

Disk Drives

In This Chapter

▶ Surveying the different types of disk controllers Linux supports

▶ Understanding disk drive concepts: cylinder, heads, and sectors (CHS)

▶ Understanding disk drive operations: partitioning and booting with LILO

▶ Understanding the 1,024-cylinder limit of BIOS

▶ Surveying SCSI disks Linux supports

▶ Troubleshooting SCSI

▶ Using Iomega Zip drives in Linux

▶ Looking at known bugs in EIDE disk controllers for the PCI bus

When it comes to disk drives and Linux, what matters is whether Linux supports the *disk controller*: the card that connects the disk drive to your PC's motherboard. Linux supports most common disk controllers. This chapter gives you information on different disk controllers and specific details on how to install and run Linux on a system that has one or more of these controllers.

Disk Controller Types

The disk controller is the adapter card that acts as an intermediary between your PC's motherboard and one or more hard disk drives. Typically, you can connect up to two hard drives and two floppy drives to a single disk controller. The Small Computer System Interface (SCSI) controller is an exception to this norm; you can connect up to seven SCSI devices (anything that has a SCSI interface, such as a disk drive, CD-ROM drive, tape drive, or scanner).

Over the years, several types of hard disk controllers have appeared for the PC. Following are some of the disk controllers you may find in a PC:

- *ST506* disk controllers, which originally appeared in IBM XT and AT computers, became the common disk controller of the PC industry in its early years (remember, the IBM PC-AT came out in 1984). Many PCs have disk controllers that are compatible with the ST506. Seagate's ST506 was the original hard drive for PCs; Western Digital's WD1003 was the controller card. Thus, these controllers are often referred to as being WD1003-compatible controllers. The original ST506 drives used a recording method known as Modified Frequency Modulation (MFM). Many ST506 disk controllers also support drives that use another type of data-recording technique, known as Run Length Limited (RLL).

- The *Integrated Drive Electronics* (IDE) interface emulates the ST506 interface. IDE drives, however, contain the necessary controller circuitry built into the drive itself. The motherboard typically contains an IDE interface for connecting the drive to the motherboard. By now, IDE drives are in widespread use in PCs. Nowadays, the term *AT Attachment* (ATA) is used to refer to IDE. The original IDE interface could support only two drives and it limited the maximum disk size to approximately 500MB. You needed third-party drivers to use disks larger than 500MB. Today's PCs with large disk drives use the Enhanced IDE interface (described next).

- The *Enhanced IDE* (EIDE) interface supports up to four internal IDE devices (which include hard drives as well as CD-ROM drives), higher-capacity drives, and higher speeds of data transfer. Typical EIDE interfaces consist of two IDE interfaces: primary and secondary, each of which is capable of supporting up to two drives. EIDE interfaces are popular because of their low cost. Many PCs use the EIDE interface to connect both the hard disk and the CD-ROM drive to the PC's motherboard.

- The *Enhanced Small Device Interface* (ESDI) controllers emulate the ST506 interface but provide higher data-transfer rates.

- *Small Computer System Interface* (SCSI) controllers provide a separate bus onto which you can connect up to seven SCSI devices. You can find hard drives, CD-ROM drives, tape drives, and scanners that support SCSI. You can connect multiple SCSI devices to the computer by daisy-chaining the devices with a SCSI cable. All UNIX workstations (such as the ones from Hewlett-Packard, IBM, and Sun Microsystems) use SCSI. Lately, SCSI is also becoming popular on PCs. The only drawback is that the SCSI controller is relatively expensive compared with EIDE controllers.

Linux supports all these common disk controllers. Even though several disk controllers appear in the preceding list, essentially two types of controllers exist: IDE (where IDE refers to all ST506-compatible interfaces) and SCSI.

Cross-
Reference

Most Pentium systems use a motherboard that supports the Peripheral
Component Interconnect (PCI) bus. These PCI systems need SCSI adapter
cards that plug into PCI bus slots and IDE interface that connects to the PCI
bus. Linux supports the PCI bus. Initially, problems occurred with specific
PCI-interface hardware, but Linux can now work around some of these
problems. The PCI bus seems poised to become the dominant bus in the PC
marketplace, replacing the old and outdated ISA bus. (Chapter 9 discusses
various buses.)

Disk Drive Concepts

When you read about disk drives, you'll run into some terms and concepts
unique to the world of hard disks. This section explains some of these
concepts.

Cylinders, heads, and sectors

The physical organization of the disk is expressed in terms of cylinders,
heads, and sectors. A hard disk consists of several platters of magnetic
material. In physical terms, you can think of *cylinder, head*, and *sector* as
meaning the following:

- A *cylinder* is one of a series of concentric rings on one side of a disk
  platter. Each side of the platter is divided into cylinders.

- The total number of *heads* is the number of sides of all the magnetic
  platters.

- A *sector* is a pie-shape wedge on the platter. Each cylinder is divided into
  sectors.

Any location on the disk can be expressed in terms of the cylinder, the head,
and the sector. Identifying a disk location in terms of cylinder (C), head (H),
and sector (S) is known as *CHS addressing*.

Wizard

The physical *geometry* of a hard disk usually is expressed in terms of
cylinders, heads, and sectors. A disk may have a geometry of
528/32/63, which means the disk has 528 cylinders, 32 heads, and 63
sectors. Usually, each sector can store 512 bytes (or half a kilobyte) of
data. Thus, the capacity of this disk is (528×32×63) / 2 kilobytes, or
532,224 kilobytes.

Note

PC hard disk controllers include a read-only memory (ROM) Basic
Input/Output System (BIOS) on the controller. By convention (and
compatibility with the original IBM PC architecture), the BIOS uses CHS
addressing to access the hard disk. The disk BIOS, however, uses a 10-bit
value as the cylinder address. Because 10 bits can hold numbers between 0
and 1,023, the BIOS can address, at most, 1,024 cylinders.

Many large disks have more than 1,024 cylinders. To accommodate the 1,024-cylinder limit, the disk controllers have to resort to some tricks to handle disks with more than 1,024 cylinders. Later, in the section on "Disks with more than 1,024 Cylinders," you read more about problems with disks that have more than 1,024 cylinders; you should be able to relate to this problem.

Master Boot Record (MBR)

The first sector of the hard disk (cylinder 0, head 0, sector 1) is called the *Master Boot Record* (MBR). This 512-byte storage area contains important information about the disk, such as the partition table and a small amount of code the PC's BIOS loads and runs when you boot the PC.

The small program in the MBR reads the partition table; determines which partition is active (that's just an attribute of a partition); reads the active partition's first sector — or *boot sector* — and runs whatever program resides in that boot sector. The program in a partition's boot sector usually loads whatever operating system is installed on that partition.

When you install the Linux Loader (LILO) on the hard disk, the LILO program resides on the hard disk's MBR or the boot sector of the partition where the Linux root directory (/) is located.

Partitions

Partitions are a way of dividing a hard disk and treating each part separately. By dividing your PC's hard disk into partitions, you can install different operating systems in different partitions. Even if you use the entire disk for Linux, you would, at minimum, need a partition Linux can use as *swap space* — an extension of memory, so you can have more virtual memory than the physical memory on your system.

The Master Boot Record contains the partition table, starting at byte 446 (0x1be, which means 1be in hexadecimal). The partition table can have up to four 16-byte entries. Each 16-byte value defines a partition. Each partition is specified by a starting and an ending cylinder number. The partition entry also includes a type that identifies the operating system that created the partition. The concept of partitions is a convention all PC-based operating systems, ranging from MS-DOS to Linux, follow.

In MS-DOS, you use the FDISK program to manipulate the partitions. Linux includes a program with the same name — fdisk (lowercase) — to alter the disk partitions.

Linux device names for disks

In Linux, each device is represented by a device file in the /dev directory. The device name for the hard disk depends on the type of disk controller. For IDE and EIDE drives, the device name is /dev/hda for the first disk, /dev/hdb for the second disk, and so on.

On an EIDE interface, if you have a hard disk on the primary interface and a CD-ROM drive on the secondary interface, the device names are /dev/hda for the hard disk drive and /dev/hdc for the CD-ROM drive.

The Linux disk drivers treat each disk partition as being a separate device. The first partition in the first IDE disk is /dev/hda1, the second partition is /dev/hda2, the third one is /dev/hda3, and so on. Similarly, the device names for the partitions on the second IDE drive are /dev/hdb1, /dev/hdb2, and so on.

The SCSI disk devices are named /dev/sda, /dev/sdb, and so on. If a SCSI device is a hard disk, its partitions are named by appending the partition number to the device name. Thus, the partitions of the first SCSI hard disk are named /dev/sda1, /dev/sda2, /dev/sda3, and so on.

Floppy Disks in Linux

Chapter 7 describes several ways to access MS-DOS floppy disks under Linux. You can mount the floppy and use Linux commands or use the mtools utility programs to read from or write to the floppy. You also can create a Linux file system on a floppy disk. In fact, you'll find Linux file systems on the boot and root floppies you use to install Linux.

Formatting and creating a Linux file system on a floppy disk is a straightforward process. To format a 3.5-inch high-density floppy in the A drive, for example, use the following command:

```
fdformat /dev/fd0H1440
```

For a 5.25-inch high-density floppy, change the device name to /dev/fd0h1200. On the B drive, change the first 0 in the device name to 1.

Wizard

After you format the floppy, use the following command to create a Linux file system on the floppy:

```
mke2fs -m 0 /dev/fd0H1440 1440
```

The -m option is used to specify what percentage of blocks should be reserved for use by the *super user* (root). By specifying the -m 0 option, you ensure mke2fs does not reserve any space on the floppy disk for the super user. If you do not explicitly specify the -m option, mke2fs reserves 5 percent of the disk space for the super user.

After you create the file system on the floppy drive, you can mount the floppy at a *mount point* (an empty directory) in the Linux file system. The following example shows how to mount the floppy drive at the /mnt directory:

```
mount /dev/fd0H1440 /mnt
```

Now you can use Linux commands, such as cp and mv, to copy or move files to the floppy disk. Before you eject the floppy disk from the drive, use the following command to dismount the floppy:

```
umount /dev/fd0H1440
```

Hard Disk Operations in Linux

You must perform some disk operations to install and use Linux on your system. Chapter 1 explains some of the disk operations you perform when you set up Linux. The next few sections provide some additional information about these disk operations.

When you first get a PC, the hard disk usually is set up as a one huge partition, and DOS and Windows are already installed on it. (If you bought your PC recently, it probably came with Windows 95 or Windows 98 preinstalled.) To install Linux, you have to start by creating at least two partitions for Linux: one for the swap space and the other for the Linux file system.

If you have original disks to reinstall the current operating system (be it Windows 95 or MS-DOS and Windows 3.1), simply go ahead and repartition the disk. To do this, boot the PC, using a DOS boot floppy, and run the MS-DOS version of FDISK program to delete the current partition and create new ones. Create three new partitions: One for DOS and Windows, one for Linux swap space, and one for the Linux file system. Then you have to reinstall DOS and Windows in their partition and install Linux on the other partition.

Cross-Reference

If you do not want to go through the trouble of reinstalling DOS and Windows or Windows 95, you have to alter the existing partition somehow. FIPS, which can split an existing DOS partition into two separate partitions, enables you to perform this task. Chapter 1 describes how to use FIPS.

Partitioning with fdisk

Partitioning the disk involves creating several smaller logical devices within a single hard disk. Under MS-DOS, you would use the FDISK program to view and alter a disk's partition table. In Linux, the partitioning program is called fdisk.

Chapter 1 explains how to use Linux and MS-DOS FDISK during Linux installation. I mention it here for the sake of completeness, to jog your memory about the `fdisk` program.

Even if you have already partitioned your hard disk, you can always run `fdisk` just to see the current partition table of a hard disk. If you have a SCSI disk drive with the device name `/dev/sda`, for example, you can look at its partition table with `fdisk` as follows:

```
fdisk /dev/sda
Command (m for help): m
Command action
   a   toggle a bootable flag
   b   edit bsd disklabel
   c   toggle the dos compatibility flag
   d   delete a partition
   l   list known partition types
   m   print this menu
   n   add a new partition
   p   print the partition table
   q   quit without saving changes
   t   change a partition's system id
   u   change display/entry units
   v   verify the partition table
   w   write table to disk and exit
   x   extra functionality (experts only)

Command (m for help): p
Disk /dev/sda: 64 heads, 32 sectors, 500 cylinders
Units = cylinders of 2048 * 512 bytes

   Device Boot  Begin   Start    End  Blocks   Id  System
/dev/sda1           1       1    301  308208    6  DOS 16-bit >=32M
/dev/sda2         302     302    499  202752   83  Linux native

Command (m for help): q
```

The `m` command shows you a list of the single-letter commands `fdisk` accepts. You can see the current partition table with a `p` command. This example's SCSI disk has two partitions: one for DOS and the other for Linux.

The `Id` field in the table of partitions printed by the `fdisk` program (when you type **p** at the `fdisk` prompt) is a number that denotes a partition type. If you want to see a list of all known partition types, type **l** (that's a lowercase *L*) at the `fdisk` prompt. Table 11-1 lists the partition types that Linux understands:

Table 11-1			Partition types known to Linux				
Type	**Description**	**Type**	**Description**	**Type**	**Description**	**Type**	**Description**
0	Empty	9	AIX bootable	75	PC/IX	b7	BSDI fs
1	DOS 12-bit FAT	a	OS/2 Boot Manager	80	Old MINIX	b8	BSDI swap
2	XENIX root	b	Win95 FAT32	81	Linux/MINIX	c7	Syrinx
3	XENIX usr	40	Venix 80286	82	Linux swap	db	CP/M
4	DOS 16-bit <32M	51	Novell?	83	Linux native	e1	DOS access
5	Extended	52	Microport	93	Amoeba	e3	DOS R/O
6	DOS 16-bit >=32	63	GNU HURD	94	Amoeba BBT	f2	DOS secondary
7	OS/2 HPFS	64	Novell Netware	a5	BSD/386	ff	BBT
8	AIX	65	Novell Netware				

Booting from the hard disk with LILO

To boot Linux from a hard disk automatically, you need the Linux Loader (LILO). LILO is a boot loader program; OS/2 has an equivalent program, called *Boot Manager.* These programs usually reside in the Master Boot Record of a disk and are the first to get loaded. The boot loader program then, in turn, prompts you for the name of a operating system to start (which typically means a disk partition from which to boot). Starting an operating system basically involves loading that operating system's main program into memory and running it. For Linux, this step involves loading the Linux kernel into memory and giving control to the kernel.

Cross-Reference

LILO is much more than just Linux Loader; it also serves as a general-purpose boot manager capable of booting MS-DOS, OS/2, or Windows 95. Chapter 1 describes how you can install LILO on your hard disk during the Linux installation process. This section summarizes the LILO installation process if you do it outside the Linux installation program described in Chapter 1.

Tip

The LILO documentation is in /usr/doc/lilo-0.20 on your system. You should consult the README file in /usr/doc/lilo-0.20 for the latest word on installing and configuring LILO. The following section provides an overview only.

Installing LILO

Typically, you install LILO as part of the Linux installation process described in Chapter 1. The only time you must repeat LILO configuration and installation is when you update the kernel or add a new operating system you want to boot through LILO.

Installing LILO involves two basic steps:

1. Prepare the LILO configuration file, which contains information necessary for installing LILO. The default LILO configuration file is /etc/lilo.conf.

2. Run the /sbin/lilo program (referred to as the *map installer* in LILO's README file) to update the boot sector and create the /boot/map file, which contains information that LILO uses during the boot process.

Cross-Reference

To prepare the LILO configuration file, you must log in as root and edit the /etc/lilo.conf file. Chapter 2 briefly describes how to edit this file. Essentially, you add or edit information about the operating systems you want to boot with Linux and the names of the disk partitions where those operating systems reside.

When the LILO configuration file — /etc/lilo.conf — is ready, you can install LILO with the following command:

```
/sbin/lilo
```

The lilo program looks for the lilo.conf file in the /etc directory, interprets its contents, prepares the necessary boot and map files, and initializes the boot record of the device specified (by the boot line) in the configuration file. If the boot device is specified as a hard disk partition, for example, LILO sets up the boot sector of that disk partition.

Tip

The files in /usr/doc/lilo-0.20, especially /usr/doc/lilo-0.20/README, contain the latest information on LILO. You may want to check out this directory if you have a unique arrangement of hard disk partitions and you want to find out whether you can use LILO to boot Linux.

Using LILO's boot prompt

As LILO starts, it displays the boot: prompt and waits for the name of a boot image to load. If you do not respond within a specified period (this value is stored in the /etc/lilo.conf file), LILO loads the default boot image (the first image in the /etc/lilo.conf file).

Wizard

When you use LILO to boot Linux, you can specify the name of the Linux boot image, followed by one or more options. LILO passes these boot command-line options directly to the Linux kernel. As you read descriptions of various disk controllers, you find information on boot command-line options you can use to specify various parameters of a device. These parameters typically include the I/O port address, IRQ, and DMA of a device. Notice boot command-line options are always case-sensitive.

Removing LILO

If you set up LILO on the hard disk's Master Boot Record, but later want to remove it, you can do so easily, provided you have MS-DOS Version 5.0 or later. All you must do is boot from a DOS boot floppy (place the boot floppy in drive A and then power up the PC) and run FDISK with the /MBR option. The FDISK /MBR command essentially restores the Master Boot Record to the format MS-DOS uses. The next time you boot the PC, MS-DOS should start immediately.

Another way to uninstall LILO is to use LILO itself as follows:

```
/sbin/lilo -u
```

LILO replaces the MBR from a saved copy of the old boot sector, which LILO saves when you first install LILO.

Caution

Use the /sbin/lilo -u command only if you have installed LILO on your hard disk's MBR. When you use the -u option, LILO simply copies a file named /boot/boot.*nnnn* (*nnnn* is the device number, such as 0300 for the /dev/hda and 0800 for /dev/sda) to the disk's MBR. If you have been playing with LILO and an old boot file happens to be left over in the /boot directory, LILO might copy that file to the MBR. A bad MBR, of course, makes the disk unbootable. In such a case, boot from a DOS floppy and use the FDISK /MBR command to restore the MBR to boot DOS.

Creating swap space

Swap space is a disk partition Linux uses as an extension of its memory. When some memory-resident data is not needed immediately, Linux stores this data in the swap space. To create the swap space, you have to create a disk partition, using fdisk. Make sure you set the type of this disk partition to Linux swap. Typically, you can set up the swap partition and turn on swapping as you install Linux from this book's Slackware Linux.

If you must set up the swap space outside the installation program, you have to follow the procedure outlined in Chapter 1. The basic steps are to use the mkswap command to initialize the swap partition. You need the size of the swap partition (in number of blocks) before you use the mkswap command. Use the Linux fdisk program to find this information.

After mkswap finishes, use the swapon command to turn on swapping. Linux then begins to use the swap space.

Wizard

To ensure Linux uses the swap space every time it boots, you need a line in the /etc/fstab file that indicates the swap partition's name. If the swap partition is /dev/hda2, for example, you would need the following line to /etc/fstab:

```
/dev/hda2        swap        swap      defaults      0 0
```

If you created a swap space when you installed Linux, the installation program adds the appropriate line in the /etc/fstab file. You may need to add such a line if you create additional swap spaces later.

Secret

If you put a partition's name in /etc/fstab, but forget to run mkswap on that partition, Linux displays the following error message:

```
Unable to find swap-space signature
```

The fix is to run mkswap to initialize the swap partition.

Creating file systems

To use a disk partition in Linux, you have to create a file system on that partition. You can think of this procedure as formatting the partition for Linux. When you install Linux by following the steps described in Chapter 1, one of the steps creates the file system; the setup program actually asks you whether you want to format a partition. For a Linux partition, the setup program uses the mk2efs command to create a Linux file system.

Linux supports several types of file systems, including the following:

- *MS-DOS file system.* This DOS file system is based on the File Allocation Table (FAT). This type is designated by the keyword msdos.

- *Minix file system.* Minix is the original UNIX clone that inspired the creation of Linux. Linux started by using the Minix file system, which limits filenames to 14 or 30 characters. The minix keyword identifies this file-system type.

- *Extended file system.* This old Linux file system goes by the keyword ext. You should not use this file system anymore.

- *Second extended file system.* This system is the latest and greatest Linux file system. The keyword ext2 refers to this file-system type. You can use longer filenames in this file system.

Wizard

The installation program creates an ext2 file system on the Linux partition automatically. To create an ext2 file system manually, you have to use the mke2fs command. To use the mke2fs command, you need the number of blocks in the disk partition where you want to create the file system. Use the fdisk program to figure out the partition's size and then use the mke2fs command as follows:

```
mke2fs -c /dev/hda3 405040
```

This command creates an ext2 file system on the /dev/hda3 partition, which contains 308,040 blocks (each block is 1,024 bytes, or 1KB). The -c option forces mke2fs to check for bad blocks (using a fast read-only test) before creating the file system.

Tip

When you install Linux on a hard disk that uses standard IDE, MFM, or RLL controllers, always install the ext2 file system and use the bad-block-checking options when you create the file system.

Specific Disk Problems in Linux

For most hard drives, installing Linux amounts to booting a Linux kernel that supports your system's hard disk controller, partitioning the disk under Linux, and loading the operating system and associated software onto the hard disk. You notice the hard disk only when you create the partitions (as explained in Chapter 1).

Whenever some aspect of the hard disk is out of the ordinary, however, you may run into problems when installing Linux. This section covers some of these problems and suggests solutions.

Windows 95 and LILO

On a PC that has both Linux and Windows 3.1 installed in separate partitions, you can use the Linux Loader (LILO) program to boot one or the other operating system. If you upgrade Windows 3.1 to Windows 95, you'll notice Windows 95 wipes out LILO. Windows 95 overwrites the Master Boot Record with its own program and LILO typically resides on the Master Boot Record. In this case, all you have to do is boot Linux, using a boot floppy (you should have created the boot floppy during Linux installation), and then run /sbin/lilo to reinstall LILO.

If you bought a new PC with Windows 95 preinstalled, all you have to do is install Linux by following the steps described in Chapter 1 (start with repartitioning the hard disk). When you come to the step that installs LILO, specify the operating systems and the disk partitions that LILO should configure for booting. When you specify partitions to boot, treat the Windows 95 disk partition as a DOS partition. After you finish installing Linux and LILO, you should be able to boot Windows 95 (assuming you left it installed) or Linux by entering the name of the appropriate boot image at LILO's boot prompt.

Disks with more than 1,024 cylinders

Disks that have more than 1,024 cylinders were a problem in older Linux kernels. The version of Linux on the companion disk, however, should work fine with EIDE disks that have more than 1,024 cylinders, so you can safely ignore the discussions in this section.

You can view a disk as being a collection of sectors, each of which is 512 bytes. The sectors are addressed in two ways:

- Linear Block Address (LBA), in which the sectors are numbered sequentially, starting at zero.

- Cylinder, Head, Sector (CHS) address, which is based on the physical construction of a hard disk, consisting of a stack of magnetic platters that rotate at high speed under read-write heads.

Old PC disk controllers and the Basic Input/Output System (BIOS) use physical CHS addresses to access the sectors on the disk. This arrangement worked fine until large disks started to appear on the market. The BIOS uses a 10-bit value as the cylinder number, which means the BIOS can access, at most, 1,024 cylinders on a hard disk (because a 10-bit value lies between 0 and 1,023). Because of this limitation, any disk that has more than 1,024 cylinders is generally referred to as a *large disk* in the PC world.

Wizard

Most current hard disks tend to have 16 heads, 63 sectors, and a large number of cylinders. With a 1,024-cylinder limitation, the maximum disk size under BIOS is 16×63×1,024 = 1,0321,192 sectors = 528,482,304 bytes (because each sector is 512 bytes long) = 504MB (1MB = 1,024×1,024 bytes). As you know, many current desktop PCs have 2 or 4GB disks. These disks typically come with the Enhanced IDE (EIDE) interface.

The EIDE interface handles large disks by playing with the number of cylinders and heads. One trick EIDE BIOS uses is to halve the actual number of cylinders and double the number of heads. When the BIOS processes a disk-access request specified by CHS address, it automatically adjusts the cylinders and heads to access the correct sector on the disk. This adjustment is called *address translation*.

Linux gets a disk's geometry (number of cylinders, heads, and sectors) from the BIOS. If the BIOS does address translation, the reported values won't match the actual physical parameters of the disk. Unfortunately, Linux does not go through the BIOS to read from or write to the disk. When accessing the disk controller, Linux has to provide the CHS address with physically correct values. In other words, Linux has to perform address translation like the BIOS. Luckily, the Linux kernel on this book's companion disk already takes care of all the details and handles large disks properly.

You still may run into problems with large disks, however, not because Linux cannot handle large disks, but because on MS-DOS PCs, many older large hard disks are handled by special software that may conflict with Linux. Some large systems come with special software known as Disk Manager. The Disk Manager usually resides in the disk's Master Boot Record and may perform some magic to allow DOS to access the entire disk.

The only clean solution for such problems involves backing up your DOS files. Set the BIOS disk parameters to the correct disk parameters and then partition the disk under Linux. You can set aside the first partition for use under DOS (because DOS won't be able to access more than the first 1,024 cylinders) and create the necessary partitions for Linux beyond the DOS partition.

Because the Linux Loader (LILO) relies on BIOS, which cannot access more than 1,024 cylinders, you should try to create the Linux boot partition within the first 1,024 cylinders.

EIDE problems on PCI systems

The current crop of Pentium PCs use the PCI bus. With this new bus come new interfaces for disks. A common interface is the PCI EIDE controller to connect EIDE devices, such as hard disks and CD-ROM drives, to the PCI motherboard.

Secret

When the PCI bus first became popular in 1995, some users reported data corruption in EIDE disks with some PCI EIDE controllers. Specifically, the affected systems have PCI motherboards with PCI EIDE controllers that use one of the following chips:

- RZ 1000

- CMD 640

To find out what type of PCI EIDE controller your system has, use the cat /proc/pci command (assuming, of course, your system has a PCI bus).

The version of Linux on the companion CD-ROM detects and works around these problems automatically. The only remaining indication of the problem is when you type cat /proc/pci, the listing shows the CMD 640 controller as being buggy. For example, here are the first few lines of output on one of my PCs with the CMD 640 interface:

```
cat /proc/pci
PCI devices found:
  Bus  0, device  13, function  0:
    IDE interface: CMD 640 (buggy) (rev 2).
      Medium devsel.  IRQ 14.
(other lines deleted)
```

Notice how the CMD 640 interface is reported to be buggy.

Error messages about inodes and blocks

If you get error messages about bad inodes or blocks during system startup, chances are you did not shut down the system properly. Before powering off a Linux system, you should always log in as root and use the shutdown command to halt the system, as follows:

```
/sbin/shutdown -h now
```

After this, you must wait until you see a message saying the system has halted. Only then you should turn off the power.

Because of our typical DOS experience of simply turning the power switch off, most us are tempted to reach for the power switch to shut down the system (although, somehow, I always remember to shut down other UNIX workstations properly, such as HP and Sun workstations).

If the system is not shut down properly, the file system may be damaged. When you boot the system the next time, it runs a file-system-check program (fsck) that may fix the file system and boot the system. In some cases, though, fsck won't be able to fix the file-system damage. You have no option but to reinitialize the file system, using the mke2fs command.

SCSI Disk Controllers and Linux

The remainder of this chapter explains using SCSI controllers under Linux.

SCSI (pronounced *scuzzy*) is an increasingly popular interface for connecting up to seven different devices on the SCSI bus. Each device, and the SCSI controller, has a unique SCSI identifier (ID) in the range 0 through 7. The controller usually is set to SCSI ID 7; the other devices use numbers between 0 and 6 (this means you can connect up to seven devices to a SCSI controller). Typically, a SCSI hard disk is set to SCSI ID 0.

Linux supports the following SCSI controllers:

Adaptec AHA-1510/152*x* (ISA)

Adaptec AHA-154*x* (ISA)

Adaptec AHA-174*x* (EISA)

Adaptec AHA-274*x* (EISA)/284*x* (VLB)

Adaptec AHA 2920

Adaptec AHA-2940/3940 (PCI)

Adaptec AVA-1505/1515 (ISA) (Adaptec 152*x*-compatible)

Always IN2000

AMI Fast Disk VLB/EISA (BusLogic-compatible)

BusLogic (ISA/EISA/VLB/PCI) (all models)

DPT PM2001 and PM2012A (EATA-PIO)

DPT Smartcache (EATA-DMA) (ISA/EISA/PCI)

DTC 329*x* (EISA) (Adaptec 154x-compatible)

Future Domain TMC-16*x*0 and TMC-3260 (PCI)

Future Domain TMC-8*xx* and TMC-950

ICP-Vortex (PCI/EISA)

Media Vision Pro Audio Spectrum 16 (ISA)

Media Vision Premium 3D

NCR 53c7*x*0 and 53c8*x*0 (PCI)

NCR 5380 generic cards

Qlogic FAS408

Quantum ISA-200S and ISA-200MG

Seagate ST-01/ST-02 (ISA)

Sound Blaster 16 SCSI (Adaptec 152*x*-compatible) (ISA)

Tekram DC-390, DC-390W/U/F

Trantor T128/T128F/T228 (ISA)

Trantor T130B (NCR 5380-compatible)

UltraStor 14F (ISA), 24F (EISA), and 34F (VLB)

Western Digital WD7000 SCSI

Linux currently does not support parallel-port SCSI adapters and non-Adaptec-compatible DTC boards (such as 327x and 328x).

Cross-Reference

When you configure the Linux kernel for SCSI support, the configuration program asks a number of questions in regard to SCSI controller cards. Consult Chapter 2 for a listing of the questions about SCSI support. You should answer Yes (type **y**) only to the question that pertains to your make and model of SCSI card.

Cable and termination problems

The SCSI bus needs terminators at both ends to work reliably. A *terminator* is a set of resistors that indicate the end of the SCSI bus. One end is the controller card itself, which typically has the terminator. Each SCSI device has two SCSI connectors, so you can *daisy-chain* (connect one device to the next) several SCSI devices. You are supposed to place a terminator on the last connector on the chain.

Secret

Some SCSI controllers — such as Adaptec AHA 154xC, 154xCF, and 274x (*x* is any digit) — are sensitive to the type of cable and terminator you use. If the cables are not perfect or the terminator is not used properly, these SCSI cards may fail intermittently or may not work at all.

To avoid problems with overly sensitive SCSI cards, use cables that come from a reputable vendor and use cables from the same vendor to connect all SCSI devices. The cables should be SCSI-2-compliant and should have an impedance of 132 ohms (a characteristic of the cable; all you have to do is make sure the specified value is 132 ohms).

Adaptec AHA151x, AHA151x, and Sound Blaster 16 SCSI

These ISA-bus SCSI cards include all SCSI controllers based on the AIC 6260 or 6360 chipset. Typical hardware parameters for these controllers include the following:

BIOS addresses: 0xd8000, 0xdc000, 0xd0000, 0xd4000, 0xc8000, 0xcc000, 0xe0000, and 0xe4000

I/O ports: 0x140 and 0x340

IRQs: 9, 10, 11, and 12

DMA channels: not used

Secret

Autoprobe works with boards that have a BIOS installed. For other boards, such as Adaptec 1510 and Sound Blaster 16 SCSI, use the boot option in this format:

```
aha152x=IOPORT,IRQ,SCSI-ID,RECONNECT
```

All right-side arguments are numbers. *IOPORT* is the I/O address, and if *RECONNECT* is nonzero, the driver is allowed to disconnect and reconnect the device. Usually, the *SCSI-ID* is 7, and *RECONNECT* is specified as 1.

Usually, *SCSI-ID* is 7, and *RECONNECT* is nonzero. If an Adaptec AHA1510 card has I/O address 0x340 and IRQ 11, the boot option is the following:

```
aha152x=0x340,11,7,1
```

Adaptec AHA154x, AMI FastDisk VLB, BusLogic, and DTC 329x

Typical hardware parameters of these ISA-bus SCSI controllers include the following:

I/O ports: 0x330 and 0x334

IRQs: 9, 10, 11, 12, 14, and 15

DMA channels: 5, 6, and 7

Autoprobe works with these controllers; there is no need for a BIOS on the controller. The BusLogic SCSI controllers are software-compatible with the Adaptec 1542. ISA, VLB, and EISA versions of BusLogic cards are available.

Secret

Adaptec AHA154xC and AHA154xCF controller cards often generate unexpected errors; these controllers are sensitive to the cable and termination details.

If you encounter infinite timeout errors Adaptec AHA154xC and 154xCF controllers, you may have to run the Adaptec setup program (which you do by pressing a specified key during power up) and enable synchronous negotiation.

Adaptec AHA 174x

This controller is an EISA-bus SCSI controller Adaptec no longer sells. Older EISA bus systems may have this card. Following are the hardware parameters of the AHA174x card:

Bus slots: 1–8

I/O ports: EISA bus does not require preassigned I/O ports

IRQs: 9, 10, 11, 12, 14, and 15

DMA channels: EISA bus does not require preassigned I/O ports

The Linux driver can detect the card automatically without any problems. The driver also expects the card to be running in enhanced mode, as opposed to standard AHA1542 mode.

Adaptec AHA274x, AHA284x, and AHA294x

The Adaptec AHA274x controller is an EISA bus card; AHA284x is a VLB card; AHA294x is a new PCI bus card. The AHA274x driver supports all three cards. You should enable the BIOS on these controller cards.

For the PCI controller to work, you must answer Yes to the following question during kernel configuration:

```
PCI bios support (CONFIG_PCI) [Y/n/?] y
```

Wizard

Allways IN2000

The Allways IN2000 is an ISA-bus controller card with the following parameters:

I/O ports: 0x100, 0x110, 0x200, and 0x220

IRQs: 10, 11, 14, and 15

DMA: not used

The driver can detect the card automatically without any need for BIOS.

EATA DPT Smartcache

The Linux `eata_dma` SCSI driver supports all SCSI controllers that support the EATA-DMA protocol. The controllers include DPT PM2011, PM2012A, PM2012B, PM2021, PM2022, PM2024, PM2122, PM2124, PM2322, PM3021, PM3222, and PM3224.

Secret

The driver's autoprobe function works with all supported DPT cards. A common problem, however, is the IDE driver detects the ST-506 interface of the EATA controller. If the IDE driver has a problem with the detected parameters and fails, you won't be able to access your IDE hardware. In this case, you should change the EATA board's parameters, such as the I/O address and the IRQ. In particular, don't use IRQs of 14 or 15, which are the IRQs of the primary and secondary IDE interfaces.

If you have a PCI controller such as DPT PM2024, PM2124, or PM3224, remember to enable PCI BIOS when you configure the kernel.

Future Domain 16x0

The Future Domain 16x0 SCSI controller uses the TMC-1800, TMC-18C30, TMC-8C50, or TMC-36C70 chip. These ISA-bus cards typically have the following configurations:

BIOS addresses: 0xc8000, 0xca000, 0xce000, and 0xde000

I/O ports: 0x140, 0x150, 0x160, and 0x170

IRQs: 3, 5, 10, 11, 12, 14, and 15

DMA: not used

The driver can probe and detect the hardware automatically, provided the controller has a BIOS installed.

NCR53c8xx SCSI Chip (PCI)

NCR53C8xx refers to NCR53c810, NCR53c815, NCR53c820, and NCR53c825 — a series of low-cost SCSI chips for PCI motherboards. The version of Linux on the companion CD-ROM supports the NCR53c8xx. The driver can detect SCSI devices automatically, provided the PCI BIOS is present. In fact, the driver needs the BIOS because it uses BIOS-initialized values in the registers of the NCR53c8xx.

Secret

A reported problem with the NCR53c8xx is the chip works under DOS but fails under Linux, because it times out on a test due to a lost interrupt. A typical cause of this error is a mismatch between the IRQ setting in the hardware (typically set with a jumper) and the IRQ value stored in the CMOS setup (the setup program of your PC, the one you can run during power-up). To correct the problem, check the following things:

- Make sure the hardware IRQ setting matches that in the CMOS setup.

- If the NCR 53c8xx is on a board that has jumpers for selecting PCI interrupt lines (PCI has interrupt lines INTA, INTB, INTC, and INTD), make sure only INTA is being used.

- If the PCI board has jumpers for selecting level-sensitive and edge-triggered interrupts, make sure the board is using "level-sensitive" interrupts.

Secret

Another reported problem is system lockup when an S3 928 or Tseng ET4000/W32 PCI video chipset is used, due to problems in the video chipsets.

Secret

On a system that has an NCR53c8xx SCSI chip, you may encounter the following message:

```
scsi%d: IRQ0 not free, detaching
```

This message indicates the PCI configuration register contains a zero. The reason may be a mismatch between the hardware IRQ and the value in CMOS, or a defective BIOS.

Because the NCR53c8xx is a PCI device, you must enable PCI support when you rebuild the Linux kernel.

Seagate ST0x and Future Domain TMC-8xx and TMC-9xx

Typical hardware parameters of these ISA-bus SCSI controllers include the following:

> BIOS addresses: 0xc8000, 0xca000, 0xcc000, 0xce000, 0xdc000, and 0xde000
>
> IRQs: 3 and 5
>
> DMA channels: not used

When it tries to probe for the controller automatically, the driver probes only the BIOS addresses; it assumes the IRQ is 5. Also, autoprobe works only if a BIOS is installed.

During boot, you can provide one of the following command lines to force detection of the controller:

```
st0x=BIOS-ADDRESS,IRQ
tmc8xx=BIOS-ADDRESS,IRQ
```

BIOS_ADDRESS is the BIOS address of the board, and *IRQ* is the interrupt-request channel.

Secret

Common problems with the ST01 or ST02 SCSI controller are time-outs when Linux accesses the disk connected to the controller, because the board's default settings disable interrupts. You should set jumpers (W3 on ST01 and JP3 on ST02) on the board to reenable interrupts. You also should select IRQ 5.

Secret

If you get errors when you try to run `fdisk` on a drive connected to Seagate or Future Domain controllers, you should use `fdisk`'s extra functions menu to specify the disk geometry (cylinders, heads, and sectors).

Pro Audio Spectrum PAS16 SCSI

The PAS16 SCSI refers to the SCSI interface on a Pro Audio Spectrum sound card. Following are the hardware-configuration parameters for the PAS16 SCSI:

> I/O ports: 0x388, 0x384, 0x38x, and 0x288
>
> IRQs: 10, 12, 14, and 15 (must be different from the IRQs used for sound)
>
> DMA: not used for the SCSI portion of the card

The autoprobe function does not require BIOS. You can specify a command line at the boot prompt to specify the parameters of your PAS 16 SCSI. For a PAS 16 SCSI at I/O address 0x388 and IRQ 10, for example, use the following command line:

```
pas16=0x388,10
```

Trantor T128, T128F, and T228

These Trantor ISA-bus SCSI cards have the following configuration parameters:

BIOS addresses: 0xcc000, 00xc8000, 0xdc000, and 0xd8000

IRQs: on all boards, none, 3, 5, and 7; on T128F, 10, 12, 14, and 15

DMA: not used

The driver can autoprobe as long as a BIOS is installed. If one of these SCSI controllers does not have BIOS, or if the BIOS is disabled, you can specify the controller through a command line like the following:

```
t128=BIOS-ADDRESS,IRQ
```

BIOS-ADDRESS is the base address (not I/O address). For a controller with a BIOS address 0xcc000 and IRQ 5, for example, the command line is:

```
t128=0xcc000,5
```

Use -1 for the IRQ if a controller does not have an IRQ; use -2 to make the driver probe the IRQ.

Ultrastor 14f (ISA), 24f (EISA), and 34f (VLB)

The Ultrastor SCSI cards have the following configuration parameters:

I/O ports: 0x130, 0x140, 0x210, 0x230, 0x240, 0x310, 0x330, and 0x340

IRQs: 10, 11, 14, and 15

DMA channels: 5, 6, and 7

The autoprobe function works in all cases except when the I/O port address is 0x310. Because I/O port 0x310 is not supported by the autoprobe code, you should select a different I/O port address for the Ultrastor controller.

If you have a sound card, I/O port address 0x330 typically is used by the MIDI device. Use a different I/O port address for the Ultrastor card if you have a sound card in your PC. A good I/O port for the Ultrastor cards is 0x340.

The Ultrastor controllers support a WD1003 emulation mode, in which they can work with ST-506-interface disk drives. If you have your Ultrastor controller in WD1003 mode, the Ultrastor SCSI driver will fail, displaying the following error message:

```
hd.c: ST-506 interface disk with more than 16 heads detected,
  probably due to non-standard sector translation.  Giving up.
  (disk %d: cyl=%d, sect=63, head=64)
```

You can fix this problem by setting the Ultrastor controller to its native SCSI mode.

Western Digital 7000

The hardware configurations for this ISA-bus SCSI controller are as follows:

BIOS address: 0xce000

I/O port: 0x350

IRQ: 15

DMA channel: 6

The driver can probe and detect the SCSI controller automatically, provided the BIOS is installed.

Some revisions of the Western Digital 7000 controller may not work with the driver. Reportedly, Revision 5 and later controllers work fine. Also, on the working controllers, the onboard SCSI chip should have an A suffix.

Iomega Zip drive (SCSI)

The Iomega Zip drive is a low-cost, removable disk drive that enables you to use floppy-like disks, each of which is capable of holding 100 million characters. If you consider a megabyte to be $1,024 \times 1,024 = 1,048,576$ bytes, 100 million characters will be about 95MB. Unlike floppies, the Zip disks do not have a hardware write-protect tab, which means you must be careful when you initialize a disk or delete files.

The Zip drive comes in three versions: SCSI interface for Macintosh or MS-DOS and a parallel-port version. The current Linux kernel supports the parallel-port version of the Zip drive.

Both the DOS and Macintosh versions of the SCSI Iomega Zip drive should work under Linux. You can use an existing Linux-supported SCSI card (preferably, a simple Adaptec AHA152x-compatible card) to connect the Zip drive to your PC. The Zip drive has switches to turn on termination (if it's the last device in the chain) and select SCSI ID (one of 5 or 6).

You also can connect the Zip drive to a separately sold Zip Zoom interface card — a low-end SCSI card compatible with the Adaptec AHA152x card. If you have a kernel that supports the AHA152x and you use LILO, you can use the Zip drive with the following line added to the /etc/lilo.conf file:

```
append="aha152x=0x340,11,7,1"
```

Tip

To prepare the Zip disk for use under Linux, you should try it under DOS. Run the \SCSI\INSTALL program on the Iomega Tools disk. After that, the Zip disk should work under Linux.

Log in as `root`, and run `/sbin/fdisk` on the SCSI device that represents the Zip drive. If the Zip drive is the only SCSI device, it'll be `/dev/sda`, so you type the following:

```
/sbin/fdisk /dev/sda
```

Check the current partition and set the type to Linux native. Then create an `ext2` file system with the following command:

```
/sbin/mke2fs /dev/sda1
```

This command assumes you are using the first partition of the Zip disk. Create the a `zip` subdirectory in `/mnt` with the `mkdir /mnt/zip` command. You then can mount the Zip disk at an appropriate mount point and use the disk, as follows:

```
mount -text2 /dev/sda1 /mnt/zip
```

The contents of the Zip disk will be in the `/mnt/zip` directory. Before ejecting the disk, use the command `umount /mnt/zip` to dismount the Zip disk.

SCSI troubleshooting

Most SCSI problems are due to bad cables or improper termination. You should check the cables and the terminator before you try anything else. The following sections list other common SCSI problems and their suggested fixes:

Problem booting with LILO

When booting from a SCSI hard disk, LILO may hang after displaying the letters `LI`. This problem occurs if the SCSI controller's BIOS and the Linux SCSI driver interpret the disk geometry differently.

Wizard

To fix this problem, add the `linear` keyword on a single line in the `/etc/lilo.conf` file. This keyword causes LILO to use Linear Block Addresses (LBA) instead of the physical cylinder-head-sector (CHS) addresses when it accesses the disk. LILO uses the disk geometry supplied by the BIOS and compute physical addresses at run time, which should work properly.

SCSI device at all SCSI IDs

If a SCSI device shows up at all possible SCSI IDs, you must have configured that device with the same SCSI ID as the SCSI controller (usually, 7). Change the ID of that device to another value. (Many devices have a simple switch for setting the SCSI ID; on many other devices, you have to change a jumper.)

SCSI device at all LUNs

If a SCSI device shows up at all possible SCSI Logical Unit Numbers (LUNs), the device probably has errors in the *firmware* — the built-in code in the device's SCSI interface. To verify these errors, first use the following command line during boot:

```
max_scsi_luns=1
```

Secret

If the device works with this option, you can add it to the list of blacklisted SCSI devices in the array of structures named `device_list` in the file `/usr/src/linux/drivers/scsi/scsi.c`. The definition of this structure and the current contents of the array are as follows:

```
struct dev_info{
    const char * vendor;
    const char * model;
    const char * revision; /* Latest revision known to be bad.  Not used yet */
    unsigned flags;
};


/*
 * This is what was previously known as the blacklist.  The concept
 * has been expanded so that we can specify other types of things we
 * need to be aware of.
 */
static struct dev_info device_list[] =
{
{"CHINON","CD-ROM CDS-431","H42", BLIST_NOLUN}, /* Locks up if polled for lun
!= 0 */
{"CHINON","CD-ROM CDS-535","Q14", BLIST_NOLUN}, /* Locks up if polled for lun
!= 0 */
{"DENON","DRD-25X","V", BLIST_NOLUN},           /* Locks up if probed for lun
!= 0 */
{"HITACHI","DK312C","CM81", BLIST_NOLUN},       /* Responds to all lun - dtg */
{"HITACHI","DK314C","CR21" , BLIST_NOLUN},      /* responds to all lun */
{"IMS", "CDD521/10","2.06", BLIST_NOLUN},       /* Locks-up when LUN>0 polled.
*/
{"MAXTOR","XT-3280","PR02", BLIST_NOLUN},       /* Locks-up when LUN>0 polled.
*/
{"MAXTOR","XT-4380S","B3C", BLIST_NOLUN},       /* Locks-up when LUN>0 polled.
*/
{"MAXTOR","MXT-1240S","I1.2", BLIST_NOLUN},     /* Locks up when LUN>0 polled
*/
{"MAXTOR","XT-4170S","B5A", BLIST_NOLUN},       /* Locks-up sometimes when
LUN>0 polled. */
{"MAXTOR","XT-8760S","B7B", BLIST_NOLUN},       /* guess what? */
{"MEDIAVIS","RENO CD-ROMX2A","2.03",BLIST_NOLUN},/*Responds to all lun */
{"MICROP", "4110", "*", BLIST_NOTQ},     /* Buggy Tagged Queuing */
{"NEC","CD-ROM DRIVE:841","1.0", BLIST_NOLUN},  /* Locks-up when LUN>0 polled.
*/
{"RODIME","RO3000S","2.33", BLIST_NOLUN},       /* Locks up if polled for lun
!= 0 */
{"SANYO", "CRD-250S", "1.20", BLIST_NOLUN},     /* causes failed REQUEST SENSE
on lun 1
              * for aha152x controller, which causes
```

```
                        * SCSI code to reset bus.*/
{"SEAGATE", "ST157N", "\004|j", BLIST_NOLUN},    /* causes failed REQUEST SENSE
on lun 1
                * for aha152x controller, which causes
                * SCSI code to reset bus.*/
{"SEAGATE", "ST296","921", BLIST_NOLUN},             /* Responds to all lun */
{"SEAGATE","ST1581","6538",BLIST_NOLUN},   /* Responds to all lun */
{"SONY","CD-ROM CDU-541","4.3d", BLIST_NOLUN},
{"SONY","CD-ROM CDU-55S","1.0i", BLIST_NOLUN},
{"SONY","CD-ROM CDU-561","1.7x", BLIST_NOLUN},
{"TANDBERG","TDC 3600","U07", BLIST_NOLUN},        /* Locks up if polled for lun
!= 0 */
{"TEAC","CD-ROM","1.06", BLIST_NOLUN},            /* causes failed REQUEST SENSE
on lun 1
                * for seagate controller, which causes
                * SCSI code to reset bus.*/
{"TEXEL","CD-ROM","1.06", BLIST_NOLUN},            /* causes failed REQUEST SENSE
on lun 1
                * for seagate controller, which causes
                * SCSI code to reset bus.*/
{"QUANTUM","LPS525S","3110", BLIST_NOLUN},        /* Locks sometimes if polled
for lun != 0 */
{"QUANTUM","PD1225S","3110", BLIST_NOLUN},        /* Locks sometimes if polled
for lun != 0 */
{"MEDIAVIS","CDR-H93MV","1.31", BLIST_NOLUN},    /* Locks up if polled for lun
!= 0 */
{"SANKYO", "CP525","6.64", BLIST_NOLUN},          /* causes failed REQ SENSE,
extra reset */
{"HP", "C1750A", "3226", BLIST_NOLUN},            /* scanjet iic */
{"HP", "C1790A", "", BLIST_NOLUN},                /* scanjet iip */
{"HP", "C2500A", "", BLIST_NOLUN},                /* scanjet iicx */

/*
 * Other types of devices that have special flags.
 */
{"SONY","CD-ROM CDU-8001","*", BLIST_BORKEN},
{"TEXEL","CD-ROM","1.06", BLIST_BORKEN},
{"IOMEGA","Io20S          *F","*", BLIST_KEY},
{"INSITE","Floptical   F*8I","*", BLIST_KEY},
{"INSITE","I325VM","*", BLIST_KEY},
{"NRC","MBR-7","*", BLIST_FORCELUN | BLIST_SINGLELUN},
{"NRC","MBR-7.4","*", BLIST_FORCELUN | BLIST_SINGLELUN},
{"NAKAMICH","MJ-4.8S","*", BLIST_FORCELUN | BLIST_SINGLELUN},
{"PIONEER","CD-ROM DRM-602X","*", BLIST_FORCELUN | BLIST_SINGLELUN},
{"PIONEER","CD-ROM DRM-604X","*", BLIST_FORCELUN | BLIST_SINGLELUN},
{"EMULEX","MD21/S2    ESDI","*", BLIST_SINGLELUN},
{"CANON","IPUBJD","*", BLIST_SPARSELUN},
{"MATSHITA","PD","*", BLIST_FORCELUN | BLIST_SINGLELUN},
{"YAMAHA","CDR100","1.00", BLIST_NOLUN},  /* Locks up if polled for lun != 0 */
{"YAMAHA","CDR102","1.00", BLIST_NOLUN},  /* Locks up if polled for lun != 0 */
{"nCipher","Fastness Crypto","*", BLIST_FORCELUN},
/*
 * Must be at end of list...
 */
{NULL, NULL, NULL}};
```

From this list, you get an idea of the types of SCSI devices with the problem of showing up at all LUNs. If you have the same problem with a SCSI device, you can add that device's name to this list before the last line. You may not want to do this, however, if you are unfamiliar with the C programming language.

Sense errors on error-free SCSI device

The cause of this problem usually is bad cables or improper termination. Check all cables and make sure the SCSI bus is terminated at both ends.

Networking kernel problems with SCSI device

If a Linux kernel with networking support does not work with SCSI devices, the problem may be the autoprobe function of the networking drivers. The *autoprobe capability* is meant to detect the type of networking hardware automatically. The network drivers read from and write to specific I/O addresses during autoprobing. If an I/O addresses is the same as that used by a SCSI device, the system may have a problem. In this case, you have to check the I/O address, IRQ, and DMA values of the network cards and of the SCSI controller, and make sure no conflicts exist. Most SCSI controllers (and even network adapters) enable you to configure these parameters (I/O address, IRQ, and DMA) through setup software that comes with the adapter.

Device detected but not accessible

If the kernel detects a SCSI device (as reported in the boot messages, which you can see with `dmesg | more`) but you cannot access the device, the device file is missing from the `/dev` directory.

To add the device file, log in as `root`, change the directory to `/dev`, and then use the MAKEDEV script to create the device file. To add a device for a SCSI tape drive, for example, you would use the following command:

```
cd /dev
./MAKEDEV st0
```

When you log in as `root`, the current directory is typically not in the PATH environment variable. This is why you need to add the `./` prefix when executing the MAKEDEV script. You can find more information about the MAKEDEV script with this command:

```
man MAKEDEV
```

SCSI lockup

If the SCSI system locks up, check the SCSI controller card, using any diagnostic software that came with the card (usually, the diagnostic software runs under DOS). Look for conflicts in I/O address, IRQ, or DMA with other cards. Some sound cards, for example, use a 16-bit DMA channel in addition to an 8-bit DMA; make sure you did not inadvertently use the same 16-bit DMA for the SCSI card.

Secret

The Linux SCSI driver for some SCSI cards supports only one outstanding SCSI command at a time. With such a SCSI card, if a device such as a tape drive is busy rewinding, the system may be unable to access other SCSI devices (such as a hard disk or a CD-ROM drive) that are daisy-chained with that tape drive. A solution to this problem is to add a second SCSI controller to take care of the tape drives.

SCSI devices not found

If the Linux kernel does not detect your SCSI devices at startup, you get the following message when Linux boots:

```
scsi : 0 hosts
```

If you see this message, but you know the SCSI devices are there (and they work under DOS), the problem may be the lack of a BIOS on the SCSI controller; the autoprobe routines that detect SCSI devices rely on the BIOS.

This problem occurs for the following SCSI cards:

- Adaptec 152x, 151x, AIC-6260, and AIC-6360

- Future Domain 1680, TMC-950, and TMC-8xx

- Trantor T128, T128F, and T228F

- Seagate ST01 and ST02

- Western Digital 7000

Secret

Even if a SCSI controller has a BIOS, jumpers often are available for disabling the BIOS. If you disabled the BIOS for some reason, you may want to re-enable it (read the documentation of your SCSI controller for directions) so Linux can detect the SCSI devices automatically.

For a SCSI card, such as the Adaptec 151x, that does not have any BIOS, use the following command line during boot to force detection of the card:

```
aha152x=0x340,11,7,1
```

Summary

You need a hard disk to install Linux on your PC. In particular, to install Linux successfully, your PC's hard disk controller must be supported by Linux. This should not be a problem because Linux supports the popular IDE and Enhanced IDE interfaces, as well as the SCSI interface. This chapter describes how to install and use hard disks in Linux. By reading this chapter, you learn the following things:

▶ Linux's support for a specific hard disk drive depends on the disk controller used to connect that drive to the PC's motherboard. Linux supports the popular IDE (Integrated Drive Electronics), Enhanced IDE (EIDE), and SCSI disk controllers for ISA, EISA, VLB, and PCI buses. These disk controllers cover nearly all types of disks that PCs typically use.

▶ You must partition a disk to install Linux and when you install Linux, you must create a swap space and set up a mechanism to boot Linux. You can use LILO to manage the boot process, even if you have multiple operating systems (such as DOS and Windows 95) on the disk.

▶ The disk controller sees the disk as being a collection of 512-byte sectors on magnetic platters mounted on a spindle and rotating under read-write heads. This physical construction of a hard disk gives rise to the view of a disk as a collection of cylinders, heads, and sectors (CHS). Linux likes to see the disk as being a sequence of sectors that can be addressed sequentially (Linear Block Address, or LBA).

▶ The PC's BIOS uses CHS addressing and limits the cylinder address to a 10-bit value, thus giving rise to a 1,024-cylinder limit on hard disk geometries. Because hardware constraints prevent disks from having more than 16 heads and 63 sectors, the BIOS can handle disks up to 504MB (1,024×16×63 sectors; each sector is 512 bytes). Newer large disks use some tricks to handle larger disks, but these tricks sometimes conflict with the way Linux addresses disks. You generally are safe if you keep the DOS settings for the disk parameters such as number of cylinders, heads, and sectors.

▶ SCSI is popular because you can connect up to seven devices through a single SCSI controller. The only drawback is the SCSI controller is relatively expensive compared with EIDE controllers.

▶ Linux supports a wide variety of SCSI controllers, including the popular Adaptec and BusLogic SCSI controllers.

▶ Many recent PCs have the PCI bus and PCI-bus EIDE controller chips built into the motherboard. Two of these EIDE controllers — RZ 1000 and CMD 640 — are reported to have some bugs that occur when you have multiple IDE devices on the EIDE controller. Linux can work around these bugs.

▶ With a little effort, you should be able to use an Iomega Zip drive with Linux.

Chapter 12

CD-ROM Drives and Sound Cards

In This Chapter

▶ Looking at the different types of interfaces for CD-ROM drives

▶ Specifying Linux device names for CD-ROM drives and sound cards

▶ Using specific CD-ROM drives in Linux

▶ Fixing common problems with CD-ROM drives in Linux

▶ Looking at the brands of sound cards Linux supports

▶ Including support for a specific sound card in Linux

▶ Testing and troubleshooting sound cards in Linux

If you have installed or you plan to install Linux from this book's companion CD-ROM, chances are good your system already has a CD-ROM drive. You probably are reading this chapter because you have questions about using your CD-ROM drive to install Linux: you should find answers to your questions here. As with other peripheral devices (such as a disk drive), the CD-ROM drive connects to your PC's motherboard through a controller board. Thus, the real issue of how to use a CD-ROM drive under Linux boils down to whether Linux includes a driver for that CD-ROM drive's interface. This chapter discusses various CD-ROM interfaces and explains which ones are supported under Linux.

I grouped CD-ROM drives with sound cards because many CD-ROM drives used to connect to the PC through interfaces built into sound cards. Initially, vendors bundled CD-ROM drives and sound cards as a package — you need both types of devices to enjoy multimedia software that uses sound, video, and animation. The CD-ROM provides the storage space needed to store the video clips, images, and sound files in a typical multimedia application. The sound card allows the PC to generate professional-quality sound — the other must-have ingredient in a multimedia application.

This chapter describes specific types of Linux-supported CD-ROM drives, categorized by interface type. You also find information about how to include support for specific sound cards in Linux.

CD-ROM Drives

Each CD-ROM can hold up to 650MB of data (the equivalent of about 450 high-density 3.5-inch floppy disks) and does not cost much to produce. The physical medium of the CD-ROM is the same as that used for audio Compact Discs (CDs): a polycarbonate disc with an aluminized layer. A laser reads the data, which is encoded in microscopic pits on the aluminized layer. CD-ROM media is more robust and reliable than other magnetic media, such as floppy disks. All these factors make CD-ROMs an attractive medium for distributing data and programs. In fact, most Linux books (including this one) bundle a CD-ROM with a complete Linux distribution that includes the operating system and lots of popular software.

In that list of good properties of a CD-ROM — high capacity, low cost, and reliability — you don't see any mention of speed, because the data-transfer rates of CD-ROM drives are not as fast as those of hard disk drives. When CD-ROM drives first appeared, the drives could transfer data at rates of approximately 150KB per second. These drives were known as *single-speed* (also referred to as *1X*) CD-ROM drives. Double-speed (2X) CD-ROM drives, which provide data-transfer rates of 300KB per second, were soon widely available. Currently, most systems come with 16X or 24X CD-ROM drives, which can sustain data-transfer rates of up to 3600KB per second and average access times of 95 milliseconds (compare this with hard drive access times of around 10 milliseconds).

Note

Most CD-ROMs contain information in an ISO-9660 file system (formerly known as High Sierra). This file system supports only the MS-DOS-style 8.3 filenames, such as README.TXT, which have an 8-character name and an optional 3-character extension. An extension to the ISO-9660 file system, called the Rock Ridge Extensions, uses unused fields to support longer filenames and additional UNIX-style file attributes, such as ownership and symbolic links.

Most CD-ROM drives also typically let you play audio CDs via an external headphone jack. There's an output line you can connect to the sound card, too, so you can play an audio CD on the speakers attached to the sound card.

Supported CD-ROM drives

As with hard disks, Linux's support for a CD-ROM drive depends on the interface through which the CD-ROM drive connects to the PC's motherboard. CD-ROM drives come with three popular types of interfaces:

■ *AT Attachment Packet Interface (ATAPI).* ATAPI is a recent specification for accessing and controlling a CD-ROM drive that is connected to the PC through the AT Attachment (ATA). ATAPI is gaining popularity because it is built on the cheaper IDE interface. (ATA is the new name for IDE.)

- *Small Computer System Interface (SCSI)*. SCSI is popular because of its relatively high data rates and its capability to support multiple devices. The only drawback is you need a relatively expensive SCSI controller card for the PC.

- *Proprietary interfaces.* Many CD-ROM vendors provide their own proprietary interface between the CD-ROM drive and the PC's motherboard. Many sound cards include a built-in CD-ROM drive interface, which typically is a proprietary interface. The problem with proprietary interfaces is someone must develop a Linux driver specifically for each interface (as opposed to using a SCSI driver, for example, to access any SCSI device).

ATAPI CD-ROM drives

ATA (AT Attachment) is the official ANSI (American National Standards Institute) standard name for the commonplace IDE interface, commonly used to connect hard disk drives to the PC. ATAPI (ATA Packet Interface) is a protocol (similar to SCSI) for controlling storage devices such as CD-ROM drives and tape drives. Although ATAPI is relatively new, it is rapidly becoming the most popular type of interface for CD-ROM drives. The reason is ATAPI is based on the ATA (or IDE) interface and doesn't need any expensive controller card or cable. Also, an ATAPI CD-ROM can simply connect as the second drive on the same interface where the PC's hard drive is connected. This means the ATAPI CD-ROM drive does not require a separate interface card.

The Linux kernel includes an ATAPI driver that should work with any ATAPI CD-ROM drive. ATAPI CD-ROM drives are available from many vendors, such as Aztech, Mitsumi, NEC, Philips, Sony, and Toshiba. Nowadays, most PCs (such as those from Gateway and Dell) come configured with ATAPI CD-ROM drives.

SCSI CD-ROM drives

Linux supports a SCSI CD-ROM drive connected to one of the supported SCSI controller cards (see Chapter 11 for more information). The only restriction is the block size (for data transfers) of the SCSI CD-ROM drive should be 512 or 2,048 bytes, which covers the vast majority of CD-ROM drives on the market.

Some CD-ROM drives include a controller with a modified interface that's not fully SCSI-compatible. This interface essentially amounts to being proprietary; you cannot use such CD-ROM drives with the SCSI driver.

SCSI CD-ROM drives are available from many vendors, such as Plextor, Sanyo, and Toshiba.

Proprietary CD-ROM drives

Although the ATAPI and SCSI CD-ROM drives fall into neat categories and work well in Linux, the situation is much more confusing when it comes to CD-ROM drives with a proprietary interface. Following are some of the sources of confusion:

■ Some vendors, such as Creative Labs (of Sound Blaster fame), have sold CD-ROM drives with all types of interfaces: ATAPI, SCSI, and proprietary interfaces on a sound card. Thus, the vendor name alone means nothing; you must know what type of interface the CD-ROM drive uses.

■ PC vendors sometimes categorize the CD-ROM drive interface as being IDE, even though the interface really is proprietary. Like the IDE (or ATAPI) interface, the proprietary CD-ROM drive interface is low-cost and popular. Often, a proprietary CD-ROM interface is incorrectly branded as an IDE interface.

As you may have guessed, proprietary CD-ROM drive interfaces are popular because they tend to be much simpler than SCSI, which was the primary alternative to proprietary interfaces before ATAPI came along. Because of the popularity of relatively inexpensive ATAPI, most new PCs do not use proprietary interfaces for CD-ROMs. Because a proprietary CD-ROM interface can be built into a sound card at little cost, however, some Linux users may have PCs with a proprietary CD-ROM drive.

Table 12-1 lists CD-ROM drives with proprietary interfaces and the name of the drivers you need to support those drives.

Table 12-1	CD-ROM drives with proprietary interfaces
Driver	*CD-ROM drive*
aztcd	Aztech CDA268, Orchid CDS-3110, Okano/Wearnes CDD-110, Conrad TXC, CyCDROM CR520ie/CR940ie
cdu31a	Sony CDU31A/CDU33A
cm206	Philips/LMS CM 206
gscd	GoldStar R420
isp16	CD-ROM drives attached to the interface on an ISP16, MAD16, or Mozart sound card
mcd	Mitsumi CRMC LU005S, FX001
optcd	Optics Storage Dolphin 8000AT, Lasermate CR328A
sbpcd	Matsushita/Panasonic (Panasonic CR-521, CR-522, CR-523, CR-562, and CR-563), Kotobuki, Creative Labs (CD-200), Longshine LCS-7260, Teac CD-55A
sjcd	Sanyo H94A
sonycd535	Sony CDU-535/CDU-531

CD-ROM troubleshooting

You need a CD-ROM drive that works under Linux to install Linux from this book's companion CD-ROM. The initial Linux kernel comes with CD-ROM driver modules for all supported CD-ROM drives, so you should not have any problem as long as your CD-ROM drive is supported by Linux. Remember, the CD-ROM drive's interface is what counts, not the brand name. For example, any brands of CD-ROM drive with the IDE interface will work under Linux because Linux supports the IDE interface.

If Linux does not seem to recognize the CD-ROM drive after you have rebuilt the kernel, try the following steps to fix the problem:

1. If you have rebuilt the kernel with support for your CD-ROM drive, verify you are, indeed, running the new kernel. To see the version number, use the `uname -a` command. Following is typical output from the `uname -a` command:

   ```
   Linux localhost 2.0.32 #1 Fri Jan 30 07:08:01 EST 1998 i586 unknown
   ```

   This output of the `uname` command shows the kernel's version number as well as the date the kernel was built. If this date does not match the date when you rebuilt the kernel, you may not be running the new kernel. Go through the steps outlined in Chapter 2 and make sure you have really installed the new kernel. One common problem is forgetting to reboot, so try that step as well.

2. Look at the contents of the `/proc/devices` file to verify the CD-ROM device is present. Use the following procedure to view the contents of a `/proc/devices` file:

   ```
   cat /proc/devices
   Character devices:
    1 mem
    2 pty
    3 ttyp
    4 ttyp
    5 cua
    7 vcs
   10 misc

   Block devices:
    1 ramdisk
    2 fd
    3 ide0
    7 loop
    8 sd
    9 md
   22 ide1
   ```

   This listing corresponds to the devices on my system. You should look for the CD-ROM device in the list of block devices. I know my CD-ROM drive is connected to the secondary IDE interface. The two IDE interfaces correspond to the devices `ide0` and `ide1` in `/proc/devices`. Because `ide1` appears in the listing, I know the CD-ROM driver is in the kernel.

If you have a CD-ROM connected to a Sound Blaster Pro or compatible interface, look for a device number of 25 and a device name of `sbpcd`.

If you don't see a device that corresponds to your CD-ROM drive, you did not configure the kernel properly to include the CD-ROM driver. Reconfigure and rebuild the kernel, making sure you include support for your CD-ROM drive.

3. Verify the CD-ROM driver detected the CD-ROM drive when the system started. Use `dmesg | more` to look at the boot messages and see whether a line reports the CD-ROM drive was found. On my system, which has an ATAPI CD-ROM drive, the message looks like this:

```
hdc: FX400_02, ATAPI, CDROM drive
```

If you find no boot message about the CD-ROM drive, make sure the CD-ROM is physically installed. For an external CD-ROM drive, make sure the drive is powered on and the cables are connected. Check any drive ID or jumpers and make sure they are set correctly. You may want to first make sure the CD-ROM drive works under DOS. If you see the CD-ROM work under DOS, you can be sure the drive is physically sound. Next, verify you have rebuilt the kernel with support for the correct CD-ROM drive interface.

4. Verify you can read from the CD-ROM drive. Try the following command and see whether the drive's activity light comes on (it should) and whether there are any error messages (there shouldn't be any):

```
dd bs=1024 count=5000 < /dev/cdrom > /dev/null
5000+0 records in
5000+0 records in
```

The `/dev/null` device is what you might call the *bit bucket*. Output directed to `/dev/null` simply vanishes.

If the `dd` command does not work, the device file for the CD-ROM device may not be set properly. Use the `ls -l` command to view detailed information about your CD-ROM device. For an ATAPI CD-ROM drive on the secondary IDE interface, for example, I would look at `/dev/hdc` as follows:

```
ls -l /dev/hdc
brw-rw----   1 root      disk     22,   0 Feb  4  1995 /dev/hdc
```

Notice the numbers 22 and 0, which are the major and minor device numbers. These numbers need to be corrected. (Later sections of this chapter list the device numbers for specific CD-ROM drivers.)

5. Verify you can mount the CD-ROM. Place a good CD-ROM (such as the CD-ROM from this book) in the CD-ROM drive and try to mount by using the following command:

```
mount -t iso9660 -r /dev/cdrom /mnt/cdrom
```

If you can read from the CD-ROM drive with the dd command, but you cannot mount the CD-ROM, you may have configured the kernel without support for the ISO-9660 file system. To verify the currently supported file systems, use the following command:

```
cat /proc/filesystems
        ext2
        msdos
nodev   proc
nodev   smbfs
        iso9660
```

If you do not see iso9660 listed, you have to rebuild the kernel and add support for the ISO-9660 file system.

6. If nothing works, you may want to read the latest CDROM-HOWTO document. To read the HOWTO documents, type cd /usr/doc/HOWTO to change to the directory where the HOWTO files are located. Then type zcat CDROM-HOWTO.gz | more to view the CDROM-HOWTO file.

If you still cannot get the CD-ROM drive to work under Linux, you may want to post a news item to one of the comp.os.linux newsgroups.

The following sections suggest solutions for a few more common problems.

Kernel configuration for specific CD-ROM drives

If you are rebuilding the kernel and you have an ATAPI CD-ROM drive, you should answer Yes to the following questions as you configure the kernel (see Chapter 2 for more on configuring the kernel):

```
Enhanced IDE/MFM/RLL disk/cdrom/tape/floppy support
(CONFIG_BLK_DEV_IDE) [Y/n/?] y
Include IDE/ATAPI CDROM support (CONFIG_BLK_DEV_IDECD) [Y/n/?] y
```

The default response is shown in brackets; y means Yes, and n means No. You can accept the default by pressing Enter.

Tip

For SCSI CD-ROM drives, answer Yes to the following questions:

```
*
* SCSI support
*
SCSI support (CONFIG_SCSI) [N/y/m/?] y
*
* SCSI support type (disk, tape, CD-ROM)
*
SCSI CD-ROM support (CONFIG_BLK_DEV_SR) [N/y/m/?] (NEW) y
```

Of course, you also must specify your SCSI controller type; otherwise, the SCSI CD-ROM won't work. If you have an Adaptec AHA1542 SCSI controller, for example, answer Yes to the following question:

```
Adaptec AHA1542 support (CONFIG_SCSI_AHA1542) [N/y/m/?] (NEW) y
```

Tip

If your CD-ROM drive has a proprietary interface, you must enable support for that specific CD-ROM drive interface. Following is a sampling of the questions from the 2.0.31 kernel:

```
*
* CD-ROM drivers (not for SCSI or IDE/ATAPI drives)
*
Support non-SCSI/IDE/ATAPI CDROM drives (CONFIG_CD_NO_IDESCSI) [Y/n/?]
Aztech/Orchid/Okano/Wearnes/TXC/CyDROM  CDROM support (CONFIG_AZTCD)
[N/y/m/?]
Goldstar R420 CDROM support (CONFIG_GSCD) [N/y/m/?]
Matsushita/Panasonic/Creative, Longshine, TEAC CDROM support
(CONFIG_SBPCD) [N/y/m/?]
Mitsumi (standard) [no XA/Multisession] CDROM support (CONFIG_MCD)
[N/y/m/?]
Mitsumi [XA/MultiSession] CDROM support (CONFIG_MCDX) [N/y/m/?]
Optics Storage DOLPHIN 8000AT CDROM support (CONFIG_OPTCD) [N/y/m/?]
Philips/LMS CM206 CDROM support (CONFIG_CM206) [N/y/m/?]
Sanyo CDR-H94A CDROM support (CONFIG_SJCD) [N/y/m/?]
Soft configurable cdrom interface card support (CONFIG_CDI_INIT)
[N/y/?]
Sony CDU31A/CDU33A CDROM support (CONFIG_CDU31A) [N/y/m/?]
Sony CDU535 CDROM support (CONFIG_CDU535) [N/y/m/?]
```

Answer Yes to the question about the specific CD-ROM drive in your PC. If you have a Mitsumi CD-ROM drive (with a proprietary interface not ATAPI), for example, type **y** as your answer to the line that starts with Mitsumi (standard).

Newer versions of the Linux kernel may support other types of proprietary CD-ROM drive interfaces. Check the prompts carefully before answering these questions posed by the kernel-configuration program.

Tip

Because most CD-ROMs use the ISO-9660 file system, you also must enable support for this file system in the kernel. To do this, answer Yes to the following question during kernel configuration:

```
ISO9660 cdrom filesystem support (CONFIG_ISO9660_FS) [M/n/y/?] y
```

IDE (ATAPI) CD-ROM troubles

When a PC has an ATAPI CD-ROM drive, its ATA (IDE) adapter has two interfaces: primary and secondary, each of which is capable of supporting two drives. In Linux, the two primary devices are /dev/hda and /dev/hdb, which typically are used for hard disk drives. The secondary IDE devices are /dev/hdc and /dev/hdd. Thus, if you have an IDE hard drive connected to the primary interface and an IDE CD-ROM drive connected to the secondary interface, the hard drive will be /dev/hda, and the CD-ROM drive will be /dev/hdc.

Of the two devices on an interface, one is designated as the master and the other as the slave. When only one IDE device is attached to an interface, it must be designated as the *master* (or *single*). Typically, the IDE device has a jumper (a connector that connects a pair of pins) to indicate whether the device is a master or a slave.

When a single IDE CD-ROM drive is connected to the secondary interface, you must set the jumper on the CD-ROM drive to make it a master. If you bought a PC with an IDE CD-ROM drive preinstalled, this jumper may already be set for you. If you run into a situation in which Linux refuses to recognize your IDE CD-ROM drive, however, you should check the CD-ROM drive's parameters, making sure it uses the secondary IDE interface (IRQ 15 and I/O address 170H) and that it is set to be the master.

Some interface cards support more than two IDE interfaces. In such a case, you should know the Linux IDE CD-ROM driver may not recognize anything but the primary and secondary IDE interfaces. The Creative Labs Sound Blaster 16 CD-ROM interface is, by default, set to be the fourth IDE interface. If you are connecting a CD-ROM drive to a Sound Blaster 16 for use in Linux, you must set the jumpers on the Sound Blaster 16, so the IDE interface is the secondary interface instead of the fourth interface.

Boot-time parameters for CD-ROM drives

Linux drivers normally find CD-ROM drives (and other peripherals) by *probing,* reading from and writing to various I/O addresses. Linux drivers also use any available information from the PC's CMOS memory. CMOS is Complementary Metal Oxide Semiconductor — a type of semiconductor. Each PC has a small amount of battery-backed, nonvolatile CMOS storage, where vital information about the PC, such as the number of types of disk drives, are stored. The real-time clock also is stored in the CMOS.

One problem with probing is it involves reading from or writing to specific I/O addresses. Depending on what device uses that I/O address, probing can cause the system to *hang* (become unresponsive). When the Sound Blaster Pro CD driver, sbpcd, probes for a CD-ROM drive, it may access an I/O address used in an NE2000 Ethernet card. If this happens, the system hangs.

To avoid probing, you can pass specific device parameters for the device corresponding to your CD-ROM drive at boot time.

If you have a CD-ROM drive with the Sound Blaster Pro CD interface, the device name is sbpcd, and you can provide settings at LILO's boot prompt as follows:

```
sbpcd=0x230,SoundBlaster
```

This command tells the `sbpcd` driver the I/O address of the CD-ROM drive is 230H. The exact boot-time parameters for a device depend on that device driver. Later sections of this chapter provide specific boot-time parameters for CD-ROM device drivers.

If you use LILO, you can put the boot-time parameters in the `/etc/lilo.conf` file in the following manner:

```
append = "sbpcd=0x230,SoundBlaster"
```

CD-ROM device names

Linux uses a unique device name for each type of CD-ROM interface. The CD-ROM devices are block devices like the disk device, such as `/dev/hda` and `/dev/sda`. Table 12-2 lists the CD-ROM device names.

Table 12-2	**CD-ROM device names in Linux**
Device name	*CD-ROM type*
`/dev/aztcd`	Aztech CD-ROM drive interface
`/dev/cdu31a`	Sony CDU31A/CDU33A CD-ROM drive interface
`/dev/cm206cd`	Philips/LMS CD-ROM drive interface
`/dev/gscd`	GoldStar CD-ROM interface
`/dev/hdc`	ATAPI CD-ROM drive on the secondary IDE interface on an EIDE controller
`/dev/mcd`	Mitsumi CD-ROM drive interface
`/dev/optcd`	Optics Storage CD-ROM drive interface
`/dev/sbpcd`	Sound Blaster Pro CD-ROM drive interface
`/dev/sjcd`	Sanyo CD-ROM drive interface
`/dev/sonycd535`	Sony CDU-535/CDU-531 CD-ROM drive interface

By convention, the generic CD-ROM device `/dev/cdrom` is set up as a link to the actual CD-ROM device on your system. On my system, which has a ATAPI CD-ROM drive, a detailed listing of `/dev/cdrom` shows the following:

```
ls -l /dev/cdrom
lrwxrwxrwx   1 root      root           3 Mar 11 15:15 /dev/cdrom -> hdc
```

The output of `ls` indicates `/dev/cdrom` is a symbolic link to `/dev/hdc`, which is the IDE block device. (The same device name is used for a disk or a CD-ROM drive connected to the interface.)

On the other hand, on my old 386 PC, the CD-ROM drive is on a Sound Blaster Pro card. In this case, a detailed listing of /dev/cdrom shows the following:

```
ls -l /dev/cdrom
lrwxrwxrwx 1 root  root   10 Sep 29 20:19 /dev/cdrom -> sbpcd
```

The convention of defining a symbolic link between the generic /dev/cdrom device to the actual CD-ROM device means programs that use the CD-ROM drive can simply refer to the CD-ROM as /dev/cdrom and not worry about the actual type of CD-ROM drive interface. Because of the symbolic link between /dev/cdrom and the actual CD-ROM device, any input or output requests go directly to the actual CD-ROM driver that knows how to handle the request.

CD-ROM drive use under Linux

If you put a new CD-ROM in the drive, you must mount the CD-ROM before you can use it. Use the following command to mount the CD-ROM:

```
mount -t iso9660 -r /dev/cdrom /mnt/cdrom
```

The -t option specifies the file system of the CD-ROM is ISO-9660 (which is true for a typical CD-ROM), and the -r option indicates the CD-ROM is mounted as read-only.

If you want to eject the CD-ROM and load a new one, you should first dismount the CD-ROM's file system by using the umount command. Type umount /mnt/cdrom.

Then you can eject the CD-ROM by pressing the CD-ROM drive's eject button.

When you use removable media such as CD-ROMs or removable disks (even floppy disks), always use the umount command before you eject the removable disk or CD-ROM. For floppy disks, you have to dismount the floppy only if you previously mounted the floppy.

Playing audio CDs in the CD-ROM drive

You need a special application to play audio CDs in the CD-ROM drive. This book's companion CD-ROM comes with xplaycd, an *X* application that provides a graphical control panel for playing audio CDs.

Before using the xplaycd program, make sure you dismount any CD-ROM currently in the drive (use the umount /dev/cdrom command) and place an audio CD in the drive.

The xplaycd program needs the X Window System to run, so you should first start *X* and then run xplaycd by typing xplaycd at the shell prompt in an xterm window. Figure 12-1 shows the graphical user interface of xplaycd.

Figure 12-1: The graphical control panel of the xplaycd program for playing audio CDs

If you want to log in as a normal user and play audio CDs on the CD-ROM drive, you should first log in as root and set the permission settings on the CD-ROM device so anyone can read the CD-ROM device. You must set the permission for the actual CD-ROM device, not the generic /dev/cdrom device. To set the permission setting, follow these steps:

1. Log in as root. If you are already logged in, use the su command to assume the identity of the root user.

2. Determine the actual device name of the CD-ROM device. Type the following command:

```
ls -l /dev/cdrom
lrwxrwxrwx   1 root       root           3 Mar 11 15:15 /dev/cdrom
-> hdc
```

In the listing, you will find the name of the actual device next to -> in the listing. In this case, the actual CD-ROM device is /dev/hdc.

3. Make the actual device readable by all users using the chmod command, as follows:

```
chmod o+r /dev/hdc
```

4. Verify the permission settings of the actual CD-ROM device. You would check the permissions of /dev/hdc as follows:

```
ls -l /dev/hdc

brw-rw-r-- 1 root       disk      22,   0 Feb  4  1995 /dev/hdc
```

Notice the last three characters (r–) of the first column, which indicate all users have read access to the device. Also notice the b at the beginning of the line, which indicates the device is a block device (in a long listing, character devices have c as the first letter).

Specific CD-ROM drive information

In the following sections, I summarize information specific to some common device drivers. This information includes the name of the device file (such as /dev/sbpcd for a CD-ROM drive with Sound Blaster Pro interface), any boot parameters the driver accepts, and any unique capabilities of the driver.

You should read the section that covers the CD-ROM interface of your CD-ROM drive.

The scd driver

The scd driver supports CD-ROM drives that connect to the PC through SCSI controller cards. The scd driver has the following characteristics:

```
Allows multiple CD-ROM drives: yes
Supports loadable module: yes
Can read audio frames: no
Performs auto-probing: yes
Name of device file: /dev/scd0, major device number = 11
Device configuration file: /usr/include/linux/cdrom.h
Kernel option during make config: SCSI CDROM support?
Name of README file: none
```

Secret

The scd driver supports multiple CD-ROM drives on the SCSI bus. The names of the device files are /dev/scd0, /dev/scd1, /dev/scd2, and so on, with corresponding minor device numbers 0, 1, 2, and so on. All devices have the same major device number: 11.

The IDE CD-ROM driver

The IDE device driver supports all types of IDE devices, ranging from hard drives to CD-ROM drives. The driver finds the drives by auto-probing and assigns device names in sequence: /dev/hda and /dev/hdb for drives on the primary IDE interface, and /dev/hdc and /dev/hdd for drives on the secondary IDE interface. A CD-ROM drive on the secondary IDE interface has the device name /dev/hdc (because the CD-ROM drive is slower than the hard disk, CD-ROM drives are connected to a separate IDE interface rather than being set up as a slave drive on the primary IDE interface).

The IDE CD driver has the following characteristics:

```
Allows multiple CD-ROM drives: yes
Supports loadable module: no
Can read audio frames: yes (on some drives)
Performs auto-probing: yes
Name of device file: /dev/hdc or /dev/hdd, major device number = 22
Device configuration file: /usr/include/linux/cdrom.h
Kernel option during make config: Include IDE/ATAPI CDROM support?
Name of README file: /usr/src/linux/Documentation/cdrom/ide-cd
```

The IDE CD driver accepts the following boot parameter:

```
hdc=cdrom
```

This parameter tells the IDE device driver the first drive on the secondary IDE interface is a CD-ROM drive. If you have another CD-ROM drive on that interface, you might include the following boot parameter:

```
hdd=cdrom
```

The same IDE driver is used for both IDE hard disk drives and IDE (ATAPI) CD-ROM drives. The boot parameters are different for a hard drive.

The sbpcd driver

The sbpcd driver supports a variety of CD-ROM drives that connect to the PC through an interface that conforms to the proprietary interface used in Creative Labs Sound Blaster Pro sound cards.

The sbpcd driver has the following characteristics:

```
Allows multiple CD-ROM drives: yes
Supports loadable module: yes
Can read audio frames: yes (CR-562, CR-563, CD-200 only)
Performs auto-probing: yes
Name of device file: /dev/sbpcd, major device number = 25
Device configuration file: /usr/include/linux/sbpcd.h
Kernel option during make config: Matsushita/Panasonic/ Creative,
Longshine, TEAC CDROM support?
Name of README file: /usr/src/linux/Documentation/cdrom/sbpcd
```

The sbpcd driver accepts a boot parameter in this format:

```
sbpcd=IOPORT,interface-type
```

IOPORT is the I/O port address of the device in hexadecimal format (such as 0x230). interface-type is a single word that indicates the type of CD-ROM interface; it must be SoundBlaster, LaserMate, or SPEA.

If the device file /dev/sbpcd is missing, create it with the following mknod command:

```
mknod /dev/sbpcd b 25 0
```

The last three parameters specify the device type (b for block device), major device number (25 is the assigned number for /dev/sbpcd), and minor device number (0 for the first CD-ROM drive on the controller).

Secret

You can *daisy-chain* (connect first to second, second to third, and so on) up to four drives per controller. Use minor device numbers 1 through 3 for the next three drives you daisy-chain to the first drive.

The sonycd535 driver

The `sonycd535` driver supports Sony CDU-535 and CDU-531 CD-ROM drives that connect to the PC through Sony's proprietary interface card.

The `sonycd535` driver has the following characteristics:

```
Allows multiple CD-ROM drives: no
Supports loadable module: yes
Can read audio frames: no
Performs auto-probing: no
Name of device file: /dev/sonycd535, major device number = 24
Device configuration file: /usr/include/linux/sonycd535.h
Kernel option during make config: Sony CDU535 CDROM support?
Name of README file: /usr/src/linux/Documentation/cdrom/sonycd535
```

This driver accepts the following boot parameter:

```
sonycd535=IOPORT
```

IOPORT is the I/O port address of the device in hexadecimal format (such as 0x320).

The aztcd driver

The `aztcd` driver supports Aztech CDA268, Orchid CD-3110, and Okano/Wearnes CDD110 CD-ROM drives that use a proprietary interface. Other CD-ROM drives from these vendors, such as Aztech CDA269, have the IDE interface. You have to use the IDE CD driver for those drives. The `aztcd` driver is only for the proprietary interface.

The `aztcd` driver has the following characteristics:

```
Allows multiple CD-ROM drives: no
Supports loadable module: yes
Can read audio frames: no
Performs auto-probing: no
Name of device file: /dev/aztcd, major device number = 29
Device configuration file: /usr/include/linux/aztcd.h
Kernel option during make config:
Aztech/Orchid/Okano/Wearnes/TXC/CyDROM  CDROM support?
Name of README file: /usr/src/linux/Documentation/cdrom/aztcd
```

This driver accepts the following boot parameter:

```
aztcd=IOPORT
```

IOPORT is the I/O port address of the device in hexadecimal format (such as 0x340).

The mcd driver

The mcd driver supports Mitsumi CRMC-LU005S and CRMC-FX001 CD-ROM drives with the proprietary Mitsumi interface. Many new PCs use the Mitsumi CD-ROM drives, but not the proprietary interface. Instead, the current trend is to use the Mitsumi drives with the IDE (ATAPI) interface, so you should check carefully before you select the mcd driver as the CD-ROM driver. If your PC has a Mitsumi CD-ROM driver, it is more likely an ATAPI drive than one with the proprietary Mitsumi interface.

The mcd driver has the following characteristics:

```
Allows multiple CD-ROM drives: no
Supports loadable module: yes
Can read audio frames: no
Performs auto-probing: no
Name of device file: /dev/mcd, major device number = 23
Device configuration file: /usr/include/linux/mcd.h
Kernel option during make config: Mitsumi (standard) [no
XA/Multisession] CDROM support?
Name of README file: /usr/src/linux/Documentation/cdrom/mcd
```

This driver accepts the following boot parameter:

```
mcd=IOPORT,IRQ
```

IOPORT is the I/O port address of the Mitsumi interface card in hexadecimal format (such as 0x340). IRQ is the interrupt request number used by that card.

Tip

Linux also comes with another Mitsumi driver, mcdx, that provides additional capabilities. To include this driver, you should answer Yes to the following question during kernel configuration:

```
Mitsumi [XA/MultiSession] CDROM support?
```

Sound Cards and Linux

Compared with those of the Apple Macintosh, the built-in sound-generation capabilities of the IBM-compatible PCs are rather limited. Essentially, all you can do with the PC's built-in speaker is play a single note. You can't even vary the loudness of the note.

You can greatly improve the sound-output capability of a PC by installing a sound card, such as the Sound Blaster, which can synthesize a wide range of sounds. The *sound card*, an adapter that plugs into a slot on your PC's motherboard, includes the electronic circuitry needed to play and record sound. You can plug in speakers and a microphone to the back of a sound card. Many sound cards also include an interface through which you can connect a CD-ROM drive.

When a microphone is hooked up to the sound card, it can convert the *analog* (continuously varying) sound waves into 8-bit or 16-bit numbers, sampling the wave at rates ranging from 4kHz to 44kHz (44,000 times a second). Higher sampling rates and a higher number of bits (16) provide better quality, but you need more disk space to store high-quality sound. In addition, the sound card can convert digital sound samples to analog signals you can play on a speaker.

Most sound cards, including the popular Sound Blaster, also support MIDI commands in addition to recording and playing back waveform sound. MIDI, which stands for *Musical Instrument Digital Interface*, is commonly used to record and play back musical sounds that can be created by a synthesizer. (Most sound cards have built-in synthesizers.)

Following is a list of sound cards currently supported by the Linux sound driver:

- 6850 UART MIDI
- Adlib (OPL2)
- ECHO-PSS cards (Orchid SoundWave32, Cardinal DSP16)
- Ensoniq SoundScape
- Gravis Ultrasound
- Gravis Ultrasound ACE
- Gravis Ultrasound 16-bit sampling daughterboard
- Gravis Ultrasound Max
- Logitech SoundMan Games (SBPro, 44-kHz stereo support)
- Logitech SoundMan Wave (Jazz16/OPL4)
- Logitech SoundMan 16 (PAS-16-compatible)
- MPU-401 MIDI (Roland)
- MediaTriX AudioTriX Pro
- Media Vision Premium 3D (Jazz16)
- Microsoft Windows Sound System (MSS/WSS)
- OAK OTI-601D cards (Mozart)
- Orchid SW32
- OPTi 82C928/82C929 cards (MAD16/MAD16 Pro)
- Personal Sound System (PSS)
- Pro Audio Spectrum 16
- Pro Audio Studio 16
- Pro Sonic 16

- Sound Blaster 1.0

- Sound Blaster 16

- Sound Blaster 16ASP

- Sound Blaster 2.0

- Sound Blaster AWE32

- Sound Blaster Pro

- Texas Instruments TM4000M notebook sound

- ThunderBoard

- Turtle Beach Tropez

- Turtle Beach Maui

- Yamaha FM synthesizers (OPL2, OPL3 and OPL4)

Secret

Many sound cards include a built-in interface through which you can attach a CD-ROM drive. Linux needs a separate device driver to access a CD-ROM drive connected to a sound card; the sound driver does not have anything to do with the CD-ROM drive, even though the drive is attached to the sound card. Neither does the sound driver have anything to do with the joystick port that many sound cards include.

Installing the sound driver

Linux needs a driver to control the sound card. The initial Linux kernel (after you install Linux from the companion CD-ROM) does not include the sound driver. The directory /usr/src/linux/drivers/sound contains the source code for the sound driver. You must rebuild the kernel to add support for your system's sound card.

Cross-Reference

Chapter 2 walks you through the process of rebuilding the Linux kernel. As those steps show, when you configure the kernel with the make config command, you are asked if you want to add the support for a sound board. If you answer Yes, the configuration process prompts you for further information about your sound card.

First, the configuration program asks whether you want to include support for specific sound cards. You should answer Yes for only for the actual brand of the sound card in your PC. After you indicate you have a specific card, the configuration program may skip other cards that cannot coexist with the card you selected.

After you select the sound cards you want the sound driver to support, the configuration program asks for specific parameters for each selected card. You have to provide the I/O address, the IRQ, and the DMA channel number of the sound card. You should provide the same values for these parameters as they are set under DOS and Windows. You should be able to find the settings by reading the sound card's manual (a new PC with a sound card typically includes a small manual for the sound card).

My system has a Sound Blaster card. Under MS-DOS, the AUTOEXEC.BAT file contains the following command:

```
SET BLASTER=A220 I5 D1 H5 P300 T6
```

From my experience with Sound Blaster boards, I could determine the following from this SET command: The I/O address is 220 (hexadecimal), the IRQ is 5, and the DMA channel is 1. Thus, I provided these values when I configured the Linux kernel for sound-card support.

After the sound driver is configured, you can finish rebuilding the kernel, following the steps in Chapter 2. The new kernel should now support your system's sound card. I offer some troubleshooting suggestions in the section "Troubleshooting sound cards" later in this chapter.

Configuring the sound driver

During configuration of the sound driver, you have to answer several questions the configuration program asks. This section provides some guidelines for answering specific questions. Notice the configuration program does not ask each question because the exact sequence of questions depends on your earlier responses.

ProAudioSpectrum 16 support? — You should answer Yes (**y**) only if you have a Pro Audio Spectrum 16 (referred to as PAS16), ProAudio Studio 16, or Logitech SoundMan 16 sound card. In particular, don't answer Yes if you have some other Media Vision or Logitech card, because those cards are not PAS16-compatible.

SoundBlaster support? — Answer Yes (**y**) if your PC's sound card is a Creative Labs Sound Blaster or one of many hardware-compatible clones, such as Thunderboard or Logitech SoundMan Games. You should also answer Yes (**y**) if a sound card claims to be Sound Blaster-compatible.

Generic OPL2/OPL3 FM synthesizer support? — You should answer Yes (**y**) if your sound card has a FM chip made by Yamaha (OPL2/OPL3/OPL4). Answering Yes usually is a safe choice.

Gravis Ultrasound support? — Answer Yes (**y**) if your system's sound card is a Gravis Ultrasound (with a name such as GUS or GUS MAX). Although you can include GUS support without conflicts with other boards, the GUS driver consumes a great deal of memory. Therefore, you should answer No (**n**) if you don't have a GUS.

MPU-401 support (NOT for SB16)? — Although the Roland MPU401 MIDI interface is supported on many sound cards, the exact way of handling this interface varies from one card to another. You should answer No (**n**) if your sound card does not have an MPU401 interface. It's safe to answer Yes (**y**) if your sound card does, indeed, have a true MPU401 MIDI interface.

6850 UART Midi support? — You probably can answer No (**n**) safely, because the 6850 UART interface is rarely used. UART stands for *Universal Asynchronous Receiver Transmitter,* a circuit that splits a byte into individual bits and recombines bits into bytes.

PSS (ECHO-ADI2111) support? — Answering Yes (**y**) includes support for sound cards based on the PSS chipset. You should answer Yes only if you have an Orchid SW32, Cardinal DSP16, or any other sound card based on the PSS chipset.

16-bit sampling option of GUS (not GUS MAX)? — The Gravis Ultrasound card has a daughterboard on which you can install a card that provides 16-bit sampling. You should answer No (**n**) if you have a GUS MAX card. If you answer Yes (**y**), support for GUS MAX is turned off automatically.

GUS MAX support? — If you have a GUS MAX sound card, answer Yes (**y**) to this question.

Microsoft Sound System support? — You should answer Yes (**y**) if you have the original Windows Sound System card made by Microsoft or Aztech SG 16 Pro (or NX16 Pro).

Ensoniq Soundscape support? — Answer Yes (**y**) if your sound card is based on the Ensoniq SoundScape chipset. Several manufacturers — such as Ensoniq, Spea, and Reveal (Reveal also makes other cards) — use this chipset.

Sound Blaster Pro support? — Answer Yes (**y**) if your card is a Sound Blaster Pro, Sound Blaster 16, or a compatible card.

Sound Blaster 16 support? — Answer Yes (**y**) to enable this support if your PC has a Sound Blaster 16 sound card.

/dev/dsp and /dev/audio support (usually required)? — Answer Yes (**y**) so the configuration program automatically creates the mount points: /dev/dsp and /dev/audio.

MIDI interface support? — Answer Yes (**y**) to enable the MIDI devices (which have names such as /dev/midiNN, in which NN is a number) and allow access to the sound card through the /dev/sequencer and /dev/music devices. Answering Yes affects any MPU401 and/or any MIDI-compatible devices.

FM synthesizer (YM3812/OPL-3) support? — You can safely answer this question Yes (**y**).

/dev/sequencer support? — If you answer No (**n**), the configuration program disables the /dev/sequencer and /dev/music devices.

Learning sound-device names

Like any other devices in Linux, the sound devices have files in the /dev directory with specific names. Table 12-3 lists the standard device filenames that provide sound capability in Linux (you may not have all devices on your system).

Table 12-3:	Standard sound device filenames in Linux
Device filename	*Description*
/dev/audio	An audio device capable of playing Sun workstation-compatible audio files (typically with a .au extension). The device does not support all capabilities of the Sun workstation audio device, but can play Sun audio files.
/dev/audio1	Sun workstation-compatible audio device for the second sound card (if any).
/dev/dsp	Digital signal-processing device that also can play Sun audio files.
/dev/midi	MIDI device.
/dev/mixer	Sound-mixer device.
/dev/mixer1	Second sound-mixer device.
/dev/pcaudio	Equivalent to /dev/audio, but plays on the PC's speaker. (You have to install a separate PC speaker driver, which is available from ftp://ftp.informatik.hu-berlin.de/pub/os/linux/hu-sound/.)
/dev/pcmixer	Equivalent to /dev/mixer, but plays on the PC's speaker. (You have to install a separate PC speaker driver, which is available from ftp://ftp.informatik.hu-berlin.de/pub/os/linux/hu-sound/.)
/dev/pcsp	Equivalent to /dev/dsp, but plays on the PC's speaker. (You have to install a separate PC speaker driver, which is available from ftp://ftp.informatik.hu-berlin.de/pub/os/linux/hu-sound/.)
/dev/sequencer	MIDI sequencer device.
/dev/sndstat	A device that provides information about the sound driver (see the example in "Checking sound driver status").

Testing the sound card

After you enable support for your sound card and rebuild the Linux kernel, you should reboot the system (log in as root, and use the command /sbin/shutdown -r now). As Linux boots, you should see a message about the sound driver.

Tip

If the boot messages scroll by too fast to see, type the command dmesg | more to see these messages one screen at a time. Look for one or more lines that start with snd. On my system, for example, I have a Sound Blaster Pro sound card. The boot messages include the following line:

```
snd2 <SoundBlaster Pro 4.13> at 0x220 irq 5 drq 1
```

In this case, the text within the angle brackets shows the name of the sound card and the version number of the digital signal-processing circuitry on that card. The boot message about the sound device also shows an I/O address of 0x220 (220 in hexadecimal notation), an IRQ of 5, and a DMA channel (reported as drq) of 1.

Sometimes, the sound driver may print error or warning messages as the system boots. When you run the dmesg command, you should also look for these messages.

Checking sound-driver status

If you see the boot message about the sound driver, you can tell the sound support is included in the kernel. The sound driver comes with another way to check the status.

Secret

A special device named /dev/sndstat enables you to get information about the status of the sound driver. All you have to do is look at the contents of /dev/sndstat. A typical output is as follows:

```
cat /dev/sndstat
Sound Driver:3.5.4-960630
Kernel: Linux localhost 2.0.32 #1 Fri Jan 30 07:08:01 EST 1998 i586
Config options: 0

Installed drivers:
Type 2: Sound Blaster

Card config:
Sound Blaster at 0x220 irq 5 drq 1
OPL-2/OPL-3 FM at 0x388 drq 0

Audio devices:
0: Sound Blaster Pro (4.13)

Synth devices:
0: Yamaha OPL-3

Midi devices:

Timers:
0: System clock

Mixers:
0: Sound Blaster
```

The messages will be different on your system, because you probably have a different sound card with different settings than mine. The /dev/sndstat device file, however, provides good diagnostic information about the sound driver.

Trying the sound card

To test the sound driver, try playing a sound file. All you must do is send the sound file to the sound device (`/dev/audio`) with the `cat` command. The sound device can play Sun's sound files, which usually have names that end with the `.au` extension. To play a sound file named `piano-beep.au`, you would type the following command:

```
cat piano-beep.au > /dev/audio
```

Tip

If you have the Red Hat Linux CD-ROM mounted, you will find several `.au` files in the directory `/mnt/cdrom/live/usr/lib/games/xboing/sounds`. Try the following command:

```
cat /mnt/cdrom/live/usr/lib/games/xboing/sounds/evillaugh.au >
/dev/audio
```

If the sound file plays, your sound card is working properly.

If you have a microphone connected to your sound card, you also can try recording a 10-second sound file with the following command:

```
dd bs=8k count=10 </dev/audio >test.au
```

The `dd` command simply copies a specified amount of data from one file to another. In this case, the input file is the audio device (which records from the microphone) and the output file is the sound file. After recording the sound file, you can play back by sending the data back to `/dev/audio` with the `cat` command.

Wizard

To use the sound card properly, you need some applications that enable you to play back and record sound files. Try one of the following Internet resources to locate sound-recording and playback applications for Linux:

- `ftp://sunsite.unc.edu:/pub/Linux/apps/sound/`
- `ftp://tsx-11.mit.edu:/pub/linux/packages/sound/`
- `ftp://nic.funet.fi:/pub/Linux/util/sound/`

Troubleshooting sound cards

After you configure the sound driver and reboot, if the sound card does not produce any sound when you copy audio files to `/dev/audio`, try the following steps to determine and fix the problem:

1. Verify you are running the kernel you rebuilt with support for the sound card. To see the version number, use the `uname -a` command. Following is typical output from the `uname -a` command:

   ```
   Linux localhost 2.0.32 #1 Fri Jan 30 07:08:01 EST 1998 i586
   unknown
   ```

Cross-Reference

This string shows the kernel's version number, as well as the date when the kernel was built. If the date does not match the date when you rebuilt the kernel, you probably are not running the new kernel. Go through the steps outlined in Chapter 2 and make sure you installed the new kernel. One common problem is forgetting to reboot, so also try this step.

2. Check to see whether the sound driver is included in the kernel. One way to check this is to look at the contents of the /proc/devices file. An example follows:

```
cat /proc/devices
Character devices:
 1 mem
 2 pty
 3 ttyp
 4 ttyp
 5 cua
 7 vcs
10 misc
14 sound

Block devices:
 1 ramdisk
 2 fd
 3 ide0
 7 loop
 8 sd
 9 md
22 ide1
```

The listing should show character device 14, named sound. If you don't see this device, you did not configure the kernel properly to include the sound driver. Reconfigure and rebuild the kernel, making sure you include support for your sound card.

3. Verify the sound driver detected the sound card when the system started. Use dmesg | more to look at the boot messages and check for a line reporting the sound card was found. If the sound driver does not report the sound card, the sound card may not be installed and configured properly.

First, make sure the sound card works under DOS or Windows. Determine the I/O address, IRQ, and DMA channel, and then reconfigure the kernel to include support for your sound card with the same parameters as under DOS.

4. If nothing works, you may want to read the latest Sound-HOWTO document. To read the HOWTO documents, type cd /usr/doc/HOWTO to change to the directory where the HOWTO files are located. Then type zcat Sound-HOWTO.gz | more to view the Sound-HOWTO file.

Cross-Reference

If you still cannot get the sound card to work under Linux, you may want to post a news item to one of the comp.os.linux newsgroups. Chapter 19 discusses how to connect to the Internet and access the newsgroups.

Solving common sound-card problems

In addition to the basic sound-card driver configuration, you may run into problems with specific sound cards. This section provides hints for solving some common problems.

Works under DOS, but not under Linux

Many Sound Blaster-compatible cards work under MS-DOS and Microsoft Windows, but do not work under Linux. A typical symptom is everything appears fine—the sound driver is installed properly and it reports the sound card with the correct parameters at startup—but you don't hear any sound when you copy a sound file to /dev/audio.

In this case, you have to initialize the sound card under DOS and Windows first. Try the following steps:

1. Boot the PC under DOS and run Windows 3.1. If you have Windows 95, start Windows 95.

2. Run the Media Player application and play some sound files under Windows.

3. Exit Windows and reboot the PC. If you are running Windows 3.1, exit Windows and press Ctrl+Alt+Delete under DOS. In Windows 95, select the Start menu's Shut Down option and select Reboot from the resulting dialog box.

4. Make sure you reboot to Linux. If you use LILO, press Shift and respond to the LILO prompt. If you use a Linux boot floppy, make sure you place the boot floppy in the A drive before rebooting the PC.

After Linux boots, the sound driver should play the sound file successfully.

Can play sound, but not record

If you can play sound but you cannot record, first make sure you can record sound under DOS and Windows. This capability indicates the sound card is capable of recording.

Then get a mixer program (from one of the FTP sites listed in "Trying the sound card"), and use the mixer program to select the appropriate recording device, such as the microphone. You also may want to adjust the input gains to see whether this adjustment helps.

Pro Audio Spectrum PAS16 and Adaptec 1542 SCSI adapter

The PAS16 sound card uses I/O address 330H (hexadecimal 330) as its MIDI port address. The Adaptec AHA 1542 SCSI card also can use I/O address 330H. Linux, however, can use the AHA 1542 with the base I/O address of 334H. To avoid I/O address conflict between the PAS16 and AHA 1542 SCSI card, set the SCSI card's I/O address to 334H.

Secret

Another problem is the DMA conflicts between the PAS16 and the AHA 1542, which may halt the system with some memory error. The solution is to adjust two parameters — BUS ON and BUS OFF times — of the AHA 1542 SCSI card. Get the SCSISEL.EXE program from Adaptec through the Internet, run SCSISEL under DOS, and reduce the BUS ON time, or increase the BUS OFF time until the problem goes away.

Sound Blaster AWE32 not supported

Linux does not support the E-mu MIDI synthesizer and the ASP chip on Sound Blaster AWE32 sound cards. The problem is Creative Labs, the maker of the AWE32 card, has not released programming information about the E-mu and ASP chips.

Summary

Unlike many UNIX workstations, a typical PC nowadays comes with a CD-ROM drive and a sound card. The popularity of multimedia software fuels the demand for CD-ROM drives and sound capability in PCs. In addition, many software packages, including Linux, come on CD-ROM. Linux supports CD-ROM drives and sound cards. This chapter describes the CD-ROM drives and sound cards Linux supports, and shows you how to detect and correct some common sound-card and CD-ROM-drive installation problems.

By reading this chapter, you learn the following:

▶ Linux's support for a specific CD-ROM drive depends on the interface used to connect that CD-ROM drive to the PC's motherboard. Linux supports the most popular ATAPI (IDE) and SCSI interfaces for CD-ROM drives, as well many proprietary CD-ROM interfaces, such as Aztech, Sony, Mitsumi, and the Sound Blaster Pro CD-ROM interface.

▶ New users often mistakenly select a CD-ROM driver based on the brand name of the CD-ROM drive. Instead, they should select the CD-ROM driver that matches the CD-ROM's interface. Thus, a Mitsumi CD-ROM drive with an ATAPI interface requires the IDE driver, not the Mitsumi driver.

▶ Sound cards often include interfaces for CD-ROM drives and joysticks. The sound driver supports only the sound card's sound capabilities. You need separate drivers for the CD-ROM drive and the joystick.

▶ To use a sound card, you have to rebuild the Linux kernel. When you configure the kernel, you have to enable support for your sound card and provide information about the card's IRQ, I/O address, and DMA.

▶ You can use the /dev/audio and /dev/sndstat devices to check the sound card after you rebuild the kernel and reboot the system with the new kernel.

Chapter 13

Keyboards and Pointing Devices

In This Chapter

▶ Adjusting the keyboard autorepeat delay and repeat rate in Linux

▶ Understanding the concept of the keyboard map

▶ Configuring the keyboard for some European languages

▶ Surveying the mouse interface types and mouse protocols Linux supports

▶ Configuring XFree86 to use various keyboards and mice

The keyboard and the mouse (or some other mouselike-pointing device, such as a *trackball*) are the basic mechanisms for providing input to the computer. As far as hardware compatibility goes, Linux works with any keyboard that works under DOS. You may want to alter some characteristics of the keyboard, though, such as how fast it repeats a character when you hold down a key. You also may want to associate a different character set with the physical keys, especially if you use a language other than English. This chapter describes the keyboard-customization facilities of Linux.

You do not need a mouse (I use the term *mouse* to mean any pointing device, including a trackball) to run Linux. If, however, you install and use XFree86 (X Window System for Linux), you need a mouse. Several popular brands of mice and several types of interfaces (such as serial mouse or busmouse) are available. In this chapter, you learn about the types of mouse interfaces and mouse protocols Linux and X support.

Keyboards and Linux

The keyboard is one of those appendages of a PC you can't do without, but that you take for granted and don't think about much. If a keyboard works under DOS, it also should work under Linux. Thus, the make and model of a keyboard are not much of an issue.

You can, of course, customize some of the physical aspects of the keyboard, such as the following:

■ *Repeat delay.* If you hold down a key, the keyboard waits this amount of time before beginning to repeat that key.

■ *Repeat rate.* The repeat rate is the rate at which the keyboard repeats a key.

Another aspect of customization has more to do with Linux than with the keyboard. This aspect determines how Linux interprets a keypress. You could make the Backspace key generate Ctrl-H by *remapping* the key, which means by changing how a physical keypress is mapped to an action.

The following sections show both types of keyboard customization: the physical characteristics and the mapping of keys to actions.

Some keyboard terminology and notations

In this chapter, you encounter references to specific keys (or combinations of keys) on the keyboard. This section provides a brief overview of the key names and other terminology associated with keyboards.

Keyboard layout

Keyboard layout refers to the way the keys are laid out in the keyboard. Most PCs use a 101-key keyboard. Figure 13-1 shows the typical keyboard layout for a 101-key PC keyboard.

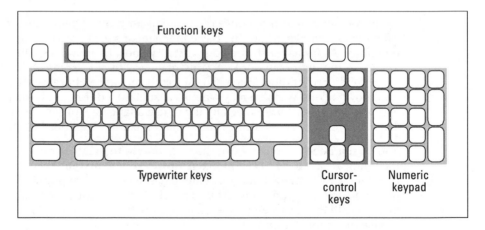

Figure 13-1: The keyboard layout for a 101-key PC keyboard

The basic alphabetic and numeric keys occupy most of the space on the keyboard. A set of 12 function keys — named F1 through F12 — appears along the top edge of the keyboard. The numeric pad is the block of keys on the right side of the keyboard.

The upper-right corner of the keyboard has three status lights, called LEDs. (*LED* stands for *light-emitting diode*, an electronic part that displays the light.) The LEDs — labeled Num Lock, Caps Lock, and Scroll Lock — indicate whether the corresponding Lock key is pressed.

Note

The Ctrl, Shift, and Alt keys are commonly referred to as the *modifier keys*. As you know, the keyboard has two of each of these keys. In Linux documentation, the right Alt key is referred to as the *AltGr key*.

Although many keys on the keyboard are labeled the same (the numbers on the number pad, for example, are the same as the numbers along the top row of the main block of keys), Linux assigns a unique keycode to each key on the keyboard. Typically, these keycodes go from number 1 through the number of keys on the keyboard.

X keyboard terminology

The X Window System (*X* for short) also assigns a keycode to each key on the keyboard. Unfortunately, the X keycodes are not the same as the Linux keycodes. Internally, *X* translates the physical keycodes to *keysyms,* which represent symbolic names for keys.

Keys such as the Shift, Ctrl, Alt, and Caps Lock keys are known as *modifier keys* because they modify the meaning of the other keys. *X* supports up to five system-dependent modifier keys.

Keyboard repeat delay and repeat rate

When Linux boots, the kernel sets the keyboard repeat rate to the maximum allowed by a keyboard. Although the maximum-repeat rate should be fine for most keyboards, in some cases, you may get multiple copies of a character all too easily because the repeat rate is too high. In such a case, you can use the kbdrate program to lower the keyboard repeat rate.

The kbdrate utility program enables you to manipulate the keyboard's repeat rate and the delay time—the amount of time for which a key must be depressed before the keyboard starts to repeat that key.

Following is the syntax of the kbdrate program:

```
kbdrate [-s] [-r rate] [-d delay]
```

All the arguments shown within brackets are optional. If you run kbdrate without any options, it works like this:

```
kbdrate
Typematic Rate set to 10.9 cps (delay = 250 mS)
```

This message from kbdrate means the keyboard repeat rate (called the typematic rate by IBM when the original PC came with these keyboards) is set to 10.9 characters per second (cps) and the repeat delay is 250 milliseconds (ms). Thus, when the program is run without any options, kbdrate sets the repeat rate and delay to these default values.

You can set the rate with the -r option; the rate can lie between 2.0 and 30.0 cps. Usually, the keyboard allows a discrete set of values. A common set of possible values is 2.0, 2.1, 2.3, 2.5, 2.7, 3.0, 3.3, 3.7, 4.0, 4.3, 4.6, 5.0, 5.5, 6.0, 6.7, 7.5, 8.0, 8.6, 9.2, 10.0, 10.9, 12.0, 13.3, 15.0, 16.0, 17.1, 18.5, 20.0, 21.8, 24.0, 26.7, and 30.0 cps. When you specify a rate, the kbdrate program selects from this set a value that's less than or equal to what you request. Thus, if you enter kbdrate -r 18.0, kbdrate selects 17.1 as the rate.

Use the -d option to set the delay, which can be between 250 and 1,000 ms (or 1 second). Only four possible values are allowed: 250, 500, 750, and 1,000 ms.

The -s option causes kbdrate to do its job without displaying any messages.

The kbdrate program may not work with some keyboards. Reportedly, the program cannot set the repeat rate on the Gateway AnyKey keyboard.

Tip

When you run the X Window System, it takes over the control of the keyboard. Under *X,* you can run kbdrate (from an xterm window) and set the delay and repeat rate. *X* also comes with the xset utility program, which enables you to alter many user preferences for the keyboard, mouse, and display screen. Although xset does not allow you to set the repeat rate, you can turn the repeat feature on or off. To turn off keyboard repeat, type the following at the shell prompt in an xterm window:

```
xset r off
```

Try holding down a key. It should not repeat at all. To turn on the autorepeat feature, use this command:

```
xset r on
```

The keyboard map

You probably don't pay much attention to how the keyboard maps the physical keys to characters because, for the English language, a one-to-one correspondence exists between the physical keys and the letters of the alphabet.

The situation is not as simple if your native language is not English and you need some special characters, such as characters with an *umlaut* (two dots above the letter) or other accented letters. To enter such letters from the keyboard, you have to change how a physical keypress is translated to characters in Linux. That conversion is referred to as the *keyboard map* or *keyboard translation*.

Note, entering special letters from the keyboard involves two steps: First, you must get Linux to interpret a keypress as the special character you want. Next, you need a program that can display the special character. How a special character is displayed depends on the font.

Note

Linux includes two programs — `loadkeys` and `xmodmap` — for modifying the way a physical keypress is mapped to an action. What you use depends on whether you are running in text mode or the X Window System. When you work in a Linux virtual console (basically, the text screen), your keypresses are handled by the keyboard driver. In this case, you should use `loadkeys` to alter the keyboard translation.

When *X* is running, it takes over both the keyboard and the mouse. Therefore, you have to use a different utility program, `xmodmap`, to change the keyboard map. *X* consults the Linux key-translation tables at startup, though, so you get some consistency in keyboard translation between text mode and *X*.

In Linux, the keyboard driver consults a keyboard table to determine how to translate a physical keycode to a string of other codes or an action. You can load a keyboard-translation (or keyboard map) table with the `loadkeys` program.

The keyboard map is defined in a text file stored in compressed format. The default keyboard map is in the `/usr/lib/kbd/keytables/` `defkeymap.map.gz` file. The keyboard driver uses this table to convert physical keypresses to actions.

Tip

You can find other keyboard-map files in the `/usr/lib/kbd/keytables` directory. Each file provides keyboard mapping for specific geographic regions or countries. The U.S. keyboard map, for example, is in the file `us.map.gz` and the map for Finland is in `fi.map.gz` (the files are stored in compressed format, so the names have an additional `.gz` extension). To load a specific keyboard map, use the `loadkeys` program and specify the file name without the `.gz` extension, as follows:

```
loadkeys /usr/lib/kbd/keytables/fi.map
```

After that, if you press the minus key, you get the plus sign — just one symptom of a different mapping of the physical keys to characters. To revert to the default keyboard map, type `loadkeys -d` (which means load the default keyboard map).

You can, in fact, change keyboard mapping interactively from the command line. Consider a useless, but illustrative, example. Suppose you want the A key to be interpreted as *Q* and vice versa. This means after remapping the keys, you have to press the key labeled *A* to enter the character *Q* (and press the Q key to enter *A*). Before the situation gets any more confusing, try typing the following at the shell prompt (this procedure won't work under *X*):

```
loadkeys
keycode 30 = +q
keycode 16 = +a
(press Ctrl+D to indicate end of input)
```

Now check the result. Press the A and Q keys a few times and verify the meanings of those two keys have switched. `loadkeys` waits for you to enter lines of text. On each line you specify the action that corresponds to a physical keypress. The left side of the equal sign (=) provides the keycode; the right side indicates the action for that keycode. A letter with a plus sign (+) simply means the keycode corresponds to that letter and the letter should change case when the Shift key or the Caps Lock key is pressed.

Tip

Linux assigns a number — a keycode — to each key on the keyboard. You can use the `showkey` command to determine the keycode of any key on the keyboard. Just type `showkey` and press the key whose keycode you want to know.

Wizard

If you're setting up Linux for a non-U.S. keyboard map, you can initialize the keyboard map at startup. All you must do is edit the file /etc/sysconfig/keyboard — this file contains a single line that specifies the keyboard map you want to load when Linux boots. To load an U.S. keyboard map, this file contains the following line:

```
KEYTABLE="/usr/lib/kbd/keytables/us.map"
```

To set up the keyboard with the Danish keyboard-translation table, you would use the following:

```
/usr/bin/loadkeys /usr/lib/kbd/keytables/dk.map
```

You can view the current keyboard-translation table with the `dumpkeys` program. If you type `dumpkeys` without any options, the program shows you the mapping from keycode to names of keys and also shows what happens when you press a key along with other modifiers (such as Ctrl, Shift, and Alt).

The keyboard and XFree86

In XFree86, the X server controls the keyboard and the mouse. Thus, the X server needs some information about the keyboard. You have to provide this information in the `Keyboard` section of the `/etc/XF86Config` file — the configuration file for XFree86. A typical `Keyboard` section might look like this:

```
Section "Keyboard"
  Protocol   "Standard"
  AutoRepeat          500 5
  LeftAlt    Meta
  RightAlt   ModeShift
EndSection
```

Table 13-1 lists the options you can specify in the `Keyboard` section.

Table 13-1 XF86Config file Keyboard section options

Option	Function
Protocol "protocol-name"	Specifies the keyboard protocol. Use Standard as the protocol-name in Linux. The other protocol name can be Xqueue, which is appropriate for other UNIX systems.
AutoRepeat delay rate	Sets the keyboard repeat delay and repeat rate (may not work on all systems). The delay is in milliseconds and the rate is in characters per second.
ServerNumLock	Makes the X server handle the Num Lock key internally. This option was needed by versions of X before X11R6. You should not have to specify this option anymore because the version of X on the companion CD-ROM is X11R6.
LeftAlt key	Maps the left Alt key to the specified key (see text for list).
RightAlt key	Maps the right Alt key to the specified key (see text for list).
AltGr key	Maps the right Alt key to the specified key (see text for list).
ScrollLock key	Maps the Scroll Lock key to the specified key (see text for list).
RightCtl key	Maps the right Ctrl key to the specified key (see text for list).
XLeds x y z	Allows X applications to take control of the status lights (LEDs). Use numbers between 1 and 3 for x, y, and z.
VTSysReq	Causes X server to reserve the Alt+SysRq+Fn (Fn denotes a function-key number n) key sequence to switch virtual terminals (VTs). If you specify this line, it disables the default key sequence to switch VT (Ctrl+Alt+Fn).
VTInit "command"	Causes the X server to run the specified command with the shell (/bin/sh -c) after the X server opens its VT (virtual terminal).

You can use one of the following key names to specify the key mapping for the left and right Alt keys, the Scroll Lock key, and the right Ctrl key (these are names the X server recognizes):

- Compose
- Control
- Meta
- ModeLock
- ModeShift
- ScrollLock

These are simply the standard names for keys in *X*. Each standard key is associated with a physical key on the keyboard. For example, what the X server calls the *Meta key* is actually the Alt key on the left-hand side of the keyboard.

Following is the default mapping for the left and right Alt keys, the Scroll Lock key, and the right Ctrl key:

- LeftAlt: `Meta`
- RightAlt (AltGr is a synonym for RightAlt): `Meta`
- RightCtl: `Control`
- ScrollLock: `Compose`

In *X*, the X server takes over the screen, the keyboard, and the mouse. The upshot is *X* has its own scheme for mapping physical keypresses to various actions. Luckily, in Linux, XFree86 uses the Linux keyboard map to initialize its own keyboard map, thus ensuring some consistency between the two keyboard maps.

The X server decides the keycode to be generated for a specific physical key. Each key, including the modifiers, has a unique keycode. Although the keycode generated for the common alphanumeric keys may be the same for many workstations, it is not guaranteed to be so. Therefore, X applications do not use the raw keycode. Instead, the X server converts the keycode to meaningful characters by a two-step process:

- In the first step, the X server translates the keycode to a symbolic name, known as `keysym`. All meaningful combinations of a key and the modifiers have unique `keysym`s, which are constants defined in the header file `/usr/include/X11/keysymdef.h` (this file is for use in X applications). The `keysym` resulting from a single keypress depends on the state of the modifier keys, as well as on the key itself. If you press the `A` key alone, you should get a lowercase `a`. If you press `A` while the Shift key is down, the result should be an uppercase `A`. The `keysym` differentiates between these cases and assigns the names `XK_a` and `XK_A`, respectively, for a lowercase and uppercase `A`.

- In the second step, the X server converts the `keysym` to an ASCII text string the X application can use for displaying (and for saving in files). For most keys, this string would have a single character, but function keys (especially programmable ones) may generate multiple-character strings.

You can use the `xmodmap` utility program to modify the mapping of keycodes to `keysym`s. Suppose you want to switch the meanings of the A and Q keys. To do this under *X,* place the following lines in a file named `xmodtest` :

```
keycode 38 = Q
keycode 24 = A
```

To make these definitions effective, type the following command in an `xterm` window:

`xmodmap xmodtest`

You'll find the A and Q keys are swapped after this command executes.

The `xmodtest` file constitutes a simple X keyboard map. As in the Linux keyboard map, the term `keycode` means a physical key. The *X* number for a physical key, however, is different from the Linux number for that key. Typically, the X keycodes are eight more than the corresponding Linux keycode.

Specific keyboard questions

When the Num Lock key is set, you can use the number pad to enter numbers. Because the 101-key keyboard already has cursor keys as well as Page Up and Page Down keys, you may want to use the number pad for entering numbers only.

CD

If you want to use the number pad this way, you may want to turn on the Num Lock key at system startup. To do this, you have to use the `setleds` (set LEDs, in which LED stands for light-emitting diode) program that comes with the `kbd` package on the CD-ROM. The `kbd` package is installed when you install Linux from this book's CD-ROM.

The `setleds` program changes the Num Lock, Caps Lock, and Scroll Lock settings. To turn on Num Lock at startup, use `setleds` in one of the script files the `init` process runs when Linux starts. You can turn on the Num Lock key (and the associated LED) by placing the following shell commands in the `/etc/rc.d/rc.local` file:

```
for t in 1 2 3 4 5 6 7 8
do
   setleds +num < /dev/tty$t > /dev/null
done
```

The `+num` option causes `setleds` to turn on the Num Lock key; `setleds -num` turns that key off.

Secret

The Gateway AnyKey keyboard has built-in key-remapping capability at a level even lower than the Linux keyboard driver. If this situation poses a problem, you should press the Ctrl+Alt+Suspend_Macro key combination to reset the keys to normal.

The Mouse in Linux

Although Linux allows you to use a mouse in text-mode display, you can do without a mouse if you plan to stick with text-mode displays only. If you want to use the graphical "point-and-click" interface provided by the X Window System, however, you must have a mouse. In fact, the X server won't start if it does not find the mouse device, so I'll discuss the mouse in the context of its use under XFree86.

Mouse interfaces

As with CD-ROM drives, the mouse interface is more important than the actual make and model of the mouse. To include support for a busmouse, you may have to rebuild the kernel. When you configure the kernel (see Chapter 2 for the procedure), the configuration program asks you to identify the type of mouse interfaces you want to include with the kernel. Following are the configuration questions related to the mouse:

```
ATIXL busmouse support (CONFIG_ATIXL_BUSMOUSE) [Y/m/n/?] n
Logitech busmouse support (CONFIG_BUSMOUSE) [Y/m/n/?] n
Microsoft busmouse support (CONFIG_MS_BUSMOUSE) [Y/m/n/?] m
PS/2 mouse (aka "auxiliary device") support (CONFIG_PSMOUSE) [Y/m/n/?] y
C&T 82C710 mouse port support (as on TI Travelmate)
(CONFIG_82C710_MOUSE) [Y/n/?] n
```

These questions essentially tell you the types of mouse interfaces Linux supports.

In addition to using these special mouse interfaces, you can connect a mouse to the PC through a serial port. Thus, Linux offers the following mouse interfaces:

- Serial interface. Basically, the mouse is connected to a serial port just like a modem; Microsoft, Logitech, and Mouse Systems mice are available with a serial interface.

- PS/2 Auxiliary Device port. This mouse interface works through the keyboard controller.

- Microsoft Busmouse. This mouse is also known as the *InPort mouse* — it connects to an interface card that plugs into the bus on your PC's motherboard.

- Logitech Busmouse. This mouse is similar to the Microsoft Busmouse, but Logitech mice follow a different protocol — the standard for data exchange between the mouse and the motherboard.

- ATI-XL Busmouse. This mouse is a variant of the Microsoft busmouse except the ATI-XL busmouse comes with the ATI-XL video card, which has a built-in interface for a mouse.

■ Chips & Technology C&T 82C710 mouse. This interface is the QuickPort interface used on some laptops, such as Toshiba and older Texas Instruments TravelMates. The C&T 82C710 interface relies on the PS/2 interface. You need to include in the kernel support for both types of interface.

Most PCs use the PS/2 Auxiliary Device interface for the mouse. Among busmice, the Microsoft Busmouse interface is popular.

If you have a busmouse or a PS/2-style mouse, the Linux kernel identifies the mouse at startup. You can see the mouse name in the boot messages the kernel displays. Check these boot messages with a `dmesg | more` command and look for the mouse type the kernel identifies. (You also can use `more /var/log/messages` to browse through the boot messages.)

All mouse interfaces require the use of an IRQ and some need an I/O port address. The serial ports COM1 and COM2 use IRQs 4 and 3, respectively. For a busmouse, the kernel uses a default IRQ of 5, which can conflict with the interrupt settings of other devices, such as sound cards and SCSI controllers.

Secret

The PS/2 Auxiliary port always uses IRQ 12. You cannot change this setting, so if any other peripheral tries to use IRQ 12, you have to change that device's IRQ.

Microsoft and Logitech busmouse interfaces

This type of mouse connects to an interface card that plugs into the bus on your PC's motherboard. The mouse cord has a round nine-pin connector with a notch on one side. This type of connector is known as a *nine-pin mini-DIN connector*.

ATI Graphics Ultra and Ultra Pro video cards include a mouse port that's compatible with the Logitech busmouse interface. If you have a mouse connected to these ATI video cards, specify your mouse as a Logitech busmouse. Despite the ATI name, these mouse interfaces are not ATI-XL busmice.

PS/2 Auxiliary Device interface

The PS/2-style mouse interface requires no expansion card. Instead, the mouse connects to the PS/2 Auxiliary Device port on the keyboard controller. The PS/2 mouse port uses a six-pin mini-DIN connector, just like the keyboard connector. The PS/2 Auxiliary device is widely used in most new PCs. The PS/2 interface also is used in some laptops.

ATI-XL mouse

The ATI-XL video cards come with a mouse interface referred to as the ATI-XL busmouse. You probably won't have to bother about the ATI-XL busmouse unless you have an ATI-XL video card.

Mouse device names

The *mouse device* is a character device just like the keyboard and the modem. *Character devices* transfer information one or more characters at a time, compared with *block devices* (such as hard disks), which transfer data in fixed-size blocks. For each supported mouse interface, Linux uses a special device name, as follows:

- `/dev/atibm`: ATI-XL busmouse

- `/dev/inportbm`: Microsoft InPort busmouse

- `/dev/logibm`: Logitech busmouse

- `/dev/psaux`: PS/2 Auxiliary port for mouse

- `/dev/ttyS0` and `/dev/ttyS1`: serial-port device names for COM1 and COM2 (used for serial mouse)

By convention, the generic mouse device `/dev/mouse` is set up as a link to the actual mouse device on your system. On my system, which has a PS/2 Auxiliary port mouse, a detailed listing of `/dev/mouse` shows the following:

```
ls -l /dev/mouse
lrwxrwxrwx  1 root     root            5 Jan 25 20:41 /dev/mouse -> psaux
```

This listing indicates `/dev/mouse` is a symbolic link to `/dev/psaux`, which represents the PS/2 Auxiliary Device interface.

On the other hand, on my old 386 PC, the mouse is on the first serial port. In this case, a detailed listing of `/dev/mouse` shows the following:

```
ls -l /dev/mouse
lrwxrwxrwx  1 root     root           10 Aug 16 11:05 /dev/mouse -> ttyS0
```

The convention of linking `/dev/mouse` to the actual mouse device allows programs that use the mouse to use `/dev/mouse` to refer to the mouse device and not worry about the actual type of mouse. Because of the symbolic link between `/dev/mouse` and the actual device, any input or output requests go directly to the actual mouse driver that knows how to handle the request.

Mouse protocols

What with the mouse interface types and device names, you may be confused enough about using a mouse in Linux. But you need yet another piece of information to specify the mouse fully to XFree86: the mouse protocol.

The *mouse protocol* is the convention the mouse uses to package information about mouse movement and button states (pressed or released). You can think of the mouse interface (such as serial, busmouse, or PS/2 Auxiliary) as being the physical data-exchange mechanism. The mouse protocol, on the other hand, is used by the recipient of the mouse data (button state or movement) to decipher that data and take action (such as moving the cursor onscreen).

The mouse protocol is important to XFree86 because the X server has to interpret and use the mouse data. You learn more about the protocols in the following section.

The mouse and XFree86

In XFree86, the recipient of the mouse data is the X server. At minimum, the X server needs two pieces of information about your mouse:

- The device name of your mouse. (You can specify /dev/mouse, provided /dev/mouse is symbolically linked to the actual mouse device.)

- The protocol the mouse uses to send reports of mouse movement and button positions.

For some mouse types, such as the Logitech serial mouse, the X server also needs information, such as BaudRate and SampleRate. You also can specify other information, such as how to simulate a third-mouse button on a two-button mouse (the typical type of mouse on PCs).

The X server expects to get this information from the /etc/XF86Config file — the configuration file for XFree86. Specifically, the Pointer section in this file specifies the mouse device and protocol. If you have a Microsoft serial mouse connected to COM1 (the first serial port on the PC), a bare-bones Pointer section in /etc/XF86Config looks like this:

```
Section "Pointer"
  Protocol "Microsoft"
  Device "/dev/ttyS0"
EndSection
```

The Device line specifies the device name for the mouse.

Protocol specification

The Protocol line indicates the mouse protocol. Following is the syntax of the Protocol line:

```
Protocol "protocol-name"
```

protocol-name is the name of a mouse protocol. (The double quotation marks are required.)

Table 13-2 lists the mouse-protocol names XFree86 recognizes.

Table 13-2	Mouse-protocol names recognized by XFree86
Protocol name	**Corresponding mouse type**
BusMouse	Specify this protocol for the Microsoft and Logitech busmouse.
Logitech	Use this protocol for older Logitech serial mice. Newer Logitech mice use Microsoft or Mouseman protocol.
Microsoft	Use this protocol for Microsoft and other serial mice.
MMSeries	Use this protocol for MMSeries serial mice.
Mouseman	Specify this protocol for the Logitech Mouseman mouse.
MouseSystems	Use this protocol for MouseSystems mice.
PS/2	Specify this protocol for any mouse connected to the PS/2 Auxiliary port.
MMHitTab	Use this protocol for the MouseMan HitTablet.
Xqueue	Use this protocol only if the Keyboard protocol also is set to Xqueue.
OSMouse	This protocol is for SCO UNIX (because XFree86 also works under SCO UNIX, a commercial brand of UNIX).

Other mouse-configuration information

Another option you can specify in the Pointer section is the way X handles the third-mouse button. Many popular brands of PC mice have only two buttons, but X applications often expect three buttons on a mouse. One option is to click the left and right mouse buttons simultaneously to simulate a middle button. To simulate a middle-button click with a simultaneous click of left and right buttons, you must specify the following line in the Pointer section of the XF86Config file:

Emulate3Buttons

Some three-button mice — such as the Logitech Mouseman — send a simultaneous left- and right-button click when you click the middle button. To alert the X server about this situation, you have to add the following line in the configuration file:

ChordMiddle

In other words, even if you have a three-button mouse, the mouse may not report three distinct button states. You may have to use the ChordMiddle flag to ensure the X server handles the middle-button click correctly.

Tip

For Logitech serial mice, you also have to specify the baud rate (the rate at which the mouse sends data) and the sample rate (how many mouse events occur per second). Following is a typical set of settings:

BaudRate 9600
SampleRate 150

Two other entries in the `Pointer` section of the `XF86Config` file are meant for MouseSystems mice that can operate in two protocol modes. Specify both of the following lines for a MouseSystems mouse:

```
ClearDTR
ClearRTS
```

Mouse use in *X*

The mouse features prominently in X applications because *X* is a graphical windowing system. How you use the mouse depends on the application. In Linux, you typically do not have many X applications (I mean applications such as word processing and spreadsheet applications). Typically, you have a window manager, such as `fvwm2` and one or more `xterm` windows on your screen. Now that Web browsers such as Netscape are all the rage, you also might have one of these graphical browsers running.

Most graphical applications respond to mouse events such as mouse clicks and double-clicks. The exact response depends on the application that receives the mouse event. You can perform several actions with the mouse. Following are the six basic actions you would use to interact with a graphical X application:

- *Press* a mouse button by holding the button down without moving the mouse.

- *Release* a mouse button you previously held down. The release of the button usually initiates some action.

- *Click* a mouse button by quickly pressing and releasing it.

- *Double-click* a mouse button by clicking it twice in rapid succession without moving the mouse.

- *Drag* the mouse pointer by pressing a mouse button and moving the mouse while holding down the button.

- *Move* the mouse pointer by moving the mouse without pressing any button.

The left mouse button commonly is used to indicate a selection. If a graphical interface shows a push button, you would activate that push button by clicking the left mouse button.

The `fvwm2` window manager displays a pop-up menu—a different one for each button—when you click a mouse button while the mouse pointer is in the X root window. The frame around each window also belongs to the window manager. Thus, the window manager controls what happens when you click the window frame by clicking any mouse button. If you click the upper-right corner of a window frame, for example, `fvwm2` displays a menu that enables you to move, resize, iconify, or even destroy the window.

If you have used Microsoft Windows or an Apple Macintosh, you probably are familiar with the cut-and-paste operation. You might select some text in one application, cut it, go to another application's window, and paste it there.

X also supports the concept of cutting and pasting, but the exact steps depend on the X toolkit used to build an application. Cutting and pasting under Motif (one of the popular graphical user interfaces) might be different under OPEN LOOK.

Tip

The `xterm` application supports cutting and pasting in a simplistic manner. If you hold down the left mouse button and drag across any text in the `xterm` window, that text becomes the current selection. Then, if you click the middle mouse button in the same or another `xterm` window, that selection is pasted.

device not found error

When you start *X* (using the `startx` command), the X server may fail, displaying a message such as this:

```
device not found (/dev/mouse or /dev/psaux)
```

This message usually means the device file (`/dev/psaux`, for example) does not exist for the mouse device.

The `device not found` error can occur if you specify the wrong kind of mouse when you install Linux. Suppose you have a Microsoft mouse that plugs into the PS/2 Auxiliary port. In this case, you must specify your mouse type as a PS/2 mouse, *not* as a Microsoft mouse (even though Microsoft may have made the mouse). Remember — what matters is the mouse interface type, not the make and model of the mouse.

device busy error

If you get a `device busy` error when you attempt to start *X,* another program may already be using the mouse device. A potential culprit is the `gpm` program, which enables you to use the mouse in text mode.

Secret

If you have a busmouse, make sure you do not run the `gpm` program (this program enables you to cut-and-paste text in text-mode display). To check if `gpm` is running, use the following command and look for a `gpm` process in the output:

```
ps ax | grep gpm
```

If `gpm` is running, use the `gpm -k` command to stop the program before you start *X.*

Mouse alternatives

Although I have not discussed other pointing devices explicitly, Linux and XFree86 can access and use other pointing devices, as long as those devices behave like mice.

The new ALPS GlidePoint pointing device, for example, works under Linux and X. All you have to do is set it up as a Microsoft serial mouse.

When you come across other pointing devices, your only problem will be determining whether that pointing device is compatible with any of the mouse types Linux and *X* can use.

Many laptops use trackballs in place of mice. Trackballs often are compatible with the PS/2 mouse. You should set up such a trackball as a PS/2 mouse and try it.

Summary

Linux works with any keyboard that works under MS-DOS and you can configure the keyboard for non-English languages. The mouse is not used much in text mode, but the XFree86 X Window System requires a mouse to run. XFree86 supports most major mouse types. This chapter describes how to use and configure the keyboard and mouse in Linux and *X*.

By reading this chapter, you learn the following:

▶ The keyboard has two configurable parameters: the repeat delay (how long a wait occurs before a key starts repeating) and the repeat rate (how fast a key repeats when it is held down). You can set these parameters with the `kbdrate` program in Linux.

▶ To handle non-English languages, you have to change the keyboard mapping — the way a physical key is interpreted as a character in an alphabet. You also have to make various applications accept and display the character. Many foreign languages use accents the standard keyboard mapping ignores. You can, however, use the `loadkeys` program in text mode and `xmodmap` in *X* to change the keyboard mapping.

▶ The mouse is a necessity when you want to run XFree86, the X Window System for Linux. XFree86 supports most popular types of mouse interfaces, such as serial port, busmouse, and PS/2 Auxiliary port. You identify the mouse interface by a device such as `/dev/psaux` for PS/2 port and `/dev/ttyS0` for the COM1 serial port.

▶ *Mouse protocol* refers to the formatting of mouse data (the way the mouse reports mouse movements and button states). XFree86 supports several common mouse protocols from busmouse, PS/2-style, Microsoft, and Logitech mice.

▶ In the XFree86 configuration file, `/etc/XF86Config`, you have to provide information about the keyboard and the mouse in the `Keyboard` and `Pointer` sections, respectively.

▶ In addition to mice, pointing devices (such as trackballs and the new GlidePoint) should work in Linux and *X*, as long as the interface and protocol are compatible with one of the mice XFree86 supports.

Chapter 14

Printers

When you set up Linux on a PC, the printer probably is the last thing on your mind. First, you want to get Linux running on the PC. Then you may decide to make the modem work to dial up your office system or your Internet service provider. When you begin to depend more on Linux, however, you want to print text or PostScript files you get from the network, and this is when you want to know how to make the printer work with Linux.

As you might guess, physically connecting a printer to the PC's parallel port is straightforward; this part does not depend on the operating system. The software setup for printing is the part that takes some effort. Accordingly, this chapter provides information on setting up the printing environment in Linux.

The PC, the Printer, and Linux

PCs typically come with one parallel port and two serial ports. The *parallel port* is so named because it can transfer 8 bits of data in parallel. The *serial port,* however, has to send data in bit-oriented serial manner. For example, an 8-bit byte is transferred as a sequence of 8 bits that go through the serial port one after another. The upshot is the parallel port is much faster than the serial port.

Although a printer can connect to the PC through either the serial port or the parallel port, most users connect the printer to the PC's parallel port.

Printer device names

In MS-DOS, the first parallel port is called *LPT1*; the second one is called *LPT2*. The serial ports are called *COM1* and *COM2*.

In Linux, the parallel ports have device names just like other devices, such as /dev/ttyS0 for the PC's first serial port or /dev/hda for the first IDE disk. The device names /dev/lp0 and /dev/lp1 refer to the first and second parallel ports, respectively.

Watch out, though — just because your PC has only one parallel port does not mean Linux will use /dev/lp0 as the device name for that parallel port. When Linux boots, it displays information about the parallel port it detects. Check the boot messages with dmesg | more to see what parallel-port device Linux detects. On my PC, which has a single parallel port, the boot message includes the following:

```
lp1 at 0x0378, using polling driver
```

Thus, for my Linux PC, the parallel port device is /dev/lp1.

Table 14-1 lists the parallel-port device names and device numbers in Linux:

Table 14-1	Parallel-port device names and numbers		
I/O address	*Device name*	*Major device number*	*Minor device number*
0x3bc	/dev/lp0	6	0
0x378	/dev/lp1	6	1
0x278	/dev/lp2	6	2

On most PCs, the LPT1 port uses the I/O address 0x378. Thus, the parallel port's device name is /dev/lp1, which is the device name you use for a printer connected to that parallel port.

Spooling and print jobs

You may already be familiar with the concept of spooling from printing under Microsoft Windows. *Spooling* refers to the capability to print in the background. When you print from a word processor in Windows, for example, the output first goes to a file on the disk. Then, while you continue working with the word processor, a background process sends that output to the printer.

The Linux printing environment, which consists of several programs I describe later in this chapter, also supports spooling. The term *spool directory* refers to the directory that contains output files intended for the printer.

Print job refers to what you print with a single print command. The printing environment queues print jobs by storing them in the spool directory. A background process then can periodically send the print jobs from the spool directory to the printer.

The Linux printing environment evolved from the printing facilities of the Berkeley Software Distribution (BSD) UNIX. As you become more knowledgeable about UNIX (or if you are a UNIX old-timer), you may find this bit of information useful because it tells you the printing commands you can use in Linux. If you don't know anything about BSD UNIX, don't worry. I explain the printing commands in the following section.

The User's View of Printing in Linux

Before I describe how to set up your Linux system for printing, I'll provide an overview of the basic printing commands. You may be unable to try the printing commands until you actually set up the printing environment, but this section should give you a sense of how you would print in Linux (or in any BSD UNIX system).

Printing with lpr

In Linux, you use the `lpr` command to queue a print job. To print the file `rfc1789.txt`, you would type the following:

```
lpr rfc1789.txt
```

The `lpr` command copies the `rfc1789.txt` file to a spool directory (located in the `/var/spool/lpd/lp` directory). Periodically, a print program known as `lpd` sends that file from the spool directory to the printer.

You can embellish that simple `lpr` command with some options. A common option is to indicate the type of printer with `-P`. If you have a Hewlett-Packard LaserJet printer named `hplj` (later, in the section "Learning about `/etc/printcap`" you'll see the printer name appears in the `/etc/printcap` file), you print with the following command:

```
lpr -Phplj rfc1789.txt
```

In addition to the `-P` option of `lpr`, you can specify the default printer through the `PRINTER` environment variable. If your printer's name is `hplj`, you would use the following command to ensure `lpr` sends all print jobs to the `hplj` printer:

```
PRINTER=hplj; export PRINTER
```

You may want to put the environment definition in the default `login` script for Bash. Just add a line like this to `/etc/profile`:

```
export PRINTER=hplj
```

This example assumes your system's printer is named `hplj`. You should replace that name with whatever name you assign to your system's printer (you learn how to name a printer in the section called "Printer name").

Because the default `login` script — `/etc/profile` — is common to all `logins` that use the Bash shell, defining the `PRINTER` environment variable in `/etc/profile` saves everyone the trouble of having to specify the printer explicitly.

Checking the print queue with lpq

When `lpr` queues a print job, it does not print any messages. If you mistakenly print a large file and want to stop the print job before you waste too much paper, you must use the `lpq` command to look at the current print jobs. Following is a typical listing of print jobs you get with `lpq`:

```
lpq
lp is ready and printing
Rank    Owner      Job  Files                          Total Size
active root         7    sendmail.cf                    30192 bytes
```

The word `active` in the Rank column indicates the job currently printing. The rest of the entries show jobs in the order in which they'll be printed. If you do not see your print job listed, it has finished printing.

Canceling the print job with lprm

To remove a job from the print queue, use the `lprm` command. To stop print job Number 1, you would type the following:

```
lprm 1
dfA001Aa00235 dequeued
cfA001Aa00235 dequeued
```

Tip

If you are in a hurry and want to cancel all print jobs you have submitted so far, use `lprm` with a minus sign as the argument, as follows:

```
lprm -
```

Checking the printer status with lpc status

To see the names of printers connected to your system, use the `/usr/sbin/lpc status` command. On a typical system, the `lpc status` command might show the following:

```
/usr/sbin/lpc status
lp:
     queuing is enabled
     printing is enabled
     no entries
     no daemon present
```

This sample output shows the status of a printer named `lp`—the default printer name used by print commands such as `lpr`, `lpq`, and `lprm` when you do not explicitly specify any printer name.

Wizard

The word `daemon` in the last line of the status message refers to the background process (called `lpd`) that takes care of the actual printing. In UNIX, the term *daemon* is used for background processes that monitor and perform many critical system functions. Typically, a daemon is started when the system boots and the daemon processes run as long as the system is up. Most daemons have the capability to restart copies of themselves to handle specific tasks. And, although this is not a rule, most daemons have names that end with d, such as `crond`, `syslogd`, `klogd`, `inetd`, `lpd` (that's the printer daemon), `named`, and `httpd`.

You should not get worried because `lpc status` reports no daemon present for a printer. The daemon controling a specific printer's queue goes away when the spool directory is empty. But there always is a master copy of the printer daemon, `lpd`, that monitors the spool directories. When you print anything on a specific printer with the `lpr` command, the master copy of `lpd` creates a new `lpd` process to take care of that printer's queue.

Employing fancy printing

So far, I've shown you the commands for sending a file to the printer. If you have a PostScript printer, you can send it a PostScript file to produce nicely formatted output.

If you want to print a text file with some additional formatting, such as a header and page number on each page, you can use the `pr` command. The idea is to use `pr` to format the text file and then send that output to `lpr`. Following is an example:

```
pr -h"Web Server Access Statistics" -l60 webstat.txt | lpr
```

This command line prints the file `webstat.txt` with the text `Web Server Access Statistics` added to the top of each page. The `-l60` option sets the length of each page to 60 lines.

Cross-Reference

To do other types of typesetting, you can use text-processing programs such as TeX (which comes with Linux on this book's CD-ROM). Chapter 24 describes these typesetting systems and explains how to print typeset pages.

PostScript is currently a common format for documentation files for software, especially software you download from the Internet. If you have PostScript files, you can preview and print them with the Ghostview program. (To try the program, type **ghostview** in an `xterm` window. You need the X Window System to run Ghostview.)

Behind-the-Scenes View of Printing

In Linux, the user's view of printing is based on the basic printing commands: `lpr`, `lpq`, `lprm`, and `lpc status`. You need a bit more information to understand how printing works behind the scenes. Like so many things in Linux, support for printing is all a matter of having the right files in the right places. This becomes apparent after you have configured Linux for networking and set up dial-in modems, for example. In each case, you must make sure several configuration files appear in the correct places. The printing environment has the same need: configuration files that specify how printing occurs.

If you have experience with MS-DOS, you may have printed files by simply copying them to the printer port (LPT1, for example). You may think a similar approach might be good enough for Linux. As you will see in the next section, such a brute force approach to copying a file to the physical printer port is not appropriate for a multiuser system like Linux. What you need is a way to queue print jobs and have a separate printing process take care of the printing.

Copying to the printer: brute-force printing

If you have a printer connected to the `/dev/lp1` parallel port (you can find this information from the boot messages), you can print a text file simply by sending the file to the printer with the following command:

```
cat webstat.txt > /dev/lp1
```

This command would, indeed, produce a printout of the file `webstat.txt`, provided the following conditions are true:

- You must be logged in as `root` (Linux allows only `root` and certain processes direct access to physical devices, such as printers).

- The printer must be connected to the `/dev/lp1` port, powered up, and online.

The problem with copying a file directly to the printer device is the command will complete only when the copying (which, in this case, is equivalent to printing) is done. For a large file, this process could take a while. In fact, if the printer is not turned on, the command will appear to hang (if this happens, press Ctrl-C to abort the command).

Spooling: a better way to print

On a multitasking and multiuser system such as Linux, a better way to print is to *spool* the data: Send the output to a file and then have a separate process send the output to the printer. This way, you can go on with your work while the printing takes place in the background. Also, if your system has more than one user, everyone can print on the same printer without worrying about whether the printer is available. The background printing process can take care of all the details.

This is how the Linux printing environment works: A directory, or *spool area*, is set up for each printer. Any data meant for a printer is stored in that printer's spool area—one file per print job. A background process called lpd—the printer daemon—constantly checks the spool area for new files. Whenever lpd finds a new file, it sends the file to the printer.

That spool area serves as the queue for the print jobs, each of which is a file in the spool directory.

Note

Although you typically would have only one printer connected to your PC, one strength of the Linux printing system and of BSD UNIX printing is the capability to print on a printer connected to another system on a network. Printing to such a remote printer is handled in the same fashion as printing to a local printer: a spool directory exists for the remote printer. The lpd program checks the remote printer's spool directory and sends any waiting files to that printer.

As explained earlier, the user-level command for spooling a file is lpr. When lpr runs, it copies the data for the printer to a file in the spool directory. Other user-level commands for working with print queues are lpq, lprm, and lpc. As this section describes, the program that completes the Linux printing environment is the printer daemon: lpd.

In addition to the five programs lpd, lpr, lpq, lprm, and lpc, a file named /etc/printcap plays a crucial role in the Linux printing environment. The "Learning about /etc/printcap" section describes that file.

Spooling with a symbolic link

When you use the lpr command to spool a file for printing, lpr copies that file to the spool directory. This situation can be a problem when you print a large file. The copying operation can take some time and you will need disk space in the spool directory (in /usr/spool). If you are low on disk space—especially in the partition that contains the /usr directory tree—you may want to avoid the copy operation.

The lpr command provides the -s option, which sets up a *symbolic link* in the spool directory, making the link refer to the file you want to print. To print a large file, you could use lpr this way:

```
lpr -s files.index
```

Instead of copying files.index to the spool directory, lpr creates a symbolic link to that file (the symbolic link will be in the spool directory). You can create a symbolic link quickly and the link uses almost no disk space compared to what the original file might use.

Caution

When you use the lpr -s command to spool a file by using a symbolic link, you must watch out for an important side effect: Because the symbolic link (in the spool directory) is only a reference to the actual file, you cannot edit or delete the original file until the printing is done.

Also, the -s option only stops lpr from copying the data file to the spool directory of the local system. If you submit a job for a remote printer, the data file is copied to the remote system's spool directory regardless of the -s option.

Controlling the printer with lpc

All users can use the lpc status command to check the status of printers. If you log in as root, you can use lpc to perform many more printer-control functions, such as starting and stopping spooling, enabling and disabling printers, and rearranging the order of print jobs. You can use the second argument to lpc to perform a specific task or run lpc in interactive mode.

To run lpc in interactive mode, type /usr/sbin/lpc at the shell prompt. At the lpc> prompt, type help to see a list of commands lpc understands. To get more help on a command, type help *command-name* (*command-name* is one of the lpc commands). Following is a sample session with lpc:

```
/usr/sbin/lpc
lpc> help
Commands may be abbreviated. Commands are:

abort    enable  disable help    restart status  topq    ?
clean    exit    down    quit    start   stop    up
lpc> help status
status           show status of daemon and queue
lpc> q
```

Tip

For a specific operation, you can simply use the single-line syntax with lpc followed by one of the lpc commands and any necessary arguments. To stop the print-spooling daemon (lpd), move print job 39 to the top of the queue and to start spooling again, you would use the following commands (the example assumes the printer's name is hplj):

```
lpc stop hplj
lpc topq 39
lpc start hplj
```

Table 14-2 lists the lpc commands anyone can use (provided the /usr/sbin directory is in the PATH environment variable; if not, type export PATH=$PATH:/usr/sbin to update PATH).

Table 14-2   lpc commands that anyone can use

Command	Description
restart *printer-name*	Tries to restart the printer daemon (lpd). A user might try this command if the printer appears to be fine but nothing is printed, even though lpq shows jobs waiting in the spool area. Use all as the printer name if you want to restart all printers.

Command	Description
`status printer-name`	Displays the status of the specified printer. If you do not provide a printer name, this command shows the status of the printer named `lp` — the default printer.
`help command-name`	Provides help information on a specific `lpc` command.
`exit`	Exits `lpc` (use in interactive mode only).
`quit`	Exits `lpc` (use in interactive mode only).

Table 14-3 lists the `lpc` commands only `root` can use.

Table 14-3   lpc commands that only root can use

Command	Description
`abort printer-name`	Behaves like `stop` but does not allow the current job to complete. When printing is restarted, this current job prints again.
`clean printer-name`	Removes all jobs, including the active job, from the printer's queue.
`disable printer-name`	Disables spooling of print jobs to a specified printer. When spooling is disabled, users can no longer use `lpr` to print.
`down printer-name message`	Disables spooling and stops the printer daemon from printing the spooled print jobs (combines the actions of `disable` and `stop`). The `message` will be displayed when users run the `lpq` command.
`enable printer-name`	Enables spooling of print jobs to a specified printer.
`start printer-name`	Enables the printer daemon so it can begin printing any jobs in that printer's spool directory.
`stop printer-name`	Waits for the current print job to complete and then disables the printer daemon so it stops printing the jobs in that printer's spool directory. When the printing is stopped, users can continue to issue `lpr` command to print, but the actual output does not appear until the printer daemon is started with the `start` command.
`topq printer-name job-id`	Moves the specified print job to the beginning of the printer's queue. If you use a user name in place of `job-id`, all jobs belonging to that user are moved to the beginning of the queue.
`up printer-name`	Reverses the action of the `down` command, enables spooling, and starts the printer daemon (combines the actions of `enable` and `start`).

Tracing a print request from lpr to the printer

A good way to understand the Linux printing environment is to trace a print request from the lpr command all the way to the actual output at the printer. Two programs, lpr and lpd, complete the printing process, as shown in Figure 14-1.

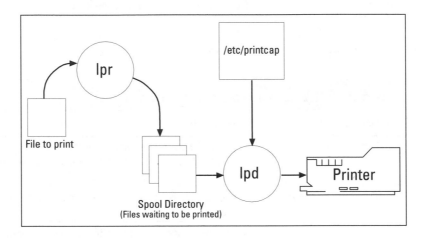

Figure 14-1: The printing process in Linux

As Figure 14-1 shows, the two steps of the printing process are the following:

1. The lpr command takes the data to be sent to the printer and puts it in a file in the spool directory.

2. The lpd program finds the file in the spool directory and sends the file to the printer.

Both the lpr and lpd programs consult the /etc/printcap file for information about the printer.

lpr spools print jobs

The lpr program is the only program in Linux that queues print jobs. All other programs that need to print files do so by sending the data to lpr — usually with the shell's pipe mechanism, in which you concatenate two commands with a vertical bar (|).

Each step involves many more details, of course. When lpr runs, it gathers information about the print job from three sources:

■ Command-line options used with the lpr command

■ Environment variables, such as PRINTER, that identify the printer where the output is to appear

- System defaults that provide information that `lpr` needs, such as the default printer name (`lp`)

After `lpr` determines the destination printer's name, it looks up that printer in the system's printer database, `/etc/printcap`. Assuming the printer has an entry in the `/etc/printcap` file, a field in that entry should tell `lpr` the name of the spool directory for that printer. Typically, the spool directory is `/usr/spool/printername`, but the directory name can be something else (although it's always in `/usr/spool`).

The `lpr` program creates two files in the spool directory:

- A file with a name that starts with `cf`, followed by an identifier (ID) for that print job. This file contains control information about the print job — information, such as who submitted the job.

- A file that contains the actual data to be printed. This file's name starts with `df`, followed by the print job's number.

After `lpr` spools the files, it sends a signal to the `lpd` process. This signal tells `lpd` a print job is waiting in a specific spool directory.

lpd sends print jobs to printer

The `lpd` process takes care of the actual printing — the act of sending a file to the printer. A copy of `lpd` is always running in the system and you can check for its existence with the following command:

```
ps ax | grep lpd
  252  ?  S    0:00 lpd
```

If you don't see an `lpd` process running, you cannot use the Linux printing environment. You have to log in as `root` and type `lpd` to start the printer daemon.

Another characteristic of `lpd` is its capability to create copies of itself to handle print jobs in specific print queues.

Secret

After `lpd` receives a signal that a print job exists for a specific printer, it checks the `/etc/printcap` file to determine whether the specified printer is on your system or on another system on the network (remote printer). For a remote printer, your system's `lpd` establishes a link to the remote system's `lpd`, transfers both the control and data files to the remote system, and deletes those files from your system's spool directory.

If the printer is, indeed, connected to your system, `lpd` checks to see whether a copy of the printer daemon (also named `lpd`) is already running for that printer's queue. If not, `lpd` makes a copy of itself and sets up that copy to process print jobs in that printer's queue. The `lpd` for a specific printer's queue sends all waiting print jobs to the printer, one at a time.

Knowing the spool directory

The *spool directory* is where data destined for a printer accumulates in separate files before the lpd printer daemon sends those files to the printer. If you installed Red Hat Linux from the companion CD-ROM, your system should have the spool directories in /var/spool.

By convention, the /var/spool directory contains queues for various UNIX programs. Mail and news programs, for example, have their spool directories here. The spool directories are named after the program that uses the directory. For example, the Mail program's spool directory is /var/spool/mail.

The printer spool directories are in /var/spool/lpd because lpd is the name of the program that spools print jobs. In /var/spool/lpd, each type of printer should have its own spool directory. You'll find it helpful to name each spool directory with the printer's name as it appears in the /etc/printcap file (described in the following section). Thus, if you have a HP LaserJet printer named hplj, the spool directory will be /var/spool/lpd/hplj. The default printer name is lp and the corresponding spool directory is /var/spool/lpd/lp.

Secret

Incidentally, a single printer may go by two different names. A HP LaserJet 4M printer, for example, might be used as a printer that understands HP's Printer Control Language (PCL) or PostScript. You might use printer names pcl and ps for the two ways in which you may access the LaserJet 4M printer. All these printer names appear in the /etc/printcap file, described in the following section.

Even remote printers need a spool directory on your system, because lpr first copies the files to the spool directory and then lpd sends those files to the remote printer.

Each printer's spool directory contains two files:

- The lock file, which contains information about the active job and ensures only one lpd process prints the contents of this spool directory. The lpd process manipulates the permission settings of the lock file to enable or disable spooling for this printer.

- The status file, which contains a one-line message that describes the printer's state. The lpq command displays the message from the status file. You can change this message when you take down the printer with the lpc down command.

When you manually set up a new printer, you must create a spool directory for the printer and set its permission appropriately. The "Printer Setup and Configuration" section later in this chapter covers printer setup and configuration steps in detail.

Learning about /etc/printcap

The /etc/printcap file is at the heart of Linux's printing environment. This text file (with cryptic syntax) describes the capabilities of various printers. The file must contain information about every printer you can access from your system (including printers on the same network as your PC). No harm is done if the /etc/printcap file contains descriptions of printers you don't actually have. The lpr and lpd programs consult the /etc/printcap file only to look up information for a specified printer.

The basic structure of /etc/printcap

The /etc/printcap file is modeled after the /etc/termcap file, which describes the capabilities of various types of terminals. To understand the syntax of entries in /etc/printcap, examine the following sample entry for an HP LaserJet printer:

```
# HP Laserjet printer
lp|hplj|Lasertjet-IRM|HP Laserjet 4M in IRM Division:\
  :lp=/dev/lp1:\
  :sd=/var/spool/lpd/lp:\
  :mx#0:\
  :if=/var/spool/lpd/lp/hplj-if.pl:\
  :lf=/var/spool/lpd/lp/hplj-log:\
  :sh:
```

This example is a reasonably readable layout of an entry in the /etc/printcap file. The entry says the following things:

- Send the print job to a printer device named /dev/lp1 (lp field).

- Store queued print jobs in the /var/spool/lpd/lp directory (sd field).

- Do not limit the size of print jobs (mx field).

- Pass the print file through the filter (a command that reads from standard input and generates output on the standard output) named /var/spool/lpd/lp/hplj-if.pl (if field).

- Log errors in a file named /var/spool/lpd/lp/hplj-log, which must already exist for the error logging to work (lf field).

- Suppress headers — a separator page between print jobs (sh field).

Notice you need a backslash (\) at the end of each line, because the entire entry is supposed to be a single line.

Caution

Make sure you do not have any extra space after the backslash character at the end of a line. If a space or tab character appears after the backslash, the printing programs (lpr, lpd, and lpc) will not consider the following line as a continuation. This error may cause printing to fail for a printer (even though the entry may look fine when you examine the /etc/printcap file).

As is true of most configuration files in Linux, the comment lines in /etc/printcap start with a pound-sign character (#).

Printer names

The first field of an entry (up to the first colon) lists the name of the printer and its aliases. Typically, each printer has three names:

- A short name with four characters at most (such as `hplj`)

- A longer name that indicates the printer's owner (such as `LaserJet-IRM`)

- A descriptive name that should fully identify the printer to the users on your system (for example, `HP LaserJet 4M in IRM Division`)

Tip

If you print something with `lpr` without specifying a printer, that print job automatically goes to the system's default printer, named `lp`. You should, therefore, provide `lp` as the first name for the default printer.

Field types

After the names, the printer's entry has a sequence of fields. If you examine the sample entry, you notice the fields are separated by colons (:). Three types of fields exist:

- *String fields*, such as `lp` (which specify the printer's device name), are specified by the following syntax:

  `:field_name=string:`

  You can embed special characters in the string by using the backslash notation from the C programming language. To specify the form-feed character (which might be used to eject a page on the printer), you would use `\f`.

- *Number fields*, such as `mx` (which specify the size of print-job files), are specified as follows:

  `:field_name#number:`

- *Boolean fields*, such as `sh` (which suppress printing of a header page separating consecutive print jobs), are true when they appear in the printer's entry; otherwise, they are false.

Each field has a specific meaning. Through these fields, you control how output appears on the printer (for example, should the data file be processed by any intermediate program before output goes to the printer) and how errors are logged. The following sections further describe the fields in `/etc/printcap`.

Although the contents of `/etc/printcap` appear cryptic at first, when you know the basic format and the meaning of the various fields, you'll be able to understand and edit the file easily.

Tip

The subsequent sections provide all the information you need to understand and add a new entry to the `/etc/printcap` file. If you need to look up information about the fields in the `/etc/printcap` file, you can do so easily with the following command:

`man printcap`

Fields in printcap entries

Before you learn about specific `printcap` fields (I refer to the `/etc/printcap` file with the generic name `printcap`), consult Table 14-4, which provides an alphabetic list of the `printcap` fields. The Field column shows the two-character name of a field. The Type column shows the type of the field (string, number, or Boolean). The Default column shows the value assumed by `lpr` and `lpd` when the `printcap` entry does not specify this field. The Description column briefly describes the field.

Table 14-4   Alphabetic List of printcap Fields

Field	Type	Default	Description
af	string	NULL	Name of accounting file
br	number	none	Baud rate (applies only if the `lp` field specifies a serial-port device)
cf	string	NULL	Name of `cifplot` data filter
df	string	NULL	Name of TeX data filter (DVI format)
fc	number	0	Flag bits to clear (applies only if the `lp` field specifies a serial-port device)
ff	string	\f (form feed)	String to send for a form feed
fo	Boolean	false	If specified, prints a form feed when device is opened
fs	number	0	Flag bits to set (applies only if the `lp` field specifies a serial port device)
gf	string	NULL	Name of graph data filter
hl	Boolean	false	If specified and if `sh` is not specified, prints the burst header page last (the *burst header page* separates one print job from another)
ic	Boolean	false	If specified, printer driver (identified by `lp`) supports control command to indent printout
if	string	NULL	Name of text filter, which is called once for each print job (you can use this to interpret the file and convert it to a format that is suitable for your printer)
lf	string	/dev/console	Name of file where errors are logged
lo	string	lock	Name of lock file
lp	string	/dev/lp	Device name to open to send output to printer
mx	number	1000	Maximum size of the print-job file (in KB); a value of 0 means unlimited size

(continued)

Table 14-4 *(Continued)*

Field	Type	Default	Description
nf	string	NULL	Name of ditroff (device-independent troff) data filter
of	string	NULL	Name of output-filtering program (called only if the `if` field is not specified, and called only once)
pc	number	200	Price per foot or page, in hundredths of cents
pl	number	66	Number of lines per page
pw	number	132	Page width, in number of characters
px	number	0	Page width in pixels (horizontal)
py	number	0	Page length in pixels (vertical)
rf	string	NULL	Name of filter for printing FORTRAN-style text files
rg	string	NULL	Restricted group; only members of listed groups can access the printer
rm	string	NULL	Name of system for remote printer
rp	string	lp	Remote printer name
rs	Boolean	false	If true, prints jobs submitted (from remote systems) by only those users with accounts on local system
rw	Boolean	false	If specified, opens the printer device for reading and writing
sb	Boolean	false	If specified, prints short banner (one line only)
sc	Boolean	false	If specified, does not print multiple copies
sd	string	/var/spool/lpd	Name of spool directory
sf	Boolean	false	If specified, does not print form feeds
sh	Boolean	false	If specified, does not print the burst page header
st	string	status	Name of status file
tf	string	NULL	Name of `troff` (typesetter) data filter
tr	string	NULL	Trailer string to print when the printer queue is emptied
vf	string	NULL	Name of raster image filter

As Table 14-4 shows, you can specify more than 35 fields for each `printcap` entry. For a typical entry in the `/etc/printcap` file, though, you have to specify only a few fields. The following nine are the most commonly used `printcap` fields:

- `if`: a string that specifies the input-filter name

- `lf`: a string that specifies the file where errors for this printer are logged

- `lp`: a string that specifies the device name for the printer (such as `/dev/lp1`)

- `mx`: a number that specifies the maximum allowable size (in 1KB blocks) of a print file

- `rm`: a string that specifies the name of a remote computer

- `rp`: a string that specifies the name of a remote printer

- `sd`: a string that specifies the name of the spool directory for this printer

- `sf`: a Boolean that suppresses the form feed at the end of each job

- `sh`: a Boolean that suppresses the burst header page that appears between jobs

The next few sections further explain a few of these fields.

Input-filter field

The *input filter* is a shell script of an executable program that reads the print data from the standard input (`stdin`) and writes output to the standard output (`stdout`). The advantage of the input filter is it enables you to process a text file and convert it to a format your printer needs.

Wizard

The print daemon calls the specified input filter once for each print job. Suppose you specified the `if` field this way:

`:if=/var/spool/lpd/lp/hplj-if.pl:`

If the file `/usr/spool/lp1/hplj-if.pl` is a Perl script, `lpd` invokes the filter with the following command line:

`/var/spool/lpd/lp/hplj-if.pl [-c] -wwidth -llength -iindent -n login -h host acct-file`

The brackets around the `-c` option indicate it's optional. The `-c` option is used only if the user invoked the `lpr` command with a `-l` option (meaning pass all characters unchanged to the printer). Thus, if you were writing the input filter, you would assume the arguments to be the following:

Argument	Description
-c	Passes control characters literally to the printer (if the first argument is -c, the filter should simply copy the standard input to the standard output)
-w*width*	Page width, in number of characters per line (from the pw field in the printcap file)
-l*length*	Page length, in number of lines per page (from the pl field in the printcap file)
-i*indent*	Indent the output by printing *indent* number of blank spaces in front of each line
-n *login*	login name of the user who submitted the print job
-h *host*	Name of system where the user submitted the print job
acct-file	Name of accounting file from the af field in printcap

You see the use of input filters in the section "How to avoid the staircase effect" that describes how to avoid a *staircase* pattern when you print UNIX text files on a PC printer, which expects a carriage return–line feed pair at the end of each line.

The printer device

The printer-device field, lp, should specify the Linux device name for the port to which you connected the printer. For a local printer on the PC's parallel port, this field is /dev/lp1 (or /dev/lp0 on some older systems).

If your printer is on a serial port, specify the serial port's device name — /dev/ttyS0 for COM1 and /dev/ttyS1 for COM2 — as the string in the lp field.

When you set up a printcap entry for a remote printer, specify an empty lp field as follows:

```
:lp=:
```

Then, of course, you must specify the rm and rp fields, which specify the host name and the printer name for the remote printer; otherwise, lpd displays an error message because it cannot find the printer device.

Another subtle use of the lp field is to set it to /dev/null — the universal *bit bucket* (nothing happens when data is sent to the null device). When you try a new printcap entry to see whether everything works and you don't want to waste paper, just set the lp field of that printcap entry this way:

```
:lp=/dev/null:
```

The log file

The log-file field, lf, specifies the file to which lpd sends error messages. If you don't specify any file, error messages go to the console. Typically, you might specify a log file in the spool directory for the printer, as follows:

```
:lf=/var/spool/lpd/lp/hplj-log:
```

You can specify any file you want, but the specified file must exist. If it does not exist, lpd will not log errors.

Suppressing headers and form feed

In the terminology of the Linux printing environment, the *burst header page* or *banner page* refers to the page preceding a print job. By default, lpd generates a banner page and also sends a form feed to make sure every print job starts on a new page.

Cross-Reference

You probably will not use header pages much if you're the only user of your Linux system. Also, most text-processing packages, such as TeX or troff (described in Chapter 24), already generate a form feed at the end of all the pages, so the form feed sent by lpd causes an extra blank page, which is wasteful.

The two Boolean options sh and sf turn off the header page and form feed, respectively. All you have to do is place the two fields in the printcap entry, as follows:

```
:sh:\
:sf:
```

Setting the maximum size of a print job

You can use the mx field to limit the size of the print job. The size refers to the number of bytes in the spooled file. Before the advent of graphics and laser printers, this limit may have made sense. Nowadays, it's better not to specify this limit, because graphics files can turn out to be huge, even though the output may be only a few pages. To make sure the size of spool files is limited only by available disk space, specify zero as the value of the mx field, as follows:

```
:mx#0:
```

If you want to make sure spool files do not take up all your available disk space, put a file named minfree in the printer's spool directory (specified by the sd field). In the minfree file, specify the number of disk blocks (1KB per block) that must be available for lpr to write spooled data in the spool directory.

Using multiple printcap entries for one printer

As you begin to understand the `printcap` entries, you'll see an entry specifies various processing options for the data that goes to the physical printer. If a printer can handle both PostScript and HP's PCL, for example, you can have two separate `printcap` entries: one for PostScript output and the other for PCL. Programs that generate PostScript could use the PostScript printer name, whereas those that *speak* PCL can send the output to the PCL printer.

Printer Setup and Configuration

When you install Linux from the companion CD-ROM following the steps outlined in Chapter 1, you also get a chance to install and set up your printers. Later on, if you want to add a new printer or change the configuration of an existing printer, log in as `root` and run the `printtool` program under *X* — start *X* and then type `printtool` in an xterm window.

In the following sections, I describe how to set up a printer manually. One of the first steps in configuring a printer is preparing the `printcap` entry for the printer. A good way to learn to prepare a `printcap` entry is to try a sample entry.

A printcap template

In this section, I write a `printcap` entry for a printer named `sample`. Because the `/var/spool/lpd/lp` directory already exists, I decide to use this directory as the spool directory. To test the `printcap` entry without actually sending output to any printer, I use `/dev/null` as the printer device name and specify an input filter that copies the input data to a file.

With these assumptions, I wrote the following `printcap` entry and added it to the `/etc/printcap` file:

```
# A sample printcap template
sample|sample-printer|A sample printer that prints to a file:\
  :sd=/var/spool/lpd/lp:\
  :lp=/dev/null:\
  :if=/var/spool/lpd/lp/sample-if.tcl:\
  :lf=/var/spool/lpd/lp/sample-log:\
  :mx#0:\
  :sh:\
  :sf:
```

For error logging, I created the `/var/spool/lpd/lp/sample-log` file with the following commands (while I was logged in as `root`):

```
cd /var/spool/lpd/lp
touch sample-log
chmod ug=rw,o=r sample-log
```

Wizard

Next, I prepare the input filter, `/var/spool/lpd/lp/sample-if.tcl`. As you may have guessed from the filename, I wrote the input filter in Tcl. You can write the filter as a shell script or in Perl—whatever language you like. In fact, you can write the filter in C or C++. If you write the filter in C or C++, of course, you must compile and link to create the executable file, the name of which you must specify in the `if` field of the `printcap` entry.

Following is the Tcl script file that serves as the input filter for the sample printer:

```
#!/usr/bin/tcl
#
# Sample input filter
#!/usr/bin/tcl
#
# Sample input filter
#
# Place in printer's spool directory and make it
# executable by world
# The filter is invoked with the following command line:
#
# <filter> [-c] -wWidth -lLength -iIndent -n Login -h Host AcctFile

# Open the file /tmp/sample.out
set outfile [open /tmp/sample.out w]

puts $outfile "----------------------------------------"
flush $outfile
exec date >@ $outfile
puts $outfile "----------------------------------------"

# Read from stdin and write to outfile

while { [gets stdin line] != -1} {
  puts $outfile $line
}

close $outfile
```

This filter simply writes the standard input to the file `/tmp/sample.out`, adding a header that shows the date and time of printing. Because the device name for the sample `printcap` entry is set to `/dev/null`, the `/tmp/sample.out` file will be the only proof that printing worked.

Note, in a real input filter, the script would copy standard input to standard output, performing any necessary conversions (such as inserting extra characters on each line or indenting a line by a specified number of blank spaces).

Make the script executable by typing the following command:

```
chmod +x sample-if.tcl
```

To see the `printcap` entry for the `sample` printer in action, try the following command:

```
ls -l /var/spool/lpd/lp | lpr -Psample
```

This command sends the directory listing of the `/usr/spool/lp1` directory to `lpr`. The `lpr` command then spools this listing for printing on the `sample` printer (because of the `-Psample` option). After the print job is spooled, the `lpd` daemon invokes the input filter for the printer named `sample`. This filter (`/var/spool/lpd/lp/sample-if.tcl`), in turn, copies the directory listing to the `/tmp/sample.out` file.

To see whether everything worked, check the contents of the `/tmp/sample.out` file, as follows:

```
cat /tmp/sample.out
-----------------------------------------
Sun May 10 02:53:22 EDT 1998
-----------------------------------------
total 16
-rwxr-xr-x   1 root     root         9334 Jan 25 20:58 filter
-rwxr-xr-x   1 root     root          189 Jan 25 20:58 general.cfg
-rw-r--r--   1 root     root           19 May 10 02:51 lock
-rwxr-xr-x   1 root     root          348 Jan 25 20:58 postscript.cfg
-rwxr-xr-x   1 root     root          617 May 10 02:49 sample-if.tcl
-rw-rw-r--   1 root     root            0 May 10 02:48 sample-log
-rw-rw-r--   1 root     root           29 May 10 02:51 status
-rwxr-xr-x   1 root     root          150 Jan 25 20:58 textonly.cfg
```

As the output of the `cat` command shows, the `/tmp/sample.out` file appears to contain the expected output: the listing of the `/var/spool/lpd/lp` directory, with a date stamp as the header.

Local-printer setup

The previous sections showed you various aspects of the Linux printing environment, including a sample `printcap` entry and an input filter. With the information from the previous sections, you should be able to set up a new printer on your Linux PC. To set up a printer that is connected to your PC's `/dev/lp1` port, follow these steps:

1. Log in as `root`, because you need superuser privileges to complete the following steps.

2. Check to see the printer daemon, `lpd`, is running. Use the command `ps ax | grep lpd` to see whether an `lpd` process is reported. If you installed Linux from this book's companion CD-ROM disk, the `lpd` daemon should be running on your system. The script file `/etc/rc.d/rc.M` starts the `lpd` program during boot.

3. Check to see whether the printing programs — `lpr`, `lpq`, `lprm`, and `lpc` — are in your system. The first three programs should be in the `/usr/bin` directory; `lpc` is in `/usr/sbin` directory.

4. Create a spool directory for the new printer or simply use `/var/spool/lpd/lp`, which should already exist in your system.

5. Open the `/etc/printcap` file and add the `printcap` entry named `sample`, shown in the preceding section. Change the name (`sample`) to your printer's name (pick a short name you can remember easily). Change the device name from `/dev/null` to `/dev/lp1` (your system's parallel port). Also remove the `if` field (you can add an input filter later, if necessary). Save the `/etc/printcap` file.

6. Make sure the printer is properly connected to the PC. Turn on its power switch and make sure the printer is online.

7. Print a test page; just try `ls -l | lpr -Pprinter_name` (replace *printer_name* with your printer's name). The printout should appear on the printer.

8. If your Linux PC is on a network and you want users from other systems to print on your printer, add the names of the remote systems to the file `/etc/hosts.lpd` (a text file). Simply add one host name per line for each remote host that can access your PC's printer.

Remote-printer setup

Suppose your Linux PC is on a network. If you have access to a printer on another system on the network, you may be able to print on that remote printer. You still must set up a `printcap` entry in your system's `/etc/printcap` file before you can send print jobs to the remote system.

To set up a `printcap` entry for a remote printer, follow these steps:

1. In the local system's `/etc/printcap` file, add a new `printcap` entry with an empty `lp` field, set the `rm` field to the name of the remote system, and set the `rp` field to the name of the printer on the remote system. On my trusty old Sun SPARCStation IPC (because it runs BSD UNIX, it uses the same printer setup as Linux), I set up the following `printcap` entry to use the `sample` printer on my Pentium, running Linux (the system name is `lnbsoft`):

```
# A remote printer
lp|lnbsoft-sample|Remote printer on lnbsoft:\
:lp=:\
:sd=/usr/spool/lpd:\
:rm=lnbsoft:\
:rp=sample:\
:mx#0:\
:sh:\
:sf:
```

2. In the remote system's `/etc/hosts.lpd` file, add the name of your local system. Thus, if I want to print on the `lnbsoft` system from my Sun workstation named `lnbsun`, I edit the `/etc/hosts.lpd` file on `lnbsoft` and add the following line:

`lnbsun`

The `/etc/hosts` file on `lnbsoft`, of course, should include the IP address of `lnbsun` (you learn more about IP addresses in Chapter 16).

After completing these steps, you should be able to print on the remote system. From my Sun workstation, I printed on the sample printer on `lnbsoft` and the result showed up in the `/tmp/sample.out` file on `lnbsoft` (because the `sample` printer is set up that way).

Specific Printing Problems and Solutions

Typically, you should be able to print text files readily. This section highlights some of the problems you may encounter and suggests appropriate solutions.

Print job submitted, but no output

This problem is one of the most frustrating. You submit a print job to a printer through `lpr` (making sure you use the `-P` option to name the printer) and no error messages are reported, but nothing comes out of the printer. Try the following steps to identify the reason for the failure to print:

1. Check the physical printer. Make sure it's connected to the PC, the power is on, and the printer is online.

2. Make sure the printer is connected to the device specified in the `lp` field of the printer's `printcap`. Also make sure the device is not `/dev/null`.

3. Run `lpq`, and make sure the printer's queue shows the job you submitted.

4. Type `lpc stat` to see the status of the printers and make sure printing and queuing are enabled for the printer.

5. Make sure the printer daemon, `lpd`, is running. If not, type **lpd** to start the daemon.

6. Make sure any input filter specified in the `printcap`'s `if` field is present in the correct directory and has execute permission. Check for error messages in the system log by using the following command:

`tail /var/log/messages`

If the messages include entries that say `cannot execv name-of-filter`, you can be sure the filter does not exist or it does not have the proper permission settings. If the filter does not have execute permission, type `chmod +x name-of-filter` to alter the permission settings.

7. Check the file you are trying to print. Some PostScript printers simply ignore plain-text files. (Filters are available that can convert plain text to PostScript. You may have to install such a filter.)

Problem printing on remote printer

If you submit a print job on a remote printer and output does not appear on the remote printer, check the following fields in the /etc/printcap file on the remote system:

■ See whether the rg field specifies groups that are allowed to print. If your user name is not in this group, it may not be processed.

■ See whether the rs field appears. If this field appears, you must have an account on the remote system to be able to print on the remote printer.

How to avoid the staircase effect

In UNIX, each line in a text file ends with a *newline* (line-feed) character. On typewriters, pressing the line-feed key advances the paper to the next line, but does not bring the carriage to the edge of the paper. You have to press the carriage-return key to make that happen. If you were to print a UNIX text file on a typewriter-like device, the result would be something like the following:

```
First line
            Second line
                       Third line
                                  Fourth line
```

As you can see, the lines of text look like a staircase—the origin of the term *staircase effect*.

MS-DOS and many PC printers behave like typewriters: each line of text must have both a carriage return and a line feed to advance properly to the next line on the paper. When you send a UNIX text file to a printer that expects a carriage-return, line-feed ending for each line, the resulting output shows the staircase effect.

Wizard

You can avoid the staircase effect in two ways, both of which require an input filter:

■ Some printers can be set to treat a line-feed (LF) character as a carriage return, followed by a line feed (CR+LF). The HP LaserJet and Deskjet family of printers, for example, can be programmed to treat a CR as CR+LF by sending the sequence Esc &k2G (the Escape key followed by &k2G). You can use an input filter to send this sequence to the printer at the beginning of the file.

■ If the printer cannot be programmed to treat LF as CR+LF, you can write an input filter that converts each LF at the end of a line to CR, followed by LF.

Following is an input filter that sends the special printer command to LaserJet printers to enable the interpretation of LF as CR+LF:

```
#!/bin/bash
# Input filter for HP LaserJet and Deskjet printers to treat LF as CR+LF

# Send command to make printer interpret LF as CR+LF
echo -ne \\033\&k2G

# Next command sends stdin to stdout
cat

# Next command sends a form feed at the end of the file
echo -ne \\f
```

If you save this shell script in the file /var/spool/lpd/lp/hplj-if.sh (and make it executable with the chmod +x command), you can use the filter by placing the following field in that printer's printcap entry:

```
:if=/var/spool/lpd/lp/hplj-if.sh:
```

Filtering a print job destined for a remote printer

After you use lpr to spool a print job for a remote printer (one that has a printcap entry on your system), your system's lpd process immediately transfers the files associated with the print job to the remote system's lpd process. This means even if you specify an input filter in the printcap for the remote printer, your system's lpd process does not apply any filter. Instead, the remote system's lpd process applies any filter specified in that system's /etc/printcap file.

If you don't have access to the remote system's /etc/printcap file to add an input filter, you can use a trick on your system to apply an input filter to the print job before it goes to the remote printer.

Create a dummy printcap entry that specifies the input filter you want to apply. In this input filter, do what you want with the data and then pipe the data to the remote printer. If you want to add the programming sequence so a remote HP printer interprets each line feed as a carriage return followed by a line feed, use a filter script such as the following:

```
#!/bin/bash
{
# Note that \033 is Esc in octal
  echo -ne \\033\&k2G
```

```
cat
echo -ne \\f
} | lpr -Php-remote -h -l
```

This example assumes your system's /etc/printcap file refers to the remote printer as hp-remote.

Avoiding truncated graphics files

Graphics files can be quite large. If you have problems printing graphics files because they get truncated, check the printcap entry for the printer. If that entry does not have an mx field, the maximum size of a file in the spool directory is 1,000 blocks. Any file larger than 1,000 blocks is truncated automatically .

To avoid the truncation problem, add the following mx field to the printcap entry:

mx#0

This entry allows spool files to be as large as necessary.

The lpr -i command does not indent output

The -i option of the lpr command is supposed to indent the output by a specified amount. For this option to work, you must provide an input filter, because lpr simply passes the -i option to the input filter. You get indented output only if the input filter handles the -i option.

Printing PostScript files

If your printer is a PostScript printer, you can print a PostScript file simply by spooling the file to the printer. If you do not have a PostScript printer, you can use the Ghostscript program to print PostScript files on many types of printers. In fact, you can preview PostScript files with the Ghostview program, which uses Ghostscript to generate output suitable for displaying in an *X* window.

CD

The Ghostscript software is included on the companion CD-ROM. You have the option to install Ghostscript when you install Linux by following the steps outlined in Chapter 1.

Table 14-5 shows the output devices the companion CD-ROM's version of Ghostscript (Version 3.33) supports. As you can see, the output devices include hardware devices such as the display screen and printer, as well as many popular image-file formats such as TIFF and PCX.

Table 14-5	Ghostscript Devices
Device Name	**Description of Output Device**
bit	Monochrome bitmap
bitcmyk	Bitmap with colors in CMYK (Cyan-Magenta-Yellow-Black) format
bitrgb	Bitmap with colors in RGB (Red-Green-Blue) format
bj10e	Canon BubbleJet BJ10e printer
bj200	Canon BubbleJet BJ200 printer
bjc600	Canon Color BubbleJet BJC-600, BJC-4000, and BJC-70 printers
cdeskjet	HP DeskJet 500C color printer in 1-bit-per-pixel mode
cdj500	HP DeskJet 500C printer (same as cdjcolor)
cdj550	H-P DeskJet 550C, 560C, 660C, and 660Cse printers
cdjcolor	HP DeskJet 500C printer with 24-bits-per-pixel color and high-quality color (Floyd-Steinberg) dithering (also good for HP DeskJet 540C and Citizen Projet IIc printers)
cdjmono	HP DeskJet 500C printer in black-and-white mode (also good for DeskJet 510, 520, and 540C in black-and-white mode)
cp50	Mitsubishi CP50 color printer
deskjet	HP DeskJet and DeskJet Plus printers
dfaxhigh	DigiFAX (from DigiBoard, Inc.) software format
dfaxlow	Low- (normal) resolution DigiFAX format
djet500	HP DeskJet 500 printer
djet500c	HP DeskJet 500C printer (does not work on 550C or 560C)
dnj650c	HP DesignJet 650C printer
eps9high	Epson-compatible 9-pin printer in triple-resolution (interleaved lines) mode
eps9mid	Epson-compatible 9-pin printer in intermediate-resolution (interleaved lines) mode
epson	Epson-compatible dot-matrix printers (9- or 24-pin)
epsonc	Epson LQ-2550 and Fujitsu 3400/2400/1200 color printers
faxg3	International Telecommunications Union (ITU) standard Group 3 FAX file with EOLs but no header or EOD
faxg32d	ITU standard Group 3 2-dimensional FAX file with EOLs but no header or EOD
faxg4	ITU standard Group 4 FAX file with EOLs but no header or EOD
ibmpro	IBM 9-pin Proprinter
jetp3852	IBM Jetprinter (Model #3852) inkjet color printer

Device Name	*Description of Output Device*
laserjet	HP LaserJet printer
ljet2p	HP LaserJet IID/IIP/III with TIFF compression
ljet3	HP LaserJet III printer with Delta Row compression
ljet3d	HP LaserJet IIID printer with duplex (2-sided printing) capability
ljet4	HP LaserJet 4 printer (default resolution of 600 dots per inch)
ljetplus	HP LaserJet Plus printer
pbm	Plain Portable Bitmap format
pbmraw	Raw Portable Bitmap format
pcx16	Older EGA/VGA 16-color PCX file format (4-bit planar format)
pcx24b	24-bit color PCX file format (3 8-bit planes)
pcx256	256-color PCX file format (8-bit chunky format)
pcxgray	8-bit gray scale PCX file format
pcxmono	Monochrome PCX file format (1-bit per pixel)
pgm	Plain Portable Graymap format
pgmraw	Raw Portable Graymap format
pj	HP PaintJet XL printer
pjxl	HP PaintJet XL color printer
pjxl300	HP PaintJet XL300 color printer (also good for PaintJet 1200C)
ppm	Plain Portable Pixmap format
ppmraw	Raw Portable Pixmap format
tiffcrle	Tagged Image File Format (TIFF) that uses ITU standard 1-dimensional Huffman Run Length Encoded (RLE) FAX format (Group 3 FAX with no End of Lines)
tiffg3	TIFF file that uses ITU standard Group 3 FAX format (Group 3 FAX with End of Lines)
tiffg32d	TIFF file that uses ITU standard 2-dimensional Group 3 FAX format
tiffg4	TIFF file that uses ITU standard Group 4 FAX format
tifflzw	Tagged Image File Format that uses Lempel-Ziv Welch (LZW) compression
tiffpack	Tagged Image File Format that uses PackBits compression
x11	X window driver (to display output in a window)
x11alpha	X window driver with 4-bit alpha (transparency) capability
x11cmyk	X window driver that accepts colors in CMYK (Cyan-Magenta-Yellow-Black) format
x11mono	Monochrome (black-and-white) X window driver

You run the Ghostscript program with the `gs` command. Use the `-sDEVICE=`*devicename* option to specify a device name. To interpret the PostScript file `testfile.ps` and produce output for an HP LaserJet 4 printer, for example, you would type the following:

```
gs -sDEVICE=ljet4 testfile.ps
```

To print PostScript files, you would define a `printcap` entry for a PostScript printer (typically, with a name such as `ps`) and specify an input filter for that entry. Then, in the input filter, you would use `gs` to create the output for your printer. If you have a HP DeskJet 550C printer, you would place the following line in the body of a shell script that serves as the input filter for the `printcap` entry for the HP DeskJet 550C:

```
/usr/bin/gs -dSAFER -dNOPAUSE -q -sDEVICE=cdj550 -sOutputFile=-
```

The `-sDEVICE=cdj550` option specifies the output device is a HP DeskJet 550C. The `-sOutputFile=-` option sends the output to `stdout`, which is what the input filter should do: send its stream of output to the standard output (the printer daemon will send that output to the physical printer).

Summary

Printing under Linux is simple, provided that the printing environment is set up properly. You do have to learn a small set of commands to submit a print job and check the status of pending print jobs. This chapter explains the Linux printing environment from the user's point of view and then explains how to set everything up as a system administrator.

By reading this chapter, you learn the following things:

- In Linux, the printer's device name depends on the port to which you connect the printer. For a typical printer connected to the parallel port, the device name is `/dev/lp0` or `/dev/lp1`, depending on the I/O address of the parallel port. If the printer is connected to the serial port, the device name is `/dev/ttyS0` (for COM1) or `/dev/ttyS1` (for COM2).

- As a user, you print with the `lpr` command, check the status of the print queue with `lpq`, cancel print jobs with `lprm`, and check the printer's status with `lpc status`.

- Behind the scenes, the `lpr` command copies the print file to a holding directory called the *spool directory*. A background process called `lpd` (the print daemon) sends the spooled print file to the printer.

- To set up the printing environment in Linux, you must have your printer defined in the `/etc/printcap` file. This file essentially specifies what to do when a print job is sent to the printer. Fields in the `/etc/printcap` file control various aspects of printing, ranging from page size to whether a burst header page is printed before each print job.

▶ In /etc/printcap, you can specify an input filter (a process that reads from standard input and writes to standard output) through which all print jobs must pass. The input filter can send special commands to the printer or alter the print file as necessary.

▶ The staircase effect refers to the appearance of the printout when you print a UNIX text file (in which each line ends with a single line-feed character) on a PC printer, which expects lines to end with a carriage return–line feed pair. You can use an input filter to avoid the staircase effect.

▶ You can set up a printer entry in the /etc/printcap file so the actual printing occurs on another system on the network.

▶ You can use the Ghostscript software (included on the companion CD-ROM) to view and print PostScript files. Many freely available software packages include documentation in PostScript format.

Chapter 15

Modems

In This Chapter

▶ Using the names of serial-port devices in Linux

▶ Understanding serial communications

▶ Looking at the RS-232C standard

▶ Understanding different types of modem standards, such as V.34 and V.90

▶ Using the Hayes-standard AT command set used by modems

▶ Dialing out with a modem in Linux

▶ Setting up Linux for dial-in use

▶ Using multiport serial I/O boards in Linux

If you have installed Linux on your home PC, you may want to use a modem to dial out to your office system or a bulletin board system (BBS). With the increasing popularity of the Internet, you also may want to connect to the Internet through the modem. To use a modem, you have to learn how Linux works with the PC's *serial ports* — the ports through which the modem communicates with the PC. You also need to get cables to connect the modem to the PC, select the proper serial device to use in Linux, and set up configuration files that control the communication parameters for the serial port.

Terminals — devices that have a display screen and a keyboard — also connect to the PC through the serial ports. In this sense, terminals are similar to modems. Terminals are ideal for simple data-entry tasks and often are used in point-of-sale systems. Linux also supports multiport serial boards that enable you to connect many terminals or modems to your PC running Linux.

This chapter explains how to connect, set up, and use modems and terminals. Much of the information applies to any device connected to the serial port, but some information is specific to modems. This chapter focuses primarily on modems because modems are more popular than terminals among Linux users.

PC and Serial Ports

If you have used communications software, such as Procomm or Crosstalk, under MS-DOS or Windows, you have used your PC's serial port. These communications programs transfer bytes of data from the PC to the modem over the serial port. The serial port is so named because each byte of data is sent *serially* — one bit at a time. Serial data communications comes with its own set of terminology. To understand how to set up the serial port, you need to understand the terminology.

UART

A chip named *Universal Asynchronous Receiver/Transmitter* (UART), which is at the heart of all serial communications hardware, takes care of converting each byte to a stream of ones and zeros. That stream of ones and zeros is then sent over the communications medium (for example, the telephone line). At the receiving end, another UART reconstitutes bytes of data from the stream of ones and zeros.

The original IBM PC's motherboard did not include any serial communications capability. Instead, the serial communications function was provided through a separate serial adapter card (or *serial board*) called the IBM Asynchronous Communications Adapter. This serial board used National Semiconductor's INS8250 UART chip.

Later, PCs began including the serial communications hardware on the motherboard, but the same 8250 or compatible UART was used for a long time. Still later, an improved version of the 8250 — the 16450 — was introduced, but the improvements were in the chip's fabrication details, not in the basic capability.

A problem with the 8250 and 16450 UARTs is they don't have any way to buffer received characters. If the PC cannot keep up with the character stream, some characters may be lost. At high data-transfer rates (more than 9,600 bits per second), the PC may have trouble keeping up with the arrival of characters, especially with operating systems that keep the PC busy (such as Microsoft Windows).

The solution was to add a first-in-first-out (FIFO) buffer on the UART so the PC can fall behind occasionally without losing any incoming characters. The newer 16550A UARTs have send and receive buffers, each of which is capable of storing up to 16 characters. The 16550A UART is compatible with the old 8250 and 16450, but it can support higher data-transfer rates because the built-in buffers can store incoming and outgoing characters directly on the UART.

On a historical note, National Semiconductor's original 16550 UART had the FIFO buffers, but the FIFO circuits had some bugs. The 16550A (and later versions of that UART) fixed the problems of the original 16550. By now, however, the 16550 name is often used in a generic manner to refer to UARTs that have onboard receive and transmit buffers. You needn't worry about the distinctions between the 16550 and 16550A except for the original 16550

UARTs from National Semiconductor; those chips are marked NS16550 (without an *A*).

Wizard

Linux supports PC serial ports and serial I/O boards that use a 8250, 16450, 16550, 16550A, or compatible UART. You need a 16550A UART to keep up with today's high-speed modems, however, which can transfer data at rates of up to 56,600 bits per second. Most new Pentium PCs should already have 16550A UARTs. If you are buying a new PC to run Linux, you should check with the vendor and make sure the serial interface uses 16550A UARTs. Nowadays, there are newer UARTs, such as 16654, that come with a 64-byte buffer. These UARTs should also work with Linux.

Communications parameters

In serial communications, the transmission medium (such as the telephone line) is kept at a logical 1 when it is idle (1 is represented by the presence of a signal on the line). In this case, the line is said to be *marking*. On the other hand, when the line is at a logical 0, it is said to be *spacing*. Thus, logical 1 and 0 are also referred to as MARK and SPACE, respectively.

A sequence of ones and zeros makes up a single 8-bit character, as shown in Figure 15-1.

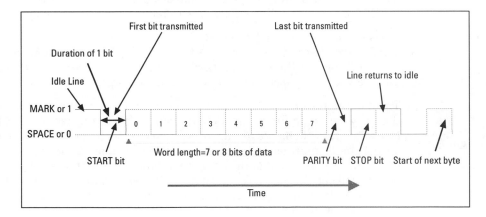

Figure 15-1: Format of a single character in serial communications

As Figure 15-1 shows, a change in the condition of the line from MARK to SPACE indicates the start of a character. This change in line condition is referred to as the START bit. Following the START bit is a pattern of bits that represents the character and then a bit known as the PARITY bit. Finally, the line reverts to its idling MARK condition, which represents the STOP bit and indicates the end of the current character. The number of bits used to represent the character is known as the *word length* and usually is either seven or eight.

The PARITY bit is used to perform rudimentary error detection. When *even parity* is selected, for example, the parity bit is set so the total number of ones in the current word is even (the logic is similar for odd parity). At the receiving end, the parity is recalculated and compared with the received parity bit. If the two disagree, the receiver declares a parity error. One problem of error detection with the parity check is it can detect only errors that affect a single bit. The bit pattern 0100 0001 0 (the ASCII code for the letter *A*), for example, transmitted with an 8-bit word length and even parity, may change (due to noise in the telephone line) to 0100 0111 0 (ASCII *G*). The receiver would not see the error, however, because the parity is still even. Thus, parity error detection is rarely used nowadays.

In serial communications, the transmitter and the receiver both must have some knowledge of how long each bit lasts; otherwise, they cannot detect the bits correctly. The duration of each bit is determined by data clocks at the receiver and the transmitter. Notice, though, although the clocks at the receiver and the transmitter must have the same frequency, they are not required to be synchronized. The START bit signals the receiver a new character follows; the receiver then begins detecting the bits until it sees the STOP bit.

A particular condition of the line is sometimes used to gain the attention of the receiver. The normal state of the line is MARK (1), and the beginning of a character is indicated by a SPACE (0). If the line stays in the SPACE condition for a period of time longer than it would have taken to receive all the bits of a character, a BREAK is assumed to have occurred. When the receiver sees the BREAK condition, it can get ready to receive characters again.

The selection of the clock frequency depends on the *baud rate* (or simply *baud*), which refers to the number of times the line changes state every second. Typically, the serial I/O hardware uses a clock rate of 16 times the baud rate so the line is sampled often enough to detect a bit reliably.

Note

The data-transfer rate is expressed in terms of *bits per second*, or *bps*. In the early days of modems, the data-transfer rate was the same as the baud rate — the rate of change of the line's state — because each line state carried a single bit of information. Nowadays, modems use different technology that can send several bits of information each time the line state changes. In other words, you can get a high bps with a relatively low baud rate. Even the fastest modems today use a baud rate of 2,400, even though the bits per second can be as high as 56,600.

Secret

Thus, the term *baud* and *bits per second* are not the same. Most of us, however, ignore the exact definition of *baud rate* and simply use the term *baud* to mean bits per second. Even though I stick to bps when I state data-transfer rates, you'll run across Linux settings that use the term *baud rate* to mean bps.

Serial-port IRQs and I/O addresses

The PC typically has two serial ports — COM1 and COM2 in MS-DOS parlance. The PC also can support two more serial ports: COM3 and COM4. Because of these port names, the serial ports are often referred to as COM ports.

Wizard

Like other devices, the serial ports need interrupt-request (IRQ) numbers and I/O port addresses. Two IRQs — 3 and 4 — are shared among the four COM ports. Table 15-1 lists the IRQs and I/O port addresses assigned to the four serial ports.

Table 15-1   IRQ and I/O port addresses assigned to serial ports

Port	IRQ	I/O Address
COM1	4	0x3f8
COM2	3	0x2f8
COM3	4	0x3e8
COM4	3	0x2e8

Serial-device names in Linux

Like other devices in Linux, the serial-port devices are represented by device files in the /dev directory. Each serial port has two names: one for incoming connections and the other for outgoing connections. Table 15-2 lists the device names for incoming and outgoing serial ports, including the major and minor device numbers.

Table 15-2   Device names for incoming and outgoing serial ports

COM Port	Device Name	Major Device Number	MinorDevice Number
Incoming COM1	/dev/ttyS0	4	64
Incoming COM2	/dev/ttyS1	4	65
Incoming COM3	/dev/ttyS2	4	66
Incoming COM4	/dev/ttyS3	4	67
Outgoing COM1	/dev/cua0	5	64
Outgoing COM2	/dev/cua1	5	65
Outgoing COM3	/dev/cua2	5	66
Outgoing COM4	/dev/cua3	5	67

If you installed Linux from this book's companion CD-ROM, all these devices should already be in your system. If you check the /dev directory, you can find the /dev/ttyS* and /dev/cua* devices, where * is 0, 1, 2, and 3.

Historically, Linux used the /dev/ttyS* devices for dialing in and the /dev/cua* devices for dialing out. The current version of the Linux kernel does not distinguish between /dev/ttyS* and /dev/cua* devices, however. My recommendation is you use the /dev/ttyS* device names wherever you need to refer to serial devices.

Modems

The term *modem* comes from *modulator/demodulator*—a device that converts digital signals, consisting of ones and zeros, to continuously varying analog signals that can be transmitted over telephone lines and radio waves. Thus, the modem is the intermediary between the digital world of the PC and the analog world of telephones.

Inside the PC, ones and zeros are represented with voltage levels, but signals carried over telephone lines usually are tones of different frequencies. The modem sits between the UART and the telephone line, and makes data communication possible over the phone lines. The modem converts information back and forth between the voltage/no voltage representation of digital circuits and analog signals that are appropriate for transmission over phone lines.

The communication between the PC and the modem follows the RS-232C standard (often stated as RS-232, without the C). The communications protocol between two modems also follows one of several international modem standards. The next few sections briefly describe these standards.

RS-232C standard

The RS-232C standard, set forth by the Electrical Industry Association (EIA), specifies a prescribed method of information interchange between the modem and the PC's serial communication hardware.

In EIA terminology, the modem is Data Communications Equipment (DCE), and the PC is considered to be Data Terminal Equipment (DTE). You see references to DCE and DTE in discussions of the RS-232C standard.

A modem can communicate in one of two modes:

- *Half-duplex mode*, in which data transmission can occur in only one direction at a time

- *Full-duplex mode*, which allows independent two-way communications

Most modems communicate in full-duplex mode.

RS-232C cables

The RS-232C standard also provides control signals, such as Request to Send (RTS) and Clear to Send (CTS), that can be used to coordinate the transmission and reception of data between the PC and the modem. The term *handshaking* refers to the coordination of the data exchange.

The handshaking signals, as well as data transmission and reception, occur through wires in the cable that connects the PC to the modem. The RS-232C specifies a 25-pin connector, with a specific function assigned to each pin.

A typical modem has a Female 25-pin, D-shell connector (called the DB-25 connector), whereas the PC's serial port provides a Male 9-pin, D-shell (DB-9) connector. To connect a PC's serial port to a modem, you need a cable with a Female DB-9 connector at one end and a Male DB-25 connector at the other end. Figure 15-2 illustrates a typical PC-to-modem cable (often sold in computer stores under the label AT Modem Cable).

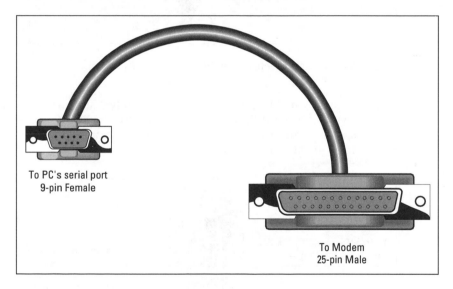

To PC's serial port
9-pin Female

To Modem
25-pin Male

Figure 15-2: A typical cable for connecting a PC's serial port to a modem

Some PCs have a DB-25 connector for the serial port. For these machines, you need a cable with DB-25 connectors on both ends.

The RS-232C standard specifies the pins for the 25-pin connector. Figure 15-3 shows the DB-25 connector and pin assignments for IBM PC-compatible DB-25 male connectors.

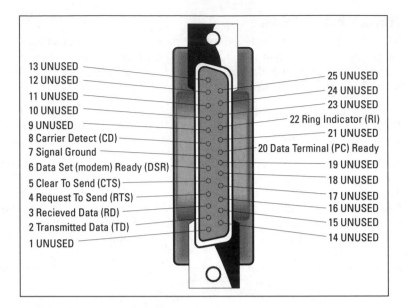

Figure 15-3: Pin assignments for the DB-25 serial connector

Of the 25 pins available in a DB-25 connector, only 9 are used in the PC's serial port. In the Serial/Parallel Adapter card for the PC-AT, IBM decided to save space by introducing a DB-9 connector. The pin assignments for the DB-9 connector are shown in Figure 15-4.

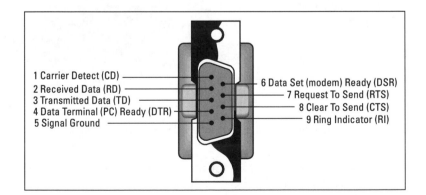

Figure 15-4: Pin assignments for the DB-9 serial connector used in PC serial ports

Using modem cables (DTE to DCE)

When you connect a PC (DTE) to a modem (DCE), the cable should connect the like signals at both ends as follows (the arrow indicates the direction of data transfer on that line):

PC (DTE)	Modem (DCE)
TD (Transmit Data) ————————>	TD (Transmit Data)
RD (Receive Data) <————————	RD (Receive Data)
RTS (Request to Send) ——————>	RTS (Request to Send)
CTS (Clear to Send) <————————	CTS (Clear to Send)
DSR (Data Set Ready) <————————	DSR (Data Set Ready)
Signal Ground ————————	Signal Ground
CD (Carrier Detect) <————————	CD (Carrier Detect)
DTR (Data Terminal Ready) ——————>	DTR (Data Terminal Ready)
RI (Ring Indicator) <————————	RI (Ring Indicator)

A cable that has such connections is often called a *straight-through cable*, because it connects like signals to each other. If the connector at one end is DB-25 and the other one is DB-9, all you have to do is look up the pin numbers for each type of connector in Figure 15-5and 15-6

Using null modem cables (DTE to DTE)

If you want to connect two PCs through the serial port, you cannot use a straight-through cable, such as the one used to connect the PC to a modem. The reason is because each PC expects to send data on the TD line and receive data on the RD line. If both PCs send data on the same line, neither PC can hear the other. A solution is to create a cable that connects one PC's output (TD) to the other one's input (RD), and vice versa. Such a cable is known as a *null modem* cable.

Figure 15-5 shows the signal interconnections in a typical null modem cable. Instead of showing the pin numbers, I have shown the RS-232C signal names. The exact pin numbers depend on the type of connectors. You should consult Figures 15-3 and 15-4 for the pin numbers.

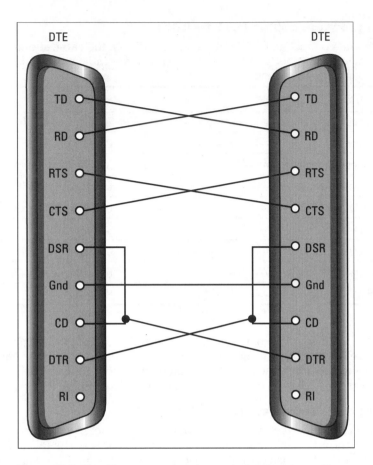

Figure 15-5: Signal interconnections in a typical null modem cable

Choosing cables

When you connect two devices that support RS-232C serial communications, the choice of cable depends on the type of each device: DTE or DCE. As I mentioned earlier, the PC is a DTE nd a modem is a DCE. Many printers and terminals are DTEs.

Use a straight-through modem cable to connect a DTE to a DCE. To connect a DTE to a DTE, you need a null modem cable. Many computer stores sell a smaller null modem adapter. You can connect two DTE devices by using a modem cable with a null modem adapter.

Secret

Notice the serial interface on the HP Laserjet family of printers is configured as a DTE. You need a null modem-style cable to connect a PC's serial port to a LaserJet printer. Unfortunately, serial interface to printers introduces a further complication. Printer manufacturers interpret some of the RS-232C signals in a printer-specific manner, so you may have to connect various signals in a specified manner to use a printer successfully with a serial interface.

Flow control

The RS-232C standard includes the RTS/CTS signals for hardware handshaking between the communicating devices (such as the PC and the modem). In addition to this hardware flow control, special ASCII control characters (Ctrl-Q/Ctrl-S, or XON/XOFF) are typically used to implement flow control in software. Flow control is necessary because sometimes either the receiver may be unable to keep up with the rate of data arrival and should be able to inform the sender to stop data transmission while it catches up.

Suppose a receiver has a buffer to store incoming characters. As the buffer gets full, the receiver can send the XOFF character (Ctrl-S) to the transmitter, indicating transmission should stop. If the transmitter understands the meaning of the XOFF character, it can stop sending data.

Then, when the receiver empties the buffer, it can send an XON character (Ctrl-Q) to indicate transmission can resume. This scheme of flow control is used in many communications programs because it is simple. Unfortunately, when the XON/XOFF protocol is used, the XON and XOFF characters cannot be part of the data because of their special meaning.

Modem standards

As the Internet and online services have grown in popularity, so has the demand for modems that offer high data-transfer rates. The early modems transferred data at the rate of 300 bits per second (bps), whereas the latest modems can transfer at rates of up to 56,600 bps — over a hundredfold increase in modem performance. To achieve these high data-transfer rates, modems use many tricks, including compressing the data before sending it. As you might expect, two modems can communicate successfully only if both modems understand how to interpret the signal being exchanged between the two. This is where the standard modem protocols come into play.

Wizard

The International Telecommunications Union (ITU) has ratified several modem standards in use today. These standards have names that start with *V*. The latest standard is V.90, which supports data-transfer rates of 56,600 bps (56Kbps or 56K for short). The V.90 standard is also called V.PCM because it uses a technique known as Pulse Coded Modulation (PCM). Table 15-3 lists some of the common modem standards used today.

Tip

If you need the exact text of the ITU Series V recommendations, as these data communication standards are called, you can purchase copies from ITU's Web site at `http://www.itu.ch/itudoc/itu-t/rec/v/`. The site offers the files in English, French, or Spanish, and in a number of file formats including Microsoft Word for Windows, Adobe's Portable Document Format (PDF), and PostScript.

Table 15-3 Modem standards	
Standard name	*Maximum data-transfer rate (bps)*
Bell 103	300
Bell 212A	1,200
V.17 (Group III Fax)	14,400
V.21	300
V.22	1,200
V.22bis	2,400
V.23	1,200
V.27ter (Group III Fax)	4,800
V.29 (Group III Fax)	9,600
V.32	9,600
V.32bis	14,400
V.34	28,800
V.90 (also called V.PCM)	56,600

When you buy a modem, make sure the modem conforms to these international standards. Nowadays, the ITU V.90-compliant 56K modems are the norm.

Modem commands (AT commands)

The now-famous AT command set first appeared in the 300-baud Hayes *Smartmodem,* a term coined and trademarked by Hayes Microcomputer Products, Inc. The Smartmodem worked in two distinct modes:

- *Command mode.* In this mode, characters sent from the PC (DTE) are interpreted as commands for the modem.

- *Online mode.* After receiving a dial command and establishing a connection, the modem sends all received data out on the phone lines.

The Hayes Smartmodem commands start with the two characters AT (for attention). The initial command set included those to dial a number, turn the modem's speaker on or off, and set the modem to answer an incoming call.

The AT command system has been widely copied by modem manufacturers, making the AT command mechanism a de facto standard. Although virtually all modems use a core command set, each modem manufacturer has its own proprietary commands that control some of the exotic and advanced features of the modem.

Tip

I have found knowing at least a few of the AT commands for controlling a modem helpful. Although many communications programs hide the details of the AT commands, you can end up in a situation in which the communications software is primitive — all the software does is send the other modem whatever you type. In such situations, you can enter AT commands to set up the modem, dial out, and establish a connection. The following sections briefly cover the AT command set.

The AT command line

As the name implies, each command in the AT command set starts with the letters AT. Following these letters, you can enter one or more valid commands, and then end the command line with a carriage return (press Enter on the PC's keyboard). Thus, the command line has the following format:

```
AT[command1][command2]...<CR>
```

[command1] and [command2] denote optional commands, each of which has appropriate arguments. The ending <CR> is a required carriage return.

Suppose you want to use the following commands:

- The E command with an argument of 1 to force the modem to echo the commands

- The V command with 1 as the argument to make the modem provide verbose result codes (instead of numeric codes)

You can send these commands to the modem with the following AT command line:

```
ATE1V1
```

As you do with any AT command line, of course, you have to end this command by pressing Enter. If you enter this command through a communications software package, you see the modem replies with the string OK.

Secret

All modems accept a minimum 40 characters per command line, in which the character count includes the AT and the final carriage return. Many modems, however, can accept up to 255 characters on an AT command line.

The A/ command

Every rule has an exception and the A/ command is an exception to the AT command syntax. If you enter **A/** as the only command on a line by itself (no need to press Enter), the modem immediately repeats the last command line that it received.

Configuration commands

These commands specify how the modem should operate and how it responds to commands. Following are some useful configuration commands:

- *Echo commands.* ATE1 causes the modem to display a command as you type it; ATE0 disables the display of the command.

- *Speaker volume.* The ATL*n* (*n* is a number between 0 and 3) command sets the volume of the modem's built-in speaker. ATL0 and ATL1 set the volume low, ATL2 sets it medium, and ATL3 sets it high.

- *Speaker control.* ATM*n*, (*n* is a number between 0 and 2) controls whether and when the modem's speaker is turned on. ATM0 turns the speaker off, ATM1 turns it on until a call is established, and ATM2 turns it on always.

- *Quiet mode.* When quiet mode is enabled, the modem does not acknowledge commands or report call status. ATQ0 disables quiet mode and causes the modem to respond to commands and show call status. ATQ1 enables quiet mode.

- *Verbose mode.* When verbose mode is enabled, the modem acknowledges commands and reports call status with words. Otherwise, the modem responds with numeric codes (which may be more suitable for communications software than for humans). The ATV1 command turns on verbose mode; ATV0 turns off verbose mode. A typical modem has the nine responses listed in Table 15-4.

Table 15-4   Responses from a typical modem

Numeric response	Word response
0	OK
1	CONNECT
2	RING
3	NO CARRIER
4	ERROR
5	CONNECT 1200
6	NO DIALTONE
7	BUSY
8	NO ANSWER

Most modems include several other responses for reporting successful connections at higher data rates.

- *Result code selection.* The ATX*n* command selects the type of reports the modem should send back. The argument *n* can be one of the following:

```
0       CONNECT
1       CONNECT bits-per-sec
2       CONNECT bits-per-sec, NO DIALTONE
3       CONNECT bits-per-sec, BUSY
4       CONNECT bits-per-sec, NO DIALTONE, BUSY
```

- *View stored profiles.* Using AT&V causes the modem to display the current values of a selected set of configuration parameters and the values of internal registers. Some modems have nonvolatile memory to store groups of settings known as *profiles.* On such modems, AT&V displays the stored profiles.

Action commands

Each action command causes the modem to perform some action immediately. The most important action command is the dial command: ATDT*number.* Two other useful action commands are ATZ*n* and AT&F*n* , which reset the modem's configuration. Following are some of the important action commands:

- *Pulse dial.* The ATDP*number* command causes the modem to use the pulse dialing system to dial a specified phone number. The pulse dialing system was used by rotary telephones. Now you typically use the ATDT command to dial a number by using the tone dialing system.

- *Tone dial.* Use the ATDT*number* command to dial a specified phone number by using the tone dialing system. To dial the number 555-1234, for example, you use the command ATDT555-1234. You should enter whatever other digits you may need to dial the number you want to reach. If you need to dial 9 to access an outside line, you simply use ATDT9,555-1234. The comma introduces a slight pause (typically, two seconds), which may be necessary to get an outside line.

- *Dial last number.* The ATDL command causes the modem to execute the last dial command.

- *Hook control.* The ATH command simulates the act of lifting or putting down the handset of a regular telephone. ATH0 hangs up the phone; ATH1 makes the modem go online (as though you had picked up the handset).

- *Answer call.* Use the ATA command to make the modem answer the phone. You can put the modem in answer mode (by setting register — a storage area in the modem — S0 to a nonzero value) so it answers the phone when someone calls. With the ATA command, you can force the modem to answer the phone even if register S0 is set to 0 (which means the modem won't answer the phone).

- *Return to online.* The ATO command returns the modem to online mode. Use this command after you press +++ (rapidly enter three plus signs in sequence with some pause before and after the sequence) to take the modem offline.

- *Software reset.* If the modem stores configuration profiles in nonvolatile memory, you can recall one of the configuration profiles with the ATZ*n* command (*n* is the number of the configuration profile). If you enter ATZ without any argument, the modem is reset. The ATZ command terminates any existing connection.

- *Factory-default setting.* The AT&F command causes the modem to restore the factory-default settings. Some modems take a numeric argument with AT&F; consult your modem's documentation for more information on the meaning of the numeric argument.

The ATS*r*=*n* commands

In addition to the AT command set, Hayes Smartmodem pioneered the use of internal modem registers to configure the modem. All current modems have a set of registers, called the *S registers*, that control many aspects of the modem (including features that may be unique to a specific brand of modem).

Secret

A typical modem has anywhere from 30 to 60 S registers, denoted by S0, S1, S2, and so on. The ATS*r*=*n* command sets the S register numbered *r* to the value *n*. To view the current contents of the S register numbered *r*, use the ATS*r*? command.

Register S0, for example, contains the number of rings after which the modem answers the phone. When S0 is zero, the modem does not answer the phone at all. Following is how you might query and set the S0 register with the ATS command:

```
ATS0?
000

OK
ATS0=1
OK
ATS0?
001
```

Wizard

The exact set of S registers varies from one brand of modem to another, but most modems seem to provide and interpret the following 13 S registers in a consistent manner:

S0 **Ring to Answer On** — The number of rings after which the modem answers the phone. When S0 is zero, the modem does not answer the phone.

S1 **Counts Number of Rings** — The count of incoming rings. When S1 equals S0, the modem answers the phone (assuming that S0 is nonzero). The modem resets S1 to zero a few seconds after the last ring.

S2 **Escape Code Character**—The character used as the escape sequence to switch the modem from online mode to command mode. The default value is 43, which is the ASCII code for the plus (+) character. To go from online mode to command mode, you have to enter this escape character three times in rapid succession.

S3 **Carriage-Return Character**—The ASCII code of the character used as the carriage return (this character terminates the AT command lines). The default value is 13.

S4 **Line-Feed Character**—The ASCII code of the character used as the line-feed character when the modem generates word responses to commands. The default value is 10.

S5 **Backspace Character**—The ASCII code of the character used as the backspace character. The modem echoes this character to implement the "erase preceding character" function. The default value is 8.

S6 **Wait Time for Dial Tone (seconds)**—The number of seconds to wait before dialing the first digit in a dial command. The default value is 2.

S7 **Wait Time for Carrier (seconds)**—The number of seconds the modem waits for a carrier. If the modem does not detect a carrier after waiting for this many seconds, it displays the NO CARRIER message. The default value depends on the modem. Typically, the default is anywhere from 30 to 60.

S8 **Comma Time (seconds)**—The number of seconds to pause when the modem finds a comma in the phone number to dial. The default value is 2.

S9 **Carrier Detect Time (tenths of a second)**—The amount of time, in tenths of seconds, the carrier must be present before the modem declares a carrier has been detected. The default value is 6, which means the carrier must be present for 0.6 seconds before the modem detects it.

S10 **Carrier Loss Time (tenths of a second)**—The amount of time, in tenths of seconds, the carrier can be lost without causing the modem to disconnect. The default value is anywhere from 7 to 15, which means the carrier can be lost for 0.7 to 1.5 seconds without causing a modem disconnect.

S11 **Dial-Tone Spacing (milliseconds)**—The duration of each dial tone and the spacing between adjacent tones. The default value typically is something between 50 and 100 milliseconds (50 is considered the minimum necessary for dial tones to be recognized by the phone system).

S12 **Escape Sequence Guard Time (fiftieths of a second)**—The amount of guard time, in fiftieths of a second, that must occur before and after the escape-code sequence (the default sequence is +++) that switches the modem from online mode to command mode. The default value is 50, which means the guard time is 1 second.

Online help

In response to the AT$ command, U.S. Robotics modems display online help information on the basic modem command sets. The help information is instructive because it shows you the breadth of commands a typical modem accepts. You can enter the command in a serial communications program such as Minicom, which I describe briefly later in the section "Dial out with a communications program" in this chapter.

Linux and Modems

If you're using Linux at home or in a small office, you probably want to use the modem for one or more of the following reasons:

- To dial out to another computer (such as a bulletin-board system), an online service (such as CompuServe), or another UNIX system, perhaps at your university or company.

- To allow other people to dial in and use your Linux system. If your home PC runs Linux and you have a modem set up, you might even dial in to your home system from work.

- To use dial-up networking with Serial Internet Protocol (SLIP) or Point-to-Point Protocol (PPP) to connect to the Internet (typically, through an Internet service provider).

Cross-Reference

In the following sections, I describe the first two uses of a modem: to dial in or dial out from your Linux PC. Dial-up networking with SLIP or PPP is an important topic in itself; Chapter 18 covers that subject in detail.

Dialing out with a modem

When you installed Linux from this book's companion CD-ROM, you automatically installed some tools you can use to dial out from your Linux system with a modem. Before you can dial out, however, you must make sure you have a modem properly connected to one of the serial ports of your PC and the Linux devices for the serial ports are set up correctly.

Examining a modem's hardware setup

Make sure your modem is properly connected to the power supply and the modem is connected to the telephone line.

Buy the right type of cable to connect the modem to the PC. As explained in earlier sections of this chapter, you need a straight-through serial cable to connect the modem to the PC. The connectors at the ends of the cable depend on the type of serial connector on your PC. The modem end of the cable needs a male DB-25 connector. The PC end of the cable often is a female DB-9 connector, but some PCs also need a female DB-25 connector at the PC end of the cable.

You can buy modem cables at most computer stores. In particular, the DB-9 to DB-25 modem cables are often sold under the label "AT Modem Cable."

Caution

If your PC's serial port is a DB-25, the connector at the back of the PC (not the one on the cable) is a male DB-25 connector. Don't confuse this connector with the parallel port's DB-25 connector, which is female. If you do use the wrong connector, no damage should occur, but serial communications won't work.

Tip

If your PC has an internal modem, all you must do is make sure the IRQ and I/O addresses are set properly (assuming the modem card has jumpers for setting these values). For COM1, set the IRQ to 4 and the I/O address to 0x3f8; for COM2, the IRQ is 3 and the I/O address is 0x2f8. You also have to connect the phone line to a phone jack at the back of the internal-modem card.

Checking Linux's serial devices

When you install Linux from this book's CD-ROM, following the directions in Chapter 1, the necessary Linux serial devices are automatically created for you. You should have two sets of devices: /dev/cua* (* is the port number), for dialing out through the modem; and /dev/ttyS*, for dialing in through the modem. You can use the /dev/ttyS* devices for both dial-in and dial-out use, though.

Wizard

The installation process creates the /dev/ttyS* and /dev/cua* file with a permission setting that does not allow everyone to read the device. If you want any user to be able to dial out with the modem, type the following command while you are logged in as root:

```
chmod o+rw /dev/ttyS*
```

This command gives all users access to the dial-out devices.

Dialing out with a communications program

After you complete the physical installation of the modem and verify the necessary Linux device files exist, you can try to dial out through the modem. The best approach is to use the minicom serial communications program included in the Linux distribution on this book's CD-ROM. The minicom program, created by Miquel van Smoorenburg, is a communications program with a text-based interface that emulates a VT102 terminal.

To run minicom, type **minicom** at the shell prompt in an xterm window or in a Virtual Terminal screen. If you run minicom as a normal user (not root), minicom may display the following error message and exit:

```
minicom
minicom: there is no global configuration file /etc/minirc.dfl
Ask your sysadm to create one (with minicom -s).
```

Log in as root and then type

```
minicom -s
```

Minicom starts and displays a dialog that enables you to configure various aspects of Minicom, including serial port and the modem dialing commands. To enter the modem initialization commands, use the arrow key to highlight the `Modem and dialing` item, as shown in Figure 15-6.

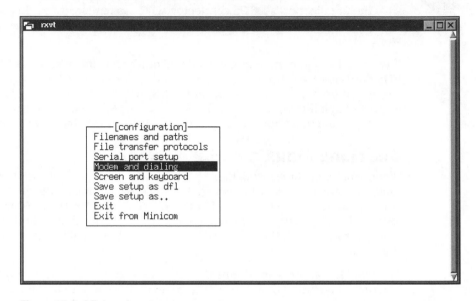

Figure 15-6: Minicom's setup menu

With the `Modem and dialing` entry highlighted, press Enter. Minicom displays another menu with a list of settings you can change. Press A to change the modem initialization string. Minicom places the cursor on the first line, as shown in Figure 15-7.

You can then use the backspace key to edit that line and type the AT command you need to initialize the modem. For example, I have a 56K modem that uses the now-outmoded x2 standard. I need to send the following AT command to connect with my Internet service provider's modem:

```
AT &F1 &K0 &I0 s33=32 s15=128 s27=64 s32=34
```

After you enter the modem initialization string, press Enter to return to the top-level menu. If you have no more changes to make, use the up and down arrow keys to highlight the item labeled `Save as dfl` (that means save as default) and then press Enter. Minicom saves the settings in the /etc/minirc.dfl file—the default configuration file for Minicom. After that, you can exit Minicom by selecting `Exit from Minicom` and pressing Enter.

```
┌─ rxvt ──────────────────────────────────────────────────────────── _□×
│                    ─[Modem and dialing parameter setup]─
│
│    A - Init string ......... AT &F1 &K0 &I0 s33=32 s15=128 s27=64 s32=34^M
│    B - Reset string ........ ^M^ATZ^M^
│    C - Dialing prefix #1.... ATDT
│    D - Dialing suffix #1.... ^M
│    E - Dialing prefix #2.... ATDP
│    F - Dialing suffix #2.... ^M
│    G - Dialing prefix #3.... ATX1DT
│    H - Dialing suffix #3.... ;X4D^M
│    I - Connect string ...... CONNECT
│    J - No connect strings .. NO CARRIER          BUSY
│                              NO DIALTONE         VOICE
│    K - Hang-up string ...... ~~+++~~ATH^M
│    L - Dial cancel string .. ^M
│
│    M - Dial time .......... 45       P - Auto baud detect .... No
│    N - Delay before redial . 5       Q - Drop DTR to hangup .. Yes
│    O - Number of tries ..... 10      R - Modem has DCD line .. Yes
│
│    Change which setting?        (Return or Esc to exit)
└──────────────────────────────────────────────────────────────────────
```

Figure 15-7: Setting up modem and dialing parameters in Minicom

You also need to do the following before any user can run `minicom`:

■ Edit the text file `/etc/minicom.users` and add a line with the word ALL to enable all users to access the `minicom` configuration file.

■ Enable any user to read from and write to the serial port where the modem is connected. For example, if the modem is on COM1 (`/dev/ttyS0`), type `chmod o+w /dev/ttyS0` to give everyone write permission for that device.

■ Establish a link between the `/dev/modem` and the serial port device where the modem is connected. If the modem is on `/dev/ttyS0`, you should type the following command:

`ln -s /dev/ttyS0 /dev/modem`

After that, you can run `minicom` as an ordinary user. When `minicom` first runs, it resets the modem. Figure 15-8 shows the result of running `minicom` in an `xterm` window.

The `minicom` program is somewhat like another shareware communications program named Telix. As in that program, you can press Ctrl-A to get the attention of the `minicom` program. After you press Ctrl-A, if you press **Z**, a help screen appears in the form of a text window, as shown in Figure 15-9.

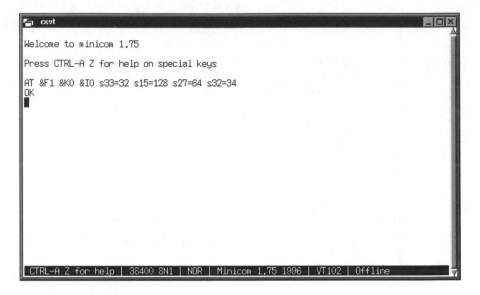

Figure 15-8: The initial minicom screen

Figure 15-9: The minicom help screen

Tip

In the help screen, you can get information about other minicom commands. From the help screen, press Enter to go back to online mode. In online mode, you can use the modem's AT commands to dial out. In particular, you can use the ATDT command to dial the phone number of another modem (for example, your Internet service provider's computer or a system at your work), as shown in Figure 15-10. Once you get the login prompt, you can log in as usual and use the remote system.

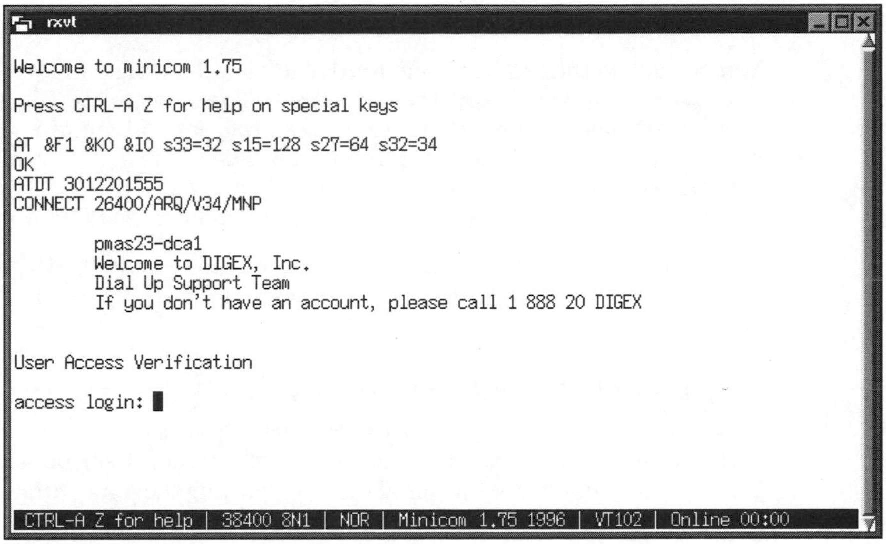

Figure 15-10: Dialing a remote system using minicom

When you log out of the other system and want to exit `minicom`, press Ctrl-A and then type *X* to exit the program. Press Enter again in response to the `minicom` prompt, as shown in Figure 15-11.

Figure 15-11: This minicom prompt appears when you press Ctrl-A and then type *X* to quit minicom.

Setting up Linux for dial-in

You can set up the same modem for dial-in as well as dial-out use (only one operation is allowed at any time, of course). The steps for setting up a modem for dial-in use involve setting up a program that monitors the serial port for any incoming calls; this program provides the login prompt. The generic name for these programs is getty. You can use the uugetty program that comes with the Linux distribution on this book's CD-ROM.

The next few sections explain how to set up a modem on COM1 for dial-in use. The Linux device name for that modem (when configured for incoming calls) is /dev/ttyS0.

Editing /etc/rc.d/rc.serial

When Linux starts, the init process executes the /etc/rc.d/rc.sysinit script, which, in turn, executes the /etc/rc.d/rc.serial script, if it exists. Thus, you can configure the serial ports by putting the appropriate commands in the /etc/rc.d/rc.serial file (simply create the /etc/rc.d/rc.serial file, if it does not exist).

If you have a high-speed modem, such as a 56K modem, you should put a command in the rc.serial file to run the setserial program and set the spd_vhi flag for the serial port. Setting the spd_vhi flag allows your PC to communicate with the modem at a much higher speed than the modem might be using to connect with a remote system. Put the following line in the rc.serial file:

```
/bin/setserial /dev/ttyS0 spd_vhi
```

Secret

If your modem supports hardware that uses the RTS (Request to Send) and CTS (Clear to Send) signals, you should make use of them. Enable hardware handshaking for the modem with the stty command by placing the following command in the rc.serial file:

```
/bin/stty crtscts < /dev/ttyS0
```

Updating the uugetty configuration file

The uugetty program checks the /etc/gettydefs file for information on the speed and settings of a serial port (often referred to as a line). The entries in /etc/gettydefs also tell uugetty what login prompt it should display.

Wizard

The existing /etc/gettydefs file should work as is. You may, however, want to edit the login prompt. I use the following setting for a modem:

```
# 38400 fixed-baud modem entry
F38400# B38400 CS8 CRTSCTS # B38400 SANE -ISTRIP HUPCL CRTSCTS #@S
login: #F38400
```

The /etc/gettydefs file has many more settings, but I use only this one. The label F38400 at the beginning of the line is what I specify when I run uugetty on the /dev/ttyS0 line.

The CRTSCTS flag indicates the modem uses hardware flow control with the RTS/CTS signals (which I enabled with the stty command in /etc/rc.d/rc.serial file).

This entry already existed in the /etc/gettydefs file. The items near the end of the last line are for the login prompt. You can use the codes listed in Table 15-5 to display specific information in the login prompt.

Table 15-5   Some useful /etc/gettydefs codes

Code	Meaning
@B	The current data-transfer rate, in bits per second.
@D	The current date, in MM/DD/YY format.
@L	The serial line to which uugetty is attached (such as ttyS0).
@S	The name of the system (as shown by the uname -n command).
@T	The current time, in HH:MM:SS (24-hour) format.
@U	The number of currently logged-on users.
@V	The value of VERSION specified in the uugetty configuration file (/etc/conf. uugetty.ttyS0 for uugetty running on the ttyS0 line).

To display a single @ character in the login prompt, use either \@ or @@. You can put other special characters in the login prompt by using the backslash escape. Table 15-6 lists some of the recognized escape characters. With these features, you can customize the login prompt to suit your needs.

Table 15-6   Escape characters in /etc/gettydefs

Character	Meaning
\\	A single backslash
\b	Backspace character (Ctrl-H)
\c	Stops newline at the end of a string
\f	Form feed (Ctrl-L)
\n	Newline character (Ctrl-J)
\r	Carriage return (Ctrl-M)
\s	Single space
\t	Single tab (Ctrl-I)
\nnn	ASCII character whose decimal value is nnn (if the number begins with 0, the value is assumed to be octal; if it begins with 0x, it's considered to be hexadecimal)

Preparing the uugetty configuration file

The uugetty program has many parameters you can tweak. In fact, you can specify separate options for uugetty on a per-line basis. These per-line configuration files are in the /etc directory. The name of each configuration file has the form uugetty.*line*, in which *line* is the device name for the line (without the /dev part). Thus, /etc/conf.uugetty.ttyS0 is the configuration file for the copy of uugetty that runs on the /dev/ttyS0 line.

Here's a typical /etc/default/uugetty.ttyS0 file on one of my Linux PCs:

```
# Line to initialize (line name should not include /dev)
INITLINE=cua0
# Alternate lock file to check (if this lock file exists,
# then uugetty is restarted so that the modem is re-initialized
ALTLOCK=cua0

# Timeout to disconnect if idle...
TIMEOUT=60

# Modem initialization string. Sets the modem not to auto-answer.
# When a call comes, uugetty will issue an ATA command to make
# the modem go online
# Format of these entries:
#   <expect> <send> ... (chat sequence)
INIT="" \d+++\dAT\r OK\r\n ATH0\r OK\r\n
AT\sM0\sE1\sQ0\sV1\sX4\sS0=0\s&C1\s&S0\r OK\r\n

# Waitfor string. If this sequence of characters is received
# over the line, a call is detected.
WAITFOR=RING

# The following line is the connect chat sequence. This chat sequence
is performed
# after the WAITFOR string is found. The \A character automatically
sets
# the baud rate to the characters that are found, so if you get the
message
# CONNECT 26400, the baud rate is set to 26400 baud.
#
# format: <expect> <send> ... (chat sequence)
CONNECT="" ATA\r CONNECT\s\A

# The next line sets the time to delay before sending the login banner
DELAY=1
```

The entries in this file control the way that uugetty initializes the modem, waits for a call, and answers with a login prompt.

The uugetty process uses the INIT string to initialize the modem. In this case, the initialization sequence issues the following modem commands:

Command	Purpose
ATM0	Turns speaker off
ATE1	Turns command echo on
ATQ0	Turns quiet mode off (so that the modem reports status)
ATV1	Turns verbose mode on
ATX4	Makes the modem report detailed result codes
ATS0=0	Turns auto-answer off (uugetty puts the modem online at the right moment with an ATA command)
AT&C1	Allows the modem to control the carrier-detect (CD) line (that line is turned on only after connect)
AT&S0	Turns the DSR (Data Set Ready) signal on and leaves it on

The uugetty process waits for the WAITFOR string before using the CONNECT string to initiate the connection. When the modem receives a call, it reports RING as the status. When uugetty receives the RING string, it issues the CONNECT string to the modem. The CONNECT string contains the command ATA, which puts the modem online.

After that, uugetty displays the contents of the file /etc/issue, followed by the login prompt. Then uugetty runs the /bin/login program to take care of the actual login.

Starting uugetty in /etc/inittab

To ensure uugetty runs when Linux starts, you have to put a line in the /etc/inittab file so the init process starts uugetty automatically. Following is what I put in the /etc/inittab file to start a copy of uugetty on the /dev/ttyS0 line (for the modem on COM1):

```
# Serial line with dial-in modem
s0:235:respawn:/sbin/uugetty ttyS0 F38400 vt100
```

Cross-Reference

This command ensures uugetty runs in run levels 2, 3, and 5. (Refer to Chapter 5 for a discussion of run levels and /etc/inittab.)

The arguments to uugetty have the following meaning:

- ttyS0 specifies the line uugetty monitors (ttyS0 means /dev/ttyS0)
- F38400 specifies the line speed (F38400 must appear in the /etc/gettydefs file)
- vt100 specifies the terminal type (the terminal type must be an entry from the /etc/termcap file)

Testing the dial-in setup

After you complete all the setup steps for uugetty and the modem, you must make sure the init process reexamines the /etc/inittab file and starts uugetty as specified in that file. To do this, log in as root and type the following command:

```
init q
```

After this command, you can test the dial-in modem. You may want to have a friend call your system and see whether login works. If you are lucky enough to have two phone lines (and more than one computer at home), you can dial out on one line and log in to the Linux system set up on the other line. On my system, here's what I get as login prompt on a PC when I dial into my Linux system:

```
Red Hat Linux release 5.0 (Hurricane)
Kernel 2.0.31 on an i586

lnbsoft login:
```

The /etc/gettydefs file on my system specifies the login prompt as follows:

```
@S login:
```

This line says the prompt should include the system name (@S) followed by the string login:, which is what I see when I call into my system.

Now your Linux system should be all set to enable users to log in through the dial-in modem.

Terminals and Multiport Serial Boards

The previous sections showed you in detail how to set up and use a modem in Linux for dialing out and letting other people dial in. The rest of this chapter briefly describes the steps involved in setting up terminals connected to the PC's serial port. You also find a list of multiport serial boards Linux supports.

Note, you might want to use other MS-DOS PCs (especially older 286 and 386 PCs) as terminals connected to your Linux system. All you need on the PC is a serial communications package such as Procomm Plus or Telix.

Setting up a terminal on a serial port

To set up a terminal on a serial port, you have to set up a getty process, just as you do when you set up a dial-in modem. Follow these steps:

1. Make sure you used the correct serial cable to connect the terminal to the serial port. Most terminals need a null modem cable in which the TD (transmit data) and RD (receive data) signal lines are reversed in going from one end of the cable to the other. (See earlier sections of this chapter for further discussions of serial cables.)

2. Set up the terminal's communication parameters. The exact steps depend on the terminal type.

3. Edit /etc/gettydefs, and add a line for the terminal. If the terminal operates at 9,600 bps, specify a line such as the following (the line that begins with a # is a comment):

```
# 9600 bps connection to a terminal
T9600# B9600 CS8 CLOCAL # B9600 SANE -ISTRIP CLOCAL #@S login:
#T9600
```

The most important part is the CLOCAL flag, which tells the getty process to ignore modem-control signals.

4. Edit the /etc/inittab file and add a line to start a getty process on the line connected to the terminal. If you have a VT100-compatible terminal on the line ttyS1 (COM2), you might add the following line to your system's /etc/inittab:

```
s2:235:respawn:/sbin/getty ttyS1 T9600 vt100
```

5. Log in as root and force the init process to reexamine the /etc/inittab file, as follows:

```
init q
```

6. A login prompt should appear on the terminal and you should be able to log in.

Setting up Multiport serial boards in Linux

If you plan to support a small business with a Linux PC and dumb terminals (terminals are cheaper than complete PCs, although you also could use old PCs as terminals), you want more than two serial ports. With another serial board, the PC can support four serial ports. If you want more than four serial ports, you have to buy special serial I/O boards known as *multiport serial boards*. These boards typically support anywhere from 4 to 32 serial ports. The serial ports share one IRQ, but each port has a unique I/O address.

Tip

Many multiport serial boards use the 16450 or 16550A UARTs. When you buy a board, you may want to make sure the UART is 16550A-compatible.

To add support for a specific multiport serial board, you have to uncomment appropriate lines in the /etc/rc.d/rc.serial file. Linux supports the following 16450 or 16550A UART-based multiport serial boards:

- AST FourPort and clones (4 ports)
- Accent Async-4 (4 ports)
- Arnet Multiport-8 (8 ports)
- Bell Technologies HUB6 (6 ports)
- Boca BB-1004 (4 ports), BB-1008 (8 ports), BB-2016 (16 ports)
- Boca IOAT66 (6 ports)
- Boca 2by4 (4 serial and 2 parallel ports)

- Computone ValuePort V4-ISA (AST FourPort-compatible)
- Digi PC/8 (8 ports)
- GTEK BBS-550 (8 ports)
- Longshine LCS-8880, Longshine LCS-8880+ (AST FourPort-compatible)
- Moxa C104, Moxa C104+ (AST FourPort-compatible)
- PC-COMM (4 ports)
- Sealevel Systems COMM-2 (2 ports), COMM-4 (4 ports), and COMM-8 (8 ports)
- SIIG I/O Expander 2S IO1812 (4 ports)
- STB-4COM (4 ports)
- Twincom ACI/550
- Usenet Serial Board II (4 ports)

Notice the Boca BB-1004 and BB-1008 boards do not support the Carrier Detect (CD) and Ring Indicator (RI) signals necessary to make dial-in modems work. Thus, you cannot use the BB-1004 and BB-1008 boards with dial-in modems.

Some multiport serial boards use special processors instead of the 16450 or 16550A UART. These intelligent multiport serial boards require special drivers. Table 15-7 lists a few multiport serial boards and the locations of the drivers for Linux.

Table 15-7   Driver locations in Linux for multiport serial boards

Name	*Ports*	*Driver Location*
Comtrol RocketPort	4, 8, 16, 32	`ftp://tsx-11.mit.edu/pub/linux/packages/comtrol`
Cyclades Cyclom-Y	8–32	Included in Linux kernel (turn on `CONFIG_CYCLADES` when configuring kernel)
Decision PCCOM8	8	`ftp://ftp.signum.se/pub/pccom8`
DigiBoard PC/Xx	2–64	Included in Linux kernel (turn on `CONFIG_DIGI` when configuring kernel)
Equinox SuperSerial	2–128	`ftp://ftp.equinox.com/library/sst`
GTEK Cyclone	6, 16, 32	`ftp://ftp.gtek.com/pub`
Hayes ESP	8	`http://www.nyx.net/~arobinso`
Maxpeed SS	4, 8, 16	`ftp://maxpeed.com/pub/ss`
Moxa C218, C320	8–32	`ftp://ftp.moxa.com.tw/drivers/c218-320/linux`

Name	Ports	Driver Location
SDL RISCom/8	8	Included in Linux kernel (turn on CONFIG_RISCOM8 when configuring kernel)
Specialix SIO	4–32	ftp://sunsite.unc.edu/pub/Linux/kernel/patches/serial
Stallion	4–64	Included in Linux kernel (turn on CONFIG_STALDRV when configuring kernel)

Tip

To learn more about setting up a multiport serial board, you may want to read the latest Serial-HOWTO document. To read the HOWTO documents, type cd /usr/doc/HOWTO to change to the directory where the HOWTO files are located. Then type zmore Serial-HOWTO.gz to view the Serial-HOWTO file.

Summary

Modems provide a convenient way to dial out and connect to other systems. You also can set up a modem to allow other people to dial into your Linux system. This chapter describes the use of modems in Linux.

By reading this chapter, you learn the following things:

▶ In Linux, the serial ports have two types of associated device files depending on whether you use the serial ports as outgoing or incoming devices. When you access the serial port to dial out with a modem, the device names are /dev/cua0 and /dev/cua1 for COM1 and COM2, respectively. On the other hand, COM1 and COM2 go by the device names /dev/ttyS0 and /dev/ttyS1 when they are used as incoming devices. Although older versions of Linux distinguished between incoming and outgoing device names, you can currently use the /dev/ttyS* devices names for both dial in and dial out.

▶ The Universal Asynchronous Receiver Transmitter (UART) is at the heart of serial communications. The UART converts outgoing bytes into individual bits the modem can convert to analog form and send over telephone lines; it also packs incoming bits into bytes. For high-speed communications, you need a National Semiconductor 16550A or compatible UART. These UARTs have 16-byte receive and transmit buffers to allow reliable data transmission in multitasking operating systems such as Linux — operating systems that may not be capable of monitoring the serial ports constantly.

▶ Serial communications involves several parameters, including baud rate (or bit rate), word length, parity, and number of stop bits. *Baud rate* actually refers to the number of times the state of the transmission line changes each second, but it is commonly used to refer to the data-transmission rate (in bits per second or bps).

▶ The RS-232C standard specifies how serial communication takes place between two devices. RS-232C refers to the modem as Data Communications Equipment (DCE), whereas the PC is called Data Terminal Equipment (DTE). The RS-232C standard also defines the pins of a serial cable.

▶ Several standards define the way modems transmit signals over telephone lines. The International Telecommunications Union (ITU) has ratified several modem standards, including V.34 for 28,800 bps, and V.90 for 56,600 bps (or 56K) operation. You need two compatible modems at two ends of a line to establish a communications path.

▶ All modern modems understand a set of commands that start with the letters AT. This AT command set was developed by Hayes Microcomputer Products, Inc. You can set up a modem and dial out by using the AT commands.

▶ To dial out from Linux, you need a communications program. The companion CD-ROM includes the minicom communications program.

▶ To allow other people to dial into your Linux system through a modem, you have to run uugetty (or some other getty process) on the serial line with the modem. You also must set up some parameters in the /etc/gettydefs file. You typically start uugetty in the /etc/inittab file.

▶ You can connect a terminal to the serial port as long as you use an appropriate cable. Linux also supports several types of multiport serial I/O boards that enable you to connect several terminals or modems to your Linux PC.

Chapter 16

Networks

In This Chapter

▶ Understanding the OSI seven-layer network model

▶ Understanding network protocols and TCP/IP

▶ Understanding network and host addresses in the Internet Protocol (IP)

▶ Getting familiar with Internet services

▶ Using Ethernet with Linux

▶ Setting up TCP/IP networking in Linux

▶ Using TCP/IP diagnostic commands in Linux

UNIX and networking go hand in hand. In particular, TCP/IP (Transmission Control Protocol/Internet Protocol) networking is practically synonymous with UNIX. As a UNIX clone, Linux includes extensive built-in networking capabilities. In particular, Linux supports TCP/IP networking over several physical interfaces, such as Ethernet cards, serial ports, and parallel ports.

You typically would use an Ethernet network for your local area network (LAN) — at your office or even your home (if you happen to have several systems at home). TCP/IP networking over the serial port allows you to connect to other networks by dialing out over a modem. Linux supports both Serial Line Internet Protocol (SLIP) and Point-to-Point Protocol (PPP).

Cross-Reference

This chapter focuses on Linux's support for Ethernet and TCP/IP. Although much of this applies to TCP/IP over the serial line, this chapter does not dwell on specific details of dial-up networking; that topic is the focus of Chapter 18.

The chapter starts with a discussion of networking in general and TCP/IP in particular; it then covers the physical setup of an Ethernet LAN, including information on specific brands of Ethernet cards. Finally, the chapter examines how to set up a TCP/IP network on a Linux system.

Cross-Reference

Laptops often use PC cards for networking. Chapter 17 describes the PC cards that Linux supports.

Networking Basics

Like any other technical subject, networking is full of terminology and jargon that a newcomer might find daunting. This section introduces some basic concepts of networking, starting with a layered model of networking and proceeding to details of Ethernet and TCP/IP network protocols.

The OSI seven-layer model

A widely used conceptual model of networking is the seven-layer Open Systems Interconnection (OSI) reference model, developed by the International Standards Organization (ISO). The OSI reference model describes the flow of data between the physical connection to the network and the end-user application. Each layer is responsible for providing particular functionality, as shown in Figure 16-1.

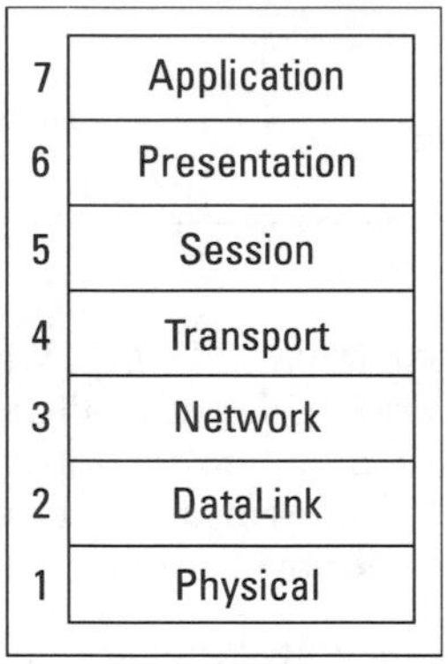

7	Application
6	Presentation
5	Session
4	Transport
3	Network
2	DataLink
1	Physical

Figure 16-1: OSI seven-layer reference model of networking

As Figure 16-1 shows, the OSI layers are numbered from bottom to top. Basic functions, such as physically sending data bits through the network cable, are at the bottom, and functions that deal with higher-level abstractions of the data are at the top. The purpose of each layer is to provide services to the next-higher layer in a manner such that the higher layer does not have to know how the services are actually implemented.

The purposes of the seven layers in the OSI reference model are as follows:

- The *physical layer* (Layer 1) transmits raw bits of data across the physical medium (the networking cable or electromagnetic waves, in the case of wireless networks). This layer carries the data generated by all the higher layers. The physical layer deals with three physical components:

- The network topology (such as bus or star), which specifies how various nodes of a network are physically connected

- The transmission medium (such as RG-58 coaxial cable, shielded or unshielded twisted pair, fiber-optic cable, and microwave) that carries the actual signals representing data

- The transmission technique (such as Carrier Sense Multiple Access with Collision Detection [CSMA/CD], used by Ethernet; and token-based techniques, used by token-ring and Fiber Distributed Data Interface [FDDI]), which defines the hardware protocols for data transfer

- The *data-link layer* (Layer 2) deals with logical packets (or *frames*) of data. This layer packages raw bits from the physical layer into frames, the exact format of which depends on the type of network, such as Ethernet or Token Ring. The frames used by the data-link layer contain the physical addresses of the sender and the receiver of data.

- The *network layer* (Layer 3) knows about the logical network addresses and how to translate logical addresses to physical ones. At the sending end, the network layer converts larger logical packets to smaller physical data frames. At the receiving end, the network layer reassembles the data frames into their original logical packet structure.

- The *transport layer* (Layer 4) is responsible for the reliable delivery of messages that originate at the application layer. At the sending end, this layer divides long messages into several packets. At the receiving end, the transport layer reassembles the original messages and sends an acknowledgment of receipt. The transport layer also checks to make sure that data is received in the correct order and in a timely manner. In case of errors, the transport layer requests retransmission of data.

- The *session layer* (Layer 5) allows applications on different computers to initiate, use, and terminate a connection (the connection is called a *session*). The session layer translates the names of systems to appropriate addresses (for example, IP addresses in TCP/IP networks).

- The *presentation layer* (Layer 6) manages the format used to exchange data between networked computers. Data encryption and decryption, for example, would be in this layer. Most network protocols do not have a presentation layer.

- The *application layer* (Layer 7) is the gateway through which application processes access network services. This layer represents services (such as file transfers, database access, and electronic mail) that directly support applications.

The OSI model is not specific to any hardware or software; it simply provides an architectural framework and gives us a common terminology for discussing various networking capabilities.

A simplified four-layer TCP/IP network model

The OSI seven-layer model is not a specification; it provides guidelines for organizing all network services. Most implementations adopt a layered model for networking services, and these layered models can be mapped to the OSI reference model. The TCP/IP networking model, for example, can be adequately represented by a simplified model.

Network-aware applications usually deal with the top three layers (session, presentation, and application) of the OSI seven-layer reference model. Thus, these three layers can be combined into a single layer called the *application layer*.

The bottom two layers of the OSI model — physical and data-link — also can be combined into a single physical layer. These combinations result in a simplified four-layer model, as shown in Figure 16-2.

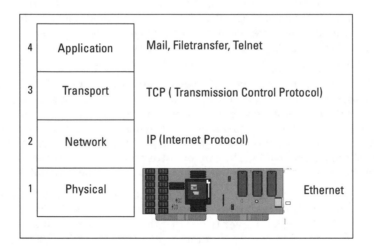

Figure 16-2: Simplified four-layer networking model

At each of these layers, information is exchanged through one of many network protocols.

Network protocols

A *network protocol* refers to a detailed process agreed upon by the sender and receiver for exchanging data at a specific layer of the networking model. Thus, you would find the following protocols in the simplified four-layer network model of Figure 16-2:

■ Physical-layer protocols, such as Ethernet, Token Ring, and FDDI.

- Network-layer protocols, such as the Internet Protocol (IP), which is part of the TCP/IP protocol suite.

- Transport-layer protocols, such as the Transmission Control Protocol (TCP) and User Datagram Protocol (UDP), that are part of the TCP/IP protocol suite.

- Application-layer protocols — such as File Transfer Protocol (FTP), Simple Mail Transfer Protocol (SMTP), Domain Name Service (DNS), Telnet, Hyper Text Transfer Protocol (HTTP), and Simple Network Management Protocol (SNMP) — that are also part of the TCP/IP protocol suite.

The term *protocol suite* refers to a collection of two or more protocols from these layers that form the basis of a network. Following are some of the well-known protocol suites:

- IPX/SPX (Internet Packet Exchange/Sequenced Packet Exchange) protocol suite, used by Novell NetWare

- NetBIOS and NetBEUI (Network BIOS Extended User Interface, used by Microsoft's operating systems)

- TCP/IP protocol suite

Note

Of these protocol suites, you would be most interested in the TCP/IP protocol suite, because that's what Linux and other UNIX systems support well.

Cross-Reference

In addition to the TCP/IP protocol, Linux also supports the IPX protocol, but not the SPX protocol necessary for NetWare. Linux's support for NetBIOS comes in the form of a software package named *Samba,* which is included in the companion CD-ROM and described in the "LAN Manager server" section of Chapter 21.

More on TCP/IP

This chapter gives you an overview of TCP/IP and Ethernet networking and then moves on to Linux-specific instructions for setting up TCP/IP networking. A single chapter simply isn't enough to provide all available information about TCP/IP. For more information on TCP/IP, consult one of the following books:

- Craig Zacker, *TCP/IP Administration,* IDG Books Worldwide, 1998

- *TCP/IP For Dummies, Second Edition,* IDG Books Worldwide, 1997

- Douglas E. Comer, *Internetworking with TCP/IP, Volume 1, Third Edition,* Prentice-Hall, 1995

- W. Richard Stevens, *UNIX Network Programming, Second Edition*, Prentice-Hall, 1998

TCP/IP and the Internet

TCP/IP has become the protocol of choice on the Internet — the "network of networks" that evolved from ARPAnet, a packet-switching network that itself evolved from research initiated by the U.S. Government's Advanced Research Projects Agency (ARPA) in the 1970s. Subsequently, ARPA acquired a *Defense* prefix and became DARPA. Under the auspices of DARPA, the TCP/IP protocols emerged as a popular collection of protocols for *internetworking* — a term used to describe communication among networks.

Note

TCP/IP has flourished for several reasons. One significant reason is that the protocol is an open protocol, which simply means that technical descriptions of the protocol appear in public documents, so anyone can build a TCP/IP on his or her hardware and software.

Another, more important reason for TCP/IP's success is the availability of sample implementation. Instead of describing network architecture and protocols on paper, each component of the TCP/IP protocol suite began life as a specification with a sample implementation.

RFCs

The details of each TCP/IP protocol are described in documents known as Request for Comments (RFCs). These documents are freely distributed on the Internet. You can get the RFCs from `http://www.cis.ohio-state.edu/hypertext/information/rfc.html` or `ftp://venera.isi.edu/in-notes/`.

In fact, this notation of naming Internet resources in a uniform manner is itself documented in an RFC. The notation, known as the Uniform Resource Locator (URL), is described in RFC 1630, "Universal Resource Identifiers in WWW," written by T. Berners-Lee, the originator of the World Wide Web (WWW).

You can think of RFCs as being the working papers of the Internet research-and-development community. All Internet standards are published as RFCs. Many RFCs do not specify any standards, however; they are informational documents only.

Important RFCs

Following are some of the RFCs that you may find interesting:

- RFC 768, "User Datagram Protocol (UDP)"

- RFC 791, "Internet Protocol (IP)"

- RFC 792, "Internet Control Message Protocol (ICMP)"

- RFC 793, "Transmission Control Protocol (TCP)"

- RFC 821, "Simple Mail Transfer Protocol (SMTP)"

- RFC 822, "Format for Electronic Mail Messages"

- RFC 950, "IP Subnet Extension"
- RFC 959, "File Transfer Protocol (FTP)"
- RFC 1034, "Domain Names: Concepts and Facilities"
- RFC 1058, "Routing Information Protocol (RIP)"
- RFC 1112, "Internet Group Multicast Protocol (IGMP)"
- RFC 1155, "Structure of Management Information (SMI)"
- RFC 1157, "Simple Network Management Protocol (SNMP)"
- RFC 1310, "The Internet Standards Process"
- RFC 1519, "Classless Inter-Domain Routing (CIDR) Assignment and Aggregation Strategy"
- RFC 1521, "Multipurpose Internet Mail Extensions (MIME)"
- RFC 1583, "Open Shortest Path First Routing V2 (OSPF2)"
- RFC 1625, "WAIS over Z39.50-1988"
- RFC 1661, "Point-to-Point Protocol (PPP)"
- RFC 1725, "Post Office Protocol, Version 3 (POP3)"

- RFC 1738, "Uniform Resource Locators (URL)"
- RFC 1739, "A Primer on Internet and TCP/IP Tools"
- RFC 1796, "Not All RFCs are Standards"
- RFC 1855, "Netiquette Guidelines"
- RFC 1866, "Hypertext Markup Language - 2.0"
- RFC 1883, "Internet Protocol, Version 6 (IPv6) Specification"
- RFC 1884, "IP Version 6 Addressing Architecture"
- RFC 1886, "DNS Extensions to support IP version 6"
- RFC 1918, "Address Allocation for Private Internets"
- RFC 2028, "The Organizations Involved in the IETF Standards Process"
- RFC 2060, "Internet Message Access Protocol - Version 4rev1 (IMAP4)"
- RFC 2200, "Internet Official Protocol Standards"
- RFC 2305, "A Simple Mode of Facsimile Using Internet Mail"

Tip The RFCs continue to evolve as new technology and techniques emerge. If you work in the networking area, you should keep an eye on the RFCs to monitor emerging networking protocols.

IP addresses

When you have many computers on a network, you need a way to identify each one uniquely. In TCP/IP networking, the address of a computer is known as the *IP address*. Because TCP/IP deals with internetworking, the address is based on the concept of a network address and a host address, which together uniquely identify a computer:

- The *network address* indicates the network on which the computer is located
- The *host address* indicates the computer on that network

Dotted-decimal addresses

The original IP address is a 4-byte (32-bit) value. The convention is to write each byte as a decimal value and to put a dot (.) after each number. Thus, you see network addresses such as 140.90.23.100. This way of writing IP addresses is known as *dotted-decimal* notation.

Address classes

The bits in an IP address are interpreted in the following manner:

```
<Network Address, Host Address>
```

In other words, a specified number of bits of the 32-bit IP address is considered to be a network address; the rest of the bits are interpreted as being a host address. The host address identifies your PC, whereas the network address identifies the LAN to which your PC is connected.

To accommodate networks of various sizes (the network size is the number of computers in that network), the IP address includes the concept of several classes of network. There are five classes of IP addresses, named class A through class E, as shown in Figure 16-3.

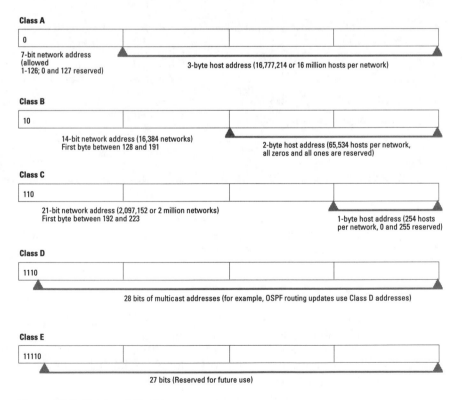

Figure 16-3: Classes of IP addresses

Of the five address classes, only classes A, B, and C are used for addressing networks and hosts; class D and E addresses are reserved for special use.

Class A addresses support 126 networks, each with up to 16 million hosts. Although the network address is 7-bit, two values (0 and 127) have special meaning; therefore, you can have only 1 through 126 as class A network addresses.

Class B addresses are for networks with up to 65,534 hosts. There can be, at most, 16,384 class B networks.

Class C addresses are for small organizations. Each class C address allows up to 254 hosts, and there can be about 2 million class C networks. If you are in a small company, you probably have one of the class C addresses.

You can tell the class of an IP address by the first number in the dotted-decimal notation, as follows:

- Class A addresses: 1.xxx.xxx.xxx through 126.xxx.xxx.xxx

- Class B addresses: 128.xxx.xxx.xxx through 191.xxx.xxx.xxx

- Class C addresses: 192.xxx.xxx.xxx through 223.xxx.xxx.xxx

Even within the five address classes, the following IP addresses have special meaning:

- An address with all zeros in the network portion of the address indicates the local network—the network where the message with this IP address originated. Thus, the address 0.0.0.200 means host number 200 on this class C network.

- The class A address 127.xxx.xxx.xxx is used for *loopback*—communications within the same host. Conventionally, 127.0.0.1 is used as the loopback address. Processes that need to communicate through TCP with other processes on the same host use the loopback address to avoid having to send packets out on the network.

- Turning on all the bits in any part of the address indicates a broadcast message. The address 128.18.255.255, for example, means all hosts on the class B network 128.18. The address 255.255.255.255 is known as a limited broadcast; all workstations on the current network will receive the packet.

IP addresses for your network

If you are setting up an independent network of your own that will be connected to the Internet, you need unique IP addresses for your network. IP addresses are administered through the Internet Network Information Center (InterNIC). For a fee, you can get a domain name (a descriptive name for your network such as mycompany.com) and a range of IP addresses for your network. To learn more about InterNIC and how to obtain a domain name, point your Web browser to http://rs.internic.net/.

If you get your Internet access through an Internet Service Provider (ISP), you need not worry about getting IP addresses for your systems; your ISP will provide the necessary IP addresses.

If you do not plan to connect your network to the Internet, you really do not need any unique IP addresses. RFC 1918 ("Address Allocation for Private Internets") provides guidance on what IP addresses you can use within private networks (the term *private internet* refers to any network that's not connected to the Internet). Three blocks of IP addresses are reserved for private internets:

- 10.0.0.0 to 10.255.255.255
- 172.16.0.0 to 172.16.255.255
- 192.168.0.0 to 192.168.255.255

You can use addresses from these blocks for your private network without having to coordinate with any organization. For example, I use the 192.168.0.0 class C address for a small private network.

Next-generation IP (IPv6)

At the time when the 4-byte IP address was created, the number of addresses seemed to be adequate. By now, however, class A and class B addresses are running out, and class C addresses are being depleted at a fast rate. In addition, the proliferation of class C addresses has introduced a unique problem. Each class C address needs an entry in the network routing tables — the tables that contain information on how to locate any network in the Internet. Too many class C addresses means too many entries in the routing tables.

The Internet Engineering Task Force (IETF) recognized this problem in 1991, and work began then on the next-generation IP addressing scheme, named IPng, which was to eventually replace the old 4-byte addressing scheme (called IPv4, for IP Version 4).

Several alternative addressing schemes were proposed and debated. The final contender, with a 128-bit (16-byte) address, was dubbed IPv6 (for IP Version 6). On September 18, 1995, the IETF declared the core set of IPv6 addressing protocols to be an IETF Proposed Standard. By now, there are over 50 RFCs dealing with various aspects of IPv6, from IPv6 over PPP to transmission of IPv6 packets over Ethernet.

The IPv6 is designed to be an evolutionary step up from IPv4. The proposed standard provides direct interoperability between hosts using the older IPv4 addresses and any new IPv6 hosts. The idea is that users can upgrade their systems to use IPv6 when they want and that network operators are free to upgrade their network hardware to use IPv6 without affecting current users of IPv4. Sample implementations of IPv6 are being developed for many operating systems, including Linux. For more information about IPv6 in Linux, consult the Linux IPv6 Frequently Asked Questions (FAQ) at http://www.terra.net/ipv6/.

A 128-bit addressing scheme allows for 170,141,183,460,469,232,000,000,000,000,000,000,000 unique hosts! That should last us for a while.

Network mask

The *network mask* is an IP address that has 1s in the bits that correspond to the network address, and 0s in all other bit positions. The class of your network address determines the network mask.

If you have a class C address, for example, the network mask is 255.255.255.0. Thus, class B networks have a network mask of 255.255.0.0, and class A networks have 255.0.0.0 as the network mask.

Network address

The *network address* is the bitwise AND of the network mask with any IP address in your network. If the IP address of a system on your network is 206.197.168.200, and the network mask is 255.255.255.0, the network address is 206.197.168.0. As you may have noticed, the network address has a zero in the host-address area. When you request a domain name and an IP address from NIC, you get a network address.

Subnets

If your site has a class B address, you get one network number, and that network can have up to 65,534 hosts. Even if you work for a megacorporation that has thousands of hosts, you may want to divide your network into smaller subnetworks (or *subnets*). If your organization has offices in several locations, for example, you may want each office to be on a separate network. You can do this by taking some bits from the host-address portion of the IP address and assigning those bits to the network address. This procedure is known as defining a subnet mask.

Essentially, you add more bits to the network mask. If you have a class B network, for example, the network mask would be 255.255.0.0. Then, if you decide to divide your network into 128 subnetworks, each of which has 512 hosts, you would designate 7 bits from the host address space as the subnet address. Thus, the subnet mask becomes 255.255.254.0.

TCP/IP routing

Routing refers to the task of forwarding information from one network to another. Consider the two class C networks 206.197.168.0 and 164.109.10.0. You need a routing device to send packets from one of these networks to the other.

Secret

Because a routing device facilitates data exchange between two networks, it has two physical network connections, one on each network. Each network interface has its own IP address, and the routing device essentially passes packets back and forth between the two network interfaces. Figure 16-4 illustrates how a routing device has a physical presence in two networks and how each network interface has its own IP address.

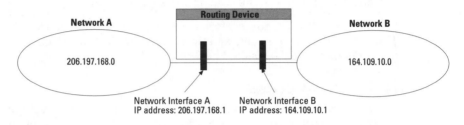

Figure 16-4: A routing device allows packet exchange between two networks

The generic term *routing device* could be a general-purpose computer with two network interfaces, or a dedicated device designed specifically for routing. Such dedicated routing devices are known as *routers*.

The generic term *gateway* also refers to any routing device. For good performance (high packet-transfer rate), you want a dedicated router, whose sole purpose is to route packets of data in a network.

Note

Later, when you learn how to set up a TCP/IP network in Linux, you'll run into the term *gateway*, which refers to a routing device regardless of whether the device is another PC or a router. All you have to specify is the gateway's IP address on your network.

A single routing device, of course, does not connect all the networks in the world; packets get around in the Internet from one gateway to another. Any network connected to another network has a designated gateway. You can even have specific gateways for specific networks. As you'll learn later, a routing table keeps track of the gateway associated with an external network and the type of physical interface (such as Ethernet or Point-to-Point Protocol over serial lines) for that network. A default gateway gets packets that are addressed to any unknown network.

In your local area network, all packets addressed to another network go to your network's default gateway. If that gateway is physically connected to the destination network, the story ends there, because the gateway can physically send the packets to the destination host. If that gateway does not know the destination network, however, it sends the packets to the next default gateway (the gateway for the other network on which your gateway also "lives"). In this way, packets travel from one gateway to the next until they reach the destination network (or you get an error message saying that the destination network is unreachable).

To send packets around the network efficiently, routers exchange information (in the form of routing tables) so that each router can have a "map" of the network in its vicinity. Routers exchange information by using a routing protocol from a family of protocols known as Interior Gateway Protocol (IGP). A commonly used Interior Gateway Protocol is the Routing Information Protocol (RIP).

Wizard

In TCP/IP routing, any time a packet passes through a router, it's considered to have made a *hop*. In RIP, the maximum size of the Internet is 15 hops. A network is considered to be unreachable from your network if a packet does not reach the destination network within 15 hops. In other words, any network more than 15 routers away is considered to be unreachable.

Within a single network, you don't need a router as long as you do not use any subnet mask to break the single IP network into several subnets. In that case, however, you'll have to set up routers to send packets from one subnet to another.

Domain Name System

You can access any host computer in a TCP/IP network with an IP address. Remembering the IP addresses of even a few hosts of interest, however, is tedious. This fact was recognized from the beginning of TCP/IP, and the association between a host name and IP address was used. The concept is similar to that of a phone book, in which you can look up a telephone number by searching for a person's name.

In the beginning, the association between names and IP addresses was maintained in a text file named HOSTS.TXT at the Network Information Center (NIC), which was located in the Stanford Research Institute (SRI). This file contained the names and corresponding IP addresses of networks, hosts, and routers on the Internet. All hosts on the Internet used to transfer that file by FTP, or File Transfer Protocol. (Can you imagine all hosts getting a file from a single source in today's Internet?) As the number of Internet hosts increased, the single file idea became intractable. The hosts file was becoming difficult to maintain, and it was hard for all the hosts to update their hosts file in a timely manner. To alleviate the problem, RFCs 881, 882, and 883 introduced the concept and plans for Domain Name in November 1983. Eventually, this led to the Domain Name System (DNS) as we know it today (documented in RFCs 1032, 1033, 1034, and 1035).

Domain-name hierarchy

DNS provides a hierarchical naming system much like your postal address, which you can read as "your name" at "your street address" in "your city" in "your state" in "your country." If I know your full postal address, I would locate you by starting with your city in your country. Then I'd locate the street address to find your home, ring the doorbell, and ask for you by name.

Note

DNS essentially provides an addressing scheme for an Internet host that is much like the postal address. The entire Internet is subdivided into several domains, such as gov, edu, com, mil, and net. Each domain is further subdivided into subdomains. Finally, within a subdomain, each host is given a symbolic name. To write a host's *fully qualified domain name (FQDN)*, you string together the host name, subdomain names, and domain name with dots (.) as separators. Following is the full domain name of a host named ADDLAB in the subdomain NWS within another subdomain NOAA in the GOV domain: ADDLAB.NWS.NOAA.GOV. Note that domain names are not case-sensitive.

Figure 16-5 illustrates part of the Internet Domain Name System, showing the location of the host ADDLAB.NWS.NOAA.GOV.

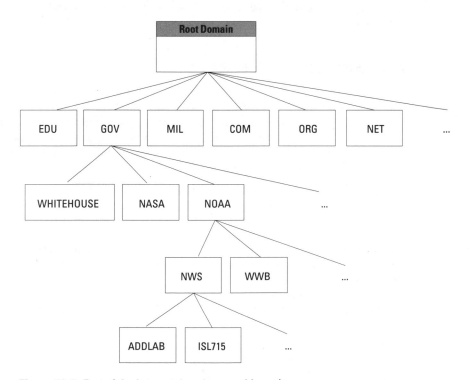

Figure 16-5: Part of the Internet domain-name hierarchy

For a commercial system in the COM domain, the name of a host might be as simple as METROLINK.COM.

Tip

You can refer to a user on a system by appending an at sign (@), followed by the host's domain name, to the user name (the name under which the user logs in). Thus, you would refer to the user named sales at the host metrolink.com as `sales@METROLINK.COM` (unlike host names, user names are case-sensitive).

That's how you refer to users when you send electronic mail.

Name servers

TCP/IP network applications resolve a host name to an IP address by consulting a *name server*, which is another host that's accessible from your network. If you decide to use the Domain Name System (DNS) on your network, you have to set up a name server in your network or indicate a name server (by an IP address).

Later sections of this chapter discuss the configuration files `/etc/host.conf` and `/etc/resolv.conf`, through which you specify how host names would be converted to IP addresses. In particular, you specify the IP addresses of a name server in the `/etc/resolv.conf` file.

If you do not use DNS, you still can have host-name-to-IP-address mapping through a text file named `/etc/hosts`. The entries in a typical `/etc/hosts` file might look like the following example:

```
# This is a comment
127.0.0.1       localhost
206.197.168.2      lnbsun
206.197.168.50     lnb386
206.197.168.100    lnb486
206.197.168.150    lnbmac
206.197.168.200    lnbsoft
```

As the example shows, the file lists a host name for each IP address. The IP address and host names will be different for your system, of course.

Secret

One problem with relying on the `/etc/hosts` file for name lookup is the fact that you have to replicate this file on each system on your network. This procedure can become a nuisance even in a network that has five or six systems.

TCP/IP Services and Client/Server Architecture

By design, a typical Internet service is implemented in two parts — a server that provides information, and one or more clients that request information. Such client/server architecture has been gaining popularity as an approach for implementing distributed information systems. The client/server architecture typically consists of a collection of computers connected by a communications network. The functions of the information system are performed by processes (computer programs) that run on these computers and communicate through the network.

In recent years, the client/server architecture has become commonplace as the mechanism that brings centralized corporate databases to desktop PCs on a network. In a client/server environment, one or more servers manage the centralized database, and clients gain access to the data through the server.

Like a database server, an Internet service such as FTP or a Web browser also provides a service using the client/server model. A user who wants to access information uses a client (for example, a Web browser) to connect to a server and download information (for example, Web pages from a Web server). In this case, the Web server acts as a database manager — the data are the HTML files (Web pages).

Client/server architecture requires clients to communicate with the servers. That's where TCP/IP comes in — TCP/IP provides a standard way for clients and servers to exchange packets of data. The next few sections explain how TCP/IP-based services communicate. From this discussion, you'll learn about the port numbers associated with many well-known Internet services.

TCP/IP and Sockets

Client/server applications such as Web servers and browsers use TCP/IP to communicate. These Internet applications perform TCP/IP communications using the Berkeley Sockets interface (so named because the socket interface was introduced in Berkeley UNIX around 1982). The sockets interface consists of a library of routines that an application developer can use to create applications that can communicate with other applications on the Internet. There is even a Windows Sockets API (Application Programming Interface — a fancy name for the library of functions) that's modeled after the Berkeley Sockets interface. The Winsock interface, as it's known, provides a standard API that Windows programmers can use to write network applications.

Even if you do not write network applications using sockets, you have to use many network applications. A knowledge of sockets can help you understand how network-based applications work, which in turn helps you find and correct any problems with these applications.

Socket definition

Network applications use sockets to communicate over a TCP/IP network. A *socket* is an abstraction that represents a bi-directional end-point of a connection. Because a socket is bi-directional, data can be sent as well as received. A socket has three attributes:

■ The network address (the IP address) of the system

■ The port number identifying the process (a process is a computer program running on a computer) that exchanges data through the socket

- The type of socket (such as stream or datagram) identifying the protocol for data exchange

Essentially, the IP address identifies a network node, the port number identifies a process on the node, and the socket type determines the manner in which data is exchanged — through a connection-oriented or connectionless protocol.

Connection-oriented protocol

The socket type indicates the protocol being used to communicate through the socket. A connection-oriented protocol works like a normal phone conversation. When you want to talk to a friend, you have to first dial your friend's phone number and establish a connection before you can have a conversation. In the same way, connection-oriented data exchange requires both the sending and the receiving processes to establish a connection before data exchange can begin.

Note

In the TCP/IP protocol suite, TCP — Transmission Control Protocol — supports a connection-oriented data transfer between two processes running on two computers on the Internet. TCP provides a reliable two-way data exchange between processes.

As the name TCP/IP suggests (and as the "Network protocols" section indicates), TCP relies on IP — Internet Protocol — for delivery of packets. IP does not guarantee delivery of packets; nor does it deliver packets in any particular sequence. IP does, however, efficiently deliver packets from one network to another. TCP is responsible for arranging the packets in the proper sequence, detecting whether errors occurred, and requesting retransmission of packets in case of any error.

TCP is useful for applications that plan to exchange large amounts of data at a time. Also, applications that need reliable data exchange use TCP. For example, FTP uses TCP to transfer files.

In the sockets model, a socket that uses TCP is referred to as a *stream socket*.

Connectionless protocol

A connectionless data exchange protocol does not require the sender and receiver to explicitly establish a connection. It's like shouting to your friend in a crowded room — you can never be sure if your friend actually heard you.

Note

In the TCP/IP protocol suite, the User Datagram Protocol (UDP) provides connectionless service for sending and receiving packets known as *datagrams*. Unlike TCP, UDP does not guarantee that datagrams ever reached their intended destination. Nor does UDP ensure that datagrams are delivered in the order they were sent.

UDP is used by applications that exchange small amounts of data at a time, or by applications that do not need the reliability and sequencing of data delivery. For example, SNMP (Simple Network Management Protocol) uses UDP to transfer data.

In the sockets model, a socket that uses UDP is referred to as a *datagram socket.*

Sockets and the client/server model

It takes two sockets to complete a communication path. When two processes communicate they use the client/server model to establish the connection. The server application listens on a specific port on the system — the server is completely identified by the IP address of the system on which it runs and the port number it listens to for connections. The client initiates connection from any available port and tries to connect to the server (identified by the IP address and port number). Once the connection is established, the client and the server can exchange data according to their own protocol.

The sequence of events in sockets-based data exchanges depends on whether the transfer is connection-oriented (TCP) or connectionless (UDP).

For a connection-oriented data transfer using sockets, the server "listens" on a specific port, waiting for clients to request connection. Data transfer begins only after a connection is established.

For connectionless data transfers, the server waits for a datagram to arrive at a specified port. The client does not wait to establish a connection; it simply sends a datagram to the server.

Client/Server communications with TCP/IP

Client/Server applications use the following basic steps to exchange data in a TCP/IP network:

1. Create a socket.
2. Bind an IP address and port to the socket.
3. Listen for connections if the application is a server using a stream socket.
4. Establish connection if the application is a client using a stream socket.
5. Exchange data.
6. Close the socket when done.

Connectionless sockets (that implement data transfer using UDP) do not require Steps 3 and 4.

Regardless of whether it's a server or a client, each application first creates a socket. Then it associates (binds) the socket with the local computer's IP address and a port number. The IP address identifies the machine (where the application is running) and the port number identifies the application that's using the socket.

Servers typically listen to a well-known port number so that clients can connect to that port to access the server. For a client application, the process of binding a socket to the IP address and port is the same as that for a server, but the client can use zero as the port number — the sockets library automatically uses an unused port number for the client.

For a connection-oriented stream socket, the communicating client and server applications have to establish a connection. The exact steps for establishing a connection depend on whether the application is a server or a client.

In the client/server model, the server has to be up and running before the client can run. After creating a socket and binding the socket to a port, the server application sets up a queue of connections, which determines how many clients can connect to the server. Typically, a server listens to anywhere from 1 to 5 connections. However, the size of the listen queue is one of the parameters you can adjust (especially for a Web server) to ensure that the server responds to as many clients as possible.

After setting up the listen queue, the server waits for a connection from a client.

Establishing the connection from the client side is somewhat simpler. After creating a socket and binding the socket to a network address, the client establishes a connection with the server. To make the connection, the client needs to know the network name or IP address of the server, as well as the port on which the server accepts connection. As the next section shows, all Internet services have well-known standard port numbers.

After a client establishes a connection to a server using a connection-oriented stream socket, the client and server can exchange data by calling appropriate socket API functions. Like a conversation between two persons, the server and client alternately send and receive data — the meaning of the data depends on the message protocol used by the server and the clients. Usually, a server is designed for a specific task and inherent in that design is a message protocol that the server and clients use to exchange the necessary data. For example, the Web server and the Web browser (client) communicate using the Hypertext Transfer Protocol (HTTP).

Internet services and port numbers

The TCP/IP protocol suite has become the lingua franca of the Internet, because many standard services are available on all systems that support TCP/IP. These services make the Internet tick by enabling the transfer of mail, news, and Web pages. These services go by well-known names such as the following:

- FTP (File Transfer Protocol) allows the transfer of files between computers on the Internet. FTP uses two ports — data is transferred on port 20, while control information is exchanged on port 21.

- HTTP (Hypertext Transfer Protocol) is a recent protocol for sending HTML documents from one system to another. HTTP is the underlying protocol of the Web. By default, the Web server and client communicate on port 80.

- SMTP (Simple Mail Transfer Protocol) for exchanging e-mail messages between systems. SMTP uses port 25 for information exchange.

- NNTP (Network News Transfer Protocol) for distribution of news articles in a store-and-forward fashion across the Internet. NNTP uses port 119.

- Telnet allows a user on one system to log into another system on the Internet (the user must provide a valid user ID and password to successfully log into the remote system). Telnet uses port 23 by default. However, the Telnet client can connect to any specified port.

- SNMP (Simple Network Management Protocol) for managing all types of network devices on the Internet. Like FTP, SNMP uses two ports: 161 and 162.

- TFTP (Trivial File Transfer Protocol) for transferring files from one system to another (typically used by X terminals and diskless workstations to download boot files from another host on the network). TFTP data transfer takes place on port 69.

- NFS (Network File System) for sharing files among computers. NFS uses Sun's Remote Procedure Call (RPC) facility, which exchanges information through port 111.

- WAIS (Wide Area Information Service) for searching data on distributed systems. WAIS uses port 210 (in the /etc/services file, you'll find information about WAIS under the service named z3950 because WAIS uses the ANSI standard Z39.50 protocol).

A well-known port is associated with each of these services. The TCP protocol uses this port to locate a service on any system. (A server *process* — a computer program running on a system — implements each service.)

Like the /etc/hosts file, which stores the association between host names and IP addresses, the association between a service name and a port number (as well as a protocol) is stored in another text file, named /etc/services. Following is a small subset of entries in the /etc/services file in a Linux system:

```
ftp-data        20/tcp
ftp             21/tcp
telnet          23/tcp
smtp            25/tcp          mail
time            37/tcp          timserver
time            37/udp          timserver
rlp             39/udp          resource        # resource location
```

```
name            42/udp          nameserver
whois           43/tcp          nicname             # usually to sri-nic
domain          53/tcp
domain          53/udp
mtp             57/tcp                              # deprecated
bootps          67/udp                              # bootp server
bootpc          68/udp                              # bootp client
tftp            69/udp
gopher          70/tcp                              # gopher server
rje             77/tcp
finger          79/tcp
http            80/tcp                              # www is used by some broken
www             80/tcp                              # progs, http is more correct
link            87/tcp          ttylink
kerberos        88/udp          kdc                 # Kerberos authentication--udp
kerberos        88/tcp          kdc                 # Kerberos authentication--tcp
```

You'll find browsing through the entries in the /etc/services file to be instructive, because they show the breadth of networking services available under TCP/IP.

Note

Note that port number 80 is designated for World Wide Web service. If you set up a Web server on your system, that server listens to port 80.

The inetd super server

The client/server model requires that the server be up and running before a client makes a request for service. A simplistic idea would be to run all the servers all the time. However, this idea is not practical because each server process would use up system resources in the form of memory and processor time. Besides, you don't need all the services up and ready at all times. A smart solution to this problem is to run a single server, inetd, that listens to all the ports and then starts the appropriate server when a client request comes in.

For example, when a client tries to connect to the FTP port, inetd starts the FTP server and lets it communicate directly with the client (and the FTP server exits when the client disconnects).

Because it starts various servers on demand, inetd is known as the Internet super server. Typically, a UNIX system starts inetd when the system boots. The inetd server reads a configuration file named /etc/inetd.conf at startup. This file tells inetd which ports to listen to and what server to start for each port. For example, on my system the entry in the /etc/inetd.conf file that starts the FTP server looks like the following:

```
ftp      stream  tcp     nowait  root    /usr/sbin/tcpd  in.ftpd -l -a
```

The first item on this line, `ftp`, tells `inetd` the name of the service. `inetd` uses this name to look up the port number from the `/etc/services` file. If you use the `grep` command to look for `ftp` in the `/etc/services` file, here's what you'll find:

```
grep ftp /etc/services
ftp-data        20/tcp
ftp             21/tcp
tftp            69/udp
sftp            115/tcp
```

From this, you can see that the port number of the FTP service is 21. This tells `inetd` to listen to port 21 for FTP service requests.

The rest of the fields on the FTP entry have the following meanings:

- The second and third fields of the entry, `stream tcp`, tell `inetd` that the FTP service uses a connection-oriented TCP socket to communicate with the client. For services that use the connectionless UDP sockets, these two fields say `dgram udp`.

- The fourth field, `nowait`, tells `inetd` to start a new server for each request. If this field says `wait`, `inetd` waits until the server exits before starting the server again.

- The fifth field provides the user ID that `inetd` uses to run the server. In this case, the server runs the FTP server as `root`.

- The sixth field specifies the program to run for this service, and the last field is the argument that `inetd` passes to the server program. In this case, the `/usr/sbin/tcpd` program is provided `in.ftpd` as argument.

Secret

Note that the `/usr/sbin/tcpd` program is an access control facility for Internet services. The `tcpd` program can start other services such as FTP and Telnet, but before starting the service, `tcpd` consults the `/etc/hosts.allow` file to see if the host requesting service is allowed that service. If there is nothing in `/etc/hosts.allow` about that host, `tcpd` checks the `/etc/hosts.deny` file to see if the service should be denied. If both files are empty, `tcpd` allows the host access to the requested service. You can place the line `ALL:ALL` in the `/etc/hosts.deny` file to deny all hosts access to any Internet services (see the "`/etc/hosts.allow`" and "`/etc/hosts.deny`" sections to learn more about these access control files).

Browse through the `/etc/inetd.conf` file on your system to find out the kinds of services that `inetd` is set up to start. Some of these services (such as `finger`, `systat`, and `netstat`) provide information that may be used by intruders to break into your system. You might want to turn off these services by placing a comment character (#) at the beginning of the lines that start these services. When you make such a change to the `/etc/inetd.conf` file, you must restart the `inetd` server by following these steps:

1. Use the `ps` command with appropriate options and determine the process identifier (ID) of `inetd`. For example, on Linux, type `ps x | grep inetd` and note the first number on the resulting line. That would be the process ID of `inetd`.

2. Type `kill -HUP` *pid,* where *pid* is the process ID (a number) of `inetd`. This restarts `inetd` and it again reads the `/etc/inetd.conf` file.

Stand-alone servers

Although starting servers through `inetd` is a smart approach, `inetd` is not efficient if a service has to be started often. The Web server typically has to be started often because every time a user clicks on a link on a Web page, a request arrives at the Web server. For such high-demand services, it's best to start the server in a stand-alone manner. Such stand-alone servers are designed to run as *daemons* — processes that run continuously. The server listens on the assigned port and whenever a request arrives, the server handles the request by making a copy of itself. In this way, the server keeps running forever. A more efficient strategy, used for Web servers, is to run multiple copies of the server and let each copy handle some of the incoming requests.

Ethernet and Linux

TCP/IP is a fine protocol suite for networking, but before you can use TCP/IP, you have to set up the physical network. Ethernet is a good choice for the physical data-transport mechanism, for the following reasons:

- Ethernet is proven technology (it has been in use since the early 1980s).

- Ethernet provides good data-transfer rates: typically 10 million bits per second (10 Mbps) although there is now 100 Mbps Ethernet.

- Ethernet hardware is relatively low-cost (PC Ethernet cards cost less than $100).

Typically, Linux supports affordable hardware, and Ethernet is no exception. The following sections describe the Ethernet cards that Linux supports and the physical setup of an Ethernet LAN.

Ethernet basics

Ethernet is a standard way to move packets of data between two or more computers connected to a single cable. (Larger networks are constructed by connecting multiple Ethernet segments with gateways.) Because a single wire is used, a protocol has to be used for sending and receiving data, because only one data packet can exist on the cable at any time. An Ethernet LAN uses a data-transmission protocol known as *Carrier Sense Multiple Access/Collision Detection* (CSMA/CD) to ensure that multiple computers can share the single transmission cable. Ethernet controllers embedded in the computers follow the CSMA/CD protocol to transmit and receive Ethernet packets.

The idea behind the CSMA/CD protocol is analogous to the way that you might have a conversation in a party. You listen for a pause (*carrier sense*) and talk when no one else is speaking. If you and another person begin talking at the same time, both of you realize the problem (*collision detection*) and pause for a moment; then one of you starts speaking again. As you know from experience, everything works out.

In an Ethernet LAN, each Ethernet controller checks the cable for the presence of signals — that's the carrier-sense part. If the signal level is low, a controller sends its packets on the cable; the packet contains information about the sender and the intended recipient. All Ethernet controllers on the LAN listen to the signal, and the recipient receives the packet. If, somehow, two controllers send out a packet simultaneously, the signal level in the cable rises above a threshold, and the controllers know that a collision occurred (two packets were sent out at the same time). Both controllers wait for a random amount of time and then send their packets again.

Ethernet was invented in the early 1970s at the Xerox Palo Alto Research Center (PARC) by Robert M. Metcalfe. In the 1980s, Ethernet was standardized through the cooperative effort of three companies: Digital Equipment Corporation (DEC), Intel, and Xerox. Using the first initials of the company names, that Ethernet standard became known as the *DIX standard*. Later, the DIX standard was included in the 802-series standards developed by the Institute of Electrical and Electronics Engineers (IEEE). The formal Ethernet specification is formally known as IEEE 802.3 CSMA/CD, but people continue to call it Ethernet.

Ethernet sends data in packets (also known as *frames*) with a standard format that consists of the following sequence of components:

- 8-byte preamble
- 6-byte destination address
- 6-byte source address
- 2-byte length of the data field
- 46- to 1,500-byte data field
- 4-byte frame-check sequence (used for error checking)

You don't need to know much about the innards of Ethernet packets except to note the 6-byte source and destination addresses. Each Ethernet controller has a unique 6-byte (48-bit) address. At the physical level, packets must be addressed with these 6-byte addresses.

Address Resolution Protocol

In an Ethernet LAN, two Ethernet controllers can communicate only if they know each other's 6-byte physical Ethernet address. You may wonder how IP addresses are mapped to physical addresses. This problem is solved by the Address Resolution Protocol (ARP), which specifies how to obtain the physical address that corresponds to an IP address. Essentially, when a packet has to be sent to an IP address, the TCP/IP protocol uses ARP to find the physical address of the destination.

When the packet is meant for an IP address outside your network, the packet is sent to the gateway that has a physical presence on your network and that, therefore, can respond to an ARP request for a physical address.

Ethernet cables

The original Ethernet standard used a thick coaxial cable, nearly half an inch in diameter. That wiring is called *thickwire* or *thick Ethernet*, although the IEEE 802.3 standard calls it 10BASE5. That designation means that the data-transmission rate is 10 megabits per second (10 Mbps), that the transmission is baseband (which simply means that the cable's signal-carrying capacity is devoted to transmitting Ethernet packets only), and that the total length of the cable can be no more than 500 meters. Thickwire was expensive, and the cable was rather unwieldy.

Nowadays, two other forms of Ethernet cabling are more popular. The first alternative to thick Ethernet cable is *thinwire*, or 10BASE2, which uses a thin, flexible coaxial cable. A thinwire Ethernet segment can be, at most, 185 meters long. The other, more recent, alternative is Ethernet over unshielded twisted-pair cable (UTP), known as 10BASET.

To set up a 10BASET Ethernet, you need an Ethernet *hub* — a hardware box with RJ-45 jacks. You build the network by running twisted-pair wires from each PC's Ethernet card to this hub.

Tip

Thinwire has a feature that makes it attractive for small offices or home offices that have more than one PC. You can daisy-chain the thinwire cable from one PC to another and construct a small Ethernet LAN, as shown in Figure 16-6.

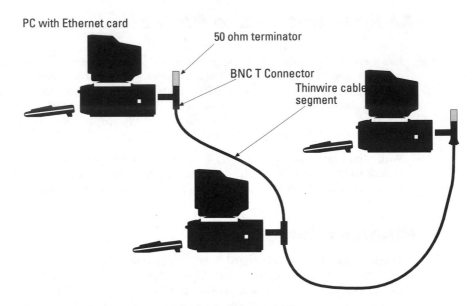

PC with Ethernet card

50 ohm terminator

BNC T Connector

Thinwire cable segment

Figure 16-6: Constructing a small thinwire Ethernet LAN

As Figure 16-6 shows, you need Ethernet cards in the PCs. The cards should have thinwire connectors, known as BNC connectors. You also need segments of thinwire cable (technically known as RG-58 thin coaxial cables with 50-ohm impedance). For each Ethernet card's BNC connector, you need a BNC T connector (so called because the connector looks like a *T*), and you need two 50-ohm terminators for the two end points of the Ethernet network. Then all you have to do to complete your own Ethernet LAN is connect the parts in the manner shown in Figure 16-6. I used this approach to connect several PCs and a workstation in my home office.

Caution

Remember that you have to use the BNC T connector and 50-ohm terminators even if you are connecting only two PCs on a LAN; you can't simply connect the two Ethernet cards with a cable.

Supported Ethernet cards

To set up an Ethernet LAN, you need an Ethernet card for each PC. Linux supports a wide variety of Ethernet cards for the PC. Following is a list of supported Ethernet cards in Linux kernel 1.2.8:

- 3Com 3C501 (obsolete and very slow)
- 3Com 3C503, 3C505, 3C507, 3C509/3C509B (ISA), 3C579 (EISA)
- 3Com Etherlink III Vortex Ethercards (3C590, 3C592, 3C595, 3C597) (PCI)
- 3Com Etherlink XL Boomerang Ethercards (3C900, 3C905) (PCI)
- 3Com 3C515 Fast EtherLink Ethercard (ISA)

- Allied Telesis AT1700 and LA100PCI-T
- AMD LANCE (79C960) and PCnet (AT1500, HP J2405A, NE1500, NE2100)
- Ansel Communications AC3200 (EISA)
- Apricot Xen-II (82596) onboard Ethernet
- AT&T GIS WaveLAN
- Cabletron E21xx
- Cogent EM110
- Danpex EN-9400
- DEC DE425 (EISA), DE434 (PCI), DE435 (PCI), DE450/DE500
- DEC DE450/DE500-XA, QSilver (Tulip driver)
- DEC DEPCA, EtherWORKS, and EtherWORKS 3
- Fujitsu FMV-181/182/183/184
- HP PCLAN (27245 and other 27xxx series)
- HP PCLAN PLUS (27247B and 27252A)
- IBM ThinkPad 300 built-in adapter
- ICL EtherTeam 16i/32 (EISA)
- Intel EtherExpress and EtherExpress Pro
- KTI ET16/P-D2, ET16/P-DC ISA
- New Media Ethernet
- Novell Eagle NE1000 and NE2000
- PureData PDUC8028, PDI8023
- Racal-Interlan NI5210 (i82586 Ethernet chip; not working well with current driver)
- Racal-Interlan NI6510 (am7990 LANCE Ethernet chip; has problems with more than 16MB RAM)
- Schneider & Koch G16
- SEEQ 8005
- SMC Ultra/EtherEZ (ISA)
- SMC 9000 series
- SMC PCI EtherPower 10/100 (Tulip driver)
- Western Digital WD8003 (same as SMC Elite) and WD8013 (SMC Elite Plus)
- Zenith Z-Note built-in adapter
- Znyx 312 etherarray (Tulip driver)

If you have upgraded the Linux kernel, the new kernel may support even more cards than the ones shown in this list.

If you have not bought an Ethernet card yet, you want to buy a 16-bit card, not an 8-bit card. A 16-bit card transfers data faster and has a larger onboard buffer. The cards come with different types of connectors, as follows:

- A DB-15 connector for thick Ethernet. (You need an additional transceiver to connect thickwire to other types of Ethernet, such as thinwire or 10BASE-T.)
- A thinwire BNC connector.
- An RJ-45 connector for 10BASE-T. (The RJ-45 connector looks like a common RJ-11 phone jack, but the RJ-45 version has eight positions instead of six.)

Nowadays, many Ethernet cards come with more than one, or all three, of these connectors. If you have a small office or a home office, I recommend you buy an Ethernet card with a thinwire connector. Then you can set up an Ethernet LAN with a few RG58 coaxial cables, BNC T connectors, and 50-ohm terminators.

Thinwire is easy to set up, but it's not convenient to connect many PCs this way. One problem is that any break in the cable causes the entire network to come down.

To set up a 10BASE-T network, you need a separate hub with telephone jacks. A wire goes from each PC's Ethernet card to the hub, and the hub sets up the proper connections for Ethernet.

You can use Ethernet cards with a DB-15 thick Ethernet connector in a thinwire or 10BASE-T network. All you need is a transceiver that attaches to the DB-15 port and provides the right type of connector (BNC for thinwire and RJ-45 for 10BASE-T).

A better choice is to buy the newer "Combo" version of Ethernet cards that come with both thinwire and 10BASE-T transceivers built in; there is a BNC connector for a thinwire network and a RJ-45 jack for a 10BASE-T network.

Unsupported Ethernet cards

As you may realize by now, most device drivers in Linux exist because someone voluntarily wrote the code and provided it free to all of us. Of course, the developer can write a device driver only if the vendor provides technical information about the device without any restrictions (remember that the GNU Public License requires all source code to be freely available). Unfortunately, some hardware vendors refuse to provide technical information about their devices without a nondisclosure agreement. Many advanced video cards fall into this category, which is why many such video cards are not supported in Linux.

A few Ethernet-card vendors also refuse to provide technical information freely. At present, Cabletron and Xircom are two such vendors. Because of the lack of programming information, Cabletron and Xircom Ethernet cards are *not* supported in Linux. You need to watch out for these cards if you plan to run Linux on your PC.

Caution

The Cabletron E2100 card is supported only because it is a generic design based on the National Semiconductor DP8390 chip. Although a driver is available for the Cabletron E2100, future fixes or enhancements may not be available for this driver.

Kernel support for Ethernet

When you follow the steps in Chapter 1 to install Linux from the companion CD-ROM, you have to select a kernel. Typically, these kernels already include support for some networking cards.

After you complete the Linux installation and reboot the system, you should check the boot messages to see whether your Ethernet card was detected. (If the boot messages flash by too quickly, you can view them at your convenience with the dmesg | more command.) My PC, for example, has a 3Com 3C509 Ethernet card, and I see the following lines in the boot messages:

```
eth0: 3c509 at 0x210 tag 1, BNC port, address  00 20 af e8 a2 25, IRQ
10.
3c509.c:1.12 6/4/97 becker@cesdis.gsfc.nasa.gov
```

The first line starts with the name of the Ethernet device (eth0 means the first Ethernet card), followed by some identifying information about the card. The message also shows the I/O port address (0x210) and IRQ (10).

The second line, which starts with 3c509, shows information about the Ethernet driver being used. The line ends with the electronic mail address of Donald J. Becker, the author of most Ethernet drivers in Linux.

Secret

If you do not see a message about your Ethernet card, you have to rebuild the kernel to enable support for your Ethernet card or load the driver module for your card. Follow the steps outlined in Chapter 2 to rebuild the kernel. When you run make config to configure the kernel, the configuration program asks several questions (you answer Yes or No) about what devices to support in the kernel. Because many devices conflict with one another, you should specify only those devices that you have installed on your system.

When I configured the kernel on my PC with a 3Com 3C509 Ethernet card, I answered the questions in the following manner:

```
3COM cards (CONFIG_NET_VENDOR_3COM) [Y/n/?] y
3c501 support (CONFIG_EL1) [M/n/y/?] n
3c503 support (CONFIG_EL2) [M/n/y/?] n
3c509/3c579 support (CONFIG_EL3) [M/n/y/?] y
3c590/3c900 series (592/595/597/900/905) "Vortex/Boomerang" support
(CONFIG_VORTEX) [M/n/y/?] n
```

```
AMD LANCE and PCnet (AT1500 and NE2100) support (CONFIG_LANCE) [Y/n/?] n
Western Digital/SMC cards (CONFIG_NET_VENDOR_SMC) [Y/n/?] n
Other ISA cards (CONFIG_NET_ISA) [Y/n/?] n
EISA, VLB, PCI and on board controllers (CONFIG_NET_EISA) [Y/n/?] n
Pocket and portable adaptors (CONFIG_NET_POCKET) [Y/n/?] n
Token Ring driver support (CONFIG_TR) [Y/n/?] n
FDDI driver support (CONFIG_FDDI) [N/y/?] n
ARCnet support (CONFIG_ARCNET) [M/n/y/?] n
```

The default response appears in uppercase in the brackets at the end of each question; simply press Enter to accept the default. Otherwise, answer by typing **y** or **n** (to indicate Yes or No, respectively). Press **m** to build the support in the form of a loadable driver module.

Answer Yes to the appropriate questions from that set of networking questions, and complete the kernel-rebuild process. The next time you boot the system, Linux should detect your Ethernet card.

Ethernet autoprobing

At boot time, a kernel with Ethernet support attempts to probe and detect the Ethernet card. The probing involves reading from and writing to specific I/O port addresses.

Although you specify a single I/O port address for a device, most devices use a block of I/O addresses for their operation. The I/O address you specify is the *base address*; the rest of the I/O addresses are consecutive I/O ports, starting at the base address.

Secret

Depending on the number of I/O addresses used by a device, two devices may end up with overlaps in the range of I/O addresses they use. The NE2000 card, for example, uses 32 I/O ports (that's 0x20 in hexadecimal notation). If you select 0x360 as the base I/O address for a NE2000 card, the card uses the ports from 0x360 to 0x37F. Unfortunately, the PC's parallel port (LPT1) uses the base I/O address of 0x378, and the secondary IDE controller uses the addresses 0x376 – 0x376. Thus, the NE2000 configured at 0x360 now has an overlap with the I/O addresses used by the first parallel port and the secondary IDE controller. In this case, you can prevent any problems by configuring the NE2000 card at a different I/O address, such as 0x280.

Such overlapping I/O port addresses cause problems because during autoprobing, the kernel may perform operations that might be harmless for some devices but that may cause another device to lock up the system. Typically, however, if your Ethernet card and other devices were working under DOS or Windows, you should have no problem with them under Linux (assuming, of course, that your Ethernet card is supported under Linux).

If your system hangs during autoprobe, you can exclude a specific range of I/O addresses from being probed. To exclude a range of addresses during autoprobing, use the `reserve` command during the LILO boot prompt. The `reserve` command has the following syntax:

```
reserve=BASE-IO-PORT1,NUMPORTS1[,BASE-IO-PORT2,NUMPORTS2,...]
```

Here, `BASE-IO-PORT1` is an I/O port address in hexadecimal notation (for example, `0x300`), and `NUMPORTS1` is the number of ports (for example, 32) to be excluded when autoprobing. The arguments in brackets are optional; they are used to specify additional exclusion regions.

If you prevent a range of I/O addresses from being autoprobed, a device at that address may not be detected. Thus, you must specify that device's parameters explicitly on the boot command-line.

For Ethernet cards, the LILO command for specifying device parameters is `ether`, which takes the following format:

```
ether=IRQ,BASE-IO-PORT,PARAM-1,PARAM-2,NAME
```

Table 16-1 explains the meanings of the arguments. All arguments are optional. The Ethernet driver takes the first non-numeric argument as `NAME`.

Table 16-1	Arguments for ether
Argument	**Meaning**
`IRQ`	The IRQ of the Ethernet card. Specify a zero `IRQ` to make the driver autodetect the IRQ.
`BASE-IO-PORT`	The base I/O port address of the Ethernet card. Specify a zero `BASE-IO-PORT` to make the driver autodetect the base I/O port address.
`PARAM-1`	The meaning depends on the Ethernet driver. Some drivers use the least significant four bits of this value as the debug message level. The default is 0; set this argument to a value of 1 to 7 to indicate how verbose the debug messages should be (7 means most verbose). A value of 8 stops debug messages. The AMD LANCE driver uses the low-order four bits as the DMA channel.
`PARAM-2`	The meaning depends on the Ethernet driver. The 3Com 3c503 drivers use this value to select between an internal and external transceiver — 0 means the internal transceiver, and 1 means that the card uses an external transceiver connected to the DB-15 thick Ethernet port.
`NAME`	The name of the Ethernet driver (`eth0`, `eth1`, and so on). By default, the kernel uses `eth0` as the name of the first Ethernet card it autoprobes. The kernel does not probe for more than one Ethernet card, because that would increase the chance of conflicts with other devices during autoprobing.

If you have an Ethernet card at the I/O address 0x300 and do not want this card to be autoprobed, use a command line such as the following at the LILO boot prompt:

```
reserve=0x300,32 ether=0,0x300,eth0
```

The `reserve` command prevents 32 I/O ports starting at 0x300 from being autoprobed, whereas the `ether` command specifies the base I/O port address for the Ethernet card. The exact I/O addresses depend on your Ethernet card and the range of addresses for which an overlap with some other device exists. Most of the time, you should not have to use these commands.

Secret

A note about PCI cards: their I/O addresses and IRQs are assigned by the PCI BIOS when the system powers up. Thus, you cannot set the I/O address or IRQ of any PCI card through the LILO command line. Even if you specify these parameters through LILO commands, they are ignored for a PCI device.

Network-device names

For most devices, Linux uses files in the /dev directory. The networking devices, however, have names that are defined internally in the kernel; no files for these devices exist in the /dev directory. Following are the common network-device names in Linux:

- `lo` — the loopback device. This device is used for efficient handling of network packets sent from your system to itself (when, for example, an X client communicates with the X server on the same system).

- `eth0` — the first Ethernet card. If you have more Ethernet cards, they get device names `eth1`, `eth2`, and so on.

- `ppp0` — the first serial port configured for a point-to-point link to another computer, using Point-to-Point Protocol (PPP). If you have more serial ports configured for PPP networking, they are assigned device names `ppp1`, `ppp2`, and so on.

- `sl0` — the first serial port configured for Serial Line Internet Protocol (SLIP) networking. SLIP is used for establishing a point-to-point link to a TCP/IP network. If you use a second serial port for SLIP, it gets the device name `sl1`.

Wizard

You always have a loopback device (`lo`), whether or not you have any network. The loopback device passes data from one process to another without having to go out to a network. In fact, the whole idea of the loopback device is to allow network applications to work as long as the communicating processes are on the same system.

Cross-Reference

PPP is popular in dial-up networks, in which you use a modem to dial in to an Internet host (typically, a system at your work or your Internet Service Provider) and establish a connection to the Internet. Chapter 18 covers this subject in detail.

If you want to see the names of installed network devices on your system, try the following command:

```
cat /proc/net/dev
```

This command shows the network-device names, as well as statistics on the number of packets sent and received for a specific device.

Multiple Ethernet cards

You might use a Linux PC as a gateway between two Ethernet networks. In that case, you might have two Ethernet cards in the PC. The Linux kernel can support more than one Ethernet card; what it does *not* do is detect multiple cards automatically. The kernel looks for only the first Ethernet card. If you happen to have two Ethernet cards, you should specify the parameters of the cards on the LILO boot command line. (The two cards must have different IRQs and I/O addresses, of course.) Following is a typical boot command line for two Ethernet cards:

```
 ether=10,0x220,eth0 ether=5,0x300,eth1
```

If you happen to have two Ethernet cards, you can place the necessary LILO boot parameters in the `/etc/lilo.conf` file so you don't have to enter the arguments every time you boot Linux. For the preceding example, the line in `/etc/lilo.conf` looks like this:

```
append="ether=10,0x220,eth0 ether=5,0x300,eth1"
```

If you plan to use a Linux PC with two network interfaces as a TCP/IP gateway, you have to recompile the kernel with IP forwarding enabled. Chapter 2 explains how to rebuild the kernel. During the rebuild process, when you use the `make config` command, the following questions appear (these are a few of many questions):

```
IP: forwarding/gatewaying (CONFIG_IP_FORWARD) [Y/n/?] y
IP: multicasting (CONFIG_IP_MULTICAST) [Y/n/?] y
IP: optimize as router not host (CONFIG_IP_ROUTER) [N/y/?] y
```

If you are using your Linux PC as a router, you should answer **y** to these questions.

TCP/IP Setup in Linux

Like almost everything else in Linux, TCP/IP setup is a matter of preparing a bunch of configuration files (text files you can edit with any text editor). Most of these configuration files are in the `/etc` directory. The Red Hat installation program helps by hiding the details of the TCP/IP configuration files. Nevertheless, it's better if you know the names of the files and their purposes so you can edit the files manually, if necessary.

Cross-Reference

The next few sections show you how to set up TCP/IP for an Ethernet LAN. Chapter 18 covers dial-up networking under Linux, including topics such as PPP.

Before you look at TCP/IP setup, make sure your system's Ethernet card is properly installed and detected by the Linux kernel.

Configuring the kernel for TCP/IP

The kernel configuration is the first step in setting up your system for TCP/IP. As shown in Chapter 2, the first step in kernel configuration involves the following commands:

```
cd /usr/src/linux
make config
```

The configuration program asks several questions about various system capabilities; some of these questions are about networking. Following are the first two sets of questions about networking (and some possible responses):

```
* Networking options
*
Network firewalls (CONFIG_FIREWALL) [Y/n/?] n
Network aliasing (CONFIG_NET_ALIAS) [Y/n/?] n
TCP/IP networking (CONFIG_INET) [Y/n/?] y
IP: forwarding/gatewaying (CONFIG_IP_FORWARD) [Y/n/?] n
IP: multicasting (CONFIG_IP_MULTICAST) [Y/n/?] n
IP: syn cookies (CONFIG_SYN_COOKIES) [Y/n/?] y
IP: accounting (CONFIG_IP_ACCT) [Y/n/?] n
IP: optimize as router not host (CONFIG_IP_ROUTER) [N/y/?] n
IP: tunneling (CONFIG_NET_IPIP) [M/n/y/?] n
*
* (it is safe to leave these untouched)
*
IP: PC/TCP compatibility mode (CONFIG_INET_PCTCP) [N/y/?] n
IP: Reverse ARP (CONFIG_INET_RARP) [M/n/y/?] m
IP: Disable Path MTU Discovery (normally enabled)
(CONFIG_NO_PATH_MTU_DISCOVERY) [N/y/?] n
IP: Drop source routed frames (CONFIG_IP_NOSR) [Y/n/?] y
IP: Allow large windows (not recommended if <16Mb of memory)
(CONFIG_SKB_LARGE) [Y/n/?] y
The IPX protocol (CONFIG_IPX) [M/n/y/?] n
```

You can accept the default answer (shown in brackets at the end of each question) for almost all of these questions. You should answer Yes to enable IP forwarding if you want to use your Linux system as a gateway (or router) between two separate networks.

The following list explains the meaning of some of these configuration questions:

Network firewalls — If you answer Yes to this question, the kernel allows networking software to selectively enable or disable access to groups of TCP/IP ports. You need additional software to control access to specific TCP/IP ports.

Network aliasing — If you answer Yes to this question, the kernel allows multiple IP addresses for a single network interface.

TCP/IP networking — This option enables support for the TCP/IP protocol suite in the kernel. You should answer Yes to this question, even if you do not plan to set up a LAN. TCP/IP can be used even within a single system; the loopback device lo provides the data-transport mechanism to support TCP/IP exchanges between processes on the same PC.

IP: forwarding/gatewaying — Answer Yes to this question if you want to use your Linux system to forward TCP/IP packets to another network. The default is to disable IP forwarding. You should turn on IP forwarding if you want to connect your LAN to the Internet with a Linux PC running PPP.

IP: multicasting — This question refers to the capability of the system to send and receive network packets addressed to a subset of hosts on the network. Some new Internet services, such as Internet Talk Radio, rely on multicasting. Even if you enable this feature, you need additional software to use the multicasting capabilities.

IP: syn cookies — If you answer Yes to this question, the kernel includes code that provides protection against a type of network attack known as SYN flooding.

IP: accounting — If you enable this feature, the kernel counts and records incoming and outgoing data volume (in bytes) on a per-port and per-address basis. You may want to use this feature if you use a Linux PC to provide Internet connectivity to other systems. You can use the IP accounting information to charge your customers based on level of use.

PC/TCP compatibility mode — If your Linux system is on a LAN with other PCs, and some of those PCs run the PC/TCP networking software, you should answer Yes to this question; it takes care of some problems that may occur when a PC running PC/TCP connects to your Linux PC.

Reverse ARP — ARP refers to Address Resolution Protocol, which is used to determine the physical Ethernet address that corresponds to an IP address. The opposite is Reverse ARP (or RARP) — a protocol that allows a system to say, "Here's my Ethernet address; somebody please give me an IP address." Some old Sun 3 workstations and other diskless workstations need RARP to work. Typically, you should not have to answer Yes to this query.

The IPX protocol — Answer Yes if you want to include support for the Internet Packet Exchange (IPX) protocol — part of the Xerox Network System (XNS) protocol. Novell NetWare uses IPX as its network layer. NetWare's transport layer is called Sequenced Packet Exchange (SPX); Linux does not include SPX support.

Running netcfg

After you make sure that the Linux kernel is properly configured for TCP/IP, you have to make sure that the appropriate configuration files exist. Red Hat Linux (which is on the companion CD-ROM) includes a program named netcfg (in the /usr/bin directory) that helps you configure various network interfaces on your system for TCP/IP networking. You can run netcfg to add a new network interface or alter information such as name servers and host names (you can also directly edit the configuration files listed in the "Using TCP/IP configuration files" section).

To run netconfig, log in as root, start the X Window System, and type the following command in an xterm window:

/usr/bin/netcfg

The netcfg program displays a dialog box, as shown in Figure 16-7.

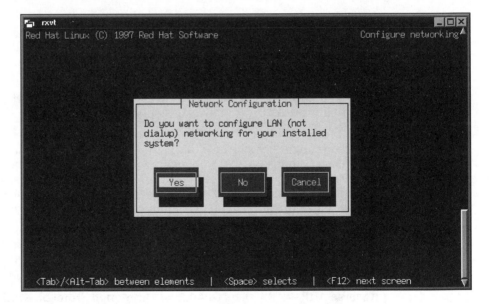

Figure 16-7: Configuring a TCP/IP network with the netcfg program

You can configure various aspects of your network through the at the top dialog box. Specifically, you can do the following:

- **Names** — lets you enter the host name for your system and enter the IP addresses of name servers. The name server addresses are stored in the /etc/resolv.conf file. The host name is stored in a variable in the /etc/sysconfig/network file.

- **Hosts**—shows you the current contents of the /etc/hosts file and lets you add, remove, or edit entries.

- **Interfaces**—lets you add a new network interface, specify the IP address of the interface, and activate the interface. This information gets stored in various files in the /etc/sysconfig directory.

- **Routine**—lets you add static routes (each route lists the gateway to use to reach a specified network).

Testing the network

After you run netcfg, you may want to check to see whether the network is up and running. If you have not rebooted your system yet, you have to run /sbin/ifconfig to configure the Ethernet interface for your IP address. On a system whose IP address is 206.197.168.200, you would type the following command (you have to be logged in as root to do this):

```
/sbin/ifconfig eth0 206.197.168 netmask 255.255.255.0 broadcast
206.197.168.255
```

Verifying another system's accessibility

Now you should use the ping utility program to verify whether another system on your network is accessible. On my PC, I might try the following:

```
ping 206.197.168.50
PING 206.197.168.50 (206.197.168.50): 56 data bytes
64 bytes from 206.197.168.50: icmp_seq=0 ttl=32 time=3.4 ms
64 bytes from 206.197.168.50: icmp_seq=1 ttl=32 time=1.8 ms
64 bytes from 206.197.168.50: icmp_seq=2 ttl=32 time=1.8 ms
64 bytes from 206.197.168.50: icmp_seq=3 ttl=32 time=1.9 ms
        (press Ctrl-C here)
--- 206.197.168.50 ping statistics ---
4 packets transmitted, 4 packets received, 0% packet loss
round-trip min/avg/max = 1.8/2.2/3.4 ms
```

If the ping command shows that other systems on your network are reachable, you can proceed to use other network programs, such as ftp and telnet.

Using TCP/IP configuration files

Running the netcfg script may be enough to get TCP/IP configured on your system. You may want to know the configuration files, however, so that you can edit the files if necessary. You can specify the name servers through the netcfg script, for example, but you may want to add an alternative name server. To do so, you need to know about the /etc/resolv.conf file, which stores the IP addresses of name servers.

The following sections describe the basic TCP/IP configuration files.

/etc/HOSTNAME

The /etc/HOSTNAME file stores your system's host name — your system's fully qualified domain name, such as addlab.nws.noaa.gov.

Secret

In Red Hat Linux, the host name is stored in a variable named HOSTNAME in the /etc/sysconfig/network file. During system startup, the initialization script (/etc/rc.d/rc.sysinit) uses the hostname command to set your system's host name to whatever the HOSTNAME variable is in /etc/sysconfig/network. The /etc/rc.d/rc.sysinit script also saves that host name in the /etc/HOSTNAME file.

/etc/hosts

The /etc/hosts text file contains a list of IP addresses and host names for your local network. In the absence of a name server, any network program on your system consults this file to determine the IP address that corresponds to a host name.

Following is the /etc/hosts file from my system, showing the IP addresses and names of other hosts on my LAN:

```
127.0.0.1     localhost

# Other hosts on the LAN
206.197.168.200      lnbsoft.com lnbsoft
206.197.168.50       lnb386
206.197.168.100      lnb486
206.197.168.150      lnbmac
206.197.168.2        lnbsun

# End of hosts.
```

As the example shows, each line in the file starts with an IP address, followed by the host name for that IP address. You can have more than one host name for a given IP address.

/etc/networks

The /etc/networks file is another text file containing the names and IP addresses of networks. These network names are commonly used in the routing command (/sbin/route) to specify a network by name instead of its IP address.

Don't be alarmed if your Linux PC does not have the /etc/networks file. Your TCP/IP network will work fine without this file. In fact, the Red Hat Linux installation program does not create any /etc/networks file.

/etc/host.conf

Linux uses a resolver library to obtain the IP address corresponding to a host name. The /etc/host.conf file specifies how names are resolved. A typical /etc/host.conf file might contain the following lines:

```
order hosts, bind
multi on
```

The entries in the /etc/host.conf file tell the resolver library what services to use, and in what order, to resolve names.

The order option indicates the order of services. The sample entry specifies that the resolver library should first consult the /etc/hosts file and then check the name server to resolve a name.

Wizard

The multi option determines whether a host in the /etc/hosts file can have multiple IP addresses. Hosts that have more than one IP address are said to be *multihomed*, because the presence of multiple IP addresses implies that the host has several network interfaces (the host "lives" in several networks simultaneously).

/etc/resolv.conf

The /etc/resolv.conf file is another text file used by the resolver — a library that determines the IP address for a host name. Following is a sample /etc/resolv.conf file:

```
domain com
nameserver 164.109.1.3
nameserver 164.109.10.23
```

The first line specifies your system's domain name. The nameserver line provides the IP addresses of name servers for your domain. If you have multiple name servers, you should list them on separate lines. They are queried in the order they appear in the file.

Note

If you do not have any name server for your network, you can safely ignore this file. TCP/IP should still work, even though you may not be able to refer to hosts by name.

/etc/hosts.allow

This file specifies which hosts are allowed to use the Internet services (such as Telnet and FTP) running on your system. As explained in the section "The inetd super server," the /usr/sbin/tcpd program consults the /etc/hosts.allow file before starting Internet services. It starts the service only if the entries in the hosts.allow file imply that the requesting host is allowed to use the services.

The entries in /etc/hosts.allow are in the form of a *server:IP address* format, where *server* refers to the name of the program providing a specific Internet service and *IP address* identifies the host allowed to use that service. For example, if you want all hosts in your local network (which has the class C address 192.168.1.0) to access the FTP service (which is provided by the in.ftpd program), you would add the following line in the /etc/hosts.allow file:

```
in.ftpd:192.168.1.
```

If you want to let all local hosts have access to all Internet services, you can use the ALL keyword and rewrite the line as follows:

```
ALL:192.168.1.
```

Finally, to open up all Internet services to all hosts, you can replace the IP address with ALL, as follows:

```
ALL:ALL
```

You can also use host names in place of IP addresses.

Tip

To learn the detailed syntax of entries in the /etc/hosts.allow file, type man hosts_access at the Linux shell prompt.

/etc/hosts.deny

This file is just the opposite of /etc/hosts.allow — whereas hosts.allow specifies which hosts may access Internet services (such as Telnet and FTP) on your system, the hosts.deny file identifies the hosts that must be denied services. As explained in the section "The inetd super server," the /usr/sbin/tcpd program consults the /etc/hosts.deny file if it does not find any rules in the /etc/hosts.allow file that applies to the requesting host. The tcpd program denies service if it finds in the hosts.deny file a rule that applies to the host.

The entries in the /etc/hosts.deny file follow the same format as those in the /etc/hosts.allow file — they are in the form of a *server:IP address* format, where *server* refers to the name of the program providing a specific Internet service and *IP address* identifies the host allowed to use that service.

If you have already set up entries in the /etc/hosts.allow file to allow access to specific hosts, you can place the following line in /etc/hosts.deny to deny all other hosts access to any service on your system:

```
ALL:ALL
```

Tip

To learn the detailed syntax of entries in the /etc/hosts.deny file, type man hosts_access at the Linux shell prompt.

Configuring networks at boot time

You want to start your network automatically every time you boot the system. For this to happen, you have to put the appropriate commands in one or more startup scripts. The init process runs immediately after Linux boots. The process consults the /etc/inittab file and then executes various commands (typically, shell scripts), depending on the current run level. In run level 3 — the multiuser level — /etc/inittab specifies that init should run the script file /etc/rc.d/rc with the argument 3.

Essentially, the startup script ends up executing the script file /etc/rc.d/init.d/network to activate all networking interfaces. If you consult the /etc/rc.d/init.d/network file, you will notice that network initialization is done by using another set of files in the /etc/sysconfig directory. The network activation script checks the variables defined in the /etc/sysconfig/network file to decide whether to activate the network. In /etc/sysconfig/network, you should see a line with the NETWORKING variable as follows:

```
NETWORKING=yes
```

The network is activated only if the NETWORKING variable is set to yes.

The /etc/rc.d/init.d/network script, in turn, executes a number of scripts in the /etc/sysconfig/network-scripts directory to activate specific network interfaces. For example, to activate the Ethernet interface eth0, the /etc/sysconfig/network-scripts/ifup script is executed with /etc/sysconfig/network-scripts/ifcfg-eth0 as the configuration file. Here is what a typical /etc/sysconfig/network-scripts/ifcfg-eth0 file contains:

```
DEVICE=eth0
IPADDR=192.168.1.1
NETMASK=255.255.255.0
NETWORK=192.168.1.0
BROADCAST=192.168.1.255
ONBOOT=yes
BOOTPROTO=none
```

As you can see, this file contains the network device name as well as the IP address of the interface and several other TCP/IP parameters. The ONBOOT variable indicates whether this network interface should be activated when Linux boots. In the case of the Ethernet card, you would want to activate the interface at boot time; therefore, ONBOOT is set to yes.

Cross-Reference

The files in the /etc/sysconfig directory are created by the Red Hat Linux installation program as you install Linux following the steps outlined in Chapter 1.

The /etc/sysconfig/network-scripts/ifup script essentially runs the following commands:

- /sbin/ifconfig, to configure the specified network interface; in this case, the Ethernet card (eth0).

- /sbin/route, to set up the routing table for the activated network interface.

TCP/IP Diagnostics

After you configure the kernel for Ethernet and TCP/IP, and you run netconfig to set up the TCP/IP network, you should be able to use various networking applications without any problem. The TCP/IP protocol suite includes several tools to help you monitor and diagnose problems.

Checking the interfaces

Use the /sbin/ifconfig command to view the currently configured network interfaces. The ifconfig command is used to configure a network interface (that is, to associate an IP address with a network device). If you run ifconfig without any command-line arguments, the command displays information about the current network interfaces. Following is a typical invocation of ifconfig and the resulting output:

```
/sbin/ifconfig
lo        Link encap:Local Loopback
          inet addr:127.0.0.1  Bcast:127.255.255.255  Mask:255.0.0.0
          UP BROADCAST LOOPBACK RUNNING  MTU:3584  Metric:1
          RX packets:1584 errors:0 dropped:0 overruns:0
          TX packets:1584 errors:0 dropped:0 overruns:0

eth0      Link encap:Ethernet  HWaddr 00:20:AF:E8:A2:25
          inet addr:192.168.1.1  Bcast:192.168.1.255
Mask:255.255.255.0
          UP BROADCAST RUNNING MULTICAST  MTU:1500  Metric:1
          RX packets:129187 errors:6 dropped:6 overruns:0
          TX packets:105955 errors:0 dropped:0 overruns:0
          Interrupt:10 Base address:0x210
```

This output shows that two interfaces — the loopback interface (lo) and an Ethernet card (eth0) — are currently active on this system. For each interface, you get to see the IP address, as well as statistics on packets delivered and sent. For the Ethernet card, ifconfig also reports the IRQ (10) and the base I/O port address (0x210).

Checking the IP routing table

The other network configuration command, /sbin/route, also provides status information when it is run without any command-line argument. If you are having trouble checking a connection to another host (that you specify with an IP address), check the IP routing table to see whether a default gateway is specified. Then check the gateway's routing table to ensure paths to an outside network appear in that routing table.

A typical output from the /sbin/route command looks like this:

```
/sbin/route
Kernel IP routing table
Destination      Gateway          Genmask          Flags Metric Ref    Use Iface
default-gateway  *                255.255.255.255  UH    0      0        0 ppp0
192.168.1.0      *                255.255.255.0    U     0      0       99 eth0
127.0.0.0        *                255.0.0.0        U     0      0       54 lo
default          default-gateway  0.0.0.0          UG    0      0       52 ppp0
```

As this routing table shows, the local network uses the eth0 Ethernet interface, and the default gateway happens to be a PPP connection (named ppp0) to the Internet.

Checking connectivity to a host

To check for a network path to a specific host, use the ping command. Ping is a widely used TCP/IP tool that uses a series of Internet Control Message Protocol (ICMP, often pronounced *eye-comp*) messages. (ICMP provides for an Echo message to which every host responds.) Using the ICMP messages and replies, Ping can determine whether the other system is alive, and compute the round-trip delay in communicating with that system.

The following example shows how I run ping to see whether one of the systems on my network is alive:

```
ping 206.197.168.50
PING 206.197.168.50 (206.197.168.50): 56 data bytes
64 bytes from 206.197.168.50: icmp_seq=0 ttl=32 time=3.4 ms
64 bytes from 206.197.168.50: icmp_seq=1 ttl=32 time=1.8 ms
64 bytes from 206.197.168.50: icmp_seq=2 ttl=32 time=1.8 ms
64 bytes from 206.197.168.50: icmp_seq=3 ttl=32 time=1.9 ms
            (press Ctrl-C here)
--- 206.197.168.50 ping statistics ---
4 packets transmitted, 4 packets received, 0% packet loss
round-trip min/avg/max = 1.8/2.2/3.4 ms
```

On some systems, ping simply reports that a remote host is alive. You can still get the timing information with appropriate command-line arguments. In Linux, ping continues to run until you press Ctrl-C to stop it; then it displays summary statistics, showing the typical time it takes to send a packet between the two systems.

Checking network status

To check the status of the network, use the netstat command. This command displays the status of network connections of various types (such as TCP and UDP connections). You can view the status of the interfaces quickly with the -i option, as follows:

```
netstat -i
Kernel Interface table
Iface    MTU Met  RX-OK RX-ERR RX-DRP RX-OVR  TX-OK TX-ERR TX-DRP TX-OVR Flags
lo      3584   0   1588      0      0      0   1588      0      0      0 BLRU
eth0    1500   0 129287      6      6      0 106008      0      0      0 BRU
```

In this case, the output shows the current status of the loopback and Ethernet interfaces. Table 16-2 describes each column's meaning.

Table 16-2   Columns in the kernel interface table

Column	Meaning
Iface	Name of the interface
MTU	Maximum Transfer Unit — the maximum number of bytes a packet can contain
RX-OK, TX-OK	Number of error-free packets received (RX) or transmitted (TX)
RX-ERR, TX-ERR	Number of packets with errors
RX-DRP, TX-DRP	Number of dropped packets
RX-OVR, TX-OVR	Number of packets lost due to overflow
Flags	A = receive multicast, B = broadcast allowed, D = debugging turned on, L = loopback interface (notice the flag on lo), M = all packets received, N = trailers avoided, O = no ARP on this interface, P = point-to-point interface, R = interface is running, and U = interface is up

Another useful netstat option is -t, which shows all active TCP connections. Following is a typical result of netstat -t on one of my Linux PCs:

```
netstat -t
Active Internet connections (w/o servers)
Proto Recv-Q Send-Q Local Address          Foreign Address        State
tcp        0      0 lnbp75:telnet          lnbp133:listen         ESTABLISHED
tcp        0    124 lnbp75:telnet          lnbp200:listen         ESTABLISHED
tcp        0      0 lnbp75:ftp             lnb486:listen          ESTABLISHED
```

In this case, the output columns show the protocol (Proto), the number of bytes in receive and transmit queues (Recv-Q, Send-Q), the local TCP port in *hostname:service* format (Local Address), the remote port (Foreign Address), and the state of the connection.

Summary

Linux has extensive built-in support for TCP/IP and Ethernet networks. Thinwire Ethernet, which uses flexible RG-58 coaxial cables, provides a convenient way to set up a small network because you can simply daisy-chain the PCs together. This chapter explains the basics of TCP/IP and Ethernet; it also shows you how to set up TCP/IP networking on your Linux PC. By reading this chapter, you learn the following things:

▶ The OSI seven-layer model provides a framework for making various networks work together. The OSI layered model also sets the stage for various networking protocols.

▶ The Transmission Control Protocol and Internet Protocol (TCP/IP) originated from research initiated by the U.S. Government's Advanced Research Projects Agency (APRA) in the 1970s. The modern Internet evolved from the networking technology developed during that time.

▶ All Internet protocols are documented in Request for Comments (RFC) documents. The RFCs are available from the Internet resource `ftp://rs.internic.net/rfc`. All standards are in RFCs, but many RFCs simply provide information to the Internet community.

▶ Internetworking is at the heart of the TCP/IP protocol; that is the purpose of the Internet Protocol. TCP/IP protocol identifies a host with an 32-bit IP address that has two parts: a network address and a host address.

▶ An IP address typically is expressed in dotted-decimal notation, in which each byte's value is written in decimal format and separated from the adjacent byte by a dot (.). A typical IP address is 140.90.23.100.

▶ IP addresses are grouped in classes. Class A addresses use a 1-byte network address and 3 bytes for the host address; class B addresses use a 2-byte network and host address; and class C addresses use a 3-byte network address and a single byte for the host address. The values of the first byte indicate the type of address: 1–126 is class A, 128–191 is class B, and 192–223 is class C.

▶ The IP address space is filling rapidly. To alleviate this problem, the Internet Engineering Task Force has adopted a new 16-byte (128-bit) addressing scheme known as IPv6 (or IP Version 6). Hosts that use the new IPv6 addresses will work with hosts that use the older IPv4 (32-bit) addresses.

▶ Ethernet is a popular physical data-transport mechanism. Several Ethernet standards exist, each of which uses a different type of cable. The 10BASE5 Ethernet (the original Ethernet) uses thick coaxial cables, 10BASE2 uses thin coaxial cables, and 10BASE-T uses unshielded twisted-pair (UTP) or telephone cables. Thinwire Ethernet (10BASE2) is easy to implement and convenient for small office networks.

▶ You need an Ethernet card on your PC to connect to an Ethernet network. Linux supports a wide variety of Ethernet cards. You should buy a 16-bit Ethernet card for good performance.

▶ Setting up TCP/IP on Linux requires setting up various configuration files. The `netcfg` program provides a convenient way to set up these files. You need some information — such as an IP address, the address of a gateway, and the address of a name server — to set up TCP/IP networking on your system. If you do not plan to connect your local network to the Internet, you can use a range of IP addresses (such as 192.168.0.0 to 192.168.255.255) without having to coordinate with any organization.

▶ Linux comes with many TCP/IP utilities, such as `ftp` (File Transfer Protocol) and `telnet` (for logging in to another system on the network).

▶ To diagnose TCP/IP networking problems, you can use the `ping`, `route`, and `netstat` commands.

Chapter 17

PC Cards

In This Chapter

PCMCIA stands for *Personal Computer Memory Card International Association*, an organization that standardized the interface for adding memory cards to laptop computers. Although originally conceived for memory cards, PCMCIA devices became popular for a wide variety of add-ons for laptops. Today, laptop computers use PCMCIA devices such as modems, network cards, SCSI controllers, and sound cards. Using Linux on a laptop means having to deal with the PCMCIA devices, or PC Cards, as they are called in the popular press nowadays. Thanks to the efforts of David Hinds, you can use PCMCIA devices under Linux with his PCMCIA Card Services for Linux. That software is available now and is being used by many people. This chapter briefly describes this PCMCIA support package for Linux.

CD

Red Hat Linux on the companion CD-ROM includes support for PCMCIA devices. The PCMCIA software is in the form of loadable driver modules. To get the latest version, you have to download the software yourself from `ftp://sunsite.unc.edu/pub/Linux/kernel/pcmcia/`.

Note

I refer to the actual cards as *PC Cards*, because that's the proper name for the devices. PCMCIA refers to the industry organization that specifies the standard for PC Cards. However, I use the term PCMCIA Card in one context — when referring to *PCMCIA Card Services for Linux* (or *Card Services*, for short), which is the software that supports PC Cards in Linux.

PC Card Basics

PC Cards originated as static random-access memory (SRAM) and flash RAM cards that were used to store data on small laptop computers. The credit-card-size cards fit into a slot on the side of the laptop. The flash memory cards used electrically erasable, programmable read-only memory (EEPROM) to provide laptops with storage capability that might have been too small for other conventional storage media.

Vendors soon realized the convenience of the memory-card slot as a general-purpose expansion slot for laptop computers. The Personal Computer Memory Card International Association (PCMCIA) standardized various aspects of PC Cards, including the electrical interface, card dimensions, and the card slot sizes. This standardization has contributed to the proliferation of PC Cards in the laptop market.

By now, PCMCIA slots are a common feature of almost all laptops. The memory card is a small part of the overall PC Card market. Most laptops provide the PCMCIA slots so users can add hardware, such as fax/modems, sound cards, network cards, and even hard disks.

To learn more about PCMCIA (the association) and PC Card specifications, point your favorite World Wide Web browser to `http://www.pc-card.com/`.

PC Card physical specifications

PC Cards are classified in three different types, according to the thickness of the card. Following are the standard physical dimensions for each type of PC Card, in terms of width by length by thickness:

- Type I PC Card: 54 mm by 85.6 mm by 3.3 mm
- Type II PC Card: 54 mm by 85.6 mm by 5 mm
- Type III PC Card: 54 mm by 85.6 mm by 10.5 mm

All three types of PC Cards have the same length and width — the size of a standard credit card, except for corner rounding; and card types are differentiated by thickness.

The term *form factor* is often used to refer to the dimensions of PC Cards.

All PC Cards use the same 68-pin connector. Because of this connector, a thinner card (Type I, for example) can be used in a thicker slot (Type II, for example). As you might guess, a thicker card cannot be used in a thinner slot.

PC Card use

Each type of PC Card is used for a specific type of application. Following are the typical applications of PC Cards, by card type:

- *Type I PC Card.* These thin cards are used for memory devices, such as static RAM (SRAM) and flash RAM.

- *Type II PC Card.* These cards are used for input and output (I/O) devices, such as fax/modems, network adapters, and sound cards.

- *Type III PC Card.* These cards are used for devices that require greater thickness, such as hard disks with rotating components (hard to believe, isn't it!).

A PC Card can have a maximum length of 135.6 mm (that's slightly longer than 5.25 inches), which means the card can extend outside the host. Extended cards are used in devices such as removable media, transceivers, and antennas.

PCMCIA standards

All these specifications are described in the PCMCIA Standard, of which there have been three major releases so far:

- *PCMCIA Standard Release 1.0 (June 1990).* The initial standard defined the 68-pin connector and Type I and Type II PC Cards. The standard also defined the Card Information Structure (CIS) that has been the basis for interoperability of PC Cards. The first release of the PCMCIA standard did not account for any I/O cards; only memory cards were considered.

- *PCMCIA Standard Release 2.0, 2.01 , 2.1 (1991–94).* The second release of the standard defined an I/O interface for the 68-pin connector. Release 2.01 added the PC Card AT Attachment (ATA) specification and provided an initial version of the Card and Socket Services (CSS) Specification. Release 2.1 further enhanced the Card and Socket Services Specification.

- *PC Card Standard (February 1995).* This release of the standard discards the old PCMCIA name and uses PC Card Standard as the name. It also adds information to improve compatibility among different types of PC Cards and includes support for features such as 3.3 volt operation, direct memory access (DMA) support, and 32-bit CardBus bus mastering.

PC Card terminology

As all laptop vendors adopt PC Card slots, the PC Card market has experienced explosive growth. Thanks to the PCMCIA standards, PC Card devices can be used in any PC Card slot. As you use PC Cards, you'll run into some terms that have special meaning for PC Cards:

- *Card Information Structure (CIS)* describes the characteristics and capabilities of a PC Card so the operating system or driver software can configure the card.

- *CardBus* is an electrical specification that describes the use of bus mastering technology and allows PC Cards to operate at up to 33MHz.

- *Direct Memory Access (DMA)* has the same meaning as in other peripherals, but now PC Cards can use DMA technology.

- *Execute In Place (XIP)* refers to the feature that allows operating-system and application software to run directly from the PC Card without having to be loaded into the system's RAM (eliminating the need for too much system RAM).

- *Low Voltage Operation* refers to the capability of PC Cards to operate at 3.3 volts (as well as 5 volts). The connector has a physical key to ensure that you cannot inadvertently insert a 3.3-volt card into a 5-volt slot.

- *Multifunction Capability* allows a PC Card to support several functions. 3Com's 3C562, for example, is a 10BASE-T Ethernet card and a 28,800-bps modem in a Type II form-factor PC Card.

- *Plug and Play* allows you to insert or remove a PC Card while the system is turned on (this is known as *hot swapping*). Such hot swapping of PC Cards is done by making the power-connection pins the longest, so the data lines disconnect before the power.

- *Power Management* refers to the capability of PC Cards to interface with the Advanced Power Management (APM) capabilities of laptops through the Card Services Specification.

- *Zoomed Video (ZV)* refers to a connection between a PC Card and the system's video controller that allows the card to write video data directly to the video controller.

PCMCIA Card Services for Linux

The standardization of PC Cards means that Linux developers can get their hands on the programming information they need to write device drivers for PC Cards. In particular, the Card Services Specification provides an Application Programming Interface (API) that's independent of the hardware controlling the PC Card sockets — the receptacles or slots for PC Cards.

A related specification is the Socket Services Specification, which also provides an API to access the hardware controlling the sockets for PC Cards.

You do not really have to learn about the PC Card and Socket Services APIs. David Hinds has already done the work in his PCMCIA Card Services for Linux, a software package you can use to access PC Card devices under Linux. All you need to do is turn on the PCMCIA support when you need it.

Activating card services

PCMCIA Card Services software should already be installed on your system because Red Hat Linux includes PCMCIA support. In Red Hat Linux, the activation of Card Services is controlled by the following files:

- `/etc/rc.d/init.d/pcmcia` is the shell script used to start the PCMCIA Card Services. Essentially, the command `/etc/rc.d/init.d/pcmcia start` is used to activate the Card Services when you boot the system. The script loads the appropriate PCMCIA driver modules using the `/sbin/insmod` command. Then the script runs the `cardmgr` program, which handles all card-insertion and card-removal events. Running the `cardmgr` program allows you to "hot swap" PC Cards, so you can insert and eject a card at any time.

- `/etc/sysconfig/pcmcia` contains a number of variables used by the `/etc/rc.d/init.d/pcmcia` script. In particular, the Card Services are not activated unless the line `PCMCIA=yes` appears in the `/etc/sysconfig/pcmcia` file. If your system does not have any PCMCIA devices, you will find the line `PCMCIA=no` in that file.

You can activate the Card Services at system startup by ensuring that the line `PCMCIA=yes` appears in the `/etc/sysconfig/pcmcia` file. Of course, you want to do this only if your PC has a PCMCIA socket on your PC (which happens to be true for most laptop PCs).

Using the cardctl program

If you have PCMCIA Card Services running, you can use the `/sbin/cardctl` program to monitor and control a PCMCIA socket. To view the status of a PCMCIA socket, type

`/sbin/cardctl status`

The output should show the current socket status flags.

The `cardctl` program takes many more arguments. With different arguments, you can suspend a card, resume it, and view the configuration parameters such as interrupts and configuration registers. You can learn more about `cardctl` from the online manual; type `man cardctl` to view the manual page.

Using supported PC cards

In the PCMCIA Card Services documentation directory, you'll find a file named SUPPORTED.CARDS (you can change to that directory by typing cd /usr/doc/pcmcia*). That file lists all the PCMCIA Cards known to work with at least one system.

The list of supported cards is becoming too numerous to include here. The categories of cards supported by the Card Services are as follows:

- **Ethernet cards:** Close to a hundred different models of Ethernet cards are supported, including popular models such as 3Com 3c589, 3c589B, 3c589C, 3c589D; Megahertz XJ10BT, CC10BT; and Xircom CreditCard CE2.

- **Fast Ethernet (10/100BASE-T) cards**: Linksys EtherFast 10/100 and Xircom CreditCard CE3 Fast Ethernet cards are supported.

- **Token Ring cards:** IBM Token Ring Adapter and 3Com 3c689 TokenLink III cards are supported.

- **Wireless network cards:** AT&T GIS / NCR WaveLAN version 2.0, DEC RoamAbout/DS, and Xircom CreditCard Netwave are supported.

- **Modem and serial cards:** All modem and serial port cards should work. The only exceptions are modems such as Compaq 192 and the New Media WinSurfer, and any other modems that require special Windows drivers.

- **Memory cards:** All static RAM (SRAM) memory cards should work.

- **SCSI adapter cards:** Over thirty different models of SCSI cards are supported, including models such as Adaptec APA-1460, APA-1460A, APA-1450A SlimSCSI; IBM SCSI; Iomega ZIP Card; NEC PC-9801N-J03R; and Toshiba NWB0107ABK, SCSC200B.

- **ATA/IDE disk drive cards:** All ATA/IDE disk drive PC Cards are supported.

- **ATA/IDE CD-ROM adapter cards:** Several ATA/IDE CD-ROM adapters are supported, including Argosy EIDE CD-ROM; Caravelle CD-36N; Creative Technology CD-ROM; Digital Mobile Media CD-ROM; some EXP models; and several IO-DATA models.

- **Multifunction cards:** Several multifunction cards are supported, including 3Com 3c562, 3c562B/C/D, 3c563B/C/D; IBM Home and Away Card; Linksys LANmodem 28.8, 33.6; Megahertz EM1144, EM3288, EM3336; Motorola Mariner and Marquis; Ositech Jack of Diamonds; and Xircom CreditCard CEM28, CEM33, CEM56 models.

- **Other cards:** The Trimble Mobile GPS card is supported through the serial/modem driver.

For the latest list of supported cards, you should consult the SUPPORTED.CARDS file in the version of PCMCIA Card Services you have installed on your system.

Notice that Xircom CE-10BT Ethernet and CE II Ethernet/Modem combo cards are not supported.

Reading further

To learn more about the PCMCIA Card Services software, you should consult the PCMCIA-HOWTO. To read this HOWTO document, type cd /usr/doc/HOWTO to change to the directory where the HOWTO file is located. Then type zmore PCMCIA-HOWTO.gz to view the PCMCIA-HOWTO file. This file contains the latest information about the Card Services software, including common problems and suggested fixes.

In particular, you should look through the PCMCIA-HOWTO file for any information that applies to your specific PC Card.

Summary

Developed as a way to attach memory cards to laptop computers, PC Cards have become a popular way to add new capabilities to laptops. If you use Linux on a laptop, you need some way to access the PC Cards. Dave Hinds's PCMCIA Card Services for Linux provides a way to use PC Cards under Linux. This chapter describes how to activate the Card Services for Linux software.

By reading this chapter, you learn the following things:

▶ PC Cards originated as credit-card-size memory devices that plugged into a slot on the side of a laptop computer and provided a data-storage medium.

▶ The Personal Computer Memory Card International Association (PCMCIA) standardized various aspects of PC Cards, including the electrical interface, the card dimensions, and the card-slot sizes.

▶ Nowadays, PC Cards are used widely in laptops as an expansion slot for many devices, such as network adapters, fax/modem cards, SCSI controllers, sound cards, and even hard disks.

▶ There are three types of PC Cards: Type I, II, and III. All cards have the same length and width (54 mm by 85.6 mm) — the size of a standard credit card. The types differ in thickness. Type I is the thinnest (3.3 mm), and Type III is the thickest (10.5 mm).

▶ Red Hat Linux includes Dave Hinds's PCMCIA Card Services for Linux. The latest version of this software is available via FTP from the /pub/Linux/kernel/pcmcia directory at sunsite.unc.edu.

▶ You will find a list of supported PC Cards in the SUPPORTED.CARDS file.

▶ For the latest information about a specific PCMCIA device, consult the PCMCIA-HOWTO file in the /usr/doc/HOWTO directory.

Part IV:

Using Linux for Fun and Profit

Chapter 18

Dial-up Networking in Linux

In This Chapter

- Understanding networking
- Understanding SLIP and PPP
- Establishing a SLIP connection
- Setting up PPP on your Linux PC
- Using PPP for data transport in TCP/IP networking
- Routing TCP/IP over a PPP connection
- Making your Linux system a PPP server

Previous parts of this book focus on Linux installation and setup on your PC. You learned how to install Linux on your system, configure the XFree86 X Window System, and set up Linux to use various types of hardware. This part of the book gets to the fun aspects of Linux (and some business, too). The seven chapters in this part show you how to connect your Linux PC to the Internet; set up various Internet services, including a World Wide Web server; develop software; and even run a small business with Linux.

This chapter covers dial-up networking — one of the first steps that many of you perform to connect your Linux PC (and perhaps your own local area network) to the Internet.

If you have a Linux system at home (or in a small office), you may want to use a modem to connect to the Internet. At the other end of the modem, you'll need a system that's already on the Internet. This system could be one at your office, your university, or a commercial Internet Service Provider (ISP). That's what I mean by *dial-up networking* — establishing a network connection between your Linux PC and a remote computer through a dial-up modem.

This chapter describes the dial-up networking facilities in Linux, with particular emphasis on Point-to-Point Protocol (PPP) as the method of exchanging network packets over a dial-up connection.

Cross-Reference

As you read this chapter, you should consult Chapter 16 for a discussion of networking, TCP/IP, the Internet, and terms such as Request for Comments (RFC).

Learning the Basics of Dial-up Networking

Dial-up networking refers to connecting a PC to a remote network through a dial-up modem. A significant difference exists between dial-up networking and plain old serial communication. Both approaches use a modem to dial up another computer and establish a communication path, but serial communication software (such as `minicom`, described in Chapter 15) makes your computer act like a terminal connected to the remote computer. The dial-up connection is used exclusively by the serial communication software. You could not run another copy of the communication software and use the same modem connection, for example.

In dial-up networking, you run TCP/IP or other network-protocol software on your PC as well as on the remote system with which your PC has a dial-up communication path. That communication path simply forms one of the layers in the OSI seven-layer network model. The network protocols exchange data packets over the dial-up connection. You can simultaneously use any number of network applications to communicate over the single dial-up connection. With dial-up networking, your PC truly becomes part of the network to which the remote computer belongs. (If the remote computer is not on a network, the dial-up networking creates a network that consists of the remote computer and your PC.) Thus, you can have any number of network applications, ranging from a Web browser to a `telnet` session, running at the same time, with all applications sharing the physical data-transport capabilities of the dial-up connection.

This chapter describes TCP/IP over a dial-up connection, because TCP/IP is the dominant protocol of the Internet, and Linux has built-in support for TCP/IP. To be more accurate, I should say that the discussion in this chapter applies to TCP/IP over any point-to-point serial communication link. The "dial-up" part simply reflects the fact that most of us use a modem to establish the point-to-point communication link to a remote computer.

Like TCP/IP networking over Ethernet, TCP/IP networking over a dial-up link is a matter of specifying the *protocol* — the convention — for packaging a network packet over the communication link. There are two popular protocols for TCP/IP networking over point-to-point serial communication links:

- Serial Line Internet Protocol (SLIP) is a simple protocol that specifies how to frame an IP packet on a serial line. SLIP is described in RFC 1055.

- Point-to-Point Protocol (PPP) is a more advanced protocol for establishing a TCP/IP connection over any point-to-point link, including dial-up serial links. RFC 1661 describes PPP.

I first provide an overview of SLIP and PPP; and then I show you how to use SLIP, as well as PPP, to set up a network connection to a remote system.

Serial Line Internet Protocol

SLIP originated as a simple protocol for framing an *IP packet*—an Internet Protocol packet that consists of an IP header (which includes the source and destination IP addresses) followed by data (the data being sent from source to destination). RFC 1055, "A Nonstandard for Transmission of IP Datagrams over Serial Lines: SLIP," Ronkey, 1988, describes SLIP. As the title of RFC 1055 suggests, SLIP is not an official Internet standard; it's a de facto standard.

SLIP defines two special characters for framing IP packets:

- SLIP-END is octal 300 (decimal 192), and it marks the end of an IP packet.

- SLIP-ESC is octal 333 (decimal 219), and it is used to "escape" any SLIP-END or SLIP-ESC characters embedded in the packet (to ensure, for example, that a packet does not end prematurely because the IP packet happens to include a byte with decimal 192).

The protocol involves sending out the bytes of the IP packet one by one and marking the end of the packet with a SLIP-END character. The following convention is used to handle any SLIP-END and SLIP ESC characters that happen to be in the IP packet:

- Replace a SLIP-END character with SLIP-ESC, followed by octal 334 (decimal 220).

- Replace a SLIP-ESC character with SLIP-ESC, followed by octal 335 (decimal 221).

That's it! Based on the most popular implementation of SLIP from Berkeley UNIX, SLIP uses a few more conventions:

- Packets start and end with the SLIP-END character to ensure that each IP packet starts anew.

- The total size of the IP packet (including the IP header and data, but without the SLIP framing characters) is 1,006 bytes.

SLIP's simplicity led to its popularity (although nowadays PPP is more widely used). SLIP has several shortcomings, however:

- Both ends of the SLIP connection have to know their IP addresses. Although some schemes have been worked out to allow the dynamic assignment of IP addresses, the protocol does not have any provisions for address negotiation.

- Both ends of SLIP must use the same packet size, because the protocol does not allow the two ends to negotiate the packet size.

- SLIP has no support for data compression. (As you will learn later in this section, Compressed SLIP, or CSLIP, introduces compression in SLIP.)

- There is no way to identify the packet type in SLIP. Accordingly, SLIP can carry only one protocol — the one that both ends of SLIP are hard-wired to use. A transport mechanism such as SLIP should be capable of carrying packets of any protocol type.

Note

The lack of data compression in SLIP was addressed by Compressed SLIP (CSLIP), which is described in RFC 1144, "Compressing TCP/IP Headers for Low-Speed Serial Links," Jacobson, 1990. CSLIP compresses TCP/IP header information, which tends to be repetitive in packets exchanged between the two ends of a SLIP connection. CSLIP does not compress the packet's data.

CSLIP is often referred to as *Van Jacobson compression*, in recognition of CSLIP's author. Incidentally, PPP also supports Van Jacobson TCP/IP header compression.

Point-to-Point Protocol

PPP fixes the shortcomings of SLIP and defines a more complex protocol. Unlike SLIP, PPP is an official Internet standard; it is documented in RFC 1661, "The Point-to-Point Protocol," Simpson, 1994 (updated in RFC 2153, "PPP Vendor Extensions," Simpson, May 1997).

PPP includes the following main components:

- A packet-framing mechanism that uses a modified version of the well-known High-Level Data Link Control (HDLC) protocol.

- A Link Control Protocol (LCP) to establish, configure, and test the data link.

- A Network Control Protocol (NCP) that allows PPP to carry more than one type of network packet — such as IP, IPX, and NetBEUI (Network BIOS Extended User Interface) — over the same connection.

PPP is gradually replacing SLIP as the protocol of choice for transporting packets over point-to-point links. In addition to the ubiquitous serial link, some versions of PPP work over several other types of point-to-point links. Some of the point-to-point links with which PPP works include Frame Relay, SONET/SDH (Synchronous Optical Network/Synchronous Digital Hierarchy), X.25, and ISDN (Integrated Services Digital Network).

The PPP frame has a more complex structure than SLIP does. The PPP frame structure is based on ISO (International Standards Organization) standard 3309, "Data Communications — High-Level Data Link Control Procedures — Frame Structure," 1979. The High-Level Data Link Control (HDLC) protocol uses a special flag character to mark the beginning and end of a frame. Figure 18-1 shows the structure of a complete PPP frame.

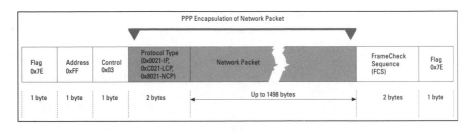

Figure 18-1: The format of a PPP frame

As Figure 18-1 shows, the PPP frames begin and end with a flag character whose value is always 0x7E (that's 7E in hexadecimal notation). The Address and Control fields come from HDLC; they have the fixed values of 0xFF and 0x03, respectively. The PPP data consists of a 2-byte protocol field. (Actually, this field can be only 1 byte; the length of the protocol field is negotiated with the Link Control Protocol.)

Within the encapsulated network packet, PPP uses 0x7D as the escape character. To send a byte that has a special meaning (such as 0x7E, which marks the beginning and end of a frame), PPP uses the following steps:

Embeds 0x7D in the data

Places the data byte being escaped

Toggles the sixth bit of that data byte

Thus, if the PPP data includes 0x7E, that byte is replaced by the 2-byte sequence 0x7D, followed by 0x5E. (If you toggle the sixth bit of 0x7E, or 0111 1110 in binary, you get 0x5E, or 0101 1110 in binary.)

When you use PPP to set up a link between your Linux PC and a remote computer, your PC first sends LCP packets to set up the data link. After the physical data link is established and any optional parameters are negotiated, your PC sends NCP packets to select one or more network protocols to be used over that link. Thereafter, any of those network protocols can send packets over the PPP link.

Tip

You don't need to know the complete details of PPP to use it effectively. Later sections of this chapter describe how you can use PPP to establish a TCP/IP network connection to another computer.

Making a SLIP Connection

To set up a SLIP connection between your Linux PC and a remote system, both systems must support SLIP. Both ends also must run some SLIP software during the time when the connection is up.

To include SLIP in your Linux kernel, you should accept the default answers to the following questions during the kernel-configuration step (in which you type **make config**):

```
SLIP (serial line) support (CONFIG_SLIP) [M/n/y/?] y
CSLIP compressed headers (CONFIG_SLIP_COMPRESSED) [Y/n/?]
Keepalive and linefill (CONFIG_SLIP_SMART) [Y/n/?]
Six bit SLIP encapsulation (CONFIG_SLIP_MODE_SLIP6) [N/y/?]
```

Cross-Reference

Chapter 2 describes how to configure and rebuild the kernel. You also need TCP/IP support in the kernel, of course.

Typically, the first step in establishing a SLIP connection is dialing up the remote system, logging in, and starting SLIP on the remote system. Then you must start SLIP at your end. After the two ends are running SLIP, you have the SLIP connection up. To use that connection, you also have to configure the interface (with the ifconfig command) and set up the routing (with the route command) so that network packets originating on your PC can reach their destination. You can do all these things through a program called dip (Dial-up IP Protocol Driver), which automates the process of setting up a SLIP connection. You learn how to use dip in the following sections.

Verifying SLIP support

Before trying SLIP, you should verify that your kernel includes SLIP support. Type **dmesg | more** to view the boot messages. If your kernel has SLIP support, you should see messages such as the following:

```
CSLIP: code copyright 1989 Regents of the University of California
SLIP: version 0.8.4-NET3.019-NEWTTY-MODULAR (dynamic channels,
max=256).
SLIP linefill/keepalive option.
```

The first two lines refer to Compressed SLIP (CSLIP) and SLIP support, respectively. If you see these lines, you can assume that your kernel supports SLIP.

If SLIP support is in the form of a loadable module, you should load the SLIP support by logging in as root and typing the following command:

```
modprobe slip
```

Type lsmod to verify that the SLIP module has been loaded.

Obtaining remote-system information

The exact mechanics of establishing a SLIP connection to a remote system depend on that system's setup. If you obtained a SLIP account from an Internet Service Provider (ISP), the ISP should give you the information you need to establish a SLIP connection. At minimum, this information includes the following:

- The phone number you must dial to connect to the remote computer.

- The user name and password that you have to use to log into the system.

- The IP addresses for both ends of the SLIP connection. Many ISPs provide a fixed (static) IP address, whereas other ISPs assign IP addresses dynamically.

You'll also get the IP addresses of name servers (a name server translates names to IP addresses), a mail server, and a news server. These IP addresses are necessary when you begin to use Internet applications on your system; you don't need them during SLIP-connection setup.

Typically, an ISP sets up a SLIP account for you in such a way that the SLIP software starts automatically after you log in. The ISP automatically starts SLIP by specifying that the SLIP software be run in place of a shell (such as /bin/bash) for that account name. An ordinary user might have an entry in /etc/passwd that looks like the following example:

```
naba:ZbWOxq2XGAO3g:501:100:Naba Barkakati:/home/naba:/bin/bash
```

Colons (:) separate the fields in this line in /etc/passwd. The first field is the user name; the last two fields are the home directory and the shell (the program to run after that user logs in), respectively. For a SLIP account, the entry might be the following:

```
slipxxx:ZbWOxq2XfLO3g:501:101:SLIP user xx:/tmp:/usr/bin/ppl
```

The user name may be something cryptic (slipxxx), the home directory might be /tmp, and the last field shows the name of the SLIP program on the remote system. On a Hewlett-Packard workstation, for example, /usr/bin/ppl is the point-to-point link software that establishes a SLIP connection.

If the remote system is at your office, you may have a separate SLIP login, or you could log in as a normal user and then start the SLIP software. You can automate this part of the process with the dip program you would run on your Linux PC.

Using dip to establish a SLIP connection

The dip (Dial-up IP Protocol Driver) program allows you to automate the steps involved in setting up a SLIP connection to a remote system. If you want, you can run dip in an interactive mode. The best way to use dip, however, is to prepare a *script file* (a text file containing commands for dip) and then run dip with that script file as input. I show you how to set up a dip script in the section "Setting up a dip script". First, however, try using some of the dip commands interactively.

Running dip interactively

To get a feel for dip's commands, run dip interactively. Start dip with the -t option, as follows:

```
/usr/sbin/dip -t
DIP: Dialup IP Protocol Driver version 3.3.7o-uri (8 Feb 96)
Written by Fred N. van Kempen, MicroWalt Corporation.

DIP> help
DIP knows about the following commands:

        beep     bootp    break    chatkey   config
        databits dec      default  dial      echo
        flush    get      goto     help      if
        inc      init     mode     modem     netmask
        onexit   parity   password proxyarp  print
        psend    port     quit     reset     send
        shell    skey     sleep    speed     stopbits
        term     timeout  wait

DIP> quit
```

Tip

When you run dip in interactive mode, you can use the help command to see a list of commands dip accepts. If you have all the information, you can use dip in interactive mode and issue appropriate commands to dial a remote system, log in, and complete the SLIP connection. Table 18-1 lists the available dip commands, showing the syntax and meaning of each. You typically would use these commands in a dip script file.

Table 18-1	The dip commands
Command	**Meaning**
beep [*times*]	Beeps a specified number of times.
bootp	Uses BOOTP protocol to determine the local IP address. (BOOTP, or Bootstrap Protocol, defined in RFC 951, provides a way for a workstation to determine its IP address. The protocol was developed to allow a diskless workstation to find a host from which to download a boot file and execute.)
break	Sends a BREAK. (Refer to Chapter 15 for an explanation of BREAK.)
chatkey *keyword* [*value*]	Adds a keyword (and an associated value) to the list of modem responses dip recognizes. chatkey RING 10, for example, associates the value 10 with the modem response RING.
config [interface| routing] [pre|up|down |post] *arguments*	Uses the specified interface and routing-table configuration parameters. By default, this command is disabled.

Command	Meaning
databits 7 | 8	Sets the number of data bits to 7 or 8 (you must specify one of the two values). The number of data bits also is referred to as *word length* in serial communications.
dec $variable [number | $var2]	Decrements the specified variable (dip uses a dollar-sign prefix with a name to denote a variable). You can provide a number or another variable to indicate the amount to be decremented. If you do not provide a number or a second variable, dip decrements the value of the variable by 1.
default	Sets up the default route to the remote system with which dip has established connection. The default route is used to forward network packets addressed to any unknown network address.
dial phonenum [num_seconds]	Dials the specified phone number and waits the specified number of seconds to receive an answer. If you do not specify a number of seconds, dip uses 60 seconds as a timeout. After issuing the modem's dial command, dip parses the modem's reply and sets the variable named $errlvl according to the reply (0=OK; 1=CONNECT).
echo on | off	The command echo on enables the display of all modem replies and text being sent to the modem. (This command can help you debug dip scripts.) The echo off command disables this feature and makes dip work in silence. I like to see what's going on, so I always use echo on in dip scripts.
exit [status]	Exits the dip script with the specified status code (leaves the current SLIP connection intact and leaves dip running). You must exit a dip script in this manner after establishing a successful SLIP connection.
flush	Flushes the input that was read from the modem or terminal.
get $variable [number | ask | r emote [timeout] | $var2]	Gets the value of a specified variable. Use the ask keyword to prompt the user for a value. Use a number to simply set the variable to that value. Use the remote keyword to read a value from the remote system. You also can provide the name of a second variable as the source of the value.
goto label	Jumps to a specified label in the script. The label marks a location in the script. The syntax for a label uses the label's text followed by a colon (:). You'll see an example of this in the section "Setting up a dip script.".
help	Prints help information (used in interactive mode).

(continued)

Table 18-1 *(Continued)*

Command	Meaning
if *expression* goto *label*	Tests the *expression* and jumps to the *label* if the expression is true. The expression is of the form $variable operator constant, in which $variable denotes a dip variable, and *operator* is ==, !=, <, >, <=, or >=. *constant* is a constant value.
inc $*variable* [*number* | $*var2*]	Increments the specified variable. You can provide a a number or another variable to indicate the amount to be incremented. If you do not provide a number or a second variable, dip increments the value of the variable by 1.
init *init_string*	Specifies the initialization string to be sent to the modem before dip executes the dial command. The default *init_string* is ATE0 Q0 V1 X1. (Refer to Chapter 15 for a list of Hayes modem commands.)
mode SLIP | CSLIP | PPP | TERM	Sets the protocol to be used for the connection. The default is SLIP. If your ISP supports Compressed SLIP, use the CSLIP mode.
modem *modem_type*	Specifies the type of modem. The only acceptable value is HAYES, which dip assumes by default.
netmask *xxx.xxx. xxx.xxx*	Specifies the netmask to be used in configuring the SLIP interface. (Refer to Chapter 16 for a discussion of TCP/IP terms, including netmask.)
parity E | O | N	Sets the parity to be used for serial communication. Use E for even, O for odd, and N for none.
password	Prompts the user for a password and then sends that password to the modem.
proxyarp	Sets up proxy ARP. (Described in RFC 1027, proxy ARP allows a host — which also must be a gateway — to stand in for other hosts.)
print *any_text* [$*variable*]	Prints the text, as well as the values, of any variables.
port *device_name*	Specifies the device name of the serial port to which the modem is connected. You must provide the device name without the /dev/ prefix. Thus, use cua0 if the modem is on COM1.
quit	Exits dip with nonzero status.
reset	Sends the string +++, followed by ATZ, to the modem. (The three plus signs are used to get the modem's attention, and ATZ resets the modem.)
securidf *fixed_part*	Stores the fixed part of a SecureID password.

Command	Meaning
`securid`	Prompts the user for the variable part of a password generated by an ACE System SecureID card.
`send` *`text`* `[$`*`variable`*`]`	Sends the text, as well as the values of any variables, to the modem.
`skey [`*`timeout`* `|` *`$variable`*`]`	Makes `dip` look for a S/Key challenge from the remote system. (S/Key is an authentication system developed by Bellcore.)
`sleep` *`num_seconds`*	Waits the specified number of seconds.
`speed` *`bits_per_second`*	Sets the serial port's speed. (Provide a number in bits-per-second units.)
`stopbits 1 | 2`	Sets the number of stop bits for serial communication.
`term`	Makes `dip` go into terminal-emulation mode. This mode allows you to interact directly through the serial connection. You can press `Ctrl-]` to exit terminal mode.
`timeout` *`num_seconds`*	Sets the timeout value to a specified number of seconds. If no activity occurs for that number of seconds, `dip` breaks the connection and exits.
`wait` *`text`* `[`*`timeout`* `|` *`$variable`*`]`	Waits for specified text to arrive. The optional argument indicates how long `dip` should wait.

In addition to the commands, `dip` provides several built-in variables. Table 18-2 lists the built-in variables in `dip`.

Table 18-2   Built-in dip variables

Variable	Description
`$errlvl`	The result code of the last executed command. Zero indicates success; any other value indicates error.
`$local`	The host name of your Linux PC (the local system).
`$locip`	The IP address of your Linux PC.
`$modem`	The name of the modem. (The only supported value is HAYES.)
`$mtu`	The Maximum Transfer Unit — the maximum number of bytes a packet can contain.
`$port`	The name of the serial device (for example, `cua0` for COM1) used for the SLIP connection.
`$remote`	The host name of the remote system — the other end of the SLIP connection.
`$rmtip`	The IP address of the remote end of the SLIP connection.
`$speed`	The data-transfer rate between your PC and the modem (in bits per second).

When you first try a SLIP connection, you may want to run dip in interactive
mode and use its term command to log in and establish the connection. The
following example shows how I log in as root on my Linux system and
establish a SLIP connection with a remote HP workstation. (My input is in
boldface; comments are in italics.)

```
lnbsoft:/home/naba/slip# dip -t
DIP: Dialup IP Protocol Driver version 3.3.7o-uri (8 Feb 96)
Written by Fred N. van Kempen, MicroWalt Corporation.

DIP> get $locip 140.90.23.195
DIP> get $rmtip 140.90.23.194
DIP> port cua0
DIP> speed 38400
DIP> term
[ Entering TERMINAL mode. Use CTRL-] to get back ]

NO CARRIER
ATZ
OK
ATDT5551212    (use appropriate phone number here)
CONNECT 28800/ARQ/V34/LAPM/V42BIS

GenericSysName [Release] (see /etc/issue)
 dialin login: naba  (use your login name here)
Password:  (type your password here)

(extraneous messages deleted)

You have mail.
TERM = (hp)  (press Enter)
/users/naba 21 % ppl
 ppl: starting for naba at Mon Apr 11 20:45:55 1998

/dev/ttyd01 38400 Linet=140.90.23.194 Rinet=140.90.23.195
Mask=255.255.255.0 SLIP
initialization complete, running protocol
  (Press Ctrl-] here)
[ Back to LOCAL mode. ]
DIP> default
DIP> mode SLIP
```

Tip

After the final mode SLIP command, dip exits, and the connection is
completed. At this point, I can use network applications such as telnet or
ftp to access the remote system. When I no longer need the SLIP connection,
I log in as root again and type **dip -k cua0** to end the connection.

Notice that in dip's interactive mode, you have to switch to a terminal mode
(with the term command) to send commands to the modem. You have to be
in terminal mode to send the dialing commands to the modem and to log into
the remote system when you see the login prompt.

After you enter any commands needed by the remote system, you should revert to `dip`'s command mode by pressing Ctrl-]. Then you can complete the SLIP setup by entering the `default` command, followed by the `mode SLIP` command. The default command causes `dip` to set up a default route by using the SLIP connection (which means that any network packet with an unknown address goes to the SLIP connection). The `mode SLIP` command makes `dip` communicate with the remote end by using the SLIP protocol.

Tip

If your ISP supports Compressed SLIP, use the `mode CSLIP` command instead of `mode SLIP`.

Setting up a dip script

As the preceding section shows, you can establish a SLIP connection by running `dip` in interactive mode with the `-t` option. That approach is not convenient, however, if you want to make a SLIP connection regularly. If your ISP provides you with fixed IP addresses for both ends of the SLIP connection, you can set up a script file that can set up the connection automatically. The script file contains commands for the `dip` program; you have to write the script according to the syntax required by the `dip` program.

Tip

If your `dip` script file is named `connect.dip` (it is common to use the `.dip` extension for script files meant for `dip`), you can use that file with `dip` by typing **dip connect**. This command causes the `dip` program to read and execute commands from the script file named `connect.dip`.

The script file itself is essentially a sequence of commands for `dip`, much like the commands you use when you run `dip` with the `-t` option. The only major difference is that you have to use the `send` command to send some text to the modem, and use the `wait` command to look for specific text coming back from the remote system. Following is a `dip` script file I use to connect to a HP workstation (I must use the `ppl` command manually to establish a point-to-point link by using the SLIP protocol):

```
# File: connect.dip
#
# Establishes a dial-up SLIP connection.
#
# Naba Barkakati, 4/11/98

main:
# Echo everything so we can debug easily
  echo on

# Set up my IP address
  get $locip 140.90.23.195

# Set up the remote IP address
# NOTE: These are test values only -- you should use
# IP addresses specific to your case
```

```
      get $rmtip 140.90.23.194

# Set the netmask on sl0 to 255.255.255.0
   netmask 255.255.255.0

# Select the serial port and speed (my modem is on COM1, which
# is /dev/cua0 -- select yours appropriately)
   port cua0
   speed 38400

# Send initialization sequence to modem
   send ATZ\r
   wait OK 2
   send ATE1M1V1X4L3S0=0\&c1Q0DT5551212\r
   wait CONNECT 75

# Check the "errlvl"
   if $errlvl != 0 goto error

# We are connected. Log in.
login:
   wait ogin: 30
if $errlvl != 0 goto no_login_prompt

# Send your user name (use your user ID on the next line)
   send your-username\r
   wait word: 10

# Send the passwrd (use your password on the next line)
   send your-password-here

# The following sequence depends on your system
# In this case, I am responding to a system's prompt for
# terminal name
   wait TERM 10
   send \r
   sleep 5
   send \r
   send \r
   wait some-text-in-the-prompt 30

# Start SLIP at the remote end
   print Sending command to start SLIP...
   send ppl\n
   wait some-text-indicating-SLIP-is-running 30

   default
   mode SLIP
# Print a message and exit
   print Connected... $locip -> $rmtip
   goto exit

no_login_prompt:
```

```
print No login prompt...
goto error

error:
  print CONNECT FAILED...
  quit 1

exit:
```

Notice that you must replace the items in italics with the text and numbers appropriate for your situation. In particular, if you obtained a SLIP account from an ISP, you must get the IP addresses and the phone number from the ISP. Also, the exact steps for logging into the remote system will vary from one system to another.

Checking the SLIP connection

After the SLIP connection is set up, you can use the `ifconfig` command to see whether the SLIP device `sl0` is configured (`dip` does this for you). Following is typical output from the `ifconfig` command after you have SLIP up and running:

```
ifconfig
lo      Link encap:Local Loopback
        inet addr:127.0.0.1 Bcast:127.255.255.255 Mask:255.0.0.0
        UP BROADCAST LOOPBACK RUNNING MTU:2000 Metric:1
        RX packets:0 errors:0 dropped:0 overruns:0
        TX packets:25 errors:0 dropped:0 overruns:0

sl0     Link encap:Serial Line IP
        inet addr:140.90.23.195 P-t-P:140.90.23.194 Mask:255.255.255.0
        UP POINTOPOINT RUNNING MTU:296 Metric:1
        RX packets:4 errors:0 dropped:0 overruns:0
        TX packets:4 errors:0 dropped:0 overruns:0

eth0    Link encap:10Mbps Ethernet HWaddr 00:20:AF:E8:A2:25
        inet addr:206.197.168.200 Bcast:206.197.168.255
Mask:255.255.255.0
        UP BROADCAST RUNNING MULTICAST MTU:1500 Metric:1
        RX packets:2087 errors:0 dropped:0 overruns:0
        TX packets:543 errors:0 dropped:0 overruns:0
        Interrupt:10 Base address:0x210
```

Secret

Additionally, if you use the `default` command, `dip` adds a default route to the SLIP connection. To verify this, type `/sbin/route` command and verify that the packets for the IP address 140.90.23.194 (which, in this case, is the remote end of the SLIP connection) are sent to the `sl0` device — the SLIP device. Packets meant for the `default` destination (any IP address other than the ones listed in the routing table) should also be sent to the IP address 140.90.23.194 — the remote end of the SLIP connection. You need these routing-table entries so that your Linux system can communicate with the remote system.

Ending a SLIP connection

To end a SLIP connection, you have to use dip itself with the -k option, followed by the serial device being used for the SLIP connection. Log in as root, and type the following command to close a SLIP connection on /dev/cua0:

```
dip -k cua0
DIP: Dialup IP Protocol Driver version 3.3.7o-uri (8 Feb 96)
Written by Fred N. van Kempen, MicroWalt Corporation.

DIP: process 951 killed.
```

Connecting to a Remote Network As a PPP Client

PPP is a more complex and more versatile protocol than SLIP, but the mechanics of connecting to a remote network with PPP are very similar to the steps you use for SLIP. You still get IP addresses for the two ends of the PPP connection, a phone number to dial, and a user name under which to log into the remote system.

Note

Just as the dip program helps you automate SLIP setup, you use two other programs — pppd and chat — to set up and configure a PPP connection. Before you try anything, your Linux kernel must include the PPP network devices.

Checking PPP support

As with SLIP, you must have the kernel configured with PPP support. In the make config step of rebuilding the Linux kernel (consult Chapter 2 for details), you should answer Yes to the following question about PPP support:

```
PPP (point-to-point) support (CONFIG_PPP) [M/n/y/?] y
```

You can use the command cat /proc/net/dev to verify that PPP devices are available on your system. Typically, you should see the ppp0 device listed in the output.

Additionally, when your system boots, the boot messages show whether PPP devices have been configured. Use the dmesg | more command to view the boot messages. You should see lines such as the following in the boot messages:

```
IP Protocols: IGMP, ICMP, UDP, TCP
PPP: version 2.2.0 (dynamic channel allocation)
TCP compression code copyright 1989 Regents of the University of
California
PPP Dynamic channel allocation code copyright 1995 Caldera, Inc.
PPP line discipline registered.
```

**Cross-
Reference** If you do not see any evidence of PPP support in the kernel, you should rebuild the kernel, using the steps in Chapter 2. Then you should make sure that you enable PPP support during the make config step.

Gathering information for a PPP connection

Many ISPs (Internet Service Providers) provide PPP access to the Internet through one or more systems that the ISP maintains. If you sign up for such a service, the ISP should provide you with the information you need to make a PPP connection to the remote system. At minimum, this information should include the following:

- The IP address for your side of the connection. (This IP address will be associated with your PC's PPP interface — the serial port.)

- The IP address of the ISP's PPP interface. (This address may be listed as the "gateway" address, because this interface is your system's gateway to the Internet.)

- The phone number to dial to connect to the remote system.

- The user name and password that you must use to log into the remote system.

Most ISPs also provide the IP addresses of a name server, mail server, and news server. These addresses, however, are not important for the mechanics of setting up a PPP connection.

Using pppd with chat to make the PPP connection

To set up a PPP networking connection between two systems, you must have PPP software running at both ends. Typically, your ISP will provide you with an account that's set up so that the PPP software runs automatically upon login. In that case, all that remains is to start the PPP software on your system after you log into the remote system.

Note Following are the two basic steps for setting up a PPP connection:

1. Dial up and log into the remote system. (I'll assume that when you log in, the remote system starts its PPP software automatically.)

2. Start the PPP software on your Linux system.

Just as the dip program supports a SLIP connection, the pppd program takes care of communicating with PPP over a dial-up line. Therefore, after you log in and start PPP software at the remote system, you have to run pppd on your Linux system.

Secret

The pppd program's name stands for Point-to-Point Protocol Daemon. (In UNIX, the term *daemon* refers to a program that runs in the background and performs some useful task.) The pppd program provides an option through which you can invoke another program that actually establishes the serial communication and completes the remote login process.

CD

In Linux, it is common practice to use pppd with the chat program. If you installed Linux from this book's companion CD-ROM, you'll find both the pppd and chat programs in the /usr/sbin directory on your Linux system.

Using the chat program

You need to understand how chat works so you can use it to automatically dial and log into the remote system. The chat program is designed to process a script that uses an *expect-send* pattern of text. The program looks for the *expect* string, and when it receives the *expect* string, chat sends the *send* string.

Suppose I want chat to look for the string login: (which is how most UNIX systems prompt for a user name), and then send my user name (naba). Following that, I want chat to expect the Password: prompt and send out my password. I would use the following *expect-send* pairs to do this:

```
ogin: naba word: my-password
```

You may notice I left out the leading l in the login prompt and some parts of the password prompt; the reason was to avoid being too specific, so that chat will succeed even if the received text is slightly different. After all, the first few characters of the login prompt or the Password: string may be garbled.

Timeouts

When it waits for an expected text string, chat uses a timeout feature. If the string does not arrive within the timeout period, chat moves to the next string. The default timeout value is 45 seconds. You can change the timeout with the TIMEOUT command, as follows:

```
TIMEOUT 10 ogin: naba TIMEOUT 5 word: my-password
```

In this case, the timeout period is 10 seconds when chat is waiting for the login: prompt. Then the timeout is changed to 5 seconds before chat looks for the Password: string.

Sub-expect sequences

The typical login sequence illustrates a simple case. A more complex case is when chat is looking for a login prompt, but none arrives within the timeout period. If you were logging in at a terminal, you would have pressed Enter to get another login prompt. You can simulate this behavior with chat's *sub-expect sequences*, which start with two dashes. Following is an example:

```
ogin:--ogin: naba word: my-password
```

In this case, if `chat` does not receive the `login:` prompt within the timeout period, `chat` sends a single return (just as if you had pressed Enter at the keyboard), and then looks for the `login:` prompt again.

ABORT strings

Most modems report the status of a connection as a string. For example, the modem might report `CONNECT` (which might be followed by the speed of connection) when successfully connected, `BUSY` if the remote phone is busy, or `NO CARRIER` if the modem does not get a dial tone from the phone.

You probably will want to stop the connection if the modem returns any status other than `CONNECT`. You can take care of this with `chat`'s `ABORT` command. The idea is to specify strings that should cause `chat` to abort the phone call. Following is an example:

```
ABORT BUSY ABORT "NO CARRIER" "" ATZ OK ATDT5551212
```

The first `ABORT BUSY` pair defines the `BUSY` string as an abort string. The next pair, `ABORT "NO CARRIER"`, defines another abort string. (Use quotation marks to enclose any string that includes spaces.)

After the two abort strings, you see two expect-send pairs. The first pair instructs `chat` to expect nothing (indicated by an empty string, "") and to send the `ATZ` command to reset the modem. The next expect-send pair causes `chat` to expect the string `OK` and to send the dialing command (`ATDT`, followed by a phone number) after the modem sends the `OK` string.

Escape sequences

You can use special characters in the expect-send strings. Most special characters are denoted by a backslash prefix, which serves as the escape character. These special character sequences are traditionally called *escape sequences*. Table 18-3 lists the escape sequences you can use in scripts for the `chat` program.

Table 18-3   chat escape sequences

Sequence	Description
" "	Two consecutive quotes indicate an empty string. If you send an empty string, `chat` sends a single carriage-return character.
\b	A backspace character.
\c	Stops the new-line character at the end of the send string. You can send \c only at the end of a string.
\d	Delays for one second. You cannot use this sequence in the expect string.
\ddd	A byte that contains the specified octal value.
\K	Sends a BREAK signal (refer to Chapter 15). You cannot use this sequence in an expect string.

(continued)

Table 18-3   *(Continued)*

Sequence	Description
\n	A new-line (line-feed) character.
\N	Sends a null character (a byte with all zero bits). You cannot use this sequence in an expect string.
\p	Pauses for a tenth of a second. You cannot use this sequence in an expect string.
\q	Suppresses writing of the string to the /var/adm/syslog file. This sequence is not valid in an expect string.
\r	A carriage return.
\s	A space character. Use this sequence when you do not want to place quotes around the string.
\t	A tab character.
^C	A control character corresponding to the letter following the caret. Thus, ^X means Ctrl-X.

You can use all these escape sequences in send strings; but as the comments indicate, you cannot use many sequences in expect strings.

Using pppd with a chat script

The actual details of PPP networking are handled by the PPP daemon program, pppd, which uses the PPP driver code in the Linux kernel to exchange TCP/IP packets over the serial port.

You need to perform two basic steps to complete a PPP connection with a remote system:

1. Dial out, using your modem, and log into the remote system, using a user name and password provided by the remote system's owner. Typically, when you log into the remote system, that action should start the necessary PPP software at the remote end.

2. Start the PPP daemon (pppd) on your system to initiate and conduct a PPP session with the remote system.

The pppd program is designed to take care of both of these steps. Essentially, you use the chat program to perform the first step: dialing up and logging into the remote system. You do not have to run chat separately. Instead, you provide a chat script in the pppd command line; pppd invokes chat to process that script.

A typical pppd command line

In its simplest form, you can run `pppd` with a long command line that might look like the following:

```
/usr/lib/ppp/pppd connect "/usr/lib/ppp/chat chat-script" crtscts modem \
defaultroute 192.168.101.111:192.168.102.1 /dev/cua0 38400
```

The backslash at the end of the first line is used to continue the command on the next line. The actual `pppd` command line is even longer, because the *chat-script* part is a sequence of *expend-send* pairs. Following is a list of what various parts of the `pppd` command line mean:

- The `connect` option instructs `pppd` to connect by executing the command within double quotes following the `connect` option. In the example, the command is shown without the enclosing quotation marks:

  ```
  /usr/lib/ppp/chat chat-script
  ```

- The *chat-script* part may be a long sequence of expect-send pairs of strings that the `chat` program processes. You might implement a simple dial-up login script by using the following command to start `chat`:

  ```
  /usr/lib/ppp/chat "" ATZ OK ATDT5551212 CONNECT "" ogin: my-
  username \
  word: my-password
  ```

- This `chat` script sends `ATZ` to reset the modem; waits for an `OK` and then sends a dial command (`ATDTphone-number`); waits for a `CONNECT` and then sends an empty string (a carriage return); waits for the `ogin:` string and sends *my-username* (which should be your PPP login name); and, finally, waits for the `word:` string and sends *my-password* (the password for your PPP login account).

- The `crtscts` option instructs `pppd` to use the Request to Send (RTS) and Clear to Send (CTS) signals for hardware handshaking with the modem. (Consult Chapter 15, "Modems," for more information on RTS and CTS signals.)

- The `modem` option causes `pppd` to use and honor the modem control signals that reflect the modem's status.

- The `defaultroute` option instructs `pppd` to set up a default route entry on your system to use the remote system as the gateway. If you already have a default route set up (for your Ethernet LAN, for example), `pppd` does not set up the default route to the remote system.

- The two IP addresses instruct `pppd` to use the IP address 192.168.101.111 for the local interface and the IP address 192.168.102.1 for the remote end of the PPP connection. If the remote host assigns IP addresses dynamically, you can use 0.0.0.0 as your local IP address; `pppd` automatically uses the IP address assigned by the remote system.

- The device name tells pppd to dial out on the device /dev/cua0 (COM1). If your modem is on COM2, use /dev/cua1 as the device name.

- The last option causes pppd to set the modem's data rate (often called the *baud rate*) to 38,400 bps.

As this list shows, that single pppd command line packs a great deal of information. At the same time, however, that command does a great deal of work. After pppd establishes the connection to the remote system, your system becomes part of the remote network (provided that the remote system adds appropriate routing-table entries).

You should note one key point about the pppd command line: The entire chat command (which follows the connect option) is enclosed in quotes, but the chat command itself uses various strings in quotes. You have to remember to use a backslash-character prefix for those embedded quotes. The following example shows how a chat script looks in a pppd command line:

```
/usr/lib/ppp/pppd connect "/usr/lib/ppp/chat \"\" ATZ OK ATDT5551212
CONNECT \"\" \
ogin: my-username word: my-password"     (rest of command line not shown)
```

As this example shows, all embedded quotes need a backslash prefix. If the modem's AT command includes an ampersand (&), you need a backslash prefix for each ampersand as well. You could use single quotes around the chat command line; then you won't need the backslash prefixes in front of the embedded double quotes.

A PPP dial-up script

If you are going to use pppd routinely, you probably do not want to type the command. You should prepare a shell script and start pppd from the script. If you save the script in a file named dial-ppp, for example, you can set up a PPP connection with the following command:

```
dial-ppp
```

That's what I do to connect my Linux PC to the Internet through my ISP. Here's a typical shell script to set up a PPP connection to a remote system:

```
#!/bin/sh
# A script to establish a dial-up PPP connection

# Shell variable with remote end's IP address
  RMTIP="192.168.102.1"

# If PPP link exists, then exit
  /sbin/ifconfig | grep $RMTIP >/dev/null && exit 0

# Other shell variables
# Set LOCIP to "" if your IP address is dynamically assigned
  LOCIP="192.168.101.111"
  PHONE="301-555-1212"
```

```
DEVICE="/dev/ttyS0"
SPEED="38400"
PPP_LOGINNAME="my-username"
PPP_PASSWORD="my-password"

/usr/sbin/pppd connect "/usr/sbin/chat -v REPORT CONNECT \
     ABORT \"NO CARRIER\" ABORT BUSY ABORT \"NO DIAL TONE\" \
     \"\" ATZ OK ATE1M1V1X4L3SO=0\&c1Q0DT$PHONE CONNECT \"\" \
     ogin:--ogin: $PPP_LOGINNAME word: $PPP_PASSWORD" \
     crtscts modem defaultroute $LOCIP:$RMTIP $DEVICE $SPEED
# End of script
```

I replaced some sensitive information (such as phone number, user name, password, and IP addresses) with phony values. In the script, this information appears in italics. You should replace these parameters with ones that apply to your situation. If you have a PPP account with an ISP, the ISP should provide you with this information (phone number, IP addresses, user name, and password). You must also edit the AT command sequence to work with your modem.

Testing the PPP connection

If you have PPP access to another system (such as an ISP or a system at your employer's organization), you can set up a script as described in the preceding section and enjoy the benefits of full TCP/IP network access to another system. After you run the script, and after pppd completes the initial protocol exchanges to set up the connection, you can verify that the connection is up by typing the ifconfig command, which should show a listing like the following:

```
/sbin/ifconfig
lo        Link encap:Local Loopback
          inet addr:127.0.0.1  Bcast:127.255.255.255  Mask:255.0.0.0
          UP BROADCAST LOOPBACK RUNNING  MTU:3584  Metric:1
          RX packets:1738 errors:0 dropped:0 overruns:0
          TX packets:1738 errors:0 dropped:0 overruns:0

eth0      Link encap:Ethernet  HWaddr 00:20:AF:E8:A2:25
          inet addr:192.168.1.1  Bcast:192.168.1.255
Mask:255.255.255.0
          UP BROADCAST RUNNING MULTICAST  MTU:1500  Metric:1
          RX packets:146900 errors:6 dropped:6 overruns:0
          TX packets:120970 errors:0 dropped:0 overruns:0
          Interrupt:10 Base address:0x210

ppp0      Link encap:Point-to-Point Protocol
          inet addr:204.192.67.100  P-t-P:204.91.204.91
Mask:255.255.255.0
          UP POINTOPOINT RUNNING  MTU:1500  Metric:1
          RX packets:492 errors:0 dropped:0 overruns:0
          TX packets:682 errors:0 dropped:0 overruns:0
```

You should find the ppp0 device listed in the output. The ifconfig output also shows the IP addresses of the local and remote ends of the PPP connection. This output confirms that the PPP device is up and running.

To verify that the routing table is set up correctly, use the /sbin/route command without any arguments, as follows:

```
/sbin/route
Kernel IP routing table
Destination      Gateway          Genmask          Flags Metric Ref    Use Iface
default-gateway  *                255.255.255.255 UH     0      0        0 ppp0
192.168.1.0      *                255.255.255.0   U      0      0      117 eth0
127.0.0.0        *                255.0.0.0       U      0      0       60 lo
default          default-gateway  0.0.0.0         UG     0      0        2 ppp0
```

In the routing table, the first line shows a route to the remote end of the PPP connection; this one should be set to the ppp0 device. Also, the default route should be set up so that the remote end of the PPP connection serves as the gateway for your system (as the last line of the routing table shows).

After checking the interface configuration (with the ifconfig command) and the routing table (with the route command), you should verify that you can reach some well-known host. If your ISP gave you the IP address of a name server or a mail server, you can try to ping those addresses. Otherwise, try to ping the IP address of a system at your workplace or your university.

The following example shows what you would see if you try the ping command:

```
ping 140.90.23.100
PING 140.90.23.100 (140.90.23.100): 56 data bytes
64 bytes from 140.90.23.100: icmp_seq=0 ttl=244 time=336.0 ms
64 bytes from 140.90.23.100: icmp_seq=1 ttl=244 time=290.2 ms
64 bytes from 140.90.23.100: icmp_seq=2 ttl=244 time=350.2 ms
64 bytes from 140.90.23.100: icmp_seq=3 ttl=244 time=300.2 ms
64 bytes from 140.90.23.100: icmp_seq=4 ttl=244 time=340.2 ms
64 bytes from 140.90.23.100: icmp_seq=5 ttl=244 time=290.2 ms

--- 140.90.23.100 ping statistics ---
6 packets transmitted, 6 packets received, 0% packet loss
round-trip min/avg/max = 290.2/317.8/350.2 ms
```

The end of each line shows the round-trip time for a packet originating at your system to reach the designated IP address (140.90.23.100, in this case) and back to your system again. For a PPP connection over dial-up lines, you'll see times in hundreds of milliseconds.

Incidentally, you do not have to have an account on a system to ping its IP address. Although a system may disable the automatic response to ping messages (ping uses Internet Control Message Protocol or ICMP messages), most systems respond to ping.

Ending the PPP connection

After pppd establishes a PPP connection, the link remains as long as the PPP software at both ends continues to run. When you no longer need the PPP connection, you can end it by stopping the pppd process.

After setting up a PPP link, pppd creates a file in the /var/run directory where it stores the process ID of pppd. The filename is based on the PPP device name. For the first PPP link, the PPP device is ppp0, and the process ID file is /var/run/ppp0.pid. You can write a shell script to kill the pppd process by using the process ID stored in the /var/run/ppp0.pid file.

Secret

In fact, you do not have to write your own shell script to end a PPP link. In the /usr/doc/ppp-2.2.0f/scripts/ directory, you'll find a script named ppp-off that performs this task for you. Whenever you want to bring down the PPP link, log in as root and type **/usr/doc/ppp-2.2.0f/scripts/ppp-off**.

This command ends the pppd process, which in turn cleans up the routing table.

The /usr/doc/ppp-2.2.0f/scripts/ppp-off script looks like the following:

```sh
#!/bin/sh

DEVICE=ppp0

#
# If the ppp0 pid file is presen, the program is running. Stop it.
if [ -r /var/run/$DEVICE.pid ]; then
    kill -INT `cat /var/run/$DEVICE.pid`
#
# If unsuccessful, ensure that the pid file is removed.
#
    if [ ! "$?" = "0" ]; then
            echo "removing stale $DEVICE pid file."
            rm -f /var/run/$DEVICE.pid
            exit 1
    fi
#
# Success. Terminate with proper status.
#
    echo "$DEVICE link terminated"
    exit 0
fi
#
# The link is not active
#
echo "$DEVICE link is not active"
exit 1
```

Notice that this script uses the command `cat /var/run/$DEVICE.pid` (`DEVICE` is defined as `ppp0`) to obtain the process ID of the `pppd` process. That process ID then is used as an argument in the `kill` command that terminates the `pppd` process.

Routing Through the PPP Connection

A common use of a PPP connection is to connect two geographically separated networks or, more commonly, to connect a small local-area network (LAN) to the Internet. In a typical scenario, you have a small Ethernet LAN you want to connect to the Internet. You can do this with a Linux PC that has both an Ethernet card and a modem. The Linux system has a presence on your Ethernet LAN through its Ethernet-card interface. If you can establish a PPP connection to a system on the Internet, you can use the Linux PC as the gateway between your LAN and the remote system (which, presumably, is already connected to the Internet). Figure 18-2 illustrates such a scenario.

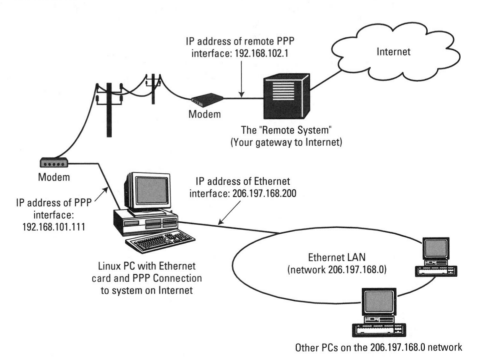

Figure 18-2: Connecting a LAN to the Internet

In this case, you have a small Ethernet LAN with a few PCs and a class C IP address of 206.197.168.0. You have assigned 206.197.168.200 as the IP address of your Linux PC's Ethernet-card interface.

The Linux PC also has a modem through which you establish a PPP connection to a remote system on the Internet. Both ends of the PPP connection have unique IP addresses. You want to ensure that the PCs on your Ethernet LAN can access the Internet. You want to use your Linux PC as a gateway to route network packets between the Ethernet LAN and the remote system, because the Linux PC is the only one with both PPP and Ethernet interfaces. You can accomplish this goal in one of the following ways:

- **Use your Linux PC as a router**: Obtain a valid Class C network address from an ISP and configure the Linux PC so that it acts as the gateway between your network and the Internet.

- **Use IP masquerading**: Set up your Ethernet LAN with private IP addresses (for example, use 192.168.1.0 as the network address) and use the Linux PC as a firewall. Enable IP masquerading in the Linux kernel and use the `ipfwadm` program to allow the Linux PC to masquerade as any of the systems in your LAN. Essentially, each system on your Ethernet LAN ends up being able to access the Internet even though it doesn't have a unique IP address.

The following sections further explain these two approaches.

Using Linux PC as a router

To use your Linux PC as a router, you have to perform the following steps:

1. Enable IP forwarding in the Linux kernel. As you reconfigure the kernel with the `make config` command (see Chapter 2), you have to answer Yes to the following (among other questions related to TCP/IP networking):

```
TCP/IP networking (CONFIG_INET) [Y/n/?] y
IP: forwarding/gatewaying (CONFIG_IP_FORWARD) [Y/n/?] y
IP: multicasting (CONFIG_IP_MULTICAST) [Y/n/?] y
IP: syn cookies (CONFIG_SYN_COOKIES) [Y/n/?] y
IP: accounting (CONFIG_IP_ACCT) [Y/n/?] y
IP: optimize as router not host (CONFIG_IP_ROUTER) [N/y/?] y
```

When IP forwarding is enabled, the Linux kernel automatically forwards packets from one interface to another.

2. Use the `route` command to set up a route to the remote system. A *route* specifies a path between two network nodes. A typical specification says something like the following: "All packets for the 206.197.168.0 network should be sent to the Ethernet interface named `eth0`." The *gateway* IP address is used as the destination for any network address without an explicit route. If you do have a PPP link, you may want to say, "Send any packet with an unresolved address to the remote IP address of the PPP link." You should use the IP address of the remote end of the PPP connection as the gateway on the Linux system. To learn more about the route command, type `man route` at the shell prompt.

3. Make sure all systems on your LAN use the Linux PC as the default gateway for TCP/IP networking.

4. Make sure the remote gateway has a route to your LAN. Without this step, TCP/IP packets from the Internet cannot reach your LAN. If you get your Internet connection from an ISP, the ISP will (for a fee, of course) provide you with properly routed IP addresses for your LAN.

Note

Although a Linux PC with a PPP connection can act as a gateway between a LAN and the Internet, a more economical solution might be to use a dial-up router specifically designed to connect your LAN to the Internet. In both cases you need an ISP to provide you access to a remote system already connected to the Internet.

Using IP masquerading

You use IP masquerading when you want to connect an Ethernet LAN with a private IP address to the Internet through a Linux PC (with an officially-assigned IP address) that has a connection to the Internet.

With IP masquerading enabled, your Linux PC acts as a stand-in for any of the other systems on the Ethernet LAN. As with the router setup, the Linux PC is designated as the gateway for the Ethernet LAN. However, masquerading involves more than simply forwarding IP packets back and forth between the LAN and the Internet.

When the Linux PC masquerades as another system on the LAN, it modifies outgoing packets so that they always appear to originate from the Linux PC. When a response to one of the outgoing packets is received, the Linux PC performs the reverse task — it modifies the packets so that they appear to come from the Internet directly to the system that sent the outgoing packet. The end result is that each system on the Ethernet LAN appears to have full access to the Internet even though the Ethernet LAN uses a non-unique private IP address.

To enable and use IP masquerading, you must perform the following steps:

1. Enable IP forwarding, IP firewalling, and IP masquerading in the Linux kernel. As you reconfigure the kernel with the `make config` command (see Chapter 2), you have to answer Yes to the following (among other questions related to TCP/IP networking):

```
*
* Networking options
*
Network firewalls (CONFIG_FIREWALL) [Y/n/?] y
Network aliasing (CONFIG_NET_ALIAS) [Y/n/?] y
TCP/IP networking (CONFIG_INET) [Y/n/?] y
IP: forwarding/gatewaying (CONFIG_IP_FORWARD) [Y/n/?] y
IP: multicasting (CONFIG_IP_MULTICAST) [Y/n/?] y
IP: syn cookies (CONFIG_SYN_COOKIES) [Y/n/?] y
```

```
IP: rst cookies (CONFIG_RST_COOKIES) [N/y/?]
IP: firewalling (CONFIG_IP_FIREWALL) [Y/n/?] y
IP: firewall packet logging (CONFIG_IP_FIREWALL_VERBOSE) [Y/n/?] y
IP: masquerading (CONFIG_IP_MASQUERADE) [Y/n/?] y
*
* Protocol-specific masquerading support will be built as modules.
*
IP: ipautofw masq support (CONFIG_IP_MASQUERADE_IPAUTOFW) [Y/n/?]
y
IP: ICMP masquerading (CONFIG_IP_MASQUERADE_ICMP) [Y/n/?] y
IP: transparent proxy support (EXPERIMENTAL)
(CONFIG_IP_TRANSPARENT_PROXY) [Y/n/
?] y
IP: always defragment (CONFIG_IP_ALWAYS_DEFRAG) [Y/n/?] y
```

2. Make sure the Linux PC has an Internet connection and a network connection to your LAN. Typically, the Linux PC has two network interfaces — an Ethernet card for the LAN and a dial-up PPP connection to the Internet (through an ISP).

3. Make sure that all systems on your LAN use the Linux PC as the default gateway for TCP/IP networking.

4. Run `ipfwadm` — the IP firewall administration program — to set up the rules that allow the Linux PC to masquerade for your LAN. For example, to enable masquerading for a LAN with the class C network address 192.168.1.0, you could use the following commands:

```
ipfwadm -F -p deny
ipfwadm -F -a m -S 192.168.1.0/24 -D 0.0.0.0/0
```

If you want the IP masquerading to be set up at system startup, you should place these commands in the `/etc/rc.d/rc.local` file.

To learn more about the `ipfwadm` program, type `man ipfwadm`. You should also read the IP-Masquerade mini-HOWTO as described in Step 6.

5. Load the modules that provide masquerading capability for specific Internet services such as File Transfer Protocol (FTP), Internet Relay Chat (IRC), and Real Audio. You should add the following lines to the `/etc/rc.d/rc.local` file:

```
/sbin/depmod -a
/sbin/modprobe ip_masq_ftp
/sbin/modprobe ip_masq_irc
/sbin/modprobe ip_masq_raudio
```

6. For more details on IP masquerading and `ipfwadm`, read the IP-Masquerade mini-HOWTO. To read this document, type `cd /usr/doc/HOWTO/mini` to change directory. Then type `more IP-Masquerade` to read the document. You can also check out the latest version of the IP-Masquerade mini-HOWTO at http://www.wwonline.com/~achau/ipmasq/.

Tip

You'll find IP masquerading a convenient way to provide Internet access to a small LAN (for example, a LAN at home or the office). At home, I use IP masquerading to connect an Ethernet LAN to the Internet through a Linux system. The Linux PC has an Ethernet card for the LAN connection and a modem to connect to the Internet via an ISP (I have a valid IP address from the ISP). With IP masquerading on the Linux PC, everyone in the family can now access the Internet from any of the other PCs on the LAN.

Setting Up a PPP Server

The preceding sections describe how your Linux PC can establish a PPP link with another system that offers PPP service. After a PPP link is set up, both ends of the PPP link behave as peers. Before a PPP link is established, you can think of the end that initiates the dial-up connection as being the client, because that system asks for the connection. The other end provides the PPP connection when needed, so it's the PPP server.

If you want to allow other people to connect to your Linux PC by using PPP over a dial-up modem, follow these steps:

1. Follow the steps outlined in Chapter 15 to enable dial-up login on your system. Test this part to make sure that everything works; dial into your system from another computer and log in as a user. This step involves adding a line such as the following to the /etc/inittab file:

   ```
   s0:235:respawn:/sbin/uugetty ttyS0 F38400 vt100
   ```

2. Add a new user for the dial-up PPP connection — the user name under which the client system logs in. Upon login, the pppd program should run automatically. Specify /usr/local/bin/ppp-login as the shell for the user.

3. Prepare the /usr/local/bin/ppp-login script. This script is the "shell" for the PPP login account, which means the script is executed when the PPP user logs in. Thus, the script should start the pppd program with appropriate options. After you prepare the script, remember to make it executable. Following is a typical /usr/local/bin/ppp-login script:

   ```
   #!/bin/sh
   # A script to start PPP service for a login account

   # Shell variables with IP addresses
     RMTIP="192.168.111.111"
     LOCIP="192.168.111.222"

     exec /usr/sbin/pppd -detach silent modem \
                crtscts $LOCIP:$RMTIP
   ```

I tested this setup from a Windows 95 PC and it worked; however, I had to type in the user name and password manually in a terminal window. In Windows 95 dial-up networking, you can turn on an option that displays a terminal window after the modems establish connection. That's the window in which I typed the PPP user name and password.

Summary

Most of us do not have a direct connection to the high-bandwidth backbones of the Internet. Instead, we rely on dial-up modem connections to Internet Service Providers (ISPs), which in turn are connected to the backbones (typically provided by large telecommunications companies, such as Sprint and MCI). TCP/IP networking over serial lines is possible with SLIP and PPP. Software for both SLIP and PPP comes with Linux. This chapter explains what SLIP and PPP are, and shows you how to configure and use both of these protocols as the data-transport mechanism for TCP/IP networking.

By reading this chapter, you learn the following things:

▶ Serial communications with software such as minicom (or something like ProComm, in the MS-DOS world) allows your PC to become a terminal to a remote host. This type of serial communication does not get you a full network connection, in which several network applications can use the same physical link to transfer data between your PC and the remote system.

▶ SLIP, or Serial Line Internet Protocol, was the first attempt at using the serial link as a data-transport layer for TCP/IP networking. Although simple, SLIP was deficient in many ways. Both ends needed to know the IP addresses, for example, and only one type of protocol could use a SLIP connection for packet transport.

▶ PPP, or Point-to-Point Protocol, is a more complex protocol for packet transport over any point-to-point link. PPP can carry packets of many protocols over the same link. PPP is the preferred way to establish a dial-up TCP/IP network connection with ISPs.

▶ A program named dip is used to establish a SLIP connection with a remote system.

▶ Setting up a PPP link involves two basic steps. First you must use a utility program to dial the modem and make the connection with the remote modem; and then you have to start the PPP software on your system. The chat program is used with the pppd program to perform these two steps.

▶ When you connect your Linux PC to a remote system by using PPP, the PPP link is used as the default route on the Linux PC, because the PPP connection becomes the gateway to the rest of the Internet.

▶ You can use IP masquerading to provide Internet access to a private LAN through a Linux PC that has a PPP connection to an ISP.

▶ You also can set up your Linux PC as a PPP server so others may dial in and establish a PPP connection with your system. This chapter describes the steps for setting up a PPP server.

Chapter 19

Setting Up a Linux Internet Host

In This Chapter

▶ Understanding Internet hosts

▶ Looking at typical Internet services: mail, news, and FTP

▶ Setting up and testing mail

▶ Setting up and using news

▶ Posting news and verifying news distribution

▶ Setting up a secure anonymous `ftp` server

xperts see the Internet as the foundation of a new wave of computing, in which information is distributed and business is conducted over the network. Web browsers such as Netscape Navigator and Microsoft Internet Explorer give us a glimpse of that new world of computing, one in which you can access information from anywhere in the world as easily as if it were right on your local disk.

You probably already are familiar with electronic mail (or e-mail) and news — the mainstay of the Internet. E-mail enables you to exchange messages and documents with anyone on the Internet. The newsgroups provide a bulletin-board system that spans the globe.

If you want to take advantage of the Internet's offerings, you need access to it. Whether you run a business or whether you are a Linux hobbyist, you'll find it beneficial to put your Linux PC on the Internet; set it up as an Internet host.

Cross-Reference

I use the term Internet host for a system that has network access to the Internet — which means the Internet host can exchange TCP/IP network packets with any other computer on the Internet. Typically, your Linux system sets up a network connection to the Internet through a dial-up line by using SLIP or PPP. Chapter 18 explains SLIP and PPP and also shows you how to connect your Linux PC to the Internet.

To be an Internet host, however, your Linux PC needs more than just the network connection to the Internet. You also need to set up e-mail, FTP, and news. If you want to provide information to other users, you may want to set up your own Web server. Additionally, you may have to worry about security. After all, your system will be on the Internet, and anyone with Internet access can (in theory, at least) get to your system.

This chapter focuses on the tasks that you might typically perform to set up your Linux PC as an Internet host. You learn how to set up e-mail, anonymous FTP (which enables anyone to download files from you, but in a reasonably secure manner), and newsgroups. This chapter also describes some ways to make your Internet host secure.

Setting up a Web server is a detailed process covered in the next chapter.

What Is an Internet Host?

The meaning of the term *Internet host* depends on what you think *Internet* means. Technically speaking, the Internet is a worldwide network of networks. The term *internet* (without capitalization) is a short form of *internetworking*—the interconnection of networks. The Internet Protocol (IP) was designed to connect networks. As you learned in Chapter 16, even IP addresses have a network part and a host part.

Physically, the Internet is similar to a network of highways and roads. This similarity has prompted the popular press to dub the Internet the *Information Superhighway*. Just as the network of highways and roads includes some interstate highways, many state roads, and many more residential streets, the Internet has some very high bandwidth networks (45-Mbps T3 backbones) and a large number of lower-capacity networks (ranging from 28,800-bps dial-up connections to 1.54-Mbps T1 links). The high-bandwidth network constitutes the backbone of the Internet.

Unlike commercial networks, such as CompuServe and America Online, the Internet is not run by a single organization; nor is it managed by any central computer. You can view the physical Internet as a "network of networks" managed collectively by hundreds of cooperating organizations. I know that a collection of networks managed by hundreds of organizations sounds incredible, but it works!

From the point of view of physical connectivity, an Internet host is any computer on a network that's part of the Internet. The user, however, judges an Internet host in terms of the services that it provides. Typically, users expect the following common services from an Internet host:

- *Electronic mail (e-mail).* From an Internet host, you can send e-mail to any other user on the Internet, using addresses such as president@whitehouse.gov.

- *Newsgroups.* You can read newsgroups and post news items to newsgroups with names such as comp.os.linux.networking or comp.os.linux.setup.

- *Information retrieval.* You can search for information with tools such as gopher and the World Wide Web browser. You also can download files with File Transfer Protocol (FTP). Reciprocally, users on other systems also can download files from your system, typically through a feature known as *anonymous FTP*. You learn how to set up anonymous FTP service in the "Secure Anonymous FTP" section of this chapter.

■ *Remote access*. You can use `telnet` to log into another computer (the remote computer) on the Internet, assuming that you have access to that remote computer.

Note

Some capabilities, such as being able to access a remote computer with `telnet` or download files with `ftp`, are free when your Linux PC is connected to the Internet. For e-mail, newsgroups, and anonymous FTP, you may have to perform some steps in Linux. Later sections of this chapter describe how to configure these Internet services.

Exchanging e-mail

One of the most common ways that people use the Internet is to keep in touch with colleagues, friends, loved ones, and even strangers through e-mail. If you have not used e-mail much, you may wonder why it is such a big deal. Even if you have used your company's internal e-mail system, you may not appreciate the convenience of Internet e-mail until you try it.

You may be surprised that you can send a message to a friend thousands of miles away and get back a reply within a couple of minutes. Essentially, you can send messages anywhere in the world from an Internet host, and that message typically makes its way to the destination within minutes — something that you cannot do with regular paper mail.

Because e-mail can be stored and forwarded, you can arrange to send and receive e-mail without making your Linux system a full-time host on the Internet. You won't get the benefits of nearly immediate delivery of messages, however, if your system is not an Internet host.

Participating in newsgroups

The Internet helps you communicate in many ways. With e-mail, you can exchange messages with people whom you already know. Sometimes, however, you may want to participate in group discussions. If you are looking for help in setting up XFree86 on an ATI Mach64 graphics card, for example, you may want to consult anyone who knows anything about this subject. For that sort of communication, you can post a message on the appropriate Internet newsgroup; someone is likely to give you an answer.

Internet newsgroups are like the bulletin boards or forums on other online systems, such as CompuServe and America Online. You'll find a wide variety of newsgroups covering subjects ranging from politics to computers. You can think of the Internet newsgroups as being a gathering place — a virtual meeting place where you can ask questions and discuss various issues.

Locating and browsing information

You may already have experienced sharing files among computers on a LAN (local area network). Typically, a LAN has a server, and any user on the LAN can access and use the information in the files stored on that server.

Being a collection of interconnected networks, the Internet also allows the Internet hosts — the computers on the Internet — to share information by using a variety of protocols. For example, the File Transfer Protocol (FTP) specifies how to select and download files from another computer on the Internet. You saw some examples of FTP in Chapter 2, where I explained how to download patches to the Linux kernel.

Cross-Reference

Another, more recent, information-sharing protocol is the Hypertext Transfer Protocol (HTTP), which allows computers to exchange documents formatted in the Hypertext Markup Language (HTML). HTML and HTTP form the foundation of the World Wide Web, where you can literally look at documents maintained on other computers on the Internet. You learn more about the World Wide Web in Chapter 20.

Using a simple mail and news strategy

Although using mail and news is reasonably simple, both mail and news require some effort on your part to set up and maintain properly. Newsgroups in particular need a great deal of disk space, and access to a news server. You need a large amount of disk space because so many newsgroups exist, and the volume of messages can be quite high. Also, the news articles must be purged periodically; otherwise, the disk will get filled. Even if you choose a small subset of newsgroups, you may need a hundred or so megabytes just to keep the news items on your system.

Tip

If you get your Internet access from an ISP (Internet Service Provider), the ISP gives you access to a mail server and a news server. Then you can use mail software that downloads messages from your mail server, and use a news reader that reads newsgroups directly from the news server. If you are the lone user of your Linux PC, I strongly recommend this strategy for reading news.

Cross-Reference

As you learn in Chapter 20, you can use a Web browser, such as Netscape, to read news and send mail, as well as access Web pages.

Installing mail and news software

During Red Hat Linux installation from this book's companion CD-ROM, you have the option to install the necessary packages for mail and news. As described in Chapter 1, select the *Mail/WWW/News Tools* component when you are prompted for the components to install.

Cross-Reference

If you install the mail and news software during Linux installation, you do not have to do much more to begin using the mail and news services. Otherwise, you can use the Red Hat Package Manager (RPM) to install individual packages. Chapter 2 describes how to use the rpm program to install new software.

To access the RPM files for mail and news, mount the CD-ROM with the following command:

```
mount /dev/cdrom /mnt/cdrom
```

Then, change directory to /mnt/cdrom/RedHat/RPMS. You will find the RPM files located in that directory. Some of the RPMs you may want to install are as follows (I show the RPM name; the actual file name starts with the RPM name, has a version number, and ends with a .rpm extension):

- anonftp (anonymous FTP setup)
- elm (a mail user agent)
- fetchmail (a mail retrieval and forwarding utility)
- ftp (FTP client)
- imap (Internet Message Access Protocol server)
- inews (Internet news program to post news)
- inn (InterNetNews, a TCP/IP-based news server)
- mailx (a mail user agent)
- metamail (software to handle MIME — Multipurpose Internet Mail Extensions)
- pine (a versatile mail and news program)
- procmail (a local mail-delivery package)
- sendmail (a complex mail-transport agent)
- sendmail-cf (configuration files for sendmail)
- sendmail-doc (documentation for sendmail)
- tin (a full-screen news reader)
- trn (a news reader for a remote news server)
- uucp (UNIX-to-UNIX Copy protocol)

You probably have installed many of these packages already. For this chapter, you need only the mail and news packages, so you should install elm, sendmail, sendmail-cf, tin and trn (as well as any other mail or news reader that you want to try).

Mail

Electronic mail — e-mail — is one of the most popular services on the Internet. Everyone likes the convenience of being able to send a message without having to play the game of "phone tag," in which two people leave phone messages for each other without successfully making contact. When you send an e-mail message, it waits in the recipient's mailbox to be read at the recipient's convenience.

E-mail started as a simple mechanism in which messages were copied to a user's mailbox file. That simple mechanism is still used. In Linux, your mail messages are stored in the /var/spool/mail directory, in a text file with the same name as your user name.

Messages are still addressed to a user name, which means that if John Doe logs in with the user name jdoe, e-mail to him is addressed to jdoe. The only other piece of information needed to uniquely identify the recipient is the fully qualified domain name of the recipient's system. Thus, if John Doe's system is named someplace.net, his complete e-mail address becomes jdoe@someplace.net. Given that address, anyone on the Internet can send e-mail to John Doe.

CD

The Linux distribution on this book's companion CD-ROM comes with the software you need to set up and use e-mail on your Linux system. The following sections guide you through various aspects of setting up and using e-mail on your Linux system.

Mail software

To set up and use e-mail on your Linux PC, you need two types of mail software:

- *Mail user agent* software allows you to read your mail messages, write replies, and compose new messages.

- *Mail transport agent* software actually sends and receives mail message text. The exact method used for mail transport depends on the underlying network. In TCP/IP networks, the mail transport agent delivers mail using the Simple Mail Transfer Protocol (SMTP). This book's Red Hat Linux CD-ROM includes sendmail, a powerful and popular mail transport agent for TCP/IP networks.

Most mail transport agents run as *daemons* — background processes that run as long as your system is up. Because you or another user on the system might send mail at any time, the transport agent has to be there to deliver the mail to its destination. The mail user agent runs only when the user wants to check mail.

Wizard

Typically, a mail transport agent is started after the system boots. The system startup files for Red Hat Linux are set up so that the sendmail mail transport agent starts when the Linux system is in multiuser mode. In the file /etc/rc.d/init.d/sendmail, you'll find the lines that start sendmail.

More on sendmail

This chapter shows you how to use a predefined sendmail configuration file to get e-mail going on your system. sendmail, however, is a very complex mail system. *sendmail,* by Bryan Costales with Eric Allman and Neil Rickert (O'Reilly & Associates, 1993), will help you learn how to configure sendmail.

Because the system is already set up to start sendmail at boot time, all you have to do is use an appropriate sendmail configuration file to get e-mail going on your Linux system.

The sendmail configuration file

You cannot send or receive e-mail until the sendmail mail transport agent is configured properly. sendmail has the reputation of being a complex but complete mail-delivery system. If you take a quick look at sendmail's configuration file, /etc/sendmail.cf, you'll immediately agree that sendmail is indeed complex. Luckily, you do not have to become an expert on the sendmail configuration file (a whole book has been written on that subject; see the sidebar "More on sendmail"). All you need is one of the predefined configuration files from this book's companion CD-ROM.

If you have installed the *Mail/WWW/News Tools* component during Red Hat Linux installation (see Chapter 1), your system should already have a working sendmail configuration file — /etc/sendmail.cf. The default file assumes an Internet connection and a name server. Provided you have an Internet connection, you should be able to send and receive e-mail from your Linux PC.

Secret

To ensure that mail delivery works correctly, you must make sure that your system's name matches what your ISP assigned to you. Although you can give your system any host name you want, other systems can successfully deliver mail to your system only if your system's name is in the ISP's name server.

A mail-delivery test

On my system, I could send and receive mail immediately after selecting a sendmail configuration file. First, I made sure that my system's host name matched what my ISP assigned for my use. Then I used the mail command to compose and send a mail message to myself at a different address, as follows:

```
mail naba@access.digex.net
Subject: Testing e-mail
This is from my Linux PC.
.
EOT
```

The `mail` command runs a simple mail user agent. In this example, I specify the addressee — naba@access.digex.net — in the command line. The mail program prompts for a subject line. Following the subject, I enter my message and end it with a line that contains only a period. After I end the message, the mail user agent passes the message to `sendmail` — the mail transport agent — for delivery to the specified address. Because my system was already connected to the Internet, `sendmail` delivered the mail message immediately.

To verify the delivery of mail, I used `telnet` to log into access.digex.net and then checked my mail, as follows:

```
access2% mail
Mail version SMI 4.0 Fri Oct 14 12:50:06 PDT 1994  Type ? for help.
"/usr/spool/mail/naba": 1 message 1 new
>N  1 naba@dcc05211.slip.digex.net Sat May 16 17:17   16/707   Testing
e-mail
Mail>  (press Enter)
Message  1:
From naba@dcc05211.slip.digex.net Sat May 16 17:17:41 1998
Date: Sun, 17 May 1998 04:22:16 -0400
From: Naba Barkakati <naba@dcc05211.slip.digex.net>
To: naba@access.digex.net
Subject: Testing e-mail

This is from my Linux PC.

Mail>r
To: naba@dcc05211.slip.digex.net
Subject: Re:  Testing e-mail

Received your message.
Cc:
Mail>q
Saved 1 message in /homea/naba/mbox
access2%
```

As you can verify from this listing, my mail message arrived at the destination. After reading the message, I pressed **r** to reply to the message. I typed a short reply and pressed Ctrl-D (that's how the mail program on access.digex.net expects messages to end). The mail program prompts for a carbon-copy list (addresses that should get a copy of the reply) with the text `Cc:`. I pressed Enter to indicate that I didn't want any carbon-copy addresses. At the mail prompt, I pressed **q** to quit the mail program.

After I logged out of access.digex.net, I checked mail again on my Linux PC to see whether my reply made its way back to the Linux PC. I used the `elm` program to read my mail on the Linux system. After I typed `elm`, a window appeared and `elm` displayed the current messages in my mailbox. I selected the message and pressed Enter. Figure 19-1 shows the terminal screen as `elm` displayed the mail message.

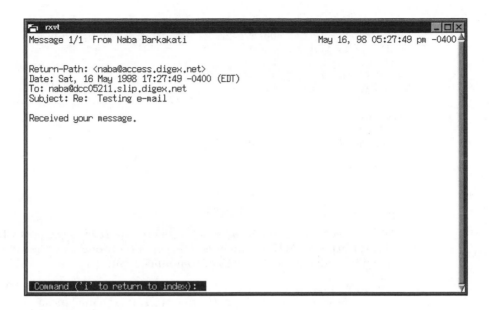

Figure 19-1: Reading mail with elm.

As the output shows, the reply from the other system reached my Linux system as well.

Thus, the initial `sendmail` configuration file from this book's companion CD-ROM should be adequate for sending and receiving e-mail, provided that your Linux system has an Internet connection.

The mail-delivery mechanism

On an Internet host, the `sendmail` mail transport agent delivers mail using the Simple Mail Transfer Protocol (SMTP). SMTP is documented in RFC 821, "Simple Mail Transfer Protocol," Jonathan Postel, 1982.

SMTP-based mail transport agents listen to the TCP port 25 and use a small set of text commands to interact with other mail transport agents. In fact, the commands are simple enough that you can use them directly to send a mail message. The following example shows how I use SMTP commands to send a mail message to my account on the Linux PC from a `telnet` session running on another system on the local area network:

```
telnet lnbp200 25
Trying 192.168.1.200...
Connected to lnbp200.
Escape character is '^]'.
220 lnbp200 ESMTP Sendmail 8.8.7/8.8.7; Sat, 16 May 1998 17:39:31 -
0400
```

```
HELO lnbp200
250 lnbp200 Hello lnbp75 [192.168.1.1], pleased to meet you
MAIL FROM: naba
250 naba... Sender ok
RCPT TO: naba
250 naba... Recipient ok
DATA
354 Enter mail, end with "." on a line by itself
Testing... 1 2 3
Sending mail by telnet to port 25
.
250 RAA00476 Message accepted for delivery
QUIT
221 lnbp200 closing connection
Connection closed by foreign host.
```

The `telnet` command opens a `telnet` session to port 25 — the port where `sendmail` expects SMTP commands. The `sendmail` process on the Linux system immediately replies with an announcement.

I type `HELO lnbp200` to initiate a session with the host named lnbp200. The `sendmail` process replies with a greeting. To send the mail message, I start with the `MAIL FROM:` command, which specifies the sender of the message (I enter the user name on the system from which I am sending the message).

Next, I use the `RCPT TO:` command to specify the recipient of the message. If I want to send the message to several recipients, all I have to do is provide each recipient's address with the `RCPT TO:` command.

To enter the mail message, I use the `DATA` command. In response to the `DATA` command, `sendmail` displays an instruction that I should end the message with a period on a line by itself. I enter the message and end it with a single period on a separate line. The `sendmail` process displays a message indicating that the message has been accepted for delivery. Finally, I quit the session with `sendmail` with the `QUIT` command.

Afterward, I log into my Linux system and check mail with the `mail` command. Following is what I see when I display the mail message that I sent through the sample SMTP session with `sendmail`:

```
mail
Mail version 5.5-kw 5/30/95.  Type ? for help.
"/var/spool/mail/naba": 1 message 1 new
>N  1 naba@lnbp200        Sat May 16 17:40   12/376
& 1
Message 1:
From naba@lnbp200  Sat May 16 17:40:29 1998
Return-Path: <naba>
Received: from lnbp200 (lnbp75 [192.168.1.1])
        by lnbp200 (8.8.7/8.8.7) with SMTP id RAA00476
        for naba; Sat, 16 May 1998 17:39:50 -0400
```

```
Date: Sat, 16 May 1998 17:39:50 -0400
From: Red Hat Linux User <naba@lnbp200>
Message-Id: <199805162139.RAA00476@lnbp200>
Status: R

Testing... 1 2 3
Sending mail by telnet to port 25
```

As you can see, the SMTP commands are simple enough to understand. This example should help you understand how a mail transfer agent uses SMTP to transfer mail on the Internet.

Newsgroups

Newsgroups originated in *Usenet*—a store-and-forward messaging network for exchanging electronic mail and news items. Usenet works like a telegraph in that news and mail are relayed from one system to another. In Usenet, the systems are not on any network; they simply dial up and use the UNIX-to-UNIX Copy (UUCP) protocol to transfer text messages.

Note

Usenet is a very loosely connected collection of computers that has worked well and continues to be used because very little expense is involved in connecting to it. All you need is a modem and a site willing to store and forward your mail and news. You have to set up UUCP on your system, but you do not need a sustained network connection; just a few phone calls are all it takes to keep the e-mail and news flowing. The downside is that you cannot use TCP/IP services, such as the World Wide Web, telnet, or ftp.

From its Usenet origins, the newsgroups have migrated to the Internet. Instead of UUCP, the news is transported by means of the Network News Transfer Protocol (NNTP), which is described in RFC 977, "Network News Transfer Protocol: A Proposed Standard for the Stream-Based Transmission of News," B. Kantor and P. Lapsley, 1986.

Even though the news transport protocol has changed from UUCP to NNTP, the store-and-forward concept of news transfer still exists. Thus, if you want to get news on your Linux system, you have to find a news server from which your system can download news.

Tip

If you have signed up with an Internet Service Provider (ISP), the ISP should provide you access to a news server. Such Internet news servers communicate by using NNTP. Then you can use an NNTP-capable news reader, such as tin, to access the news server and read selected newsgroups. This is the easiest way to access news on your Linux Internet host.

For the following discussion, I'll assume that you have obtained access to a news server from your ISP.

How to read news

To read news, you need a *news reader*—a program that allows you to select a newsgroup and view the items in that newsgroup. You also need to understand the newsgroup hierarchy and naming convention, which I describe in the section "The newsgroup hierarchy". First, I want to show you how to read news from a news server.

Like mail programs, quite a few news readers are available. Most news readers support *threading*, which means organizing the replies to each article as a separate thread (sequence) of articles. Of these programs, the following two are most popular:

- The *threaded read news* program, trn, which is an improved version of rn, the venerable *read news* program. This news reader is called "threaded" because it interconnects an article with any replies.

- The full-screen news reader program, tin. Like trn, tin supports *threading*.

CD

This book's companion CD-ROM includes several news readers, including both trn and tin. Both newsreaders should be installed, provided you selected the *Mail/WWW/News Tools* component during Red Hat Linux installation.

Setting the NNTPSERVER environment variable

To read news from a news server by using NNTP, you have to define the NNTPSERVER environment variable. Define this environment variable to your news server's name. Both tin and trn news readers look up the NNTPSERVER environment variable for the name of the news server to contact.

For example, my news server's name is news.digex.net. Therefore, I define the NNTPSERVER variable as follows:

```
NNTPSERVER=newsreader.digex.net; export NNTPSERVER
```

Creating a .newsrc file

Far too many newsgroups exist on the Internet. When a news reader starts, it has to know which newsgroups you want to read. Both the tin and trn news readers expect to find a list of the newsgroups in a file named .newsrc in your home directory.

To prepare the .newsrc file, you need to know how to name the newsgroups. You learn more about naming newsgroups in the section "The newsgroup hierarchy."

If you are interested in information about Linux, you might create a .newsrc file, specifying the following newsgroups:

```
comp.os.linux.networking:
comp.os.linux.answers:
comp.os.linux.misc:
```

```
comp.os.linux.announce:
comp.os.linux.setup:
comp.os.linux.hardware:
```

Each line shows the name of a newsgroup, followed by a colon. After you begin to read news, the news-reader program fills in article numbers following the newsgroup name.

Running tin -r to read news

As long as you have set the NNTPSERVER environment variable to your news server's name, you can use either of the news readers — `trn` or `tin` — to read the news. You can try reading the news with each of the news readers to decide which one you like best.

To read news with `tin`, use the following command:

```
tin -r
tin 1.2 PL2 [UNIX] (c) Copyright 1991-93 Iain Lea.
Connecting to newsreader.digex.net...
Reading news active file...
Reading attributes file...
Reading newsgroups file...
```

Tip

The `-r` option causes `tin` to read news from a remote news server (the one you specify through the NNTPSERVER environment variable). After `tin` starts, it connects to the news server and communicates by using NNTP. The `tin` news reader displays status messages as it progresses to the point at which it gathers the newsgroups listed in the `.newsrc` file in your home directory.

After obtaining information about the newsgroups from the news server, `tin` displays those newsgroups in a full-screen text menu, as shown in Figure 19-2.

```
rxvt                                                                    _□×
                     Group Selection (newsreader.digex.net  6)         h=help
     1    663  comp.os.linux.networking
     2      1  comp.os.linux.answers
     3   1068  comp.os.linux.misc
     4     55  comp.os.linux.announce
     5    946  comp.os.linux.setup
     6    552  comp.os.linux.hardware




          <n>=set current to n, TAB=next unread, /=search pattern, c)atchup,
         g)oto, j=line down, k=line up, h)elp, m)ove, q)uit, r=toggle all/unread,
           s)ubscribe, S)ub pattern, u)nsubscribe, U)nsub pattern, y)ank in/out
                             *** End of Groups ***
```

Figure 19-2: A typical newsgroup selection screen displayed by tin.

The list of newsgroups that you see, of course, depends on the contents of the `.newsrc` file in your home directory. Figure 19-2 shows `tin`'s initial screen for my `.newsrc` file.

In `tin`'s newsgroup selection screen, you see the list of newsgroups at the top of the screen, and some help information at the bottom of the screen. Initially, the first newsgroup is selected (it appears highlighted). Press **j** to go down the list; press **k** to go up. (Yes, the movement keys are the same as those used by the `vi` editor.) You also can press the up and down arrow keys to select a new newsgroup.

After you select a newsgroup to read, press Enter to view the list of articles in that newsgroup. Figure 19-3 shows the screen after I selected the `comp.os.linux.announce` newsgroup and pressed **j** to move down the list to an item of interest.

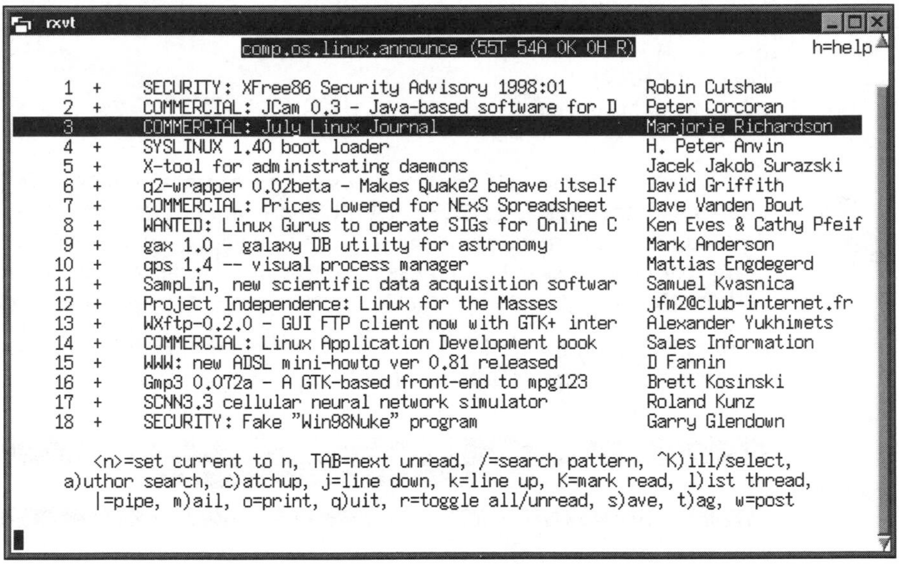

Figure 19-3: List of articles in a newsgroup (comp.os.linux.announce) as displayed by `tin`

As the highlighted item in Figure 19-3 shows, I am interested in an item about the July 1998 issue of *Linux Journal*. To read the item, I press Enter. The `tin` news reader downloads the article's text from the news server and displays it, as shown in Figure 19-4.

You can read the article's text one screen at a time. To view the next screen, press the space bar or Page Down. To return to the article selection menu, press **q**.

Pressing **q** again takes you back to the newsgroup selection screen. To quit `tin`, press **q** in the newsgroup selection screen.

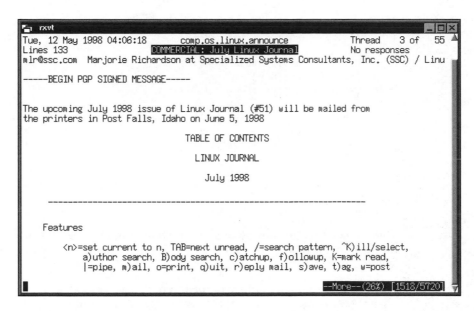

Figure 19-4: The `tin` news reader, displaying the text of a news article

Although using `tin -r` to read news from a remote news server is painless, it can take a painfully long time for the news reader to download news overviews and news items over a slower link. Even if you are using a PPP connection over a 56Kbps modem, news reading over that PPP link is slow enough to make you wish for at least a 1.54Mbps T1 link to your ISP.

Using an alternative news reader: trn

It's easy to read news with the `trn` news reader as well. To read news from an NNTP news server, you need a version of `trn` configured for NNTP news access. The `trn-nntp` package on disk set N of the companion CD-ROM includes the appropriate version of `trn`.

After you set the NNTPSERVER environment variable to the name of your news server, run `trn` as follows:

```
trn
                        *** NEWS NEWS ***

Welcome to trn 3.6, which continues on the feature trail, adding support
for slow net connections, and squashing some bugs.  Trn is "threaded read
news", based on rn.

You can type 'h' at any prompt to display a summary of the commands that
are available.
```

```
This message will not be displayed again unless it is updated with new
information.

Wayne Davison  <davison@borland.com>
[Type space to continue]
Unread news in comp.os.linux.networking               665 articles
Unread news in comp.os.linux.answers                    1 article
Unread news in comp.os.linux.misc                    1072 articles
Unread news in comp.os.linux.announce                  55 articles
Unread news in comp.os.linux.setup                    949 articles
etc.


====== 665 unread articles in comp.os.linux.networking -- read now?
[+ynq]
Getting overview file.
```

The trn news reader downloads information about the newsgroups listed in
the .newsrc file in your home directory. Then trn displays the number of
articles for some of the newsgroups.

Tip

Because of the chaotic nature of the Internet, new newsgroups (especially the
ones whose names begin with alt) are being added continually. If your
.newsrc file does not contain the names of any recently added newsgroups,
trn asks whether you want to subscribe to the newsgroup. I generally press **N**
(capital N) to indicate that I do not want to add any new newsgroups.

After displaying some messages about new newsgroups, trn prompts you
with the name of the first newsgroup. To read that newsgroup, press **y** or
Enter; to skip it, press **n**. To quit trn, press **q**.

If you select a newsgroup to read, trn gets an overview file for that
newsgroup (that's the file with the list of articles in threaded order, so that
each article is grouped with its replies). Then trn displays the list of articles
in the selected newsgroup. Each thread is identified by a letter that appears
in the first column. To view a thread, use the arrow keys to select a thread
letter and then press Enter. The trn news reader downloads and displays the
first article of that thread.

While you read articles, you can use several trn commands to navigate the
articles. The commands typically are single letters.

To see the trn commands that are available at any time, press **h**.

If you press **q** while you are reading an article, trn returns to the newsgroup
selection level and displays a prompt such as the following:

```
======  55 unread articles in comp.os.linux.announce -- read now?
[+ynq]
```

If you press **h** at this point, trn displays a list of article selection commands.

To quit trn, press **q** at the article selection prompt.

The newsgroup hierarchy

News items are organized into a hierarchy of newsgroups for ease of maintenance as well as ease of use. A typical newsgroup name looks like the following:

```
comp.os.linux.announce
```

This name says that `comp.os.linux.announce` is a newsgroup for announcements (`announce`) about the Linux operating system (`os.linux`) and that these subjects fall under the broad category of computers (`comp`).

As you can see, the format of a newsgroup name is a sequence of words separated by periods. These words denote the hierarchy of the newsgroup.

To understand the newsgroup hierarchy, compare the newsgroup name with the path name of a file (such as `/usr/lib/news/bin/nntpget`) in Linux. Just as a file's path name shows the directory hierarchy of the file, the newsgroup name shows the newsgroup hierarchy. In filenames, a slash (/) separates the names of directories; in a newsgroup's name, a period separates the different levels in the newsgroup hierarchy.

In a newsgroup name, the first word represents the newsgroup category. The `comp.os.linux.announce` newsgroup, for example, is in the `comp` category, whereas `alt.books.technical` is in the `alt` category.

Table 19-1 lists some of the major newsgroup categories.

Table 19-1   Major newsgroup categories

Category	Subject
alt	"Alternative" newsgroups (not subject to any rules), running the gamut from the mundane to the bizarre
bionet	Biology newsgroups
bit	Bitnet newsgroups
biz	Business newsgroups
clari	Clarinet news service (daily news)
comp	Computer hardware and software newsgroups
ieee	Newsgroups for the Institute of Electrical and Electronics Engineers
k12	Newsgroups devoted to elementary and secondary education
misc	Miscellaneous newsgroups
news	Newsgroups about Internet news administration
rec	Recreational and art newsgroups
sci	Science and engineering newsgroups
soc	Newsgroups for discussing social issues and various cultures
talk	Discussions of current issues (such as "talk radio")

This short list of categories is deceptive because it doesn't show you the wide-ranging variety of newsgroups available in each category. Because each newsgroup category contains several levels of subcategories, the overall count of newsgroups runs into several thousands. The `comp` category alone has more than 500 newsgroups.

Typically, you have to narrow your choice of newsgroups according to your interests. If you are interested in Linux, for example, you can pick one or more of the following newsgroups:

- `comp.os.linux.admin`: Information about Linux system administration

- `comp.os.linux.advocacy`: Discussions about promoting Linux

- `comp.os.linux.announce`: Important announcements about Linux. This newsgroup is *moderated*, which means that you must mail the article to the moderator, who then posts it to the newsgroup.

- `comp.os.linux.answers`: Questions and answers about Linux. All the Linux HOWTOs (see Chapter 1 for a list of Linux HOWTOs) are posted in this moderated newsgroup.

- `comp.os.linux.development`: Current Linux development work

- `comp.os.linux.development.apps`: Linux application development

- `comp.os.linux.development.system`: Linux operating-system development

- `comp.os.linux.hardware`: Discussions about Linux and various types of hardware

- `comp.os.linux.help`: Help with various aspects of Linux

- `comp.os.linux.misc`: Miscellaneous Linux-related topics

- `comp.os.linux.networking`: Networking under Linux

- `comp.os.linux.setup`: Linux setup and installation

- `comp.os.linux.x`: Discussions about setting up and running the X Window System under Linux

You have to be selective about what newsgroups you read, because it's impossible to keep up with all the news, even in a specific area such as Linux. When you first install and set up Linux, you might read newsgroups such as `comp.os.linux.setup.comp.os.linux.hardware`, and `comp.os.linux.x` (especially if you run *X*). After you get Linux up and running, you may want to learn only about new things that are happening in Linux. For such information, you would read the `comp.os.linux.announce` newsgroup.

Newsgroup subscriptions

Unlike magazines or newspapers, newsgroups do not require you to actually subscribe to them; you can essentially read any newsgroup available on the news server. The news-server administrator may decide to exclude certain newsgroups, however, in which case you cannot read the excluded newsgroups.

The only thing that comes close to "subscribing" is the .newsrc file in your home directory. All news readers consult this file to determine which newsgroups you want to read. From inside the news reader, you can use a command such as g, followed by the newsgroup name (in the trn news reader), to subscribe to a newsgroup. When you subscribe to the newsgroup, the news reader simply adds the name of that newsgroup to the .newsrc file.

How to post news

You can use a news reader to post a news item (a new item or a reply to an old posting) to one or more newsgroups. The exact command for posting a news item depends on the news reader. In the trn news reader, follow these steps to post an article:

1. While you are reading an article in trn, press **f**. The news reader asks whether you are posting an unrelated topic (unrelated to the article that you were reading when you pressed **f**). Press **y** to answer Yes, as follows:

   ```
   Are you starting an unrelated topic? [ynq] y
   ```

2. The news reader then prompts you for the subject of the new posting and the distribution. For this test posting, type a subject line with the word *ignore* in it. Otherwise, any site that receives your article will reply by mail to tell you that the article has reached the site; that's in keeping with the purpose of the misc.test newsgroup. For distribution, enter **na** to indicate North America, as follows:

   ```
   Subject: ignore no reply test
   Distribution: na
   ```

3. The newsreader uses the Pnews program to post an article to the newsgroups. If you are posting an article for the first time, you see the following message:

   ```
   (leaving cbreak mode; cwd=/usr/etc)

   I see you've never used this version of Pnews before. I will give you extra
   help this first time through, but then you must remember what you learned.
   If you don't understand any question, type h and a CR (carriage return) for
   help.
   ```

```
If you've never posted an article to the net before, it is HIGHLY
recommended
that you read the netiquette document found in news.announce.newusers so
that you'll know to avoid the commonest blunders. To do that, interrupt
Pnews, get to the top-level prompt of [t]rn, and use the command
"g news.announce.newusers" to go to that group.
```

4. **After the message, the news reader asks whether you really want to post an article. Press y to continue.**

   ```
   This program may post news to many machines.
   Are you absolutely sure that you want to do this? [ny] y
   ```

5. **The news reader asks whether you have a file that you want to include as the news item with the following prompt:**

   ```
   Prepared file to include [none]:
   ```

   Press Enter to continue.

6. **The news reader prompts you for the name of your editor (the default is vi) with the following explanation and prompt:**

   ```
   A temporary file has been created for you to edit. Be sure to leave at
   least one blank line between the header and the body of your message.
   (And until a certain bug is fixed all over the net, don't start the body of
   your message with any indentation, or it may get eaten.)

   Within the header may be fields that you don't understand. If you don't
   understand a field (or even if you do), you can simply leave it blank, and
   it will go away when the article is posted.

   Type return to get the default editor, or type the name of your favorite
   editor.

   Editor [/usr/bin/vi]:
   ```

   Press Enter to compose the news article with vi.

7. **The news reader starts the vi editor. In the editor, you can fill in the name of the newsgroup and any other fields in the news article (including the body of the article). Following is what I filled in (shown in boldface):**

   ```
   Newsgroups: misc.test
   Subject: ignore no reply test
   Summary:
   Expires:
   Sender:
   Followup-To:
   Distribution: na
   Organization:
   Keywords: test ignore
   ```

```
Cc:

Testing ignore
```

Notice that there is no entry for the name of the organization. You can edit the field to show your organization's name or define the `ORGANIZATION` environment variable (set it to your organization's name) before you start `trn`. After you finish editing the article, save it with the `:wq` command.

8. The news reader shows you the name (and a description) of the newsgroup to which you are about to post the article. Then `trn` prompts you for a command. Press **s** to send the article. The interaction with the news reader goes like this:

```
Your article's newsgroup:
misc.test                  [no description available]

Check spelling, Send, Abort, Edit, or List? s
```

9. The `trn` news reader returns you to the article that you were reading when you started to post this article. Press **q** to quit the newsgroup that you have been reading.

10. Type **g misc.test** to subscribe to the `misc.test` newsgroup (that's where you just posted the new article).

11. Look at the latest article in `misc.test`, which should be the article that you just posted.

Did the article get out?

If you post an article and read the newsgroup immediately, you'll see the new article, but that does not mean the article has reached other sites on the Internet. After all, your posting shows up on your news server immediately because that's where you posted the article. Because of the store-and-forward model of news distribution, the news article gradually propagates from your news server to others around the world.

Secret

The `misc.test` newsgroup provides a way to see whether your news posting is really getting around. If you post to that newsgroup and do not include the word *ignore* in the subject, news servers will acknowledge receipt of the article by sending an e-mail message to the address listed in the `Reply-To` field of the article's header.

If you have your Linux host on the Internet, try posting to the `misc.test` newsgroup to verify that articles are getting out. You should be prepared to receive a dozen or so replies from various sites, acknowledging the arrival of your article.

Secure Anonymous FTP

Besides mail and news, anonymous FTP is a common service on an Internet host. You may be familiar with FTP (File Transfer Protocol), which you can use to transfer files from one system to another. When you use FTP to transfer files to or from a remote system, you have to log into the remote system before you can use FTP.

Cross-Reference

Anonymous FTP refers to the use of the user name `anonymous`, which anyone can use with FTP to transfer files from a system. Anonymous FTP is a common way to share files on the Internet. Chapter 2, "Upgrading Linux," explains how you can use anonymous FTP to download patches to Linux kernels from the Internet host named ftp.funet.fi.

If you have used anonymous FTP to download files from various Internet sites, you already know the convenience of that service. With anonymous FTP, you can make information available to anyone on the Internet. If you have a new Linux application that you want to share with the world, set up anonymous FTP on your Linux PC and place the software in an appropriate directory. After that, all you need to do is announce to the world (probably through a posting in the `comp.os.linux.announce` newsgroup) that you have a new program available. Now anyone can get the software from your system at his or her convenience.

Even if you run a for-profit business, you can use anonymous FTP to support your customers. If you sell some hardware or software product, you may want to provide technical information or software "fixes" through anonymous FTP.

Unfortunately, the convenience of anonymous FTP comes at a price. If you do not configure the anonymous FTP service properly, intruders and pranksters may gain access to your system. Some intruders may simply use your system's disk as a temporary holding place for various files; others may fill your disk with junk files, effectively making your system inoperable. At the other extreme, an intruder may gain user-level (or, worse, root-level) access to your system and do much more damage.

Note

If you installed Red Hat Linux from this book's companion CD-ROM, you already have anonymous FTP installed on your system. The default setup also employs the necessary security precautions.

Following are the key features of the anonymous FTP setup:

- There is a user named `ftp` whose home directory is `/home/ftp`. The user does not have any shell assigned. Here is what you get when you search for ftp in the `/etc/passwd` file:

```
grep ftp /etc/passwd
ftp:*:14:50:FTP User:/home/ftp:
```

Note the asterisk in the second field — that means no one can actually log in with the user name `ftp`.

■ Here is the full permission setting and owner information of the `/home/ftp` directory:

```
drwxr-xr-x   6 root      root            1024 Mar 11 14:58 ftp
```

As this line shows, the `/home/ftp` directory is owned by `root` and the permission is set to 755 (only root can read and write; everyone else can only read).

■ You can view the contents of the `/home/ftp` directory with the `ls -la` command. The result is as follows:

```
total 6
drwxr-xr-x   6 root      root            1024 Mar 11 14:58 .
drwxr-xr-x   6 root      root            1024 Feb  6  1996 ..
d--x--x--x   2 root      root            1024 Mar 11 14:58 bin
d--x--x--x   2 root      root            1024 Mar 11 14:58 etc
drwxr-xr-x   2 root      root            1024 Mar 11 14:58 lib
dr-xr-sr-x   2 root      ftp             1024 Nov  6  1997 pub
```

Note that the permission settings of the `bin` and `etc` directories are 111 (execute only). All files inside the `bin` directory are also execute only (permission setting 111). All files in the `etc` directory are read-only (permission setting 444).

■ The `pub` directory is where you place any files that you want others to download from your system through anonymous FTP.

More on Internet Security

The latest information on securing an Internet host is available on the Internet itself. For this information, and to keep up with the latest security problems, visit the CERT home page (`http://www.cert.org/`) and read the CERT advisories, bulletins, and summaries posted periodically at CERT's FTP site (`ftp://info.cert.org/pub/`). (CERT used to stand for Computer Emergency Response Team, but nowadays it is simply CERT — a service mark of Carnegie Mellon University.)

Another good source of information is the Computer Incident Advisory Capability (CIAC) of the U.S. Department of Energy. From their Web page at http://ciac.llnl.gov/, you'll be able to find many Internet resources on security.

Summary

The Internet's growing popularity has resulted in Internet Service Providers (ISPs) springing up all over the United States and in much of the world. Online services such as America Online and CompuServe now offer Internet mail and Web browsing, bringing even more people to the Internet. Because of its support for TCP/IP networking — the universal language of the Internet — a Linux PC is ideal as an Internet host. This chapter describes the typical services available on an Internet host and shows you how to configure these services — mail, news, and anonymous `ftp` — on a Linux PC.

By reading this chapter, you learn the following things:

▶ Although the Internet essentially is a "network of networks," it manifests itself differently, depending on how people use its capabilities. For most people, the Internet is the World Wide Web and electronic mail (e-mail), whereas many other people use it to read the newsgroups. Still other people use Internet applications such as `telnet` and `ftp` to access remote computers.

▶ The World Wide Web, e-mail, newsgroups, and anonymous FTP are some of the important services available on an Internet host. This chapter describes the e-mail, newsgroup, and anonymous FTP services available on a Linux PC. (The World Wide Web is covered in the next chapter.)

▶ E-mail software comes in two parts: a mail transport agent, which physically sends and receives mail messages; and a mail user agent, which reads messages and prepares new messages.

▶ The companion CD-ROM includes several mail transfer agents and mail user agents. This chapter describes how to use `sendmail` as a mail transport agent.

▶ The `sendmail` configuration is complex, but you can get going with the sample file provided on the CD-ROM. All you may need to do is set your Linux PC's host name properly.

▶ To read e-mail, you can use `mail` or `elm`.

▶ Newsgroups originated in Usenet, which is a store-and-forward network. News items travel around the world from one system to another. Nowadays, news is transported over the Internet by means of the Network News Transport Protocol (NNTP).

▶ Because thousands of newsgroups exist, storing numerous news articles takes a great deal of disk space. Also, the articles must be purged periodically; otherwise, the disk will get filled. It's best to read news from a news server maintained by an Internet Service Provider (ISP).

▶ The companion CD-ROM includes several news readers, such as `tin` and `trn`. This chapter shows you how to use these news readers to read news from a designated news server.

▶ To read newsgroups from a news server, you should set the environment variable NNTPSERVER to the name of the news server.

▶ Anonymous FTP is another popular Internet service for distributing files. With anonymous FTP, anyone can use FTP with the `anonymous` user ID and download files from your system. Although anonymous FTP is useful for distributing data, it also poses a security risk if it is not set up properly.

▶ The default Linux installation includes an FTP server with anonymous FTP capabilities. The default anonymous FTP setup incorporates the necessary security precautions.

Chapter 20

Running a World Wide Web Server on Linux

Chapters 18 and 19 showed you how to connect your Linux PC to the Internet (through an Internet Service Provider) and set up common Internet services — such as mail, news, and anonymous FTP — on your system. This chapter turns to one of the reasons why the Internet has become so popular in recent years: the World Wide Web (WWW, W3, or simply the Web), which provides a easy graphical way to browse and retrieve information from the Internet.

As a host on the Internet, all your Linux system needs is a *Web browser* — an application that "knows" how to download and display Web documents — so you can begin enjoying the benefits of the Web. You also can make information available to other users through *Web pages* — the common term for Web documents.

This chapter first explains what the World Wide Web is and describes the Hypertext Transfer Protocol (HTTP) — the information exchange protocol that makes the Web work. Then the chapter shows you how to download the Netscape Web browser, set up the browser, and use it.

Next, the chapter turns to the use of the Web as a popular way to publish information on the Internet. Red Hat Linux includes the Apache HTTP server (that's the technical term for a Web server), which you can use simply by placing your HTML files in the appropriate directory. I'll show you where various files are supposed to go and how you can configure the server.

Discovering the World Wide Web

If you have used a network file server of any kind, you know the convenience of being able to access files that reside at a shared location. Using a word processing application that runs on your computer, you can easily open a document that physically resides on the file server.

Now imagine a word processor that allows you to open and view a document that resides on any computer on the Internet. You can view the document in its full glory, with formatted text and graphics. If the document makes a reference to another document (possibly residing on yet another computer), you can open that linked document by clicking the reference. That kind of easy access to distributed documents is essentially what the World Wide Web provides.

Of course, the documents have to be in a standard format, so that any computer (with appropriate Web software) can access and interpret the document. Additionally, a standard protocol is necessary for transferring Web documents from one system to another.

The standard Web document format is Hypertext Markup Language (HTML), and the standard protocol for exchanging Web documents is Hypertext Transfer Protocol (HTTP).

Note

A Web server is the software that provides HTML documents to any client making the appropriate HTTP requests. A Web browser is the client software that actually downloads an HTML document from a Web server and displays the contents graphically.

Like a giant spider's web

The World Wide Web is the combination of Web servers and HTML documents that contain the information. Imagine the Web as a giant book whose pages are scattered throughout the Internet. You use a Web browser running on your computer to view the pages, as illustrated in Figure 20-1.

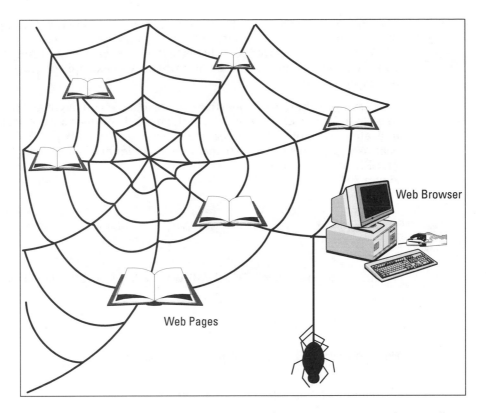

Figure 20-1: The World Wide Web is like millions of pages, scattered across the network, that you can read from your computer by using a Web browser.

As Figure 20-1 shows, the pages — the HTML documents — are linked by network connections that resemble a giant spider's web, so you can see why the Web is called the Web. The "World Wide" part comes from the fact that the Web pages are linked around the world.

Links and URLs

Like the pages of real books, Web pages contain text and graphics. Unlike real books, however, Web pages can contain multimedia information, such as video clips, digitized sound, and links to other Web pages that can actually take the user to the referenced Web page.

The *links* in a Web page are references to other Web pages that you can follow to go from one page to another. The Web browser displays these links as underlined text (in a different color), or images. Each link is like an instruction to the reader — something like "for more information, please consult Chapter 20," which you might find in a real book. In a Web page, all you have to do is click the link; and the Web browser brings up the referenced page, even if it's on a different computer.

The term *hypertext* refers to the nonlinear organization of text (as opposed to the sequential, linear arrangement of text in a book or a magazine). The links in a Web page are referred to as hypertext links because by clicking a link, you can jump to a different Web page, which is an example of the nonlinear organization of text.

This arrangement raises a question. In a real book, you might ask the reader to go to a specific chapter or page in the book. How does a hypertext link indicate the location of the referenced Web page? In the World Wide Web, each Web page has a special name, called a *Uniform Resource Locator (URL)*. An URL uniquely specifies the location of a file on a computer, as shown in Figure 20-2.

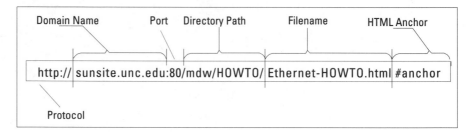

Figure 20-2: Various parts of a Uniform Resource Locator (URL)

As Figure 20-2 illustrates, an URL has the following sequence of components:

1. *Protocol.* The first field in the URL is the name of the protocol to be used to access the data residing in the file specified by the URL. In Figure 20-2, the protocol is http://, which means the URL specifies the location of a Web page. Following are the common protocol types and their meanings:

   - file:// specifies the name of a local file that is to be opened and displayed. You can use this file to view HTML files without having to connect to the Internet.

   - ftp:// specifies a file accessible through File Transfer Protocol (FTP).

   - gopher:// specifies a document and the name of a host system that runs the Gopher server from which the document is to be retrieved. (Gopher servers provide information by using a simple protocol.)

   - http:// specifies an HTML document that is accessible through Hypertext Transfer Protocol (HTTP).

   - mailto:// specifies an e-mail address that should be used to send an e-mail message.

   - news:// specifies a newsgroup to be read by means of Network News Transfer Protocol (NNTP).

- `telnet://` specifies a user name and a system name for remote login.

- `wais://` specifies the name of a Wide Area Information Server (WAIS) from which information is to be retrieved.

2. *Domain name.* This part of the URL contains the fully qualified domain name of the computer on which the file specified by this URL resides. You also can specify an IP address in this field (see Chapter 16 for more information on IP addresses). The domain name is not case-sensitive.

3. *Port address.* This is the port address of the server that implements the protocol listed in the first part of the URL (see Chapter 16 for a discussion of port addresses). This part of the URL is optional, because there are default ports for all protocols. The default port for HTTP, for example, is 80. Some sites, however, may configure the Web server to listen to a different port. In such a case, the URL must include the port address.

4. *Directory path.* This field is the directory path of the file being referenced in the URL. For Web pages, this field is the directory path of the HTML fil. The directory path is case-sensitive.

5. *File name.* This field is the name of the file. For Web pages, the filename typically ends with `.htm` or `.html`. If you omit the filename, the Web server returns a default file (often named `index.html`). The file name is case-sensitive.

6. *HTML anchor.* This optional part of the URL is used to make the Web browser jump to a specific location in the file. If this part starts with a question mark (?) instead of a pound sign (#), the text following the question mark is taken to be a query. The Web server returns information based on such queries.

Hypertext Transfer Protocol

Hypertext Transfer Protocol (HTTP) — the protocol that underlies the World Wide Web — is called *Hypertext* because Web pages include hypertext links. The *Transfer Protocol* part refers to the standard conventions for transferring a Web page across the network from one computer to another. Although you don't have to understand HTTP to set up a Web server or use a Web browser, I think you'll find it instructive to know how the Web works.

Before I explain anything about HTTP, you should get a firsthand taste of it. On most systems, the Web server listens to port 80 and responds to any HTTP requests sent to that port. Therefore, you can use the `telnet` program to connect to port 80 of a system (that has a Web server) and try out some HTTP commands.

To see an example of HTTP at work, follow these steps:

1. Make sure that your Linux PC's connection to the Internet is up and running. (If you use SLIP or PPP, for example, make sure you have established the connection.)

2. Type the following command:

   `telnet www.idgbooks.com 80`

3. After you see the `Connected...` message, type the following HTTP command:

   `GET / HTTP/1.0`

   and press Enter twice. In response to this HTTP command, the Web server returns some useful information, followed by the contents of the default HTML file (usually called `index.html`).

Following is what I got when I tried the GET command on the IDG Books Web site:

```
telnet www.idgbooks.com 80
Trying 206.80.51.140...
Connected to leland.idgbooks.com.
Escape character is '^]'.
GET / HTTP/1.0
........(Press Enter once more to send a blank line)
HTTP/1.1 200 OK
Date: Sun, 17 May 1998 22:35:19 GMT
Server: Apache/1.3b3
Connection: close
Content-Type: text/html

<html>

<head>
<meta http-equiv="Content-Type"content="text/html; charset=iso-
8859-1">

...... (lines deleted)

<title>IDG Books Online</title>
</head>

<body  background="http://www.idgbooks.com//images/background.5.gif"
text="#0000
00" link="#0201FE" vlink="#000087" alink="#FF0000">

...... (lines deleted)

</body>

</html>
Connection closed by foreign host.
```

When you try this example with `telnet`, you see exactly what the Web server sends back to the Web browser. The first few lines are administrative information for the browser. The server returns the following information:

- A line showing that the server uses HTTP protocol version 1.1 and a status code of 200 indicating success: `HTTP/1.1 200 OK`

- The current date and time. A sample date and time string looks like `Date: Sun, 17 May 1998 22:35:19 GMT`

- The name and version of the Web server software. For example, for a site running the Apache HTTPD Version 1.3b3, the server returns the following string: `Server: Apache/1.3b3`

- The type of document being returned by the Web server. For HTML documents, the content type is reported as follows: `Content-type: text/html`

The document itself follows the administrative information. An HTML document has the following general layout:

```
<title>Document's title goes here</title>
<html>
<body optional attributes go here >
... The rest of the document goes here
</body>
</html>
```

You can identify this layout by looking through the listing that shows what the Web server returns in response to the `GET` command. Because the example uses a `telnet` command to get the document, you see the HTML content as lines of text. If you were to access the same URL (`http://www.idgbooks.com`) with a Web browser (such as Netscape Navigator), you would see the page in its graphical form, as shown in Figure 20-3.

If you don't have a Web browser, you learn how to download and set up a Web browser in the next few sections.

The example of `HTTP` commands shows the result of the `GET` command. `GET` happens to be the most common `HTTP` command, because `GET` causes the server to return a specified HTML document.

The other two `HTTP` commands are `HEAD` and `POST`. The `HEAD` command is almost like `GET`; it causes the server to return everything in the document except the body. The `POST` command is used to send information to the server; it's up to the server to decide how to act on the information.

Figure 20-3: The home page from www.idgbooks.com, viewed with the Netscape Navigator Web browser.

Is HTTP an Internet Standard?

Despite its widespread use in the World Wide Web since 1990, Hypertext Transfer Protocol (HTTP) was not an Internet standard until recently. All Internet standards are distributed as Request for Comments (RFC) documents. The first HTTP-related RFC was RFC 1945, "Hypertext Transfer Protocol — HTTP/1.0," T. Berners-Lee, R. Fielding, and H. Frystyk, May 1996. However, RFC 1945 is considered an informational document, not a standard.

RFC 2068, "Hypertext Transfer Protocol — HTTP/1.1," R. Fielding, J. Gettys, J. Mogul, H.

Frystyk, T. Berners-Lee, January 1997, is the proposed Internet standard for HTTP.

To read these RFCs, point your Web browser to http://www.cis.ohio-state.edu/htbin/rfc/rfc-index.html.

To learn more about HTTP/1.1 and other Web-related standards, use a Web browser to access http://www.w3.org/pub/WWW/Protocols/.

Surfing the Net

Like anything else, the World Wide Web is easier to understand after you have seen how it works. One of the best ways to learn about the Web is to "surf the Net" with a Web browser. Browsing Web pages is fun, because the typical Web page contains both text and images. Also, browsing has an element of surprise; you can click the links and end up in unexpected Web pages. These links are the most curious aspect of the Web. You can start by looking at a page that shows today's weather; and a click later, you can be reading this week's issue of *Time* magazine online.

Before you can try anything, of course, you need a Web browser. (You also must have an Internet connection for your Linux system, but I am assuming that you have already taken care of that part.)

Downloading the Netscape Web browser

In January 1998, Netscape Communications Corporation announced the free availability of their Netscape Communicator product (Netscape Communicator is an integrated Web browser, e-mail and news reader, and Web page composer — the Web browser is called Navigator). That means you can now download, install, and use the Netscape Web browser on your system without paying any fee.

To download and install Netscape Communicator, follow these steps:

1. Log in as `root` and create the `/usr/local/netscape` directory and change to that directory with the following commands:

   ```
   mkdir /usr/local/netscape
   cd /usr/local/netscape
   ```

2. Make sure that your Linux system's Internet connection is up and running.

3. Type the following command (shown in boldface):

   ```
   ftp ftp2.netscape.com
   Connected to ftp.netscape.com.
   220 ftp25 FTP server (UNIX(r) System V Release 4.0) ready.
   Name (ftp2.netscape.com:root): anonymous
   331 Guest login ok, send your complete e-mail address as password.
   Password:  (type your e-mail address)
   230-Welcome to the Netscape Communications Corporation FTP server.
   230-
   230-If you have any odd problems, try logging in with a minus sign
   (-)
   230-as the first character of your password.  This will turn off a
   feature
   230-that may be confusing your ftp client program.
   ```

```
230-
230-Please send any questions, comments, or problem reports about
230-this server to ftp@netscape.com.
230-
230 Guest login ok, access restrictions apply.
Remote system type is UNIX.
Using binary mode to transfer files.
```

4. At the `ftp>` prompt, type the following command (shown in boldface):

```
ftp> cd /pub/communicator/4.05/shipping/english/unix/linux20
250 CWD command successful.
```

5. Type the `ls` command to view the file listing:

```
ftp> ls
200 PORT command successful.
150 Opening ASCII mode data connection for *ls.
drwxr-xr-x   1 ftp        ftp          512 Apr 01 22:39 base_install
drwxr-xr-x   1 ftp        ftp          512 Apr 01 22:40
navigator_standalone
drwxr-xr-x   1 ftp        ftp          512 May 07 16:11
professional_edition
226 ASCII Transfer complete.
```

As you can see, several versions of Netscape browsers are available.

6. To download the professional edition of Netscape Communicator, first change directory with the `cd` command:

```
ftp> cd professional_edition
```

7. Set the file type to binary with the following command:

```
ftp> binary
200 Type set to I.
```

8. Get the Netscape Communicator with the following command:

```
ftp> mget communicator*
mget communicator-v405-export.x86-unknown-linux2.0.tar.gz? y
```

If you have a SLIP or PPP connection over a modem, this step will take a while, because that command downloads 11,314,759 bytes (about 11MB). (The file size may be different by the time you download Netscape.) With a 28,800bps link, you can expect to download about 3KB per second; at this rate, 11MB will take about 1 hour. With a higher speed connection, your download time will be proportionately less.

9. Type **bye** to quit `ftp`.

10. The downloaded file is a compressed archive (the `.gz` at the end of the filename indicates that the file is compressed). Use the following command to extract the contents of the archive:

```
tar zxvf communicator*.gz
```

A number of messages will appear as files and are extracted from the archive.

11. You should see a file named README.install (the file name may change in future versions of Netscape Communicator). Type the following command to read that file:

    more README.install

12. Follow the instructions in the README.install file to install Netscape Communicator on your Linux system. Netscape's recommended way to install the software is to run a shell script named ns-install (the script name may change in future versions of Netscape Communicator).

That's it! You should be able to start the Netscape browser by typing netscape in an xterm window. (Remember that you have to start X before running netscape, because Netscape uses the X Window System.)

Taking Netscape Navigator for a spin

Netscape Navigator started as a successor to Mosaic, the original Web browser from the National Center for Supercomputing Applications (NCSA) at the University of Illinois in Urbana-Champaign. One of Mosaic's primary developers, Marc Andreessen, was the force behind Netscape Navigator as well. Netscape Navigator improved on Mosaic in several ways, the most significant being the way that Netscape Navigator loads a Web page.

When a Web page includes embedded images, the browser has to download each image separately. Mosaic displays a Web page only after everything on that page has been downloaded. Netscape Navigator, on the other hand, begins displaying the page as soon as parts of it are available.

Netscape Navigator also finishes downloading a page faster, because it makes multiple connections with the Web server to download separate parts of the page in parallel. (This process puts more load on the Web server, but it's beneficial to the user.)

Starting Netscape

To run Netscape, type netscape at the command line in an xterm window (you must start X before running Netscape). When Netscape starts, it automatically loads the Web page identified by the URL http://home.netscape.com/.

Secret

If you compare this syntax with the URL syntax shown earlier in this chapter, you'll notice that this URL does not appear to have a filename. When an URL does not have a filename, the Web server sends a default HTML file named index.html (that's the default filename for the popular UNIX-based Apache and NCSA Web servers; Windows NT-based Web servers use a different default filename).

Typically, Web servers contain many Web pages, which are organized in such a way that you can start at a main page and jump to the other pages. The main Web page on a Web server is known as the *home page*.

The URL `http://home.netscape.com/` represents the home page of Netscape Communications — the company that developed Netscape Communicator. Without a Web page, a Web browser cannot show anything.

Learning Netscape Navigator's user interface

Figure 20-4 shows a Web page from the IDG Books Web site, as well as the main elements of the Netscape Navigator window.

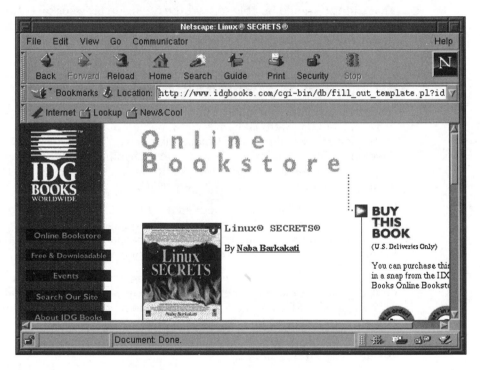

Figure 20-4: Elements of the Netscape Navigator window

The Netscape Navigator window sports a Motif user interface with a title bar showing the current document title, as well as a menu bar containing all the standard menus (such as File and Edit).

The most important part of the Netscape window is the document window — the large area in which Netscape displays the Web page with its text and images.

Immediately above the document window are three items you can turn on or off from the View menu:

- The *Navigation Toolbar* gives you quick access to some common menu items. The Back and Forward buttons are for moving between Web pages you've already seen; the Home button takes you to the default home page (which is initially set to Netscape's home page); Reload forces the browser to download the current page again; Search takes you to the page from which you can search for information on the Internet; Guide lets you view a number of helpful online guides; the Print button prints the current page; Security shows security information; and the Stop button allows you to stop loading the current Web page.

- The *Location Toolbar* displays the location of the current Web page in the form of an URL and lets you access your bookmarks (saved URLs). You can also click in this area and type in the URL of any page you want to see.

- The *Personal Toolbar* offers shortcuts to items accessible via the Guide button in the Navigation Toolbar. These buttons allow you to access specific Web pages quickly. The Internet button, for example, brings up a Web page from which you can browse information organized by categories, such as Business, Computers, Entertainment, and Headline News.

In the top-right corner of the Netscape window is the Activity Indicator button (marked with a large *N*). Netscape animates the Activity Indicator while it downloads a Web page. You can go to Netscape's home page by clicking this button.

Secret

In the bottom-left corner of the Netscape window is a padlock — the security padlock. Netscape supports a secure version of the HTTP protocol. When Netscape connects to a Web server that supports secure HTTP, the security padlock appears locked. Otherwise, the security padlock is open, signifying an insecure connection.

Netscape displays status messages in a large area to the right of the security key. When Netscape is busy downloading a Web page, it displays what percentage of the document has downloaded.

Along the bottom-right edge of the window, Netscape Navigator displays a number of icons. By clicking on these icons, you can open other windows to perform tasks such as reading e-mail messages or reading a newsgroup. To learn more about any of these icons, simply move the mouse pointer over the button and Netscape Navigator displays a help message in a small pop-up window (and also in the status message area).

Setting Up a Web Server

You probably already know how it feels to use the Web, but you may not know how to set up a Web server so that you, too, can provide information to the world through Web pages. To become an information provider on the Web, you have to run a Web server on your Linux PC on the Internet. You also have to prepare the Web pages — a task that may turn out to be more demanding than the server setup.

Note

Web servers provide information by using HTTP. Web servers are also known as HTTP daemons (because continuously running server processes are called *daemons* in UNIX) or HTTPD, for short. The Web server program usually is named `httpd`.

Among the freely available Web servers, the Apache Web server happens to be the most popular. The Apache Web server started out as an improved version of the NCSA HTTPD server, but soon grew into a separate development effort. Like NCSA HTTPD, the Apache server is developed and maintained by a team of collaborators. Apache is freely available over the Internet.

The following sections describe the Apache Web server.

Installing the Apache Web server

During Red Hat Linux installation from this book's companion CD-ROM, you have the option to install the Apache Web server. As described in Chapter 1, simply select the *Mail/WWW/News Tools* component when you are prompted for the components to install. The WWW in the name of the component refers to the World Wide Web and it includes the Apache Web server. As you proceed with the installation steps in Chapter 1, you get to a part where you have to specify which services to start automatically whenever you boot your Linux system. At this step, you should select `httpd` — this ensures that the Apache Web server is started automatically.

Perform the following steps to verify that the Web server software is installed on your system:

1. Use the rpm -q command to check if the Apache package is installed:

```
rpm -q apache
apache-1.2.4-4
```

If the output shows an Apache package name, you have installed the Apache software.

2. Type the following command to check if the `httpd` process (the name of the Apache Web server program is `httpd`) is running:

```
ps ax | grep httpd
```

The output should show a number of `httpd` processes. It is common to run several Web server processes — one parent and several child processes — so several HTTP requests can be handled efficiently by assigning each request to an `httpd` process.

3. Use the `telnet` program from any system with a network connection to your Linux system and use the `HTTP HEAD` command to query the Web server as follows:

```
telnet 192.168.1.1  80  (use your system's IP address)
Trying 192.168.1.1...
Connected to 192.168.1.1.
Escape character is '^]'.
HEAD / HTTP/1.0
... Press Enter once more to type a blank line
HTTP/1.1 200 OK
Date: Tue, 19 May 1998 11:07:19 GMT
Server: Apache/1.2.4
Last-Modified: Thu, 06 Nov 1997 18:20:06 GMT
ETag: "a014-792-34620a56"
Content-Length: 1938
Accept-Ranges: bytes
Connection: close
Content-Type: text/html
Connection closed by foreign host.
```

If you get a response such as the above, your system already has the Apache Web server installed and set up correctly. All you have to do is understand the configuration so you can place the HTML documents in the proper directory.

Tip

Use a Web server to load the home page from your system. If your system's IP address is 192.168.1.100, use the URL `http://192/168.1.100/` and see what happens. You should see a Web page with the title "Test Page for Red Hat Linux's Apache Installation."

Why is it called "Apache?"

According to the information about the Apache Web server project on `http://www.apache.org/info.html`, the Apache group was formed in March 1995 by a number of people who provided patch files that had been written to fix bugs in NCSA HTTPD 1.3. The result, after applying the patches to NCSA HTTPD, was what they called *A PAtCHy* server; that's how the name Apache came about.

According to the May 1998 Netcraft Web Server Survey at `http://www.netcraft.co.uk/Survey/`, the Apache Web server is the most popular—48.26% of 2,308,502 sites reported using the Apache server. Microsoft Internet Information Server (IIS) is a distant second with 21.34% percent of the sites.

Configuring the Apache Web server

Red Hat Linux configures the Apache Web server software to use the following directories:

- The Web server program — `httpd` — is installed in the `/usr/sbin` directory.

- The Apache Web server configuration files are located in the `/etc/httpd/conf` directory. The three configuration files — `access.conf`, `httpd.conf`, and `srm.conf.` — are described in the next four sections.

- The Apache Web server is set up to serve the HTML documents from the `/home/httpd/html` directory. Therefore, you should place your Web pages in the `/home/httpd/html` directory.

- If you have any Common Gateway Interface (CGI) programs — programs that can be invoked by the Web server to access other files and databases — you should place these in the `/home/httpd/cgi-bin` directory.

- The `/var/log/httpd` directory is meant for Web server log files (access logs and error logs).

- The `/etc/rc.d/init.d/httpd` script starts the `httpd` process as your Linux system boots.

Apache configuration files

The Apache server's operation is controlled by three configuration files located in the `/etc/httpd/conf` directory. The configuration files control how the server runs, what documents it serves, and who can access these documents.

Following are descriptions of the three configuration files:

Filename	Purpose
`httpd.conf`	Configuration file for the Apache server. It specifies general attributes of the server such as the port number and the directory in which the server's directories are located.
`srm.conf`	Configuration file for the server resources — documents and other information the Web server provides to users. For example, the `srm.conf` file specifies where the documents are located. (Note that `srm` stands for *server resource map*.)
`access.conf`	Configuration file that controls access to the Web server. You can control access to the entire Web server as well as to specific directories.

The next few sections provide key information about each configuration file. Typically, you do not have to change anything in the configuration files to use the Apache Web server. However, it is useful to know the format of the configuration files and the meaning of various keywords used in them.

As you study the configuration files in the `/etc/httpd/conf` directory, keep the following syntax rules in mind:

- Each configuration file is a text file that you can edit with your favorite text editor and view with the `more` command.

- All comment lines begin with a #.

- Each line can have only one directive.

- Extra spaces and blank lines are ignored.

- All entries except pathnames and URLs are case-insensitive.

The httpd.conf configuration file

The `/etc/httpd/conf/httpd.conf` file is the basic HTTP daemon configuration file — it controls how the Apache Web server runs. For example, the `httpd.conf` file specifies the port number the server uses, the name of the Web site, and the e-mail address to which mail is sent in case of any problems with the server.

Following are two interesting items from the `httpd.conf` file:

- `ServerAdmin` is the e-mail address the Web server provides to clients in case any errors occur. The default value for ServerAdmin is `root@localhost`. You should set this to a valid e-mail address that anyone on the Internet can use to report errors with your Web site.

- `ServerName` specifies the hostname of your Web site (of the form `www.your.domain`). The name should be a registered domain name that others can locate through their name server. Here is an example:

`ServerName   www.myhost.com`

Many more directives control the way the Apache Web server works. The following list summarizes some of the directives you can use in the `httpd.conf` file. You can leave most of them at their default settings, but it's important to know about these directives if you are maintaining a Web server.

`ServerType` *type* — **Specifies how the HTTP server is executed by Linux. The** *type* **can be** `inetd` **(to run the server through the** `inetd` **daemon) or** `standalone` **(to run the server as a stand-alone process). You should run the server stand-alone for better performance.**

`Port` *num* — Specifies that the HTTP daemon should listen to port *num* (a number between 0 and 65,535) for requests from clients. The default port for HTTPD is 80. You should leave the port number at its default value, because clients assume the HTTP port to be 80. If your server does not use port 80, the URL for your server must specify the port number.

`User` *name* [*#id*] — Specifies the user name (or ID) used by the HTTP daemon when running in stand-alone mode. You can leave this directive at the default setting (`nobody`). If you specify a user ID, use a pound-sign (#) prefix for the numeric ID.

Group *name* [*#id*]—Specifies the group name (or ID) of the HTTP daemon when running in stand-alone mode. The default group name is nobody.

ServerAdmin *webmaster@company.com*—Provides the server with the e-mail address of the person who maintains the Web server. In case of errors, the server provides this address so users can report errors.

ServerRoot *pathname*—Specifies the directory where the Web server is located. By default, the configuration and log files are expected to reside in subdirectories of this directory.

ServerName *www.company.com*—Sets the server's hostname to *www.company.com* instead of its real hostname. You cannot simply invent a name; the name must be a valid name from the Domain Name System (DNS) for your system.

StartServers *num*—Sets the number of child processes that start as soon as the Apache Web server runs.

MaxSpareServers *num*—Sets the desired maximum number of idle child server processes (a child process is considered to be idle if it is not handling an HTTP request).

TimeOut *numsec*—Sets the number of seconds the server waits for a client to send a query after the client establishes connection. The default TimeOut is 300 seconds (5 minutes).

ErrorLog *filename*—Sets the file where httpd logs the errors it encounters. If the file name does not begin with a /, the name is taken to be relative to ServerRoot. The default ErrorLog is /var/log/httpd/error_log. Typical error log entries include events such as server restarts and any warning messages, such as the following:

```
[Sun Apr 19 01:02:03 1998] Server configured -- resuming normal
operations
[Wed Apr 22 01:24:29 1998] httpd: caught SIGTERM, shutting down
```

TransferLog *filename*—Sets the file where httpd records all client accesses (including failed accesses). The default TransferLog is /var/log/httpd/access_log. The following example shows how a typical access is recorded in the TransferLog file:

```
192.168.1.200 - - [19/May/1998:06:22:15 -0400] "GET / HTTP/1.0"
200 1938
192.168.1.200 - - [19/May/1998:06:22:15 -0400] "GET /apache_pb.gif
HTTP/1.0" 200 2326
```

The first entry is for the text of the file; the second entry is for an embedded image. The last two items in each line show the status code returned by the server, followed by the number of bytes sent by the server.

PidFile *filename*—Sets the file where httpd stores its process ID. The default PidFile is /var/run/httpd.pid. You can use this information to kill or restart the HTTP daemon. The following example shows how you would restart httpd:

```
kill -HUP `cat /var/run/httpd.pid `
```

TypesConfig *filename* — Specifies the file containing the mapping of file extensions to MIME data types. (MIME stands for *Multipurpose Internet Mail Extensions*, which defines a way to package attachments in a single message file.) The server reports these MIME types to clients. If you do not specify a TypesConfig directive, httpd assumes that the TypesConfig file is /etc/mime.types. Following are a few lines from the default /etc/mime.types file:

```
(many lines deleted...)
text/html                       html
image/ief                       ief
image/jpeg                      jpe jpeg jpg
application/x-latex             latex
application/x-troff-man         man
```

Each line shows the MIME type (such as text/html), followed by the file extensions for that type (html).

The srm.conf configuration file

The resource configuration file, /etc/httpd/conf/srm.conf, specifies the location of the Web pages, as well as how to specify the data types of various files. To get started, you can leave the directives at their default settings. Following are some of the resource configuration directives for the Apache Web server:

DocumentRoot *pathname* — Specifies the directory where the HTTP server finds the Web pages. In Red Hat Linux, the default DocumentRoot is /home/httpd/html. If you place your HTML documents in another directory, set DocumentRoot to that directory.

UserDir *dirname* — Specifies the directory below a user's home directory, where the HTTP server looks for the Web pages when a user name appears in the URL (in an URL such as http://www.access.digex.net/~naba/, for example, which includes a user name with a tilde prefix). The default UserDir is public_html, which means that a user's Web pages will be in the public_html subdirectory of that user's home directory. If you do not want to allow users to have any Web pages, specify disabled as the directory name in the UserDir directive.

DirectoryIndex *filename* — Indicates the default file to be returned by the server when the client does not specify any document. The default DirectoryIndex is index.html. If httpd does not find this file, it returns an index (basically, a nice-looking listing of the files) of that directory.

AccessFileName *filename* — Specifies the filename that may appear in each directory containing documents, and indicates who has permission to access the contents of that directory. The default AccessFileName is .htaccess. The syntax of this file is the same as that of the access.conf file, discussed in the following section.

AddType `type/subtype extension`—Associates a file extension with a MIME data type (of the form `type/subtype`, such as `text/plain` or `image/gif`). Thus, if you want the server to treat files with the `.lst` extension as plain-text files, you would specify the following:

AddType text/plain lst

The default MIME types and extensions are listed in the `/etc/mime.types` file.

AddEncoding type `extension`—Associates an encoding type with a file extension. If you want the server to mark files ending with `.gz` as encoded with the `x-gzip` encoding method (the standard name for the GZIP encoding), you would specify the following:

AddEncoding x-gzip gz

DefaultType `type/subtype`—Specifies the MIME type the server should use if it cannot determine the type from the file extension. If you do not specify `DefaultType`, `httpd` assumes the MIME type to be `text/html`. In the default `srm.conf` file you get from the companion CD-ROM, `DefaultType` is specified as `text/plain`.

Redirect `requested-file actual-URL`—Specifies that any requests for `requested-file` be redirected to `actual-URL`.

Alias `requested-dir actual-dir`—Specifies that the server use `actual-dir` to locate files in the `requested-dir` directory (in other words, `requested-dir` is an alias for `actual-dir`). If you want requests for `/icons` directory to go to `/home/httpd/icons`, you would specify the following:

Alias /icons/ /home/httpd/icons/

ScriptAlias `requested-dir actual-dir`—Specifies the real name of the directory where scripts for the Common Gateway Interface (CGI) are located. The default `srm.conf` file contains the following directive:

ScriptAlias /cgi-bin/ /home/httpd/cgi-bin/

This directive means that when a Web browser requests a script such as `/cgi/bin/test-cgi`, the HTTP server runs the script `/home/httpd/cgi-bin/test-cgi`.

FancyIndexing on [off]—Enables or disables the display of fancy directory listings, with icons and file sizes.

DefaultIcon `iconfile`—Specifies the location of the default icon that the server should use for files with no icon information. By default, `DefaultIcon` is `/icons/unknown.gif`.

ReadmeName `filename`—Specifies the name of a README file whose contents are added to the end of an automatically generated directory listing. The default `ReadmeName` is README.

`HeaderName` *filename* — Specifies the name a header file whose contents are prepended to an automatically generated directory listing. The default `HeaderName` is HEADER.

`AddDescription` *"file description" filename* — Specifies that the *file description* string be displayed next to the specified *filename* in the directory listing. You can use a wildcard, such as *.html, as the *filename*.

`AddIcon` *iconfile extension1 extension2 ...* — Associates an icon with one or more file extensions. The following directive associates the icon file /icons/movie.xbm with the file extensions .mpeg and .qt:

`AddIcon /icons/text.gif .txt`

`AddIconByType` *iconfile MIME-types* — Associates an icon with a group of file types specified as a wildcard form of MIME types (such as text/* or image/*). To associate an icon file of /icons/text.xbm with all text types, you would specify the following:

`AddIconByType (TXT,/icons/text.gif) text/*`

This directive also tells the server to use TXT in place of the icon for clients that cannot accept images. (Browsers tell the server what types of data they can accept.)

`AddIconByEncoding` *iconfile encoding1 encoding2 ...* — Specifies an icon to be displayed for one or more encoding types (such as x-compress or x-tar).

`IndexIgnore` *filename1 filename2 ...* — Instructs the server to ignore the specified filenames (they typically have wildcards) when preparing a directory listing. To leave out README, HEADER, and all files with a leading period (.), you would specify the following:

`IndexIgnore */.??* *~ *# */HEADER* */README* */RCS`

`IndexOptions` *option1 option2 ...* — Indicates the options you want in the directory listing prepared by the server. Options can include one or more of the following:

- `FancyIndexing` turns on the fancy directory listing.
- `IconsAreLinks` makes the icons act like links.
- `ScanHTMLTitles` shows a description of HTML files.
- `SuppressLastModified` stops display of the last date of modification.
- `SuppressSize` stops display of the file size.
- `SuppressDescription` stops display of any file description.

`ErrorDocument` *errortype filename* — Specifies a file that the server should send when an error of a specific type occurs. If you do not have this directive, the server sends a built-in error message. The *errortype* can be one of the following:

- 302 - REDIRECT
- 400 - BAD_REQUEST
- 401 - AUTH_REQUIRED
- 403 - FORBIDDEN
- 404 - NOT_FOUND
- 500 - SERVER_ERROR
- 501 - NOT_IMPLEMENTED

The access.conf configuration file

The `/etc/httpd/conf/access.conf` file allows you to control who can access different directories in the system. This file is the global access configuration file. In each directory, you can have another access configuration file, with the name specified by the `AccessFileName` directive in the `srm.conf` file. (That per-directory access configuration file is named `.htaccess` by default.)

Stripped of most of the comment lines, the `access.conf` file has the following format:

```
# The following directory name should
# match DocumentRoot in srm.conf
<Directory /home/httpd/html>
    Options Indexes FollowSymLinks
    AllowOverride None
    order allow,deny
    allow from all
</Directory>

# The directory name should match the
# location of the cgi-bin directory
<Directory /home/httpd/cgi-bin>
AllowOverride None
Options ExecCGI
</Directory>
```

Note that the `access.conf` file uses a different syntax than the `httpd.conf` and `srm.conf` files. If you know HTML, you can see that the syntax is similar to that of HTML. Various access control directives are enclosed within pairs of tags, such as `<Directory> ... </Directory>`.

The following list describes some of the access control directories. In particular, notice the `AuthUserFile` directive; you can have password-based access control for specific directories.

Options *opt1 opt2 ...* —Specifies the access control options for the directory section in which this directive appears. The options can be one or more of the following:

- `None` disables all access control features.
- `All` turns on all features for the directory.

- `FollowSymLinks` enables the server to follow symbolic links.

- `SymLinksIfOwnerMatch` follows symbolic links only if the linked directory is owned by the same user as this directory.

- `ExecCGI` allows execution of CGI scripts in the directory.

- `Includes` allows server-side include files in this directory.

- `Indexes` allows clients to request indexes (directory listings) for this directory.

- `IncludesNoExec` disables the exec feature.

`AllowOverride` *directive1 directive2 ...* —Specifies which access control directives can be overridden on a per-directory basis. The directive list can have one or more of the following:

- `None` stops any directive from being overridden.

- `All` allows overriding of any directive on a per-directory basis.

- `Options` allows the use of the `Options` directive in the directory-level file.

- `FileInfo` allows the use of `AddType` and `AddEncoding` directives.

- `AuthConfig` allows the use of the `AuthName`, `AuthType`, `AuthUserFile`, and `AuthGroupFile` directives.

- `Limit` allows the use of `Limit` directives in a directory's access configuration file.

`AuthName` *name* —Specifies the authorization name for a directory.

`AuthType` *type* —Specifies the type of authorization to be used. The only supported authorization type is `Basic`.

`AuthUserFile` *filename* —Specifies the file in which user names and passwords are stored for authorization. The following directive sets the authorization file to `/etc/httpd/conf/.htpasswd`:

`AuthUserFile /etc/httpd/conf/.htpasswd`

You have to create the authorization file with the `/usr/sbin/htpasswd` support program, located in the `/etc/httpd/support` directory. To create the authorization file and add the password for a user named `jdoe`, you would specify the following:

```
/usr/sbin/htpasswd -c /etc/httpd/conf/.htpasswd jdoe
Adding password for jdoe.
New password: (type the password)
Re-type new password: (type the same password again)
```

`AuthGroupFile` *filename* —Specifies the file to consult for a list of user groups for authentication.

`order` *ord* — This directive specifies the order in which two other directives — `allow` and `deny` — are evaluated. The order can be one of the following:

- `deny,allow` evaluates the `deny` directive before `allow`.

- `allow,deny` evaluates the `allow` directive before `deny`.

- `mutual-failure` allows only those hosts that are in the `allow` list.

    `deny from` *host1 host2...* — This directive specifies the hosts that are denied access.

    `allow from` *host1 host2...* — This directive specifies the hosts that are allowed access. If you want all hosts in a specific domain to access the Web documents in a directory, you would specify the following:

```
order deny,allow
allow from .nws.noaa.gov
```

`require` *entity en1 en2...* — This directive specifies which users can access a directory. The *entity* can be one of the following:

- `user` allows only a list of named users.

- `group` allows only a list of named groups.

- `valid-user` allows all users listed in the `AuthUserFile` access to the directory (provided they enter the correct password).

Summary

The World Wide Web (WWW or the Web) has propelled the Internet into the mainstream, because Web browsers make it easy for users to browse documents stored on various Internet hosts. Whether you run a small business or manage computer systems and networks for a company, chances are good that you have to set up and maintain a Web server. Because of its built-in networking support, a Linux PC makes an affordable World Wide Web server. This chapter describes how to set up and configure a Web server on a Linux PC.

By reading this chapter, you learn the following things:

▶ The World Wide Web is possible because a standard format exists for documents, and a standard protocol exists for transferring documents across the network. The document format is Hypertext Markup Language, or HTML. The standard document exchange protocol is Hypertext Transfer Protocol, or HTTP.

▶ The Web has a client-server architecture, with Web servers providing the HTML documents (often referred to as *Web pages*) to Web browser clients.

▶ To uniquely identify Web pages and other network resources, the Uniform Resource Locator (URL) syntax is used. An URL identifies the location of the document (machine name and directory), as well as the protocol to be used to transfer the document (such as `http` or `ftp`).

▶ This chapter shows you how to download and set up Netscape Navigator. You should try a browser before setting up a Web server.

▶ The most popular Web server is the Apache Web server. You can install the Apache Web server during Red Hat Linux installation. This chapter describes the Apache Web server configuration files.

Chapter 21

Running a Business with Linux

In This Chapter

▶ Understanding the role Linux can play in business

▶ Looking at tasks that are best suited for Linux

▶ Using a Linux PC as a LAN Manager server

▶ Printing from Linux on a LAN Manager printer

▶ Looking at business opportunities with Linux

▶ Using Linux in specific businesses

Because Linux is freely available, many people think that it must not be good enough for a business. Some of the common reasons cited are the unsupported nature of Linux and the lack of business applications. These may be good reasons for some businesses to avoid Linux, but many small businesses can actually run entirely on Linux. By running a business, I mean taking care of all of your business chores such as keeping records and writing business correspondence.

Note

Smaller technology companies with in-house UNIX expertise, for example, can manage to run the business with Linux. If you are a consultant providing a complete turnkey system for a point-of-sale application, you may use Linux and keep the cost low enough to gain a competitive advantage. You may even consider providing the support necessary to assure your clients that they can count on the solution you provide.

The situation has changed in other ways as well. A company named Caldera, Inc., sells a commercial Linux distribution called OpenLinux that includes a graphical desktop; productivity applications including WordPerfect for Linux and StarOffice; Netscape Internet server and browser; and the capability to access NetWare servers. Granted, all these features cost you some money, but the cost is still less than what you have to pay for a comparable package that does not use Linux. Incidentally, Caldera, Inc., was started by Ray Noorda of Novell fame.

I won't describe the Caldera products in this chapter; you can find out more at the URL `http://www.caldera.com`. Instead, I focus on businesses that inherently have the types of technical personnel who can manage well with a "self-supported" operating system like Linux. In fact, many of the discussions in this chapter should give you ideas for new types of businesses — ones that build on the current popularity of the Internet and the World Wide Web.

This Chapter's Strategy

This chapter is not about a specific technical subject. After all, running a business has many aspects, and in each area of business, you have many ways to do the job. Although this chapter focuses on areas that can benefit from the use of Linux, you still can use many different tools for each job. You, as the decision-maker, have to decide what's right for your business.

To make this chapter's information more useful in your decision-making process, I use the following strategy:

- *Role of Linux in a business.* I briefly describe the types of business needs that Linux can address well and the ones for which Linux may not be the most cost-effective or appropriate solution.

- *Specific tasks for Linux.* I discuss several specific uses of Linux. You can think of these uses as being the menu from which you can pick and choose how you use Linux in your business.

- *Linux in specific businesses.* I home in on a few specific businesses for which Linux may work particularly well.

With the information presented this way, you should be able to decide how much of your business and exactly which parts you run with Linux.

The Role of Linux in a Business

Many types of business exist, and within a given business are many areas that can benefit from Linux PCs. If you are serious about using Linux in your business, think carefully about the areas in which you can best use Linux. Most businesses, for example, need productivity applications: word processors, spreadsheets, and the like. Initially Linux was lacking in this area, but now Linux users can choose from several office productivity applications such as WordPerfect for Linux (http://www.sdcorp.com), **Applixware Office Suite** (http://www.redhat.com/products/), and StarOffice Office Suite (http://www.caldera.com/ivp/onlinecatalog/staroffice.html). These products do cost some money, but the cost may be similar to that for Microsoft's office suite.

On the other hand, when it comes to TCP/IP networking or UNIX software development, Linux provides all necessary software at no extra cost. Clearly, it makes sense to use Linux as a platform for networking, software development, or a Web server.

One attractive aspect of Linux is the fact that it runs on the same PCs that you might use for Windows 95 or OS/2. In other words, you can standardize your business on low-cost and powerful PC hardware. Then choose Linux and other popular operating systems you'll need on your network (such as Windows 95, Windows NT, or OS/2) for the operating system. What you run on a specific PC depends on how that PC is used.

Linux is not for every kind of business; nor is it appropriate for all aspects of a business. Think of Linux as a tool for your business. Linux cannot be the one and only tool that your business uses. Just as a single tool does not work in all situations, Linux cannot solve all problems for a business. Even if you are a proponent of Linux, you should not try to make Linux the sole operating system for your entire business. Remember the phrase "the right tool for the right job." Select Linux for the jobs it can do well.

What Linux offers

To decide what business needs Linux might fulfill in your business, you need to know exactly what Linux offers. When I talk about Linux, I mean a typical Linux software distribution, such as the one on this book's companion CD-ROM. Such a distribution includes much more than the basic operating system: utility programs; applications; entire add-on systems, such as the XFree86 X Window System; and compilers and interpreters for software development.

The Red Hat Linux distribution includes the following major components:

- Linux kernel 2.0.32, with built-in TCP/IP networking support and support for a wide variety of hardware, such as disk controllers, CD-ROM drives, Ethernet cards, and sound boards.

- Internet services such as SLIP/PPP networking, the Apache Web server, electronic mail (BSD `sendmail`, `elm`, `pine`), news (`tin`, `trn`, and `inn`), `telnet`, and `ftp`.

- Samba LAN Manager software for networking with PCs.

- XFree86 3.3.1 X Window System for graphical user interface and graphical applications.

- Executable and Linking Format (ELF) for binaries and shared libraries (important because ELF is the binary format used by Sun's Solaris and UNIX System V Release 4).

- Compilers and interpreters for many programming languages: GNU `gcc` 2.7.2 C and C++ compiler, BASIC, Perl 5.004, Tcl 8.0 and Tk 8.0 scripting languages, Berkeley Yacc and GNU bison parser generators, and `flex` 2.5.4a lexical analyzer generator.

- The Intel Binary Compatibility Specification (iBCS) module, which allows binaries from several other operating systems to run on Linux. Currently, you can run binaries from the following systems on Linux: System V Release 4 UNIX (such as Interactive, Unixware, and Dell UNIX), any System V Release 3 UNIX system, SCO UNIX, Xenix V/386, and Xenix 286.

- A plethora of applications and utilities, including the GNU Emacs editor, the `seyon` and `minicom` serial communication programs, and games.

- Text processing and typesetting software, such as TeX, LaTeX, and `groff`.

As you can see from this list, Linux clearly excels in two broad technology areas:

- TCP/IP networking and Internet services, including the World Wide Web
- UNIX and *X* software development

These two areas have a common theme: the people who work in these areas tend to be computer-savvy. Thus, they are not worried about the apparent lack of technical support for Linux. In the next section, you'll see why I use the term *apparent* to describe the lack of a single source of technical support for Linux.

What Linux (apparently) lacks

I didn't write this section to complain about Linux's shortcomings. After all, you could pick any operating system or product (be it commercial or freeware), and find real or apparent shortcomings in each product. My goal is to point out the perceived shortcomings of Linux and explain how even those shortcomings can become business opportunities for someone like you — someone who has the technical knowledge necessary to install and configure Linux.

Lack of personal-productivity applications

When I mention using Linux in a business, the immediate reaction I get is that Linux does not have personal-productivity applications like the ones in Microsoft Office. (Microsoft Office is a collection of several applications: Microsoft Word, for word processing; Microsoft Excel, for spreadsheets; Microsoft PowerPoint, for presentation graphics; and Microsoft Access, for databases.)

This used to be true, but not any more. As I mentioned earlier in this chapter, you can now take your pick from several office productivity suites for Linux. The fact remains, however, that the Linux office application suites are not as popular as Windows-based office suites.

I do not consider this situation to be a problem, however. If you follow the philosophy of selecting the right tool for the job, you may as well select the mainstream Windows applications for the word processing and spreadsheet tasks.

Lack of technical support

Another commonly cited shortcoming of Linux is that it requires someone with a reasonable level of computer knowledge to install and configure Linux. I would argue that all UNIX operating systems require installation and maintenance by a knowledgeable person. In that respect, Linux is no different from the other UNIX systems.

The real complaint is that no single source of technical support for Linux is available. You cannot pick up the phone, dial a number, and talk to someone about any technical difficulties that you might have with Linux. Many businesses prefer a commercial product that comes with technical support.

In reality, the technical support for a commercial product often means the privilege of being put on hold every time you call. Then, after you explain your problem, all you may get is a promise that someone will call you back. Nevertheless, many businesses turn away from Linux because it lacks technical support.

I consider this situation to be an apparent problem, rather than a real one, because the Linux newsgroups on the Internet typically have the answers to any questions you might have. You can start by reading the Frequently Asked Questions (FAQ) for the Linux newsgroups. If your question has not yet been asked, you can simply post a news item, explaining your problem. Typically, you'll hear from someone within a day — probably the same amount of time it takes for some of the commercial technical support people to get back to you with an answer.

Furthermore, this business need for technical support can become the basis for your own business venture. You could be a consultant who provides technical support for Linux installation, setup, and configuration. It's up to you to decide what you want to offer through your business. You may want to sell preconfigured Linux workstations with several levels of technical support, for example.

Specific Tasks for Linux

Linux shines in many specific tasks that apply to various types of businesses. The next few sections briefly describe how you can use Linux for the following purposes:

■ *Personal UNIX workstation.* If your organization uses UNIX workstations, and you cannot afford Sun or HP workstations for everyone, equip everyone with Linux PCs. They are affordable, and they make powerful UNIX machines.

■ *Workgroup server.* Linux PCs can easily be configured for file and print sharing.

■ *Internet host.* Linux itself originated in the Internet, and its internetworking capabilities make it an ideal Internet host. You can easily set up and use a Linux PC as a server on the Internet with mail, news, `ftp`, and `telnet` services.

■ *World Wide Web server.* Red Hat Linux comes with the Apache Web server. You can have a Web server up and running on your system as soon as you finish installing Linux. All you have to do is opt to install the Web server (see Chapter 1 for information on how to select different packages to install during Red Hat Linux installation).

■ *LAN Manager server/client.* With Samba (which comes on the companion CD-ROM), you can set up a Linux PC as a LAN Manager server. Samba makes it easy to use a Linux PC in a business that relies on LAN Manager for file and print sharing. Conversely, if you already have a LAN Manager server, you can make the Linux PC (with Samba) a client.

■ *Developer's workstation.* A Linux PC makes an ideal workstation for UNIX and X developers. You can use your choice of languages, ranging from C and C++ to Tcl/Tk.

Workgroup server

A 486 or Pentium PC configured with Linux 2.0.34 (from this book's companion CD-ROM) makes a very capable workgroup server. By *workgroup*, I mean a small LAN of perhaps a dozen or so PCs. If all the PCs run Linux, you can configure one Linux PC to be the file and print server, and have the other Linux PCs be the clients. The file sharing can be through Network File Sharing (NFS), which is built into Linux.

Sharing files through NFS is simple, involving two basic steps:

■ On the Linux server, export one or more directories by listing them in the `/etc/exports` file (`man exports` shows you the syntax).

■ On each client Linux PC, mount the directories exported by the server. Use the `mount` command to do this.

Cross-Reference

You can enable print sharing by configuring a remote printer on each client Linux PC and setting up the physical printer as a local printer on the server. Chapter 14 describes how to set up remote and local printers in Linux.

If your LAN includes PCs running Windows for Workgroups, for example, you have to configure the Linux PC as a LAN Manager server. Later, the "LAN Manager Server" section of this chapter briefly discusses what software you should use to configure a Linux PC to work with LAN Manager.

Tip

Instead of simply using a Linux workgroup server for your business, of course, you could start a business that sells preconfigured Linux "workstations." The basic idea is to configure the Linux PC with appropriate hardware and software (Linux operating system, plus XFree86 and any necessary networking software) and to sell it bundled with on-site service.

Because Linux is freely available, this idea of selling a ready-to-run Linux workstation is a common one; therefore, you can expect quite a bit of competition in this area. You may be able to build up the business in your own area, however, because you'll have the advantage of being able to provide in-person service. Of course, you can also provide support to businesses or individuals who run Linux on PCs purchased elsewhere.

Internet host

Chapter 19 describes how you can configure a Linux PC as a host on the Internet. With an appropriate network connection to an Internet Service Provider, such a Linux PC can give your business an Internet presence.

An Internet host performs a collection of tasks. At minimum, those tasks include the following:

■ *Electronic mail*, so users can send and receive messages

■ *News,* so users can read and participate in discussions in various newsgroups

■ *World Wide Web server*, to provide Web pages to other users on the Internet

■ *Anonymous* `ftp`, so other users can download information you provide (software fixes and technical information about your products, for example)

The Linux distribution on this book's CD-ROM comes with all the software necessary to set up these Internet services. For the most part, you have to do only minimal configuration to get everything going.

Secret

The primary reason for selecting Linux as an Internet host is the price/performance advantage that Linux holds over other UNIX systems. Linux runs on commodity PCs — a market in which the competition is intense, and powerful Pentium PCs cost much less than comparable UNIX workstations. Install Linux from a distribution such as the one on this book's CD-ROM, and the Pentium PC is transformed into a powerful UNIX workstation comparable to ones from vendors such as Sun, HP, and IBM. My experience is that a Linux PC has more built-in capabilities than a commercial UNIX workstation, on which many features are options available at extra cost.

The bottom line is that a fully configured Linux PC costs much less than a similarly configured commercial UNIX workstation, yet the Linux PC offers performance comparable to that of other UNIX workstations. That's why a Linux PC is attractive as an Internet host.

In addition to the price/performance advantage, a Linux PC can be configured as a *firewall* — a system that isolates two networks, allowing only selected types of network data packets to pass between the two networks. When you connect a local area network (LAN) to the Internet, you can use a firewall to isolate the LAN from the Internet at large.

World Wide Web server

A Linux PC with an Internet connection serves as an ideal Web server for your business. Chapter 20 gives you detailed information on how to set up the Web server. Essentially, the task is as simple as setting up the configuration files of the Apache Web server and starting to use it. Red Hat Linux already comes with the Apache Web server. (The tougher job is developing the Web pages — the content for the World Wide Web.)

Nowadays most businesses have a Web presence. For some businesses, the Web is a profitable venture because of the online sales that it generates. For example, businesses such as online flower shops and bookstores are doing well on the Web. For other businesses, sales have not been up to expectation. Many companies are using the Web to distribute technical information (such as bug fixes, patches, and documentation) to their customers. The consensus is that the Web certainly is a good tool for marketing and customer service.

Using a Web server in an intranet

Businesses are now using Web servers on internal networks to distribute information to employees. The term *intranet* refers to such internal networks, which employ the TCP/IP protocol suite and provide information services such as the Web and FTP.

Information published on a typical intranet includes employee information, corporate policies and procedures, upcoming events, job openings, and much more. On your business intranet, you might share documents — technical documents, status reports, meeting notes, and anything else — through a Web server, assuming that you have a TCP/IP network and Web browsers installed on all systems in the network.

You can conveniently set up a Web server on a Linux PC that serves as your workgroup server, and place the documents on that server. You'll have to convert formatted documents to HTML format; many popular word processing programs, including WordPerfect and Microsoft Word, allow you to save documents in HTML format. Then, users will be able to access the documents from their desktops through a Web browser.

Following are some ideas for using a Web server within a private LAN:

- Provide an online phone directory, which employees can search through a form on a Web page.

- Let employees submit time and attendance reports, travel requests, and travel expense reports through the Web browser.

- Provide access to any corporate databases through forms on a Web page.

- Distribute announcements on upcoming meetings and other events.

- Implement an electronic suggestion box, enabling employees to submit suggestions through a form on a Web page.

- Maintain a list of action items for various projects. Provide a form through which everyone can track the disposition of assigned work.

- Make important technical papers available through the Web server.

Linux makes efficient use of hardware, so you can implement a Linux-based Web server on very affordable PC hardware.

Providing Web service

If you are an Internet Service Provider, you might use Linux PCs to provide Web services to customers. Following are several possible Web services:

- *Web server at customer site.* Provide the customer a Linux PC and a dial-up PPP connection. Configure the Linux PC with a Web server. Also offer to prepare the Web pages for the customer. In this case, the limited bandwidth of the dial-up connection to the customer's site may be a bottleneck that limits the number and frequency of accesses the Web server can support.

- *Dedicated Web server at ISP site.* Offer the customer a dedicated Linux PC with a high-speed connection to the Internet located at your site. (I am assuming that, as an ISP, you have a high-bandwidth connection to the Internet.) This scenario should provide much better performance, because the network connection can sustain many Web accesses simultaneously. The drawback is that you have to charge the customer for a complete Linux PC; you also have to charge for the high-bandwidth Internet access, because you are offering a dedicated system to the customer. Although high-priced, this service may appeal to large businesses that want a Web presence without the hassles of maintaining an Internet connection.

- *Individual Web pages.* Provide individual Web pages on a shared Linux PC that runs the Web server and that has the high-bandwidth Internet connection. In this case, you can spread the cost of the Linux PC and the Internet connection over several customers, so this service may be appropriate for individuals or small businesses that want a Web presence on the Internet without spending too much money.

LAN Manager server

If your business relies on LAN Manager for file and print sharing, you probably use Windows for Workgroups, Windows NT, or OS/2 in your servers and clients. You can move to a Linux PC as your server without losing the LAN Manager file and printer sharing, because a Linux PC can be set up as a LAN Manager server. When you install Red Hat Linux from this book's companion CD-ROM, you also get a chance to install the Samba software package, which performs that task.

Tip

After you install and configure Samba on your Linux PC, client PCs (running Windows for Workgroups, Windows 95, Windows NT, or OS/2) can access disks and printers on the Linux PC by using the Server Message Block (SMB) protocol, which is the underlying protocol in LAN Manager.

With the Samba package installed, you also can make your Linux PC a LAN Manager client, which means that the Linux PC can access disks and printers managed by a LAN Manager server. For example, I have my printer physically connected to a PC running Windows 95, and other PCs use that printer through LAN Manager print sharing. I use Linux, however, on a PC that does not have its own printer. To print from the Linux PC, I use the Samba client to access the printer on the PC running Windows 95.

The Samba software package has the following major components:

- `smbd`: the SMB server, which accepts connections from LAN Manager clients and provides file and print sharing services

- `nmbd`: the NetBIOS name server, which clients use to look up servers. (NetBIOS stands for Network Basic Input/Output System — an interface that applications use to communicate with network transports such as TCP/IP.)

- `smbclient`: the LAN Manager client, which runs on Linux and allows Linux to access the files and printers on any LAN Manager server

- `/etc/smb.conf`: the Samba configuration file used by the SMB server

- `testparm`: a program that makes sure the Samba configuration file is correct

Because I have not covered Samba elsewhere, the following sections describe how to install Samba from the companion CD-ROM and how to set up a printer on the Linux PC to print through LAN Manager.

Installing Samba

If you already installed Samba during Red Hat Linux installation, you should skip this section. Otherwise, follow these steps to install Samba from this book's companion CD-ROM:

1. Log in as `root` and make sure that the companion CD-ROM is in the drive and mounted. If not, use the `umount /dev/cdrom` command to dismount the current CD-ROM, replace it with the companion CD-ROM, and then mount it with the `mount -r /dev/cdrom /cdrom` command.

2. Change the directory to the CD-ROM — specifically to the directory where the Red Hat Package Manager (RPM) packages are located:

   `cd /cdrom/RedHat/RPMS`

3. Use the following `rpm` command:

   `rpm -ivh samba*`

If Samba is already installed, this command returns an error message. Otherwise the `rpm` command installs Samba on your system by copying various files to their appropriate locations.

These steps complete the unpacking and installation of the Samba software. Now all you have to do to use Samba is configure it.

Configuring Samba

To set up the LAN Manager file and print sharing services, you have to provide a configuration file named /etc/smb.conf. The configuration file looks like a Microsoft Windows 3.1 INI file, in case you are familiar with those files. Just to refresh your memory, the following example shows what part of a Windows 3.1 WIN.INI file looks like:

```
[windows]
; This is the "windows" section
; Comment lines start with a semicolon
NullPort=None
load=
run=
device=HP LaserJet 4/4M PostScript,PSCRIPT,LPT1:

[Desktop]
; This is the "Desktop" section
Wallpaper=(None)
TileWallpaper=0
WallpaperStyle=0
Pattern=(None)
Many lines deleted...
```

Secret

Like the Windows INI files, the /etc/smb.conf file consists of sections, with a list of parameters in each section. Each section of the smb.conf file begins with the name of the section in brackets. The section continues until the next section begins or the file ends.

Each line in a section specifies the value of a parameter, with the following syntax:

name = value

As in Windows INI files, comment lines begin with a semicolon (;). Following are a few typical sections of the Samba configuration file:

```
[homes]
; This section shares the home directory of each user
   comment = Home Directories
   browseable = no
   read only = no
   preserve case = yes
   short preserve case = yes
   create mode = 0750

[printers]
; This section specifies sharing of the printers
   comment = All Printers
   path = /var/spool/samba
   browseable = no
```

```
      printable = yes
; Set public = yes to allow user 'guest account' to print
      public = no
      writable = no
      create mode = 0700
Lines deleted...
```

Notice the similarity of these entries with those in Windows INI files.

The Samba software comes with a configuration file you can edit to get started. To prepare the configuration file, follow these steps:

1. Log in as `root`.

2. Use your favorite text editor to edit `/etc/smb.conf`.

3. In the `global` section, change the `workgroup` line, as follows:

   ```
   ; set this to your workgroup's name
   workgroup = LNB SOFTWARE
   ```

4. Uncomment the lines in one of the `public` sections to provide access to a shared directory on the Linux PC, as follows:

```
[public]
path = /home/public
public = yes
only guest = yes
writable = yes
printable = no
```

Testing the Samba configuration file

To ensure that the Samba configuration file is correct, run the `testparm` program that comes with the Samba software. Following is the result of running `testparm` on my configuration file:

```
testparm
Load smb config files from /etc/smb.conf
Processing section "[homes]"
Processing section "[printers]"
Loaded services file OK.
Press enter to see a dump of your service definitions(Press Enter)
(Long list of parameters and services deleted...)
```

If `testparm` reports syntax errors in the `smb.conf` file, you should edit the file to fix the problem. For detailed information about the contents of the `smb.conf` file, consult its online help by typing `man smb.conf`.

Tip

Another good source of information about Samba configuration is the SMB-HOWTO file. To read this HOWTO file, change directory to `/usr/doc/HOWTO` and then type `zcat SMB-HOWTO | more` to view the file.

Testing with smbclient

You should use the `smbclient` program to ensure that the LAN Manager server is working. One quick way to check is to use the `-L` option to view the list of services. Following is what I get when I run `smbclient` on my Linux PC:

```
smbclient -L dcc05211
Server time is Fri May 22 07:11:40 1998
Timezone is UTC-4.0
Password:
Domain=[LNB SOFTWARE] OS=[Unix] Server=[Samba 1.9.17p4]
security=user

Server=[DCC05211] User=[naba] Workgroup=[LNB SOFTWARE] Domain=[LNB
SOFTWARE]

        Sharename       Type        Comment
        ---------       ----        -------
        IPC$            IPC         IPC Service (Samba 1.9.17p4)
        lp              Printer
        naba            Disk        Home Directories
        sample          Printer     A sample printer that prints to a
file


This machine has a browse list:

        Server                  Comment
        ---------               -------
        DCC05211                Samba 1.9.17p4


This machine has a workgroup list:

        Workgroup               Master
        ---------               -------
        LNB SOFTWARE            DCC05211
```

The server name comes from the name associated with the IP address of my Linux PC's Ethernet interface. That name appears in the `/etc/hosts` file.

If you have other LAN Manager servers around, you can look at their services with the `smbclient` program. Following here is what I get when I view the services on my 486 PC running Windows 95:

```
smbclient -L lnb486
Server time is Thu May 21 19:34:52 1998
Timezone is UTC-4.0
security=share
```

```
Server=[LNB486] User=[] Workgroup=[LNB SOFTWARE] Domain=[LNB SOFTWARE]

        Sharename        Type        Comment
        ---------        ----        -------
        A                Disk
        C                Disk
        D                Disk
        E                Disk
        F                Disk
        HPLJ4M           Printer     Hp Laserjet 4M on Dell 486
        IPC$             IPC         Remote Inter Process Communication
        PRINTER$         Disk


This machine has a workgroup list:

        Workgroup                Master
        ---------                -------
        LNB SOFTWARE             LNB486
```

Secret

You can do much more than simply look at resources with the smbclient program; you also can use smbclient to access a disk on a LAN Manager server, as well as send a file to a LAN Manager printer. The smbclient program is somewhat like ftp — you connect to a LAN Manager server and then use commands to get or put files and to send files to the printer.

The following example shows how I used smbclient to access a disk on my Windows 95 PC and view its directory:

```
smbclient \\\\lnb486\\f username password
Server time is Thu May 21 21:04:50 1998
Timezone is UTC-4.0
security=share
smb: \> dir
  ~MSSTFQF.T              DHR           0  Mon Jan 16 10:12:42 1995
  WINDOWS.000             D             0  Fri Nov 25 18:09:14 1994
  MSVCRT20.DLL            A        243200  Fri Oct 28 12:00:00 1994
  RECYCLED                DHS           0  Sat Nov 26 22:51:00 1994
  autoexec.bat            A            54  Sun Mar  9 12:16:22 1997
  ffastun.ffl             AH        32768  Thu Feb 12 20:00:42 1998
  Program Files           DR            0  Sat Mar 18 16:44:38 1995
  ffastun0.ffx            AH       114688  Thu Feb 12 20:00:42 1998
  ffastun.ffo             AH        24576  Thu Feb 12 20:00:42 1998
  ffastun.ffa             AH         4379  Thu Feb 12 20:00:42 1998

        51141 blocks of size 4096. 3440 blocks available
smb: \> quit
```

To see a list of smbclient commands, type help at the prompt. Table 21-1 briefly summarizes smbclient commands.

Table 21-1   Some smbclient commands

Command	Description
!	Executes a shell command (remember that you run `smbclient` on Linux)
? cmd	Displays a list of commands or help on a specific command
cancel id	Cancels a print job identified by its ID
cd dir	Changes the remote directory
del file	Deletes the specified file
dir file	Displays the directory listing
exit	Logs off the LAN Manager server
get rfile lfile	Copies a remote file (`rfile`) to a local file (`lfile`)
help cmd	Provides help on a command (or displays a list of commands)
lcd newdir	Changes the local directory (on the Linux PC)
lowercase	Toggles automatic lowercase conversion of filenames when executing the `get` command
ls files	Lists files on the server
mask name	Applies a mask (such as `*.c`) to all file operations
md dirname	Makes a directory on the server
mget name	Gets all files with matching names (such as `*.doc`)
mkdir dirname	Makes a directory
mput name	Copies files from the Linux PC to the server
newer file	Gets only the files that are newer than the specified file
print name	Prints the named file
printmode *mode*	Sets the print mode (the *mode* must be `text` or `graphics`)
prompt	Toggles prompt mode off (similar to the command in `ftp`)
put lfile rfile	Copies a local file (`lfile`) to a remote file (`rfile`)
queue	Displays the print queue
quit	Logs off the LAN Manager server
rd dir	Deletes the specified directory on the server
recurse	Toggles directory recursion during file get and put operations
rm name	Deletes all files with the specified name
rmdir name	Deletes the specified directory
translate	Toggles text translation (converts a line feed to a carriage return–line-feed pair)

LAN Manager client

If you bring a Linux PC into an existing LAN Manager environment, you may have to use the Linux PC as a LAN Manager client, because a server may already exist. As the preceding sections explain, the Samba software package includes the smbclient program, which allows your Linux PC to be a client in a LAN Manager network.

Cross-Reference

In this section, I show you how to set up a printer on your Linux PC so that print jobs are sent to a specified LAN Manager server by means of the smbclient program. Chapter 14 describes how the printing system works in Linux. If you have questions about printing while reading this section, please consult that chapter.

Setting up the printer in two steps

The basic idea is to define a new printer on your Linux PC so that when you print on that printer with the lpr command, the output actually appears on a specified network printer (managed by a LAN Manager server). This process involves two steps:

1. Add an entry for the printer to the /etc/printcap file, and specify an *input filter* (a script that gets to process the file being printed).

2. Write the script that runs smbclient and prints the file on a designated LAN Manager server.

Adding the printcap entry

Note two key items when you prepare the printcap entry that prints on a LAN Manager printer:

- Specify /dev/null as the printer device name, because the actual printing occurs on a network printer.

- Specify an input filter that copies the input data to a file and then uses smbclient to send that file to the printer on a selected LAN Manager server.

Secret

Following is the printcap entry (in the /etc/printcap file) I used on my Linux PC to specify this printer:

```
lp|smbpr|Prints on a LAN Manager printer:\
    :sd=/var/spool/lpd/lp:\
    :lp=/dev/null:\
    :if=/var/spool/lpd/lp/smbprint.tcl:\
    :lf=/var/spool/lpd/lp/smbprint.log:\
    :mx#0:\
    :sh:\
    :sf:
```

For error logging, I created the /var/spool/lpd/lp/smbprint.log file with the following commands (while I was logged in as root):

```
cd /var/spool/lpd/lp
touch smbprint.log
chmod ug=rw,o=r smbprint.log
```

Writing a script to print with smbclient

The next important step is writing the input filter — `/var/spool/lpd/lp/` `smbprint.tcl`, which performs the actual printing. As the extension suggests, I used Tcl to write the input filter. You could write the script in Perl or bash.

In the `smbprint.tcl` script, I decided to make a copy of the print job in a temporary file and then run `smbclient` to print that file. Following is the complete `/uvar/spool/lpd/lp/smbprint.tcl` script:

```
#!/usr/bin/tcl
#
# Tcl script to print on a LAN manager printer using smbclient.
# Place in printer's spool directory and make it executable
# by world.

# Open the file /tmp/smbprint.out
set outfile [open /tmp/smbprint.out w]

# Read from stdin and write to outfile

while { [gets stdin line] != -1} {
 puts $outfile $line
}

close $outfile

# Now prepare a script to run smbclient and print the file
set server "lnb486"
set printer "hplj4m"
set password "mypassword"

set outfile [open /tmp/printit w]
puts $outfile "#\!/bin/sh"
puts $outfile "echo print /tmp/smbprint.out | /usr/bin/smbclient
\\\\\\\\$serve
r\\\\$printer $password -N -P"
close $outfile

# Make the script executable
exec chmod +x /tmp/printit

# Now execute the script
exec /tmp/printit
# Delete the script
exec rm /tmp/printit
```

I wrote the script in a simple way: copy the print job to a temporary file, create a script that runs `smbclient` to print that file, and then run that script. I have used this printer setup to print directly from Linux programs (such as Netscape) on that network printer.

This chapter gives you an overview of Samba, but there simply isn't enough space to provide all the available information. For more information on how to use Samba, consult John Blair's *Samba: Integrating UNIX and Windows*, SSC, 1998.

Linux in Specific Businesses

In previous sections, I described several specific tasks for which Linux is an appropriate choice. The next few sections focus on specific businesses for which Linux makes the most sense. When I describe the use of Linux in a business, I also mention which tasks you might consider performing with Linux.

Internet Service Provider

The Internet Service Provider (ISP) is a relatively new type of business that has emerged as more and more individuals and businesses want to connect to the Internet. Many ISPs began by offering dial-up modem accounts to individual users in the early 1990s. Then, as the Internet became more popular, ISPs switched to offering SLIP and PPP over ISDN (Integrated Services Digital Network — an offering of the phone companies), and other high-speed connections that offer full TCP/IP networking. (Consult Chapter 18 for more information on SLIP and PPP.)

Nowadays, most ISPs maintain one or more T1 lines to larger telecommunications companies, such as Sprint and MCI. (A T1 link is capable of transmitting 1.54 million bits of data per second — more than 50 times faster than the data-transfer rate of 28,800-bps modems). Individual customers typically have SLIP/PPP connections over high-speed dial-up modems.

In addition to various telecommunications equipment (including modems), the ISP needs Internet hosts — the servers that handle the SLIP/PPP, as well as simple dial-in, connections. This is where Linux comes in. With the built-in TCP/IP networking capabilities of Linux and its support for all types of network hardware, Linux PCs are ideal for this core aspect of the ISP business. Many ISPs around the country are finding Linux PCs to be very capable Internet hosts.

I have used Windows NT, SunOS, HP-UX, and Linux, and I have found Linux to be the most flexible and fully featured operating system. The other operating systems aren't necessarily bad, but almost everything — from a C or C++ compiler to PPP support — typically is an option. As you might guess, each option costs money. If you want to get started as an ISP within your budget, you can't go wrong with Linux PCs.

Tip

Although I briefly describe some aspects of the ISP business in this section, you should browse the Internet and read the available information before deciding to take the plunge as an ISP. A good place to start is "Internet Access Frequently Asked Questions (FAQ)," maintained by David Dennis at http://www.amazing.com/internet/.

In that Web page, you'll find detailed information on all aspects of the ISP business, from viable types of network connections to accounting and billing practices.

You can't run the ISP business on Linux PCs alone. Following is a typical assortment of equipment you'll need to start business as an ISP:

- *A high-bandwidth connection to the Internet.* As an ISP, you'll go to one of the major telecommunication carriers for this service. For a small startup, this connection may be 56Kbps, but a 1.54Mbps T1 connection is more appropriate for a typical ISP.

- *A router* to direct network packets between your system and the rest of the Internet. Although Linux can serve as a router, that job is best left to a dedicated router.

- *Networking equipment* (such as CSU/DSU) you may need to connect to your communications provider.

- *A terminal server* to handle the dial-up modems as well as SLIP/PPP connections. A Linux PC with a multiple-port serial board can handle this task, but the "right tool for the job" philosophy dictates that you use a terminal server for this task. Handling multiple dial-up modems requires the constant attention of the processor. If the Linux PC is busy responding to arrival of data at the modem lines, it cannot adequately perform other tasks. On the other hand, a terminal server with a dedicated processor can easily handle the dial-up modems.

- *Phone lines for dial-up access*, which is how most of your customers access the system. For a small set of users, you need one phone line for every six to eight users; for a larger user base, 1 line for every 10 users is reported to be adequate.

- *Server PCs* (Internet hosts) for news, mail, the World Wide Web, and user logins. This area is where Linux PCs come into play.

- *Uninterruptible Power Supply* (UPS) to continue operation or to gracefully shut down during power outages.

As this list of equipment shows, Linux PCs are most useful as servers. You typically need quite a few servers, each of which is dedicated to a specific service such as the World Wide Web and Usenet newsgroups.

UNIX software developer

If your business develops applications for UNIX and X Window System, you should have the in-house technical know-how to install and set up Linux on PCs. Because Linux comes with a full set of software-development tools, a Linux PC can serve as the development workstation for each software developer.

Although the Linux software distribution comes with many programming languages, a Linux PC is ideal for developing UNIX applications. Nowadays, most applications are graphical, and on Linux, you'd use the XFree86 X Window System for graphics. The Linux distribution on the companion CD-ROM includes all necessary header files and libraries for developing X applications.

Tip

One item that you won't find on the companion CD-ROM is Motif — the graphical user interface that is built on top of X. Unfortunately, Motif is a licensed product of Open Software Foundation, and you have to buy it separately. Several vendors sell Motif for Linux; prices range from $100 to $200. (See Chapter 23 for further information.)

Incidentally, Linux PCs make ideal low-cost UNIX workstations for university students. Instead having to share a VAX or some other large system with other users, each student can have a complete "UNIX workstation" with Linux PCs.

Acting as a consultant

As I explained earlier in this chapter, many businesses shy away from Linux because no single source of technical support exists for it. You could set yourself up as a Linux consultant to sell businesses on using Linux and then provide the necessary technical support.

Following are some of the ways you can provide Linux-related service to businesses:

- Offer short courses on Linux installation and setup, as well as setting up a Linux Internet host and Web server

- Provide Linux PCs with bundled technical support as solutions to specific customer needs, such as Internet connectivity or a Web presence

Tip

Instead of offering Linux technical support only, you might consider packaging a business solution based on Linux. For a given business need, you should be able to configure a Linux PC with appropriate free software from the Internet. Then you can sell that business system as a package that includes the hardware, the software, and support.

If you work with businesses that rely on Windows for Workgroups, propose a Linux PC with Samba software as a replacement LAN Manager server for the business. Again, sell the Linux LAN Manager server as a turnkey system with support.

Summary

Businesses are often reluctant to use Linux, because it's not a supported product. Linux also has the reputation of being a hacker's dream, and no mainstream personal-productivity applications (such as word processors and spreadsheets) are available for Linux. Despite these perceived shortcomings, Linux actually has a great deal to offer, as long as it is used for the appropriate task. This chapter describes the role of Linux in business and describes some business uses of Linux.

By reading this chapter, you learn the following things:

▶ Although Linux initially lacked office productivity applications, such as word processing and spreadsheet software, the situation has changed. Now you can choose from several office application suites, including StarOffice, ApplixWare, and WordPerfect for Linux.

▶ Linux excels in networking and software-development tools. To top it off, Linux can run on commodity PCs, which are much less expensive than Sun and HP workstations. Thus, Linux PCs are ideal as Internet hosts and as software-development workstations.

▶ The Red Hat Linux distribution on the companion CD-ROM includes nearly all the networking and software-development tools that a business needs, for a nominal price (in this case, the price of this book).

▶ For PC networks using LAN Manager, you can configure a Linux PC as a LAN Manager server; all you have to do is use the Samba software package from the companion CD-ROM. This chapter shows you how to install and use Samba.

▶ A Linux PC also can act as a LAN Manager client. As an example, this chapter describes how to use a LAN Manager printer from a Linux PC.

▶ Linux PCs are especially well-suited to be servers in the Internet Service Provider (ISP) business. The built-in TCP/IP networking of Linux is a big plus in the ISP business.

▶ The perceived lack of Linux support can be a business opportunity for those who can install and maintain Linux. Another potential business is to sell Linux PCs configured with custom-developed or free software and designed to meet a specific business need. If they are bundled with technical support, such Linux PCs can be positioned as business solutions instead of just low-cost UNIX boxes.

Chapter 22

Developing Software in Linux

In This Chapter

▶ Looking at GCC: the GNU C and C++ compiler

▶ Using GNU `make` to automate software builds

▶ Using the GNU debugger: `gdb`

▶ Using RCS for version control

▶ Understanding GPL and LGPL

▶ Understanding ELF

▶ Dynamically loading and using a shared library

Many Linux users happen to be software developers. If you want to develop software as a hobby or want to add features to Linux, you'll find that Linux includes everything you need to create UNIX and X applications. You can use the GNU C and C++ compilers to write conventional programs (that you compile and link into an executable). Alternatively, you can use the Tcl/Tk scripting language to write interpreted graphical applications.

This chapter covers the general subject of software development on a Linux PC. The focus is not on any specific programming language. Instead, this chapter describes how to use various software development tools, such as compilers, makefiles, and version-control systems.

The chapter also describes the implications of Free Software Foundation's GNU Public License on any plans you might have to develop Linux software. You need to know this because you'll be using GNU tools and GNU libraries to develop software in Linux.

I also cover the subject of dynamic linking and the recently adopted Executable and Linking Format (ELF), which makes dynamic linking easier. These topics are of interest to Linux programmers because dynamic linking reduces the size of executables and may allow you to distribute your software in binary form, even if your software uses the GNU libraries.

Cross-Reference

Developing X applications is a complex-enough subject to deserve an entire chapter. Accordingly, X programming on Linux is covered in Chapter 23.

Software Development Tools in Linux

As expected, being a UNIX look-alike, Linux includes the traditional UNIX software development tools. By traditional tools, I mean the following:

- A text editor, such as `vi` or `emacs`, for editing the source code (described in Chapter 24)

- A C compiler for compiling and linking programs written in C — the programming language of choice for writing UNIX applications (although nowadays, many programmers are turning to C++). Linux includes GCC: the GNU C and C++ compiler.

- The GNU `make` utility for automating the *software build* process — the process of combining object modules into an executable or a library

- A debugger for debugging programs. Linux includes the GNU debugger `gdb`, as well as `xxgdb`, a graphical interface to `gdb`.

- A version-control system to keep track of various revisions of a source file. Linux comes with RCS (Revision Control System).

CD

All these tools are installed automatically if you install Linux from this book's companion CD-ROM, following the steps outlined in Chapter 1. The next few sections briefly describe how to use these tools to write applications for Linux.

info: The authoritative help on GNU tools

You may already have noticed that most of the Linux software development tools are from the Free Software Foundation's GNU project. The online documentation for all these tools come as `info` files. The `info` program is GNU's hypertext help system.

Tip

To see `info` in action, type **info** at the shell prompt or type **Esc-x** followed by **info** in GNU Emacs. I typically access `info` from GNU Emacs, because that way, I can look up online help while editing a program. Figure 22-1 shows the GNU Emacs window after I typed **Esc-x info**.

In `info`, the online help text is organized in nodes; each node represents information on a specific topic. The first line shows the header for that node.

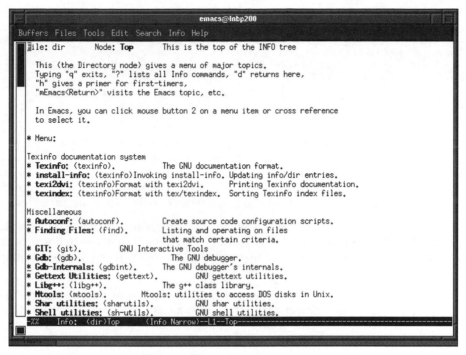

Figure 22-1: The GNU Emacs window, showing the result of the command Esc-x **info**

Figure 22-1 shows the initial `info` screen, with a directory of topics. This directory itself is an `info` file, `/usr/info/dir`, a text file containing some embedded special characters. Following are a few lines from the `/usr/info/dir` file corresponding to the screen shown in Figure 22-1:

```
$Id: dir,v 1.2 1996/09/24 18:43:01 karl Exp $
This is the file .../info/dir, which contains the topmost node of the
Info hierarchy.  The first time you invoke Info you start off
looking at that node, which is (dir)Top.
^_   (This is the Ctrl+_ character)
File: dir       Node: Top       This is the top of the INFO tree

  This (the Directory node) gives a menu of major topics.
  Typing "q" exits, "?" lists all Info commands, "d" returns here,
  "h" gives a primer for first-timers,
  "mEmacs<Return>" visits the Emacs topic, etc.

  In Emacs, you can click mouse button 2 on a menu item or cross
reference
  to select it.

* Menu:
```

```
Texinfo documentation system
* Texinfo: (texinfo).            The GNU documentation format.
* install-info: (texinfo)Invoking install-info. Updating info/dir
entries.
* texi2dvi: (texinfo)Format with texi2dvi.      Printing Texinfo
documentation.
* texindex: (texinfo)Format with tex/texindex.  Sorting Texinfo index
files.
(...Lines deleted...)
```

If you compare this listing with the screen shown in Figure 22-1, you notice that info displays only the lines following the Ctrl+_ character. In your system, the /usr/info directory contains this info file as well as others, with the text for each topic. These info files usually are stored in compressed format. You don't have to know these details to use the info files.

Tip

You have to use several single-letter commands to navigate info files. The best way to learn the commands is to type **h** from the initial info directory, shown in Figure 22-1. After reading the help screens, type **d** to return to the initial directory of topics.

From the directory screen of Figure 22-1, type **m**, followed by the name of a menu item (shown in boldface with an asterisk prefix). To view the online help for GCC, for example, type **m** and then **gcc**. The info system in turn displays the top-level menu of items for GCC, as shown in Figure 22-2.

```
                              emacs@lnbp200
Buffers Files Tools Edit Search Info Help

File: gcc.info,  Node: Top,  Next: Copying,  Up: (DIR)

Introduction

    This manual documents how to run, install and port the GNU compiler,
as well as its new features and incompatibilities, and how to report
bugs.  It corresponds to GNU CC version 2.7.2.

* Menu:

* Copying::           GNU General Public License says
                      how you can copy and share GNU CC.
* Contributors::      People who have contributed to GNU CC.
* Funding::           How to help assure funding for free software.
* Look and Feel::     Protect your freedom--fight "look and feel".

* G++ and GCC::       You can compile C or C++ programs.
* Invoking GCC::      Command options supported by `gcc'.
* Installation::      How to configure, compile and install GNU CC.
* C Extensions::      GNU extensions to the C language family.
* C++ Extensions::    GNU extensions to the C++ language.
* Trouble::           If you have trouble installing GNU CC.
* Bugs::              How, why and where to report bugs.
* Service::           How to find suppliers of support for GNU CC.
* VMS::               Using GNU CC on VMS.

* Portability::       Goals of GNU CC's portability features.
* Interface::         Function-call interface of GNU CC output.
* Passes::            Order of passes, what they do, and what each file is for.
* RTL::               The intermediate representation that most passes work on.
-%%   Info:  (gcc)Top      (Info Narrow)--L1--Top------------------------------
```

Figure 22-2: The GNU Emacs window, showing the top-level help for GCC.

You can explore further by typing **m**, followed by one of the menu items shown in Figure 22-2.

While you're at it, you may want to press the spacebar from the screen shown in Figure 22-2. That action displays the GNU General Public License (GPL), shown in Figure 22-3.

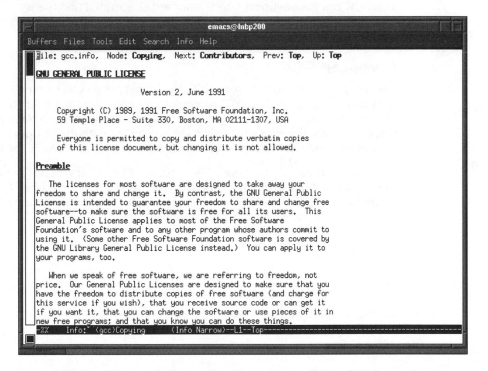

Figure 22-3: The GNU Emacs window, showing the first page of the GNU General Public License (GPL).

Linux and the `gcc` compiler itself are covered by the GPL, which requires distribution of the source code (that's why all Linux distributions come with source code). In the "Implications of GNU Licenses" section, you learn that you can still use GNU tools to develop commercial applications and distribute the applications in binary form (without source code) as long as they link with selected GNU libraries only.

At any time in `info`, you can type **d** to go back to the `info` topic directory shown in Figure 22-1. From that screen, you can view help on other GNU tools, such as `make` and the GNU debugger.

To quit `info`, type **q**. If you accessed `info` from the Emacs editor, press Ctrl+X@(Ctrl+C to quit the Emacs editor.

GNU C and C++ compilers

The most important software development tool in Linux is GCC, which is the GNU C and C++ compiler. In fact, GCC can compile three languages: C, C++, and Objective-C (a language that has object-oriented extensions to C). You'd use the same gcc command to compile and link both C and C++ source files. The GCC compiler supports ANSI standard C, so you'll find it easy to port any ANSI C program to Linux. Additionally, if you've ever used a C compiler on other UNIX systems, you'll be right at home with GCC.

Invoking GCC

Use the gcc command to invoke GCC. By default, when you use the gcc command on a source file, GCC preprocesses, compiles, and links the executable. You can use GCC options to stop this process at an intermediate stage, however. For example, you might invoke gcc with the -c option to compile a source file and generate an object file, but not perform the link step.

Using GCC to compile and link a few C source files is easy. Suppose you want to compile and link a simple program made up of two source files. The following listing shows the file area.c: the main program that computes the area of a circle whose radius is specified through the command line:

```c
#include <stdio.h>
#include <stdlib.h>

/* Function prototype */
double area_of_circle(double r);

void main(int argc, char **argv)
{
  if(argc < 2)
  {
    printf("Usage: %s radius\n", argv[0]);
    exit(1);
  }
  else
  {
    double radius = atof(argv[1]);
    double area = area_of_circle(radius);
    printf("Area of circle with radius %f = %f\n",
        radius, area);
  }
}
```

The following listing shows the file circle.c, which provides a function that computes the area of a circle.

```c
#include <math.h>

#define SQUARE(x) ((x)*(x))

double area_of_circle(double r)
{
```

```
   return 4.0 * M_PI * SQUARE(r);
}
```

For such a simple program, of course, I could have placed everything in a single file, but this contrived example shows you how to handle multiple files.

To compile these two programs and create an executable file named `area`, you might use the following command:

```
gcc -o area area.c circle.c
```

This particular invocation of GCC uses the `-o` option to specify the name of the executable file. (If you don't specify the name of an output file, GCC creates a file named `a.out`.)

If you have numerous source files to compile and link, you want to compile the files individually and generate object files (with the `.o` extension). That way, when you change a source file, you need to compile only that single file and then link all the object files. The following example shows how you can separate the compile and link steps for the example program:

```
gcc -c area.c
gcc -c circle.c
gcc -o area area.o circle.o
```

The first two invocations of `gcc` with the `-c` option compile the source files. The third invocation links the object files into an executable named `area`.

In case you are curious, here's how you run the sample program (to compute the area of a circle with a radius of 1):

```
area 1
Area of circle with radius 1.000000 = 12.566371
```

Compiling C++ programs

GNU CC is a combined C and C++ compiler, so the `gcc` command also can compile C++ source files. GCC uses the file extension to determine whether a file is C or C++. C files have a lowercase `.c` extension, whereas C++ files end with `.C` or `.cpp`.

Although the `gcc` command can compile a C++ file, that command does not automatically link with various class libraries that C++ programs typically require. That's why it's easier to compile and link a C++ program with the `g++` command, which invokes `gcc` with appropriate options.

Suppose you want to compile the following simple C++ program stored in a file named `hello.C` (it's customary to use an uppercase `C` extension for C++ source files):

```
#include <iostream.h>

void main(void)
{
  cout << "Hello from Linux!" << endl;
}
```

To compile and link this program into an executable program named `hello`, you use the following command:

```
g++ -o hello hello.C
```

This command creates the `hello` executable, which you then can run as follows:

```
hello
Hello from Linux!
```

As you see in the following section, a host of GCC options control various aspects of compiling C++ programs.

Exploring GCC options

Following is the basic syntax of the `gcc` command:

```
gcc options filenames
```

Each option starts with a hyphen (-) and usually has a long name, such as `-funsigned-char` or `-finline-functions`. Many commonly used options are short, however, such as `-c` to compile only, and `-g` to generate debugging information (needed to debug the program with the GNU debugger).

Tip

You can view a summary of all GCC options using `info`. Type `info` at the shell prompt and press `m` followed by `gcc`. Then follow the menu items: Invoking GCC -> Option Summary. Usually, you do not have to specify GCC options explicitly; the default settings are fine for most applications. Table 22-1 lists some of the GCC options you might use.

Table 22-1	Commonly used GCC options
Option	*Meaning*
`-ansi`	Support ANSI standard C syntax only. (This option disables some GNU C–specific features, such as the `asm` and `typeof` keywords.)
`-c`	Compile and generate object file only
`-DMACRO`	Define the macro with the string "1" as its value.
`-DMACRO=DEFN`	Define the macro as *DEFN*.
`-E`	Run only the C preprocessor.
`-fallow-single-precision`	Perform all math operations in single precision.
`-fpack-struct`	Pack all structure members without any padding.
`-fpcc-struct-return`	Return all `struct` and `union` values in memory, rather than in registers. (Returning values this way is less efficient, but compatible with other compilers.)

Option	*Meaning*
`-fPIC`	Generate position-independent code (PIC) suitable for use in a shared library
`-freg-struct-return`	Return `struct` and `union` values in registers, when possible.
`-g`	Generate debugging information. (The GNU debugger can use this information.)
`-IDIRECTORY`	Search the specified directory for files that you include with the `#include` preprocessor directive.
`-LDIRECTORY`	Search the specified directory for libraries.
`-lLIBRARY`	Search the specified library when linking.
`-m486`	Optimize code for a 486. (This code also will run on a 386.)
`-o FILE`	Generate the specified output file (used to designate the name of an executable file).
`-O0`	Do not optimize.
`-O` or `-O1`	Optimize the generated code.
`-O2`	Optimize even more.
`-O3`	Perform optimizations beyond those done for `-O2`.
`-pedantic`	Generate errors if any non-ANSI standard extensions are used.
`-pg`	Add extra code to the program so that, when run, it generates information that the `gprof` program can use to display timing details for various parts of the program.
`-shared`	Generate a shared object file (typically used to create a shared library).
`-traditional`	Support traditional Kernighan and Ritchie C syntax only.
`-UMACRO`	Undefine the specified macro.
`-v`	Display the version number of GCC.
`-w`	Don't generate any warning messages.
`-Wl,OPTION`	Pass the `OPTION` string (containing multiple comma-separated options) to the linker. To create a shared library named `libXXX.so.1`, for example, you use the following flag: `-Wl,-soname,libXXX.so.1`

The GNU make utility

When an application is made up of more than a few source files, compiling and linking the files by manually typing the gcc command is no longer convenient. Additionally, you do not want to compile every file whenever you change something in a single source file. This situation is what makes the GNU make utility so helpful.

The make utility works by reading and interpreting a *makefile*: a text file you have to prepare according to a specified syntax. The makefile describes which files constitute a program, and explains how to compile and link the files to build the program. Whenever you change one or more files, make determines which files should be recompiled and then issues the appropriate commands for compiling those files and rebuilding the program.

The make utility is, in fact, specified in Section 6.2 of the POSIX.2 standard (IEEE Standard 1003.2-1992) for shells and tools. GNU make conforms with the POSIX.2 standard.

Makefile names

By default, GNU make looks for a makefile with one of the following names, in the order shown:

- GNUmakefile

- makefile

- Makefile

In UNIX systems, it is customary to use Makefile as the name of the makefile because it appears near the beginning of directory listing, where uppercase names appear before lowercase ones.

When you download software from the Internet, you usually will find a Makefile together with the source files. To build the software, all you have to do is type **make** at the shell prompt; make takes care of all the steps necessary to build the software.

If your makefile does not have a standard name, such as Makefile, you have to use the -f option to specify the makefile's name. If your makefile is called webprog.mak, for example, you have to run make with the following command line:

```
make -f webprog.mak
```

GNU make also accepts several other command-line options, which are summarized in the "How to run make" section of this chapter.

The makefile

For a program consisting of several source and header files, the makefile specifies the following:

- The items to be created by make — usually, the object files and the executable. The term *target* is used for an item to be created.

- How the items (created by make) depend on other files

- What commands should be executed to create each target

Suppose you have a C++ source file named form.C that contains the following preprocessor directive:

```
#include "form.h"  // Include header file
```

The object file form.o clearly depends on the source file form.C and the header file form.h. In addition to these dependencies, you must specify how make should convert the form.C file to the object file form.o. Suppose you want make to invoke g++ (because the source file is in C++) with the following options:

- -c (compile only)

- -g (generate debugging information)

- -O2 (optimize some)

In the makefile, you can express this with the following rule:

```
# This a comment in the makefile
# The following lines indicate how form.o depends
# form.C and form.h and how to create form.o.

form.o: form.C form.h
  g++ -c -g -O2 form.C
```

In this example, the first noncomment line shows form.o as the *target* and form.C and form.h as the *dependent* files. The line following the dependency indicates how to build the target from its dependents. This line must start with a Tab.

The benefit of using make is that it prevents unnecessary compilations. After all, you could invoke g++ (or gcc) in a shell script to compile and link all the files that make up your application, but the shell script will compile everything, even if the compilations are unnecessary. GNU make, on the other hand, builds a target only if one or more of its dependents has changed since the last time the target was built. make verifies this change by examining the time of the last modification of the target and the dependents.

Note

Notice that make treats the target as the name of a goal to be achieved; the target does not have to be a file. You can have a rule such as the following:

```
clean:
  rm -f *.o
```

This rule specifies an abstract target named clean that does not depend on anything. This dependency statement says that to make clean, GNU make should invoke the command rm -f *.o, which deletes all files with the .o extension (these are the object files). Thus, the net effect of creating the target named clean is to delete the object files.

Variables (or macros)

In addition to the basic service of building targets from dependents, GNU make includes many nice features that make it easy for you to express the dependencies and rules for building a target from its dependents. If you need to compile a large number of C++ files with the same GCC options, for example, typing the options for each file would be tedious. You can avoid this task by defining a variable or macro in make as follows:

```
# Define macros for name of compiler
CXX= g++

# Define a macro for the GCC flags
CXXFLAGS= -O2 -g -m486

# A rule for building an object file
form.o: form.C form.h
    $(CXX) -c $(CXXFLAGS) form.C
```

In this example, CXX and CXXFLAGS are make variables. GNU make prefers to call them variables, but most UNIX make utilities call them macros.

To use a variable anywhere in the makefile, start with a dollar sign ($), followed by the variable within parentheses. GNU make replaces all occurrences of a variable with its definition; thus, it replaces all occurrences of $(CXXFLAGS) with the string -O2 -g -m486.

GNU make has several predefined variables that have special meanings. Table 22-2 lists these variables. In addition to the variables shown in Table 22-2, GNU make considers all environment variables to be predefined variables.

Table 22-2 Some predefined variables in GNU make

Variable	Meaning
$%	Member name for targets that are archives. If the target is libDisp. a(image.o), for example, $% is image.o, and $@ is libDisp.a.
$*	Name of the target file without the extension
$+	Names of all dependent files with duplicate dependencies, listed in their order of occurrence
$<	The name of the first dependent file
$?	Names of all the dependent files (with spaces between the names) that are newer than the target.
$@	Complete name of the target
$^	Names of all the dependent files, with spaces between the names. Duplicates are removed from the dependent filenames.

Variable	Meaning
AR	Name of the archive-maintaining program. (Default value: `ar`.)
ARFLAGS	Flags for the archive-maintaining program. (Default value: `rv`.)
AS	Name of the assembler program that converts the assembly language to object code. (Default value: `as`.)
ASFLAGS	Flags for the assembler
CC	Name of the C compiler. (Default value: `cc`.)
CFLAGS	Flags to be passed to the C compiler
CO	Name of the program that extracts a file from RCS. (Default value: `co`.)
COFLAGS	Flags for the RCS `co` program
CPP	Name of the C preprocessor. (Default value: `$(CC) -E`.)
CPPFLAGS	Flags for the C preprocessor
CXX	Name of the C++ compiler. (Default value: `g++`.)
CXXFLAGS	Flags to be passed to the C++ compiler
FC	Name of the FORTRAN compiler. (Default value: `f77`.)
FFLAGS	Flags for the FORTRAN compiler
GET	Name of the program to extract a file from SCCS. (Default value: `get`.)
GFLAGS	Flags for the SCCS `get` program
LDFLAGS	Flags for the compiler when it is supposed to invoke the linker `ld`.
LEX	Name of the program to convert Lex grammar to C program. (Default value: `lex`.)
LFLAGS	Flags for Lex
MAKEINFO	Name of the program that converts Texinfo source files to `info` files. (Default value: `makeinfo`.)
RM	Name of the command to delete a file. (Default value: `rm -f`.)
TEX	Name of the program to generate TeX DVI files from TeX source files. (Default value: `tex`.)
TEXI2DVI	Name of the program to generate TeX DVI files from the Texinfo source. (Default value: `texi2dvi`.)
YACC	Name of the program to convert YACC grammars to C programs. (Default value: `yacc -r`.)
YFLAGS	Flags for `yacc`

Implicit rules

GNU make also includes built-in, or implicit, rules that define how to create specific types of targets from various dependencies. An example of an implicit rule is the command that make should execute to generate an object file from a C source file.

GNU make supports two types of implicit rules:

■ *Suffix rules.* Suffix rules are the old-fashioned way to define an implicit rule for make. A suffix rule defines how to convert a file with a given extension to a file that has another extension. Each suffix rule is defined with the target showing a pair of suffixes (file extensions). The suffix rule for converting a .c (C source) file to a .o (object) file, for example, might be written as follows:

```
.c.o:
$(CC) $(CFLAGS) $(CPPFLAGS) -c -o $@ $<
```

This rule uses the predefined variables CC, CFLAGS, and CPPFLAGS. For filenames, the rule uses the variables $@ (the complete name of the target) and $< (the name of the first dependent file).

■ *Pattern rules.* These rules are more versatile, because you can specify more complex dependency rules with pattern rules. A pattern rule looks just like a regular rule, except that a single percent sign (%) appears in the target's name. The dependencies also use % to indicate how the dependency names relate to the target's name. The following pattern rule specifies how to convert any file X.c to a file X.o:

```
%.o: %.c
$(CC) $(CFLAGS) $(CPPFLAGS) -c -o $@ $<
```

GNU make has a large set of implicit rules, defined as both suffix and pattern rules. To see a list of all known variables and rules, run make with the following command:

```
make -p -f/dev/null
# GNU Make version 3.76.1, by Richard Stallman and Roland McGrath.
# Copyright (C) 1988, 89, 90, 91, 92, 93, 94, 95, 96, 97
#       Free Software Foundation, Inc.
# This is free software; see the source for copying conditions.
# There is NO warranty; not even for MERCHANTABILITY or FITNESS FOR A
# PARTICULAR PURPOSE.

# Report bugs to <bug-gnu-utils@prep.ai.mit.edu>.

make: *** No targets.  Stop.

# Make data base, printed on Sat May 23 15:25:04 1998
(lines deleted...)

# default
```

```
CC = cc
# default
OUTPUT_OPTION = -o $@
# default
COMPILE.c = $(CC) $(CFLAGS) $(CPPFLAGS) $(TARGET_ARCH) -c (lines
deleted...)

# Implicit Rules
 %.o: %.c
# commands to execute (built-in):
    $(COMPILE.c) $< $(OUTPUT_OPTION)
(lines deleted...)
```

This listing shows selected parts of the output displayed by GNU make when
you use the -p option. The output includes the names of variables as well as
implicit rules.

A sample makefile

You can write a makefile easily if you use GNU make's predefined variables
and built-in rules. Consider, for example, a makefile that creates the
executable xdraw from three C source files (xdraw.c, xviewobj.c, and
shapes.c) and two header files (xdraw.h and shapes.h). Assume that each
source file includes one of the header files. Given these facts, a sample
makefile might look like the following:

```
##############################################################
# Sample makefile
# Comments start with '#'
#
##############################################################

# Use standard variables to define compile and link flags

CFLAGS= -g -O2

# Define the target "all"

all: xdraw

OBJS=xdraw.o xviewobj.o shapes.o

xdraw: $(OBJS)

# Object files
xdraw.o: Makefile xdraw.c xdraw.h

xviewobj.o: Makefile xviewobj.c xdraw.h

shapes.o: Makefile shapes.c shapes.h
```

This makefile relies on GNU make's implicit rules. The conversion of .c files to .o files uses the built-in rule. The flags to the C compiler are passed by defining the variable CFLAGS.

Secret

The target named all is defined as the first target for a reason — if you run GNU make without specifying any targets in the command line (see the make syntax described in the following section), it builds the first target it finds in the makefile. By defining the first target, all, as xdraw, you can ensure that make builds this executable file even if you do not explicitly specify it as a target. UNIX programmers traditionally use all as the name of the first target, but the target's name is immaterial; what matters is that it is the first target in the makefile.

If you have a directory containing the appropriate source files and header files, you can try the makefile. Here's what happens when I try the sample makefile:

```
make
cc -g -02  -c xdraw.c -o xdraw.o
cc -g -02  -c xviewobj.c -o xviewobj.o
cc -g -02  -c shapes.c -o shapes.o
cc xdraw.o xviewobj.o shapes.o  -o xdraw
```

As the output of make shows, it uses the cc command (which happens to be a symbolic link to GCC in your Linux system) with appropriate options to compile the source files and, finally, to link the objects to create the xdraw executable.

How to run make

Typically, you run make with a single command in the command line; that is, by typing make. When run this way, GNU make looks for a file named GNUmakefile, makefile, or Makefile — in that order. If make finds one of these makefiles, it builds the first target specified in that makefile. However, if make does not find an appropriate makefile, it displays the following error message and exits:

```
make: *** No targets.  Stop.
```

If your makefile happens to have a different name from the default ones, you have to use the -f option to specify the makefile. The syntax of this make option is

```
make -f filename
```

where filename is the name of the makefile.

Even when you have a makefile with a default name such as Makefile, you may want to build a specific target out of several targets defined in the makefile. In that case, you have to run make with the following syntax:

```
make target
```

If the makefile contains the target named clean, you can build that target with the following command:

```
make clean
```

Another special syntax overrides the value of a `make` variable. For example, GNU `make` uses the `CFLAGS` variable to hold the flags used when compiling C files. You can override the value of this variable when you invoke `make`. Following is an example of how you can define `CFLAGS` to be the options `-g -O2`:

```
make CFLAGS="-g -O2"
```

In addition to these options, GNU `make` accepts several other command-line options. Table 22-3 lists the GNU `make` options.

Table 22-3   Options for GNU make

Option	Meaning
`-b`	Ignored, but accepted for compatibility with other versions of `make`
`-C DIR`	Change to the specified directory before reading the makefile
`-d`	Print debugging information
`-e`	Allow environment variables to override definitions of similarly named variables in the makefile
`-f FILE`	Read `FILE` as the makefile
`-h`	Display the list of `make` options
`-i`	Ignore all errors in commands executed when building a target
`-I DIR`	Search specified directory for included makefiles (the capability to include a file in a makefile is unique to GNU `make`)
`-j NUM`	Specifies the number of commands `make` can run simultaneously
`-k`	Continue to build unrelated targets even if an error occurs when building one of the targets
`-l LOAD`	Don't start a new job if load average is at least `LOAD` (a floating-point number)
`-m`	Ignored, but accepted for compatibility with other versions of `make`
`-n`	Print the commands to be executed, but do not execute them
`-o FILE`	Do not rebuild the file named `FILE`, even if it is older than its dependents
`-p`	Display the `make` database of variables and implicit rules
`-q`	Do not run anything, but return zero if all targets are up-to-date; one if anything needs updating; and two if an error occurs
`-r`	Get rid of all built-in rules
`-s`	Work silently (without displaying the commands as they are executed)
`-t`	Change the timestamp of the files without actually changing them
`-v`	Display the version number of `make` and a copyright notice
`-w`	Display the name of the working directory before and after processing the makefile
`-W FILE`	Assume that the specified file has been modified

The GNU debugger

Although make automates the process of building a program, that task is the least of your worries when a program does not work correctly or when a program suddenly quits with an error message. You need a debugger to find the cause of program errors. This book's companion CD-ROM includes gdb: the versatile GNU debugger with a command-line interface. The CD-ROM also includes xxgdb, an X Window System–based graphical front end for gdb.

Like any debugger, gdb allows you to perform typical debugging tasks, such as the following:

- Set breakpoint so program execution stops at a specified line
- Watch the values of variables in the program
- Step through the program one line at a time
- Change variables in an attempt to fix errors

The gdb debugger can debug C and C++ programs.

Preparing a program for debugging

If you want to debug a program with gdb, you have to ensure that the compiler generates and places debugging information in the executable. The debugging information contains the names of variables in your program and the mapping of addresses in the executable file to lines of code in the source file. gdb needs this information to perform its functions, such as stopping after executing a specified line of source code.

Tip

To ensure that the executable is properly prepared for debugging, use the -g option with GCC. You can do this by defining the variable CFLAGS in the makefile as follows:

```
CFLAGS= -g
```

Running gdb

The most common way to debug a program is to run gdb with the command

```
gdb progname
```

where *progname* is the name of the program's executable file. After it runs, gdb displays the following message and prompts you for a command:

```
GDB is free software and you are welcome to distribute copies of it
 under certain conditions; type "show copying" to see the conditions.
There is absolutely no warranty for GDB; type "show warranty" for
details.
GDB 4.16 (i386-redhat-linux), Copyright 1996 Free Software Foundation,
Inc...
(gdb)
```

To see a list of gdb commands, type **help** at the prompt, as follows:

```
(gdb) help
```

```
List of classes of commands:

running -- Running the program
stack -- Examining the stack
data -- Examining data
breakpoints -- Making program stop at certain points
files -- Specifying and examining files
status -- Status inquiries
support -- Support facilities
user-defined -- User-defined commands
aliases -- Aliases of other commands
obscure -- Obscure features
internals -- Maintenance commands

Type "help" followed by a class name for a list of commands in that
class.
Type "help" followed by command name for full documentation.
Command name abbreviations are allowed if unambiguous.
(gdb)
```

The initial message displays the classes of gdb commands. You can get further help on a specific class of commands or a specific command by following the instructions. To see the list of commands you would use to run the program you are debugging, for example, type help running at the gdb prompt.

To quit gdb, type **q** and then press Enter.

gdb has a large number of commands, but you need only a few to find the cause of an error quickly. Table 22-4 lists the commonly used gdb commands.

Table 22-4   Commonly used gdb commands

Command	Description
break *NUM*	Set a breakpoint at the specified line number (the debugger stops at breakpoints).
bt	Display a trace of all stack frames. (This command shows you the sequence of function calls so far.)
clear *FILENAME:NUM*	Delete the breakpoint at a specific line in a source file. clear xdraw.c:8, for example, clears the breakpoint at line 8 of file xdraw.c.
continue	Continue running the program being debugged. (Use this command after the program has stopped due to a signal or breakpoint.)
display *EXPR*	Display value of expression (consisting of variables defined in the program) each time the program stops.
file *FILE*	Load specified executable file for debugging.
help *NAME*	Display help on the command named *NAME*.

(continued)

Table 22-4 *(Continued)*

Command	Description
info break	Display a list of current breakpoints, including information on how many times each breakpoint has been reached.
info files	Display detailed information about the file being debugged.
info func	Display all function names.
info local	Display information about local variables of the current function.
info prog	Display the execution status of the program being debugged.
info var	Display all global and static variable names.
kill	End the program you are currently debugging.
list	List a section of the source code.
make	Run the make utility to rebuild the executable without leaving gdb.
next	Advance one line of source code in the current function without stepping into other functions.
print *EXPR*	Show the value of the expression *EXPR*.
quit	Quit gdb.
run	Start running the currently loaded executable.
set variable *VAR=VALUE*	Set the value of the variable *VAR* to *VALUE*.
shell *CMD*	Execute a UNIX command *CMD* without leaving gdb.
step	Advance one line in the current function, stepping into other functions, if any.
watch *VAR*	Show the value of the variable named *VAR* whenever the value changes.
where	Display the call sequence. You can use this command to locate where your program died.
x/*F ADDR*	Examine the contents of the memory location at address *ADDR* in the format specified by the letter *F*, which can be o (octal), x (hex), d (decimal), u (unsigned decimal), t (binary), f (float), a (address), i (instruction), c (char), or s (string). You can append a letter indicating the size of the data type to the format letter. Size letters are b (byte), h (halfword, 2 bytes), w (word, 4 bytes), and g (giant, 8 bytes). Typically, *ADDR* is the name of a variable or pointer.

Finding bugs with gdb

To understand how you can find bugs with gdb, it is easiest to look at an example, so I'll start with a rather contrived program that contains a typical bug.

Following is the program, which I stored in the file dbgtst.c:

```
#include <stdio.h>

static char buf[256];
void read_input(char *s);

void main(void)
{
  char *input = NULL; /* Just a pointer, no storage for string */

  read_input(input);

/* Process command. */
  printf("You typed: %s\n", input);

/* ... */
}

void read_input(char *s)
{
  printf("Command: ");
  gets(s);
}
```

This program's main function calls the read_input function to get a line of input from the user. The read_input function expects a character array in which it returns what the user types. In this example, however, main calls read_input with an uninitialized pointer — that's the bug in this simple program.

Build the program using gcc with the -g option, as follows:

```
gcc -g -o dbgtst dbgtst.c
```

To see the problem with this program, run it, as follows:

```
dbgtst
Command: test
Segmentation fault
```

The program dies with the Segmentation fault message. For this small program, you could find the cause by examining the source code. In a real-world application, however, you may not immediately know what caused the error. That's when you can use gdb to find the cause of the problem.

To use gdb to locate a bug, follow these steps:

1. **Load the program under** gdb. To load a program named dbgtst in gdb, type the following:

```
gdb dbgtst
GDB is free software and you are welcome to distribute copies of
it
 under certain conditions; type "show copying" to see the
conditions.
There is absolutely no warranty for GDB; type "show warranty" for
details.
GDB 4.16 (i386-redhat-linux), Copyright 1996 Free Software
Foundation, Inc...
(gdb)
```

2. **Run the program under** gdb **with the** run **command. If the program prompts for input, type the input text. The program should fail as it did before. Here's what happens with the** dbgtst **program:**

```
(gdb) run
Starting program: /home/naba/lxs2/test/dbgtst
Command: test

Program received signal SIGSEGV, Segmentation fault.
0x40046d10 in _IO_gets (buf=0x0) at iogets.c:62
iogets.c:62: No such file or directory.
(gdb)
```

3. **Use the** where **command to determine where the program died. For the** dbgtst **program, this command yields the following output:**

```
(gdb) where
#0  0x40046d10 in _IO_gets (buf=0x0) at iogets.c:62
#1  0x80484f5 in read_input (s=0x0) at dbgtst.c:21
#2  0x80484c6 in main () at dbgtst.c:10
(gdb)
```

The output shows the sequence of function calls. Function call #0 — the most recent one — is to a C library function, gets. The gets call originated in the read_input function, which in turn was called from the main function.

4. **Use the** list **command to inspect the lines of suspect source code. In** dbgtst, **you might start with line 21 of** dbgtst.c **file, as follows:**

```
(gdb) list dbgtst.c:21
16      }
17
18      void read_input(char *s)
19      {
20        printf("Command: ");
21        gets(s);
22      }
23
(gdb)
```

After looking at this listing, you should be able to tell that the problem may have been in the way that read_input was called. Then you'd list the lines around line 10 in dbgtst.c (which is where the read_input call originated), as follows:

```
(gdb) list dbgtst.c:10
5
6        void main(void)
7        {
8          char *input = NULL; /* Just a pointer, no storage for
string */
9
10          read_input(input);
11
12      /* Process command. */
13        printf("You typed: %s\n", input);
14
(gdb)
```

At this point, you should be able to narrow the problem down to the variable named input.

Fixing bugs in gdb

Sometimes, you can try a bug fix directly in gdb. For the example program in the preceding section, you can try this fix immediately after the problem dies with an error. Because the example is a contrived one, I have an extra buffer named buf defined in the dbgtst program, as follows:

```
static char buf[256];
```

I can fix the problem of the uninitialized pointer by setting the variable input to buf. The following session with gdb corrects the problem of the uninitialized pointer (this example picks up immediately after the program has run and died due to the segmentation fault):

```
(gdb) file dbgtst
A program is being debugged already. Kill it? (y or n) y

Load new symbol table from "dbgtst"? (y or n) y
Reading symbols from dbgtst...
done.
(gdb) list
1    #include <stdio.h>
2
3    static char buf[256];
4    void read_input(char *s);
5
6    void main(void)
7    {
8      char *input = NULL; /* Just a pointer, no storage for string */
9
10      read_input(input);
(gdb) break 9
```

```
Breakpoint 1 at 0x80484bd: file dbgtst.c, line 9.
(gdb) run
Starting program: /home/naba/lxs2/test/dbgtst

Breakpoint 1, main () at dbgtst.c:10
10      read_input(input);
(gdb) set var input=buf
(gdb) cont
Continuing.
Command: test
You typed: test

Program exited with code 020.
(gdb)
```

As the listing shows, if I stop the program just before read_input is called and set the variable named input to buf (which is a valid array of characters), the rest of the program runs fine.

After you try a fix that works, you can make the necessary changes to the source files and make the fix permanent.

Implications of GNU Licenses

You have to pay a price for the bounty of Linux — to protect its developers and users, Linux is distributed under the GNU GPL (General Public License), which stipulates the distribution of the source code.

This does not mean, however, that you can't write commercial software for Linux that you want to distribute (either for free or for a price) in binary form only. You can actually follow all the rules and still sell your Linux applications in binary form.

When writing applications on Linux, you should be aware of two licenses:

- The GNU General Public License (GPL) governs many Linux programs, including the Linux kernel and GCC.

- The GNU Library General Public License (LGPL) covers many Linux libraries.

Caution

The following sections provide an overview of these licenses and some suggestions for how to meet the requirements of the licenses. Because I am not a lawyer, however, you should not take anything in this book as constituting legal advice. As you'll see, the full text for these licenses is in text files on your Linux system; show these licenses to your legal counsel for a full interpretation and an assessment of applicability to your business.

The GNU General Public License

You'll find the text of the GPL in a file named `COPYING` in various directories in your Linux system. For example, type `cd /usr/doc/ghostscript*` and then type `more COPYING` to read the GPL.

The GPL has nothing to do with whether you charge for the software or distribute it for free; its thrust is to keep the software free for all users. The GPL does this by requiring that the software be distributed in source-code form, and stipulating that any user can copy and distribute the software to anyone else in source-code form. Additionally, everyone is reminded that the software comes with absolutely no warranty.

Software covered by the GPL is not in the public domain; such software is always copyrighted, and the GPL spells out the restrictions on the software's copying and distribution. From a user's point of view, of course, the GPL's restrictions are not really restrictions; they are benefits, because the user is guaranteed access to the source code.

Caution

If your application uses parts of any software covered by the GPL, your application is considered to be a derived work, and it becomes covered by the GPL, which means you must distribute the source code to your application.

Although the Linux kernel is covered by the GPL, the GPL does not cover any applications that use the kernel services through system calls. Those applications are considered to be normal use of the kernel.

If you plan to distribute your application in binary form (as most commercial software is distributed), you must make sure your application does not use any parts of any software covered by the GPL. Your application may end up using parts of other software when it calls functions in a library. Most libraries, however, are covered by a different GNU license, which is described in the following section.

You have to watch out for only a few library and utility programs covered by the GPL. The GNU `dbm` (`gdbm`) database library is one of the prominent libraries covered by GPL. The GNU `bison` parser-generator tool is another utility covered by the GPL. If you allow `bison` to generate code, that code is covered by the GPL.

Secret

For the GNU `dbm` and the GNU `bison`, you have other alternatives not covered by the GPL. For a database library, you can use the Berkeley database library `db` in place of `gdbm`. For a parser-generator, you might use `yacc` instead of `bison`.

The GNU Library General Public License

You'll find the text of the GNU LGPL in a file named `COPYING.LIB`. If you have the kernel source installed, you'll find a copy of the `COPYING.LIB` file in one of the source directories. To locate a copy of the `COPYING.LIB` file, use the following `find` command:

```
find /usr -name "COPYING*" -print
```

This command lists all occurrences of `COPYING` and `COPYING.LIB` in your system. The `COPYING` file contains the GPL, whereas `COPYING.LIB` has the LGPL.

The LGPL is intended to allow the use of libraries in your applications even if you do not distribute source code for your application. The LGPL stipulates, however, that users must have access to the source code of the library you used, and that users can make use of modified versions of those libraries.

Most Linux libraries, including the C library (`libc.a`), are covered by the LGPL. Thus, when you build your application on Linux with the GCC compiler, your application links with code from one or more libraries covered by the LGPL. If you want to distribute your application in binary form only, you need to pay attention to the LGPL.

Secret

One way to meet the intent of the LGPL is to provide the object code for your application and a makefile that relinks your object files with any updated Linux libraries covered by the LGPL.

Wizard

A better way to satisfy the LGPL is to use *dynamic linking*, in which your application and the library are separate entities even though your application calls functions in the library when it runs. With dynamic linking, users immediately get the benefit of any updates to the libraries without having to relink the application.

Version Control

When you write applications with a few files, it might be simple enough to prepare a makefile to automate the software build process and not worry about keeping track of changes. Typically, for small projects, you might keep track of changes through comments at the beginning of a file.

While this approach works well for a small project, for larger software projects you should use some tools that help you manage different versions of your applications. In fact, you can benefit from version-control tools even if you are the sole author of a small application. After some time passes, you may have trouble remembering what changes you made. Software version control can help you figure out these changes.

The Linux software distribution comes with RCS (Revision Control System), which is a collection of tools to help you control software revisions. The next few sections provide an overview of RCS and show you how to use it with some simple examples.

Source-control tools in RCS

Source control refers to the concept of saving a version of the source code so you can recover a specific version or revision of a file whenever you need it. Essentially, when you modify a source file, the sequence goes something like this:

1. When you have an initial version of the source file, you archive it — place it under source control.

2. When you want to make any changes in the file, you first get a copy of the current revision. (When you get it this way, the tools should ensure that no one else can modify that revision.)

3. You make the changes in the source file, test the code, and store the modified file as a new revision.

4. The next time you want to make changes in the file, you start with the latest revision of the file.

Note

RCS provides the tools that allow to you archive file revisions and update them in a controlled manner. Table 22-5 lists the tools.

Table 22-5   RCS tools

Tool	Purpose
ci	Creates a new revision of a file or adds a working file to an RCS file
co	Gets a working version of a file for reading. (co -1 provides a working file and locks the original so that you can modify the working file.)
ident	Searches for identifiers in a file
merge	Incorporates changes from two files into a third one
rcsdiff	Compares a working file with its RCS file
rcsmerge	Merges different revisions of a file
rlog	Views the history of changes in a file

Beginner's RCS

Suppose you have just finished developing the initial working version of an application, and you want to use RCS to manage the revisions from now on. The following sections outline the steps you'd follow to use RCS for your development effort.

Creating initial RCS files

The first step in managing source-file revisions with RCS is to allow RCS to archive the current revision of your files. Follow these steps to put the source file under the control of RCS:

1. In the directory where you keep your application's source files, create a subdirectory named RCS by typing `mkdir RCS`. If the RCS subdirectory exists, RCS archives file revisions in this directory.

2. In each file you plan to place under revision control, add a comment with the following RCS identification keyword:

   `$Header$`

   In a C source file, for example, add the following:

   ```
   /*
    * $Id$
    */
   ```

   In a makefile, on the other hand, use the following:

   `# $Id$`

   RCS later expands these identifier keywords to include information about the file revision and date.

3. Check in each file with RCS, use the `ci` command, and provide a brief description of each file as prompted by `ci`. Following is how you might check in `Makefile`:

   ```
   ci Makefile
   RCS/Makefile,v <-- Makefile
   enter description, terminated with single '.' or end of file:
   NOTE: This is NOT the log message!
   > Makefile for sample programs.
   >.
   initial revision: 1.1
   done
   ```

   When a file is checked in, the `ci` command creates a corresponding RCS file in the RCS subdirectory. The RCS file's name is the same as the original file except for a `,v` appended to the name. Thus, the RCS file for `Makefile` is `Makefile,v`. Also, `ci` deletes the original source file after it creates the RCS file. To use or edit the file again, you have to extract it with the `co` command.

After you follow these steps, all your files will be safely stored in RCS files in the RCS subdirectory.

Using archived files

Now suppose you want to edit one of the files (for example, to add a new feature) and rebuild the application again. For starters, you need all the source files and the makefile for the compile and link step.

You should extract all these files with the `co` command for read-only access only (except for the file you want to change, as you'll see soon). The `co` command is straightforward to use. To get a working copy of `Makefile` for read-only use, for example, use the following command:

```
co Makefile
RCS/Makefile,v --> Makefile
revision 1.1
done
```

By default, this command looks for an RCS file named `RCS/Makefile,v` and creates a read-only working copy of it named `Makefile`.

You'll find a copy of `Makefile` in the directory. Examine that copy of `Makefile` to see what happened to that `$Id$` keyword you added as a comment. Here's what my example `Makefile` shows:

```
# $Id: Makefile,v 1.1 1998/05/24 08:19:07 naba Exp $
```

As this example shows, RCS expands each identifier keyword into a string with information. The exact information depends on the identifier.

If you want to modify a file, you have to check it out with the `-l` option. If you want to check out a copy of the file `xmutil.c` for editing, use the following command:

```
co -l xmutil.c
RCS/xmutil.c,v --> xmutil.c
revision 1.1 (locked)
don
```

If you compare this output with that from the previous example of `co`, you notice that the current output confirms that the RCS file is locked. No one else can modify the archived file until you check in the copy you checked out for editing.

When you check out a file and put a lock on it, no one else can check out the same file for editing. Anyone can get a copy of the file for read-only use, however.

After you make changes in a file, you can check it in again with the `ci` command, just as you did when you created the RCS file.

Using identification keywords

You can use the RCS identification keywords — each of which is a string delimited by dollar signs (`$...$`) — to record information in source files. RCS expands the `$Id$` keyword, for example, into summary information about the file, including the filename, revision number, date, and author. All you have to do is put the keyword in the file; RCS takes care of expanding that keyword into the appropriate information. Table 22-6 lists the identification keywords RCS supports.

Table 22-6	Identification keywords supported by RCS
Keyword	*Purpose*
`$Author$`	Login ID of the user who checked in the revision
`$Date$`	Date and time when the revision was checked in
`$Header$`	Expands to summary information, including full path name of the RCS file, revision number, date, author, and the state of file revision
`$Id$`	Same as `$Header$`, except that the RCS filename does not have any directory prefix
`$Locker$`	Login ID of the user who locked the file (empty if the file is not currently locked)
`$Log$`	Expands to a log of changes made in the file
`$RCSfile$`	Name of the RCS file without the directory names
`$Revision$`	Revision number of the RCS file
`$Source$`	Expands to the full path name of the RCS file
`$State$`	Indicates the state of the file revision (whether it is locked or not)

Tip

At minimum, you may want to use the `$Id$` keyword in your files to include summary information about the latest revision.

Wizard

RCS expands the identifier keywords anywhere in a file. Thus, you might "mark" an object file (and the executable using that object file) by placing the identifier keyword in a string variable. A common practice is to define a string named `rcsid` as follows:

```
static const char rcsid[] =
  "$Id";
```

Defining the `rcsid` string causes the object and executable file to contain a string such as the following:

```
$Id: xmutil.c,v 1.2 1998/05/24 08:31:20 naba Exp $
```

Other RCS commands

Most of the time, you will use the `ci` and `co` commands to maintain file revisions by using RCS. RCS, however, includes several other tools for managing various aspects of version control, such as comparing two revisions, viewing the history of changes, and examining identifiers in files.

Viewing the changes made so far

If you checked out a file for modification, you may want to know what changes you have made thus far. You can use the `rcsdiff` program to see a list of changes. If you've been editing a file named `xmutil.c`, for example, you can compare the working file against its RCS file with the following command:

```
rcsdiff xmutil.c
```

The `rcsdiff` program runs the UNIX `diff` utility to find the differences between the working file and the RCS file.

If necessary, you can even find the differences between two specific revisions of a file, with a command such as the following:

```
rcsdiff -r1.1 -r1.2 xmutil.c
```

This command lists the differences between revision 1.1 and 1.2 of the file `xmutil.c`.

Discarding changes made so far

Sometimes, after you make some changes in a file, you realize that the changes are either wrong or unnecessary. In such a case, you want to discard the changes you have made so far.

To discard changes, all you have to do is unlock the RCS file and then delete the working copy of the file. To unlock an RCS file, use the `rcs` command with the `-u` (unlock) option. The following command discards the current changes in the file named `xmutil.c`:

```
rcs -u xmutil.c
```

Another, more convenient, way to discard changes is to overwrite the current working file with a copy of the old RCS file. To do this, use the `co` command with `-u` and `-f` flags, as follows:

```
co -f -u xmutil.c
```

The `-u` option unlocks the checked-out revision, and `-f` forces `co` to overwrite the working file with the older revision of that file.

Viewing the change log

As you make changes in a file and keep checking in revisions, RCS maintains a log of changes. You can view this log with the `rlog` command. The following example shows how to view the log of changes for the file `xmutil.c`:

```
rlog xmutil.c

RCS file: RCS/xmutil.c,v
Working file: xmutil.c
head: 1.2
branch:
locks: strict
access list:
```

```
symbolic names:
keyword substitution: kv
total revisions: 2;    selected revisions: 2
description:
Utility functions
----------------------------
revision 1.2
date: 1998/05/26 06:31:20; author: naba; state: Exp; lines: +15 -1
minor revisions
----------------------------
revision 1.1
date: 1998/05/26 05:55:23; author: naba; state: Exp;
Initial revision
========================================================================
```

The first part of the `rlog` output displays some summary information about the RCS file. The lines following the `description:` line show the description I entered when I created the RCS file. Following this description, you see an entry for each revision, with the most recent revision appearing first. Each revision's entry shows the date, the author, and a brief description entered by the author.

Examining identifier keywords

If you have any identifier keywords embedded in a file, you can view them with the `ident` command. If `Makefile` contains the `$Id$` keyword, you can examine the keyword with the following command:

```
ident Makefile
Makefile:
    $Id: Makefile,v 1.2 1998/05/24 08:25:47 naba Exp $
```

If you define a string variable with a keyword that eventually gets embedded in a binary file (an object file or an executable file), you can use `ident` to view those identifiers as well. You can try `ident` in any binary file to see whether it contains any embedded keywords. Following is what I found when I tried `ident` in the file `/usr/bin/co` (the executable program for the `co` command):

```
ident /usr/bin/co
/usr/bin/co:
    $Id: rcsbase.h,v 5.20 1995/06/16 06:19:24 eggert Exp $
    $Id: co.c,v 5.18 1995/06/16 06:19:24 eggert Exp $
    $Id: rcslex.c,v 5.19 1995/06/16 06:19:24 eggert Exp $
    $Id: rcssyn.c,v 5.15 1995/06/16 06:19:24 eggert Exp $
    $Id: rcsgen.c,v 5.16 1995/06/16 06:19:24 eggert Exp $
    $Id: rcsedit.c,v 5.19 1995/06/16 06:19:24 eggert Exp $
    $Id: rcskeys.c,v 5.4 1995/06/16 06:19:24 eggert Exp $
    $Id: rcsmap.c,v 5.3 1995/06/16 06:19:24 eggert Exp $
    $Id: rcsrev.c,v 5.10 1995/06/16 06:19:24 eggert Exp $
    $Id: rcsutil.c,v 5.20 1995/06/16 06:19:24 eggert Exp $
    $Id: rcsfnms.c,v 5.16 1995/06/16 06:19:24 eggert Exp $
    $Id: maketime.c,v 5.11 1995/06/16 06:19:24 eggert Exp $
    $Id: partime.c,v 5.13 1995/06/16 06:19:24 eggert Exp $
    $Id: rcstime.c,v 1.4 1995/06/16 06:19:24 eggert Exp $
    $Id: rcskeep.c,v 5.10 1995/06/16 06:19:24 eggert Exp $
```

From this output, you can tell the exact versions of source files that were used to build this version of the co program.

Linux Programming Topics

Developing software under Linux is quite similar to developing software under any UNIX system. Most C and UNIX programming issues are generic and apply to all UNIX systems. There are, however, a few topics you want to know about if you are developing software for Linux.

This section covers the most significant topic: the new Executable and Linking Format (ELF) binary in Linux. The other topic — the use of dynamic linking in applications — is related to ELF. I also describe how you can exploit dynamic linking and how to create a dynamically linked library in Linux.

The Executable and Linking Format (ELF)

If you have programmed in UNIX, you probably know that when you compile and link a program, the default executable file is named a.out. What you may not have realized is that a file format is associated with the a.out file. The operating system has to know this file format so it can load and run an executable. Linux has been using the a.out format for its binaries ever since it originated.

Although the a.out format has served its purpose adequately, it has two shortcomings:

■ Shared libraries are difficult to create.

■ Dynamically loading a shared library is cumbersome.

Using shared libraries is desirable because a shared library allows many executable programs to share the same block of code. Also, the dynamic loading of modules is becoming increasingly popular because it allows an application to load blocks of code only when needed, thus reducing the memory requirement of the application.

Meanwhile, the UNIX System Laboratories (USL) has developed a new binary format named Executable and Linking Format (ELF) for use in System V Release 4 (SVR4). The ELF format is much more flexible than the a.out format. In particular, ELF has the following advantages over the a.out format in Linux:

■ Shared libraries for the ELF format are simpler to create. You compile all source files with the gcc -fPIC -c command and then link with a command such as the following, which creates the library libXXX.so.1.0:

```
gcc -shared -Wl,-soname,libXXX.so.1 -o libXXX.so.1.0 *.o
```

■ Dynamic loading (wherein a program loads code modules at run time) is simpler. With dynamic loading, you can design an application to be extensible, so users can add new code in the form of shared libraries.

Because of ELF's increased flexibility, Linux developers (in particular, the GCC developers) decided to move to ELF as the standard binary-format Linux. By default, the new GCC compiler — gcc Version 2.7 — generates ELF binaries.

Secret

Notice that GCC Version 2.7 continues to use a.out as the default name of the executable file (used only if you do not specify an output filename with the -o option). Although the executable may be named a.out, the binary format is ELF and not the old a.out format.

Wizard

If you want to check the binary format of an executable file, use the file command. The following example shows how you would check the file type of /bin/ls (the executable file for the ls command):

```
file /bin/ls
/bin/ls: ELF 32-bit LSB executable, Intel 80386, version 1,
dynamically linked,stripped
```

On the other hand, the file command reports the following for an older a.out format executable, as follows:

```
file a.out
a.out: Linux/i386 demand-paged executable (QMAGIC)
```

Shared libraries in Linux applications

Most Linux programs use shared libraries. At minimum, most C programs use the C shared library libc.so.X , wherein X is a version number. When a program uses one or more shared libraries, you need the program's executable file, as well as all the shared libraries, to run the program. In other words, your program won't run if all shared libraries are not available on a system.

If you sell an application, you need to make sure that all necessary shared libraries are distributed with your software.

Examining a program's shared libraries

Use the ldd utility to determine what shared libraries an executable program needs. Following is what ldd reports for a typical C program compiled with gcc Version 2.7.2 (the program uses the ELF binary format):

```
ldd a.out
        libc.so.6 => /lib/libc.so.6 (0x40003000)
        /lib/ld-linux.so.2 => /lib/ld-linux.so.2 (0x00000000)
```

For a more complex program such as xv (ELF version), ldd shows more shared libraries, as follows:

```
ldd /usr/X11/bin/xv
        libX11.so.6 => /usr/X11R6/lib/libX11.so.6 (0x40003000)
        libjpeg.so.6 => /usr/lib/libjpeg.so.6 (0x4009a000)
        libpng.so.0 => /usr/lib/libpng.so.0 (0x400b8000)
        libz.so.1 => /usr/lib/libz.so.1 (0x400d1000)
        libm.so.6 => /lib/libm.so.6 (0x400de000)
        libc.so.6 => /lib/libc.so.6 (0x400f7000)
        /lib/ld-linux.so.2 => /lib/ld-linux.so.2 (0x00000000)
```

In this case, the program uses several shared libraries including the X11 library (libX11.so.6), the JPEG library (libjpeg.so.6), the Portable Network Graphics (PNG) library (libpng.so.0), the Math library (libm.so.6), and the C library (libc.so.6).

Thus, almost any Linux application requires shared libraries to run. Additionally, the shared libraries must have the same binary format as that used by an application.

Creating a shared library

With ELF, creating a shared library for your own application is simple enough. Suppose you want to implement an object in the form of a shared library. A set of functions in the shared library will represent the object's interfaces. To use the object, you load its shared library and then invoke its interface functions (you learn how to do this in the following section).

Following is the C source code for this simple object, implemented as a shared library (you might also call it a dynamically linked library):

```c
/*------------------------------------------------------*/
/* File: dynobj.c
 *
 * Demonstrate use of dynamic linking.
 * Pretend this is an object that can be created by calling
 * init and destroyed by calling destroy.
 */
#include <stdio.h>
#include <stdlib.h>
#include <string.h>

/* Data structure for this object */
typedef struct OBJDATA
{
  char *name;
  int version;
} OBJDATA;

/*------------------------------------------------------*/
/* i n i t
 *
 * Initialize object (allocate storage).
 *
 */
void* init(char *name)
{
  OBJDATA *data = (OBJDATA*)calloc(1, sizeof(OBJDATA));
  if(name)
    data->name = malloc(strlen(name)+1);
  strcpy(data->name, name);

  printf("Created: %s\n", name);

  return data;
}
/*------------------------------------------------------*/
```

```
/* s h o w
 *
 * Show the object.
 *
 */
void show(void *data)
{
  OBJDATA *d = (OBJDATA*)data;
  printf("show: %s\n", d->name);
}
/*-------------------------------------------------------*/
/* d e s t r o y
 *
 * Destroy the object (free all storage).
 *
 */
void destroy(void *data)
{
  OBJDATA *d = (OBJDATA*)data;
  if(d)
  {
    if(d->name)
    {
      printf("Destroying: %s\n", d->name);
      free(d->name);
    }
    free(d);
  }
}
```

The object offers three interface functions:

- `init` to allocate any necessary storage and initialize the object
- `show` to display the object (here, it simply prints a message)
- `destroy` to free any storage

To build the shared library named `libdobj.so`, follow these steps:

1. Compile all source files with the `-fPIC` flag. In this case, compile the `dynobj.c` file with the following command:

   ```
   gcc -fPIC -c dynobj.c
   ```

2. Link the objects into a shared library with the `-shared` flag, and provide appropriate flags for the linker. To create the shared library named `libdobj.so.1`, use the following:

   ```
   gcc -shared -Wl,-soname,libdobj.so.1 -o libdobj.so.1.0 dynobj.o
   ```

3. Set up a sequence of symbolic links so that programs using the shared library can refer to it with a standard name. For the sample library, the standard name is `libdobj.so`, and the symbolic links are set up with the following commands:

   ```
   ln -s libdobj.so.1.0 libdobj.so.1
   ln -s libdobj.so.1 libdobj.so
   ```

4. When you test the shared library, define and export the `LD_LIBRARY_PATH` environment variable with the following command:

```
export LD_LIBRARY_PATH=`pwd`:$LD_LIBRARY_PATH
```

After you test the shared library and are satisfied that the library works, you should copy it to a standard location, such as `/usr/local/lib`, and run the `ldconfig` utility to update the link between `libdobj.so.1` and `libdobj.so.1.0`. Following are the commands you use to install your shared library for everyone's use (you have to be `root` to perform these steps):

```
cp libdobj.so.1.0 /usr/local/lib
/sbin/ldconfig
cd /usr/local/lib
ln -s libdobj.so.1 libdobj.so
```

Dynamically loading a shared library

ELF makes it simple to load a shared library in your program and use the functions within the shared library. The header file `<dlfcn.h>` declares the functions for loading and using a shared library. Four functions are declared in the file `dlfcn.h` for dynamic loading:

- `void *dlopen(const char *filename, int flag);` — Loads the shared library specified by `filename` and returns a handle for the library. The flag can be `RTD_LAZY` (resolve undefined symbols as the library's code is executed); or `RTD_NOW` (resolve all undefined symbols before `dlopen` returns and fail if all symbols are not defined). If `dlopen` fails, it returns `NULL`.

- `const char *dlerror (void);` — If `dlopen` fails, call `dlerror` to get a string that contains a description of the error.

- `void *dlsym (void *handle, char *symbol);` — Returns the address of the specified `symbol` (function name) from the shared library identified by the `handle` (which was returned by `dlopen`).

- `int dlclose (void *handle);` — Unloads the shared library if no one else is using it.

When you use any of these functions, include the header file `<dlfcn.h>` with the following preprocessor directive:

```
#include <dlfcn.h>
```

Following is a simple test program that shows how to load and use the object defined in the shared library `libdobj.so`, which you created in the preceding section:

```
/*-------------------------------------------------------*/
/* File: dltest.c
 *
 * Test dynamic linking.
 *
 */
#include <dlfcn.h>   /* For the dynamic loading functions */
```

```
#include <stdio.h>

void main(void)
{
  void *dlobj;
  void * (*init_call)(char *name);
  void (*show_call)(void *data);
  void (*destroy_call)(void *data);

/* Open the shared library and set up the function pointers */
  if(dlobj = dlopen("libdobj.so.1",RTLD_LAZY))
  {
    void *data;

    init_call=dlsym(dlobj,"init");
    show_call=dlsym(dlobj,"show");
    destroy_call=dlsym(dlobj,"destroy");

/* Call the object interfaces */
    data = (*init_call)("Test Object");
    (*show_call)(data);
    (*destroy_call)(data);
  }
}
```

The program is straightforward: It loads the shared library, gets the pointers to the functions in the library, and calls the functions through the pointers.

You can compile and link this program in the usual way, except you must link with the `-ldl` option so you can use the functions declared in `<dlfcn.h>`. Following is how you build the program `dltest`:

```
gcc -o dltest dltest.c -ldl
```

To see the program in action, run `dltest` as follows:

```
dltest
Created: Test Object
show: Test Object
Destroying: Test Object
```

Although this procedure does not seem exciting, you now have a sample program that uses a shared library.

To see the benefit of using a shared library, go back to the preceding section and make some changes in the shared library (print some other message in a function, for example). Rebuild the shared library alone and run `dltest` again. The resulting printout should show the effect of the changes you made in the shared library, which means you can update the shared library independently of the application.

Summary

Your Linux system comes loaded with all the tools you need to develop software. In particular, you'll find all the GNU software development tools, such as GCC, the GNU debugger, GNU make, and the RCS version-control utility. This chapter describes these software development tools and shows you how to use them. By reading this chapter, you learn the following:

▶ The GNU tools comprise the software development environment on your Linux PC. These tools include GNU Emacs for text editing, GCC for compiling C and C++ programs, GNU make for automating software builds, the GNU debugger for debugging, and the RCS for version control.

▶ A utility named info provides online help information on the GNU tools. You can run info alone or under GNU Emacs with the Ctrl+h i command.

▶ GCC is the GNU C and C++ compiler. You can use the gcc command to compile and link C programs. Use g++ to compile and link C++ programs.

▶ GCC has a plethora of options, but you need to use only a few. Some of the common options are -c (for compiling only) and -o (for specifying the name of the output executable file).

▶ The GNU make utility allows you to automate the build process. You specify the modules that comprise an executable as well as any dependencies; make takes care of compiling only those files that need recompilation. The input file for make is known as a *makefile* and is commonly named Makefile.

▶ The GNU debugger allows you to locate errors in your programs. Use the gdb command to run the debugger. You have to compile the program with GCC's -g option to generate debugging information that the GNU debugger can use.

▶ When you use GNU tools to develop software (as you would in Linux), you should be aware of the GNU licenses: the GNU General Public License (GPL) and the GNU Library General Public License (LGPL). The GNU libraries are covered by the LGPL. If you distribute your software in binary form, you should use dynamic linking to comply with the terms of the LGPL. You should not take anything in this book as constituting legal advice, of course; always consult your own legal counsel for a definitive answer.

▶ Version control is an important aspect of software development. In Linux, you get the RCS (Revision Control System) to manage revisions of source files. With the RCS, you use commands such as ci and co to manage source files. You can embed strings such as Id or $Header$ to mark the revision and date in your source files.

▶ Shared libraries are commonly used in Linux applications to reduce the memory requirement of executables. Applications are dynamically linked with a shared library at run time, and many applications can share a single shared library.

▶ The Linux development community has adopted the Executable and Liking Format (ELF) for binaries. ELF makes dynamic linking simpler to program. This chapter shows you how to use dynamic linking in your own applications.

Chapter 23

X Programming in Linux

Chapter 22 showed you how to use the software development tools in Linux and described how to exploit dynamic linking in your applications. This chapter turns to another important programming topic: how to write applications with graphical user interfaces. This means writing X applications, because the X Window System happens to be the underlying windowing system on Linux.

The primary programming interface to the X Window System is the Xlib library of C functions. You can use Xlib functions to build graphical user interfaces with menus and buttons, using a hierarchy of windows; and display graphics, text, and images in these windows. Although you can do a great deal with Xlib, building complete programs using Xlib functions alone is tedious. To build user interfaces without getting mired in details, you need utility functions and a collection of prefabricated user-interface components, such as buttons, menus, and scrollbars. Luckily, several X toolkits provide the tools that help you build user interfaces easily.

The current crop of X toolkits includes Open Software Foundation's Motif toolkit, Sun's XView and OPEN LOOK Intrinsics Toolkit (OLIT), and the Athena Widgets, to name but a few. Of these, Motif happens to be the most popular toolkit for creating graphical user interfaces.

Unfortunately, Motif is a licensed product of the Open Software Foundation, so the companion CD-ROM does not include Motif. If you want to develop Motif applications, you'll have to buy Motif separately. Nevertheless, I cover Motif programming in this chapter because if you are developing X applications at all, chances are good you'll have to use Motif.

This chapter provides a brief introduction to the Motif toolkit, which is based on Xt Intrinsics. This chapter shows you how to create and manipulate widgets through the functions provided by Xt Intrinsics. The latter part of the chapter provides an overview of the Motif widget set and describes how to use Xlib functions to draw in a Motif application.

If you have not yet purchased Motif for your Linux system, Chapter 4 lists a few vendors of Motif for Linux.

Basic Motif Programming

The Motif toolkit provides a set of user interface components called *widgets*. You can think of each widget as a window with some associated information, such as window dimensions and color. A layer of data structures and functions built with Xlib, *Xt Intrinsics,* provides the necessary data structures for a widget. Xt Intrinsics also automatically handles redrawing a widget's contents when needed.

Just as windows in X are organized in a parent–child hierarchy, with child windows contained within a parent's borders, Motif widgets are organized in a parent–child hierarchy.

If you have never written any applications with graphical user interfaces, you'll have to adapt to a new programming style when you write Motif applications. That new programming style is known as *event-driven programming*.

In an event-driven program, you do not specify the exact sequence of tasks the program must perform. Instead, you define many small functions, each of which is responsible for responding to an event, such as "user has clicked the Save button." The event-driven program waits for events and processes each event by calling the corresponding event-handler function.

You can understand event-driven programming best by going through the simple example presented in the following section.

Step-by-step Motif programming

To write any Motif program, you follow these steps:

1. Include the Motif header files, as follows:

```
#include <Xm/Xm.h>

/* Include header file of each widget you plan to use.
 * For example, here are the necessary header files
```

```
 * for Form, Label, and PushButton widgets.
 */

#include <Xm/Form.h>
#include <Xm/Label.h>
#include <Xm/PushB.h>
```

2. Call the XtAppInitialize function to initialize the toolkit and create a top-level widget. This function returns an identifier (of the data type Widget) that represents the top-level widget.

3. Call XtVaCreateManagedWidget to create each widget and set the widget's internal variables, known as *resources*.

4. Call XtAddCallback to indicate what functions should be called to handle specific events occurring in a widget. These functions are known as *callback functions*. In a Motif program, all work is done in callback functions.

5. Call XtRealizeWidget with the identifier of the top-level widget as the argument. This action realizes (creates) all the widgets.

6. Call the XtAppMainLoop function to begin processing events. This action gets the Motif program running.

A simple Motif program

The following listing shows a simple Motif program that displays a button. The program quits when the user clicks the button.

```
/*------------------------------------------------------*/
/* File: xmquit.c
 *
 * An example program that displays a PushButton
 * inside a Form widget.
 *
 */

#include <Xm/Xm.h>
#include <Xm/Form.h>
#include <Xm/PushB.h>

/* Label for the push button */
static char label[] = "Press here to quit...";

/* Prototype of callback function */
static void cb_quit(Widget w, XtPointer client_data,
             XtPointer call_data);

/*------------------------------------------------------*/
void main(int argc, char **argv)
{
  XtAppContext app;
  Widget    toplevel, quit_button, form;
  XmString    xmlabel;
```

```
    /* Initialize toolkit and create the top-level widget */
      toplevel = XtAppInitialize(&app, "XMquit", NULL, 0,
                    &argc, argv, NULL, NULL, 0);

    /* Create the Form widget */
      form = XtCreateManagedWidget("Form", xmFormWidgetClass,
                    toplevel, NULL, 0);

    /* Create the push button widget as a child of the Form
     * and set its label at the same time. This also shows
     * how to create a "Motif String (XmString)" and use it.
     */

      xmlabel = XmStringCreateLtoR(label,
                    XmSTRING_DEFAULT_CHARSET),
      quit_button = XtVaCreateManagedWidget("Exit",
              xmPushButtonWidgetClass, form,
              XmNlabelString, xmlabel,
              NULL);
      XmStringFree(xmlabel);

    /* Set the callback function for this pushbutton */
      XtAddCallback(quit_button, XmNactivateCallback,
            cb_quit, NULL);

    /* Realize the widgets */
      XtRealizeWidget(toplevel);

    /* Start the event loop */
      XtAppMainLoop(app);
    }
    /*-----------------------------------------------------------*/
    /* c b _ q u i t
     *
     * Function to be called when user presses and releases
     * button in the pushbutton.
     */
    static void cb_quit(Widget w, XtPointer client_data,
                    XtPointer call_data)
    {
      XtCloseDisplay(XtDisplay(w));
      exit(0);
    }
```

Makefile for a Motif program

Use the makefile shown in the following listing to compile and link the xmquit
program. (You need Motif installed on your system.)

```
###############################################################
# Makefile to compile and link a Motif program on Linux

LDFLAGS= -lXm -lXt -lX11 -lXext

all: xmquit
```

```
xmquit.o: xmquit.c

xmquit: xmquit.o
    cc -o xmquit xmquit.o $(LDFLAGS)
```

Type make to build the program, as follows:

```
make
cc  -c xmquit.c -o xmquit.o
cc -o xmquit xmquit.o -lXm -lXt -lX11 -lXext
```

To test the program, first make sure that X is running on your Linux PC. From an xterm window, type xmquit to run the program. Figure 23-1 shows the graphical interface displayed by the xmquit program.

Figure 23-1: Output of the sample Motif program xmquit.

When you click the push button (by pressing and releasing the left mouse button with the pointer inside the push button's window), the program exits.

Widget resources

When you use a Motif widget in an application, you do not need to know details about the widget's data structure. What you need is information about the configurable parameters of the widget. These parameters, known as the widget's *resources*, control its appearance and behavior. A widget's resources simply means any configurable data used by that widget.

To be useful as a building block of user interfaces, a widget has to be highly configurable. A widget that allows the programmer to pick the foreground and background colors, for example, is much more useful than one that hard-wires these values.

As a programmer, you can set a widget's resources through an argument list. To do this, you first have to consult the widget's documentation and learn the names of the resources you want to set. The resource names are constants, such as XmNwidth and XmNheight. You use the constants XmNwidth and XmNheight to refer to the width and height resources of a widget.

To set the values of resources through an argument list, specify the value of each resource in an Arg structure, which is defined in <X11/Intrinsic.h> with the following typedef statement:

```
typedef struct
{
  String  name; /* Name of resource */
  XtArgVal value; /* Its value     */
} Arg, *ArgList;
```

The value of the resource is stored as an XtArgVal — a system-dependent data type capable of holding a pointer to any C variable. If the value of a resource is less than the size of XtArgVal, it is stored directly in the value field of Arg. Otherwise, the value field is a pointer to the resource's value.

When you create a widget, you can specify an array of Arg structures with the values of the resources you want to set. You can prepare the array of resource values in two ways:

- Use a statically initialized array of Arg structures.

- Assign values at run time by using the XtSetArg macro.

To see how to set resources, consider the PushButton widget. Suppose you want to set the push button's width and height as well as its *label* — the text displayed on the button. The documentation of the PushButton widget tells you that the names of the resources are XmNwidth, XmNheight, and XmNlabelString. You also have to know that the string for XmNlabelString is not a simple C character array; it is a *compound string*, a special data type you create by passing the string as an argument to a Motif utility routine (XmStringCreateLtoR).

With that information in hand, you can set the resource values with an Arg array as follows:

```
Arg    args[20];
Cardinal nargs;
XmString cstr;
.

.
cstr = XmStringCreateLtoR("WarnGen",
                          XmSTRING_DEFAULT_CHARSET);
XtSetArg(args[nargs], XmNwidth, 160);    nargs++;
XtSetArg(args[nargs], XmNheight, 80);    nargs++;
XtSetArg(args[nargs], XmNlabelString, cstr); nargs++;
XmStringFree(cstr);
```

There is a reason why nargs++ is not used in XtSetArg to increment the count of arguments; XtSetArg is defined as a macro in such a way that it uses the first argument twice. If you use nargs++ in the first argument, the macro ends up incrementing nargs twice in each call. This result is why most toolkit applications define the argument list as shown.

After you prepare the argument list, call the XtCreateManagedWidget function to create a widget and set its resources, as follows:

```
Arg    args[20];
Cardinal nargs;
Widget  toplevel, /*Previously-created top-level shell */
        pb1;      /* New push-button                  */

pb1 = XtCreateManagedWidget("WarnGen", xmPushButtonWidgetClass,
toplevel,
                            args, nargs);
```

This procedure creates a new push button named WarnGen whose parent widget is toplevel and whose initial resource settings are in the array args.

Tip You can avoid the tedious steps of specifying the resources one by one and then creating the widget. The Xt Intrinsics library includes the XtVaCreateManagedWidget function, which allows you to specify the resources and create the widget with a single function call. You can create a push button with a specified width, height, and label, for example, by using the following call to XtVaCreateManagedWidget:

```
Widget  toplevel, /*Previously-created top-level shell */
        pb1;      /* New push-button                   */
XmString label;   /* Compound string to store label    */

/* First, create the compound string for the label */
xmlabel = XmStringCreateLtoR("WarnGen", XmSTRING_DEFAULT_CHARSET),

h_button = XtVaCreateManagedWidget("WarnGen",
           xmPushButtonWidgetClass, toplevel,
           XmNwidth,    200,
           XmNheight,   100,
           XmNlabelString, xmlabel,
           NULL);

/* Free the compound string (the Motif toolkit
   makes a copy) */
XmStringFree(xmlabel);
```

As the code fragment shows, XtVaCreateManagedWidget accepts a variable number of arguments, as follows:

■ The first three arguments are required and are the same as those required by XtCreateManagedWidget. The first argument is the name of the widget, the second one is the widget class, and the third one specifies the parent widget.

■ Following the three compulsory arguments is a list of resource specifications. Each specification is in the form of a resource name followed by the value of that resource.

■ A NULL resource name marks the end of this list.

Callback registration

Most Motif widgets include a class of resources known as *callbacks*, which are pointers to functions. You can set such a resource to one of your functions and have the widget call that function in response to one or more events. These functions go by the name of *callback functions* because the Motif toolkit calls them back when appropriate.

A widget typically has more than one type of callback resource, with each type meant for functions to be called in a specific situation. A widget's callback resource actually is a list of functions, rather than a single function.

The widget calls all the callbacks when the conditions for that callback resource are met. The calling order is the same as the order in which you register the callbacks.

In the program listed under the heading "A simple Motif program," the function cb_quit is a callback function for the push button widget's XmNactivateCallback resource. According to the PushButton documentation, the widget calls the functions in the XmNactivateCallback resource when the user clicks the button. In addition to XmNactivateCallback, PushButton has two more callback resources:

- XmNarmCallback functions, called when the user clicks the button

- XmNdisarmCallback list, called when the user releases the button

As the example shows, you use the XtAddCallback function to add a function to a callback list of a widget. To add the cb_quit function to the XmNactivateCallback resource of the quit_button widget, use the following:

```
XtAddCallback(quit_button, XmNactivateCallback, cb_quit, NULL);
```

The last argument of XtddCallback — declared to be of type XtPointer — is a pointer to data you want passed to the callback function when the widget calls it. The callback function, cb_quit, has the following prototype:

```
static void cb_quit(Widget w, XtPointer client_data, XtPointer call_data);
```

When the widget calls this function, the second argument will be whatever you passed to XtAddCallback as the last argument. The last argument passed to the callback function is the pointer to an XmAnyCallbackStruct structure, which is defined in <Xm/Xm.h> (refers to the file /usr/include/Xm/Xm.h) as follows:

```
typedef struct
{
  int    reason;  /* Indicates why callback was called  */
  XEvent *event; /* Info on event triggering callback  */
} XmAnyCallbackStruct;
```

Note

The reason field indicates why the widget called the callback function. You have to consult the widget's documentation to interpret the value of this field. The event field is a pointer to an XEvent structure with information on the event that triggered the callback.

Event-handler registration

Suppose you want to allow the user to draw in a widget's window with the mouse. (Motif provides an XmDrawingArea widget for this purpose.) To program this capability, you want to catch the mouse click in the widget's window. The Motif toolkit allows you to do this by using a method similar to the callback resources used by widgets. Essentially, you can register your own event handler for selected events in a widget's window. Thereafter, when these events occur, the widget calls the registered event handler, giving you a chance to take some action.

Use the Xt Intrinsics function `XtAddEventHandler` to add an event handler. To add a function named `event_handler` as the handler for `ButtonPress` events in the `drawing` widget, you would use the following:

```
XtAddEventHandler(drawing, ButtonPressMask, FALSE,
        event_handler, NULL);
```

The first argument of `XtAddEventHandler` is the widget for which you are setting up an event handler. The second argument is an *event mask* (a bit pattern represented by a named constant value) that specifies the events for which the handler is invoked. The third argument is a Boolean value that should be set to `True` if you are setting the event handler for one of the X events — `ClientMessage`, `MappingNotify`, `SelectionClear`, or `SelectionRequest` — for which there is no event mask. In this case, set the second argument to `NoEventMask`. As in `XtAddCallback`, the last argument is a pointer to any data you want passed back to the event handler when it is called.

Note

You have to write the `event_handler` function according to the following prototype:

```
void event_handler(Widget w, XtPointer client_data, XEvent *event);
```

As this function prototype shows, the widget calls the event handler with three arguments:

- The first argument is the widget's ID.

- The second argument is the same pointer you passed as the last argument of `XtAddEventHandler` when you registered this event handler.

- The third argument is a pointer to the `XEvent` structure that triggered the function call.

You'll find a summary of X events in the "X event summary" section.

Motif Widgets

A widget set is like any toolbox; before using the tools, you have to know what each one does. This section provides an overview of the Motif widgets so you can learn the widget categorie and what each category can do. You also should learn how to use important widgets in each category. Then you'll be able to pick the widgets that meet your application's needs. The next few sections provide an overview of the Motif widgets.

There are three distinct categories of Motif widgets:

- *Shell widgets* provide the top-level window for a Motif application. Pop-up dialog boxes also use shell widgets.

- *Primitive widgets* represent the stand-alone widgets, such as labels, push buttons, and scrollbars.

- *Manager widgets* can contain other widgets as children and manage the layout of the child widgets. This category includes forms, message boxes, and scrolled windows.

Note

All Motif widgets inherit the resources of a widget named `Core`. Knowing the resources of the `Core` widget is important, because its resources apply to every widget. Following is a list of the `Core` resources:

- `XmNaccelerators` is the translation table that binds a sequence of keyboard and mouse events to specific actions.

- `XmNancestorSensitive` is a Boolean variable indicating whether the immediate parent of a widget receives input events. To alter this resource setting, call the `XtSetSensitive` function.

- `XmNbackground` is the background pixel value for the widget's window. The pixel value translates to an actual RGB (red-green-blue) color through the current colormap.

- `XmNbackgroundPixmap` is a pixmap (a block of memory that stores an array of pixel values) used to tile the widget's window.

- `XmNborderColor` and `XmNborderPixmap` are the colormap and pixmap for the border of the widget's window.

- `XmNborderWidth` is the width of the border of the widget's window.

- `XmNcolormap` is the colormap to be used by the widget's window.

- `XmNdepth` is the number of bits used for each pixel value in the widget's window. This value is set by Xt Intrinsics when the window is created.

- `XmNdestroyCallback` is the list of functions to be called when you destroy the widget by calling the `XtDestroyWidget` function.

- `XmNheight` and `XmNwidth` are the height and width of the widget's window, excluding the border width.

- `XmNmappedWhenManaged` is a flag that, when set to `True`, maps the widget's window as soon as the widget is realized and managed (the `XtCreateManagedWidget` function manages the widget). You can alter this flag by calling the `XtSetMappedWhenManaged` function.

- XmNscreen is a pointer to the Screen data structure that contains information about the physical display screen where the widget's window is displayed.

- XmNsensitive is a Boolean variable that, when True, causes Xt Intrinsics to dispatch mouse and keyboard events to the widget. To alter this resource, use the function XtSetSensitive.

- XmNTranslations is the *translation table* — a list of events with corresponding functions that are called when the specified events occur.

- XmNx and XmNy are the *x* and *y* coordinates of the upper-left corner of the widget's window, excluding the border. The coordinates are specified in the parent widget's coordinate frame.

Shell widgets

A shell widget manages only one child; its primary purpose is to set up the top-level window of an application. Xt Intrinsics provides several classes of shell widgets, the most important of which are as follows:

- TopLevelShell

- OverrideShell

- TransientShell

When you call XtAppInitialize, Xt Intrinsics creates an instance of the ApplicationShell widget, a subclass of TopLevelShell. The ApplicationShell and TopLevelShell widgets are used for normal top-level windows of applications. The window manager interacts with these top-level windows.

The TransientShell class is used for pop-up dialog boxes, which are top-level windows the user can move but not resize to an icon. To create a dialog box, you actually use a subclass of TransientShell called DialogShell. Motif includes several convenience functions that enable you to create a DialogShell widget and place inside it another widget, such as a selection box or message box. These convenience functions have names that start with XmCreate and end with Dialog (for example, XmCreateFileSelectionDialog or XmCreateMessageDialog).

The OverrideShell widget is a type of Shell widget that completely bypasses the window manager. The window manager does not put any frames around an OverrideShell widget. Motif defines a subclass of OverrideShell — XmMenuShell — to display pop-up menus. You can use the function XmCreatePopupMenu to create a MenuShell with a menu inside it.

Motif versions

The latest version of Motif is 2.0. Much of the UNIX world, however, still uses Motif version 1.2.x. One reason for the persistence of the older version of Motif is the Common Desktop Environment (CDE), which uses X11R5 and Motif 1.2 as the foundation. Motif 2.0 is what you get when you buy one of the commercially available versions of Motif for Linux.

Most Motif distributions include a sample program named `periodic` that displays a periodic table of widgets (remember the periodic table of elements in chemistry?). Following is a screen shot of the periodic table of widgets for Motif 2.0.

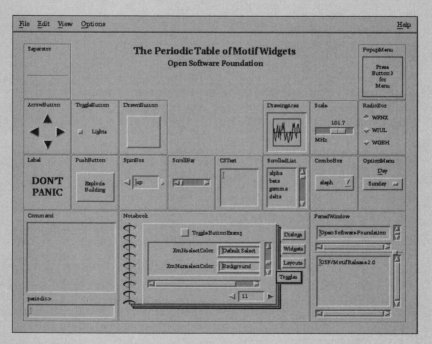

Compared with version 1.2.x, Motif 2.0 has the following new features:

- The addition of six new widgets: `CSText` (compound text editing), `ComboBox` (just like the Microsoft Windows `ComboBox`, a drop-down list with a text-editing area), `SpinButton` (two arrow buttons to cycle through options), `IconGadget` (icon- and text-based list browser), `Container` (manages `IconGadget` widgets), and `Notebook` (displays information in a book with tabbed pages)

- Support of the X Pixmap (XPM) image format for defining color icons

- Unified support for cut and paste as well as drag and drop, through the Uniform Transfer Model (UTM)

- Keyboard support for drag-and-drop operation

- Use of the `XmRenderTable` property to support multiple fonts, colors, underlining, and tab stops in the `XmString` data type

- Inclusion of the C++ classes `XmCxxPrimitive` and `XmCxxManager`, from which you can derive other C++ widget classes

Primitive widgets

All Motif primitive widgets are derived from the XmPrimitive class, which in turn is defined as a subclass of the Core class. The XmPrimitive class defines a standard set of resources inherited by all primitive widgets. In particular, the XmPrimitive class is responsible for the 3-D shading effect of Motif widgets.

Note

The following eight primitive widgets are derived directly from the XmPrimitive class:

- ArrowButton displays a button with an arrow. You can specify the direction of the arrow.

- CSText displays and edits multiple lines of compound strings. The text can include multiple fonts, colors, underlined text, and embedded tabs.

- Label displays a string or a pixmap inside a window.

- List displays a list of text items from which the user can select one or more.

- Sash is used as a separator between two panes. The user can drag the sash to adjust the size of the panes.

- ScrollBar is a scrollbar with arrows at the two ends and a slider. Scrollbars can be horizontal or vertical.

- Separator is used to separate items in a menu.

- Text widget acts as a single- or multiple-line editor.

TextField displays a single line of editable text.

The functionality of the Label class is further specialized by the following subclasses:

- CascadeButton displays an associated pull-down menu when the user clicks the CascadeButton.

- DrawnButton is a button that allows you to draw on it (so you can display whatever you want on the button).

- PushButton is a standard push button.

- TearOffButton is a special push button that displays a tear-off menu.

- ToggleButton displays a string or a pixmap next to a small button. The button represents a state with two values: on or off. When the user clicks the button, it changes state.

All primitive widgets inherit the resources of the XmPrimitive class. Following are some of the important resources of the XmPrimitive class:

- XmNbottomShadowColor is the pixel value used to draw the bottom and right side of a primitive widget's shadow. These two sides are collectively called the *bottom shadow*.

- `XmNbottomShadowPixMap` is the pixmap used to draw the bottom shadow.

- `XmNforeground` is the foreground color to be used in the primitive widgets.

- `XmNhelpCallback` is the list of callbacks that can be bound to functions that provide context-sensitive help.

- `XmNhighlightColor` is the color used to highlight the widget's window. A push button, for example, is highlighted when the user clicks it.

- `XmNhighlightOnEnter` is a Boolean variable that, when set to `True`, asks the widget to highlight its window when the cursor enters the window (provided that the input focus follows the pointer; the window with the input focus gets the keyboard input). This resource is ignored if the user has to click to indicate input focus.

- `XmNhighlightPixmap` is the pixmap used to highlight the widget's window.

- `XmNhighlightThickness` is the thickness of the rectangle used to highlight the widget's window.

- `XmNnavigationType` is a constant that specifies how focus is assigned to the widget during keyboard traversal (keyboard traversal refers to the way the input focus moves from one widget to another as the user presses the Tab key); it can be `XmNONE`, `XmTAB_GROUP`, `XmSTICKY_TAB_GROUP`, or `XmEXCLUSIVE_TAB_GROUP`.

- `XmNshadowThickness` is the thickness of the shadow.

- `XmNtopShadowColor` is the color for the top shadow. Used only if `XmNtopShadowPixmap` is `NULL`.

- `XmNtopShadowPixmap` is the pixmap for the top shadow.

- `XmNtraversalOn` is a Boolean value indicating whether the widget accepts keyboard inputs.

- `XmNunitType` is the measurement unit used for all values that specify dimensions in the widget. The default value is copied from a manager that owns the widget. Usually, the default unit is pixels (specified by the constant `XmPIXELS`). Motif allows you to work in device-independent units, if you prefer. You specify the unit with one of the constants: `XmPIXELS`, `Xm100TH_MILLIMETERS`, `Xm1000TH_INCHES`, `Xm100TH_POINTS`, or `Xm100TH_FONT_UNIT`, defined in the header file `<Xm/Xm.h>`. You can set `XmNunitType` to `Xm100TH_FONT_UNIT`, for example, to indicate that all dimensions are defined in terms of one hundredth of a font's unit. You can explicitly set the font unit with the `XmSetFontUnits` function.

- `XmNuserData` is a pointer not used internally. You can store a pointer to your own widget-specific data in this resource.

Manager widgets

The manager widgets are derived from the XmManager class — a subclass of the Constraint class that in turn inherits from the Composite class. A manager widget can act as a container for other child widgets and manage the layout of the children. Some manager widgets, such as Form, allow you to specify the layout in terms of constraints such as "attach this child widget to the left edge of the container."

All manager widgets inherit their resources from the XmManager class. The XmManager resources are similar to those of the XmPrimitive class.

Following are a few important manager widgets:

- The Command widget is a type of SelectionBox that provides a command-history mechanism. A command-entry area allows the user to type commands. When you execute a command by pressing Enter, that command string is saved in a history buffer, which is displayed in a scrollable list area. You can use the Command widget to accept user input for your command-driven applications.

- The DrawingArea widget provides an empty window in which you can draw graphics or text (using Xlib functions as described in the "Xlib function overview" section later in this chapter).

- The FileSelectionBox widget is a special type of SelectionBox that displays a list of filenames in a list box. The widget has an area in which the user can enter a *file filter*, which is a search string used to locate the files of interest. (.*c , for example, displays all filenames that end with .c.) The user's current selection is displayed in another box. At the bottom of the widget are four buttons labeled OK, Filter, Cancel, and Help.

- The Form widget supports complex layouts specified through certain resources that the widget attaches to each of its children. These resources are known as *constraint resources*; in effect, they provide a layout language you can use to indicate how the child widgets are placed in the Form. Each constraint resource indicates the spatial relationship of a child widget to the Form or to another existing child widget.

- The Frame widget displays a frame (with 3-D shading) around a single child widget.

- The MainWindow widget provides a standard layout for the main window of an application. The MainWindow widget manages a combination of a menu bar, a Command widget, a DrawingArea widget, and scrollbars.

- The MessageBox widget displays a message and a row of three buttons labeled OK, Cancel, and Help.

- The `PanedWindow` widget lays out its children in panes, arranged vertically.

- The `RowColumn` widget arranges its children in rows and columns. You can use `RowColumn` widgets in menu bars and pull-down menus.

- The `Scale` widget displays an elongated rectangle with a slider that allows the user to enter a numerical value. You can set the minimum and maximum values for the scale and for floating-point values; you can specify the number of digits to follow the decimal point.

- The `ScrolledWindow` widget manages a work area (that can contain other widgets) and two scrollbars (horizontal and vertical).

- The `SelectionBox` widget displays a list of items in a scrollable box and provides an area where the current selection is displayed. The widget has three buttons labeled `OK`, `Cancel`, and `Help`. You can optionally turn on or off a fourth button labeled `Apply`.

Xlib and Motif

You can use the Motif widgets to build the user interface of a Motif application, but you cannot build most real-world applications with the Motif widgets alone. Suppose your application is for viewing satellite images for weather forecasting. You can use Motif widgets to allow the user to select a satellite image and even prepare a scrollable viewing area to display the image. To actually display the image, however, you have to rely on Xlib functions. You use Xlib functions for displaying image, graphics, and text in Motif applications. Additionally, you may have to write code that responds to an X event.

Note

The bottom line is that you have to learn the basics of X programming with Xlib functions, even if you use the Motif toolkit to write most of your applications. The next few sections provide an overview of Xlib and X events. You'll also see an example of how to use Xlib drawing functions in a Motif application.

An overview of Xlib

The X Window System uses a client/server model to provide its services. The X server takes care of input and output at the display. X applications are the clients that use the capabilities of the server by sending X protocol requests. The X protocol requests are delivered over a communication link between the clients and the X server. If client and server are running on different machines, this link is a network connection. If both client and server are on the same machine, the communication may be through a shared block of memory or some other interprocess communication (IPC) mechanism supported by the operating system.

Although you could conceivably write an X application that performs all input and output by sending X protocol requests to the server, doing so would be like programming a microprocessor directly in its machine language. To ease the programmer's job, the X Window System includes *Xlib*, a set of C language functions and macros that X applications can use to access the facilities of the X server.

Because Motif is based on X, a Motif application also is an X client; under the hood, a Motif application works by calling Xlib functions.

The primary purpose of Xlib is to provide an easy way for C programmers to send X protocol requests to the server. Xlib, however, is much more than just a set of functions with a one-to-one correspondence to all possible X protocol requests; it also includes many convenience functions to ease the burden of handling common tasks, while hiding the X protocol completely from the programmer. For example, only one X protocol request exists to create a window, but Xlib has two routines for creating windows: `XCreateSimpleWindow` and `XCreateWindow`, of which the first one is simpler than the second. Similarly, the foreground and background colors for a window are specified in a graphics context (GC). To set these colors, you simply call the Xlib routines `XSetForeground` and `XSetBackground`. Xlib takes care of setting up the proper protocol requests to change only these colors in the specified GC.

Xlib also includes many utility functions that don't have anything to do with interacting with the X server. Xlib utility functions help you get the user's choices from a resource file, manipulate screen images and bitmaps, translate names of colors to pixel values, and use the resource manager.

More Information on Xlib and Motif Programming

This chapter provides an overview of Motif programming and how Xlib functions are used in Motif applications. However, a single chapter is not enough to provide all the information that you need to fully exploit the power of Xlib and the Motif toolkit. Because of X and Motif's popularity, there are quite a few books on Xlib and Motif programming. For a more complete discussion of Xlib and the Motif toolkit, consult any of the following books:

- Volume 1: *Xlib Programming Manual*, O'Reilly & Associates, 1993

- Volume 2: *Xlib Reference Manual*, O'Reilly & Associates, 1993

- Volume 6A: *Motif Programming Manual*, Second Edition, Dan Heller, Paula Ferguson, and David Brennan, O'Reilly & Associates, 1994

- *Volume 6B: Motif Reference Manual,* Paula Ferguson and David Brennan, O'Reilly & Associates, 1993

An Xlib function overview

Broadly speaking, Xlib functions allow an application to open the X display (connect to the X server), create windows and draw in them, retrieve events, and finally close the display. If you are developing a Motif application, you can get by with a reasonably small number of Xlib functions. You do not have to worry about opening the display, for example, if you are using the Motif toolkit. In a Motif application, you primarily use the Xlib graphics, image, and text-output functions.

Table 23-1 summarizes the commonly used Xlib functions, grouped according to task. This list is by no means complete, yet it is rather long. As a Motif programmer, you do not have to learn all these functions; I provide this list just to give you an overview of Xlib's capabilities. For complete coverage of Xlib functions, consult the books listed in the "More Information on Xlib and Motif Programming" sidebar.

Table 23-1   Common Xlib functions grouped according to task

Task	Commonly used Xlib functions
Open/close X display	`XOpenDisplay XCloseDisplay`
Get user's choices	`XGetDefault XrmInitialize XrmGetResource XrmParseCommand`
Create/manage windows	`XCreateSimpleWindow XCreateWindow XDestroyWindow XMapRaised XMapWindow XUnmapWindow XGetWindowAttributes XChangeWindowAttributes`
Control window's size and position	`XGeometry XGetGeometry XMoveWindow XResizeWindow XMoveResizeWindow XLowerWindow XRaiseWindow XCirculateSubWindows`
Interact with window manager	`XSetStandardProperties XGetWMHints XSetWMHints`
Get and process events	`XSelectInput XEventsQueued XNextEvent XPeekEvent`
Synchronize with server	`XFlush XSync XSynchronize`
Handle errors	`XGetErrorText XSetErrorHandler XSetIOErrorHandler`
Manipulate graphics contexts	`XCreateGC XChangeGC XCopyGC XFreeGC XSetForeground XSetState XSetBackground XSetFunction`
Draw graphics	`XDrawArc XDrawArcs XDrawLine XDrawLines XSetDashes XSetArcMode XDrawPoints XDrawPoint XDrawRectangle XDrawRectangles XFillArc XFillArcs XSetFillRule XFillRectangle XFillRectangles XFillPolygon XSetLineAttributes`

Task	Commonly used Xlib functions
Clear and copy areas	XClearWindow XClearArea XCopyArea XCopyPlane
Draw text	XLoadFont XLoadQueryFont XSetFont XUnloadFont XDrawString XDrawImageString XDrawText XTextWidth XListFonts
Use color	XDefaultColorMap XDefaultVisual XGetVisualInfo XParseColor XAllocColor XGetStandardColorMap XSetWindowColorMap XFreeColors
Display images	XCreatePixmap XFreePixmap XCreatePixmapFromBitmapData XReadBitmapFile XWriteBitmapFile XCreateImage XDestroyImage XGetImage XPutImage XGetPixel XPutPixel
Handle mouse and keyboard input	XQueryPointer XTranslateCoordinates XCreateFontCursor XDefineCursor XFreeCursor XUndefineCursor XGetMotionEvents XLookupString XRefreshKeyboardMapping XRebindKeysym
Interapplication communication	XInternAtom XChangeProperty XGetWindowProperty XDeleteProperty XSendEvent XGetSelectionOwner XSetSelectionOwner XConvertSelection

Common Xlib features

Although Xlib has a large number of functions, they share some common features. Knowing these common features can help you use Xlib effectively. The common features fall into the following categories:

- Common header files
- Function and data-structure naming conventions
- Order of arguments in function calls

Header files

If you use Xlib functions in a program, you have to include the following header files:

```
#include <X11/Xlib.h>
#include <X11/Xutil.h>
```

The first header file declares the Xlib functions and data structures. The second header file is used by the utility functions of Xlib. Additionally, you may need to include other header files, such as <X11/cursorfont.h>, if you use the standard cursor shapes.

When a header file is named this way (<X11/Xlib.h>), the compiler expects to find the file in the X11 subdirectory of the standard location for header files: the /usr/include directory. Thus, you'll find the file <X11/Xlib.h> in the /usr/include/X11 directory of your system.

Naming conventions

Xlib follows a consistent naming convention for all functions, macros, and data structures. When you know this naming scheme, you can often guess function names and avoid common typing errors. Following are the naming conventions:

- *Functions and macros.* The names of Xlib functions and macros are built by concatenating one or more words, with the first letter of each word capitalized (see Table 23-1 for examples). The names of functions begin with a capital X, but macro names never start with X. In fact, if a function and a macro work identically, the function's name is derived by adding an X prefix to the macro's name. The macro that returns the name of the current X display is `DisplayString`, for example; and the equivalent function is named `XDisplayString`.

- *Data structures.* User-accessible data structures are named just like functions; their names begin with a capital X. Data-structure members are named in lowercase, with underscore characters (_) separating multiple words. The `XImage` data structure, for example, has an integer field named `bits_per_pixel`. This rule does not apply to data structures whose members are not to be accessed by the user. An example is the `Display` data structure, whose name does not begin with X because the user is not supposed to access the internals of this structure directly.

You can use these conventions to select names for your own data structures and functions so they do not conflict with names in Xlib. You can use lowercase names for your variables, and uppercase names for your macros. To be safe, you may decide to add a unique prefix (perhaps your organization's or your project's initials) to all your external functions and variables.

Argument order in Xlib function calls

In addition to the naming conventions, Xlib functions and macros order their arguments in a consistent manner. The arguments appear in the following order:

- *Display.* The display is the first argument of a function or a macro.

- *Windows, fonts, and other X server resources.* X server resources — such as window, font, and pixmap — appear immediately after the display argument. When several resources are used, windows and pixmaps precede all others. The graphics context (GC) appears last among the resources.

- *Source and destination.* Many functions perform tasks that involve taking something from one or more arguments (the source) and storing the result in other arguments (the destination). In these cases, the source arguments always precede the destination arguments.

- *x, y, width, and height.* Many functions take the position (x, y) and size (*width, height*) of windows or pixmaps as arguments. Among x and y, the x argument always precedes y, whereas *width* always comes before *height*. When all four arguments are present, the order is x, y, *width*, and *height*.

- *Bit mask.* Some Xlib functions selectively change one or more members in a structure. You indicate the members being changed by setting bits in a *bit mask* (an integer variable in which each bit position corresponds to a member of the structure). When a function takes a bit mask as an argument, the mask always precedes the pointer to the structure.

Tip

Knowing the convention for argument order is even more helpful than knowing how functions are named. After you get familiar with a few Xlib functions, you can often guess the argument list for a function simply because you know these rules.

X server resources

Chapter 5 uses the term *resource* to mean user-customizable parameters in an application. In the context of the X server, however, *resource* signifies anything created at the request of an application. Thus, X resources include the following:

- Window
- Graphics context (GC)
- Font
- Cursor
- Colormap
- Pixmap

A large part of X programming involves creating and using these resources, because that is how an X or Motif application generates output in windows and accepts input from the mouse and keyboard.

Applications create resources by calling Xlib functions. When your program creates any of these resources, the Xlib function returns a resource ID — a 32-bit identifier (of type `unsigned long` in the C programming language). For your convenience, the header file `<X11/X.h>` uses the C `typedef` statement to define several synonyms — such as `Window`, `Font`, `Pixmap`, `Cursor`, and `Colormap` — for the resource identifiers. Thus, when you create a window, you can refer to the returned resource ID as a `Window`.

Windows

Among the resources of the X server, windows are the most important. Windows are the lifeblood of the X Window System. In X, a *window* is an area of the display screen where an application displays output and accepts input (mouse and keyboard). X allows windows to be nested in a parent–child hierarchy, with all child windows clipped at the boundary of the parent. Whenever an X application draws text or graphics, it must specify a window. Also, all inputs from the mouse and the keyboard are associated with a window. Xlib includes many functions for controlling the size, color, and hierarchy of windows.

Graphics contexts (GC)

To avoid repeatedly sending graphics attributes to the server, X uses the concept of a *graphics context* (GC) — an X server resource that holds all graphics attributes, such as colors and font, necessary for drawing in a window. These graphics attributes control the appearance of the output. The advantage of this approach is that an application can create one or more GCs at the server, initialize them, and later use them for drawing in a window. Because a GC is identified by a resource identifier, you can ask the server to use a specific set of attributes by including a single graphics-context identifier in the drawing request, instead of a variable number of graphics attributes.

To perform text output using the Xlib text-output routine, XDrawString, you have to create the GC and set up the font and colors before calling XDrawString. You can use Xlib routines such as XCreateGC and XChangeGC to create and manipulate GCs.

Fonts

In X, a *font* refers to a collection of bitmaps (a pattern of ones and zeros) representing the size and shape of characters from a set. The X server uses a font to display text in a window. When you call an Xlib function such as XDrawString to draw one or more characters, the server retrieves and draws the image corresponding to each character from the current font.

Cross-Reference

X provides a large number of fonts with a standard naming convention. You have to load one of these fonts before drawing text in a window; otherwise, the server uses a default font. To specify a font, use a resource identifier of type Font. Chapter 5 summarizes the font-naming convention of X.

Cursors

The *cursor* represents the shape of the onscreen pointer that indicates the current position of the mouse. As you move the mouse, the cursor tracks the movement onscreen. A cursor is somewhat similar to a single character from a font. In fact, you can call Xlib's XCreateFontCursor function to create a new cursor by selecting one of the characters from a special cursor font. As with any other resource, when you create a cursor, you get back a resource identifier of type Cursor. After creating a cursor, you can assign it to a window using the function XDefineCursor. If you do not define any cursor for a window, the X server uses the cursor of its parent.

Changing cursors is a useful way to inform users about the special purpose of a particular window. If a window manager allows you to resize a window by dragging the corners of a window's frame, for example, the window manager changes the cursor when the user has the mouse at the corners.

Colormaps

An X display screen uses a block of memory, known as the *frame buffer* (or *video memory*), that is capable of storing a fixed number of bits (usually, 8) for each pixel on the screen. This number is the so-called *pixel value*. The color displayed at each pixel, on the other hand, is the result of varying the intensities of three closely located dots of the basic colors: red (R), green (G), and blue (B). The intensity of these three components is often referred to as the *RGB value* or the *RGB triplet*.

The *colormap* is the key to generating an RGB triplet from a pixel value — it maps a pixel value to an RGB color. For example, if the video memory stores 8-bit pixel values, a pixel can take one of 2^8, or 256, possible values. Thus, the colormap must have 256 entries, and each entry must show the intensities of the R, G, and B components.

When an X application uses colors, it works with pixel values. To ensure that a pixel value appears as the correct color, the application has to identify the colormap used to translate that pixel value to a color. The application does so through the colormap resource.

The video card in most systems can use only one colormap at a time — a situation that led to the concept of installing a colormap. If multiple applications install colormaps independently, the result will be chaos. The convention is that X applications should never install their own colormaps; instead, they should inform the window manager of the colormaps they need. Given the right hints, the window manager will take care of installing the right colormap for each application.

Pixmaps

A *pixmap* is a block of memory in the X server in which you can draw just as you would in a window. In fact, window and pixmap resources are collectively known in X as *drawables*. All drawing functions accept drawables as arguments. What you draw in a pixmap does not appear on the display; to make the contents of a pixmap visible, you have to copy from the pixmap to a window. You can think of a pixmap as an offscreen window — a two-dimensional array of pixel values that can be used to hold graphics images and fill patterns. If each pixel value in a pixmap is represented by a single bit, the pixmap is known as a *bitmap*.

X event summary

Everything in an X application happens in response to events received from the X server. When an application creates a window and makes it visible by mapping it, for example, the application cannot tell whether the server has actually finished preparing the window for output. To draw in that window, the application must wait for a specific event — an Expose event — from the server. All mouse and keyboard inputs from the user also arrive at the X application in the form of events.

Because the basic design of X does not impose any particular style of user interface, X events contain an extraordinary amount of detail. For example, you can get one mouse event when a mouse button is clicked and another when that button is released. For each event, you can find out (among other things) which button was involved, the window that contains the cursor, the time of the event, and the x and y coordinates of the cursor location. This level of detailed event reporting allows programmers to use X to implement any type of user interface.

X provides 33 events for handling everything from mouse and keyboard input to messages from other X clients. Table 23-2 summarizes the X events.

Table 23-2   Summary of X events

Event Name	Meaning
Mouse Events	
ButtonPress	Mouse button clicked with pointer in the window
ButtonRelease	Mouse button released with pointer in the window
EnterNotify	Mouse pointer enters the window
LeaveNotify	Mouse pointer leaves the window
MotionNotify	Mouse moved after stopping
Keyboard Events	
FocusIn	Window receives input focus (all subsequent keyboard events come to that window)
FocusOut	Window loses input focus
KeyMapNotify	Occurs after an EnterNotify or FocusIn event (this is how the X server informs the application of the state of the keys after these events)
KeyPress	Key pressed (when window has focus)
KeyRelease	Key released (when window has focus)
MappingNotify	Keyboard reconfigured (the mapping of a key to a string has changed)
Expose Events	
Expose	Previously obscured window or part of window becomes visible
GraphicsExpose	During graphics copy operations, parts of the source image are obscured (which means that the copied image is not complete)
NoExpose	Graphics copy is successfully completed

Event Name	Meaning
Colormap Notification Event	
ColormapNotify	Window's colormap has changed
Interclient Communication Events	
ClientMessage	Another client has sent a message, using the XSendEvent function
PropertyNotify	Property associated with the window has changed
SelectionClear	Window loses ownership of selection
SelectionNotify	Selection successfully converted
SelectionRequest	Selection needs conversion
Window-State Notification Events	
CirculateNotify	Window raised or lowered in the stacking order
ConfigureNotify	Window moved or resized, or position in the stacking order changed
CreateNotify	Window created
DestroyNotify	Window destroyed
GravityNotify	Window moved because its parent's size changed
MapNotify	Window mapped
ReparentNotify	Window's parent changed
UnmapNotify	Window unmapped
VisibilityNotify	Window's visibility changed (became visible or invisible)
Window-Structure Control Events	
CirculateRequest	Request to raise or lower the window in the stacking order (used by window managers)
ConfigureRequest	Request to move, resize, or restack window (used by window managers)
MapRequest	Window about to be mapped (used by window managers)
ResizeRequest	Request to resize window (used by window managers)

The 33 X events shown in Table 23-2 can be broadly grouped in the following seven categories:

■ *Mouse events*. The X server generates mouse events when the user clicks a mouse button or moves the mouse.

- *Keyboard events.* The server generates keyboard events when the user presses or releases any key on the keyboard. These events are delivered to an application only if a window owned by the application has the input focus. Usually, the window manager decides how the focus is transferred from one window to another. There are two common focus models: clicking a window to type in it (used by the Macintosh and Microsoft Windows), or allowing the focus to follow the mouse pointer (which means the focus is assigned to the window containing the mouse pointer).

- *Expose events.* Of all X events, an `Expose` event is the most crucial; applications draw in their windows in response to this event. Almost all X applications request and process this event. (In Motif applications, most `Expose` events are handled behind the scenes, but you do have to take care of `Expose` events in `DrawingArea` widgets.) The `GraphicsExpose` and `NoExpose` events involve copying from one part of a window or a pixmap to another. These events allow applications to handle situations in which the source of the copy operation is obscured by another window and the contents of the obscured area are unavailable for copying.

- *Colormap notification event.* The server generates a `ColorMapNotify` event whenever an application changes the colormap associated with a window or installs a new colormap. Well-behaved X applications should handle colormap changes through the window manager.

- *Interclient communication events.* These events send information from one X application to another. The concepts of property and selection are used for this purpose.

- *Window-state notification events.* The server generates these events whenever a window is moved or resized, or when its place in the stacking order is altered. These events are useful for keeping track of changes in the layout of windows onscreen. Typically, window managers use these events for this purpose; your application can use them, too, if you want to alter the size and position of the subwindows when the user resizes the topmost window.

- *Window-structure control events.* These events are used almost exclusively by window managers to intercept an application's attempt to change the layout of its windows. By monitoring the `MapRequest` event, for example, the window manager can tell when an application maps its topmost window. When this happens, the window manager can add its own frame to the window and place it at an appropriate location onscreen.

Xlib programming topics

When you write Motif applications, the Motif toolkit takes care of many window-creation and event-handling details for you. All you typically provide are callback functions that perform application-specific tasks. You need to use only a small set of Xlib functions in a Motif application. The following sections provide an overview of the types of Xlib programming you have to perform in a Motif application.

Setting cursor shape and color

The cursor determines the onscreen appearance of the mouse pointer. In X, a cursor is defined by the following parameters:

- Source bitmap

- Mask bitmap

- Foreground and background colors, specified as RGB values

- Hotspot (the point in the cursor's bitmap that defines the location of the pointer on-screen)

The bitmaps are small rectangular arrays of ones and zeros (usually, 16×16 or 32×32). When drawing the cursor, the X server paints the pixels corresponding to ones by using the foreground color, whereas pixels at locations with zeros appear in the background color. The mask bitmap determines the outline within which the cursor shape is drawn. The hotspot determines the pointer location. For many cursor shapes, the hotspot is at the center of the cursor's bitmap. For an arrow cursor, the hotspot is the point of the arrow.

You can assign a cursor to any window in your Motif application. The following example shows how you might create a new cursor from a standard cursor font and assign it to the window of a `DrawingArea` widget in a Motif application:

```
#include <X11/cursorfont.h>
Cursor xhair_cursor;
.
.
.
/* Create a cross-hair cursor for the drawing area. Assume that
"drawing_area"
 * is the name of the DrawingArea widget.
 */
  xhair_cursor = XCreateFontCursor(XtDisplay(drawing_area),
                XC_crosshair);
.
.
/* Change the cursor shape in the DrawingArea (call this after the
 * widgets are realized.
 */
/* Realize all widgets */
  XtRealizeWidget(top_level);

/* Set the cursor for the DrawingArea widget's window */
  XDefineCursor(XtDisplay(drawing_area), XtWindow(drawing_area),
        xhair_cursor);

/* Free the cursor */
  XFreeCursor(XtDisplay(drawing_area), xhair_cursor);
```

After this is done, the cursor shape changes to the cross-hair cursor whenever the pointer enters the window `my_window`. This selection remains in effect until you undefine the cursor for that window by calling `XUndefineCursor`. When you remove the cursor from a window, the server displays the cursor of its parent when the pointer is in that window with an undefined cursor.

Notice that the second argument of `XCreateFontCursor` specifies the cursor shape with a symbolic name. These names are defined in the header file `<X11/cursorfont.h>`.

After assigning a cursor to a window, if you do not intend to refer to it anymore, you can free the cursor by calling `XFreeCursor`. Any window displaying this cursor will continue to do so; the server will get rid of the cursor only after that cursor is not defined for any window. After you undefine a cursor, you must not refer to that cursor's ID again.

When a cursor is created, it has, by default, a black foreground and a white background. To change the color of a cursor, use the `XRecolorCursor` function, as follows:

```
XColor fgcolor, bgcolor; /* Colors in XColor structure */
Cursor arrow_cursor;     /* Cursor whose color is set */

XRecolorCursor(theDisplay, arrow_cursor, &fgcolor, &bgcolor);
```

You have to allocate the foreground and background colors before using them in the `XRecolorCursor` function call.

You also can use your own source and mask bitmaps to define a custom cursor. After you have the two pixmaps (bitmaps are pixmaps of depth 1), you can use `XCreatePixmapCursor` to create a new cursor. This function needs the two pixmaps, the foreground and background colors, and the coordinates of the hotspot, as shown in the following example:

```
Display    *theDisplay;
Cursor     my_cursor;
Pixmap     source, mask;
XColor     fgcolor, bgcolor;
unsigned int x_hot, y_hot;

my_cursor = XCreatePixmapCursor(theDisplay, source, mask,
            &fgcolor, &bgcolor, x_hot, y_hot);
```

Another way to get a cursor is to select a specific character from a font and use the bitmap of that character as a cursor. Before using the font, you have to load the font by calling the `XLoadFont` function. Then you can create the cursor by using the function `XCreateGlyphCursor`.

Drawing graphics and text

To draw graphics or text in an X window, you have to create a *graphics context* (GC) — a data structure (resource) in which the X server stores graphics attributes such as background and foreground colors, line style, and font. The appearance of graphics and text is controlled by these attributes.

Creating a GC

To create a GC, use the Xlib function XCreateGC. This function takes four arguments, in the following order:

- A pointer to the X display

- The ID of a drawable (a Window or a Pixmap variable)

- An unsigned long bit mask that indicates which attributes of the GC you want to specify

- The address of a XGCValues structure

You specify various graphics attributes in the XGCValues structure and use the bit mask to indicate which members of the structure have valid values. Following is an example of how to call XCreateGC:

```
Display    *disp;
Drawable   win;
unsigned long mask;
XGCValues   xgcv;
GC       gc;

/* Set values of selected members of xgcv, as needed.
 * Then set mask. This example sets the foreground and
 * the background pixels to the default white and black
 * colors for the screen.
 */
xgcv.foreground = WhitePixel(disp, DefaultScreen(disp));
xgcv.background = BlackPixel(disp, DefaultScreen(disp));
mask = GCForeground | GCBackground;

gc = XCreateGC(disp, win, mask, &xgcv);
```

Because a GC is a resource, it consumes memory in the X server. Therefore, you should free a GC when it is no longer needed. You can do so with the XFreeGC function, as follows:

```
Display *disp;
GC    gc;

XFreeGC(disp, gc);
```

The X server automatically frees all your application's resources (including GCs) when the application exits, so you need to explicitly destroy a GC only when you have created one for a temporary purpose.

GC attributes

The X server maintains the GC, so you don't need to know the internal details of the GC. You specify the values of a GC's attributes through a XGCValues structure. The basic idea is to set the values of the attributes you want and then create a bit mask to indicate which attributes you are specifying. The X server uses the XGCValues structure together with the bit mask to determine which parts of a GC to change.

The definition of the XGCValues structure gives you an idea of which graphics attributes you can control. Following is how that structure is defined in the <X11/Xlib.h> header file:

```
typedef struct
{
  int        function;          /* Operation on pixels     */
  unsigned long plane_mask;     /* Bit planes affected     */
  unsigned long foreground;     /* Foreground pixel value  */
  unsigned long background;     /* Background pixel value  */
  int        line_width;        /* Line width (0 or more)  */
  int        line_style;        /* One of: LineSolid,
                                           LineOnOffDash,
                                           LineDoubleDash */
  int        cap_style;         /* One of: CapNotLast,
                                   CapButt, CapRound,
                                   CapProjecting            */

  int        join_style;        /* One of: JoinMiter,
                                   JoinRound, JoinBevel     */
  int        fill_style;        /* One of: FillSolid,
                                   FillTiled, FillStippled,
                                   FillOpaqueStippled       */
  int        fill_rule;         /* One of: EvenOddRule,
                                           WindingRule      */
  int        arc_mode;          /* One of: ArcChord,
                                           ArcPieSlice      */
  Pixmap     tile;              /* Pixmap for tiling       */
  Pixmap     stipple;           /* Bitmap for stippling    */
  int        ts_x_origin;       /* x and y offset for tile*/
  int        ts_y_origin;       /* or stipple operations   */
  Font       font;              /* Default font            */
  int        subwindow_mode;    /* One of: ClipByChildren,
                                   IncludeInferiors         */
  Bool       graphics_exposures;/*True=generate exposures*/
  int        clip_x_origin;     /* Origin of clip_mask     */
  int        clip_y_origin;
  Pixmap     clip_mask;         /* Bitmap for clipping     */
  int        dash_offset;       /* Controls dashed line    */
  char       dashes;            /* Pattern of dashes       */
} XGCValues;
```

To set these attributes, you also need the name of the bit mask associated with each member of the XGCValues structure. Table 23-3 lists the bit masks used to select specific members of XGCValues. When you set multiple attributes, use a bitwise-OR (indicated by the C operator |) combination of the masks corresponding to the attributes you want to set.

Table 23-3 also shows the default value of each attribute. When you create a GC without specifying any attribute values, the X server initializes the GC with the default attribute values.

Table 23-3   Bit-mask constants for GC attributes

Attribute name	Bit-mask constant	Description
function	GCFunction	Operation on pixels (Default: overwrite existing pixels)
plane_mask	GCPlaneMask	Bit planes affected (Default: all bitplanes affected)
foreground	GCForeground	Foreground pixel (Default: 0)
background	GCBackground	Background pixel (Default: 1)
line_width	GCLineWidth	Line width (Default: 0)
line_style	GCLineStyle	Line style (Default: solid line)
cap_style	GCCapStyle	How lines end (Default: ends at end point without any projection)
join_style	GCJoinStyle	How lines join (Default: miter join)
fill_style	GCFillStyle	Fill style (Default: solid fill)
fill_rule	GCFillRule	How figures are filled (Default: fill using the even-odd rule, in which a point is inside if a line drawn from outside the figure crosses its edges an odd number of times)
arc_mode	GCArcMode	Appearance of filled arcs as pie slices or closed with a chord (Default: arcs filled as pie slices)
tile	GCTile	Pixmap for tiling (Default: pixmap filled with foreground pixel)
stipple	GCStipple	Bitmap for stippling (Default: bitmap of all ones). The stipple pattern is like a stencil through which the foreground color is applied to a drawable.
ts_x_origin	GCTileStipXOrigin	x-offset for tiling or stippling (Default: 0)
ts_y_origin	GCTileStipYOrigin	y-offset for tiling or stippling (Default: 0)
font	GCFont	Default font for text output (Default: depends on X server)
subwindow_ mode	GCSubwindowMode	Draw into children or not (Default: do not draw into child windows)
graphics_ exposures	GCGraphics Exposures	Graphics exposure events generated if True (Default: True)
clip_x_origin	GCClipXOrigin	x-origin of clip_mask (Default: 0)

(continued)

Table 23-3 *(Continued)*

Attribute name	Bit-mask constant	Description
clip_y_origin	GCClipYOrigin	y-origin of clip_mask (Default: 0)
clip_mask	GCClipMask	Bitmap for clipping (Default: no clip mask used)
dash_offset	GCDashOffset	Starting point in dash pattern (Default: 0)
dashes	GCDashList	Pattern of dashes (Default: pattern of 4 pixels on and then 4 off)

Drawing points

The simplest graphics operation in X is drawing a point in a window or pixmap. You can draw a single point at the coordinates x, y with the following call:

```
Display *disp; /* The connection to the X server   */
Window win;    /* The drawable--a window           */
GC   thisGC;   /* Graphics context for the drawing */
int  x, y;     /* Point to be drawn                */

XDrawPoint(disp, win, thisGC, x, y);
```

The pixel at the location is set to the foreground color specified in the GC. Other attributes in the GC control the final appearance of the point. For example, the point is not drawn if it lies outside the clip mask.

Tip

If you want to draw a large number of points, all using the same GC, you can use the XDrawPoints function to draw them all at the same time with a single X protocol request. Store the points in an array of XPoint structures. The XPoint structure is defined in <X11/Xlib.h>, as follows:

```
typedef struct
{
  short x, y;  /* x and y coordinates of the point */
} XPoint;
```

You call XDrawPoints in the usual manner with a display, a drawable, and a GC as the first three arguments:

```
XPoint pt[10];
int    numpt = 10;
...
XDrawPoints(p_disp, window_1, thisGC, pt, numpt,
            CoordModeOrigin);
```

The array of points and number of points follow the three standard arguments. The last argument tells the server how to interpret the coordinates of the points in the array. You can specify one of the following constants:

- CoordModeOrigin **means that the coordinates are relative to the origin of the window or the pixmap.**

- CoordModePrevious **is used when the coordinate of each point is given in terms of the x and y displacements from the preceding point. The first point is assumed to be relative to the origin of the window.**

Drawing lines

Xlib includes three line-drawing functions:

- **XDrawLine**

- XDrawSegments

- XDrawLines

The XDrawLine **function has the following calling syntax:**

```
XDrawLine(disp, win, thisGC, x1, y1, x2, y2);
```

This function draws a line between the points (x1, y1) and (x2, y2) in the drawable named win, **using the line attributes specified in the GC (**thisGC**).**

XDrawSegments **draws several possibly disjointed line segments, using the same graphics attributes. The segments are specified by means of the** XSegment **structure, which is defined in** <X11/Xlib.h> **as follows:**

```
typedef struct
{
  short x1, y1; /*Coordinates of start-point of segment*/
  short x2, y2; /*Coordinates of end-point of segment  */
} XSegment;
```

The following example shows how to use the XDrawSegments **function to draw several line segments:**

```
Display  *disp;
Window    window_1;
GC        thisGC;
XSegment lines[] =
{
  {50, 80, 150, 200},
  {10, 20, 35, 60},
  {250, 10, 200, 100}
};
int numsegs = sizeof(lines) / sizeof(XSegment);

XDrawSegments(disp, window_1, thisGC, lines, numsegs);
```

The XDrawLines **function is similar to** XDrawPoints, **with one difference:** XDrawPoints **draws points, whereas** XDrawLines **connects them with a line. Call** XDrawLines **with the same arguments you use for** XDrawPoints.

Drawing and filling rectangles

Xlib includes several functions for drawing rectangles. The `XDrawRectangle` function is for drawing a rectangle, given the coordinates of its upper-left corner and its width and height. The function call is of the following form:

```
XDrawRectangle(disp, window, thisGC, x, y, width, height);
```

To draw the outline around the rectangle, this function draws the following lines:

- (x, y) to (x+width, y)
- (x+width, y) to (x+width, y+height)
- (x+width, y+height) to (x, y+height)
- (x, y+height) to (x,y)

You can use the same GC to draw several rectangles by calling `XDrawRectangles`, which expects an array of rectangles and their number as arguments, as follows:

```
XRectangle rects[]; /* Array of rectangles  */
int        nrects;  /* Number of rectangles */

XDrawRectangles(disp, window, thisGC, rects, nrects);
```

The `XRectangle` function is a structure for storing the parameters of a rectangle. The function is defined in `<X11/Xlib.h>` as follows:

```
typedef struct
{
  short      x, y;                 /* Upper-left corner */
  unsigned short width, height; /* Width and height  */
} XRectangle;
```

You can draw a filled rectangle by calling the `XFillRectangle` function. Call this function the same way you call `XDrawRectangle`, with exactly the same arguments. Notice that when you draw a filled rectangle, the width and height of the filled area are exactly the width and height specified in the call to `XFillRectangle`.

`XFillRectangles` is the function for drawing multiple filled rectangles. The function is analogous to `XDrawRectangles` and is called with the same arguments.

Drawing polygons

A *polygon* is a figure enclosed by multiple lines. To draw the outline of a polygon, use the `XDrawLines` function. For filled polygons, Xlib provides the `XFillPolygon` function, which has the following usage:

```
int shape; /* One of: Convex, NonConvex, or Complex */
int mode;  /* One of: CoordModeOrigin or
                       CoordModePrevious           */
```

```
XPoint points[];  /* Vertices of the polygon */
int  numpoints;   /* How many vertices        */

XFillPolygon(disp, win, thisGC, points, numpoints,
              shape, mode);
```

You have to specify the vertices of the polygon in an array of XPoint structures, just as you do when drawing multiple points with XDrawPoints. Also, the mode argument is interpreted the same way as it is for XDrawPoints.

The shape argument helps the server optimize the filling algorithm. Specify Convex for this argument only if your polygon is such that a line drawn between any two internal points lies entirely inside the polygon. (Triangles and rectangles, for example, are convex shapes.)

If the shape is not convex but none of the edges intersect, you should use NonConvex as the shape argument. For polygons with intersecting edges, use Complex. Notice that if you are not sure about a polygon, you can safely specify Complex as the shape. The drawing process may be a bit slower, but the result will be correct.

The fill rule in the GC determines which points are filled by XFillPolygon. You can set the fill rule by calling XSetFillRule.

Drawing arcs, circles, and ellipses

In X, arcs, ellipses, and circles are handled by the arc-drawing functions: XDrawArc and XDrawArcs. The former function is for a single arc, and the latter is for several arcs. Call the XDrawArc function like this:

```
XDrawArc(disp, window, gc, x, y, width, height, angle1, angle2);
```

You can think of an arc as being a part of an ellipse. Drawing an arc involves specifying the *bounding rectangle*, which is the smallest rectangle that completely encloses the ellipse to which the arc belongs. Specify the rectangle with the coordinates of the upper-left corner (x,y) and the dimensions of the rectangle (width and height). Indicate the angle where the arc starts (angle1), as well as its angular extent (angle2).

The X server draws the arc by starting at a point on the ellipse along the angle1 line, where angle1 is measured counterclockwise, with zero degrees along the three o'clock line. Then the server traces over the ellipse in a counterclockwise direction until it covers the angular extent specified by angle2.

The angles angle1 and angle2 are integer values specifying angles in units of $1/64$-degree. Thus, to draw a 60-degree-wide arc starting at 30 degrees from the three o'clock direction, you would use the following call:

```
XDrawArc(p_disp, window, thisGC, x, y, width, height, 30*64, 60*64);
```

You can draw an ellipse by starting at zero degrees and specifying an extent of 360*64. If the width and height of the bounding rectangle are equal, you get a circle.

Drawing text

To display text, you first need to select a font. In X, fonts are resources residing in the server. Applications have to load a font before using it. When the X server successfully loads a font, it returns a resource ID that the application subsequently uses to refer to that font. In Chapter 5, you learned how to name a font. When the name is known, you can load a font by calling the XLoadFont function as follows:

```
Display *disp; /* Identifies connection to X server   */
char   fontname[]="*helvetica-bold-r*140*";/*Font Name */
Font   helvb14;                            /* Font id   */
.
.
.
if((helvb14 = XLoadFont(disp, fontname)) == None)
{
  fprintf(stderr, "Cannot load font: %s\n", fontname);
/* Handle error. Probably just use the default font */
/* ... */
}
```

When the XLoadFont function returns a nonzero value (meaning that the function is successful), you can start using the 14-point, bold Helvetica font, shown in the example, by setting the font attribute of a GC. To do this, call XSetFont as follows:

```
XSetFont(disp, thisGC, helvb14);
```

Subsequently, whenever any text is drawn with this GC, the output will be in 14-point, bold Helvetica.

Because fonts are server-resident resources, when your application no longer needs a font, you should release the font with the XUnloadFont function. This function call has the following form:

```
XUnloadFont(p_disp, helvb14);
```

Notice that if you have a GC with helvb14 as the font, and you unload that font, the X server does not actually unload the font until that GC is destroyed.

After you have a GC with the appropriate font, your application can call one of the following functions to display text:

- XDrawString(Display* display, Drawable d, GC gc, int x, int y, const char* string, int length); — Draws text string in foreground color only.

- XDrawImageString(Display* display, Drawable d, GC gc, int x, int y, const char* string, int length); — Draws characters using both foreground and background colors.

- XDrawText(Display* display, Drawable d, GC gc, int x, int y, XTextItem* items, int nitems); — Draws several text strings on a line.

Each function draws several characters on a single line. The first two functions draw all the characters using the font specified in the GC you provide as an argument. The functions are called in the same way, as follows:

```
char string[]; /* String to be displayed       */
int  nchars;   /* Number of characters in string */

XDrawString(disp, window, thisGC, x, y, string, nchars);
XDrawImageString(disp, window, thisGC, x, y, string, nchars);
```

You specify a starting position, where the server places the origin of the first character's bitmap. Then the server copies the foreground pixel value (from the GC) to all pixels corresponding to ones in the bitmap. XDrawString does not alter the pixels where the bitmap is zero. XDrawImageString, on the other hand, also fills the pixels corresponding to zeros in each character's bitmap with the GC's background color (using the stipple or tile, if any).

Tip

If you want to use more than one font on the same line of text, use the XDrawText function. This function accepts information about the string segments in a XTextItem structure, which is defined in <X11/Xlib.h> as follows:

```
typedef struct
{
    char *chars;  /* Pointer to the string to be drawn   */
    int nchars;   /* Number of characters in string       */
    int delta;    /* Dist. from last char of prev. string*/
    Font font;    /* Font = None means use GC's font      */
} XTextItem;
```

Each XTextItem structure contains information about a single block of text. The first two members identify the string and its length. The member named delta is an offset, in pixels, applied before drawing this string. The last member specifies the font to be used when drawing this string. When calling XDrawText, you have to provide the usual Display pointer, drawable, and GC, followed by the location where the string should appear and the strings in an array of XTextItem structures, as follows:

```
XTextItem text_chunks[]; /*Array of strings to display */
int numchunks;          /* Number of XTextItem structures  */

/* Initialize "text_chunks" first ... */


XDrawText(disp, window, thisGC, x, y, text_chunks, numchunks);
```

XDrawText displays each string using the font specified in the font field of the corresponding XTextItem structure. The function does so by loading the font into the GC you provide in the function call. If the font field in the XTextItem is set to None, XDrawText uses whatever font the GC happens to have.

Using drawing functions in Motif

To use Xlib functions in any application, you need the `Display` pointer; the window ID; and, for drawing functions, a graphics context (GC). Xt Intrinsics (the foundation on which Motif is built) provide macros and functions to get these parameters for any widget.

Display and window ID

Motif applications work with widgets, but most Xlib functions require a pointer to the `Display` structure and a window identifier as arguments. Given a widget ID, you can get the pointer to its `Display` structure by using the `XtDisplay` function. Similarly, the `XtWindow` function returns the ID of the window associated with a widget.

Suppose you want to use the Xlib function `XClearWindow` to clear a widget's window. Given the widget ID `w`, you can do this with the following code fragment:

```
#include <X11/Intrinsics.h>

Widget  w;
Display *p_disp;
Window  win;

p_disp = XtDisplay(w);
win = XtWindow(w);
XClearWindow(p_disp, win);
```

The window ID returned by `XtWindow` will be `NULL` if the widget has not been realized. The `Display` pointer, however, is valid immediately after the widget is created if you call `XtCreateWidget` or another equivalent function.

GC creation in Motif

To draw text and graphics in a widget's window, you have to create one or more GCs. When using Xlib alone, you use functions such as `XCreateGC`, `XCopyGC`, and `XChangeGC` to create and manipulate GCs. Xt Intrinsics provides the function `XtGetGC` for creating GCs. This function tries to minimize the number of GC creations by keeping track of the GCs created by all the widgets in an application. Xt Intrinsics creates a new GC only when none of the existing ones has attributes matching what you request in the `XtGetGC` call.

When creating a GC for a widget, you should get the foreground and background pixel values from the widget's resources. That way, you will be using the foreground and background colors the user may have specified for that widget in a resource file.

You get the value of a widget's resources by calling `XtGetValues`. The steps are similar to those involved in setting resource values. Suppose you want the foreground and background colors for the `DrawingArea` widget named `drawing_area`. The following example shows how you can get these values and set up a GC with these attributes:

```
Arg     args[20];
Cardinal  narg;
```

```
  Widget   drawing_area;
  XGCValues xgcv;
  GC       theGC;
  int      fg, bg;

/* Retrieve the background and foreground
 * colors from the widget's resources.
 */
  narg = 0;
  XtSetArg(args[narg], XmNforeground, &fg); narg++;
  XtSetArg(args[narg], XmNbackground, &bg); narg++;
  XtGetValues(drawing_area, args, narg);

/* Now, define a GC with these colors */
  xgcv.foreground = fg;
  xgcv.background = bg;
  theGC = XtGetGC(drawing_area, GCForeground | GCBackground,
        &xgcv);
```

Notice that when you retrieve a resource's value, you provide the address of a variable in which XtGetValues places the value.

After you create the GC, you can manipulate it with Xlib functions. Note, however, that the GC returned by XtGetGC is read-only; hence, you cannot change it. Use XCreateGC if you need a GC you can change.

A Motif line-drawing program

The following listing shows xmlines, a Motif line-drawing program. The program can draw rubber-band figures. When the user first clicks the left mouse button in the drawing area, one corner of the line is marked. As the user moves the mouse while holding down the mouse button, the line appears to move in keeping with the mouse movement. The final line is drawn when the user releases the button.

```
/*-----------------------------------------------------*/
/* File: xmlines.c
 *
 * A Motif program that draws lines.
 */
 /*-----------------------------------------------------*/
#include <stdio.h>

#include <X11/Xlib.h>
#include <X11/Xutil.h>
#include <X11/cursorfont.h>

#include <Xm/Xm.h>
#include <Xm/RowColumn.h>
#include <Xm/MainW.h>
#include <Xm/DrawingA.h>

#define MAXARGS    20
#define MAXLINES   100
#define WIDTH      400
#define HEIGHT     300
```

```c
static char message[] =
 "Hold down left mouse button, move, and then release.";
static int msglen = XtNumber(message) - 1;

/* Array of lines */

XSegment lines[MAXLINES];
int    numlines = 0;
int    curline = 0;

GC  theGC;   /* GC for regular drawing */
GC  xorGC;   /* GC used for rubber-band drawing */

Cursor xhair_cursor;

/* Function prototypes */

/* These are callbacks */
void start_rubberband(Widget w, XtPointer data, XEvent *p_event,
          Boolean *cdispatch);
void continue_rubberband(Widget w, XtPointer data, XEvent *p_event,
          Boolean *cdispatch);
void end_rubberband(Widget w, XtPointer data, XEvent *p_event,
          Boolean *cdispatch);

void handle_expose(Widget w, XtPointer client_data, XtPointer other);

/* This function draws the lines */
static void draw_line(Display *d, Window w, GC gc, int curline);

/*-----------------------------------------------------------*/
void main(int argc, char **argv)
{
  Widget    top_level, main_window, drawing_area;
  Arg       args[MAXARGS];
  Cardinal  argcount;
  int       fg, bg;
  XGCValues xgcv;
  XtAppContext app;

/* Create the top-level shell widget and initialize the toolkit*/
  top_level = XtAppInitialize(&app, "XMlines", NULL, 0,
                &argc, argv, NULL, NULL, 0);

/* Next, the main window widget */
  argcount = 0;
  XtSetArg(args[argcount], XmNwidth, WIDTH);  argcount++;
  XtSetArg(args[argcount], XmNheight, HEIGHT); argcount++;
  main_window = XmCreateMainWindow(top_level, "Main",
                    args, argcount);
  XtManageChild(main_window);

/* Create the drawing area */
  argcount = 0;
  XtSetArg(args[argcount], XmNresizePolicy, XmRESIZE_ANY);
  argcount++;
```

```
  drawing_area = XmCreateDrawingArea(main_window,
              "drawing_area", args, argcount);
  XtManageChild(drawing_area);

/* Attach the drawing area to main window */
  XmMainWindowSetAreas(main_window, NULL, NULL, NULL,
            NULL, drawing_area);

/* Create the GCs. First retrieve the background and foreground
 * colors from the widget's resources.
 */
  argcount = 0;
  XtSetArg(args[argcount], XmNforeground, &fg); argcount++;
  XtSetArg(args[argcount], XmNbackground, &bg); argcount++;
  XtGetValues(drawing_area, args, argcount);

/* Define a GC with these colors */
  xgcv.foreground = fg;
  xgcv.background = bg;
  theGC = XtGetGC(drawing_area, GCForeground | GCBackground,
          &xgcv);
/* Set up a GC with exclusive-OR mode (for rubber-band drawing)*/
  xgcv.foreground = fg ^ bg;
  xgcv.background = bg;
  xgcv.function = GXxor;
  xorGC = XtGetGC(drawing_area, GCForeground |
          GCBackground | GCFunction, &xgcv);

/* Add callback to handle expose events for the drawing area */
  XtAddCallback(drawing_area, XmNexposeCallback, handle_expose,
        &drawing_area);

/* Create a cross-hair cursor for the drawing area */
  xhair_cursor = XCreateFontCursor(XtDisplay(drawing_area),
                  XC_crosshair);

/* Add event handlers for button events to handle the drawing */
  XtAddEventHandler(drawing_area, ButtonPressMask, False,
          start_rubberband, NULL);
  XtAddEventHandler(drawing_area, ButtonMotionMask, False,
          continue_rubberband, NULL);
  XtAddEventHandler(drawing_area, ButtonReleaseMask, False,
          end_rubberband, NULL);

/* Realize all widgets */
  XtRealizeWidget(top_level);

/* Change the cursor for the drawing area */
  XDefineCursor(XtDisplay(drawing_area), XtWindow(drawing_area),
        xhair_cursor);

/* Set up a grab so that the cursor changes to a cross-hair and
 * is confined to the drawing_area while the mouse button is
 * pressed. This is done through what is known as a "grab"
 */
  XGrabButton(XtDisplay(drawing_area), AnyButton, AnyModifier,
```

```
            XtWindow(drawing_area), True, ButtonPressMask|
            ButtonMotionMask | ButtonReleaseMask,
            GrabModeAsync, GrabModeAsync,
            XtWindow(drawing_area), xhair_cursor);

/* Free the cursor */
  XFreeCursor(XtDisplay(drawing_area), xhair_cursor);

/* Start the main event-handling loop */
  XtAppMainLoop(app);
}
/*------------------------------------------------------------*/
/* s t a r t _ r u b b e r b a n d
 *
 * Start of rubber-band line
 */
void start_rubberband(Widget w, XtPointer data, XEvent *p_event,
          Boolean *cdispatch)
{
  int x = p_event->xbutton.x,
    y = p_event->xbutton.y;

/* Crude check to ensure that we don't exceed array's capacity */
  if(numlines > MAXLINES-1) numlines = MAXLINES-1;
  curline = numlines;
  numlines++;

  lines[curline].x1 = x;
  lines[curline].y1 = y;
  lines[curline].x2 = x;
  lines[curline].y2 = y;
  draw_line(XtDisplay(w), XtWindow(w), xorGC, curline);
}
/*------------------------------------------------------------*/
/* c o n t i n u e _ r u b b e r b a n d
 *
 * Handle mouse movement while drawing a rubber-band line
 */
void continue_rubberband(Widget w, XtPointer data, XEvent *p_event,
          Boolean *cdispatch)
{
  int x = p_event->xbutton.x,
    y = p_event->xbutton.y;

/* Draw once at old location (to erase line) */
  draw_line(XtDisplay(w), XtWindow(w), xorGC, curline);

/* Now update end-point and redraw line */
  lines[curline].x2 = x;
  lines[curline].y2 = y;
  draw_line(XtDisplay(w), XtWindow(w), xorGC, curline);
}
/*------------------------------------------------------------*/
/* e n d _ r u b b e r b a n d
 *
 * End of rubber-band drawing
```

```
   */
void end_rubberband(Widget w, XtPointer data, XEvent *p_event,
          Boolean *cdispatch)
{
  int x = p_event->xbutton.x,
    y = p_event->xbutton.y;

/* Draw once at old location (to erase line) */
  draw_line(XtDisplay(w), XtWindow(w), xorGC, curline);

/* Now update end-point and redraw line in normal GC */
  lines[curline].x2 = x;
  lines[curline].y2 = y;
  draw_line(XtDisplay(w), XtWindow(w), theGC, curline);
}
/*-------------------------------------------------------*/
/* h a n d l e _ e x p o s e
 *
 * Expose event-handler for the drawing area
 */
void handle_expose(Widget w, XtPointer data, XtPointer other)
{
  XmDrawingAreaCallbackStruct *call_data =
          (XmDrawingAreaCallbackStruct*)other;
  XEvent *p_event = call_data->event;
  Window win = call_data->window;
  Display *p_display = XtDisplay(w);

  if(p_event->xexpose.count == 0)
  {
    int i;
/* Clear the window and draw the lines in the "lines" array*/
    XClearWindow(p_display, win);

    if(numlines > 0)
    {
      XDrawSegments(p_display, win, theGC, lines, numlines);
    }
  }

/* Display the message (this is an example of text output) */
  XDrawImageString(p_display, win, theGC, 50, 30, message,
          msglen);
}
/*-------------------------------------------------------*/
/* d r a w _ l i n e
 *
 * Draw a specified line from the lines array.
 */
static void draw_line(Display *d, Window w, GC gc, int curline)
{
  int x1 = lines[curline].x1, y1 = lines[curline].y1,
    x2 = lines[curline].x2, y2 = lines[curline].y2;

  XDrawLine(d, w, gc, x1, y1, x2, y2);
}
```

Tip

To build the `xmlines` program, use the following command:

```
gcc -o xmlines xmlines.c -lXm -lXt -lX11 -lXext
```

Figure 23-2 shows the output of the `xmlines` program.

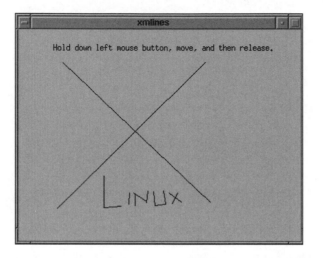

Figure 23-2: Output of the `xmlines` program, showing some lines.

Using color

X incorporates an abstract color model that captures most of the capabilities of common color graphics hardware. To use color in an X application, you need to understand the color model X uses.

Visuals

X encapsulates the common features of the display hardware in a data structure called the `Visual`. X adds an important twist to encourage the sharing of colormaps, however, by allowing colormaps to be read-only or read-write. Cells in the read-write colormaps can be changed dynamically, whereas read-only colormaps are fixed.

The class member of the `Visual` structure indicates the color capabilities of the underlying graphics display. Based on the classification of color and gray-scale displays together with X's notion of read-write and read-only colormaps, there are six distinct classes of `Visual`s, identified by the following names (defined in `<X11/X.h>`):

- `DirectColor` visual represents a display in which the pixel value is decomposed into bit fields that index into individual colormaps for the R, G, and B components. The colormap entries can be changed dynamically. This visual class is common among displays that have 24-bit planes.

- `TrueColor` displays are the same as `DirectColor`, but their colormaps are fixed.

- The PseudoColor visual class models a common type of display hardware — one in which each pixel value looks up an RGB value and in which the colormap can be modified at any time.

- StaticColor displays are similar to PseudoColor, except that the colormap cannot be modified.

- GrayScale visual represents a gray-scale monitor that allows the intensity map to be modified. The GrayScale visual is the gray-scale equivalent of the PseudoColor visual.

- StaticGray is similar to GrayScale but has a fixed gray-level map. Black-and-white (monochrome) displays are modeled by a StaticGray visual with a depth of 1.

Each screen in an X display has at least one associated visual structure. Many servers provide more than one visual for a screen. The server for an 8-bit display, for example, might provide a PseudoColor visual of depth 8 and a StaticGray visual of depth 1. Thus, windows on the same screen can be used as a color window or, in the case of StaticGray, as a monochrome window.

Note

Even if a server supports multiple visuals, one of them is the default visual. You can refer to this default visual by using the macro DefaultVisual(display,screen), which returns a pointer to the Visual structure of the specified screen in the X display identified by display.

Available visuals

To see a list of visuals supported by the X server on your system, start X (use the startx command) and then type the following command at the shell prompt:

```
xdpyinfo -display :0.0
```

The xdpyinfo program displays a great deal of information about the X server, including the number of visuals. Typically, the X server supports six visuals, the default one being an 8-bit PseudoColor visual.

Typically, you do not have to select any visual, because the default visual is adequate for most applications. If your system has a 24-bit graphics card and the default visual is 8-bit, however, you may want to explicitly select and use a 24-bit visual.

Secret

To use a nondefault visual in a Motif application, you have to specify three resources — visual type, colormap, and depth — of the top-level shell before the widget is realized.

X colormap

In X, each window has an associated colormap that determines how the pixel values are translated into colors (or gray levels, in gray-scale monitors). Although the hardware may allow only one colormap, X allows each window to have its own colormap, as long as the visual class of the screen is not TrueColor, StaticColor, or StaticGray. Before the pixel values in a window are interpreted according to such a *virtual colormap*, that colormap has to be installed in the hardware colormap. You need a window manager to take care of this chore. By convention, most window managers implement a policy of installing a window's colormap in the hardware as soon as the window gains input focus.

A colormap is a resource of the X server. Normally, you do not have to create a new colormap for your application. When the server is started, it creates and installs a default colormap. The server normally defines only two color cells in this default colormap. The rest of the cells can be allocated and used by any X application.

Note

To use colors from a colormap, you first have to find the colormap's identifier, which is a variable of type `Colormap`. When you create a new colormap, you get back an ID. For the default colormap, the colormap's ID is returned by the macro `DefaultColormap(display,screen)`, which requires you to identify the display and the screen. You can use `DefaultScreen(display)` as the screen argument for `DefaultColormap`.

Colors from a colormap

When you use color in a Motif application, you have to specify a pixel value. The pixel value implies a particular color, depending on the contents of the colormap cell it references. The first step in using a color in X is to obtain the index of a colormap cell containing the red, green, and blue intensities appropriate for the color you want. To do this, you request that the X server allocate a colormap cell (in a specified colormap) with your color. When requesting a colormap cell, you provide the desired red, green, and blue levels; the X server returns an index you can use as the pixel value corresponding to that color.

Note

Because many applications may use similar colors, X provides two ways to allocate colormap cells:

■ Shared read-only cells

■ Private read-write cells

Shared read-only color cells

You can allocate shared read-only cells in any visual class, but to allocate read-write cells, the visual class must allow the colormap to be altered. That means the visual class has to be `DirectColor`, `PseudoColor`, or `GrayScale`.

For each colormap, the X server keeps track of the cells currently in use. When the server receives a request for a shared read-only cell in a colormap, it determines the closest color that the hardware can support; then it searches any previously allocated read-only cells in that colormap for one that may already contain that color. If the server finds such a cell, it returns the information about it. Otherwise, if the visual class permits writing to the colormap, the server allocates a new cell for read-only use, loads the requested color into the cell, and returns that information.

The nice thing about shared read-only colormap cells is that you can use them on any visual; to allocate private read-write colormap cells, you have to make sure the visual is DirectColor, PseudoColor, or GrayScale.

Private read-write color cells

Private read-write cells also have some advantages. These cells allow you to alter the mapping of pixel to color at any time. This capability can be useful for displaying images; you can change the colors of an image by altering the colormap entries without having to redraw the image with new pixel values.

Also, private colormap cells can be allocated in a single contiguous block so that the pixel values are in sequence. This capability can be useful if the application requires the displayed colors to relate to the pixel values in a well-defined way. An example is a satellite image displayed in a gray scale that associates a gray level to each data level in the satellite image.

XColor structure

When you are allocating colors or defining new colormap entries, you provide information about the color in an XColor structure, which is defined in <X11/Xlib.h> as follows:

```
typedef struct
{
  unsigned long pixel; /*Pixel value (after allocation)*/
  unsigned short red,   /* Red intensity (0 - 65,535)   */
              green,   /* Green intensity (0 - 65,535) */
              blue;    /* Blue intensity (0 - 65,535)  */
  char      flags;    /* Used when storing colors    */
  char      pad;  /* Added to make structure size even */
};
```

You should specify a color by indicating the intensities of the RGB components in the fields red, green, and blue. These intensities range from 0 to 65,535; 0 implies no intensity, and 65,535 means full intensity. The server automatically scales these values to the range of intensities needed by the display screen's hardware.

The field named pixel is the pixel value you use to display the color corresponding to the RGB value in red, green, and blue. When allocating a color, you provide the RGB values for the color; the X server returns the pixel value corresponding to the colormap cell with that color.

Read-only colormap cell allocation

Xlib provides two functions for allocating shared read-only colormap cells:

- XAllocColor
- XAllocNamedColor

The XAllocColor function requires that you define a XColor structure and then fill in the red, green, and blue fields with the RGB levels for the color you want. You also have to specify the colormap in which you want to allocate the color. Typically, you use XAllocColor in conjunction with XParseColor, which accepts the name of a color and sets up the corresponding RGB values in an XColor structure.

To allocate a light cyan color in the default colormap and use it as the background of a window, for example, you might use the following code (see Chapter 5 for information on naming colors in X applications):

```
Display    *disp;
  XColor    color;
  Colormap   default_cmap;
  unsigned long bgpixel;

  default_cmap = DefaultColormap(disp,
                        DefaultScreen(disp));

/* Try to allocate a "light cyan" colormap cell */

  if (XParseColor(disp, default_cmap, "light cyan",
               &color) == 0 ||
    XAllocColor(disp, default_cmap, &color) == 0)
  {
/* Use white background in case of failure */
    bgpixel = WhitePixel(disp, DefaultScreen(disp));
  }
  else
  {
/* Colormap cell successfully allocated */
    bgpixel = color.pixel;
  }
.
.
/* Use "bgpixel" as background when creating the window */
```

First, XParseColor sets up the RGB values for the color named light cyan. Then XAllocColor requests a read-only color cell with that RGB value. If all goes well, both functions return nonzero values, and the pixel member of color contains the pixel value you should use wherever you need the light cyan color. If the functions fail, you must include some means to handle the situation. In this example, if the allocation fails, the white color is used as the background color. The server always allocates the white and black colors in the default colormap. You can refer to these colors by using the macros WhitePixel(display,screen) and BlackPixel(display,screen), respectively.

The X server provides a color database that applications can use to translate the textual names of colors into red, green, and blue intensities appropriate for that particular display screen. The functions XParseColor and XAllocNamedColor use this database.

XAllocNamedColor is similar to XAllocColor, except that it directly takes the name of a color as a string. When you use XAllocNamedColor, the earlier example of allocating a light-cyan cell becomes the following:

```
XColor exact; /* Exact RGB definition of color */

if (XAllocNamedColor(disp, default_cmap, "light cyan",
        &exact, &color) == 0)
{
/* Use white background in case of failure */
    bgpixel = WhitePixel(disp, DefaultScreen(disp));
}
else
{
/* Colormap cell successfully allocated */
    bgpixel = color.pixel;
}
```

XAllocNamedColor requires two XColor arguments. In the XColor structure named exact, XAllocNamedColor returns the exact RGB value for the requested color (from the database); in color, it returns the closest color supported by the hardware and the pixel value corresponding to the allocated colormap cell (when allocation succeeds).

Read-write colormap cell allocation

Some applications need colors to be allocated in the colormap in a specific way. You can, for example, display a two-dimensional array of weather-satellite data as an image in which the color of each pixel represents a data point. When you display such an image, you may want all pixel values to appear in sequence so you can easily map the data into colors. You also may want to alter the mapping of data to colors to bring out features of the data. This type of need is best handled by allocating a contiguous block of private read-write colormap cells.

To allocate read-write color cells, call the XAllocColorCells function. Before you use this function, of course, you must make sure that the screen's visual class allows alterations to the colormap (the class must be DirectColor, PseudoColor, or GrayScale).

Following is how you should call XAllocColorCells:

```
Display    *disp;
Colormap   cmap;  /* Colormap where cells are allocated*/
Bool       contig;  /* True = allocate contiguous planes */
unsigned long planes[]; /* Array to hold plane masks    */
unsigned int nplanes;   /* Number of planes to allocate*/
unsigned long pixels[]; /* Array to hold pixel values   */
unsigned int npixels;   /* Number of pixels to allocate*/

if(!XAllocColorCells(disp, cmap, contig, planes, nplanes, pixels,
npixels))
{
/* Error allocating color cells */
/* ... */
}
```

X requires you to specify the read-write colormap cells in a unique manner. You specify the number of pixel values (`npixels`) and the number of planes (`nplanes`); `npixels` must be positive, whereas `nplanes` can be zero or positive. In return, the server reserves `npixels*`$2^{nplanes}$ colormap cells and returns the information about the usable cells in the arrays named `pixels` and `planes`. `npixels` values are returned in `pixels`, and `nplanes` bit masks are returned in the `planes` array.

If you want to allocate a single read-write colormap cell, you call `XAllocColorCells` as follows:

```
Display    *disp;
Colormap   cmap;    /* Colormap where cells are allocated*/
unsigned long pixels[1];

if(!XAllocColorCells(disp, cmap, False, NULL, 0, pixels, 1))
{
/* Error allocating color cells */
/* ... */
}
/* Successfully allocated color cell. The pixel value is pixels[0] */
```

After you call `XAllocColorCells` to allocate private read-write colormap cells, you must store colors in these cells before using them. Use `XStoreColor` to change the RGB value corresponding to a single pixel value; you have to use an `XColor` structure to do this. Set the `red`, `green`, and `blue` fields to the desired levels of the primary color. Set `pixel` to the pixel value of an allocated (read-write) cell. Then call `XStoreColor` as follows:

```
  Colormap colormap;
  XColor   color;
/* Assume that colorcell is a previously allocated read-
 * writecell. The following code stores "red" in
 * this cell
 */
  color.pixel = colorcell;
  color.red = 65535;
  color.green = 0;
  color.blue = 0;
  color.flags = DoRed | DoGreen | DoBlue;
  XStoreColor(disp, colormap, &color);
```

The `flags` field in `color` indicates which of the primary color levels in the colormap cell should be updated.

Tip

To set a single colormap cell with a color identified by a name, rather than the RGB components, you can use `XStoreNamedColor`. To set pixel value `colorcell` to red, you use the following:

```
XStoreNamedColor(p_disp, colormap, "red", colorcell,
        DoRed | DoGreen | DoBlue);
```

If you have several read-write colormap cells to initialize, you can use XStoreColors to store colors in them at the same time. As expected, this function takes an array of XColor structures and the number of such structures as arguments, as follows:

```
XColor colors[]; /* Array of colors      */
int  ncolors;    /* Number in colors array */
.

.
/* Set up the "colors" array before calling XStoreColors */

XStoreColors(p_disp, colormap, colors, ncolors);
```

Freeing colors

Whether you use shared or private colormap cells, you should free the colors when they are no longer needed. When an application terminates, the X server automatically frees the colors used by that application. If your application allocates colors often (it may allocate colors every time an image is displayed in a window, for example), you should call XFreeColors to free the colors that you no longer need, as follows:

```
Display    *disp;
Colormap   colormap;   /* Cells freed in this colormap */
unsigned long pixels[];/* Identifies cells being freed */
int        numpix;     /* Number of cells being freed  */
unsigned long planes;  /* Identifies planes being freed*/

XFreeColors(disp, colormap, pixels, numpix, planes);
```

XFreeColors frees colors allocated by any of the following functions: XAllocColor, XAllocNamedColor, XAllocColorCells, and XAllocColorPlanes. When you are freeing one or more read-only cells allocated by XAllocColor or XAllocNamedColor, provide the array of pixel values, their number, and a zero for the planes argument.

For private read-write cells, use a logical OR of the plane masks that were returned by an earlier call to XAllocColorCells.

Displaying an image

The X server supports images through pixmaps and bitmaps, whereas Xlib supports the XImage structure that allows you to manipulate images locally —on the system where your application is running, not at the server.

Creating a pixmap

A *pixmap* is a drawable, which means you can draw into a pixmap just as you would in a window. Like a window, a pixmap can be thought of as a rectangular array of pixels (a *raster*), with each location capable of holding a pixel value. You also can view a pixmap as several rectangular bit planes, with as many planes as there are bits in the pixel value.

For windows, the pixel values in the raster are being displayed constantly. The hardware reads the pixel values and translates them to colors or gray levels, depending on the capabilities of the display.

By contrast, the contents of a pixmap are not visible until they are copied into a window. Thus, you can think of a pixmap as an offscreen drawing area — an area of memory where you can save a drawing or an image. In fact, you can prepare drawings in a pixmap and display them whenever they are needed by using the XCopyArea function.

Pixmaps are used primarily to draw images and to store patterns for tiling. Pixmaps used as tiles are small (usually, no larger than 32×32 pixels), but those used to store images may be quite large.

Like windows, pixmaps are resources maintained at the X server. Before using a pixmap, you have to create it by calling the Xlib function XCreatePixmap. This function returns a resource identifier of type Pixmap, which you use when referring to the pixmap in subsequent drawing requests.

Suppose you want to create a pixmap to draw some figures offscreen. You can create a pixmap with the following code:

```
Display     *disp;      /* Identifies the X display   */
Window      root_win;   /* Root window's ID           */
Pixmap      pmap1;      /* Pixmap being created       */
unsigned int width,     /* Width of pixmap (pixels)   */
             height,    /* Height of pixmap (pixels)  */
             depth;     /* Bits per pixel value       */
  .
  .
  .
/* Create a pixmap */
  width = 100;
  height = 50;
  depth = DefaultDepth(disp, DefaultScreen(disp));
  root_win = RootWindow(disp, DefaultScreen(disp);

  pmap1 = XCreatePixmap(disp, root_win, width, height, depth);
```

When you create a pixmap, you specify its dimensions (*width* and *height*) and its *depth* (the number of bits in the pixel values that the pixmap should be able to store).

The second argument of XCreatePixmap must be an identifier of a previously created drawable. The X server uses this argument to determine the screen for which you are creating the pixmap. You can use the ID of any valid window or pixmap. A simple solution is to use the root window's ID.

Caution

In X, every window and pixmap is created for a specific screen. In a multiple-screen X display, you cannot copy a pixmap from one screen to a window in another, even if both have the same depth.

Drawing into a pixmap

When a valid pixmap is available, you can draw into it just as you would in a window. Following is how you draw some figures in a pixmap:

```
/* Draw into the pixmap (assume that the GC has been set up) */
  XFillRectangle(disp, pmap1, theGC, 10, 10, 20, 20);
  XFillArc(disp, pmap1, theGC, 30, 30, 20, 20, 0, 360*64);
```

As you do with windows, you have to provide a graphics context (GC) with all the graphics attributes, such as foreground and background colors. You use the same coordinate system with pixmaps as you do with windows —with the origin at the upper-left corner, the x-axis pointing to the right, and the y-axis pointing down.

Secret

A few minor differences exist between drawing into pixmaps and drawing in windows. Windows are always displayed onscreen, but pixmaps are never displayed. One of the main differences is that windows have an associated background color, but pixmaps do not. Thus, you cannot fill the pixmap with the background color by calling XClearArea. Instead, you must use XFillRectangle to fill all pixels in the pixmap with the current background color. When you create a pixmap, its contents are undefined, so you should always fill it with a known value, such as the background color.

Pixmaps do not generate any events other than GraphicsExpose and NoExpose events that occur during copying between windows and pixmaps.

Displaying a pixmap

After you have created and drawn in a pixmap, you can display it by using the XCopyArea function. To display the pixmap pmap1 in the window win at coordinates x, y, for example, you use the following code:

```
/* Copy drawing from pixmap to the window */
  XCopyArea(p_disp, pmap1, win, theGC, 0, 0, width, height, x, y);
```

Freeing pixmaps

Because most X displays have limited offscreen memory, you should release pixmap resources as soon as you finish using them. You can free a pixmap by calling XFreePixmap as follows:

```
Pixmap pmap1;

/* Create pixmap "pmap1" and use it */
/* ... */
XFreePixmap(p_disp, pmap1);
```

All resources (including pixmaps) used by your application are automatically freed when your application exits. You have to free pixmaps explicitly only if you use several large pixmaps.

Using bitmaps

A *bitmap* is a pixmap of depth 1. You create a bitmap by specifying depth 1 when you call the `XCreatePixmap` function. Because only 1 bit exists in each location of the bitmap, a bitmap is a pattern of ones and zeros.

Bitmaps are used somewhat differently from pixmaps. Because pixmaps store the entire pixel value, they usually are copied directly into windows and displayed. Bitmaps, however, are mostly used as stencils (or stipples) through which the background and foreground pixel values are applied to a drawable's raster. First, the bitmap is laid down over the raster of the drawable (repeating the bitmap, if necessary, to cover the entire raster). Then the foreground color is applied to all pixels where the bitmap (the stencil) has a one.

Another use of bitmaps is as a clip mask. The operation is similar to using the bitmap as a stencil, except that the graphics operations are performed only for those pixels in the raster that have a one in the bitmap pattern being used as the stencil.

Because of the special use of bitmaps, they are widely used even when the displays support more than one plane.

Although bitmaps are often used as stipples and clip masks, you also can display a bitmap directly in a window or copy it into a pixmap. Because the bitmap is depth 1 and the drawable (pixmap or window) may have a depth greater than 1, you cannot use the `XCopyArea` function to do this. Xlib provides another function, `XCopyPlane`, just for this purpose.

`XCopyplane` requires you to specify a rectangular area in a source bitmap and a destination drawable. The server copies the bitmap into the destination pixmap as follows: It uses the bitmap as a stencil and, using the foreground color (specified in a GC), draws those pixels in the drawable where the bitmap has ones.

You can identify the bitmap as being one of the planes in an arbitrary pixmap. To do this, you specify a mask with exactly 1 bit set to 1. That mask identifies a bit plane in the source pixmap. This bit plane is used as the stencil for the copy operation.

Following is some code that copies the bitmap read in by `XReadBitmapFile` into a window, using the current foreground color in a GC:

```
Display     disp;           /* Identifies the X display  */
Window      win;            /* Destination window        */
GC          theGC;          /* GC used for copying        */
Pixmap      my_bmp;         /* Bitmap created by function*/
int      xh_bmp, yh_bmp;    /* Coordinates of hotspot     */
unsigned int w_bmp, h_bmp;/* Width and height of bitmap*/
unsigned long planemask;  /* Identifies source bitmap  */
int      xsrc, ysrc;       /* Corner of source rectangle*/
int      xdest, ydest;     /* Copy to this point        */
.
.
/* Read in bitmap using "XReadBitmapFile" Assume
```

```
 * that bitmap data is in a file named "testicon.xbm"
 */
root_win = RootWindow(disp, DefaultScreen(disp);

if(XReadBitmapFile(disp, root_win, "testicon.xbm",
        &w_bmp, &h_bmp, &my_bmp,
        &xh_bmp, &yh_bmp) != BitmapSuccess)
{
  fprintf(stderr, "Failed to read bitmap file!\n");
/* Exit if you cannot proceed */
.
.
}
/* Bitmap "my_bmp" is ready to be used */

xsrc = 0;
ysrc = 0;
xdest = 10;
ydest = 10;
planemask = 1;

XCopyPlane(disp,my_bmp, win, theGC, xsrc, ysrc,
      w_bmp, h_bmp, xdest, ydest, planemask);
```

Notice that the mask identifying the bitmap from `my_bmp` is set to 1, because `my_bmp` is already a bitmap and, as such, has only 1 bit plane.

Summary

Nowadays, users expect most software to come with an easy-to-use graphical interface. In Linux, the graphical interface happens to be the X Window System —the standard for all UNIX workstations. X provides the basic windowing capability and graphical output capability, but not much more than that. The actual "look and feel" come from toolkits such as Motif. Motif is the de facto standard graphical user interface for UNIX workstations. Although Linux does not come with Motif, you can buy Motif for as little as $100. Because Motif is the most commonly used graphical interface, this chapter provides an introduction to Motif programming. By reading this chapter, you learn the following:

▶ Xlib is the C function library that provides access to the basic capabilities of the X Window System. With Xlib, it's tedious to create even simple user-interface elements, such as buttons and menus. You need a higher-level toolkit, such as Motif, to easily build graphical user interfaces. (Some people would say that you need even a higher level of abstraction than Motif provides.)

▶ Motif relies on the X Toolkit Intrinsics, or Xt Intrinsics, which are a set of convenience functions for managing widgets—graphical user interface objects. Xt Intrinsics provides a basic set of widgets on which other widget sets (such as Motif) are built.

▶ Motif programs rely on widgets to implement the user interface. The look and feel of widgets are controlled by the settings of variables known as *resources*.

▶ A typical Motif program creates several widgets, sets their resources, and then runs a loop that processes events (such as input from the mouse and keyboard or the request to redraw the contents of a window). This style of programming is known as *event-driven programming*.

▶ Motif widgets employ an object-oriented architecture (even though they were implemented in C) that uses inheritance to build on a basic set of widgets. The three basic types of widgets are shell, primitive, and manager.

▶ Most Motif distributions come with a sample program called `periodic`. You can view the widgets by running this demo program.

▶ Although Motif widgets make it easy to build user-interface elements such as buttons, menu bars, and list boxes, you still need to use the basic Xlib functions for displaying text, graphics, and images.

▶ The graphics context (GC) is at the heart of any graphics output that uses the X Window System. You specify all graphics attributes, such as color and font, through the GC.

▶ Pixmaps are offscreen blocks of memory where you can draw graphics and text just as you would in a window on the display screen. The X server manages the pixmaps.

▶ When you use Xlib drawing calls in Motif programs, you have to obtain an appropriate graphics context before making the Xlib calls.

Chapter 24

Text Processing in Linux

In This Chapter

▶ Editing text in Linux

▶ Using ed, the line editor

▶ Using vi, the full-screen text editor

▶ Editing text files with GNU Emacs

▶ Getting online help in GNU Emacs

▶ Understanding the format of a man page

▶ Preparing a man page with groff

Text processing refers to all aspects of creating, editing, and formatting textual documents. The simplest form of text processing is preparing a plain-text file, which you have to do often, because most Linux configuration files are plain-text files. For this purpose, Linux offers a choice of text editors, ranging from the UNIX standard vi to the all-powerful GNU Emacs.

To prepare formatted text in Linux, you have to use a markup language such as groff. With a markup language, you place special formatting commands in a plain-text file, and a formatting program processes the marked-up text file to generate the formatted document for printing or viewing. You may already be familiar with a more recent markup language called Hypertext Markup Language (HTML), which is used as the standard document format in the World Wide Web.

Note

Even if you use a Microsoft Windows- or Macintosh-based "what you see is what you get" (often referred to as "whizzy whig" for the acronym WYSIWYG) application to prepare formatted text, you have to learn the rudiments of a markup language if you want to prepare a man page — online help text available through the man command.

This chapter describes the text-processing facilities in Linux. The chapter starts with the ed, vi, and GNU Emacs text editors. The latter half of the chapter describes how to use the groff text-formatting program to prepare a man page.

Text Editing with ed and vi

Text editing is an important part of all operating systems, including Linux. In Linux, you need to create and edit a variety of text files:

- System configuration files, including /etc/fstab, /etc/hosts, /etc/inittab, /etc/X11/XF86Config, and many more
- User files, such as .newsrc and .bash_profile
- Mail messages and news articles
- Shell script files
- Perl and Tcl/Tk scripts
- C or C++ programs

All UNIX systems, including Linux, come with two text editors:

- ed, a line-oriented text editor
- vi, a full-screen text editor that supports the command set of an earlier editor named ex

In Linux, vi and ex are emulated by another text editor named vim, but you can invoke the editor with the vi command.

Tip

Although ed and vi may be more cryptic than other, more graphical text editors, you should learn the basic editing commands of these two editors, because there are times when these may be the only editors available. When you run into some system problem and Linux refuses to boot from the hard disk, for example, you may have to boot from a floppy. In this case, you have to edit system files with the ed editor, because that editor is small enough to fit on the floppy.

As you see in the following sections, learning the basic text-editing commands of ed and vi isn't hard.

Using ed

The ed text editor works with a *buffer*—an in-memory storage area where the actual text resides until you explicitly store the text in a file. You have to use ed only when you boot a minimal version of Linux (for example, from a boot floppy) and the system does not support full-screen mode.

Invoking ed

To invoke ed, use the following command syntax:

```
ed [-] [-G] [-s] [-pprompt-string] [filename]
```

The arguments shown in brackets are optional. The following list explains the arguments:

- ■ - suppresses the printing of character counts and diagnostic messages

- ■ -G forces backward compatibility

- ■ -s means the same as the single hyphen

- ■ -p *prompt-string* sets the prompt string (the default is a null prompt string)

- ■ *filename* is the name of the file to be edited

Learning ed

When you use the ed editor, you work in one of two modes:

- ■ *Command mode* is what you get by default. In this mode, anything you type is interpreted as a command. As you see in the "Summarizing ed commands" section, ed has a simple command set wherein each command consists of a single character.

- ■ *Text-input mode* allows you to enter text into the buffer. You can enter text-input mode with the commands a (append), c (change), or i (insert). After entering lines of text, you can leave text-input mode by entering a period (.) on a line by itself.

The ed editor works with the concept of the *current line* — the line to which ed applies the commands you type. Each line has an address: the line number. You can apply a command to a range of lines by prefixing the command with an address range. The p command, for example, prints (displays) the current line. To see the first 10 lines, you use the following command:

```
1,10p
```

In a command, the period (.) refers to the current line, and the dollar sign ($) refers to the last line. Thus, the following command deletes all the lines from the current line to the last one:

```
.,$d
```

Examining a sample session with ed

The following example shows how you might begin editing a file in ed:

```
ed -p: /etc/fstab
532
:
```

This example uses the -p option to set the prompt to the colon character (:) and opens the file /etc/fstab for editing. You may find turning on a prompt character to be helpful, because without the prompt, it's difficult to tell whether ed is in text-input mode or command mode.

The ed editor opens the file, reports the number of characters in the file (532), displays the prompt (:), and waits for a command.

After ed opens a file for editing, the current line is the last line of the file. To
see the current line number, use the .= command, as follows:

```
:.=
7
```

This output tells you that the /etc/fstab file has seven lines. (Your system's
/etc/fstab file, of course, may have a different number of lines.) The
following example shows how you can see all these lines:

```
:1,$p
/dev/hda1               /                     ext2    defaults    1 1
/dev/sda1               /usr/local            ext2    defaults    1 2
/dev/hda2               swap                  swap    defaults    0 0
/dev/sda2               swap                  swap    defaults    0 0
/dev/fd0                /mnt/floppy           ext2    noauto      0 0
/dev/cdrom              /mnt/cdrom            iso9660 noauto,ro   0 0
none                    /proc                 proc    defaults    0 0
:
```

To go to a specific line, type the line number, as follows:

```
:1
/dev/hda1                                     ext2    defaults    1 1
:
```

The editor responds by displaying that line.

Suppose you want to delete the line that contains dosc. To search for a string,
type a slash (/), followed by the string you want to locate, as follows:

```
:/cdrom
/dev/cdrom              /mnt/cdrom            iso9660 noauto,ro    0 0
:
```

The editor locates the line that contains the string and then displays it. That
line becomes the current line. To delete the line, use the d command, as
follows:

```
:d
:
```

To replace a string with another, use the s command. To replace cdrom with
the string cd, for example, use the following command:

```
:s/cdrom/cd/
/dev/cd                /mnt/cdrom            iso9660 noauto,ro    0 0
:
```

To insert a line in front of the current line, use the i command, as follows:

```
:i
    (type the line you want to insert)
.   (type a single period)
:
```

You can enter as many lines as you want. After the last line, enter a period (.) on a line by itself. That period marks the end of text-input mode, and the editor switches over to command mode. In this case, you can tell that ed has switched to command mode because you see the prompt (:).

Tip

When you are happy with the changes, you can write them out to the file with the w command. If you want to save the changes and exit, you can simply type **wq** to perform both steps at the same time, as follows:

```
:wq
535
```

The ed editor saves the changes in the file, displays the number of characters that it has saved, and exits.

If you want to quit the editor without saving any changes, use the Q command.

Summarizing ed commands

The sample session should give you an idea of how to use ed commands to perform the basic tasks of editing a text file. Table 24-1 lists all commonly used ed commands:

Table 24-1	Commonly used ed commands
Command	**Meaning**
!command	Execute a shell command
$	Go to last line in the buffer
%	Apply command that follows to all lines in the buffer (for example, %p prints all lines)
+	Go to next line
+N	Go to N-th next line (N is a number)
,	Apply command that follows to all lines in the buffer (for example, ,p prints all lines); similar to %
-	Go to preceding line
-N	Go to N-th previous line (N is a number)
.	Refer to the current line in the buffer
/regex/	Search forward for the specified regular expression; see Chapter 6 for an introduction to regular expressions
;	Refer to a range of lines: current through last line in the buffer
=	Print line number
?regex?	Search backward for the specified regular expression; see Chapter 6 for an introduction to regular expressions

(continued)

Command	Meaning
Table 24-1	*(Continued)*
Command	*Meaning*
^	Go to the preceding line; also see the - command
^*N*	Go to the *N*-th previous line (where *N* is a number); also see the -*N* command
a	Append after current line
c	Change specified lines
d	Delete specified lines
e *file*	Edit file
f *file*	Change default filename
h	Display explanation of last error
H	Turn on verbose-mode error reporting
i	Insert text before current line
j	Join contiguous lines
k*x*	Mark line with letter *x* (later, the line can be referred to as '*x*)
l	Print (display) lines
m	Move lines
N	Go to line number *N*
Newline	Display next line and make that line current
P	Toggle prompt mode on or off
q	Quit editor
Q	Quit editor without saving changes
r *file*	Read and insert contents of file after the current line
s/*old*/*new*/	Replace *old* string with *new*
Space N	A space, followed by *N*; *N*th next line (*N* is a number)
u	Undo the last command
W *file*	Append contents of buffer to the end of the specified file
w *file*	Save buffer in the specified file (if no file is named, save in the default file —the file whose contents ed is currently editing)

Tip

Notice that you can prefix most editing commands with a line number or an address range, expressed in terms of two line numbers separated by a comma; the command then applies to the specified lines. To append after the second line in the buffer, for example, you use the following command:

```
2a
(Type lines of text. End with single period on a line.)
```

To print lines 3 through 15, use this command:

```
3,15p
```

Although you may not use ed often, much of the command syntax carries over to the vi editor. As the following section on vi shows, in its command mode, vi accepts the commands you use with ed.

Using vi

The vi editor is a full-screen text editor that allows you to view a file several lines at a time. Most UNIX systems, including Linux, comes with vi. Therefore, if you learn the basic features of vi, you'll be able to edit text files on almost any UNIX system.

Like the ed editor, vi works with a buffer. When vi edits a file, it reads the file into a buffer — a block of memory — and allows you to change the text in the buffer. The vi editor also uses temporary files during editing, but the original file is not altered until you save the changes with a specific vi command.

Setting the terminal type

Before you start a full-screen text editor such as vi, you have to set the TERM environment variable to the terminal type (such as vt100 or xterm). The vi editor uses the terminal type to look up the terminal's characteristics in the /etc/termcap file and then control the terminal in full-screen mode.

When you run X, you can use vi in an xterm window. The xterm window's terminal type is xterm. When you start xterm, it automatically sets the TERM environment variable to xterm. Therefore, you should be able to use vi in an xterm window without explicitly setting the TERM variable.

Starting vi

On your Linux system, the vim editor emulates what you see as vi on most other UNIX systems. You can, however, continue to use the vi name to run the editor, because a symbolic link exists between vi and vim. To see this link, type the following ls command:

```
ls -l /usr/bin/vi
lrwxrwxrwx   1 root      root           13 Mar 11 15:04 /usr/bin/vi ->
../../bin/vim
```

If you want to consult the online manual pages for vi, type the following command:

```
man vi
```

To start the editor, use the vi name and run it with the following command syntax:

```
vi [flags] [+cmd] [filename]
```

The arguments shown in brackets are optional. The following list explains the arguments:

■ *flags* are single-character flags that control the way vi runs.

■ *+cmd* causes vi to run the specified command after it starts. (You learn more about the commands in the "Summarizing vi commands" section.)

■ *filename* is the name of the file to be edited.

The *flags* arguments can be one or more of the following:

■ -c *cmd* executes the specified command before editing begins.

■ -e starts in colon command mode (described in the following section).

■ -i starts in input mode (described in the following section).

■ -m causes the editor to search through the file for something that looks like an error message from a compiler.

■ -R makes the file read-only so you cannot accidentally overwrite the file.

■ -s runs in safe mode, wherein many potentially harmful commands are turned off.

■ -v starts in visual command mode (described in the following section).

Most of the time, however, you start vi with a filename as the only argument, as follows:

```
vi /etc/hosts
```

Another common way to start vi is to jump to a specific line number right at startup. To begin editing at line 296 of the file /etc/X11/XF86Config, for example, use the following command:

```
vi +296 /etc/X11/XF86Config
```

This way of starting vi is useful when you edit a source file after the compiler reports an error at a specific line number.

Learning vi concepts

When you edit a file with vi, the editor loads the file into a buffer, displays the first few lines of the file in a full-screen window, and positions the cursor on the first line. When you type the command **vi /etc/fstab** in an xterm window, for example, you get a full-screen text window, as shown in Figure 24-1.

The last line shows information about the file, including the number of lines and the number of characters in the file. Later, this area is used as a command-entry area. The rest of the lines are used to display the file. If the file contains fewer lines than the window, vi displays the empty lines with a tilde (~) in the first column.

```
                               rxvt
/dev/hda3          /                ext2      defaults    1 1
/dev/hda1          /dosc            msdos     defaults    0 0
/dev/hda5          /dosd            msdos     defaults    0 0
/dev/hda4          swap             swap      defaults    0 0
/dev/fd0           /mnt/floppy      ext2      noauto      0 0
/dev/cdrom         /mnt/cdrom       iso9660   noauto,ro   0 0
none               /proc            proc      defaults    0 0
~
~
~
~
~
~
~
~
~
~
~
~
~
~
~
~
~
"/etc/fstab" [readonly] 7 lines, 532 characters
```

Figure 24-1: A file displayed in a full-screen text window by the vi editor.

The current line is marked by the cursor, which appears as a small black rectangle. The cursor appears on top of a character. In Figure 24-1, the cursor is on the first character of the first line.

In vi, you work in one of three modes:

- *Visual command mode* is what you get by default. In this mode, anything you type is interpreted as a command that applies to the line containing the cursor. The vi commands are similar to those of ed and are listed in the "Summarizing vi commands" section.

- *Colon command mode* allows you to read or write files, set vi options, and quit. All colon commands start with a colon (:). When you enter the colon, vi positions the cursor at the last line and allows you to type a command. The command takes effect when you press Enter.

- *Text input mode* allows you to enter text into the buffer. You can enter input mode with the command a (insert after cursor), A (append at end of line), or i (insert after cursor). After entering lines of text, you have to press Esc to leave input mode and re-enter visual command mode.

One problem with all these modes is the fact that you cannot easily tell vi's current mode. It can be frustrating to begin typing, only to realize that vi is not in input mode. The converse situation also is common: You may be typing text when you want to enter a command. If you want to make sure that vi is in command mode, just press Esc a few times. (Pressing Esc more than once doesn't hurt.)

Tip

To view online help in vi, type :help while in command mode.

Examining a sample session with vi

To begin editing the file /etc/fstab, enter the following command:

```
vi /etc/fstab
```

Figure 24-1 shows the resulting display, with the first few lines of the file displayed in a full-screen text window. The last line shows the file's name and statistics: the number of lines and characters.

The vi editor initially positions the cursor on the first character. One of the first things you need to learn is how to move the cursor around. First, try the following commands (each command is a single letter; just type the letter, and vi responds):

- j moves the cursor one line down
- k moves the cursor one line up
- h moves the cursor one character to the left
- l moves the cursor one character to the right

Instead of moving one line or one character at a time, you can move around a word at a time. Try the following single-character commands for word-size cursor movement:

- w moves the cursor a word forward
- b moves the cursor a word backward

The last type of cursor movement is several lines at a time. Try the following commands, and see what happens:

- Ctrl-D moves down half a screen
- Ctrl-U scrolls up half a screen

The last two commands, of course, are not necessary when the file contains only a few lines. When you are editing large files, you'll find it handy to move around several lines at a time.

At any time, you can go to a specific line number. This situation is where a colon command comes in. To go to line 1, for example, type the following and then press Enter:

```
:1
```

When you type the colon, vi displays the colon on the last line of the screen. From then on, vi uses the text you type as a command. You have to press Enter to submit the command to vi. In colon command mode, vi accepts all the commands the ed editor accepts — and then some.

To search for a string, first type a slash (/). The vi editor displays the slash on the last line of the screen. Type the search string and then press Enter. The vi editor locates the string and positions the cursor at the beginning of that string. Thus, to locate the string dosc in the file /etc/fstab, type the following:

```
/dosc
```

To delete the line containing the cursor, type **dd** (two lowercase *d*s). The vi editor deletes that line of text and makes the next line the current one.

To begin entering text in front of the cursor, type **i** (a lowercase *i* all by itself). The vi editor switches to text-input mode. Now you can enter text. When you finish entering text, press Esc to return to visual command mode.

After you finish editing the file, you can save the changes in the file with the :w command. If you want to save the changes and exit, you can type **:wq** to perform both steps at the same time. The vi editor saves the changes in the file and exits.

If you want to quit the editor without saving any changes, use the :q! command.

Summarizing vi commands

The sample editing session should give you a feel for the vi commands, especially the three modes:

- visual command mode (the default)
- input mode, which you enter by typing **a, A**, or **i**
- colon command mode, in which you enter commands followed by a colon (:)

In addition to the few commands illustrated in the sample session, vi accepts a large number of other commands. Table 24-2 lists the basic vi commands, organized by task.

Table 24-2   Basic vi commands

Command	Meaning
Insert text	
a	Insert text after the cursor
A	Insert text at the end of the current line
I	Insert text at the beginning of the current line
i	Insert text before cursor
o	Open a line below the current line
O	Open a line above the current line
Ctrl-v	Insert any special character in input mode

(continued)

Table 24-2   *(Continued)*

Command	*Meaning*
Delete text	
D	Delete up to the end of the current line
dd	Delete the current line
dw	Delete from the cursor to the end of the following word
x	Delete the character on which the cursor rests
Change text	
C	Change up to the end of the current line
cc	Change the current line
cw	Change the word
J	Join the current line with the next one
r*x*	Replace the character under the cursor with *x* (*x* is any character)
~	Change character under the cursor to the opposite case
Move cursor	
$	Move to the end of the current line
;	Repeat last f or F command
^	Move to the beginning of the current line
e	Move to the end of the current word
f*x*	Move cursor to the first occurrence of character *x* on the current line
F*x*	Move cursor to the last occurrence of character *x* on the current line
H	Move cursor to the top of the screen
h	Move one character to the left
j	Move one line down
k	Move one line up
L	Move cursor to the end of the screen
l	Move one character to the right
M	Move cursor to the middle of the screen
N|	Move cursor to column *N* on current line
*N*G	Place cursor on line *N*
w	Move to the beginning of the following word

Command	Meaning
Mark a location	
'x	Move cursor to the beginning of the line that contains mark x
`x	Move cursor to mark x
mx	Mark the current location with the letter x
Scroll text	
Ctrl-b	Scroll backward by a full screen
Ctrl-d	Scroll forward by half a screen
Ctrl-f	Scroll forward by a full screen
Ctrl-u	Scroll backward by half a screen
Refresh screen	
Ctrl-l	Redraw screen
Cut and paste text	
"xNdd	Delete N lines and move them to buffer x (x is any single lowercase character)
"XNyy	Same as "xNyy, except that the yanked lines are appended to buffer x
"xNyy	Yank N (a number) lines into buffer x (x is any single uppercase character)
"xp	Put the yanked lines from buffer x after the current line
P	Put yanked line above the current line
p	Put yanked line below the current line
yy	Yank (copy) current line into an unnamed buffer
Colon commands	
:!command	Execute shell command
:e filename	Edit file
:f	Display filename and current line number
:N	Move to line N (N is a number)
:q	Quit editor
:q!	Quit without saving changes
:r filename	Read file and insert after current line
:w filename	Write buffer to file
:wq	Save changes and exit

(continued)

Table 24-2	*(Continued)*
Command	*Meaning*
Search text	
/string	Search forward for string
?string	Search backward for string
n	Find next string
View file information	
Ctrl-g	Show filename, size, and current line number
Miscellaneous	
u	Undo last command
Esc	End input mode and enter visual command mode
U	Undo recent changes to current line

Working with GNU Emacs

Text editors are a matter of personal preference, and many UNIX users swear by GNU Emacs. Although it is intimidating at first, GNU Emacs is one of those software packages that grow on you; it has so many features that many users and programmers often perform all their tasks directly from within GNU Emacs.

A significant advantage of GNU Emacs is its availability on nearly every computer system imaginable, from MS-DOS PCs to any UNIX system. If a system does not have GNU Emacs, you can get it from one of many sites on the Internet. For your Linux system, you get GNU Emacs on the companion CD-ROM; you can choose to install it when you install Linux on your system. If you are just getting started with UNIX text editors, I would recommend that you learn to use GNU Emacs. That way, you acquire a skill you can use on any UNIX system.

Note

Because GNU Emacs is so versatile and powerful, describing it in detail could easily take an entire book, and in fact, quite a few books on GNU Emacs are on the market. Most notably, O'Reilly & Associates has a GNU Emacs book, *Learning GNU Emacs*, that you may find to be useful.

On a text terminal, GNU Emacs runs in text-mode full-screen display. Under X, GNU Emacs runs in a window. Either way, the basic commands remain the same. The X version also allows you to position the cursor with the mouse.

The next few sections provide a brief introduction to the text-editing features of GNU Emacs.

Starting GNU Emacs

On the Linux console, you can start GNU Emacs by typing **emacs**. If you are running X, type **emacs &** in an xterm window to start GNU Emacs: This command launches the X window version of GNU Emacs in the background and allows you to continue other work in the xterm window.

When first started, GNU Emacs creates a buffer named *scratch* and displays a help message followed by a copyright message in a window, as shown in Figure 24-2.

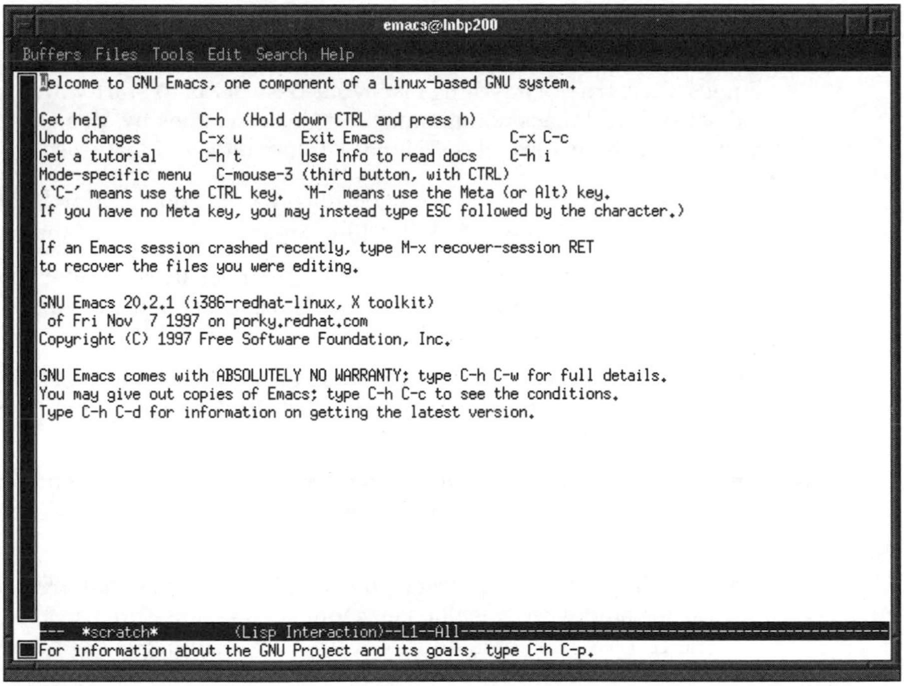

```
                              emacs@lnbp200
 Buffers Files Tools Edit Search Help
 Welcome to GNU Emacs, one component of a Linux-based GNU system.

 Get help          C-h  (Hold down CTRL and press h)
 Undo changes      C-x u      Exit Emacs         C-x C-c
 Get a tutorial    C-h t      Use Info to read docs   C-h i
 Mode-specific menu   C-mouse-3 (third button, with CTRL)
 (`C-' means use the CTRL key. `M-' means use the Meta (or Alt) key.
 If you have no Meta key, you may instead type ESC followed by the character.)

 If an Emacs session crashed recently, type M-x recover-session RET
 to recover the files you were editing.

 GNU Emacs 20.2.1 (i386-redhat-linux, X toolkit)
  of Fri Nov  7 1997 on porky.redhat.com
 Copyright (C) 1997 Free Software Foundation, Inc.

 GNU Emacs comes with ABSOLUTELY NO WARRANTY; type C-h C-w for full details.
 You may give out copies of Emacs; type C-h C-c to see the conditions.
 Type C-h C-d for information on getting the latest version.




 --- *scratch*        (Lisp Interaction)--L1--All-------------------------------
 For information about the GNU Project and its goals, type C-h C-p.
```

Figure 24-2: The initial window displayed by the X version of GNU Emacs.

The initial GNU Emacs window also shows helpful information in the area where you normally edit the contents of a file. That information offers the following suggestions:

- Press C-h t (press Ctrl-h, followed by t) to view an online tutorial on GNU Emacs.

- Press C-h i to start info, the online help system for all GNU software. Chapter 22 describes how to use info (Hint: Type **m** and then **emacs** to see the information on GNU Emacs.)

The message also tells you that to quit GNU Emacs, you should press `C-x C-c` (that's Ctrl-x, followed by Ctrl-c). As you'll learn in the "Typing GNU Emacs commands" section, all GNU Emacs command keystrokes start with a control character or Escape (which is referred to as Meta and abbreviated as `M` in Emacs documentation).

Note

To be consistent with the GNU Emacs notation, I'll use the notation `C-x` for Ctrl-x and `M-x` for Escape-x (x is any character).

Learning GNU Emacs

I have used GNU Emacs extensively for years, but I feel that I have barely scratched the surface when it comes to using the full capabilities of GNU Emacs. As is true of anything else, your best bet is to start with a small subset of GNU Emacs commands. Then, as time goes by, you can gradually add to your repertoire of GNU Emacs commands and features.

GNU Emacs is built around some basic concepts you'll find helpful to learn. Following are some of these concepts:

- Like other text editors (`vi` or `ed`), GNU Emacs uses a buffer to maintain the text you enter and change. You have to explicitly save the buffer to update the contents of a file.

- Unlike `vi` and `ed`, GNU Emacs does not require you to type any special command to enter text into the buffer. By default, anything you type goes into the buffer.

- GNU Emacs uses a cursor marked by a block shape. When you type text, GNU Emacs inserts that text in front of the character on which the cursor rests.

- GNU Emacs has long, descriptive command names that are *bound to* (associated with) specific key sequences — these are the *key bindings* for the GNU Emacs commands. `C-x C-c`, for example, is bound to the GNU Emacs command `save-buffers-kill-emacs`.

- All GNU Emacs key bindings start with a control character (for which you simultaneously press Ctrl and a character) or Escape.

- GNU Emacs uses several modes, each of which provides a specific type of editing environment. (In C mode, for example, GNU Emacs helps you by indenting the braces.)

- In the GNU Emacs window, the last screen line is called the *minibuffer;* it displays all commands and filenames you type. The line second to the bottom is called the *mode line*. On this line, GNU Emacs displays the name of the buffer and the current mode (the default mode is called *fundamental*).

■ You do not have to start GNU Emacs each time you want to edit a file. Rather, you start GNU Emacs and then open one or more files for editing. You save and close files that you finish editing.

■ You can use many buffers in GNU Emacs, and you can cut and paste between buffers.

Typing GNU Emacs commands

GNU Emacs has an extensive set of commands, and each one has a long descriptive name, such as the following:

```
save-buffer save-buffers-kill-emacs scroll-up previous-line
```

Most of the commands, however, are bound to somewhat cryptic keystrokes. Otherwise, you'd have to type these long commands and wouldn't get much editing done.

Although you can enter any of the descriptive commands in the minibuffer (at the bottom of the GNU Emacs window), the basic means of entering the commands is through special keystrokes. These keystrokes begin with one of the following characters:

■ A control character that you enter by simultaneously pressing the Ctrl key and the character. In GNU Emacs documentation, each control character is abbreviated as C-*x* (*x* is a letter). This book uses the notation Ctrl-*x* to denote the control character that corresponds to the letter *x*. In GNU Emacs online help, Ctrl-v is written as C-v.

■ An Escape character. In GNU Emacs, the Escape key is abbreviated as the Meta key, or M. Thus, Esc v (Escape, followed by the letter v) is written as M-v.

Most of the time, you'll be entering the control commands, which require you to press the Ctrl key together with a letter. Ctrl-v or C-v, for example, causes GNU Emacs to move forward one screen.

The commands with an Esc prefix are easier to enter, because you press the keys in sequence: first the Escape key and then the letter. Esc v or M-v, for example, causes GNU Emacs to move backward one screen of text. To enter this command, you press Escape first and then press **v**. Although the Ctrl and Esc commands may sound complicated, you can learn a basic set very quickly.

Getting help

The best source of information on GNU Emacs is GNU Emacs itself. For starters, GNU Emacs includes an online tutorial that teaches you the basics of GNU Emacs. To use the tutorial, type **C-h t**. GNU Emacs displays the initial screen of the tutorial in its window, as shown in Figure 24-3.

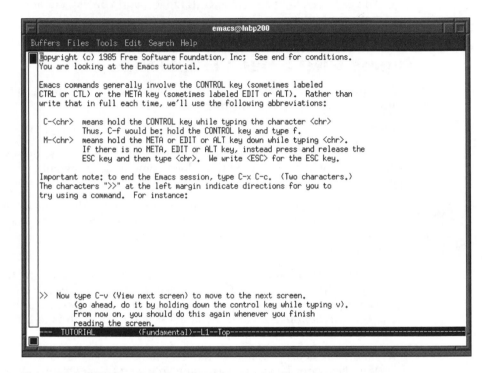

Figure 24-3: GNU Emacs displays the online tutorial when you press C-h t.

As the instructions toward the bottom of Figure 24-3 show, the tutorial guides you through the steps and asks you to try GNU Emacs commands. If you are new to GNU Emacs, you should go through the tutorial. Because the tutorial is hands-on, you'll get a good feel for GNU Emacs after going through it.

In addition to the tutorial, you can look up the key bindings for various GNU Emacs commands. To see the key bindings, type **C-h b**. GNU Emacs splits the window and displays a list of key bindings in the bottom half, as shown in Figure 24-4.

Each line in the key binding shows the name of the key and the GNU Emacs command associated with that key. If you press the key, GNU Emacs executes the command bound to that key.

Figure 24-4 illustrates another feature of GNU Emacs: the capability to split its window into two or more parts. After splitting, each part becomes a separate window with its own buffer.

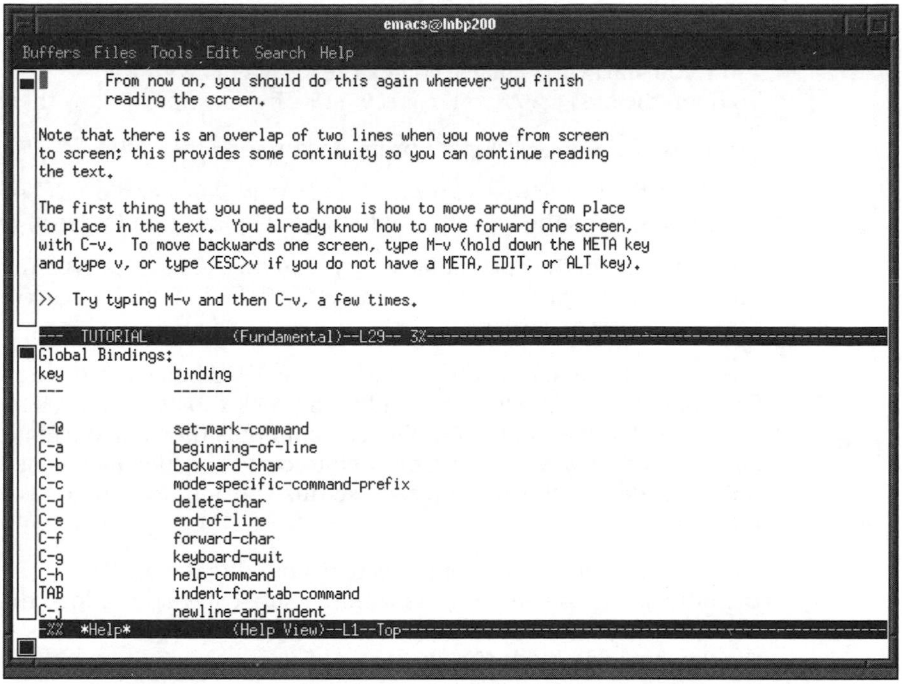

Figure 24-4: GNU Emacs displays the key bindings in a split window when you press C-h b.

In Figure 24-4, you can scroll the key-bindings list with the following keystrokes:

- C-x o switches to the other window (the bottom window, which shows the Help buffer with its key-bindings list)
- C-v scrolls the contents of the Help buffer

Table 24-3 lists other GNU Emacs help commands.

Table 24-3   GNU Emacs help commands

Command	Meaning
C-h c	Prompts you for a key sequence and describes that sequence briefly
C-h f	Prompts you for a GNU Emacs command name and describes that command
C-h k	Prompts you for a key sequence and describes what that sequence does
C-h l	Displays the last 100 characters typed
C-h m	Displays current GNU Emacs mode
C-h s	Displays the syntax table for the current buffer
C-h v	Prompts for a variable name and describes that variable
C-h w	Prompts for a command and shows that command's key binding

Reading a file

After you start GNU Emacs, you can read in a file with the C-x C-f command. To open the file /usr/src/linux/COPYING, for example, follow these steps:

1. Press **C-x C-f**. GNU Emacs prompts you for a filename.

2. Type the filename — /usr/src/linux/COPYING — and press Enter. GNU Emacs reads the file into a buffer and displays that buffer in the window.

To open a file in the current directory, you do not have to type the full directory name; just type the filename. By default, GNU Emacs looks for the file in the current working directory.

Tip

You do not have to type the full filename in GNU Emacs; just enter the first few characters of the filename and then press Tab. If the partial name uniquely identifies a file, GNU Emacs completes the filename for you. Thus, all you need to type is the first few characters of a filename — just enough to uniquely identify the file. You can use this shortcut feature to avoid typing long filenames.

Suppose the current working directory contains the file Makefile, which is the only file whose name starts with the substring Mak. To load that file in GNU Emacs, press C-x C-f, type Mak, and press Tab. GNU Emacs completes the filename and reads the file Makefile.

Moving around the buffer

One of the first things you have to do is move around in the buffer. The cursor marks the current spot in the buffer; anything you type goes into the buffer in front of the character under the cursor. Thus, to insert text into a file, you have to read in the file, move the cursor to the desired spot, and type the text.

To move around the buffer, you need to move the cursor. You have to use control keys to move the cursor in any direction. Following are the six basic cursor-movement commands:

- C-b moves the cursor backward one character

- C-f moves the cursor forward one character

- C-n moves the cursor to the following line (while trying to maintain the same column position as in the current line)

- C-p moves the cursor to the preceding line (while trying to maintain the same column position as in the current line)

- C-a moves the cursor to the beginning of the current line

- C-e moves the cursor to the end of the current line

If moving one character at a time is too slow, you can move one word at a time, using the following commands:

- M-f moves the cursor forward a word

- M-b moves the cursor backward a word

You can move in even bigger chunks through the buffer. The following commands allow you to move one screen at a time:

- C-v moves forward one screen

- M-v moves backward one screen

You can use two other simple cursor-movement commands for really big jumps:

- M-< (Escape, followed by the less-than key) moves the cursor to the beginning of the buffer

- M-> (Escape, followed by the greater-than key) moves the cursor to the end of the buffer

A time-saving feature of GNU Emacs enables you to repeat a command a specified number of times. Suppose you want to move 13 characters forward. You can do so by pressing C-f 13 times or by typing **C-u 13 C-f**. The C-u command accepts a repeat count and repeats the next command that many times. If you don't provide a count and simply type a command after C-u, GNU Emacs repeats the command four times. Thus, C-u C-f means "move forward four characters."

Secret

One exception to the behavior of the C-u command exists: When you use C-u with the M-v or C-v command, GNU Emacs does not repeat the screen-scrolling commands. Instead, GNU Emacs scrolls the screen up or down by the specified count. Thus, if you press C-u 10 C-v, GNU Emacs scrolls down 10 lines (not 10 screens).

Inserting and deleting text

Because GNU Emacs does not have special command and insert modes like vi, to insert text in GNU Emacs, just begin typing. GNU Emacs inserts the text in front of the cursor. GNU Emacs, of course, interprets control characters and Esc as being the beginning of a command.

You can take advantage of the repeat-count feature to insert many copies of a character. I typically use the following line to separate sections of a C program:

```
/*-----------------------------------------------*/
```

I enter this line with the following key presses:

```
/* C-u 51 - */
```

Ignore the spaces; I don't really type them. I first type **/***. Then I press **C-u** and type **51**. Finally, I press the hyphen (-), followed by the ending ***/**.

You can delete text in GNU Emacs in the following ways:

- To delete the character in front of the cursor, press the Delete key.
- To delete the character on which the cursor rests, press C-d.
- To delete the word after the cursor, press M-d.
- To delete the word immediately before the cursor, press M-Delete.
- To delete from the cursor to the end of the line, press C-k. (GNU Emacs refers to this command as "kill the line.")

Tip

Whenever you delete anything more than a character, GNU Emacs saves it for you. Simply press C-y to get back the saved text.

You can undo a change with the C-x u command. Each time you press C-x u, GNU Emacs performs the undo operation for a previous command. To undo the effects of the last two commands, for example, press C-x u twice.

Searching and replacing

Every text editor has search-and-replace capability, and GNU Emacs is no exception. The two most common search commands are

- C-s *string*: incrementally search forward for *string*
- C-r *string*: incrementally search backward for *string*

When you press C-s to search forward, GNU Emacs prompts you for a search string in the minibuffer (the last line in the GNU Emacs window). As you enter the characters for the string, GNU Emacs jumps to the first occurrence of the string you have typed so far. By the time you finish typing the search string, GNU Emacs will have positioned the cursor at the end of the next occurrence of the search string (provided, of course, that GNU Emacs finds the string).

To find the next occurrence of the string, simply press C-s again. To end the search, press Enter. You also can halt the search with cursor control commands, such as C-f or C-b.

Searching in the reverse direction works similarly; just press C-r instead of C-s.

GNU Emacs also allows you to replace an occurrence of one string with another. The two basic commands for replacing strings are replace-string and query-replace. The replace-string command replaces all occurrences of one string with another. The `query-replace` command works similarly, but GNU Emacs prompts you each time it's about to replace a string, allowing you to decide which strings actually get replaced.

The `query-replace` command is bound to the `M-%` (Escape, followed by %) key sequence. To perform a `query-replace` operation, first press `M-%`. GNU Emacs displays the following prompt in the minibuffer:

```
Query replace:
```

Enter the string you want to replace — suppose that it's **1998** — and then press Enter. GNU Emacs prompts you for the replacement string, as follows:

```
Query replace 1998 with:
```

Enter the replacement string — say, **1999** — and press Enter. GNU Emacs moves the cursor to the next occurrence of the string to be replaced and displays a prompt in the minibuffer, as follows:

```
Query replacing 1998 with 1999: (? for help)
```

Type **y** or press the spacebar to allow GNU Emacs to replace the string. Otherwise, press **n** or Delete to stop GNU Emacs from replacing the string. In either case, GNU Emacs moves to the next occurrence of the string and repeats the prompt. When no more strings are left, GNU Emacs displays a message in the minibuffer informing you how many occurrences of the string were replaced.

No key binding exists for the `replace-string` command. You can type any GNU Emacs command, however, by following these steps:

1. Type **M-x**. GNU Emacs displays `M-x` in the minibuffer and waits for more text.

2. Type the GNU Emacs command and press Enter. To use the `replace-string` command, for example, type **replace-string** and then press Enter.

3. For some commands, GNU Emacs prompts for further input; enter that input. When you use `replace-string`, for example, GNU Emacs first prompts for the string to be replaced and then for the replacement string.

When you type a GNU Emacs command with `M-x`, you can press the spacebar or the Tab key for command completion. To enter the `replace-string` command, for example, you might start by typing **repl** and pressing the spacebar. That action causes GNU Emacs to display `replace-` and then pause. Type **s** and press the spacebar again. GNU Emacs displays `replace-string`. You then can use the command by pressing Enter. Try it; you'll see what I mean.

Copying and moving

Another common editing function is copying blocks of text and moving that text to another location in the buffer. The first step in working with a block of text is defining the block.

Note

In GNU Emacs, a *block* is defined as the text between a mark and the current cursor position. You can think of the *mark* as a physical marker placed in the buffer to mark a location. To set the mark, move the cursor to the beginning of the block and then press C-@ or C-Space (press the Ctrl key together with the spacebar). GNU Emacs sets the mark at the current location and displays the following message in the minibuffer:

```
Mark set
```

After you set the mark, GNU Emacs treats the text between the mark and the current cursor location as a block. To copy the block, type the following:

```
M-w
```

That command copies the block to an internal storage area without deleting the block from the current buffer.

If you actually want to cut the block of text, use the following command:

```
C-w
```

That command deletes the block of text from the buffer and moves it to an internal storage area.

To insert the cut (or copied) text at any location, move the cursor to the insertion point and type the following:

```
C-y
```

That command causes GNU Emacs to paste the previously cut text in front of the cursor.

Between the cut and paste operations, you may switch from one buffer to another, and thereby cut from one file and paste in another. To cut from one file and paste into another, follow these steps:

1. Open the first file with the Cx C-f command. For this exercise, assume that the first file's name is first.txt.

2. Open the second file with the C-x C-f command. For this exercise, assume that the second file's name is second.txt.

3. Change to the first buffer with the C-x b first.txt command.

4. Move the cursor to the beginning of the text to be copied and press C-Space.

5. Move the cursor to the end of the block, and press `C-w` to cut the text.

6. Change to the second buffer with the `C-x b second.txt` command.

7. Move the cursor to the location where you want to insert the text, and press `C-y`. GNU Emacs inserts the previously cut text from the first buffer into the second one.

Saving changes

After you edit a buffer, you have to write those changes to a file to make them permanent. The GNU Emacs command for saving a buffer to its file is `C-x C-s`. This command saves the buffer to the file with the same name.

To save the buffer in another file, use the command `C-x C-w`. GNU Emacs prompts you for a filename. Type the filename and press Enter to save the buffer in that file. Unlike many DOS or Windows word processors, GNU Emacs does not automatically add a file extension. You have to provide the full filename.

Running a shell in GNU Emacs

GNU Emacs is versatile enough to allow you to access anything in Linux from within a GNU Emacs session. One way to access something in Linux is to run a shell session. You can do so with the GNU Emacs command named `shell`. To see how the `shell` command works, use `M-x` (press Escape, followed by **x**). GNU Emacs displays `M-x` in the minibuffer and waits for further input. Type **shell** and press Enter. GNU Emacs starts a new shell process and displays the shell prompt in the GNU Emacs window. Type any shell command you want. The output appears in the GNU Emacs window.

You can continue to use the shell as long as you need it. All outputs from the commands go into the window where the shell prompt appears. When you no longer need the shell, type **exit**. That command terminates the shell process and returns you to GNU Emacs.

If you want to run a single shell command, use the `M-!` key binding. When you use `M-!`, GNU Emacs displays the following prompt in the minibuffer:

```
Shell command:
```

Type a shell command (such as **ls -l**) and press Enter. GNU Emacs executes that command and displays the resulting output in a separate window. To revert to a single-window display, type **C-x 1**. That command is Ctrl-x, followed by the number 1. The command instructs GNU Emacs to delete the other windows (excluding the one that contains the cursor).

Writing Man Pages with groff

Before the days of graphical interfaces, typesetting with the computer meant preparing a text file with embedded typesetting commands and then processing that marked-up text file with a computer program that generated commands for the output device: a printer or some other typesetter.

As you know, such markup languages still exist. A prime example is Hypertext Markup Language (HTML), which is used to prepare World Wide Web pages.

In the late seventies and early eighties, I prepared all my correspondence and reports on a DEC VAX/VMS system, using a program named RUNOFF. It formatted output for a line printer or a daisy-wheel printer. That VAX/VMS RUNOFF program accepted embedded commands like the following:

```
.page size 58,80
.spacing 2
.no autojustify
```

As you might guess, the first command sets the number of lines per page and the number of characters on each line. The second command generates double-spaced output. The last command turns off justification. Essentially, I would pepper a text file with these commands, run it through RUNOFF, and send RUNOFF's output to the line printer. The resulting output looked as good as a typewritten document, which was good enough for most work in those days.

UNIX came with a more advanced typesetting program called `troff` (which stands for *typesetting runoff*) that could send output to a special device called a *typesetter*. A typesetter could produce much better output than a line printer. `troff` allows you to choose different fonts and to print text in bold and italic.

To handle output on simpler printers, UNIX also included `nroff` (which stands for *nontypesetting runoff*) to process `troff` files and generate output, ignore fancy output commands, and generate output on a line printer. `troff` typesetting is versatile enough that many computer books have been typeset with it.

Now that nearly every computer has some sort of graphical interface (Microsoft Windows, Apple Macintosh, or the X Window System), most word-processing programs work in "what you see is what you get" mode, in which you get to work directly with the formatted document. Therefore, you probably won't have any reason to use `troff` for typesetting. `nroff` is still used for one important task, however: preparing man pages. The remainder of this chapter focuses on that aspect of using `nroff`.

Note

The `groff` program is the GNU version of `troff` and `nroff`. With appropriate flags, you can use `groff` to typeset for several output devices, including any typewriterlike device.

Even if you do not use `groff` to prepare formatted documents (because using a PC-based word processor is more convenient), you may end up using `groff` to write the man page for any program that you write.

Man pages are the files containing the information that users can view by typing the command `man progname`. This command shows online help information on `progname`. The subject of a man page can be anything from an overview of a software package to the programming information for a specific C function (for example, try `man fopen` on your Linux system).

After you go through an example, you'll realize that writing man pages in `groff` is quite simple.

Note

Before I describe the man-page preparation process, I should make it clear that you do not use the `groff` program to prepare the man page. The man page is just a text file containing embedded commands that `groff` recognizes. You might use `groff` to view a man page during preparation, but you can prepare a man page without ever running `groff`.

Trying an existing man page

Before you write a man page, you should look at an existing one. A brief example is the man page for `nroff`. Figure 24-5 shows the man page of `nroff` in an `xterm` window.

```
                              xterm

NROFF(1)                                           NROFF(1)

NAME
       nroff - emulate nroff command with groff

SYNOPSIS
       nroff [ -h ] [ -i ] [ -mname ] [ -nnum ] [ -olist ] [ -rcn
       ] [ -Tname ] [ file... ]

DESCRIPTION
       The nroff script emulates the nroff command using groff.
       The -T option with an argument other than ascii and latin1
       will be ignored.  The -h option is equivalent to the
       grotty -h option.  The -i, -n, -m, -o and -r options have
       the effect described in troff(1).  In addition nroff
       silently ignores options of -e, -q or -s.

SEE ALSO
       groff(1), troff(1), grotty(1)

Groff Version 1.11        26 June 1995                    1

(END)
```

Figure 24-5: Output of the `man nroff` command in an `xterm` window.

In this case, you don't really have to pay attention to the exact content of the man page; all you care about is the layout. Take a moment to look over the layout. You'll notice the following things:

- The name of the command appears at the top of the man page. The number 1 that appears in parentheses next to the command's name denotes the section of the UNIX manual where this command belongs.

- The man page contains several sections, each of which appears in boldface. The text within the section is indented.

- In this example, the sections are NAME, SYNOPSIS, DESCRIPTION, and SEE ALSO. If you try a few more man pages, you'll see that some have many more sections. Almost all man pages, however, have these four sections.

- Some text appears in boldface.

Looking at a man-page source

After you view a man page with the man command, you should look at the original source file from which the man command generates output. In your Linux system, the man-page source files are in several directories. These directory names are defined in the /etc/man.config file.

The source file for the nroff man page is /usr/man/man1/nroff.1. You should look at this file to see how the man page appears in its final form, as shown in Figure 24-5. Here is how you can look at the source file for the gnroff man page:

```
cd /usr/man/man1
more nroff.1
... Some lines deleted here
.TH NROFF 1 "26 June 1995" "Groff Version 1.11"
.SH NAME
nroff \- emulate nroff command with groff
.SH SYNOPSIS
.B nroff
[
.B \-h
]
[
.B \-i
]
        ... Some lines deleted here
[
.I file\|.\|.\|.
]
.SH DESCRIPTION
The
.B nroff
script emulates the
```

```
.B nroff
command using groff.
The
.B \-T
option with an argument other than
.B ascii
and
.B latin1
will be ignored.
        ... Some lines deleted here
.SH "SEE ALSO"
.BR groff (1),
.BR gtroff (1),
.BR grotty (1)
```

One interesting feature of the marked-up text file for the man page is the haphazard manner in which lines break. The formatting program groff (the man command uses groff to process the marked-up text file) fills up the lines of text and makes everything presentable.

Most groff commands have to be on a line by themselves, and each such command starts with a period. You can, however, embed some groff font-control commands in the text; these embedded commands start with a backslash (\).

Following is a summary of the commands you see in the gnroff man-page source file:

- .B turns on boldface

- .BI turns on boldface and then switches to italic

- .BR turns on boldface and then changes to roman

- .I turns on italic

- .SH is the start of a new section

- .TH indicates the document title

If you use these dot commands (by *dot commands*, I mean the commands that begin with a period or dot) to change the font, the man-page source file tends to have many short lines, because each dot command has to appear on a separate line. As the following section shows, you can use embedded font-change commands to produce a more readable source file.

Writing a sample man page

This section shows you how to write a man page for a sample application named satview. Assume that the satview program displays a satellite image in a window. The program has some options for specifying the map projection, the zoom level, and the name of the file that contains the satellite-image data.

Use a text editor to type the man-page source code shown in the following listing, and save it in a file named satview.1.

```
.TH SATVIEW 1 "May 25, 1998" "Satview Version 4.01"
.SH NAME
satview \- View satellite images.
.SH SYNOPSIS
\fBsatview\fP [-p \fIprojection\fP] [-m] [-z \fIzoomlevel\fP]
\fIfilename\fP
.SH DESCRIPTION
\fBsatview\fP displays the satellite image from \fIfilename\fP.
.SS Options
.TP
\fB-p \fIprojection\fR
Set the map projection (can be \fBL\fR for Lambert Conformal or
\fBP\fR for Polar Stereographic). The default is Lambert Conformal.
.TP
\fB-m\fP
Include a map in the satellite image.
.TP
\fB-z \fIzoomlevel\fR
Set the zoom level (can be one of: 2, 4, or 8). The default
zoomlevel is 1.
.TP
\fIfilename\fR
File containing satellite data.
.SH FILES
.TP
\fC/etc/awips/satview.rc\fR
Initialization commands for \fBsatview\fR
.SH SEE ALSO
nexrad(1), contour(1)
.SH Bugs
At zoom levels greater than 2, map is not properly aligned with image.
```

The source file has the following significant features:

- The .TH tag indicates the man-page title, as well as the date and a version-number string. In the formatted man page, the version and date strings appear at the bottom of each page.

- This man page has six sections — NAME, SYNOPSIS, DESCRIPTION, FILES, SEE ALSO, and Bugs — each of which starts with the .SH tag.

- The DESCRIPTION has an Options subsection. The .SS tag indicates the beginning of a subsection.

- In the Options subsection, each item is listed with the .TP tag.

- The \fB command changes the font to boldface.

- The \fI command changes the font to italic.

- The \fR command changes the font to roman.

- The \fP command changes the font to its preceding setting.

With this information in hand, you should be able to understand the man-page source listing.

Testing and installing the man page

As you prepare the man-page file, you want to make sure it is formatted correctly. To view the formatted output, you should use the following command:

```
groff -Tascii -man satview.1 | more
```

This command runs the `groff` command with the `ascii` typesetting device (which means produce plain ASCII output) and with the man-page macro set (that's what the `-man` option does).

If you find any formatting discrepancies, check the dot commands and any embedded font-change commands, and make sure that everything looks right.

After you are satisfied with the man-page format, you can make the man page available to everyone by copying the file to one of the directories where all man pages are located. You could install the man page with the following copy command:

```
cp satview /usr/man/man1
```

After that, try the man page with the following command:

```
man satview
```

Figure 24-6 shows the resulting output. Compare the output with the source file in Listing 24-1 to see the effects of the commands on the final output. Notice that the italic command generates underlined output, because the terminal window cannot display an italic font.

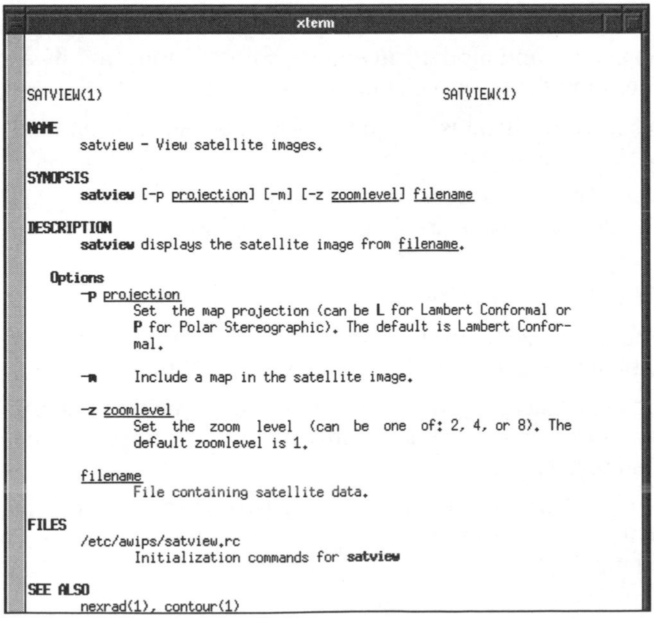

Figure 24-6: Output of the `man satview` command in an `xterm` window.

With the listing in this section as a guideline, you should now be able to write your own man pages.

Summary

The configuration of many Linux features depends on settings stored in text files. Therefore, you have to know how to edit text files to set up and maintain a Linux system. Another form of text processing involves typesetting and formatting text documents. Linux includes `groff` for this purpose. Nowadays, you're likely to use a PC to prepare formatted documents, but you still need to prepare one kind of formatted document: the man pages that provide online help about any software you may write. Accordingly, this chapter shows you how to use several text editors, and shows you how to prepare man pages by using `groff`. By reading this chapter, you learn the following:

▶ Linux includes a variety of text editors. It's important to learn `ed` and `vi`, because all UNIX systems come with these editors. Although the `ed` editor may be cryptic, you sometimes may have to edit files when no other editor is available.

▶ The `ed` editor works on a text file one line at a time (which is why it's called a line editor). Each command takes the form of a range of lines, followed by a one-character command that applies to that range of lines.

▶ The `vi` editor is a full-screen editor that allows you to view a file several lines at a time. The `vi` editor has three modes: visual command mode, colon command mode, and text-input mode.

▶ In text-input mode, you can enter text. To change to input mode, press **i, a**, or **A**. To return to command mode, press Escape.

▶ In `vi`'s colon command mode, you enter a colon (:) followed by a command that has the same syntax as `ed` commands.

▶ GNU Emacs is more than just an editor — it's also an environment from which you can perform most routine tasks.

▶ As an editor, GNU Emacs does not have any modes; whatever you type goes into the file. Commands begin with a control character (such as `Ctrl-x`) or Escape.

▶ To view the online tutorial, type `Ctrl-h t` in GNU Emacs.

▶ The `groff` utility is useful for formatting documents. `groff` provides the functionality of the standard UNIX `nroff` and `troff` utilities.

▶ Even though you may not prepare formatted documents in Linux (because it's easier to do so on a PC or a Macintosh), you still need to use `groff` to prepare man pages.

▶ The best way to learn to prepare a man page is to study an existing man page and mimic its style in your own man page. This chapter provides an example of how you might prepare a typical man page.

Appendixes

Appendix A

Linux Applications Roundup

The Red Hat Linux distribution on this book's companion CD-ROM includes many applications. Many more Linux applications are available on the Internet. This chapter briefly describes many of the Linux applications on the companion CD-ROM. The purpose of this chapter is to introduce some of the applications so you know they are available on the CD-ROM.

Following is a selected set of Linux applications from the CD-ROM, organized by category:

Category	Applications
Editors	GNU Emacs, JED, Joe, `vim`
Utilities	DOSEMU, GNU `bc`, `gzip`, `ispell`, Midnight Commander, `patch`, `xfm`
Graphics and images	XV, XPaint, Xfig, Gnuplot, Ghostscript, Ghostview, GIMP, ImageMagick, `xanim`
Internet	`dip`, `elm`, `imap`, `ircii`, `inn`, `pine`, `pppd`, `rdist`, `sendmail`, `tin`, `trn`, `x3270`, Netscape Communicator
Serial communications	Minicom, Seyon
Programming	Bison, `f2c`, `flex`, Gawk, GCC, `p2c`, Perl, Python, RCS, Tcl/Tk, `yacc`
Text formatting	`groff`, TeX
Games	GNU Chess, `xtetris`, `acm`, `colour-yahtzee`, `flying`, `fortune-mod`, `mysterious`, `paradise`, `xchomp`, `xevil`, `xgalaga`, `xgammon`, `xpilot`

This list is by no means comprehensive. The Linux distribution comes with a plethora of standard UNIX commands, for example, not shown in the list.

This chapter provides a brief summary of a smaller subset of these applications. In particular, I focus on some of the utility programs not covered in earlier chapters. Some applications, such as GNU Emacs and DOSEMU, are covered in detail elsewhere in this book. Also, entire categories of important applications, such as Internet applications, are covered in great detail in individual chapters.

Quite a few of the listed applications are automatically installed during the Linux installation process. For a few applications, you have to go through the trouble of installing them from the CD-ROM.

Notice some of these applications are shareware. You are expected to register and pay a shareware fee if you plan to use the applications for your work. This information is noted where appropriate.

Editors

You can find the following text editors on the companion CD-ROM:

- GNU Emacs, the one and only original Emacs
- JED, a GNU Emacs-like editor
- Joe, a text editor with commands similar to those of WordStar
- Vim, a `vi`-like editor

As you can see, most of these editors aspire to be either GNU Emacs or `vi`. The look-alikes typically are smaller in size and have less features.

GNU Emacs

The companion CD-ROM includes GNU Emacs Version 20.2.1. GNU Emacs, which is one of the best-known GNU products, is distributed by Free Software Foundation. The CD-ROM includes two versions of GNU Emacs:

- The full version of GNU Emacs that works under *X* and provides menus for editing operations. You must have *X* installed to run this version. The binary is configured with the following options:

  ```
  --with-x11 --with-x-toolkit --prefix=/usr
  ```

- A version that is about 330KB smaller than the full version of GNU Emacs, with the same functionality, but without the support for *X*.

You can run the non-*X* version of GNU Emacs in an `xterm` window under *X*. The non-*X* version, however, is mainly for those users who do not have the X Window System installed on their systems.

Chapter 24 describes the features of GNU Emacs and shows how to use GNU Emacs for text-editing tasks.

JED

Like several of the other freely available text editors, this editor is named after its author, John E. Davis. JED is a powerful but small GNU Emacs-like editor that supports editing modes — such as GNU Emacs — and can read info files, like GNU Emacs. JED also can emulate other text editors, such as WordStar and the EDT editor of VAX/VMS systems. One of the unique features of JED is that you can actually edit binary files in JED.

You will find the RPM file for JED in the `RedHat/RPMS` directory of the companion CD-ROM.

Joe

The companion CD-ROM includes the Joe text editor Version 2.2. Joe is named after its creator, Joseph H. Allen. The Joe editor uses commands similar to those of the popular PC word processor of yesteryear, WordStar.

You will find the RPM file for the Joe editor in the `RedHat/RPMS` directory of the companion CD-ROM.

Vim

Vim stands for *Vi IMproved*. As the name implies, Vim is supposed to be an improved version of the standard UNIX text editor `vi`. The companion CD-ROM includes Version 3.0 of Vim. In addition to the standard `vi` commands, Vim includes several new features, such as several levels of undo, command-line history, and filename completion.

Cross-Reference

Chapter 24 shows you how to use the `vi` editor. If you know `vi`, you can use Vim easily.

Utilities

This category is a catchall category for many helpful applications that come with the Linux distribution. The list is not exhaustive, because I included only the most popular applications. The applications summarized in the following sections are:

- DOSEMU, a DOS emulator for Linux
- GNU `bc`, an arbitrary precision calculator
- `gzip`, a utility for compressing and expanding files
- `ical`, an X-based calendar program
- `ispell`, a full-screen interactive spelling checker
- Midnight Commander, a file manager with a text-based interface
- `patch`, a utility for applying changes to a text file
- `xfm`, an X-based file manager

DOSEMU

DOSEMU is a freely distributed DOS emulator — a program you can run under Linux to get an MS-DOS environment. With DOSEMU, you can run DOS applications under Linux. DOSEMU is not installed by default. You will find the DOSEMU software distribution in the `contrib` directory of the companion CD-ROM.

Cross-Reference

To use DOSEMU, you first have to install it from the CD-ROM. Chapter 7 shows you how to install and use DOSEMU.

GNU bc

GNU bc enables you to enter arbitrary precision numbers and perform various calculations with these numbers. GNU bc implements the arbitrary precision-calculation capability specified by the POSIX P1003.2/D11 draft standard.

You'll get a chance to install GNU bc as part of a package during Linux installation from the companion CD-ROM.

If you have GNU bc installed, you should be able to run it with the following command:

```
bc
bc 1.04
Copyright (C) 1991, 1992, 1993, 1994, 1997 Free Software Foundation,
Inc.
This is free software with ABSOLUTELY NO WARRANTY.
For details type `warranty'.
```

After displaying the banner, bc waits for your input. Then you can enter numbers and expressions, using a syntax similar to that of the C programming language.

Numbers are the basic elements in bc. A number is treated as an arbitrary precision number with an integral and fractional part. You can enter numbers and evaluate expressions just the way you write expressions in C, as the following example shows:

```
1.000000000000000033 + 0.1
1.100000000000000033
```

As soon as you enter an expression, bc evaluates the expression and displays the result.

You also can define variables and use them in expressions, as follows:

```
cost=119.95
tax_rate=0.05
total=(1+tax_rate)*cost
total
125.94
```

If you check this result with your calculator, you notice bc truncates the result of multiplication (it does the same with division). If you want, you can retain more significant digits by setting the scale variable, as follows:

```
scale=10
total=(1+tax_rate)*cost
total
125.9475
```

In this case, the result has more significant digits.

The bc utility supports an entire programming language with a C-style syntax. You can write loops and conditional statements, and even define new functions with the define keyword. The following example shows how you might define a factorial function:

```
define factorial (n) {
  if(n <= 1) return (1);
  return (factorial(n-1)*n);
}
```

As you can see, the factorial function is recursive; it calls itself. Entering the lines as shown in the example is important. In particular, bc needs the open brace on the first line because that brace tells bc to continue reading input until it gets a closing brace.

After you define the factorial function, you can use it just as you might call a C function. Following are some examples:

```
factorial(3)
6
factorial(4)
24
factorial(10)
3628800
factorial(40)
815915283247897734345611269596115894272000000000
factorial(50)
30414093201713378043612608166064768844377641568960512000000000000
factorial(100)
93326215443944152681699238856266700490715968264381621468592963895217\
5\
999932299156089414639761565182862536979208272237582511852109168640000\
00000000000000000000
```

As the example shows, you can use bc to represent as large a number as you want; no limit exists. When necessary, bc displays the result on multiple lines, with each continuation line ending in a backslash followed by a new line.

To quit bc, type the following command:

```
quit
```

To learn more about bc, consult its man pages by using the man bc command. After you learn about new features of bc, try them interactively.

gzip

The `gzip` program is the GNU zip compression utility used to compress all Linux software distributions. When you run `gzip` with a filename as argument, it reduces the file's size by using the Lempel-Ziv (LZ77) compression algorithm and stores the result in a file with the same name but with an additional `.gz` extension. Thus, if you compress a file with the `gzip files.tar` command, the result is a compressed file with the name `files.tar.gz.`

The same `gzip` program can decompress any file previously compressed by `gzip`. To decompress the file `files.tar.gz`, for example, you can simply type the following:

```
gzip -d files.tar
```

Notice you needn't explicitly type the `.gz` extension; `gzip` automatically appends a `.gz` extension when it is looking for the compressed file. After decompressing, the utility creates a new file with the name `files.tar`.

Instead of `gzip -d`, you can use the `gunzip` command to decompress a file, as follows:

```
gunzip files.tar
```

This command also looks for a file named `files.tar.gz` and decompresses the file, if found.

By default, `gzip` stores the original filename and timestamp in the compressed file. You can decompress a file with the `-N` option to restore the original filename and time stamp.

Following is the basic syntax of the `gzip` command:

```
gzip [-cdfhlLnNrtvV19] [-S .xxx] [file ...]
```

The options have the following meanings:

- `-c` writes output to standard output
- `-d` decompresses the file
- `-f` forces compression or decompression, even if file has multiple links or the corresponding file already exists
- `-h` displays a help screen and quits
- `-l` lists files sizes before and after compression
- `-L` displays the `gzip` license and quits
- `-n` stops `gzip` from storing the original filename in the compressed file
- `-N` restores original filename during decompression
- `-q` suppresses all warnings
- `-r` causes `gzip` to traverse the directory structure recursively and operate on all files

- -S .xxx causes gzip to use the suffix .xxx instead of .gz

- -t tests the integrity of a compressed file

- -v displays the name and percentage compression for each file

- -V displays version number and the compiler options used to build that version of gzip

- -1 uses the fastest compression method (even though compression may not be as much)

- -9 uses the slowest compression method (provides the most compression)

- *file* ... are one or more filenames (the files to be compressed or decompressed)

The gzip utility is installed automatically when you install Linux from the companion CD-ROM.

ical

The ical utility is an interactive, *X* window-based calendar program. When you install Linux from the companion CD-ROM, you also install ical.

To use ical, type **ical** from an xterm window or use the menu selections Start->Programs->Utilities->Ical. The program displays a full-screen window where you can click a date to view that day's schedule. Figure A-1 shows a typical calendar.

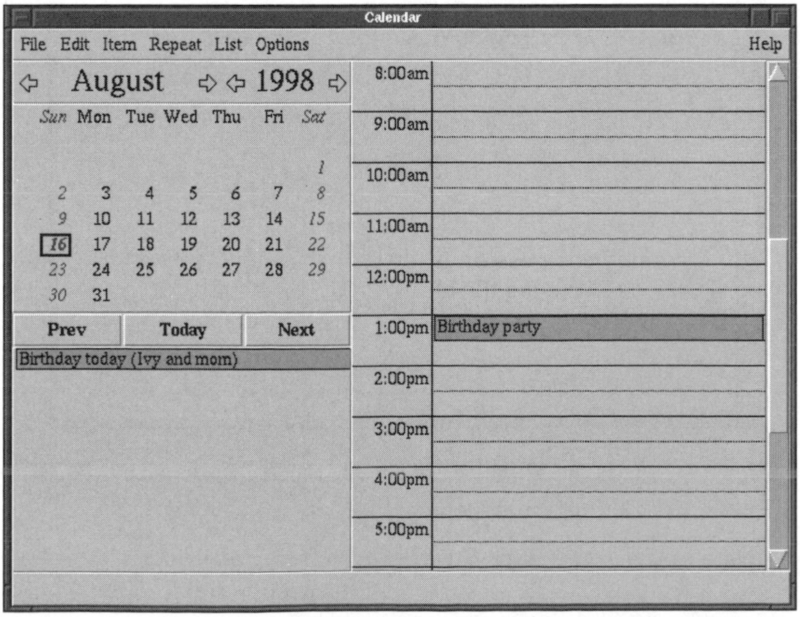

Figure A-1: Viewing the calendar with ical

You can go to a different month or year by clicking the arrows next to the month and the year. For a specific date, you can add events in the area underneath the month's calendar.

To add appointments for a specific time, click the time and type a brief description of the appointment.

After you finish adding events and appointments, select Save from the File menu to save the calendar.

ispell

The `ispell` utility is an interactive spelling checker. When you install Linux from the companion CD-ROM, you get a chance to install `ispell`.

Using `ispell` is simple. Most of the time, you use `ispell` to check the spelling of words in a text file. To do so, simply type **ispell** *filename*. Suppose you typed some notes and stored them in a text file named `notes`. To run the spelling checker on that file, type the following command:

```
ispell notes
```

After `ispell` runs, it scans the file named `notes` until it finds a misspelled word (any word not in `ispell`'s dictionary). In the `notes` file, `ispell` may find the misspelled word *concensus*. Figure A-2 shows how `ispell` reports this misspelling in the full-screen text window.

Figure A-2: A misspelled word with suggested spellings reported by `ispell`

As Figure A-2 shows, `ispell` shows you the misspelled word highlighted within the sentence where it occurs. Below that sentence, `ispell` lists possible corrections. In this case, the utility lists *consensus* — the right choice — as the first correction for *concensus*.

At the bottom of the screen, `ispell` displays the commands you can enter. Following are the meanings of the items on the last line in Figure A-2:

- `Space` means accept the word this time.
- `<number>` refers to the number of the suggested correction you want to use. To replace the misspelled word with the correction numbered 0, simply type **0**.
- `R` means replace. `ispell` prompts for a replacement word.
- `A` means accept. `ispell` accepts the word for the rest of the file.
- `I` means insert. `ispell` accepts the word and also adds it to the user's private dictionary.
- `L` causes `ispell` to look up words in the system dictionary.
- `U` means accept the word and add a lowercase version to the user's private dictionary.
- `Q` causes `ispell` to quit immediately.
- `X` causes `ispell` to save the rest of the file, ignoring misspellings.
- `?` displays a help screen.

In addition, you can enter a shell command with an exclamation-mark (`!`) prefix. If the screen gets messed up for any reason, press Ctrl-L to refresh the screen.

Midnight Commander

Midnight Commander is a file manager with a text-based interface, similar to Norton Commander for MS-DOS. You can use Midnight Commander to manage files and directories without having to learn UNIX commands. If you are uncertain about all the UNIX commands, you may want to use Midnight Commander to perform file operations such as copy, rename, and delete. You can even view or edit a file with Midnight Commander.

When you install Linux from the companion CD-ROM, you get a chance to install Midnight Commander.

You can run Midnight Commander from the console or an `xterm` window. To start Midnight Commander, type **mc**.

Figure A-3 shows typical output from Midnight Commander. In this case, the current directory happens to be the root directory (/).

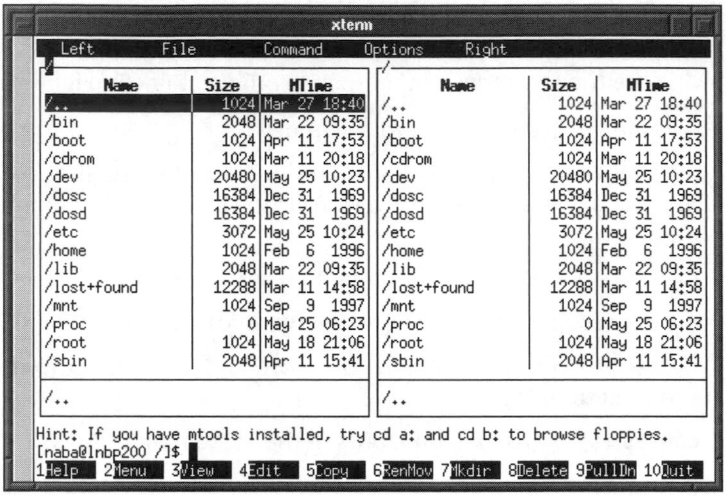

Figure A-3: Midnight Commander display in an `xterm` window

The display has two side-by-side directory listings. You can change the directory on either listing. The two side-by-side views enable you to perform operations such as copy or move between two directories.

At the bottom of the Midnight Commander display are ten commands that vaguely resemble buttons in a graphical interface. These commands are the common operations you can perform in the Midnight Commander window.

Midnight Commander responds to mouse input in a console window as well as an `xterm` window. This means you can double-click a directory name to view that directory's contents in the Midnight Commander display. Also, you can click the commands (displayed in reverse video on the bottom edge of the Midnight Commander display) to activate them.

patch

The GNU `patch` utility is designed to apply *patches* (corrections) to files. The basic idea behind `patch` is, when you want to distribute changes in a file, you run the standard UNIX `diff` command and generate a `diff` file that indicates how the file should be changed. Then you distribute that `diff` file to everyone who has the original file. The recipient runs the `patch` utility with the `diff` file as input and `patch` makes the changes in the original files.

The `patch` utility is installed automatically when you install Linux from the companion CD-ROM. Chapter 2 shows you how to use `patch` to apply changes to the Linux kernel sources when you upgrade the kernel from one version to the next.

You can learn more about `patch` through a simple example. Assume you have a file named `original.txt` that contains the following text:

```
Version: 1.0

Revision history:
  5/25/98: Original file (NB)

This text file used as an example to illustrate how to
use diff and patch to update a file.
```

Suppose you already distributed this file to several users. (Pretend the file is the source file of a computer program.) After a while, you make some changes in this file. The new file, named `revised.txt`, looks like this:

```
Version: 1.1

Revision history:
  5/25/98: Original file (NB)
  6/15/98: Added a new line (LB)

This text file used as an example to illustrate how to
use diff and patch to update a file.

Something new added...
```

Now you want to provide these changes to your users so they can use the new file. Your first task is to create a `diff` file that captures the changes you have made.

To create the `diff` file, run `diff` with the `-u` option and specify the two filenames as arguments — the original file, followed by the revised one. Thus, the following command creates the `diff` file for the current example:

```
diff -u original.txt revised.txt > patch-1.1
```

This command creates the file `patch-1.1`, which is what you would distribute to your users who are currently using the file `original.txt`. This `diff` file also is referred to as the *patch file*.

When users receives the patch file, all they need to do is put the patch file in the same directory where the file `original.txt` resides and then type the following command:

```
patch < patch-1.1
Hmm... Looks like a unified diff to me...
The text leading up to this was:
--------------------------
|--- original.txt      Mon May 25 11:27:24 1998
|+++ revised.txt       Mon Jun 15 11:30:00 1998
--------------------------
Patching file original.txt using Plan A...
Hunk #1 succeeded at 1.
done
```

The `patch` utility reports some helpful messages and applies the changes from the patch file. First, `patch` copies the `original.txt` file to `original.txt.orig`; then it applies the changes directly to the file `original.txt`. After `patch` finishes, you'll find the content of the `original.txt` file matches that of `revised.txt`. This example should give you a good idea of how to use the `patch` utility to update text files.

xfm

The `xfm` program is an X-based file- and application-manager utility. When you first install Linux from this book's companion CD-ROM, you have the option to install `xfm`.

Before you use `xfm`, you should run a script file — `/usr/X11R6/bin/xfm.install` — that installs some default configuration files in the `.xfm` subdirectory of your home directory (the script creates a `.xfm` directory, if it does not exist). Because the `/usr/X11R6/bin` directory usually is in your `PATH` environment variable, you should be able to run the `xfm` installation script with the following command:

```
xfm.install
Default configuration files installed.
```

After completing this step, you can start `xfm` in an `xterm` window by typing **xfm &**. Figure A-4 shows the initial set of `xfm` windows.

The `File Manager` window shows the directories and files in the user's home directory. The directories appear as folders — a metaphor popular in many file managers, including recent ones such as the Explorer in Microsoft Windows 95.

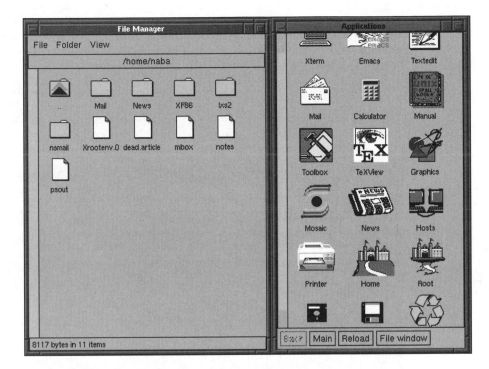

Figure A-4: Initial windows of the `xfm` program

The `Applications` window displays a set of icons that represent applications. The contents of the window depend on a text-configuration file named `Apps` (located in the `.xfm` subdirectory of your home directory). The default `Apps` file contains the following code:

```
#XFM
Xterm:::terminal.xpm:exec xterm:
Emacs:::emacs.xpm:exec emacs:exec emacs $*
Textedit:::edit.xpm:exec textedit:exec textedit $*
Mail:::mailtool.xpm:exec xmailtool:
Calculator:::calc.xpm:exec xcalc:
Manual:::man2.xpm:exec xman:
Toolbox:~/.xfm:Toolbox:tools.xpm:LOAD:
TeXView:::tex-view.xpm::exec xdvi $1
Graphics:~/.xfm:Graphics:drawing.xpm:LOAD:
Mosaic:::xmosaic.xpm:exec mosaic:
News:::news.xpm:exec xrn:
Hosts:~/.xfm:Hosts:rlogin.xpm:LOAD:
Printer:::printer.xpm:lpq -Plaser:exec lpr -Plaser $*
Home:::..citadel.xpm:OPEN:
Root:/:::citadelroot.xpm:OPEN:
A\::/disk:a:floppy.xpm:OPEN:
B\::/disk:b:disk.xpm:OPEN:
Trash:::.trash:recycle.xpm:OPEN:shift; mv -f -b -V numbered $* ~/.trash
```

You should be able to guess the syntax of the Apps file from this listing. Lines that begin with the pound sign (#) are comments. Other lines list a label, a pixmap icon file (with the .xpm extension), and a command to execute when the user double-clicks that icon.

You needn't learn the syntax of the Apps file because you can edit its contents directly from the Applications window. When you right-click anywhere in the Applications window, a context-sensitive pop-up menu appears. If you right-click an icon, xfm displays the pop-up menu shown in Figure A-5.

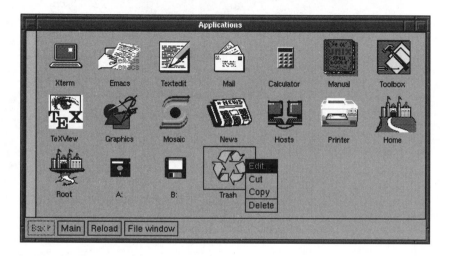

Figure A-5: This pop-up menu appears when you right-click an icon in the Applications window.

The pop-up menu enables you to perform one of several operations on the icon. If you right-click the Trash icon and then choose Edit from the pop-up menu, for example, xfm displays another dialog box from which you can edit the action performed by the Trash icon.

To add a new application to the Applications window, right-click an empty spot in the window. Figure A-6 shows the pop-up menu that appears.

As Figure A-6 shows, the pop-up menu allows you to add or remove applications. If you select Install from the pop-up menu, xfm displays a dialog box where you can fill in the requested information and then click the Install button.

You have to double-click an icon in the Applications window to launch the associated application.

In the File Manager window, xfm does not, by default, show any file or directory whose name begins with a period. By convention, these files are considered to be hidden files in UNIX. To view these hidden files, click the View label along the top edge of the window (the menu bar). From the pull-down View menu that appears, select Show hidden files. After that, xfm displays all files and directories, including the ones whose names begin with a period.

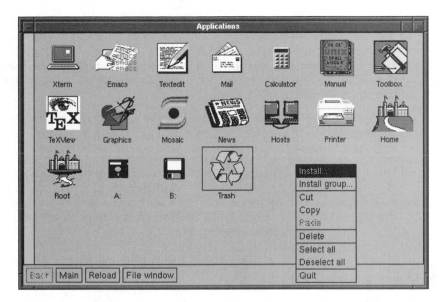

Figure A-6: This pop-up menu appears when you right-click an empty spot in the `Applications` window.

To view the contents of a directory, double-click that directory's name. The `File Manager` window shows the contents of that directory. To go back to the parent directory, double-click the folder that has two periods (..) as its label.

The `File Manager` window also supports context-sensitive pop-up menus that appear when you right-click an icon. Figure A-7 shows the pop-up menu that appears when you right-click a file icon.

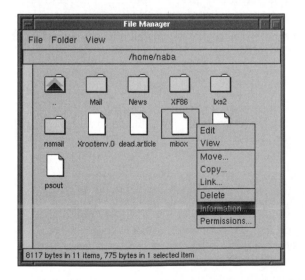

Figure A-7: This pop-up menu appears when you right-click an icon in the `File Manager` window.

You can use this pop-up menu to perform file operations such as copy, move, and delete. You also can view detailed information about the file and change its permission settings. To view file information, for example, select Information from the pop-up menu. A dialog box appears with information about the file you right-clicked. After viewing the file information, click the Ok button to dismiss the dialog box.

Finally, to quit xfm, select Quit from the File menu in the File Manager window. When xfm asks for confirmation, click the Continue button (if you really want to quit).

This brief overview does not do justice to all xfm can do. You can, for example, configure the Applications window with your favorite applications by dragging and dropping icons of applications and scripts into the window. The best way to learn more about xfm is to start using it. If you plan to rely on a file manager, you should give xfm a try.

Graphics and Images

The applications in this category enable you to prepare, view, modify, and print graphics and images. The following applications are summarized in the following sections:

- XV, a shareware program for viewing and manipulating many kinds of images
- XPaint, a bitmap painting program patterned after MacPaint
- Xfig, a drawing program capable of producing engineering drawings
- Gnuplot, a plotting package
- Ghostscript, a PostScript interpreter capable of producing output on many devices, including output in various image-file formats
- Ghostview, an X application that serves as a front end to Ghostscript

XV

XV is an impressive shareware program for viewing nearly any kind of image (GIF, JPEG, PostScript, Windows BMP, TIFF, PCX, and X11 Bitmap File, to name a few) on an *X* display. If you are interested in using the program, you should read the license information that appears in the accompanying documentation.

When you install Linux from the companion CD-ROM, you can choose to install XV as well; it's in the *Graphics Manipulation* package.

If XV is installed, you'll find its documentation in the /usr/doc/xv-3.10a directory. In particular, you should find the file /usr/doc/xv-3.10a/xvdocs.

ps. This file happens to be a PostScript file, which is nearly 4MB in size. That PostScript file is the XV manual.

XV has so many features, a brief description does not do it justice. You should find a PostScript printer and print the xvdocs.ps file. The documentation is nearly 130 pages long and contains many images, so printing it may take a while.

You'll also find the license in the XV documentation. You should read the license to determine what you must do if you plan to use XV for your work. Because XV is shareware, the author encourages you to it and even distribute it to other users.

To try XV, type **xv &** in an xterm window (you must run *X* to use XV). From the X window desktop, you can also follow the menu selection Start->Programs->Graphics->xv. XV starts and displays its logo in an initial image window, as shown in Figure A-8.

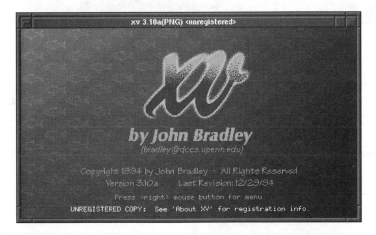

Figure A-8: The initial XV image window

The image window's title bar shows the XV version number and indicates this copy is unregistered. The text in the window tells you to right-click to get the menu. If you right-click the image window, XV brings up the XV Controls window, shown in Figure A-9.

As the name implies, the XV Controls window is the control center for XV; you perform all operations from this window.

If you have not read the license agreement already, click the About XV button in the XV Controls window. XV opens a text viewer window that displays the XV licensing information.

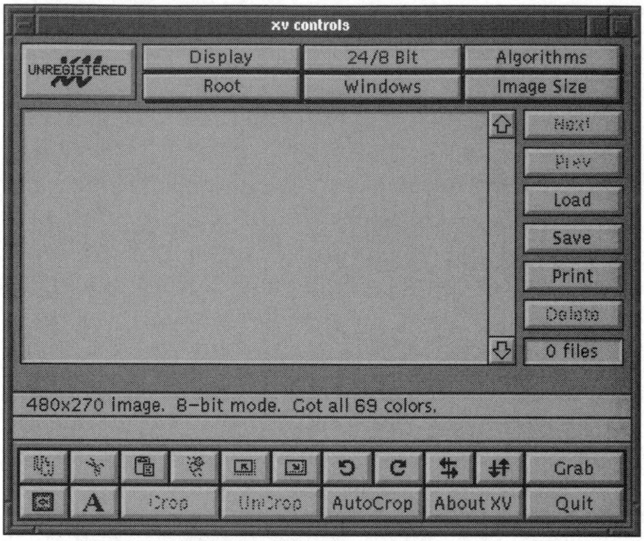

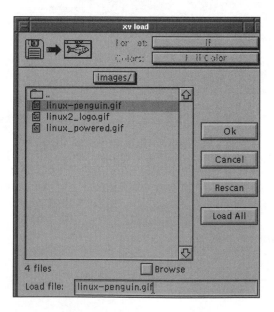

Figure A-9: The XV Controls window

One common operation is loading an image. To do this, click the Load button in XV Controls window. XV displays a file-selection dialog box, as shown in Figure A-10.

Figure A-10: Selecting an image file to view in XV

Through the dialog box of Figure A-10, you can select an image file from a directory. In Figure A-10, the linux-penguin.gif file is selected. From the .gif extension, you probably can guess this is a GIF file, which XV can display.

To view the selected image file, click the Ok button. That action causes XV to load the image into the image window and to list the file's name in the XV Controls window, as shown in Figure A-11.

Figure A-11: Loading the image file into the image window in XV

The XV Controls window shows some detailed information about the image, which is in GIF87 format and has 191 colors. The image size is 256×116 pixels.

You can do much more than just load and view images in XV, but describing all that would require hundreds of pages. If you want to try the other features of XV, please print the PostScript documentation (as described in this section) and use that documentation to learn more about XV. Another, equally effective, approach is simply to dive right in and try various buttons and menu selections in the XV Controls window.

XPaint

XPaint is an image-display and -editing program patterned after the venerable MacPaint program for the Apple Macintosh. XPaint runs under the X Window System and enables you to view and edit bitmapped images in several formats, including GIF, X11 Pixmap (xpm), X11 Bitmap (xbm), and TIFF.

XPaint is included on this book's companion CD-ROM. You can choose to install XPaint when you install Linux from the companion CD-ROM; it's in the *Graphics Manipulation* package.

To run XPaint, type **xpaint &** in an `xterm` window. From the X window desktop, you can also follow the menu selection Start->Programs->Graphics->xpaint. XPaint runs and displays its toolbox window, as shown in Figure A-12.

Figure A-12: The image-editing toolbox in XPaint

All image-loading and -editing operations start at the toolbox window. If you have used any image-editing program, you should not have any problem with the tools in the toolbox.

A menu bar that contains four items — `File`, `Line`, `Font`, and `Help` — appears at the top edge of the XPaint toolbox window. If you click any of these items, a pull-down menu appears, from which you can make further selections. The `Help` menu offers some online help information.

Figure A-13 shows the result of selecting `About` from the `Help` menu.

The same window provides information on how to use various features of XPaint. Click the `Next` and `Previous` buttons (at the bottom edge of the Help window) to select a topic and look at its help information.

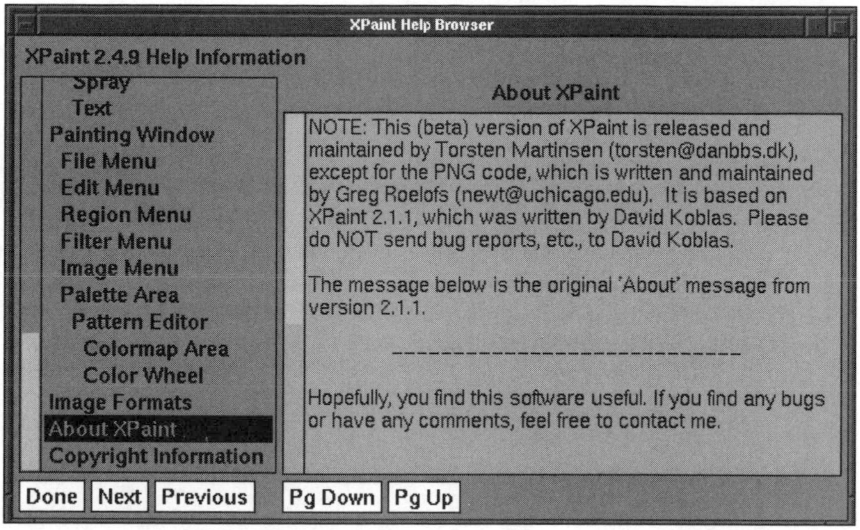

Figure A-13: About XPaint window

xfig

The xfig program is an interactive drawing program that runs under *X* and can generate encapsulated PostScript files suitable for inclusion in documents. On the companion CD-ROM, xfig is in the RedHat/RPMS subdirectory in two Red Hat Package Manager (RPM) files: xfig-3.2-3.i386.rpm and transfig-3.2-4.i386.rpm.

To install xfig, follow these steps:

1. Log in as root and mount the CD-ROM with the following command:

   ```
   mount /dev/cdrom /mnt/cdrom
   ```

2. Change to the appropriate directory with the following command:

   ```
   cd /mnt/cdrom/RedHat/RPMS
   ```

3. Install the transfig program with the rpm command, as follows:

   ```
   rpm -ivh transfig*.rpm
   ```

4. Install the xfig program with the rpm command, as follows:

   ```
   rpm -ivh xfig*.rpm
   ```

To try xfig, type **xfig &** in an xterm window. This command causes a rather large xfig window to appear. At the top edge of the window, you'll find a menu bar. To open an xfig drawing, click the File button. This action brings up a file-selection dialog box, through which you can change directories and locate xfig files (they usually have the .fig extension).

The Linux Loader (LILO) program uses a few xfig drawings in its documentation. You can find these files in the /usr/doc/lilo-0.20/doc directory. Use xfig's file-selection dialog box to locate this directory and select one of the files. Figure A-14 shows the xfig window after loading a drawing file.

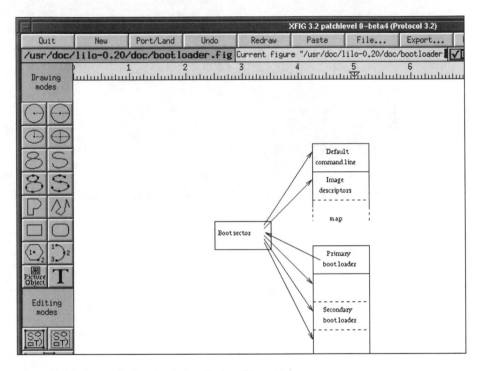

Figure A-14: A sample drawing being displayed by xfig

As Figure A-14 shows, in the hands of a skilled illustrator, xfig can produce impressive drawings.

As is true of any other tool, learning to use all the features of xfig takes some practice. If you are familiar with other drawing software, such as MacDraw (Macintosh) or CorelDRAW (PC), you should be able to use xfig without much trouble.

Gnuplot

Gnuplot is an interactive plotting utility. You need to run Gnuplot under the X Window System, because it uses an *X* window as the output device. Gnuplot is a command-line-driven program; it prompts you and accepts your input commands. In response to those commands, Gnuplot displays various types of plots. The output appears in an *X* window.

Incidentally, even though Gnuplot has *Gnu* in its name, it has nothing to do with GNU or the Free Software Foundation.

On the companion CD-ROM, Gnuplot is in the `RedHat/RPMS` sub directory in the `gnuplot-3.5-8.i386.rpm` file.

To install Gnuplot, follow these steps:

1. Log in as `root` and mount the CD-ROM with the following command:

   `mount /dev/cdrom /mnt/cdrom`

2. Change to the appropriate directory with the following command:

   `cd /mnt/cdrom/RedHat/RPMS`

3. Install Gnuplot with the following `rpm` command:

   `rpm -ivh gnuplot*.rpm`

After installing Gnuplot, you should be able to run it by typing **gnuplot** in an `xterm` window. Gnuplot displays an opening message and waits for further input at a prompt, as shown in Figure A-15.

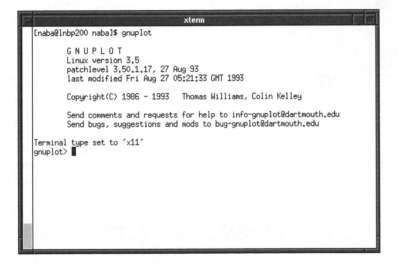

Figure A-15: Running Gnuplot in an `xterm` window

To see an immediate result, type the following Gnuplot command at the prompt:

`plot sin(x)`

Gnuplot opens an output window and displays a plot of the sine function, as shown in Figure A-16.

To quit Gnuplot, click the `xterm` window to make it active and then type **quit**. This example is a simple illustration of Gnuplot's capabilities.

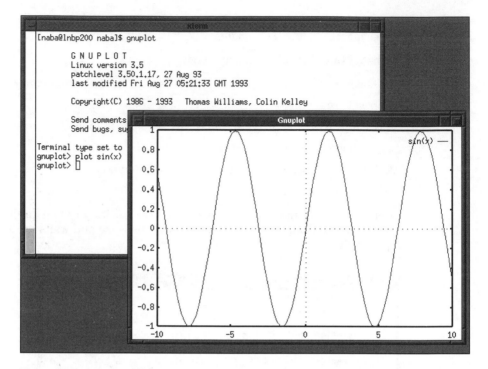

Figure A-16: Plotting sin(x) in Gnuplot

At any time in Gnuplot, you can ask for online help. The help is similar to that in DEC's VAX/VMS system. To learn more about the plot command, for example, type **help plot** at the Gnuplot prompt. Figure A-17 shows the resulting help information.

```
gnuplot> help plot
`plot` and `splot` are the primary commands of the program. They plot
functions and data in many, many ways. `plot` is used to plot 2-d
functions and data, while `splot` plots 3-d surfaces and data.

Syntax:

        plot {ranges} {<function> | {"<datafile>" {using ...}}}
                    {title} {style} {, <function> {title} {style}...}

        splot {ranges} {<function> | {"<datafile>" {index i} {using ...}}}
                    {title} {style} {, <function> {title} {style}...}

where either a <function> or the name of a data file enclosed in quotes is
supplied.  A function is a mathematical expression, or a pair (`plot`) or
triple (`splot`) of mathematical expressions in the case of parametric
functions.  User-defined functions and variables may also be defined here.

`plot` and `splot` commands can be as simple as

        plot sin(x)

and
Press return for more:
```

Figure A-17: Online help in Gnuplot

Ghostscript

Ghostscript is a utility for previewing and printing PostScript documents. Ghostscript enables you to print PostScript documents on many non-PostScript devices.

At heart, Ghostscript is a nearly complete implementation of the PostScript language. Ghostscript includes the interpreter that processes PostScript input and generates output on an output device. A Ghostscript device can be a printer (or display screen), as well as an image-file format, such as BMP or PCX

Ghostscript is distributed under the GNU General Public License but is copyrighted and maintained by Aladdin Enterprises. You can find the latest contact information in the README file in /usr/doc/ghostscript-3.33 directory. That directory also contains Ghostscript documentation.

The documentation in the /usr/doc/ghostscript-3.33 directory includes the files listed in Table A-1. All of these files are text files you can view using the more command.

Table A-1   Ghostscript documentation in /usr/doc/ghostscript-3.33 directory

File	Description
devices.doc	Detailed description of a few printers for which Ghostscript can produce output.
drivers.doc	Description of the interface between Ghostscript and device drivers.
fonts.doc	Description of the fonts and font facilities supplied with Ghostscript.
hershey.doc	Information about the Hershey fonts.
history1.doc	History of changes to older versions of Ghostscript.
history2.doc	Recent changes to Ghostscript.
humor.doc	Humorous message about Ghostscript.
language.doc	Description of the Ghostscript language.
lib.doc	Description of the Ghostscript library — a collection of C functions that implement the primitive graphic capabilities of the Ghostscript language.
make.doc	Description of how to install Ghostscript and how to build Ghostscript executables from source code.
NEWS	Summary of recent changes to Ghostscript.
ps2epsi.doc	Description of the ps2epsi utility, which converts a Ghostscript file to Adobe's Encapsulated Postscript Interchange or EPSI format. (You can insert EPSI files into many word processors.)
psfiles.doc	Description of the .ps files in the Ghostscript distribution. (These files are in the /usr/share/ghostscript/3.33 directory.)

(continued)

Table A-1	*(Continued)*
File	*Description*
use.doc	Description of how to use the Ghostscript language interpreter.
xfonts.doc	Description of the interface between Ghostscript and the routines that access externally supplied font and text-output facilities

This list of documentation should give you an idea of Ghostscript's capabilities and what you get with the Ghostscript software distribution.

To run Ghostscript, type **gs** in an xterm window. Ghostscript brings up an empty window and displays the following text in the xterm window:

```
Aladdin Ghostscript 3.33 (4/10/1995)
Copyright (C) 1995 Aladdin Enterprises, Menlo Park, CA.  All rights
reserved.
This software comes with NO WARRANTY: see the file COPYING for
details.
GS>
```

At this point, you are interacting with the Ghostscript interpreter. Unless you know the Ghostscript language (which is like PostScript), you'll feel lost at this prompt. It's like the C:> prompt under MS-DOS or the UNIX shell prompt at a terminal.

If you do have a PostScript file available, you can load and view it with a simple command. For example, try the following:

```
GS> (/usr/share/ghostscript/3.33/examples/golfer.ps) run
```

What you typed is a Ghostscript command that should cause Ghostscript to load the file /usr/share/ghostscript/3.33/examples/golfer.ps and process it. The result is a picture in Ghostscript's output window. After that, press Enter and type **quit** to exit Ghostscript.

Fortunately, you needn't use Ghostscript at the interpreter level (unless you know PostScript well and want to try PostScript commands interactively). You typically use Ghostscript to load and view a PostScript file.

Ghostscript takes several command-line arguments, including the file to be loaded. To see a list of Ghostscript options, type the following command:

```
gs -h
Copyright (C) 1995 Aladdin Enterprises, Menlo Park, CA.  All rights
reserved.
Usage: gs [switches] [file1.ps file2.ps ...]
Available devices:
        x11 x11alpha x11cmyk x11mono deskjet djet500 djet500c dnj650c
```

```
          laserjet ljetplus ljet2p ljet3 ljet3d ljet4 cdeskjet cdjcolor
          cdjmono cdj500 cdj550 pj pjxl pjxl300 bj10e bj200
          bjc600 epson eps9mid eps9high epsonc ibmpro jetp3852 dfaxhigh
          dfaxlow faxg3 faxg32d faxg4 cp50 tiffg3 tiffg32d tiffg4
          pcxmono pcxgray pcx16 pcx256 pcx24b pbm pbmraw pgm
          pgmraw ppm ppmraw bit bitrgb bitcmyk tiffcrle tiffg3
          tiffg32d tiffg4 tifflzw tiffpack
Language interpreters:
          PostScript PostScriptLevel1 PostScriptLevel2 PDF
Search path:
   .
     /usr/share/ghostscript/3.33:/usr/share/ghostscript/fonts
Most frequently used switches: (you can use # in place of =)
    -c quit               (as the last switch) exit after processing
files
    -d<name>[=<token>]    define name as token, or true if no token
given
    -dNOPAUSE             don't pause between pages
    -g<width>x<height>    set width and height (`geometry'), in pixels
    -q                    `quiet' mode, suppress most messages
    -r<res>               set resolution, in pixels per inch
    -s<name>=<string>     define name as string
    -sDEVICE=<devname>    select initial device
    -sOutputFile=<file>   select output file: embed %d or %ld for page
#,
                          - means stdout, use |command to pipe
     -                    read from stdin (e.g., a pipe) non-
interactively
For more information, see the (plain text) file  use.doc  in the
directory
          /usr/doc/ghostscript-3.33.
```

To see how Ghostscript renders a PostScript document, you can use any PostScript document you may have available. One good solution is to use one of the sample PostScript files in the `/usr/share/ghostscript/3.33/examples` directory. Type the following command, for example, in an `xterm` window:

```
gs /usr/share/ghostscript/3.33/examples/golfer.ps
```

Ghostscript opens that file, processes its contents, and displays the output in another window, as shown in Figure A-18.

In this case, the output happens to be a picture of a golfer. After displaying the output, Ghostscript displays the following message:

```
>showpage, press <return> to continue<<
```

Press Enter to continue. For a multiple-page PostScript document, Ghostscript then shows the next page. After all the pages are displayed, you return to the Ghostscript prompt. Type **quit** to exit Ghostscript.

Figure A-18: Ghostscript displaying the file `/usr/share/ghostscript/3.33/examples/golfer.ps`

Ghostview

Ghostview is a X-based graphical front end to the Ghostscript interpreter. Ghostview is ideal for viewing and printing PostScript documents. For a long document, you can even print selected pages. You also can view the document at various levels of magnification (you can zoom in or out).

To run Ghostview, type **ghostview &** in an `xterm` window. This command causes the Ghostview window to appear. The window is divided into three parts:

- Along the top edge, you'll find eight buttons. The first five buttons are menu buttons — when you click any of these buttons, a menu appears.

- On the left side are several more buttons, text boxes for information display, and scroll bars for scrolling the image.

- The large area occupying most of the Ghostview window is the work area, where Ghostview displays the PostScript document.

To load and view a PostScript document in Ghostview, click the `File` button and select `Open` from the pop-up menu. This action causes Ghostview to display a file-selection dialog box. Use this dialog box to select the file `tiger.ps` in the `/usr/share/ghostscript/3.33/examples` directory, as shown in Figure A-19.

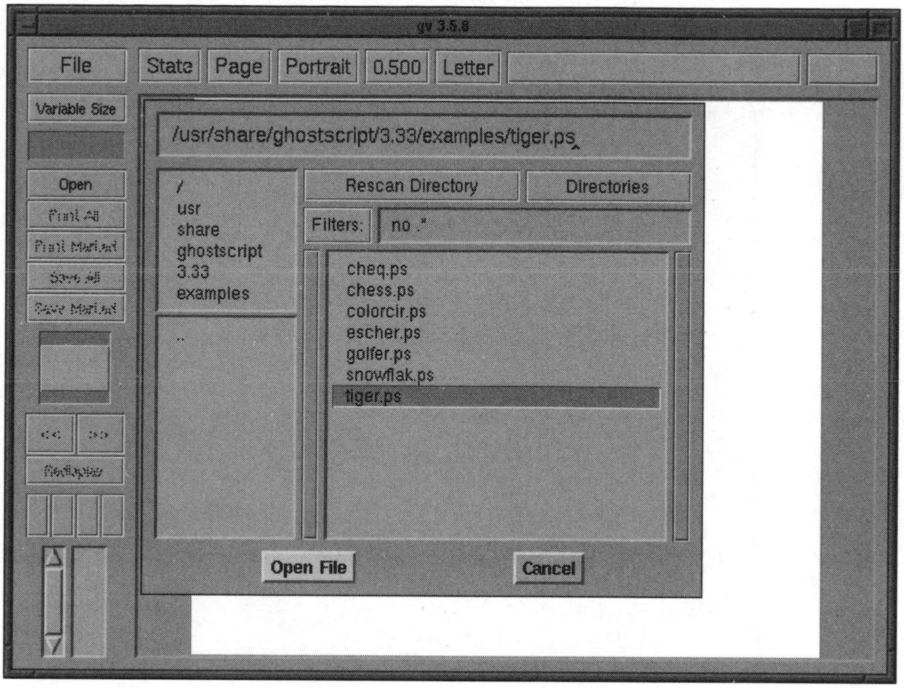

Figure A-19: Selecting a file to open in Ghostview

In Figure A-19, you see the file-selection dialog box in the foreground; the Ghostview window appears in the background.

To open the selected file, click the Open File button in the file-selection dialog box shown in Figure A-19. Ghostview opens the selected file, processes its contents, and displays the output in its window, as shown in Figure A-20.

In the last two buttons on the upper-right corner of the window, Ghostview displays the current filename and date the file was created. Ghostview takes this information from the comments in the PostScript file itself, not from the timestamp of the file.

As you move the mouse over the image, Ghostview displays the coordinates of the mouse pointer in a button along the upper-left corner of the window.

Ghostview is useful for viewing various documentation that comes in PostScript format (these files typically have the .ps extension in their names). For example, I used Ghostview to view the documentation for the XV program; that documentation comes in a PostScript file (/usr/doc/xv-3.10a/xvdocs. ps). When viewing such documents in Ghostview, I use the magnification button—the button labeled 0.500 in Figure A-20. If you click this button, a menu appears with a number of magnification factors from 0.1 to 10.0. I had to select a magnification of 2.000 to make the document legible onscreen.

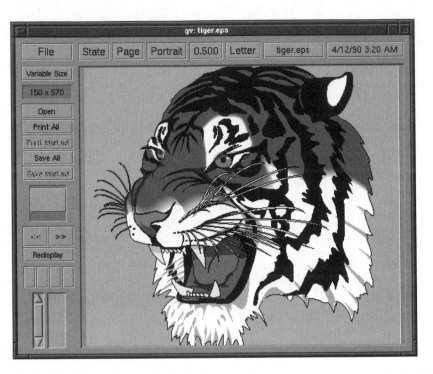

Figure A-20: Ghostview displaying the file `/usr/share/ghostscript/3.33/examples/tiger.ps`

Appendix B

Linux Commands

This appendix presents an alphabetically arranged reference of the most important Linux commands. The goal is to provide you with an overview of all commands needed to manage files and directories, start and stop processes, find files, work with text files, and access online help.

If you are looking for a command for a specific task, but don't know which command to use, you may find it helpful to browse through the commands by category. Table B-1 shows the Linux commands organized by category.

Table B-1   Linux commands grouped by category

Command Name	Action
Getting online help	
apropos	Find man pages for a specified keyword
info	Display online help information about a specified command
man	Display online help information
whatis	Similar to apropos, but searches for complete words only
Making commands easier	
alias	Define an abbreviation for a long command
type	Show the type and location of a command
unalias	Delete an abbreviation defined using alias
Managing files and directories	
cd	Change current directory
chmod	Change file permissions
chown	Change file owner and group
cp	Copy files
ln	Create symbolic links to files and directories
ls	Display the contents of a directory
mkdir	Create a directory
mv	Rename file as well as move file from one directory to another
rm	Delete files
rmdir	Delete directories

(continued)

Table B-1 *(Continued)*

Command Name	Action
Managing files and directories	
pwd	Display the current directory
touch	Update a file's time stamp
Finding files	
find	Find files based on specified criteria such as name, size, and so on.
locate	Find files using a periodically updated database
whereis	Find files based in the typical directories where executable (also known as binary) files are located
which	Find files in the directories listed in the PATH environment variable
Processing files	
cat	Display a file on standard output (can be used to concatenate several files into one big file)
cut	Extract specified sections from each line of text in a file
dd	Copy blocks of data from one file to another (used to copy data from devices)
diff	Compare two text files and finds any differences
expand	Convert all tabs into spaces
file	Display the type of data in a file
fold	Wrap each line of text to fit a specified width
grep	Search for regular expressions within a text file
less	Display a text file, one page at a time (can go backward also)
lpr	Print files
more	Display a text file, one page at a time (goes forward only)
nl	Number all nonblank lines in a text file and print the lines to standard output
paste	Concatenate corresponding lines from several files
patch	Update a text file using the differences between the original and revised copy of the file
sed	Copy a file to standard output while applying specified editing commands
sort	Sort lines in a text file

Processing files

`split`	Break up a file into several smaller files with specified size
`tac`	Reverse a file (last line first, and so on)
`tail`	Display last few lines of a file
`tr`	Substitute one group of characters for another throughout a file
`uniq`	Eliminate duplicate lines from a text file
`wc`	Count the number of lines, words, and characters in a text file
`zcat`	Display a compressed file (after decompressing)
`zless`	Display a compressed file one page at a time (can go backward also)
`zmore`	Display a compressed file one page at a time

Archiving and compressing files

`compress`	Compress files
`cpio`	Copy files to and from an archive
`gunzip`	Uncompress files compressed with GNU ZIP (`gzip`) or `compress`
`gzip`	Compress files (more powerful than `compress`)
`tar`	Create an archive of files in one or more directories (originally meant for archiving on tape)
`uncompress`	Uncompress files compressed with `compress`

Managing processes

`bg`	Run an interrupted process in the background
`fg`	Run a process in the foreground
`free`	Display amount of free and used memory in the system
`halt`	Shut down Linux and halts the computer
`kill`	Send a signal to a process (usually used to terminate a process)
`ldd`	Display the shared libraries needed to run a program
`nice`	Run a process with lower priority (referred to as nice mode)
`ps`	Display list of currently running processes
`printenv`	Display the current environment variables
`pstree`	Similar to `ps`, but shows parent-child relationships clearly
`reboot`	Stop Linux and then restarts the computer
`shutdown`	Shut down Linux
`top`	Display list of most processor- and memory-intensive processes
`uname`	Display information about the system and the Linux kernel

(continued)

Table B-1 *(Continued)*	
Command Name	**Action**
Managing users	
chsh	Change the shell (command interpreter)
groups	Print the list of groups that includes a specified user
id	Display the user and group ID for a specified user name
passwd	Change the password
su	Become another user or root (when invoked without any argument)
Managing the file system	
df	Summarize free and available space in all mounted storage devices
du	Display disk usage information
fdformat	Format a diskette
fdisk	Partition a hard disk
fsck	Check and repair a file system
mkfs	Create a new file system
mknod	Create a device file
mkswap	Create swap space for Linux in a file or a disk partition
mount	Mount a device (for example, the CD-ROM) on a directory in the file system
swapoff	Deactivate a swap space
swapon	Activate a swap space
sync	Write buffered data to files
tty	Display the device name for the current terminal
umount	Unmount a device from the file system
Working with the date and time	
cal	Display a calendar for a specified month or year
date	Show current date and time or set a new date and time

The rest of this appendix presents individual reference entries for each command shown in Table B-1. Each reference entry has a standard appearance with the following sections:

■ *Purpose*: Tells you when to use the command.

■ *Syntax*: Shows the syntax of the command with a few common options. Typical option values are also shown. All optional items are shown in square brackets.

- *Options*: Lists most options, along with a brief description of each option. For many commands, you will find all options listed in this section. However, some commands have too many options to list. For those commands, I show the most commonly used options.

- *Description*: Describes the command and provides more details about how to use the command.

---

alias

Purpose	Define an abbreviation for a long command or view the current list of abbreviations
Syntax	`alias [abbrev=command]`
Options	None
Description	If you type `alias` alone, you get a listing of all currently defined abbreviations. Typically, you use `alias` to define easy-to-remember abbreviations for longer commands. For example, if you type `ls -l` often, you might add a line with `alias ll='ls -l'` in the `.bashrc` file in your home directory. Then you can type `ll` instead of `ls -l` to see a detailed listing of a directory. `alias` is a built-in command of the Bash shell and is described in Chapter 6.

apropos

Purpose	View a list of all man pages containing a specific keyword
Syntax	`apropos keyword`
Options	None
Description	The `apropos` command looks up the keyword in a database (known as the `whatis` database) created by the `/usr/sbin/makewhatis` program. The `whatis` database is an index of keywords contained in all the man pages in the system. Unfortunately, when you try `apropos` with a simple keyword such as *find,* you may end up with a long listing of man pages because the word *find* appears in many man pages.

bg

Purpose	Run an interrupted process in the background
Syntax	`bg`
Options	None
Description	After you type a command that takes a long time to finish, you can press Ctrl+Z to interrupt the process. Then, you can type `bg` to continue that command in the background while you type other commands at the shell prompt. `bg` is a built-in command of the Bash shell.

---

cal

Purpose	View the calendar of any month in any year
Syntax	`cal` `cal [-jy] [[month_number] year]]`
Options	`-j` displays Julian dates (the day number between 1 and 366) `-y` displays the calendar for all months of the current year

Description   If you type `cal` without any options, it prints a calendar for the current month. If you type `cal` followed by a number, `cal` treats the number as the year and prints the calendar for that year. To view the calendar for a specific month in a specific year, provide the month number (1 = January, 2 = February, and so on) followed by the year. Thus, to view the calendar for January 2000 type the following:

cal 1 2000
```
    January 2000
Su Mo Tu We Th Fr Sa
                   1
 2  3  4  5  6  7  8
 9 10 11 12 13 14 15
16 17 18 19 20 21 22
23 24 25 26 27 28 29
30 31
```

---

cat

Purpose	Copy contents of a file to standard output (the screen)
Syntax	`cat [-benstvA] files`
Options	`-b` numbers nonblank lines `-e` shows end of line (as $) and all nonprinting characters `-n` numbers all output lines starting with number 1 `-s` replaces multiple blank lines with a single blank line `-t` shows tabs as `^I` `-v` shows nonprinting characters `-A` shows all characters (including nonprinting ones)
Description	Typically, `cat` is used to display the contents of a file or to concatenate several files into a single file. For example, `cat file1 file2 file3 > all` combines three files into a single file named `all`.

---

cd

Purpose	Change current directory
Syntax	`cd [directory]`
Options	None
Description	Typing `cd` without a directory name changes the current directory to your home directory. Otherwise, `cd` changes to the specified directory. `cd` is a built-in command of the Bash shell.

chmod	
Purpose	Change the permission settings of one or more files
Syntax	`chmod [-cfvR] permission files`
Options	`-c` lists only files whose permissions changed `-f` stops any error message displays `-v` verbosely displays permission changes `-R` recursively changes permission of files in all subdirectories
Description	To use `chmod` effectively, you have to learn how to specify the permission settings. One way is to concatenate one letter from each of the following tables in the order shown (*who, action, permission*):

Who		Action		Permission	
u	user	+	add	r	read
g	group	-	remove	w	write
o	others	=	assign	x	execute
a	all			s	set user ID

To give everyone read access to all files in a directory, you would type `chmod a+r *`. On the other hand, to make a specific file executable by everyone, you would type `chmod +x filename`.

Another way to specify permission settings is to use a three-digit sequence of octal numbers. In a detailed listing, the read, write, and execute permission settings for the user, group, and others appear as the sequence `rwxrwxrwx` (with dashes in place of letters for disallowed operations). Think of `rwxrwxrwx` as three occurrences of the string `rwx`. Now, assign the values $r=4$, $w=2$, and $x=1$. To get the value of the sequence `rwx`, simply add the values of r, w, and x. Thus, `rwx` = 7. Using this formula, you can assign a three-digit value to any permission setting. For example, if the user can read and write the file and everyone else can only read the file, the permission setting is `rw-r--r-` (that's how it appears in the listing) and the value is 644. Thus, if you wanted all files in a directory to be readable by everyone, but writable by only the user, you would use the command `chmod 644 *`.

chown	
Purpose	Change the user and group ownership of a file
Syntax	`chown [cvfR] username.groupname files`
Options	`-c` lists only files whose ownership changed `-f` stops any error message displays `-v` verbosely displays ownership changes `-R` recursively changes ownership of files in all subdirectories
Description	To make a user the owner of one or more files, invoke `chown` with the user name followed by the file names. To change the group ownership as well, append the new group name to the user name with a period as separator. For example, to make user `naba` the owner of all files in a directory, I type `chown naba *`. Note that you have to be logged in as `root` to change the ownership of files.

---

chsh

Purpose	Change the default shell that is started at login
Syntax	`chsh [-s shell] [username]`
Options	`-s` shell specifies the name of the shell executable to use (shell can be any program listed in the `/etc/shells` file, such as `/bin/bash` and `/bin/csh`)
Description	A user's default shell is stored in the `/etc/passwd` file. The `chsh` command lets you change the default shell to any of the shells listed in the `/etc/shells` file. If you type `chsh` without any arguments, `chsh` prompts you for the name of a shell.

compress

Purpose	Compress one or more files using Lempel-Ziv compression
Syntax	`compress [-cdrvV] files`
Options	`-c` writes compressed file to the standard output and retains original `-d` decompresses the file `-r` recursively compresses files in all subdirectories `-v` displays a message as each file is compressed `-V` prints version number and exits
Description	The `compress` command compresses each specified file and replaces the original with the compressed version (with a `.Z` suffix appended to the name). You can uncompress the file with the `compress -d` command or the `uncompress` command.

cp

Purpose	Copy files and directories
Syntax	`cp [options] source_files destination_directory` `cp [options] source_file destination_file`
Options	`-a` preserves all file attributes `-b` makes backup copy before copying `-d` copies a link but not the file pointed to by the link `-i` asks for confirmation before overwriting files `-l` creates hard links instead of copying files `-p` preserves ownership, permissions, and file time stamp `-R` recursively copies files in all subdirectories `-s` creates soft links instead of copying files `-u` copies only when the file being copied is newer than the destination `-v` displays verbose messages as copying progresses `—help` displays a help message about `cp`
Description	The `cp` command copies one file to another. You can also copy several files from one directory to another.

---

cpio

Purpose	Copy files in from or out to an archive that can be on a storage medium such as tape or a file on the disk
Syntax	cpio [-icdv] *pattern* cpio [-ocBv] *pattern* cpio [-padm] *pattern*
Options	-i extracts files whose names match the *pattern* -o copies to archive files whose names are provided on standard input -p copies files to another directory on the same system -a resets access times of input files -B copies using 5,120 bytes per record (default is 512 bytes per record) -c reads or writes header information as ASCII characters -d creates directories as needed -m retains previous file modification time -v prints a list of file names
Description	The cpio command copies files in from and out to archives. There are three distinct variants of the cpio command: cpio -o creates an archive; cpio -i extracts from an archive; and cpio -p copies from one directory to another. cpio is not that popular among Linux users; tar is much more commonly used. However, some installation programs use cpio during the installation process.

---

cut

Purpose	Copy selected parts of each line of text from a file to standard output
Syntax	cut [options] *file*
Options	-b *list* extracts the characters at positions specified in the *list* -f *list* extracts the fields (assumed to be tab-separated) specified in *list* -d *char* specifies the character that delimits the fields (default is the tab) -s skips lines that do not contain delimited fields (see -f option)
Description	The cut command specifies parts from each line of text in a file and writes those lines out to standard output. You can either extract a range of characters (specified by their positions) from each line or specific fields, where the fields are separated by a special character such as the tab. For example, to extract characters 1 through 11 and the 56th character onward from a detailed directory listing, use the following command:

```
ls -l | cut -b 1-11,56- | more
-rw-r--r-- DIR_COLORS
-rw-r--r-- HOSTNAME
-rw-r--r-- Muttrc
-drwxr-xr-x X11
-rw-r--r-- adjtime
-rw-r--r-- aliases
-rw-r--r-- aliases.db
-rw------- at.deny
(... lines deleted)
```

---

date

Purpose	Display current date and time or set new date and time
Syntax	`date [options] [+format]` `date [-su] [MMDDHHMM[[CC]YY][.SS]]`
Options	`-s` sets the date and/or time `-u` displays or sets time using Greenwich Mean Time
Description	The `date` command alone displays the current date and time. Using the `+format` argument, you can also specify a display format for the date and time. For a complete listing of the format specification, type `man date`.
	To set the date, use date -s followed by the date and time in the `MMDDHHMM` format, where each character is a digit (`MM` is the month number, `DD` is the day, `HH` is the hour, and `MM` are the minutes). You can optionally specify the year (`YY`) and century (`CC`) as well.

---

dd

Purpose	Copy blocks of data from standard input to standard output (and optionally convert the data from one format to another).
Syntax	`dd option1=value1 option2=value2 option3=value3 ...`

Options	`if=file` reads from specified file instead of standard input
	`of=file` writes to specified file instead of standard output
	`ibs=nbytes` reads blocks of *n* bytes at a time
	`obs=nbytes` writes blocks of *n* bytes at a time
	`bs=nbytes` reads and writes blocks of *n* bytes at a time
	`cbs=nbytes` converts blocks of *n* bytes at a time
	`skip=nblocks` skips *n* input blocks from beginning of input file
	`seek=nblocks` skips *n* output blocks in the output file
	`count=nblocks` copies *n* blocks from input to output
	`conv=code` performs conversion; *code* can be one of following:
	    `ascii` converts EBCDIC to ASCII
	    `ebcdic` converts ASCII to EBCDIC
	    `lcase` converts to lowercase
	    `ucase` converts to uppercase
	    `swab` swaps every pair of input bytes
	    `noerror` continues after read errors
	    (Note: EBCDIC is an encoding format used in IBM mainframes.)

Description	The `dd` command copies blocks of data from standard input to standard output, optionally converting the data as the copying proceeds. Typically, `dd` is used to copy data directly from one device to another. For example, you can copy the Linux kernel (`/boot/vmlinuz`) to a diskette with the following command: `dd if=/boot/vmlinuz of=/dev/fd0`

---

df

Purpose	Display the amount of free and used storage space on all mounted file systems.
Syntax	`df [options] [filesystem]`
Options	`-a` displays information for all file systems `-i` displays inode information (the disk is organized into inodes) `-T` prints the type of file system `-t type` displays information about specified types of file systems only `-x type` excludes specified types of file systems from the output `—help` displays a help message
Description	The `df` command returns the amount of free and used space on a specified file system. If you want to know how full your disks are, use the `df` command without any arguments. The `df` command then displays information about used and available storage space on all currently mounted file systems.

diff

Purpose	Show the difference between two text files (or all files with same names in two directories)
Syntax	`diff [options] from_file  to_file`

Options	`-a` treats all files as text even if they do not seem to be text files
	`-b` ignores blank lines and repeated blanks
	`-c` produces output in a different format
	`-d` tries to find a smaller set of changes (this makes `diff` slower)
	`-e` produces a script for `ed` editor to convert `from_file` to `to_file`
	`-f` produces output similar to that in `-e`, but in reverse order
	`-i` ignores case
	`-l` passes the output to the pr command to paginate it
	`-n` works like `-f`, but counts the number of changed lines
	`-r` recursively compares files with same name in all subdirectories
	`-s` reports when two files are the same
	`-t` expands tabs to spaces in the output
	`-u` uses the unified output format
	`-v` displays version of `diff`
	`-w` ignores spaces and tabs when comparing lines

Description	The `diff` command compares `from_file` with `to_file` and displays the lines that differ. The output can be in a format that the patch command can use to convert `from_file` to `to_file`.

du	
Purpose	Display summary information about disk usage (in kilobytes)
Syntax	`du [options] [directories_or_files]`
Options	`-a` displays usage information for all files (not just directories) `-b` displays usage in bytes (instead of kilobytes) `-c` displays a grand total of all usage information `-k` displays usage information in kilobytes (default) `-s` displays total disk usage without per-directory details

Description	The `du` command displays the disk space (in kilobytes) used by the specified files or directories. By default, `du` displays the disk space used by each directory and subdirectory. A common use of `du` is to type `du -s` to view the total space used by the current directory. For example, here is how you might check the details of disk space used by the `/usr/doc/HOWTO` directory:
	
	`du /usr/doc/HOWTO`
	
	`480      /usr/doc/HOWTO/mini/other-formats/html`
	`278      /usr/doc/HOWTO/mini/other-formats/sgml`
	`762      /usr/doc/HOWTO/mini/other-formats`
	`2998     /usr/doc/HOWTO/mini`
	`4742     /usr/doc/HOWTO`

expand	
Purpose	Write files to standard output after expanding each tab into an appropriate number of spaces
Syntax	`expand [options] [files]`
Options	`-n` (where *n* is a number) sets the tabs *n* spaces apart `-n1 [n2, ...]` (where *n1*, *n2*,... are numbers) specifies the tab stops `-i` converts only the initial tab into spaces
Description	The `expand` command reads from the specified files (or standard input, if no files are specified) and writes them to standard output, with each tab character expanded an appropriate number of spaces. By default, `expand` assumes that the tab positions are eight spaces apart (this is equivalent to the `-8` option).
fdformat	
Purpose	Format a diskette specified by device name (such as `/dev/fd0H1440` for a 3.5-inch, high-density diskette in drive A).
Syntax	`fdformat [-n] device_name`
Options	`-n` disables the verification performed after formatting
Description	The `fdformat` command formats a diskette. Use an appropriate device name to identify the diskette drive (see Chapter 7 for naming conventions for diskette drives). After formatting a diskette with `fdformat`, you can use `mkfs` to install a Linux file system, or `tar` to store an archive.

fdisk	
Purpose	Partition a disk or display information about existing partitions
Syntax	`fdisk [options] [device_name]`
Options	`-l` displays partition tables and exits `-s` *device* displays the size of the specified partition `-v` displays the version number of the `fdisk` program
Description	The `fdisk` command partitions a specified hard disk (see Chapter 11 for disk-drive naming conventions). You can also use `fdisk` to display information about existing partitions. You should never run `fdisk` and alter the partitions of a hard disk while one or more of its partitions are mounted on the Linux file system. Instead, you should boot from an installation diskette (or a boot diskette) and then perform the partitioning. Remember that partitioning typically destroys all existing data on a hard disk.
fg	
Purpose	Continue an interrupted process in the foreground
Syntax	`fg`
Options	None
Description	After you interrupt a process by typing Ctrl+Z, you can continue that process in foreground by typing the `fg` command. Note that `fg` is a built-in command of the Bash shell.
file	
Purpose	Display the type of data in a file based on rules defined in the `/usr/lib/magic` file (also known as the "magic file")
Syntax	`file [options] files`
Options	`-c` displays a parsed form of a magic file (or the default one) and exits `-m` *file1[:file2:...]* specifies other magic files `-v` displays version number and exits `-z` looks inside compressed files

Description	The `file` command uses rules specified in the /usr/lib/magic file to determine the type of data in the specified files. For example, you can use the `file` command to check the type of each file in the `/usr/lib` directory, as follows:
	
	`file *
		more`
		<pre>Mcrt1.o: ELF 32-bit LSB relocatable, Intel
		80386, version 1, not stripped
		X11: symbolic link to ../X11R6/lib/X11
		autoconf: directory
		bison.hairy: C program text
		bison.simple: C program text
		cracklib_dict.hwm: ASCII text
		cracklib_dict.pwd: ASCII text
		cracklib_dict.pwi: ASCII text
		(... lines deleted)</pre>

find	
Purpose	Display a list of files that match a specified set of criteria
Syntax	`find [path] [options]`

Options	`-depth` processes current directory first, and then subdirectories
	`-maxdepth` *n* restricts searches to *n* levels of directories
	`-follow` processes directories included through symbolic links
	`-name` *pattern* finds files whose names match the *pattern*
	`-ctime` *n* matches files modified exactly *n* days ago
	`-user` *uname* finds files owned by the specified user
	`-group` *gname* finds files owned by the specified group
	`-path` *pattern* finds files whose pathname matches the *pattern*
	`-perm` *mode* finds files with specified permission setting
	`-size` +*n*K finds files bigger than *n* kilobytes
	`-type` *x* finds files of specified type where *x* is one of the following:
	    f matches files
	    d matches directories
	    l matches symbolic links
	`-print` displays the name of files found
	`-exec` *command* `[options] {} \;` executes specified command by passing it the name of the found file

Description	The `find` command is useful for finding all files that match a specified set of criteria. If you type `find` without any arguments, the output is a listing of every file in all subdirectories of the current directory. To view all files whose names end with `.gz`, you would type `find . -name "*.gz"`.

fold	
Purpose	Wrap lines of text to a specified width (default is 80 characters)
Syntax	`fold [options] [files]`
Options	`-b` counts bytes instead of columns, so backspaces and tabs are counted `-s` breaks lines at word boundaries `-w` *N* (where *N* us a number) sets line width to *N* characters
Description	The `fold` command wraps each input line to a specified number of characters and displays the results on the screen (standard output). If you do not specify any file name, `fold` reads lines from the standard input.

free	
Purpose	Display amount of free and used memory in the system
Syntax	`free [options]`
Options	`-b` displays memory in number of bytes `-k` displays memory in kilobytes (default) `-m` displays memory in megabytes `-s` *n* repeats the command every *n* seconds `-t` displays a line containing a summary of the total amounts
Description	The `free` command displays information about the physical memory (RAM) and the swap area (on the disk). The output shows the total amount of memory as well as the amount used and the amount free.

fsck	
Purpose	Check and repair a Linux file system
Syntax	`fsck [options] device_name`
Options	`-A` checks all file systems listed in the `/etc/fstab` file `-R` skips the root file system (when checking all file systems) `-T` does not show the title on startup `-N` shows what might be done, but does not actually do anything `-V` produces verbose output `-t fstype` specifies the file system type (such as `ext2`) `-n` answers all confirmation requests with no (only for `ext2` file system) `-p` carries out all repairs without asking for confirmation (for `ext2`) `-y` answers all confirmation requests with no (only for `ext2` file system)
Description	The `fsck` command checks the integrity of a file system and carries out any necessary repairs. Depending on the type of file system, `fsck` runs an appropriate command to perform the actual task of checking and repairing the file system. For example, to check an `ext2` file system, `fsck` runs the `e2fsck` program. You have to run `fsck` when you power down your system without running the shutdown command. Typically, `fsck` is automatically run during system startup.

grep	
Purpose	Search one or more files for lines that match a regular expression (a search pattern)
Syntax	`grep [options] pattern  files`
Options	`-N` (where *N* is a number) displays *N* lines around the line containing *pattern* `-c` shows the number of lines that contain the search pattern `-f file` reads options from specified file `-i` ignores case `-l` displays the filenames that contain *pattern* `-n` displays the line number next to lines that contain *pattern* `-q` returns a status code, but does not display any output `-v` displays the lines that do not contain *pattern* `-w` matches only whole words
Description	The `grep` command searches the specified files for a pattern. The pattern is a regular expression, which has its own rules. Typically, you use `grep` to search for a specific sequence of characters in one or more text files.

groups	
Purpose	Show the groups to which a user belongs
Syntax	`groups [username]`
Options	None
Description	The `groups` command displays the names of groups to which a user belongs. If you do not specify a username, the command displays your groups.

gunzip	
Purpose	Uncompress files compressed by the `gzip` or the `compress` command
Syntax	`gunzip [options] files`
Options	See the options for `gzip`
Description	The `gunzip` command uncompresses compressed files (these files have the .gz or .Z extension). After uncompressing, `gunzip` replaces the compressed files with their uncompressed versions and removes the `.gz` or `.Z` extension in the filenames. The `gunzip` command is the same as `gzip` with the `-d` option.
gzip	
Purpose	Compress one or more files
Syntax	`gzip [options] files`
Options	`-c` writes output to standard output and retains original file `-d` uncompresses file (same as `gunzip`) `-h` displays a help message `-l` lists contents of a compressed file `-n` does not save original name and time stamp `-r` recursively compresses files in all subdirectories `-v` displays verbose output `-V` displays version number
Description	The `gzip` command compresses files using Lempel-Ziv (LZ77) coding, which produces better compression than the algorithm used by the `compress` command. After compressing a file, `gzip` replaces the original file with the compressed version and appends a `.gz` to the filename.
halt	
Purpose	Terminate all processes and halt the system (you must log in as `root`)
Syntax	`halt [options]`
Options	`-n` does not flush out in-memory buffers to disk before halting system `-f` forces halt without calling the `/sbin/shutdown` command `-i` shuts down all network interfaces before halting system
Description	The `halt` command lets the super user (root) terminate all processes and halt the system. The `halt` command invokes `/sbin/shutdown` with the `-h` option.
id	
Purpose	List the user ID, group ID, and groups for a user
Syntax	`id [options] [username]`
Options	`-g` displays group ID only `-n` displays group name instead of ID `-u` displays user ID only
Description	The `id` command displays the user ID, group ID, and groups for a specified user. If you do not provide any user name, `id` displays information about the current user.

info	
Purpose	View online help information about any Linux command
Syntax	`info [options] command`
Options	`-d dirname` adds a directory to the list of directories to be searched for files `-f infofile` specifies file to be used by `info` `-h` displays usage information about info
Description	The `info` command displays online help information about a specified command in a full-screen text window. You can use Emacs commands to navigate the text displayed by `info`. To learn more about `info`, type `info` without any arguments.

kill	
Purpose	Send a signal to a process
Syntax	`kill [options] process_id`
Options	`-signum` (where `signum` is a number or name) sends the specified signal `-l` lists the signal names and numbers
Description	The `kill` command sends a signal to a process. Typically, the signal is meant to terminate the process. For example, `kill -9 123` terminates the process with ID `123`. To see process IDs, use the `ps` command. To see a list of signal names and numbers, type `kill -l` (that's lowercase "ell").

ldd	
Purpose	Display names of shared libraries required to run a program
Syntax	`ldd [options] programs`
Options	`-v` prints the version number of `ldd` `-V` prints the version number of the dynamic linker (`ld.so`) `-d` relocates functions and reports missing functions `-r` relocates both data and functions and reports missing objects

Description	The `ldd` command lets you determine which shared libraries are needed to run the specified programs. For example, to determine what you need to run the Bash shell (/bin/bash), type the following:
	`ldd /bin/bash`
	`        libtermcap.so.2 => /lib/libtermcap.so.2 (0x40003000)`
	`        libc.so.6 => /lib/libc.so.6 (0x40006000)`
	`        /lib/ld-linux.so.2 => /lib/ld-linux.so.2 (0x00000000)`

less	
Purpose	View text files one screen at a time (and scroll back if needed)
Syntax	`less [options] filenames`
Options	`-?` displays a list of commands you can use in `less` `-p text` displays the first line where `text` is found `-s` reduces multiple blank lines to a single blank line
Description	The `less` command displays the specified files one screen at a time. Unlike `more`, you can press b, Ctrl+B, or Esc+V to scroll backward. To view the commands you can use to interact with `less`, press h while you are viewing a file in `less`.

ln	
Purpose	Set up a hard or symbolic link (pseudonyms) to files and directories
Syntax	`ln [options]` *`existing_file new_name`*
Options	`-b` makes backup copy of files about to be removed `-d` creates a hard link to a directory (only `root` can do this) `-f` removes existing file with *`new_name`* `—help` displays a help message `-s` creates a symbolic link `-v` displays verbose output
Description	The `ln` command assigns a new name to an existing file. With the `-s` option, you can create symbolic links that can exist across file systems. Also, with symbolic links, you can see the link information with the `ls -l` command. Otherwise, `ls -l` shows two distinct files for a file and its hard link.

locate	
Purpose	From a periodically updated database, list all files that match a specified pattern
Syntax	`locate` *`pattern`*
Options	None

Description	The `locate` command searches a database of files for any name that matches a specified pattern. Your Linux system is set up to periodically update the file database. If you are not sure about the location of a file, just type `locate` followed by a part of the filename. For example, here's how you might search for the `XF86Config` file:
	`locate XF86Config`
	`/usr/X11R6/lib/X11/XF86Config`
	`/usr/X11R6/lib/X11/XF86Config.eg`

lpr	
Purpose	Print one or more files
Syntax	`lpr [options] [`*`files`*`]`
Options	`-P`*`printer`* prints to the specified printer (the name appears in `/etc/printcap`) `-#`*`N`* (where *N* is a number) prints that many copies of each file `-h` suppresses the burst page (the first page with user information) `-m` sends mail upon completion of print job `-r` removes the file after printing `-J` *`jobname`* prints this job name on the burst page `-U` *`username`* prints this user name on the burst page
Description	The `lpr` command prints the specified files by using your system's print spooling system. If no filenames are specified, `lpr` reads input from the standard input. You can print to a specific printer with the `-P` option.

---

ls

Purpose	List the contents of a directory
Syntax	`ls [options] [directory_name]`
Options	`-a` displays all files, including those that start with a period (.) `-b` displays unprintable characters in filenames with octal code `-c` sorts according to file creation time `-d` lists directories like any other file (rather than listing their contents) `-f` lists directory contents without sorting (exactly as they are in the disk) `-i` shows the inode information `-l` shows the file listing in the long format with detailed information `-p` appends a character to the filename to indicate type `-r` sorts listing in reverse alphabetical order `-s` shows the size (in kilobytes) of each file next to the filename `-t` sorts listing according to file's time stamp `-1` displays a one-column listing of filenames `-R` recursively lists the files in all subdirectories
Description	The `ls` command displays the listing of a specified directory. If you omit the directory name, `ls` displays the contents of the current directory. By default `ls` does not list files whose names begin with a period (.); to see all files, type `ls -a`. You can see full details of files (including size, user and group ownership, and read-write-execute permissions) with the `ls -l` command.

---

man

Purpose	View online manual pages (also called *man pages*).
Syntax	`man [options] [section] command`
Options	`-C cfile` specifies man configuration file (default is `/etc/man.config`) `-P pager` specifies program to use to display one page at a time (for example, `less`) `-a` displays all man pages matching a specific `command` `-h` displays a help message and exits `-w` shows the location of man pages to be displayed
Description	The `man` command displays the man pages for the specified command. If you know the section for a man page, you can provide the section as well. For example, all Tcl/Tk man pages are in section n. Thus, you can view the man page for the Tcl/Tk command pack with the command `man n pack`.

---

mkdir

Purpose	Create a directory
Syntax	`mkdir [options] directory_name`
Options	`-m mode` assigns the specified permission setting to the new directory `-p` creates the parent directories if they do not already exist
Description	The `mkdir` command creates the specified directory.

mkfs	
Purpose	Create a Linux file system on a hard disk partition or a diskette
Syntax	`mkfs [-V] [-t] [options] device_name [blocks]`
Options	`-V` produces verbose output needed for testing `-t fstype` specifies the file system type (such as `ext2`) `-c` checks the device for bad blocks before creating the file system `-l filename` reads bad block list from specified file
Description	The `mkfs` command creates a Linux file system on the specified device. The device is typically a hard disk partition or a diskette (that has been formatted with `fdformat`).

mknod	
Purpose	Create a device file with specified major and minor numbers
Syntax	`mknod device_file {b|c} major minor`
Options	None
Description	The `mknod` command creates a device file (such as the ones in the `/dev` directory) through which the operating system accesses physical devices such as the hard disk, serial port, keyboard, and mouse. To create a device file, you have to log in as `root` and have to know the major and minor numbers of the device for which you are creating the device file. Additionally, you must specify one of the letters `b` or `c` to indicate whether the device is block- or character-oriented. Typically, you perform this step following specific instructions in a HOWTO document.

mkswap	
Purpose	Create a swap space for Linux
Syntax	`mkswap device_or_file numblocks`
Options	None
Description	The `mkswap` command creates a swap space for use by the Linux kernel. If you are creating swap space in a disk partition, specify the partition's device name (such as `/dev/hda2`) as the second argument to `mkswap`. If you want to use a file as swap space, create the file with a command such as `dd if=/dev/zero of=swapfile bs=1024 count=16384`. Then type `mkswap swapfile 16384` to create the swap space. You have to use the command `swapon` to activate a swap space.

more	
Purpose	View text files one screen at a time
Syntax	`more [options] filenames`
Options	`+N` (where *N* is a number) displays file starting at specified line number `+/pattern` begins displaying 2 lines before the *pattern* `-s` reduces multiple blank lines to a single blank line

more	
Description	The `more` command displays the specified files one screen at a time. To view the commands you can use in `more`, press h while you are viewing a file using `more`. For more advanced file viewing, use the `less` command.

mount	
Purpose	Associate a physical device to a specific directory in the Linux file system
Syntax	`mount [options]` *device directory*
Options	`-a` mounts all devices listed in the `/etc/fstab` file `-h` displays a help message and exits `-r` mounts the device for read-only (no writing allowed) `-t` *fstype* specifies the file system type on the device `-v` displays verbose messages `-V` displays the version number and exits
Description	The mount command attaches the contents of a physical device to a specific directory on the Linux file system. For example, you may mount a CD-ROM at the `/cdrom` directory. Then, you can access the contents of the CD-ROM at the `/cdrom` directory (in other words, the root directory of the CD-ROM appears as `/cdrom` after the mount operation). To see the listing of the `RedHat` directory on the CD-ROM, you would type `ls /cdrom/RedHat`.

mv	
Purpose	Rename files and directories or move them from one directory to another
Syntax	`mv [options]` *source destination*
Options	`-b` makes backup copies of files being moved or renamed `-f` removes existing files without prompting `-i` prompts before overwriting any existing files `-v` displays name of file before moving it
Description	The `mv` command either renames a file or moves it to another directory. The command works on either plain files or directories. Thus, you could rename the file `sample` to `sample.old` with the command `mv sample sample.old`. On the other hand, you can move the file `/tmp/sample` to `/usr/local/sample` with the command `mv /tmp/sample /usr/local/sample`.

nice	
Purpose	Run a program at a lower or higher priority level
Syntax	`nice [options]` *program*
Options	+*n* (*n* = number) adds *n* to nice value (positive values are lower priority) -*n* (*n* = number) subtracts *n* to nice value (negative means higher priority)
Description	The `nice` command allows you to run a program at lower or higher priority. By default, programs run at the nice value of zero. Adding to the nice value decreases the priority while subtracting from the nice value increases the program's priority. Only `root` can decrease the nice value.

---

nl

Purpose	Add line numbers to nonblank lines of text in a file and write to standard output
Syntax	`nl [options] [file]`
Options	`-ba` numbers all lines `-bt` numbers text lines only (default) `-sc` separates text from line numbers with the character *c* (default is tab) `-wn` uses *n* columns to show the line numbers

Description	The `nl` command adds a line number to each nonblank line of text from a file and writes the lines to standard output. Suppose the file `sample.txt` has the following lines:
	`A line followed by a blank line and`
	
	`then another non-blank line.`
	
	Applying the `nl` command to this file produces the following result:
	`nl sample.txt`
	`    1  A line followed by a blank line and`
	
	`    2  then another non-blank line.`

---

passwd

Purpose	Change password
Syntax	`passwd [username]`
Options	None
Description	The `passwd` command changes your password. It prompts for the old password followed by the new password. If you log in as `root`, you can change another user's password by specifying the user name as an argument to the `passwd` command.

---

paste

Purpose	Write to standard output corresponding lines of each file, separated by a tab
Syntax	`paste file1 file2 [...]`
Options	`-s` pastes the lines from one file at a time instead of one line from each file `-d delim` uses delimiters from the list of characters instead of a tab `-` causes paste to use standard input as a file
Description	The `paste` command takes one line from each of the listed files and writes them out to standard output, separated by a tab. With the `-s` option, the `paste` command can also concatenate all lines from one file into a single gigantic line.

patch

Purpose	Apply the output of the `diff` command to an original file
Syntax	`patch [options] < patch_file`

Options	`-c` causes patch file to be interpreted as a context `diff`
	`-e` forces patch file to interpret the patch file as an `ed` script
	`-f` forces patch file to be applied regardless of any inconsistencies
	`-n` causes patch file to be interpreted as a normal `diff`
	`-pN` strips everything up to *N* slashes in the pathname
	`-R` indicates that patch file was created with new and old files swappped
	`-u` causes patch file to be interpreted as a unified `diff`
	`-v` displays the version number

Description	The `patch` command is used to update an original file by applying all the differences between the original and revised version. The differences are in the form of an output from the `diff` command, stored in the *patch_file*. Changes to Linux kernel source code is distributed in the form of a patch file. Chapter 2 discusses how to apply patches to the kernel source.

printenv

Purpose	View a list of environment variables
Syntax	`printenv`
Options	None
Description	The `printenv` command displays a list of all current environment variables.

ps

Purpose	Display status of processes (programs) running in the system
Syntax	`ps [options]`
Options	[Note: Unlike other commands, `ps` options do not have a `-` prefix.] `a` displays processes of other users `f` displays family tree of processes `j` displays output using jobs format `l` displays in long format with many details for each process `m` displays memory usage information for each process `u` displays user name and start time `x` displays processes not associated with any terminal
Description	The `ps` command displays the status of processes running in the system. Typing `ps` alone produces a list of processes you are running. To see a list of all processes in the system, type `ps ax` (or `ps aux`, if you want more details about each process).

---

pstree

Purpose	Display all running processes in the form of a tree
Syntax	`pstree [options] [pid]`
Options	-a shows command-line arguments -c does not compact subtrees -l displays long lines -n sorts processes by process ID (instead of name) -p shows process IDs
Description	The `pstree` command shows all processes in the form of a tree, which makes it easy to understand the parent-child relationships among the processes. The following is typical output from `pstree`:

```
 pstree
init-+-atd
     |-crond
     |-gpm
     |-httpd---10*[httpd]
     |-inetd-+-in.telnetd---bash---pstree
     |       `-2*[in.telnetd---bash---su---bash]
     |-kerneld
     |-kflushd
     |-klogd
     |-kswapd
     |-10ve
     |-lpd
     |-lpnetd
     |-6*[mingetty]
     |-nmbd
     |-postmaster
     |-pppd
     |-sendmail
     |-smbd
     |-syslogd
     `-update
```

---

pwd

Purpose	Display current working directory
Syntax	`pwd`
Options	None
Description	The `pwd` command prints the current working directory. `pwd` is a built-in command of the Bash shell.

reboot

Purpose	Terminate all processes and reboot the system (you must log in as `root`)
Syntax	`reboot [options]`
Options	`-n` does not flush out in-memory buffers to disk before rebooting system `-f` forces halt without calling the `/sbin/shutdown` command `-i` shuts down all network interfaces before rebooting system
Description	The `reboot` command lets the super user (`root`) terminate all processes and reboot the system. The `reboot` command invokes `/sbin/shutdown` with the `-r` option.

rm

Purpose	Delete one or more files
Syntax	`rm [options]` *files*
Options	`-f` removes files without prompting `-i` prompts before removing a file `-r` recursively removes files in all subdirectories, including the directories `-v` displays name of each file before removing it
Description	The `rm` command deletes the specified files. To remove a file you must have write permission to the directory containing the file.

rmdir

Purpose	Delete a specified directory (provided the directory is empty)
Syntax	`rmdir [options]` *directory*
Options	-p removes any parent directories that become empty
Description	The `rmdir` command deletes empty directories. If a directory is not empty, you should use the `rm -r` command to delete the files as well the directory.

sed

Purpose	Copy a file to standard output after editing according to a set of commands
Syntax	`sed [options] [`*editing_commands*`] [`*file*`]`
Options	-e'instructions' applies the editing instructions to the file `-f` *scriptfile* applies editing commands from *scriptfile* -n suppresses default output
Description	The `sed` command is known as the *stream editor* — it copies a file to standard output while applying specified editing commands. If you do not specify a file, it reads from the standard input. To use the stream editor, you have to learn its editing commands, which are very similar to the ones used by the `ed` editor (described in Chapter 24).

shutdown	
Purpose	Terminate all processes and shutdown (or reboot) the system
Syntax	`shutdown [options]` *`time`* `[`*`messages`*`]`
Options	`-t` specifies the time between the message and the kill signal `-h` halts the system after terminating all the processes `-r` reboots the system after terminating all the processes `-f` performs a fast reboot `-k` sends warning messages but does not actually shut down system `-c` cancels a shutdown in progress
Description	The `shutdown` command (the full pathname is `/sbin/shutdown`) brings down the Linux system in an orderly way. You must specify a time when shutdown begins; use the keyword `now` to shutdown immediately. You must be logged in as `root` to run the `shutdown` command.

sort	
Purpose	Sort or merge lines from a file and then write to standard output
Syntax	`sort [options] [`*`files`*`]`
Options	`-c` checks if files are already sorted and prints error message if not `-m` merges files by sorting them as a group `-b` ignores leading blanks `-d` sorts in phone directory order (uses only letters, digits, and blanks) `-f` treats lowercase letters as equivalent uppercase letters `-k` *`POS1`*`[`*`,POS2`*`]` specifies the sort field as characters between the two positions *POS1* and *POS2* `-o` *`file`* writes output to specified file instead of standard output `-r` sorts in reverse order `-g` sorts numerically but uses conversion to real number `-i` ignores unprintable characters `-n` sorts numerically (used when number begins each line) `-t`*C* specifies the separator character `+`*N* only considers characters from position *N* onwards (0=first position)
Description	The `sort` command sorts the lines in one or more files and writes them out to the standard output. The same command can also merge several files (when used with the `-m` option) and produce an appropriately sorted and merged output.

split	
Purpose	Split a file into several smaller files
Syntax	`split [options]` *`file`* `[`*`prefix`*`]`
Options	`-l` *N* (where *N* is a number) puts *N* lines in each file `-`*N* (where *N* is a number) puts *N* lines in each file `-b` *N*k (where *N* is a number) splits the file every *N* kilobytes `-C` *N*k (where *N* is a number) puts as many lines as possible without exceeding *N* kilobytes per file

split

Description	The `split` command breaks up a large file into smaller files. By default, `split` puts 1,000 lines into each file. The files are named by groups of letters `aa`, `ab`, `ac`, and so on. You can specify a prefix for the filenames. For example, to split a large archive into smaller files that fit into several high-density 3.5-inch diskettes, use split as follows: `split -C 1440k bigfile.tar disk.` This creates files named `disk.aa`, `disk.ab`, and so on.

su

Purpose	Become another user
Syntax	`su [options] [username]`
Options	`-c COMMAND` passes the `COMMAND` to the shell `-f` prevents reading the startup file (`.cshrc`) when the shell is csh or tcsh `-l` makes this a login shell by reading the user's startup file `-p` preserves the environment variables `HOME`, `USER`, `LOGNAME`, and `SHELL` `-s SHELL` runs the specified `SHELL` instead of the user's default shell
Description	The `su` command lets you assume the identity of another user. You have to provide the password of that user before you can continue. If you do not provide a user name, `su` assumes you want to change to the `root` user.

swapoff

Purpose	Deactivate the specified swap device or file
Syntax	`swapoff device`
Options	None
Description	The `swapoff` command stops Linux from using the specified device or file as a swap space.

swapon

Purpose	Activate the specified swap device or file
Syntax	`swapon [-a] device`
Options	`-a` enables all swap devices listed in the `/etc/fstab` file
Description	The `swapon` command activates the specified device or file as a swap space. During system startup, all swap spaces are activated by the `swapon -a` command, which is invoked by the script file `/etc/rc.d/rc.sysinit`.

sync

Purpose	Write buffers to disk
Syntax	`sync`
Options	None
Description	When you cannot shut down your Linux system in an orderly manner (for example, when you cannot execute `shutdown`, `halt`, or `reboot` commands), you should type `sync` before switching off the computer.

---

tac

Purpose	Copy a file, line by line, to the standard output in reverse order (last line first)
Syntax	`tac file`
Options	`-b` places the separator at the beginning of each line `-r` treats the separator string specified by -s as a regular expression `-s sep` specifies a separator (instead of the default newline character)
Description	The `tac` command displays the specified text file in reverse order, copying the lines to standard output in reverse order. By default `tac` treats each line as a record and uses the newline character as the record separator. However, you can specify a different separator character, in which case, `tac` will copy those records to standard output in reverse order.

---

tail

Purpose	View the last few lines of a file
Syntax	`tail [options] file`
Options	`-N` (where N is a number) displays last N lines `-n N` (where N is a number) displays last N lines `-f` reads the file at regular intervals and displays all new lines
Description	The `tail` command displays lines from the end of the specified file. By default, `tail` displays the last 10 lines from the file. To view the last 24 lines from a file named `messages`, type `tail -24 messages`.

---

tar

Purpose	Create an archive of files or extract files from an archive
Syntax	`tar [options] files_or_directories`

Options	`-c` creates a new archive
	`-d` compares files in an archive with files in current directory
	`-r` extends the archive with more files
	`-t` lists contents of an archive
	`-x` extracts from the archive
	`-C directory` extracts files into the specified directory
	`-f file` uses the specified file as the archive instead of a tape
	`-L n` specifies capacity of tape as n kilobytes
	`-N date` only archives files newer than the specified date
	`-T file` archives or extracts the filenames specified in `file`
	`-v` displays verbose messages
	`-z` compresses or uncompresses archive with `gzip`

Description	The `tar` command creates an archive of files or extracts files from an existing archive. By default, `tar` assumes the archive to be on a tape. However, you can use the `-f` option to specify a file as the archive.

---

top	
Purpose	List currently running processes, arranged in order of their share of CPU time
Syntax	`top [q] [d delay]`
Options	`q` causes `top` to run with highest possible priority (you have to be `root`) `d delay` specifies the delay between updates in seconds
Description	The `top` command produces a full-text screen with the processes arranged according to their share of CPU time. By default, `top` updates the display every five seconds. Press `q` or Ctrl+C to quit `top`.
touch	
Purpose	Change a file's time stamp
Syntax	`touch [options] files`
Options	`-c` stops `touch` from creating a file that does not exist `-d time` uses the specified time `-r file` uses the time stamp from the specified file `-t MMDDhhmm[[CC]YY][.ss]` uses the specified date and time
Description	The `touch` command lets you change the date and time of a file's last modification (this information is stored with the file). If you use `touch` without any options, the current date and time is used as the time stamp for the file. If the specified file does not exist, `touch` creates a new file of size 0 bytes.
tr	
Purpose	Copy from standard input to standard output while substituting one set of characters with another
Syntax	`tr [options] string1 [string2]`
Options	`-c` complements characters in `string1` with ASCII codes 001–377 `-d` deletes from the input all characters specified in `string1` `-s` replaces repeated sequences of any character in `string1` with a single character

Description	The `tr` command substitutes all characters in `string1` in the input with the corresponding characters in `string2`. For example, to convert the file `sample.lc` to all uppercase and store in `sample.uc`, you would type:
	`tr [a-z] [A-Z] < sample.lc > sample.uc`
	
	To replace repeated occurrences of newlines in a file with a single newline character, you would type
	`tr -s '\n' < infile > outfile`

tty	
Purpose	Display the device name of the terminal
Syntax	`tty`
Options	None
Description	The `tty` command displays the name of the terminal connected to the standard input. This is useful in shell scripts that may need the terminal name.

type	
Purpose	Display the type of a command (whether it is a built-in shell command or a separate executable program)
Syntax	`type command`
Options	None

Description	The `type` command tells you the type of a command — whether it is a built-in shell command, an alias, or an executable program. For example, I used `alias ll='ls -l'` to define the alias `ll`. Here is what I get when I check the type of the command `ll`:
	`type ll`
	`` ll is aliased to `ls -l' ``

umount	
Purpose	Disassociate a device from the Linux file system
Syntax	`umount device`
Options	None
Description	The `umount` command removes the association between a device and a directory in the Linux file system. Only the `root` can execute the `umount` command.

unalias	
Purpose	Delete an abbreviation defined earlier with `alias`
Syntax	`unalias abbreviation`
Options	None
Description	The `unalias` command removes an abbreviation defined earlier with the `alias` command. `unalias` is a built-in command of the Bash shell.

uname	
Purpose	Display system information such as type of machine and operating system
Syntax	`uname [options]`

uname

Options	-a displays all information -m displays the hardware type (for example, i586) -n displays machine's host name -p displays the processor type (this appears as unknown) -r displays the operating system release (for example, 2.0.32) -s displays the operating system name -v displays the operating system version (shown as date of compilation)
Description	The uname command displays a variety of information about your machine and the operating system (Linux).

uncompress

Purpose	Uncompress one or more files that have been compressed using the compress command
Syntax	uncompress [-cdrvV] *files*
Options	-c writes result to the standard output and retains original -r recursively uncompresses files in all subdirectories -v displays a message as each file is uncompressed -V prints version number and exits
Description	The uncompress command uncompresses each specified file and replaces the compressed version with the original (and removes the .Z suffix appended to the name of the compressed file). The uncompress command is the same as running compress with the -d option.

uniq

Purpose	Write all unique lines from an input file to standard output
Syntax	uniq [options] *file*
Options	-*N* (where *N* is a number) ignores the first *N* fields on each line +*N* (where *N* is a number) ignores the first *N* characters on each line -c writes number of times each line occurred in file -d writes only duplicate lines -u writes only unique lines (default)
Description	The uniq command removes duplicate lines from an input file and copies the unique lines to the standard output. If you do not specify an input file, uniq reads from standard input.

wc

Purpose	Display byte, word, and line count of a file
Syntax	wc [options] [*files*]
Options	-c displays only the byte count -w displays only the word count -l displays only the line count
Description	The wc command displays the byte, word, and line count of a file. If you do not specify an input file, wc reads from standard input.

whatis	
Purpose	Search whatis database (see `apropos`) for complete words
Syntax	`whatis keyword`
Options	None
Description	The `whatis` command searches the whatis database (see the entry for `apropos`) for the specified keyword and displays the result. Only complete word matches are displayed.
whereis	
Purpose	Find the source, binary, and man page for a command
Syntax	`whereis [options] command`
Options	-b searches only for binaries -m searches only for man pages -s searches only for sources

Description	The `whereis` command searches the usual directories (where binaries, man pages, and source files are located) for binaries, man pages, and source files for a command. For example, here is the result of searching for the files for rpm command:
	`whereis rpm`
	`rpm: /bin/rpm /usr/include/rpm /usr/man/man8/rpm.8`

which	
Purpose	Search the directories in the PATH environment variable for a command
Syntax	`which command`
Options	None
Description	The `which` command searches the directories in the PATH environment variable for the file that will be executed when you type the command. This is a good way to check what you would execute when you type a specific command.
zcat, zless, zmore	
Purpose	View the contents of a compressed text file without having to first decompress the file

Syntax	`zcat filename`
	`zless filename`
	`zmore filename`

Options	None
Description	The `zcat`, `zless`, and `zmore` commands work the same way as `cat`, `less`, and `more`. The only difference is that the z commands can directly read files compressed with `gzip` or `compress` (without having to first uncompress the files with `gunzip`). These commands are particularly useful for reading the compressed HOWTO files in `/usr/doc/HOWTO` directory.

Appendix C

Linux Resources

This appendix lists some resources where you can get more information on specific topics. Most of the resources are on the Internet because that's where you can get the latest information. You can often download the files necessary for a specific task.

Some Internet resources appear in the standard Uniform Resource Locator (URL) syntax — Chapter 20 explains URLs. If you have used a Web browser — such as Netscape Navigator or Microsoft Internet Explorer — you are probably already familiar with URLs.

Web Pages

If you browse the Internet, you may have noticed quite a few Web pages exist with Linux-related information. A good starting point is the following Linux page:

`http://www.linuxresources.com/`

This page is maintained by SSC, Inc., the publisher of the *Linux Journal*. This page provides a starting point for locating information about Linux. You can click the large buttons to access more information on the topic identified by that button's label. At this page, you can also find an organized collection of links to Linux-related Web sites.

Another popular and definitive source of Linux information is the home page of the Linux Documentation Project (LDP) at the following URL:

`http://sunsite.unc.edu/LDP/`

On this Web site you'd find many more pointers to other Linux resources on the Internet. In particular, you can browse and download the latest HOWTO documents from `http://sunsite.unc.edu/LDP/HOWTO/`.

Newsgroups

To keep up with Linux developments, you need access to the Internet and especially to the newsgroups. You can find discussions on specific Linux-related topics in the following newsgroups:

- `comp.os.linux.admin` — Information about Linux system administration
- `comp.os.linux.advocacy` — Discussions about promoting Linux
- `comp.os.linux.announce` — Important announcements about Linux (this is a moderated newsgroup, which means you must mail the article to the moderator who then posts it to the newsgroup)

- `comp.os.linux.answers` — Questions and answers about Linux (all the Linux HOWTOs are posted in this moderated newsgoup)

- `comp.os.linux.development` — Current Linux development work

- `comp.os.linux.development.apps` — Linux application development

- `comp.os.linux.development.system` — Linux operating system development

- `comp.os.linux.hardware` — Discussions about Linux and various hardware

- `comp.os.linux.help` — Help with various aspects of Linux

- `comp.os.linux.misc` — Miscellaneous topics about Linux

- `comp.os.linux.networking` — Networking under Linux

- `comp.os.linux.setup` — Linux setup and installation

- `comp.os.linux.x` — Discussions about setting up and running the X Window System under Linux

Linux FTP Archive Sites

You can download Red Hat Linux and other Linux distributions from one of several FTP sites around the world. In addition to the Linux distribution itself, these sites also contain many other software packages that run under Linux.

For the latest list of Red Hat Linux FTP sites around the world, visit the following Web page maintained by Red Hat:

`http://www.redhat.com/mirrors.html`

To download specific Red Hat Package Manager (RPM) files for the latest Red Hat Linux version (for Intel-based PCs), you may want to access Red Hat's FTP site at the following URL:

`ftp://ftp.redhat.com/pub/redhat/current/i386/RedHat/RPMS/`

Magazine

The *Linux Journal* is the only magazine devoted entirely to Linux. On the Web, the magazine home page is at `http://www.linuxjournal.com/`. Here's the contact information for this magazine:

LINUX JOURNAL
P.O. BOX 500
Missouri City, TX 77459-0500
Phone (voice): 888-66-LINUX, 281-261-2581
FAX: 281-261-5999
E-mail: `subs@ssc.com`

Appendix D

About the CD-ROM

The companion CD-ROM contains Red Hat Linux 5.1 with the Linux 2.0.34 kernel, which is the latest version of Linux currently available (fall 1998). Linux is a complete UNIX operating system for your 486 or Pentium PC. The Red Hat Linux distribution includes over 300MB of source and binary files. By installing Linux on a PC, you can turn your PC into a full-fledged UNIX workstation.

Note

Please note, the software contained in this CD-ROM is distributed under a variety of license agreements. Some of the software (such as the Linux kernel) is distributed in full source and binary format under the GNU General Public License. A few software packages are distributed as shareware and you are expected to pay a nominal fee if you decide to use the software in your work. In all cases, the software is copyrighted by the respective authors. After installing Red Hat Linux, you should consult the README.* files (or files by names such as COPYING and COPYRIGHT) in various subdirectories of the /usr/doc directory for information on the license terms for each software package.

Installation can be one of the tricky steps in Linux, especially if you have a no-name IBM-compatible PC. You need some specific information about hardware, such as disk controller, video card, and CD-ROM drive. Linux controls the hardware through drivers, so you must make sure the current release of Linux includes drivers for your hardware. Because Linux is free, you cannot demand — or expect — support for some specific hardware. Linux is, however, continually growing through collaboration among programmers throughout the world. If your hardware is popular enough, a good chance exists that someone has developed a driver for it. In any case, the Red Hat Linux on the companion CD-ROM already supports such a wide variety of hardware, all your PC's peripherals probably are supported.

Cross-
Reference

The CD-ROM Installation Instructions that face this book's CD-ROM show the general procedure to install and configure Linux and the X Windows System.

Red Hat Linux 5.1 is a complete Linux distribution with the 2.0.34 kernel (operating system) plus a large selection of Linux software. In particular, you will find the following software on the Red Hat Linux 5.1 CD-ROM:

- Linux kernel 2.0.34 with driver modules for all major PC hardware configurations including IDE/EIDE and SCSI drives, PCMCIA devices, and CD-ROMs.

- Complete set of installation and configuration tools for setting up devices (such as keyboard and mouse) and services

- Graphical user interface based on the XFree86 3.3.2 package with fvwm2 and AfterStep window managers

- Full TCP/IP networking for Internet, LANs, and intranets

- Tools for connecting your PC to your Internet service provider using PPP, SLIP, or dialup serial communications programs

- Complete suite of Internet applications including electronic mail (sendmail, elm, pine, mailx), news (inn, tin, trn), Internet Relay Chat (ircii), telnet, FTP, and NFS

- Apache Web server 1.2.6 to turn your PC into a Web server and Netscape Communicator 4.05 to surf the Net

- Samba 1.9 LAN Manager software for Microsoft Windows connectivity

- Several text editors (GNU Emacs 20.2, JED, Joe, vim)

- Graphics and image manipulation software such as XV, XPaint, Xfig, Gnuplot, Ghostscript, Ghostview, GIMP, ImageMagick, and xanim

- Programming languages (GNU C and C++ 2.7.2.3, Perl 5.004, Tcl/Tk 8.0.2, Python 1.5.1, GNU AWK 3.0.3) and software development tools (GNU Debugger 4.17, RCS 5.7, GNU Bison 1.25, flex 2.5.4a, TIFF and JPEG libraries)

- Support for industry standard Executable and Linking Format (ELF) and Intel Binary Compatibility Specification (iBCS)

- Complete suite of standard UNIX utilities

- Tools to access and use DOS files and applications (DOSEMU 0.66.7, mtools 3.8)

- Text formatting and typesetting software (groff, TeX, and LaTeX)

- Games such as GNU Chess, xtetris, acm, colour-yahtzee, flying, fortune-mod, mysterious, paradise, xchomp, xevil, xgalaga, xgammon, xpilot

Index

continued

continued

continued

continued

GNU General Public License

Version 2, June 1991
Copyright © 1989, 1991 Free Software Foundation, Inc.
675 Mass Ave., Cambridge, MA 02139, USA

Preamble

The licenses for most software are designed to take away your freedom to share and change it. By contrast, the GNU General Public License is intended to guarantee your freedom to share and change free software—to make sure the software is free for all its users. This General Public License applies to most of the Free Software Foundation's software and to any other program whose authors commit to using it. (Some other Free Software Foundation software is covered by the GNU Library General Public License instead.) You can apply it to your programs, too.

When we speak of *free software*, we are referring to freedom, not price. Our General Public Licenses are designed to make sure that you have the freedom to distribute copies of free software (and charge for this service if you wish), that you receive source code or can get it if you want it, that you can change the software or use pieces of it in new free programs; and that you know you can do these things.

To protect your rights, we need to make restrictions that forbid anyone to deny you these rights or to ask you to surrender the rights. These restrictions translate to certain responsibilities for you if you distribute copies of the software, or if you modify it.

For example, if you distribute copies of such a program, whether gratis or for a fee, you must give the recipients all the rights that you have. You must make sure that they, too, receive or can get the source code. And you must show them these terms so they know their rights.

We protect your rights with two steps: (1) copyright the software, and (2) offer you this license, which gives you legal permission to copy, distribute, and/or modify the software.

Also, for each author's protection and ours, we want to make certain that everyone understands that there is no warranty for this free software. If the software is modified by someone else and passed on, we want its recipients to know that what they have is not the original, so that any problems introduced by others will not reflect on the original authors' reputations.

Finally, any free program is threatened constantly by software patents. We wish to avoid the danger that redistributors of a free program will individually obtain patent licenses, in effect making the program proprietary.

To prevent this, we have made it clear that any patent must be licensed for everyone's free use or not licensed at all.

The precise terms and conditions for copying, distribution and modification follow.

Terms and Conditions for Copying, Distribution, and Modification

0. This License applies to any program or other work that contains a notice placed by the copyright holder saying it may be distributed under the terms of this General Public License. The "Program," below, refers to any such program or work, and a "work based on the Program" means either the Program or any derivative work under copyright law: that is to say, a work containing the Program or a portion of it, either verbatim or with modifications and/or translated into another language. (Hereinafter, translation is included without limitation in the term "modification.") Each licensee is addressed as "you."

   Activities other than copying, distribution, and modification are not covered by this License; they are outside its scope. The act of running the Program is not restricted, and the output from the Program is covered only if its contents constitute a work based on the Program (independent of having been made by running the Program). Whether that is true depends on what the Program does.

1. You may copy and distribute verbatim copies of the Program's source code as you receive it, in any medium, provided that you conspicuously and appropriately publish on each copy an appropriate copyright notice and disclaimer of warranty; keep intact all the notices that refer to this License and to the absence of any warranty; and give any other recipients of the Program a copy of this License along with the Program.

   You may charge a fee for the physical act of transferring a copy, and you may at your option offer warranty protection in exchange for a fee.

2. You may modify your copy or copies of the Program or any portion of it, thus forming a work based on the Program, and copy and distribute such modifications or work under the terms of Section 1 above, provided that you also meet all of these conditions:

   a) You must cause the modified files to carry prominent notices stating that you changed the files and the date of any change.

   b) You must cause any work that you distribute or publish, that in whole or in part contains or is derived from the Program or any part thereof, to be licensed as a whole at no charge to all third parties under the terms of this License.

   c) If the modified program normally reads commands interactively when run, you must cause it, when started running for such interactive use in the most ordinary way, to print or display an announcement including an appropriate copyright notice and a notice that there is no warranty (or else, saying that you provide a warranty) and that users may redistribute the program under these conditions, and telling the user how to view a copy of this License. (Exception: If the Program itself is interactive but does not normally print such an announcement, your work based on the Program is not required to print an announcement.)

These requirements apply to the modified work as a whole. If identifiable sections of that work are not derived from the Program, and can be reasonably considered independent and separate works in themselves, then this License, and its terms, do not apply to those sections when you distribute them as separate works. But when you distribute the same sections as part of a whole that is a work based on the Program, the distribution of the whole must be on the terms of this License, whose permissions for other licensees extend to the entire whole, and thus to each and every part regardless of who wrote it.

Thus, it is not the intent of this section to claim rights or contest your rights to work written entirely by you; rather, the intent is to exercise the right to control the distribution of derivative or collective works based on the Program.

In addition, mere aggregation of another work not based on the Program with the Program (or with a work based on the Program) on a volume of a storage or distribution medium does not bring the other work under the scope of this License.

3. You may copy and distribute the Program (or a work based on it, under Section 2) in object code or executable form under the terms of Sections 1 and 2 above provided that you also do one of the following:

   a) Accompany it with the complete corresponding machine-readable source code, which must be distributed under the terms of Sections 1 and 2 above on a medium customarily used for software interchange; or,

   b) Accompany it with a written offer, valid for at least three years, to give any third party, for a charge no more than your cost of physically performing source distribution, a complete, machine-readable copy of the corresponding source code, to be distributed under the terms of Sections 1 and 2 above on a medium customarily used for software interchange; or,

   c) Accompany it with the information you received as to the offer to distribute corresponding source code. (This alternative is allowed only for noncommercial distribution and only if you received the program in object code or executable form with such an offer, in accord with Subsection b above.)

The source code for a work means the preferred form of the work for making modifications to it. For an executable work, complete source code means all the source code for all modules it contains, plus any associated interface definition files, plus the scripts used to control compilation and installation of the executable. However, as a special exception, the source code distributed need not include anything that is normally distributed (in either source or binary form) with the major components (compiler, kernel, and so forth) of the operating system on which the executable runs, unless that component itself accompanies the executable.

If distribution of executable or object code is made by offering access to copy from a designated place, then offering equivalent access to copy the source code from the same place counts as distribution of the source code, even though third parties are not compelled to copy the source along with the object code.

4. You may not copy, modify, sublicense, or distribute the Program except as expressly provided under this License. Any attempt otherwise to copy, modify, sublicense, or distribute the Program is void, and will automatically terminate your rights under this License.

   However, parties who have received copies, or rights, from you under this License will not have their licenses terminated so long as such parties remain in full compliance.

5. You are not required to accept this License, since you have not signed it. However, nothing else grants you permission to modify or distribute the Program or its derivative works. These actions are prohibited by law if you do not accept this License. Therefore, by modifying or distributing the Program (or any work based on the Program), you indicate your acceptance of this License to do so, and all its terms and conditions for copying, distributing or modifying the Program or works based on it.

6. Each time you redistribute the Program (or any work based on the Program), the recipient automatically receives a license from the original licensor to copy, distribute, or modify the Program subject to these terms and conditions. You may not impose any further restrictions on the recipients' exercise of the rights granted herein. You are not responsible for enforcing compliance by third parties to this License.

7. If, as a consequence of a court judgment or allegation of patent infringement or for any other reason (not limited to patent issues), conditions are imposed on you (whether by court order, agreement or otherwise) that contradict the conditions of this License, they do not excuse you from the conditions of this License. If you cannot distribute so as to satisfy simultaneously your obligations under this License and any other pertinent obligations, then as a consequence you may not distribute the Program at all. For example, if a patent license would not

permit royalty-free redistribution of the Program by all those who receive copies directly or indirectly through you, then the only way you could satisfy both it and this License would be to refrain entirely from distribution of the Program.

If any portion of this section is held invalid or unenforceable under any particular circumstance, the balance of the section is intended to apply and the section as a whole is intended to apply in other circumstances.

It is not the purpose of this section to induce you to infringe any patents or other property right claims or to contest validity of any such claims; this section has the sole purpose of protecting the integrity of the free software distribution system, which is implemented by public license practices. Many people have made generous contributions to the wide range of software distributed through that system in reliance on consistent application of that system; it is up to the author/donor to decide if he or she is willing to distribute software through any other system and a licensee cannot impose that choice.

This section is intended to make thoroughly clear what is believed to be a consequence of the rest of this License.

8. If the distribution and/or use of the Program is restricted in certain countries either by patents or by copyrighted interfaces, the original copyright holder who places the Program under this License may add an explicit geographical distribution limitation excluding those countries, so that distribution is permitted only in or among countries not thus excluded. In such case, this License incorporates the limitation as if written in the body of this License.

9. The Free Software Foundation may publish revised and/or new versions of the General Public License from time to time. Such new versions will be similar in spirit to the present version, but may differ in detail to address new problems or concerns.

   Each version is given a distinguishing version number. If the Program specifies a version number of this License which applies to it and "any later version," you have the option of following the terms and conditions either of that version or of any later version published by the Free Software Foundation. If the Program does not specify a version number of this License, you may choose any version ever published by the Free Software Foundation.

10. If you wish to incorporate parts of the Program into other free programs whose distribution conditions are different, write to the author to ask for permission. For software which is copyrighted by the Free Software Foundation, write to the Free Software Foundation; we sometimes make exceptions for this. Our decision will be guided by the two goals of preserving the free status of all derivatives of our free software and of promoting the sharing and reuse of software generally.

No Warranty

11. BECAUSE THE PROGRAM IS LICENSED FREE OF CHARGE, THERE IS NO WARRANTY FOR THE PROGRAM, TO THE EXTENT PERMITTED BY APPLICABLE LAW. EXCEPT WHEN OTHERWISE STATED IN WRITING, THE COPYRIGHT HOLDERS AND/OR OTHER PARTIES PROVIDE THE PROGRAM "AS IS" WITHOUT WARRANTY OF ANY KIND, EITHER EXPRESSED OR IMPLIED, INCLUDING, BUT NOT LIMITED TO, THE IMPLIED WARRANTIES OF MERCHANTABILITY AND FITNESS FOR A PARTICULAR PURPOSE. THE ENTIRE RISK AS TO THE QUALITY AND PERFORMANCE OF THE PROGRAM IS WITH YOU. SHOULD THE PROGRAM PROVE DEFECTIVE, YOU ASSUME THE COST OF ALL NECESSARY SERVICING, REPAIR, OR CORRECTION.

12. IN NO EVENT UNLESS REQUIRED BY APPLICABLE LAW OR AGREED TO IN WRITING WILL ANY COPYRIGHT HOLDER, OR ANY OTHER PARTY WHO MAY MODIFY AND/OR REDISTRIBUTE THE PROGRAM AS PERMITTED ABOVE, BE LIABLE TO YOU FOR DAMAGES, INCLUDING ANY GENERAL, SPECIAL, INCIDENTAL, OR CONSEQUENTIAL DAMAGES ARISING OUT OF THE USE OR INABILITY TO USE THE PROGRAM (INCLUDING BUT NOT LIMITED TO LOSS OF DATA OR DATA BEING RENDERED INACCURATE OR LOSSES SUSTAINED BY YOU OR THIRD PARTIES OR A FAILURE OF THE PROGRAM TO OPERATE WITH ANY OTHER PROGRAMS), EVEN IF SUCH HOLDER OR OTHER PARTY HAS BEEN ADVISED OF THE POSSIBILITY OF SUCH DAMAGES.

End of Terms and Conditions

How to Apply These Terms to Your New Programs

If you develop a new program, and you want it to be of the greatest possible use to the public, the best way to achieve this is to make it free software that everyone can redistribute and change under these terms.

To do so, attach the following notices to the program. It is safest to attach them to the start of each source file to most effectively convey the exclusion of warranty; and each file should have at least the "copyright" line and a pointer to where the full notice is found:

<One line to give the program's name and a brief idea of what it does.>

Copyright (c) 19yy (name of author)

This program is free software; you can redistribute it and/or modify it under the terms of the GNU General Public License as published by the Free Software Foundation; either Version 2 of the License, or (at your option) any later version.

This program is distributed in the hope that it will be useful, but WITHOUT ANY WARRANTY; without even the implied warranty of MERCHANTABILITY or FITNESS FOR A PARTICULAR PURPOSE. See the GNU General Public License for more details.

You should have received a copy of the GNU General Public License along with this program; if not, write to the Free Software Foundation, Inc., 675 Mass Ave., Cambridge, MA 02139, USA.

Also add information on how to contact you by electronic and paper mail.

If the program is interactive, make it output a short notice like this when it starts in an interactive mode:

```
Gnomovision version 69, Copyright (c) 19yy name of author
Gnomovision comes with ABSOLUTELY NO WARRANTY; for details type 'show w'
This is free software, and you are welcome to redistribute it under
certain conditions; type 'show c' for details.
```

The hypothetical commands show w and show c should show the appropriate parts of the General Public License. Of course, the commands you use may be called something other than show w and show c; they could even be mouse-clicks or menu items—whatever suits your program.

You should also get your employer (if you work as a programmer) or your school, if any, to sign a "copyright disclaimer" for the program, if necessary. Here is a sample; alter the names:

Yoyodyne, Inc., hereby disclaims all copyright interest in the program "Gnomovision" (which makes passes at compilers) written by James Hacker.

(signature of Ty Coon), 1 April 1989

Ty Coon, President of Vice

This General Public License does not permit incorporating your program into proprietary programs. If your program is a subroutine library, you may consider it more useful to permit linking proprietary applications with the library. If this is what you want to do, use the GNU Library General Public License instead of this License.

my2cents.idgbooks.com

LINUX JOURNAL

CD-ROM Installation Instructions

Installing Linux is a big job — too big to describe adequately in the space available here. For complete instructions, see Chapter 1.

Although these instructions do not provide detailed installation instructions for Linux, you can use the following general procedure to install and configure Linux and the X Window System, which is the graphical user interface for Linux. Follow these steps:

1. Gather information about your PC's hardware before you install Linux. Linux accesses and uses various PC peripherals through software components called *drivers*. You must make sure the version of Linux you are about to install has the necessary drivers for your system's hardware configuration. Conversely, if you do not have a system yet, look at the list of hardware supported by Linux and make sure you buy a PC with components Linux supports.

2. You may have to perform a process known as *partitioning* to allocate parts of your hard disk for use by Linux. If you are lucky enough to have a spare hard disk, you may decide to keep MS-DOS and Windows on the first hard disk and install Linux on the second hard disk. With a spare second disk, you needn't worry about partitioning under DOS or Windows. If you have only one hard disk, however, you must partition that disk into several parts. Use a part for DOS and Windows and leave the rest for Linux.

3. Under DOS or Windows, create a *Linux boot disk* (or just *boot disk*). The boot disk is used to boot your PC and to start an initial version of Linux operating system. If you boot your PC under MS-DOS (it must be MS-DOS only, not an MS-DOS window in Windows 95), you can skip this step — instead, you can boot Linux directly from the CD-ROM.

4. Boot your PC with the Linux boot disk (or start MS-DOS and run a command from the CD-ROM). This procedure automatically runs the Red Hat Linux installation program. From this point on, you will respond to a number of dialog boxes as the Red Hat installation program takes you through the steps.

5. Respond to a dialog box that asks you if you have a color monitor. From subsequent dialog boxes, you select the keyboard type and indicate where Red Hat Linux is located (in the CD-ROM drive).

6. Prepare the hard disk partitions where you plan to install Linux. If you have created space for Linux by reducing the size of an existing DOS partition, now you have to create the partitions for Linux. Typically, you need at least two partitions: one for the Linux files and the other for use as the *swap partition*, a form of virtual memory. To perform this step, the installation program gives you the option of using the Linux `fdisk` command or Red Hat's new disk management utility called *Disk Druid*.

7. Format the hard disk partitions, indicate which partition is the swap partition, and specify the partition where to install Linux (this is called the *root partition*). You also get a chance to mount other disk partitions. Mounting a partition associates a physical disk partition with a directory in the Linux file system.

8. Select various software components to install. Each component represents a part of Linux, from the base operating system to components such as the emacs editor, programming tools, the Perl scripting language, and the X Window System (a graphical windowing system). You simply select the components you need and let the Red Hat installation program do its job.

9. If you installed the X Window System, the installation program configures the mouse and then runs the Xconfigurator program that creates a configuration file (/etc/X11/XF86Config) used by the X Window System. In response to dialogs presented by the Xconfigurator program, you provide information about your video card and monitor.

10. If you installed the networking software, the installation program lets you configure the network. You specify a number of parameters including an IP address, host name, and domain name.

11. Specify the local time zone.

12. Configure any printers you have. You can configure a printer connected directly to the PC or a remote printer on the network. Red Hat even lets you configure a printer connected to a PC running Windows 95 or Windows NT.

13. Select a root password. The root user is the *super user*—a user who can do anything—in Linux.

14. Install the Linux Loader (LILO) program on your hard disk so you can boot Linux when you power up your PC after shutting it down.

15. If you find Linux does not work properly with one or more of your system components (such as the CD-ROM drive or sound card), you may have to reconfigure the Linux operating system to add support for those system components.

Limited Warranty